ADVENTURES
IN APPRECIATION

The ADVENTURES IN LITERATURE Program

ADVENTURES FOR READERS: BOOK ONE
Teacher's Manual
Tests
Reading/Writing Workshop A

ADVENTURES FOR READERS: BOOK TWO
Teacher's Manual
Tests
Reading/Writing Workshop B

ADVENTURES IN READING
Teacher's Manual
Tests
Reading/Writing Workshop C

ADVENTURES IN APPRECIATION
Teacher's Manual
Tests
Reading/Writing Workshop D

ADVENTURES IN AMERICAN LITERATURE
Teacher's Manual
Tests

ADVENTURES IN ENGLISH LITERATURE
Teacher's Manual
Tests

CURRICULUM
AND
WRITING

Fannie Safier
Formerly teacher of English
New York City Schools, New York, New York
Kathleen T. Daniel
Secondary English Editorial Staff
Harcourt Brace Jovanovich, Publishers

ADVENTURES
IN APPRECIATION

HERITAGE EDITION REVISED

HBJ **Harcourt Brace Jovanovich, Publishers**
Orlando New York Chicago San Diego Atlanta Dallas

Copyright © 1985, 1980 by Harcourt Brace Jovanovich, Inc.

All rights reserved. No part of this publication may be reproduced or transmitted in any form or by any means, electronic or mechanical, including photocopy, recording, or any information storage and retrieval system, without permission in writing from the publisher.

Requests for permission to make copies of any part of the work should be mailed to:
Permissions, Harcourt Brace Jovanovich, Publishers, Orlando, FL 32887

Printed in the United States of America

ISBN 0-15-335043-1

Acknowledgments

For permission to reprint copyrighted material, grateful acknowledgment is made to the following sources:

American Council for Nationalities Service: "Chee's Daughter" by Juanita Platero and Siyowin Miller from *Common Ground*, Vol. 8, Winter 1948.

Arizona Quarterly and Mrs. Chester Seltzer: "María Tepache" by Amado Muro from *Arizona Quarterly*, 1969.

Brandt & Brandt: "Shaving" by Leslie Norris. Copyright © 1977 by the Atlantic Monthly Company. "The Quiet Man" by Maurice Walsh. Copyright 1933 by Curtis Publishing Company; renewed © 1969 by Maurice Walsh.

Curtis Brown Ltd., on behalf of Doris Lessing: "Through the Tunnel" from *The Habit of Loving* by Doris Lessing. Copyright 1954 by Doris Lessing.

Cambridge University Press: From commentary by John Dover Wilson to *Julius Caesar* by William Shakespeare, edited by John Dover Wilson.

Don Congdon Associates, Inc.: "Contents of the Dead Man's Pockets" by Jack Finney. Copyright © 1956 by Jack Finney.

Delacorte Press/Seymour Lawrence: "Harrison Bergeron" from *Welcome to the Monkey House* by Kurt Vonnegut, Jr. Copyright © 1961 by Kurt Vonnegut, Jr. Originally published in *Fantasy and Science Fiction*.

Devin Adair Publishers: "The Trout" by Sean O'Faolain. Copyright © 1948 by the Devin Adair Company; renewed 1976.

Doubleday & Company, Inc.: "Little Elegy" from *Nude Descending a Staircase* by X. J. Kennedy. Copyright © 1960 by X. J. Kennedy. Originally appeared in *The New Yorker*. "Big Wind" from the *Collected Poems of Theodore Roethke*. Copyright 1947 by the United Chapters of Phi Beta Kappa.

Egon Dumler, attorney for producer: Excerpts from the play *The Belle of Amherst* by William Luce. Copyright © 1976 by Creative Image Company—A Dome/Creative Image Production. All rights reserved. No part of this work may be reproduced or transmitted in any form by any means, electronic or mechanical, including photocopying and recording or by any information storage or retrieval system, without permission in writing from the publisher. *Caution:* Professionals and amateurs are hereby warned that *The Belle of Amherst*, being fully protected under the copyright laws of the United States of America, the British Empire, including the Dominion of Canada, and all other countries of the Berne and Universal Copyright Conventions, is subject to royalty. All rights, including professional, amateur, motion picture, recitation, lecturing, public readings, radio and television broadcasting, phonograph recording rights, and rights of translation into foreign languages, are strictly reserved. All inquiries regarding this play should be addressed to the author's agent, Dome Productions, 9200 Sunset Boulevard, Los Angeles, California 90069.

E. P. Dutton: "Emily Dickinson" from *A Chilmark Miscellany* by Van Wyck Brooks. Copyright 1948 by Van Wyck Brooks; renewed © 1976 by Gladys Brooks.

Norma Millay Ellis: "Autumn Chant" from *Collected Poems* by Edna St. Vincent Millay, Harper & Row. Copyright 1923, 1951 by Edna St. Vincent Millay and Norma Millay Ellis. "Recuerdo" from *Collected Poems* by Edna St. Vincent Millay, Harper & Row. Copyright 1922, 1950 by Edna St. Vincent Millay. "Oh, Oh, You Will Be Sorry for That Word" from *Collected Poems* by Edna St. Vincent Millay, Harper & Row. Copyright 1923, 1951 by Edna St. Vincent Millay and Norma Millay Ellis. "I Shall Go Back" and a line from "On Hearing a Symphony of Beethoven" from *Collected Poems* by Edna St. Vincent Millay, Harper & Row. Copyright 1923, 1928, 1951, 1955 by Edna St. Vincent Millay and Norma Millay Ellis.

Ann Elmo Agency, Inc.: "Leiningen Versus the Ants" by Carl Stephenson.

Mari Evans: From "When in Rome" from *I Am a Black Woman* by Mari Evans. Published by William Morrow & Company, 1970.

Farrar, Straus and Giroux, Inc.: "One Art" from *The Complete Poems 1927–1979* by Elizabeth Bishop. Copyright © 1976 by Elizabeth Bishop; renewed © 1983 by Alice Helen Methfessel. "Musician" from *The Blue Estuaries* by Louise Bogan. Copyright © 1937; renewed © 1968 by Louise Bogan. From "Los Angeles Notebook" from *Slouching Towards Bethlehem* by Joan Didion. Copyright © 1967, 1968 by Joan Didion. "Clean Fun at Riverhead" from *The Kandy-Kolored Tangerine Flake Steamline Baby* by Tom Wolfe. Copyright © 1963, 1964, 1965 by Thomas K. Wolfe, Jr. Copyright © 1963 by New York Herald Tribune, Inc. "The Beginning of Grief" from *Beyond the Bedroom Wall* by Larry Woiwode. Copyright © 1965, 1966, 1967, 1968, 1969, 1970, 1971, 1972, 1973, 1974, 1975 by Larry Woiwode. Originally appeared in *The New Yorker.* From the Introduction to *The Acts of King Arthur and His Noble Knights* by John Steinbeck. Copyright © 1976 by Elaine Steinbeck. From "Invitation to Miss Marianne Moore" and from "Varick Street" from *The Complete Poems* by Elizabeth Bishop. Copyright 1947, 1949, 1969 by Elizabeth Bishop; renewed © 1974, 1976 by Elizabeth Bishop.

Victor Gollancz Ltd.: "Autumn" by T. E. Hulme from *The Life and Opinions of T. E. Hulme,* edited by A. R. Jones. Published by Victor Gollancz Ltd.

Harcourt Brace Jovanovich, Inc.: "Splinter" from *Good Morning, America* by Carl Sandburg. Copyright 1928, 1956 by Carl Sandburg. "Antigone," with some deletions, from *The Antigone of Sophocles: An English Version* by Dudley Fitts and Robert Fitzgerald. Copyright 1939 by Harcourt Brace Jovanovich, Inc.; renewed 1967 by Dudley Fitts and Robert Fitzgerald. *Caution:* All rights, including professional, amateur, motion picture, recitation, lecturing, performance, public reading, radio broadcasting, and television, are strictly reserved. Inquiries on all rights should be addressed to Harcourt Brace Jovanovich, Inc., Orlando, FL 32887. "Running" from *Walking to Sleep* by Richard Wilbur. Copyright © 1968 by Richard Wilbur. "Julius Caesar," with adapted notes and stage directions, from *Shakespeare: The Complete Works,* edited by G. B. Harrison. Copyright 1948, 1952 by Harcourt Brace Jovanovich, Inc.; renewed 1976 by G. B. Harrison. "Road to the Isles" from *Cress Delahanty* by Jessamyn West. Copyright 1948; renewed 1976 by Jessamyn West. Originally appeared in *The New Yorker* in somewhat different form. From *Character and Conflict: An Introduction to Drama,* Second Edition by Alvin B. Kernan. Copyright © 1969 by Harcourt Brace Jovanovich, Inc. From The *Oedipus Rex of Sophocles,* translated by Dudley Fitts and Robert Fitzgerald. Copyright 1949 by Harcourt Brace Jovanovich, Inc.; renewed 1977 by Cornelia Fitts and Robert Fitzgerald. *Caution:* All rights, including professional, amateur, motion picture, recitation, lecturing, public reading, radio broadcasting and television are strictly reserved. Inquiries on all rights should be addressed to Harcourt Brace Jovanovich, Inc., Orlando, FL 32887. "The

Piece of Yarn" by Guy de Maupassant, translated by Newbury LeB. Morse from the original French of Guy de Maupassant's story, "La Ficelle."

Harper & Row, Publishers, Inc.: "Fifteen" and "Report from a Far Place" from *Stories That Could Be True: New and Collected Poems* by William Stafford. Copyright © 1964, 1970 by William E. Stafford. "For My Grandmother" and "Sonnet" ("Some for a little . . . ") from *On These I Stand* by Countee Cullen. Copyright 1925, 1935 by Harper & Row, Publishers, Inc.; renewed 1953, 1963 by Ida M. Cullen. From *Black Boy* by Richard Wright. Copyright 1937, 1942, 1944, 1945 by Richard Wright. From *A Tree Grows in Brooklyn* by Betty Smith. Copyright 1943, 1947 by Betty Smith. "The Sonnet-Ballad" and lines from "The Ballad of Rudolph Reed" from *The World of Gwendolyn Brooks* (1971) by Gwendolyn Brooks. Copyright 1949 by Gwendolyn Brooks Blakely. Copyright © 1960 by Gwendolyn Brooks. From pp. 194–200 (Titled: "I Find Fool Gold") in *Roughing It,* Vol. I, by Mark Twain. Selections included in the play *The Belle of Amherst* by William Luce, abridged and adapted, from the following sources: *Letters of Emily Dickinson* by Mabel Loomis Todd. Copyright 1931 by The Trustees of Amherst College. *Ancestors' Brocades* by Millicent Todd Bingham. Copyright 1945 by The Trustees of Amherst College. *Emily Dickinson–A Revelation* by Millicent Todd Bingham. Copyright 1954 by The Trustees of Amherst College. *Emily Dickinson's Home* by Millicent Todd Bingham. Copyright © 1956 by The Trustees of Amherst College. *Bolts of Melody: New Poems of Emily Dickinson* by Mabel Loomis Todd and Millicent Todd Bingham. Copyright 1945 by The Trustees of Amherst College.

Harper & Row, Publishers, Inc. and Olwyn Hughes: "Mirror" from *Crossing the Waters* by Sylvia Plath. Copyright © 1963, 1971 by Ted Hughes. Originally appeared in *The New Yorker.* Published in Britain by Faber and Faber.

Harvard University Press and The Trustees of Amherst College: Poems 67, 108, 150, 254, 301, 303, 318, 321, 441, 443, 508, 657, 712, 1052, 1123, 1129, 1212, 1549, 1755 or parts thereof, included in the play *The Belle of Amherst* by William Luce and "The Saddest Noise, The Sweetest Noise" (Poem 1764) and a part of Poem 125 from *The Poems of Emily Dickinson,* edited by Thomas H. Johnson, Cambridge, Mass.: The Belknap Press of Harvard University Press. Copyright © 1951, 1955 by the President and Fellows of Harvard College.

David Higham Associates, Ltd.: "The Life of Caesar" from *Plutarch's Lives,* translated by Rex Warner.

Holt, Rinehart and Winston, Publishers: "To the Thawing Wind." "The Tuft of Flowers," "Birches," "Once by the Pacific," from "Stopping by Woods on a Snowy Evening" from *The Poetry of Robert Frost,* edited by Edward Connery Lathem. Copyright 1916, 1923, 1928, 1934, © 1969 by Holt, Rinehart and Winston. Copyright 1944, © 1951, 1956, 1962 by Robert Frost.

Holt, Rinehart and Winston, Publishers, and The Society of Authors as the literary representative of the Estate of A. E. Housman: "To an Athlete Dying Young" and a selection from "Loveliest of trees, the cherry now" quoted in I Never Sang for My Father by Robert Anderson from "A Shropshire Lad"—Authorised Edition—from The Collected Poems of A. E. Housman. Copyright 1939, 1940, © 1965 by Holt, Rinehart and Winston. Copyright © 1967, 1968 by Robert E. Symons. Published in Britain by Jonathan Cape Ltd.

Houghton Mifflin Company: "Eleven" from New and Collected Poems 1917-1976 by Archibald MacLeish. Copyright © 1976 by Archibald MacLeish. From A Wizard of Earthsea by Ursula K. Le Guin. Copyright 1968 by Ursula K. Le Guin. "Welcome Morning" from The Awful Rowing Toward God by Anne Sexton. Copyright © 1975 by Loring Conant, Jr. From "Venus Transiens" from The Complete Poetical Works of Amy Lowell. Copyright 1955 by Houghton Mifflin Company. Four quotes included in the play The Belle of Amherst by William Luce, reprinted from Emily Dickinson Face to Face by Martha Dickinson Bianchi, 1932.

Olwyn Hughes: "The Lake" by Ted Hughes. Copyright © 1961, 1963, 1965 by Ted Hughes. Originally appeared in The New Yorker. Copyright © 1961 The New Yorker Magazine, Inc.

Hutchinson Publishing Group Ltd.: "A Recollection" from Collected Poems of Frances Cornford. Published by Cresset Press Ltd.

Indiana University Press: "Snake Hunt" by David Wagoner from Sleeping in the Woods. Copyright © 1974 by Indiana University Press. Originally appeared in The New Yorker.

International Creative Management, 40 W. 57th St., New York, New York 10019: I Never Sang for My Father by Robert Anderson. Copyright © 1968 by Robert Anderson; © 1966 by Robert Anderson, as an unpublished dramatic composition. "Invasion from Mars" from The Panic Broadcast by Howard Koch. Copyright © 1940 by Princeton University Press. Copyright © 1966 by Howard Koch.

Alfred A. Knopf, Inc.: "Dreams" from The Dream Keeper and Other Poems by Langston Hughes. Copyright 1932 by Alfred A. Knopf, Inc.; renewed 1960 by Langston Hughes. "The Duke's Children" from Domestic Relations by Frank O'Connor. Copyright © 1956 by Frank O'Connor. Originally appeared in The New Yorker. "Ex-Basketball Player" from The Carpentered Hen and Other Tame Creatures by John Updike. Copyright © 1957, 1982 by John Updike.

Little, Brown and Company: "Kindly Unhitch That Star, Buddy" from Verses from 1929 On by Ogden Nash. Copyright 1935 by Ogden Nash. From "Julia" from Pentimento: A Memoir by Lillian Hellman. Copyright © 1973 by Lillian Hellman. "End of Summer" from Selected

Poems: 1928-1958 by Stanley Kunitz. Copyright © 1953 by Stanley Kunitz. "The Centaur" from New & Selected Things Taking Place by May Swenson. Copyright © 1956 by May Swenson. Originally appeared in The Western Review. "She Sweeps with Many-Colored Brooms," "I Years Had Been from Home," "Nature the Gentlest Mother Is," "My Life Closed Twice Before Its Close," and "Lightly Stepped a Yellow Star" from Poems by Emily Dickinson, edited by Martha Dickinson Bianchi and Alfred Leete Hampson. Copyright 1914, 1942 by Martha Dickinson Bianchi. Poems 443 and 657 included in the play The Belle of Amherst by William Luce, reprinted from The Complete Poems of Emily Dickinson, edited by Thomas H. Johnson. Copyright 1929 by Martha Dickinson Bianchi. Copyright © 1957 by Mary L. Hampson.

Liveright Publishing Corporation: "Thy fingers make early flowers of" from Tulips & Chimneys by E. E. Cummings. Copyright 1923, 1925; renewed 1951, 1953 by E. E. Cummings. Copyright © 1973, 1976 by the Trustees for the E. E. Cummings Trust. Copyright © 1973, 1976 by George James Firmage. "Reapers" from Cane by Jean Toomer. Copyright 1923 by Boni & Liveright; renewed 1951 by Jean Toomer. "Fear" from The Complete Poems and Selected Letters and Prose of Hart Crane, edited by Brom Weber. Copyright 1933, © 1958, 1966 by Liveright Publishing Corporation.

Macmillan Publishing Company, Inc.: "The Long Hill" from Collected Poems by Sara Teasdale. Copyright 1920 by Macmillan Publishing Company, Inc.; renewed 1948 by Mamie T. Wheless. "Sea Fever" from Poems by John Masefield.

Macmillan Publishing Company, Inc. and Michael B. Yeats: "The Lake Isle of Innisfree" from The Collected Poems of William Butler Yeats. Copyright 1906 by Macmillan Publishing Company, Inc.; renewed 1934 by William Butler Yeats.

Monica McCall, on behalf of International Creative Management: "Boy with His Hair Cut Short" from U.S. 1 by Muriel Rukeyser. Copyright © 1938, 1965 by Muriel Rukeyser.

McIntosh and Otis, Inc.: "Socrates—His Life" from The Book of Courage by Hermann Hagedorn. Copyright © 1933, 1938 by Hermann Hagedorn.

National Council of Teachers of English: "The Pearl: Realism and Allegory" by Harry Morris from the English Journal LII, no. 7. Copyright © 1963 by the National Council of Teachers of English.

The New American Library, Inc.: From the Introduction to "Julius Caesar" by William Shakespeare, edited by William and Barbara Rosen. Copyright © 1963 by William and Barbara Rosen. From "The Tale of Sir Gareth" and "The Tale of Sir Launcelot du Lake" from Le Morte d'Arthur: King Arthur and the Legends of the Round Table by Sir Thomas Malory, a new rendition by Keith Baines. Copyright © 1962 by Keith Baines.

New Directions and David Higham Associates, Ltd.: "A Child's Christmas in Wales" from *Quite Early One Morning* by Dylan Thomas. Copyright 1954 by New Directions Publishing Corporation. Published in Britain by J. M. Dent.

The New Yorker Magazine, Inc.: "Glass World" by Dorothy Donnelly. Copyright © 1960 by The New Yorker Magazine, Inc. "Love" by William Maxwell. Copyright © 1983 by William Maxwell. Originally appeared in *The New Yorker.*

Harold Ober Associates Incorporated: "A Black Man Talks of Reaping" from *Personals* by Arna Bontemps. Copyright © 1963 by Arna Bontemps. "Epigram" ("O, God of dust . . .") by Langston Hughes from *New Poems by American Poets,* edited by Rolfe Humphries. Copyright © 1957 by Langston Hughes.

Simon J. Ortiz: "A Pretty Woman" by Simon J. Ortiz. Previously appeared in *Carriers of the Dream Wheel,* Harper & Row, Publishers, Inc.

Penguin Books Ltd.: "The Death of Socrates," from *Plato: The Last Days of Socrates* by Plato, translated by Hugh Tredennick. Copyright © 1954, 1959, 1969 by Hugh Tredennick.

G. P. Putnam's Sons and David Higham Associates Ltd.: Adapted from *The Once and Future King* by T. H. White. Copyright 1939, 1940, © 1958 by T. H. White. Published in Britain by Collins Ltd.

Random House, Inc.: From "The Ring" from *Anecdotes of Destiny* by Isak Dinesen. Copyright © 1958 by Isak Dinesen. "Blues Ain't No Mockin Bird" from *Gorilla, My Love* by Toni Cade Bambara. Copyright © 1971 by Toni Cade Bambara. "Miss Rosie" from *Good Times* by Lucille Clifton. Copyright © 1969 by Lucille Clifton. From *Shadow and Act* by Ralph Ellison (Titled: "Living with a Name"). Copyright © 1964 by Ralph Ellison. "Blue Girls" from *Selected Poems,* Third Edition, Revised and Enlarged, by John Crowe Ransom. Copyright 1927; renewed 1955 by John Crowe Ransom. "Riders to the Sea' by John Millington Synge from *The Complete Plays of John M. Synge.*

Random House, Inc. and Faber and Faber Ltd.: "But in the Evening" ("Embassy") from *Collected Poems* by W. H. Auden, edited by Edward Mendelson. Copyright 1945 by W. H. Auden.

Paul R. Reynolds, Inc., 12 East 41st Street, New York, N.Y. 10017: "The Hawk Is Flying" by Harry Crews. Copyright © 1977 by Harry Crews. Originally published in *Esquire* Magazine.

Rothco Cartoons, Inc.: "Learn with BOOK" by R. J. Heathorn (Punch Publications). Copyright © 1962 by Punch/Rothco.

Russell & Volkening, Inc., as agents for the author: From

"The Key" from *A Curtain of Green and Other Stories* by Eudora Welty. Copyright 1936, 1937, 1938, 1939, 1941, © 1965, 1966, 1967, 1969 by Eudora Welty.

Saturday Review: "Advice to Travelers" by Walker Gibson from *Saturday Review,* May 5, 1956. Copyright © 1956 by Saturday Review. All rights reserved.

Louise H. Sclove: "Motto for a Dog House" from *Lyric Laughter* by Arthur Guiterman.

Gary Snyder: "Above Pate Valley" by Gary Snyder. Copyright © 1965 by Gary Snyder.

The Society of Authors as the literary representative of the Estate of W. W. Jacobs: "The Monkey's Paw" by W. W. Jacobs.

May Swenson: "Ornamental Sketch with Verbs" from *To Mix With Time, New and Selected Poems* by May Swenson. Copyright © 1963 by May Swenson.

Helen Thurber: "The Scotty Who Knew Too Much" from *Fables for Our Time* by James Thurber, published by Harper & Row. Copyright © 1940 by James Thurber. Copyright © 1968 by Helen Thurber. Originally printed in *The New Yorker.*

The University of Chicago Press: "Summer Remembered" by Isabella Gardner. Copyright © 1961 by The University of Chicago. Originally published in *The Looking Glass.*

The University of Massachusetts Press: A quote included in the play *The Belle of Amherst* by William Luce reprinted from *The Lyman Letters: New Light on Emily Dickinson and Her Family* by Richard B. Sewall (University of Massachusetts Press, 1965). Copyright © 1965, The Massachusetts Review.

The University of Nebraska Press: "The Sentimentality of William Tavener" from *Willa Cather's Collected Short Fiction, 1892–1912* (Rev. Ed.) with introduction by Mildred R. Bennett. Edited by Virginia Faulkner by permission of University of Nebraska Press. Copyright © 1965, 1970 by the University of Nebraska Press.

Viking Penguin, Inc.: "First Lesson" from *Letter from a Distant Land* by Philip Booth. Copyright © 1957 by Philip Booth. "The Creation" from *God's Trombones* by James Weldon Johnson. Copyright 1927 by The Viking Press, Inc.; renewed © 1955 by Grace Nail Johnson. "The Storyteller" from *The Complete Short Stories of Saki* (H. H. Munro). All Rights Reserved. "One Perfect Rose" from *The Portable Dorothy Parker.* Copyright 1926; renewed 1954 by Dorothy Parker. "The Phoenix" from *The Cat's Cradle Book* by Sylvia Townsend Warner. Copyright 1940; renewed © 1968 by Sylvia Townsend Warner. From *Travels with Charley* by John Steinbeck. Copyright © 1961, 1962 by The Curtis Publishing Company, Inc. Copyright © 1962 by John Steinbeck. *The Pearl* by John Steinbeck. Copyright 1945 by John Steinbeck; renewed © 1973 by Elaine Steinbeck, John Steinbeck IV, Thom Steinbeck. All Rights Reserved. From *The Log from the Sea of Cortez* by John Steinbeck. Copyright © renewed 1969 by John Steinbeck and Edward F. Ricketts, Jr. All Rights Reserved. "Amanda Is Shod" from *House, Bridge, Fountain, Gate* by Maxine Kumin. Copyright © 1975 by Maxine Kumin. All Rights Reserved. From "A Youth Mowing" from *The Complete Poems of D. H. Lawrence.* Copyright © 1964, 1971 by Angelo Ravagli and C. M. Weekley, Executors of the Estate of Frieda Lawrence Ravagli. From "Notes Written on a Damp Veranda" from *Times Three* by Phyllis McGinley. Copyright 1952 by Phyllis McGinley. Originally appeared in *The New Yorker.* "Arthur Mitchell" from *The Complete Poems of Marianne Moore.* Published by Viking Penguin, Inc. "Song" from *Collected Poems* by Marya Zaturenska. Copyright © 1965 by M. Z. Gregory.

A. P. Watt Ltd. and The Estate of Constance Garnett: "The Bet" by Anton Chekhov, translated by Constance Garnett.

Wesleyan University Press: "Simple-Song" from *Hard Loving* by Marge Piercy. Copyright © 1969 by Marge Piercy. "The Base Stealer" from *The Orb Weaver* by Robert Francis. Copyright © 1948 by Robert Francis. "A Blessing" from *The Branch Will Not Break* by James Wright. Copyright © 1961 by James Wright.

Design and Production: Kirchoff/Wohlberg, Inc.

Cover: Asher B. Durand, *Progress*, 1853.
Warner Collection of the Gulf States Paper Corporation, Tuscaloosa, Alabama

Critical Readers and Contributors

Francelia Butler, University of Connecticut, Storrs, Connecticut

Henry E. Deluzain, Mosley High School, Panama City, Florida

Nicki Economy, Kansas City Public Schools, Kansas City, Kansas

Dorothy D. Hendry, Huntsville High School, Huntsville, Alabama

Carol Kuykendall, Houston Independent School District, Houston, Texas

Irene M. Reiter, Northeast High School, Philadelphia, Pennsylvania

Araminta Seal, John H. Reagan High School, Austin, Texas

William Shewan, Warren High School, Downey, California

Jane C. Tygard, Pittsburgh Public Schools, Pittsburgh, Pennsylvania

Robert F. Workman, Evanston Township High School, Evanston, Illinois

Lee A. Jacobus, University of Connecticut, Storrs, Connecticut

Gerald Levin, University of Akron, Akron, Ohio

Contents

See page xv for the contents of *Reading and Writing About Literature*

SHORT STORIES

There are two reasons for reading imaginative literature and two tests for judging it: pleasure and insight. The first and most important test of a story, poem, or play is, "Does it bring enjoyment?" If it doesn't, we want no more of it. But we must also ask, "Enjoyment to whom?" The best story in the world will bring no enjoyment to a person who doesn't know how to read it. Many excellent stories bring no enjoyment to us because we are unskilled as readers, or because we haven't experienced enough, or are lacking in imagination, sympathy, or compassion—because we're not human enough. Thus, not only do *we* judge literature, but good literature judges *us*. We say to a story or poem, "Are you enjoyable? If not, go away." But a great story or poem says to us, "Can you enjoy me? If not, go away, perfect yourself, then come back and try again."

The second test for the worth of imaginative literature is, "Does it yield insight? Do we know more, after reading it, about the world we live in, about our fellow human beings, about ourselves?" The paradox of imaginative literature is that, though it deals with imaginary events and imaginary people, it can communicate real truth—not just facts, but essential truths about living, delivered whole to our senses, our emotions, our imaginations, and our minds.

Reading good literature is thus a source of enjoyment and a means of enlarging our experience, extending our sympathies, and deepening our understanding. As such, it is both a means and an end of education, for though we read imaginative literature for enjoyment, we also read it to make ourselves more fully human.

Plot

In order to read stories well—to get from them all that they are capable of giving—we need to be aware of the elements the stories are composed of, and the techniques a writer uses to reach the reader. Among the most important of these elements and techniques are *plot, character, setting, point of view, symbol, irony,* and *theme.*

Plot is the sequence of incidents or actions in a story. Whatever the characters do, or whatever happens to them, constitutes *plot.*

The most important element in plot is usually *conflict.* Conflict may be *external* or *internal;* it may be physical, intellectual, emotional, or moral. A story may pit a character against the environment, against another person, or against some inner impulses or desires. Many stories have more than one conflict. A story ordinarily ends when its main conflict is *resolved,* that is, when one side or the other triumphs, and the main character either succeeds or fails. In some stories, however, the conflict is left unresolved, just as conflicts in real life often have no definite conclusions.

A plot may be realistic or fantastic. It may start from an ordinary, everyday situation or from a strange, even supernatural one. All the succeeding events should proceed logically from that initial situation, and all the characters' actions should be consistent with their personalities. A good plot is governed by an inner logic. It may begin with a far-fetched coincidence, but it will not ordinarily end with one.

Leiningen Versus the Ants

Carl Stephenson

"Unless they alter their course, and there's no reason why they should, they'll reach your plantation in two days at the latest."

Leiningen sucked placidly at a cigar about the size of a corncob and for a few seconds gazed without answering at the agitated District Commissioner. Then he took the cigar from his lips, and leaned slightly forward. With his bristling gray hair, bulky nose, and lucid eyes, he had the look of an aging and shabby eagle.

"Decent of you," he murmured, "paddling all this way just to give me the tip. But you're pulling my leg of course when you say I must do a bunk. Why, even a herd of saurians[1] couldn't drive me from this plantation of mine."

The Brazilian official threw up lean and lanky arms and clawed the air with wildly distended fingers. "Leiningen!" he shouted. "You're insane! They're not creatures you can fight—they're an elemental—an 'act of God'! Ten miles long, two miles wide—ants, noth-

---

1. **saurians** (sôr′ē-əns): lizards, crocodiles, and other reptiles.

ing but ants! And every single one of them a fiend from hell; before you can spit three times they'll eat a full-grown buffalo to the bones. I tell you if you don't clear out at once there'll be nothing left of you but a skeleton picked as clean as your own plantation."

Leiningen grinned. "Act of God, my eye! Anyway, I'm not going to run for it just because an elemental's on the way. And don't think I'm the kind of fathead who tries to fend off lightning with his fists, either. I use my intelligence, old man. With me, the brain isn't a second blind gut;[2] I know what it's there for. When I began this model farm and plantation three years ago, I took into account all that could conceivably happen to it. And now I'm ready for anything and everything—including your ants."

The Brazilian rose heavily to his feet. "I've done my best," he gasped. "Your obstinacy endangers not only yourself, but the lives of your four hundred workers. You don't know these ants!"

Leiningen accompanied him down to the river, where the government launch was moored. The vessel cast off. As it moved downstream, the exclamation mark neared the rail and began waving its arms frantically. Long after the launch had disappeared round the bend, Leiningen thought he could still hear that dimming, imploring voice. "You don't know them, I tell you! *You don't know them!*"

But the reported enemy was by no means unfamiliar to the planter. Before he started work on his settlement, he had lived long enough in the country to see for himself the fearful devastations sometimes wrought by these ravenous insects in their campaigns for food. But since then he had planned measures of defense accordingly, and these, he was convinced, were in every way adequate to withstand the approaching peril.

Moreover, during his three years as a planter, Leiningen had met and defeated drought, flood, plague, and all other "acts of God" which had come against him—unlike his fellow settlers in the district, who had made little or no resistance. This unbroken success he attributed solely to the observance of his lifelong motto: *The human brain needs only to become fully aware of its powers to conquer even the elements.* Dullards reeled senselessly and aimlessly into the abyss; cranks, however brilliant, lost their heads when circumstances suddenly altered or accelerated and ran into stone walls; sluggards drifted with the current until they were caught in whirlpools and dragged under. But such disasters, Leiningen contended, merely strengthened his argument that intelligence, directed aright, invariably makes man the master of his fate.

Yes, Leiningen had always known how to grapple with life. Even here, in this Brazilian wilderness, his brain had triumphed over every difficulty and danger it had so far encountered. First he had vanquished primal forces by cunning and organization, then he had enlisted the resources of modern science to increase miraculously the yield of his plantation. And now he was sure he would prove more than a match for the "irresistible" ants.

That same evening, however, Leiningen assembled his workers. He had no intention of waiting till the news reached their ears from other sources. Most of them had been born in the district; the cry "The ants are coming!" was to them an imperative signal for instant, panic-stricken flight, a spring for life itself. But so great was the Indians' trust in Leiningen, in Leiningen's word, and in Leiningen's

---

2. **blind gut:** an allusion to the appendix, for which there is no known function.

wisdom, that they received his curt tidings, and his orders for the imminent struggle, with the calmness with which they were given. They waited, unafraid, alert, as if for the beginning of a new game or hunt which he had just described to them. The ants were indeed mighty, but not so mighty as the boss. Let them come!

They came at noon the second day. Their approach was announced by the wild unrest of the horses, scarcely controllable now either in stall or under rider, scenting from afar a vapor instinct with horror.

It was announced by a stampede of animals, timid and savage, hurtling past each other; jaguars and pumas flashing by nimble stags of the pampas;[3] bulky tapirs, no longer hunters, themselves hunted, outpacing fleet kinkajous;[4] maddened herds of cattle, heads lowered, nostrils snorting, rushing through tribes of loping monkeys, chattering in a dementia of terror; then followed the creeping and springing denizens of bush and steppe, big and little rodents, snakes, and lizards.

Pell-mell the rabble swarmed down the hill to the plantation, scattered right and left before the barrier of the water-filled ditch, then sped onward to the river, where, again hindered, they fled along its bank out of sight.

This water-filled ditch was one of the defense measures which Leiningen had long since prepared against the advent of the ants. It encompassed three sides of the plantation like a huge horseshoe. Twelve feet across, but not very deep, when dry it could hardly be described as an obstacle to either man or beast. But the ends of the "horseshoe" ran into the river which formed the northern boundary, and fourth side, of the plantation.

And at the end nearer the house and outbuildings in the middle of the plantation, Leiningen had constructed a dam by means of which water from the river could be diverted into the ditch.

So now, by opening the dam, he was able to fling an imposing girdle of water, a huge quadrilateral with the river as its base, completely around the plantation, like the moat encircling a medieval city. Unless the ants were clever enough to build rafts, they had no hope of reaching the plantation, Leiningen concluded.

The twelve-foot water ditch seemed to afford in itself all the security needed. But while awaiting the arrival of the ants, Leiningen made a further improvement. The western section of the ditch ran along the edge of a tamarind[5] wood, and the branches of some great trees reached over the water. Leiningen now had them lopped so that ants could not descend from them within the "moat."

The women and children, then the herds of cattle, were escorted by peons on rafts over the river, to remain on the other side in absolute safety until the plunderers had departed. Leiningen gave this instruction, not because he believed the noncombatants were in any danger, but in order to avoid hampering the efficiency of the defenders.

Finally, he made a careful inspection of the "inner moat"—a smaller ditch lined with concrete, which extended around the hill on which stood the ranch house, barns, stables, and other buildings. Into this concrete ditch emptied the inflow pipes from three great petrol[6] tanks. If by some miracle the ants managed to cross the water and reach the plantation, this "rampart of petrol" would be

---

3. **pampas** (păm′pəz): vast treeless plains.
4. **kinkajous** (kĭng′kə-jōōz′): three-foot-long mammals with long tails, which live in South America.

5. **tamarind** (tăm′ə-rĭnd′): tropical tree with featherlike leaves.
6. **petrol** (pĕt′rəl): a British term for gasoline.

an absolutely impassable protection for the besieged and their dwellings and stock. Such, at least, was Leiningen's opinion.

He stationed his men at irregular distances along the water ditch, the first line of defense. Then he lay down in his hammock and puffed drowsily away at his pipe until a peon came with the report that the ants had been observed far away in the south.

Leiningen mounted his horse, which at the feel of its master seemed to forget its uneasiness, and rode leisurely in the direction of the threatening offensive. The southern stretch of ditch — the upper side of the quadrilateral — was nearly three miles long; from its center one could survey the entire countryside. This was destined to be the scene of the outbreak of war between Leiningen's brain and twenty square miles of life-destroying ants.

It was a sight one could never forget. Over the range of hills, as far as eye could see, crept a darkening hem, ever longer and broader, until the shadow spread across the slope from east to west, then downward, downward, uncannily swift, and all the green herbage of that wide vista was being mown as if by a giant sickle, leaving only the vast moving shadow, extending, deepening, and moving rapidly nearer.

When Leiningen's men, behind their barrier of water, perceived the approach of the long-expected foe, they gave vent to their suspense in screams and imprecations. But as the distance began to lessen between the "sons of hell" and the water ditch, they relapsed into silence. Before the advance of that awe-inspiring throng, their belief in the powers of the boss began to steadily dwindle.

Even Leiningen himself, who had ridden up just in time to restore their loss of heart by a display of unshakable calm, even he could not free himself from a qualm of malaise. Yonder were thousands of millions of voracious jaws bearing down upon him and only a suddenly insignificant narrow ditch lay between him and his men and being gnawed to the bones "before you can spit three times."

Hadn't his brain for once taken on more than it could manage? If the blighters decided to rush the ditch, fill it to the brim with their corpses, there'd still be more than enough to destroy every trace of that cranium[7] of his. The planter's chin jutted; they hadn't got him yet, and he'd see to it they never would. While he could think at all, he'd flout both death and the devil.

The hostile army was approaching in perfect formation; no human battalions, however well-drilled, could ever hope to rival the precision of that advance. Along a front that moved forward as uniformly as a straight line, the ants drew nearer and nearer to the water ditch. Then, when they learned through their scouts the nature of the obstacle, the two outlying wings of the army detached themselves from the main body and marched down the western and eastern sides of the ditch.

This surrounding maneuver took rather more than an hour to accomplish; no doubt the ants expected that at some point they would find a crossing.

During this outflanking movement by the wings, the army on the center and southern front remained still. The besieged were therefore able to contemplate at their leisure the thumb-long, reddish-black, long-legged insects; some of the Indians believed they could see, too, intent on them, the brilliant, cold eyes, and the razor-edged mandibles,[8] of this host of infinity.

It is not easy for the average person to imagine that an animal, not to mention an insect, can *think*. But now both the brain of Leiningen and the brains of the Indians began to stir with the unpleasant foreboding that inside every single one of that deluge of insects dwelled a thought. And that thought was: Ditch or no ditch, we'll get to your flesh!

Not until four o'clock did the wings reach the "horseshoe" ends of the ditch, only to find these ran into the great river. Through some kind of secret telegraphy, the report must then have flashed very swiftly indeed along the entire enemy line. And Leiningen, riding —no longer casually—along his side of the ditch, noticed by energetic and widespread movements of troops that for some unknown reason the news of the check had its greatest effect on the southern front, where the main army was massed. Perhaps the failure to find a way over the ditch was persuading the ants to withdraw from the plantation in search of spoils more easily obtainable.

An immense flood of ants, about a hundred yards in width, was pouring in a glimmering black cataract down the far slope of the ditch. Many thousands were already drowning in the sluggish creeping flow, but they were followed by troop after troop, who clambered over their sinking comrades, and then themselves served as dying bridges to the reserves hurrying on in their rear.

Shoals of ants were being carried away by the current into the middle of the ditch, where gradually they broke asunder and then, exhausted by their struggles, vanished below the surface. Nevertheless, the wavering, floundering hundred-yard front was remorselessly if slowly advancing toward the besieged on the other bank. Leiningen had been wrong when he supposed the enemy would first have to fill the ditch with their bodies before they could cross; instead, they merely needed to act as steppingstones, as they swam and sank, to the hordes ever pressing onward from behind.

---

7. **cranium** (krā′nē-əm): skull.
8. **mandibles** (măn′də-bəls): jaws.

Near Leiningen a few mounted herdsmen awaited his orders. He sent one to the weir[9] — the river must be dammed more strongly to increase the speed and power of the water coursing through the ditch.

A second peon was dispatched to the outhouses to bring spades and petrol sprinklers. A third rode away to summon to the zone of the offensive all the men, except the observation posts, on the nearby sections of the ditch, which were not yet actively threatened.

The ants were getting across far more quickly than Leiningen would have deemed possible. Impelled by the mighty cascade behind them, they struggled nearer and nearer to the inner bank. The momentum of the attack was so great that neither the tardy flow of the stream nor its downward pull could exert its proper force; and into the gap left by every submerging insect, hastened forward a dozen more.

When reinforcements reached Leiningen, the invaders were halfway over. The planter had to admit to himself that it was only by a stroke of luck for him that the ants were attempting the crossing on a relatively short front: had they assaulted simultaneously along the entire length of the ditch, the outlook for the defenders would have been black indeed.

Even as it was, it could hardly be described as rosy, though the planter seemed quite unaware that death in a gruesome form was drawing closer and closer. As the war between his brain and the "act of God" reached its climax, the very shadow of annihilation began to pale to Leiningen, who now felt like a champion in a new Olympic game, a gigantic and thrilling contest, from which he was determined to emerge victor. Such, indeed, was his aura of confidence that the Indians forgot their fear of the peril only a yard or two away; under the planter's supervision, they began fervidly digging up to the edge of the bank and throwing clods of earth and spadefuls of sand into the midst of the hostile fleet.

The petrol sprinklers, hitherto used to destroy pests and blights on the plantation, were also brought into action. Streams of evil-reeking oil now soared and fell over an enemy already in disorder through the bombardment of earth and sand.

The ants responded to these vigorous and successful measures of defense by further developments of their offensive. Entire clumps of huddling insects began to roll down the opposite bank into the water. At the same time, Leiningen noticed that the ants were now attacking along an ever-widening front. As the numbers both of his men and his petrol sprinklers were severely limited, this rapid extension of the line of battle was becoming an overwhelming danger.

To add to his difficulties, the very clods of earth they flung into that black floating carpet often whirled fragments toward the defenders' side, and here and there dark ribbons were already mounting the inner bank. True, wherever a man saw these they could still be driven back into the water by spadefuls of earth or jets of petrol. But the file of defenders was too sparse and scattered to hold off at all points these landing parties, and though the peons toiled like madmen, their plight became momently more perilous.

One man struck with his spade at an enemy clump, did not draw it back quickly enough from the water; in a trice the wooden haft swarmed with upward scurrying insects. With a curse, he dropped the spade into the ditch; too late, they were already on his body. They lost no time; wherever they encountered bare flesh they bit deeply; a few, bigger

---

9 **weir** (wîr): dam on a river or stream.

than the rest, carried in their hindquarters a sting which injected a burning and paralyzing venom. Screaming, frantic with pain, the peon danced and twirled like a dervish.[10]

Realizing that another such casualty, yes, perhaps this alone, might plunge his men into confusion and destroy their morale, Leiningen roared in a bellow louder than the yells of the victim: "Into the petrol, idiot! Douse your paws in the petrol!" The dervish ceased his pirouette as if transfixed, then tore off his shirt and plunged his arm and the ants hanging to it up to the shoulder in one of the large open tins of petrol. But even then the fierce mandibles did not slacken; another peon had to help him squash and detach each separate insect.

Distracted by the episode, some defenders had turned away from the ditch. And now cries of fury, a thudding of spades, and a wild trampling to and fro showed that the ants had made full use of the interval, though luckily only a few had managed to get across. The men set to work again desperately with the barrage of earth and sand. Meanwhile an old Indian, who acted as medicine man to the plantation workers, gave the bitten peon a drink he had prepared some hours before, which, he claimed, possessed the virtue of dissolving and weakening ants' venom.

Leiningen surveyed his position. A dispassionate observer would have estimated the odds against him at a thousand to one. But then such an onlooker would have reckoned only by what he saw — the advance of myriad battalions of ants against the futile efforts of a few defenders — and not by the unseen activity that can go on in a man's brain.

For Leiningen had not erred when he decided he would fight elemental with elemental. The water in the ditch was beginning to rise; the stronger damming of the river was making itself apparent.

Visibly the swiftness and power of the masses of water increased, swirling into quicker and quicker movement its living black surface, dispersing its pattern, carrying away more and more of it on the hastening current.

Victory had been snatched from the very jaws of defeat. With a hysterical shout of joy, the peons feverishly intensified their bombardment of earth clods and sand.

And now the wide cataract down the opposite bank was thinning and ceasing, as if the ants were becoming aware that they could not attain their aim. They were scurrying back up the slope to safety.

All the troops so far hurled into the ditch had been sacrificed in vain. Drowned and floundering insects eddied in thousands along the flow, while Indians running on the bank destroyed every swimmer that reached the side.

Not until the ditch curved toward the east did the scattered ranks assemble again in a coherent mass. And now, exhausted and half-numbed, they were in no condition to ascend the bank. Fusillades of clods drove them round the bend toward the mouth of the ditch and then into the river, wherein they vanished without leaving a trace.

The news ran swiftly along the entire chain of outposts, and soon a long scattered line of laughing men could be seen hastening along the ditch toward the scene of victory.

For once they seemed to have lost all their native reserve, for it was in wild abandon now they celebrated the triumph — as if there were no longer thousands of millions of merciless, cold, and hungry eyes watching them from the opposite bank, watching and waiting.

---

10. **dervish** (dûr'vĭsh): member of a Moslem sect. Some dervishes use whirling movements as part of their religious rituals.

The sun sank behind the rim of the tamarind wood and twilight deepened into night. It was not only hoped but expected that the ants would remain quiet until dawn. But to defeat any forlorn attempt at a crossing, the flow of water through the ditch was powerfully increased by opening the dam still further.

In spite of this impregnable barrier, Leiningen was not yet altogether convinced that the ants would not venture another surprise attack. He ordered his men to camp along the bank overnight. He also detailed parties of them to patrol the ditch in two of his motor cars and ceaselessly to illuminate the surface of the water with headlights and electric torches.

After having taken all the precautions he deemed necessary, the farmer ate his supper with considerable appetite and went to bed. His slumbers were in no wise disturbed by the memory of the waiting, live, twenty square miles.

Dawn found a thoroughly refreshed and active Leiningen riding along the edge of the ditch. The planter saw before him a motionless and unaltered throng of besiegers. He studied the wide belt of water between them and the plantation, and for a moment almost regretted that the fight had ended so soon and so simply. In the comforting, matter-of-fact light of morning, it seemed to him now that the ants hadn't the ghost of a chance to cross the ditch. Even if they plunged headlong into it on all three fronts at once, the force of the now powerful current would inevitably sweep them away. He had got quite a thrill out of the fight — a pity it was already over.

He rode along the eastern and southern sections of the ditch and found everything in order. He reached the western section, opposite the tamarind wood, and here, contrary to the other battle fronts, he found the enemy very busy indeed. The trunks and branches of the trees and the creepers of the lianas,[11] on the far bank of the ditch, fairly swarmed with industrious insects. But instead of eating the leaves there and then, they were merely gnawing through the stalks, so that a thick green shower fell steadily to the ground.

No doubt they were victualing columns sent out to obtain provender[12] for the rest of the army. The discovery did not surprise Leiningen. He did not need to be told that ants are intelligent, that certain species even use others as milch cows, watchdogs, and slaves. He was well aware of their power of adaptation, their sense of discipline, their marvelous talent for organization.

His belief that a foray to supply the army was in progress was strengthened when he saw the leaves that fell to the ground being dragged to the troops waiting outside the wood. Then all at once he realized the aim that rain of green was intended to serve.

Each single leaf, pulled or pushed by dozens of toiling insects, was borne straight to the edge of the ditch. Even as Macbeth watched the approach of Birnam Wood in the hands of his enemies,[13] Leiningen saw the tamarind wood move nearer and nearer in the mandibles of the ants. Unlike the fey Scot, however, he did not lose his nerve; no witches had prophesied his doom, and if they had, he would have slept just as soundly. All the same, he was forced to admit to himself that the situation was now far more ominous than that of the day before.

---

11. **lianas** (lē-ăn′əs): tropical climbing vines that root in the ground.
12. **provender** (prŏv′ən-dər): food.
13. **Macbeth . . . enemies:** a reference to William Shakespeare's play *Macbeth.* Macbeth's enemies disguise themselves with boughs from Birnam Wood and creep up to his castle. From Macbeth's vantage point, it looks as if the forest is moving. This event fulfills a prophecy made by three witches.

He had thought it impossible for the ants to build rafts for themselves—well, here they were, coming in thousands, more than enough to bridge the ditch. Leaves after leaves rustled down the slope into the water, where the current drew them away from the bank and carried them into midstream. And every single leaf carried several ants. This time the farmer did not trust to the alacrity of his messengers. He galloped away, leaning from his saddle and yelling orders as he rushed past outpost after outpost: "Bring petrol pumps to the southwest front! Issue spades to every man along the line facing the wood!" And arrived at the eastern and southern sections, he dispatched every man except the observation posts to the menaced west.

Then, as he rode past the stretch where the ants had failed to cross the day before, he witnessed a brief but impressive scene. Down the slope of the distant hill there came toward him a singular being, writhing rather than running, an animallike blackened statue with a shapeless head and four quivering feet that knuckled under almost ceaselessly. When the creature reached the far bank of the ditch and collapsed opposite Leiningen, he recognized it as a pampas stag, covered over and over with ants.

It had strayed near the zone of the army. As usual, they had attacked its eyes first. Blinded, it had reeled in the madness of hideous torment straight into the ranks of its persecutors, and now the beast swayed to and fro in its death agony.

With a shot from his rifle Leiningen put it out of its misery. Then he pulled out his watch. He hadn't a second to lose, but for life itself he could not have denied his curiosity the satisfaction of knowing how long the ants would take—for personal reasons, so to speak. After six minutes the white polished bones alone remained. That's how he himself would look before you can—Leiningen spat once, and put spurs to his horse.

The sporting zest with which the excitement of the novel contest had inspired him the day before had now vanished; in its place

was a cold and violent purpose. He would send these vermin back to the hell where they belonged, somehow, anyhow. Yes, but how was indeed the question; as things stood at present, it looked as if the devils would raze him and his men from the earth instead. He had underestimated the might of the enemy; he really would have to bestir himself if he hoped to outwit them.

The biggest danger now, he decided, was the point where the western section of the ditch curved southward. And arrived there, he found his worst expectations justified. The very power of the current had huddled the leaves and their crews of ants so close together at the bend that the bridge was almost ready.

True, streams of petrol and clumps of earth still prevented a landing. But the number of floating leaves was increasing ever more swiftly. It could not be long now before a stretch of water a mile in length was decked by a green pontoon over which the ants could rush in millions.

Leiningen galloped to the weir. The damming of the river was controlled by a wheel on its bank. The planter ordered the man at the wheel first to lower the water in the ditch almost to vanishing point, next to wait a moment, then suddenly to let the river in again. This maneuver of lowering and raising the surface, of decreasing then increasing the flow of water through the ditch was to be repeated over and over again until further notice.

This tactic was at first successful. The water in the ditch sank, and with it the film of leaves. The green fleet nearly reached the bed and the troops on the far bank swarmed down the slope to it. Then a violent flow of water at the original depth raced through the ditch, overwhelming leaves and ants, and sweeping them along.

This intermittent rapid flushing prevented just in time the almost completed fording of the ditch. But it also flung here and there squads of the enemy vanguard simultaneously up the inner bank. These seemed to know their duty only too well, and lost no time accomplishing it. The air rang with the curses of bitten Indians. They had removed their shirts and pants to detect the quicker the upward-hastening insects; when they saw one, they crushed it; and fortunately the onslaught as yet was only by skirmishers.

Again and again, the water sank and rose, carrying leaves and drowned ants away with it. It lowered once more nearly to its bed; but this time the exhausted defenders waited in vain for the flush of destruction. Leiningen sensed disaster; something must have gone wrong with the machinery of the dam. Then a sweating peon tore up to him —

"They're over!"

While the besieged were concentrating upon the defense of the stretch opposite the wood, the seemingly unaffected line beyond the wood had become the theater of decisive action. Here the defenders' front was sparse and scattered; everyone who could be spared had hurried away to the south.

Just as the man at the weir had lowered the water almost to the bed of the ditch, the ants on a wide front began another attempt at a direct crossing like that of the preceding day. Into the emptied bed poured an irresistible throng. Rushing across the ditch, they attained the inner bank before the Indians fully grasped the situation. Their frantic screams dumbfounded the man at the weir. Before he could direct the river anew into the safeguarding bed he saw himself surrounded by raging ants. He ran like the others, ran for his life.

When Leiningen heard this, he knew the plantation was doomed. He wasted no time bemoaning the inevitable. For as long as there was the slightest chance of success, he had stood his ground, and now any further resistance was both useless and dangerous. He fired three revolver shots into the air—the prearranged signal for his men to retreat instantly within the "inner moat." Then he rode toward the ranch house.

This was two miles from the point of invasion. There was therefore time enough to prepare the second line of defense against the advent of the ants. Of the three great petrol cisterns near the house, one had already been half emptied by the constant withdrawals needed for the pumps during the fight at the water ditch. The remaining petrol in it was now drawn off through underground pipes into the concrete trench which encircled the ranch house and its outbuildings.

And there, drifting in twos and threes, Leiningen's men reached him. Most of them were obviously trying to preserve an air of calm and indifference, belied, however, by their restless glances and knitted brows. One could see their belief in a favorable outcome of the struggle was already considerably shaken.

The planter called his peons around him.

"Well, lads," he began, "we've lost the first round. But we'll smash the beggars yet, don't you worry. Anyone who thinks otherwise can draw his pay here and now and push off. There are rafts enough and to spare on the river, and plenty of time still to reach 'em."

Not a man stirred.

Leiningen acknowledged his silent vote of confidence with a laugh that was half a grunt. "That's the stuff, lads. Too bad if you'd missed the rest of the show, eh? Well, the fun won't start till morning. Once these blighters turn tail, there'll be plenty of work for everyone and higher wages all round. And now run along and get something to eat; you've earned it all right."

In the excitement of the fight the greater part of the day had passed without the men once pausing to snatch a bite. Now that the ants were for the time being out of sight, and the "wall of petrol" gave a stronger feeling of security, hungry stomachs began to assert their claims.

The bridges over the concrete ditch were removed. Here and there solitary ants had reached the ditch; they gazed at the petrol meditatively, then scurried back again. Apparently they had little interest at the moment for what lay beyond the evil-reeking barrier, the abundant spoils of the plantation were the main attraction. Soon the trees, shrubs, and beds for miles around were hulled with ants zealously gobbling the yield of long weary months of strenuous toil.

As twilight began to fall, a cordon of ants marched around the petrol trench, but as yet made no move toward its brink. Leiningen posted sentries with headlights and electric torches, then withdrew to his office, and began to reckon up his losses. He estimated these as large, but, in comparison with his bank balance, by no means unbearable. He worked out in some detail a scheme of intense cultivation which would enable him, before very long, to more than compensate himself for the damage now being wrought to his crops. It was with a contented mind that he finally betook himself to bed where he slept deeply until dawn, undisturbed by any thought that next day little more might be left of him than a glistening skeleton.

He rose with the sun and went out on the flat roof of his house. And a scene like one from Dante[14] lay around him; for miles in every direction there was nothing but a black, glittering multitude, a multitude of rested, sated, but nonetheless voracious ants: yes,

---

14. **Dante** (dän'tā): Dante Alighieri (ä'lē-gyä'rē) (1265–1321), author of *The Divine Comedy*. This allusion is to Dante's description of the horrors of the inferno, or hell.

look as far as one might, one could see nothing but that rustling black throng, except in the north, where the great river drew a boundary they could not hope to pass. But even the high stone breakwater, along the bank of the river, which Leiningen had built as a defense against inundations, was, like the paths, the shorn trees and shrubs, the ground itself, black with ants.

So their greed was not glutted in razing that vast plantation? Not by a long chalk; they were all the more eager now on a rich and certain booty—four hundred men, numerous horses, and bursting granaries.

At first it seemed that the petrol trench would serve its purpose. The besiegers sensed the peril of swimming it, and made no move to plunge blindly over its brink. Instead they devised a better maneuver; they began to collect shreds of bark, twigs, and dried leaves and dropped these into the petrol. Everything green, which could have been similarly used, had long since been eaten. After a time, though, a long procession could be seen bringing from the west the tamarind leaves used as rafts the day before.

Since the petrol, unlike the water in the outer ditch, was perfectly still, the refuse stayed where it was thrown. It was several hours before the ants succeeded in covering an appreciable part of the surface. At length, however, they were ready to proceed to a direct attack.

Their storm troops swarmed down the concrete side, scrambled over the supporting surface of twigs and leaves, and impelled these over the few remaining streaks of open petrol until they reached the other side. Then they began to climb up this to make straight for the helpless garrison.

During the entire offensive, the planter sat peacefully, watching them with interest, but not stirring a muscle. Moreover, he had ordered his men not to disturb in any way whatever the advancing horde. So they squatted listlessly along the bank of the ditch and waited for a sign from the boss.

The petrol was now covered with ants. A few had climbed the inner concrete wall and were scurrying toward the defenders.

"Everyone back from the ditch!" roared Leiningen. The men rushed away, without the slightest idea of his plan. He stooped forward and cautiously dropped into the ditch a stone which split the floating carpet and its living freight, to reveal a gleaming patch of petrol. A match spurted, sank down to the oily surface—Leiningen sprang back; in a flash a towering rampart of fire encompassed the garrison.

This spectacular and instant repulse threw the Indians into ecstasy. They applauded, yelled, and stamped. Had it not been for the awe in which they held the boss, they would infallibly have carried him shoulder high.

It was some time before the petrol burned down to the bed of the ditch, and the wall of smoke and flame began to lower. The ants had retreated in a wide circle from the devastation, and innumerable charred fragments along the outer bank showed that the flames had spread from the holocaust in the ditch well into the ranks beyond, where they had wrought havoc far and wide.

Yet the perseverance of the ants was by no means broken; indeed, each setback seemed only to whet it. The concrete cooled, the flicker of the dying flames wavered and vanished, petrol from the second tank poured into the trench—and the ants marched forward anew to the attack.

The foregoing scene repeated itself in every detail, except that on this occasion less time was needed to bridge the ditch, for the petrol was now already filmed by a layer of ash. Once again they withdrew; once again petrol flowed into the ditch. Would the creatures never learn that their self-sacrifice was utterly senseless? It really was senseless, wasn't it? Yes, of course it was senseless—provided the defenders had an *unlimited* supply of petrol.

When Leiningen reached this stage of reasoning, he felt for the first time since the arrival of the ants that his confidence was deserting him. His skin began to creep; he loosened his collar. Once the devils were over the trench, there wasn't a chance for him and his men. What a prospect, to be eaten alive like that!

For the third time the flames immolated the attacking troops, and burned down to extinction. Yet the ants were coming on again as if nothing had happened. And meanwhile Leiningen had made a discovery that chilled him to the bone—petrol was no longer flowing into the ditch. Something must be blocking the outflow pipe of the third and last cistern—a snake or a dead rat? Whatever it was, the ants could be held off no longer, unless petrol could by some method be led from the cistern into the ditch.

Then Leiningen remembered that in an outhouse nearby were two old disused fire engines. The peons dragged them out of the shed, connected their pumps to the cistern, uncoiled and laid the hose. They were just in time to aim a stream of petrol at a column of ants that had already crossed and drive them back down the incline into the ditch. Once more an oily girdle surrounded the garrison, once more it was possible to hold the position —for the moment.

It was obvious, however, that this last resource meant only the postponement of defeat and death. A few of the peons fell on their knees and began to pray; others, shrieking insanely, fired their revolvers at the black, advancing masses, as if they felt their despair

was pitiful enough to sway fate itself to mercy.

At length, two of the men's nerves broke: Leiningen saw a naked Indian leap over the north side of the petrol trench, quickly followed by a second. They sprinted with incredible speed toward the river. But their fleetness did not save them; long before they could attain the rafts, the enemy covered their bodies from head to foot.

In the agony of their torment, both sprang blindly into the wide river, where enemies no less sinister awaited them. Wild screams of mortal anguish informed the breathless onlookers that crocodiles and sword-tooth piranhas[15] were no less ravenous than ants, and even nimbler in reaching their prey.

In spite of this bloody warning, more and more men showed they were making up their minds to run the blockade. Anything, even a fight midstream against alligators, seemed better than powerlessly waiting for death to come and slowly consume their living bodies.

Leiningen flogged his brain till it reeled. Was there nothing on earth could sweep this devils' spawn back into the hell from which it came?

Then out of the inferno of his bewilderment rose a terrifying inspiration. Yes, one hope remained, and one alone. It might be possible to dam the great river completely, so that its waters would fill not only the water ditch but overflow into the entire gigantic "saucer" of land in which lay the plantation.

The far bank of the river was too high for the waters to escape that way. The stone breakwater ran between the river and the plantation; its only gaps occurred where the "horseshoe" ends of the water ditch passed

---

15. **piranhas** (pĭ-rän′yəz): meat-eating South American fish. A school of piranhas can devour a human or an animal in a matter of minutes.

into the river. So its waters would not only be forced to inundate into the plantation, they would also be held there by the breakwater until they rose to its own high level. In half an hour, perhaps even earlier, the plantation and its hostile army of occupation would be flooded.

The ranch house and outbuildings stood upon rising ground. The foundations were higher than the breakwater, so the flood would not reach them. And any remaining ants trying to ascend the slope could be repulsed by petrol.

It was possible — yes, if one could only get to the dam! A distance of nearly two miles lay between the ranch house and the weir — two miles of ants. Those two peons had managed only a fifth of that distance at the cost of their lives. Was there an Indian daring enough after that to run the gauntlet five times as far? Hardly likely; and if there were, his prospect of getting back was almost nil.

No, there was only one thing for it, he'd have to make the attempt himself; he might just as well be running as sitting still, anyway, when the ants finally got him. Besides, there was a bit of a chance. Perhaps the ants weren't so almighty, after all; perhaps he had allowed the mass suggestion of that evil black throng to hypnotize him, just as a snake fascinates and overpowers.

The ants were building their bridges. Leiningen got up on a chair. "Hey, lads, listen to me!" he cried. Slowly and listlessly, from all sides of the trench, the men began to shuffle toward him, the apathy of death already stamped on their faces.

"Listen, lads!" he shouted. "You're frightened of those beggars, but I'm proud of you. There's still a chance to save our lives — by flooding the plantation from the river. Now one of you might manage to get as far as the weir — but he'd never come back. Well, I'm not going to let you try it; if I did, I'd be worse than one of those ants. No. I called the tune, and now I'm going to pay the piper.

"The moment I'm over the ditch, set fire to the petrol. That'll allow time for the flood to do the trick. Then all you have to do is to wait here all snug and quiet till I'm back. Yes, I'm coming back, trust me" — he grinned — "when I've finished my slimming cure."

He pulled on high leather boots, drew heavy gauntlets over his hands, and stuffed the spaces between breeches and boots, gauntlets and arms, shirt and neck, with rags soaked in petrol. With close-fitting mosquito goggles he shielded his eyes, knowing too well the ants' dodge of first robbing their victims of sight. Finally, he plugged his nostrils and ears with cotton wool, and let the peons drench his clothes with petrol.

He was about to set off, when the old Indian medicine man came up to him; he had a wondrous salve, he said, prepared from a species of chafer whose odor was intolerable to ants. Yes, this odor protected these chafers from the attacks of even the most murderous ants. The Indian smeared the boss's boots, his gauntlets, and his face over and over with the extract.

Leiningen then remembered the paralyzing effect of ants' venom, and the Indian gave him a gourd full of the medicine he had administered to the bitten peon at the water ditch. The planter drank it down without noticing its bitter taste; his mind was already at the weir.

He started off toward the northwest corner of the trench. With a bound he was over — and among the ants.

The beleaguered garrison had no opportunity to watch Leiningen's race against death. The ants were climbing the inner bank again — the lurid ring of petrol blazed aloft. For the fourth time that day the reflection from the

fire shone on the sweating faces of the imprisoned men, and on the reddish-black cuirasses[16] of their oppressors. The red and blue, dark-edged flames leaped vividly now, celebrating what? The funeral pyre of the four hundred, or of the hosts of destruction?

Leiningen ran. He ran in long equal strides, with only one thought, one sensation, in his being—he *must* get through. He dodged all trees and shrubs; except for the split seconds his soles touched the ground, the ants should have no opportunity to alight on him. That they would get to him soon, despite the salve on his boots, the petrol in his clothes, he realized only too well, but he knew even more surely that he must, and that he would, get to the weir.

Apparently the salve was some use after all; not until he had reached halfway did he feel ants under his clothes, and a few on his face. Mechanically, in his stride, he struck at them, scarcely conscious of their bites. He saw he was drawing appreciably near the weir—the distance grew less and less—sank to five hundred—three—two—one hundred yards.

Then he was at the weir and gripping the ant-hulled wheel. Hardly had he seized it when a horde of infuriated ants flowed over his hands, arms, and shoulders. He started the wheel—before it turned once on its axis the swarm covered his face. Leiningen strained like a madman, his lips pressed tight; if he opened them to draw breath. . . .

He turned and turned; slowly the dam lowered until it reached the bed of the river. Already the water was overflowing the ditch. Another minute, and the river was pouring through the nearby gap in the breakwater. The flooding of the plantation had begun.

---

16. **cuirasses** (kwĭ-răs'əs): originally, close-fitting armor for the back and chest; here, bony plates protecting the bodies of the ants.

Leiningen let go the wheel. Now, for the first time, he realized he was coated from head to foot with a layer of ants. In spite of the petrol, his clothes were full of them, several had got to his body or were clinging to his face. Now that he had completed his task, he felt the smart raging over his flesh from the bites of sawing and piercing insects.

Frantic with pain, he almost plunged into the river. To be ripped and slashed to shreds by piranhas? Already he was running the return journey, knocking ants from his gloves and jacket, brushing them from his bloodied face, squashing them to death under his clothes.

One of the creatures bit him just below the rim of his goggles; he managed to tear it away, but the agony of the bite and its etching acid drilled into the eye nerves; he saw now through circles of fire into a milky mist, then he ran for a time almost blinded, knowing that if he once tripped and fell. . . . The old Indian's brew didn't seem much good; it weakened the poison a bit, but didn't get rid of it. His heart pounded as if it would burst; blood roared in his ears; a giant's fist battered his lungs.

Then he could see again, but the burning girdle of petrol appeared infinitely far away; he could not last half that distance. Swift-changing pictures flashed through his head, episodes in his life, while in another part of his brain a cool and impartial onlooker informed this ant-blurred, gasping, exhausted bundle named Leiningen that such a rushing panorama of scenes from one's past is seen only in the moment before death.

A stone in the path . . . too weak to avoid it . . . the planter stumbled and collapsed. He tried to rise . . . he must be pinned under a rock. . . . It was impossible . . . the slightest movement was impossible. . . .

Then all at once he saw, starkly clear and

huge, and, right before his eyes, furred with ants, towering and swaying in its death agony, the pampas stag. In six minutes—gnawed to the bones. He *couldn't* die like that! And something outside him seemed to drag him to his feet. He tottered. He began to stagger forward again.

Through the blazing ring hurtled an apparition which, as soon as it reached the ground on the inner side, fell full length and did not move. Leiningen, at the moment he made that leap through the flames, lost consciousness for the first time in his life. As he lay there, with glazing eyes and lacerated face, he appeared a man returned from the grave. The peons rushed to him, stripped off his clothes, tore away the ants from a body that seemed almost one open wound; in some places the bones were showing. They carried him into the ranch house.

As the curtain of flames lowered, one could see in place of the illimitable host of ants an extensive vista of water. The thwarted river had swept over the plantation, carrying with it the entire army. The water had collected and mounted in the great "saucer," while the ants had in vain attempted to reach the hill on which stood the ranch house. The girdle of flames held them back.

And so imprisoned between water and fire, they had been delivered into the annihilation that was their god. And near the farther mouth of the water ditch, where the stone mole had its second gap, the ocean swept the lost battalions into the river, to vanish forever.

The ring of fire dwindled as the water mounted to the petrol trench and quenched the dimming flames. The inundation rose higher and higher: because its outflow was impeded by the timber and underbrush it had carried along with it, its surface required some time to reach the top of the high stone breakwater and discharge over it the rest of the shattered army.

It swelled over ant-stippled shrubs and bushes, until it washed against the foot of the knoll whereon the besieged had taken refuge. For a while an alluvial[17] of ants tried again and again to attain this dry land, only to be repulsed by streams of petrol back into the merciless flood.

Leiningen lay on his bed, his body swathed from head to foot in bandages. With fomentations[18] and salves, they had managed to stop the bleeding, and had dressed his many wounds. Now they thronged around him, one question in every face. Would he recover? "He won't die," said the old man who had bandaged him, "if he doesn't want to."

The planter opened his eyes. "Everything in order?" he asked.

"They're gone," said his nurse. "To hell." He held out to his master a gourd full of a powerful sleeping draught. Leiningen gulped it down.

"I told you I'd come back," he murmured, "even if I am a bit streamlined." He grinned and shut his eyes. He slept.

---

17. **alluvial** (ə-lōō′vē-əl): deposit left by a flood.
18. **fomentations** (fō′mən-tā′shəns): lotions or warm compresses.

FOR STUDY AND DISCUSSION

1. This story is narrated as a series of major battles between an army of ants and a group of beleaguered humans. Describe each battle. How are the invaders finally defeated?

2. Find some of the words and phrases in the story that characterize the ants as "demons." How does this characterization affect your feelings as you read the story? Does the author ever lead you to feel sympathy or admiration for the ants? Explain.

3. After the first day, Leiningen "almost regretted that the fight had ended so soon and so simply.... He had got quite a thrill out of the fight—a pity it was already over." When does Leiningen first lose this feeling of superiority? When does he realize that the ants may indeed succeed?

4. At the beginning of the story, Leiningen's lifelong motto is quoted. What is this motto? Do the events of this story support the motto, or do they reveal that it is not necessarily true? Explain.

CONFLICT, CLIMAX, RESOLUTION

In most short stories, the main character undergoes a *conflict,* or a struggle of some kind. The conflict may be internal or external. An external conflict may involve the main character in a struggle against another character or against a force of nature. An internal conflict may take the form of a mental struggle, in which the main character tries to make a difficult decision or overcome a fear.

The nature of Leiningen's external conflict is clear from the title: "Leiningen Versus the Ants." At what point in the story does Leiningen also wage a mental battle?

The point at which the outcome of the conflict is decided is called the *climax.* The climax is usually the most exciting and tense part of the story. When does the climax occur in "Leiningen Versus the Ants"?

A story ordinarily ends when its main conflict is *resolved*—that is, when one side or the other finally triumphs. When are the conflicts of this story resolved? Would you describe this resolution as satisfying, or would you describe its effect in some other way?

How would you evaluate the resolution of this plot—is it believable? Explain.

FOR COMPOSITION

Responding to a Story

In a brief essay, discuss your response to this story. Tell first if the story held your interest, and if so, why. Then tell if you believe the ending was logical—did it seem believable or did it seem contrived? Tell what you thought of the character Leiningen. Did you find him admirable, or not? Finally, tell whether you enjoyed the story. Give reasons for your response.

Contents of the Dead Man's Pockets

Jack Finney

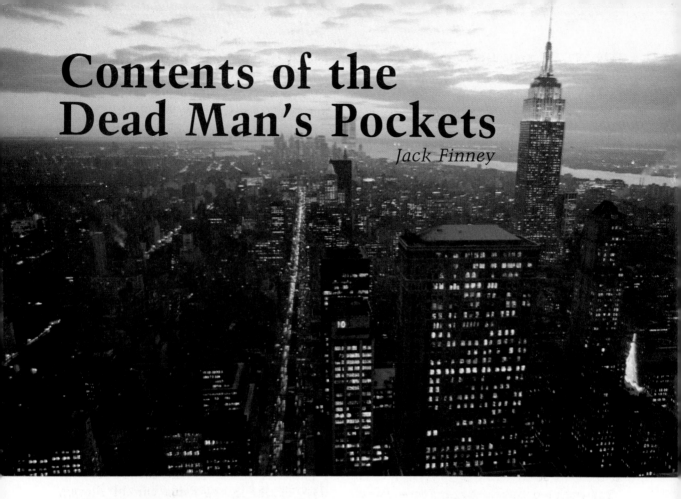

At the little living-room desk Tom Benecke rolled two sheets of flimsy[1] and a heavier top sheet, carbon paper sandwiched between them, into his portable. *Interoffice Memo*, the top sheet was headed, and he typed tomorrow's date just below this; then he glanced at a creased yellow sheet, covered with his own handwriting, beside the typewriter. "Hot in here," he muttered to himself. Then, from the short hallway at his back, he heard the muffled clang of wire coat hangers in the bedroom closet, and at this reminder of what his wife was doing he thought: Hot, no—guilty conscience.

He got up, shoving his hands into the back pockets of his gray wash slacks, stepped to the living-room window beside the desk, and stood breathing on the glass, watching the expanding circlet of mist, staring down through the autumn night at Lexington Avenue,[2] eleven stories below. He was a tall, lean, dark-haired young man in a pullover sweater, who looked as though he had played not football, probably, but basketball in college. Now he placed the heels of his hands against the top edge of the lower window frame and shoved upward. But as usual the window didn't budge, and he had to lower his hands and then

---

1. **flimsy:** thin paper used for typing carbon copies.

2. **Lexington Avenue:** one of the main streets in New York City.

shoot them hard upward to jolt the window open a few inches. He dusted his hands, muttering.

But still he didn't begin his work. He crossed the room to the hallway entrance and, leaning against the doorjamb, hands shoved into his back pockets again, he called, "Clare?" When his wife answered, he said, "Sure you don't mind going alone?"

"No." Her voice was muffled, and he knew her head and shoulders were in the bedroom closet. Then the tap of her high heels sounded on the wood floor and she appeared at the end of the little hallway, wearing a slip, both hands raised to one ear, clipping on an earring. She smiled at him — a slender, very pretty girl with light brown, almost blonde, hair — her prettiness emphasized by the pleasant nature that showed in her face. "It's just that I hate you to miss this movie; you wanted to see it too."

"Yeah, I know." He ran his fingers through his hair. "Got to get this done though."

She nodded, accepting this. Then, glancing at the desk across the living room, she said, "You work too much, though, Tom — and too hard."

He smiled. "You won't mind though, will you, when the money comes rolling in and I'm known as the Boy Wizard of Wholesale Groceries?"

"I guess not." She smiled and turned back toward the bedroom.

At his desk again, Tom lighted a cigarette; then a few moments later as Clare appeared, dressed and ready to leave, he set it on the rim of the ashtray. "Just after seven," she said. "I can make the beginning of the first feature."

He walked to the front-door closet to help her on with her coat. He kissed her then and, for an instant, holding her close, smelling the perfume she had used, he was tempted to go with her; it was not actually true that he had

to work tonight, though he very much wanted to. This was his own project, unannounced as yet in his office, and it could be postponed. But then they won't see it till Monday, he thought once again, and if I give it to the boss tomorrow he might read it over the weekend. . . . "Have a good time," he said aloud. He gave his wife a little swat and opened the door for her, feeling the air from the building hallway, smelling faintly of floor wax, stream past his face.

He watched her walk down the hall, flicked a hand in response as she waved, and then he started to close the door, but it resisted for a moment. As the door opening narrowed, the current of warm air from the hallway, channeled through this smaller opening now, suddenly rushed past him with accelerated force. Behind him he heard the slap of the window curtains against the wall and the sound of paper fluttering from his desk, and he had to push to close the door.

Turning, he saw a sheet of white paper drifting to the floor in a series of arcs, and another sheet, yellow, moving toward the window, caught in the dying current flowing through the narrow opening. As he watched, the paper struck the bottom edge of the window and hung there for an instant, plastered against the glass and wood. Then as the moving air stilled completely, the curtains swinging back from the wall to hang free again, he saw the yellow sheet drop to the window ledge and slide over out of sight.

He ran across the room, grasped the bottom edge of the window, and tugged, staring through the glass. He saw the yellow sheet, dimly now in the darkness outside, lying on the ornamental ledge a yard below the window. Even as he watched, it was moving, scraping slowly along the ledge, pushed by the breeze that pressed steadily against the building wall. He heaved on the window with all his strength and it shot open with a bang, the window weight rattling in the casing. But the paper was past his reach and, leaning out into the night, he watched it scud steadily along the ledge to the south, half-plastered against the building wall. Above the muffled sound of the street traffic far below, he could hear the dry scrape of its movement, like a leaf on the pavement.

The living room of the next apartment to the south projected a yard or more farther out toward the street than this one; because of this the Beneckes paid seven and a half dollars less rent than their neighbors. And now the yellow sheet, sliding along the stone ledge, nearly invisible in the night, was stopped by the projecting blank wall of the next apartment. It lay motionless, then, in the corner formed by the two walls—a good five yards away, pressed firmly against the ornate corner ornament of the ledge by the breeze that moved past Tom Benecke's face.

He knelt at the window and stared at the yellow paper for a full minute or more, waiting for it to move, to slide off the ledge and fall, hoping he could follow its course to the street, and then hurry down in the elevator and retrieve it. But it didn't move, and then he saw that the paper was caught firmly between a projection of the convoluted corner ornament and the ledge. He thought about the poker from the fireplace, then the broom, then the mop—discarding each thought as it occurred to him. There was nothing in the apartment long enough to reach that paper.

It was hard for him to understand that he actually had to abandon it—it was ridiculous—and he began to curse. Of all the papers on his desk, why did it have to be this one in particular! On four long Saturday afternoons he had stood in supermarkets counting the people who passed certain displays, and the results were scribbled on that yellow sheet.

From stacks of trade publications, gone over page by page in snatched half-hours at work and during evenings at home, he had copied facts, quotations, and figures onto that sheet. And he had carried it with him to the Public Library on Fifth Avenue, where he'd spent a dozen lunch hours and early evenings adding more. All were needed to support and lend authority to his idea for a new grocery-store display method; without them his idea was a mere opinion. And there they all lay in his own improvised shorthand—countless hours of work—out there on the ledge.

For many seconds he believed he was going to abandon the yellow sheet, that there was nothing else to do. The work could be duplicated. But it would take two months, and the time to present this idea was *now*, for use in the spring displays. He struck his fist on the window ledge. Then he shrugged. Even though his plan were adopted, he told himself, it wouldn't bring him a raise in pay—not immediately, anyway, or as a direct result. It won't bring me a promotion either, he argued —not of itself.

But just the same, and he couldn't escape the thought, this and other independent projects, some already done and others planned for the future, would gradually mark him out from the score of other young men in his company. They were the way to change from a name on the payroll to a name in the minds of the company officials. They were the beginning of the long, long climb to where he was determined to be, at the very top. And he knew he was going out there in the darkness, after the yellow sheet fifteen feet beyond his reach.

By a kind of instinct, he instantly began making his intention acceptable to himself by laughing at it. The mental picture of himself sidling along the ledge outside was absurd—it was actually comical—and he smiled. He imagined himself describing it; it would make a good story at the office and, it occurred to him, would add a special interest and importance to his memorandum, which would do it no harm at all.

To simply go out and get his paper was an easy task—he could be back here with it in less than two minutes—and he knew he wasn't deceiving himself. The ledge, he saw, measuring it with his eye, was about as wide as the length of his shoe, and perfectly flat. And every fifth row of brick in the face of the building, he remembered—leaning out, he verified this—was indented half an inch, enough for the tips of his fingers, enough to maintain balance easily. It occurred to him that if this ledge and wall were only a yard above ground—as he knelt at the window staring out, this thought was the final confirmation of his intention—he could move along the ledge indefinitely.

On a sudden impulse, he got to his feet, walked to the front closet, and took out an old tweed jacket; it would be cold outside. He put it on and buttoned it as he crossed the room rapidly toward the open window. In the back of his mind he knew he'd better hurry and get this over with before he thought too much, and at the window he didn't allow himself to hesitate.

He swung a leg over the sill, then felt for and found the ledge a yard below the window with his foot. Gripping the bottom of the window frame very tightly and carefully, he slowly ducked his head under it, feeling on his face the sudden change from the warm air of the room to the chill outside. With infinite care he brought out his other leg, his mind concentrating on what he was doing. Then he slowly stood erect. Most of the putty, dried out and brittle, had dropped off the bottom edging of the window frame, he found, and the flat wooden edging provided a good gripping surface, a half-inch or more deep, for the tips of his fingers.

Now, balanced easily and firmly, he stood on the ledge outside in the slight, chill breeze, eleven stories above the street, staring into his own lighted apartment, odd and different-seeming now.

First his right hand, then his left, he carefully shifted his fingertip grip from the puttyless window edging to an indented row of bricks directly to his right. It was hard to take the first shuffling sideways step then—to make himself move—and the fear stirred in his stomach, but he did it, again by not allowing himself time to think. And now—with his chest, stomach, and the left side of his face pressed against the rough cold brick—his lighted apartment was suddenly gone, and it was much darker out here than he had thought.

Without pause he continued—right foot, left foot, right foot, left—his shoe soles shuffling and scraping along the rough stone, never lifting from it, fingers sliding along the exposed edging of brick. He moved on the balls of his feet, heels lifted slightly; the ledge was not quite as wide as he'd expected. But leaning slightly inward toward the face of the building and pressed against it, he could feel his balance firm and secure, and moving along the ledge was quite as easy as he had thought it would be. He could hear the buttons of his jacket scraping steadily along the rough bricks and feel them catch momentarily, tugging a little, at each mortared crack. He simply did not permit himself to look down, though the compulsion to do so never left him; nor did he allow himself actually to think. Mechanically—right foot, left foot, over and again—he shuffled along crabwise, watching the projecting wall ahead loom steadily closer. . . .

Then he reached it and, at the corner—he'd

decided how he was going to pick up the paper —he lifted his right foot and placed it carefully on the ledge that ran along the projecting wall at a right angle to the ledge on which his other foot rested. And now, facing the building, he stood in the corner formed by the two walls, one foot on the ledging of each, a hand on the shoulder-high indentation of each wall. His forehead was pressed directly into the corner against the cold bricks, and now he carefully lowered first one hand, then the other, perhaps a foot farther down, to the next indentation in the rows of bricks.

Very slowly, sliding his forehead down the trough of the brick corner and bending his knees, he lowered his body toward the paper lying between his outstretched feet. Again he lowered his fingerholds another foot and bent his knees still more, thigh muscles taut, his forehead sliding and bumping down the brick V. Half squatting now, he dropped his left hand to the next indentation and then slowly reached with his right hand toward the paper between his feet.

He couldn't quite touch it, and his knees now were pressed against the wall; he could bend them no farther. But by ducking his head another inch lower, the top of his head now pressed against the bricks, he lowered his right shoulder and his fingers had the paper by a corner, pulling it loose. At the same instant he saw, between his legs and far below, Lexington Avenue stretched out for miles ahead.

He saw, in that instant, the Loew's theater sign, blocks ahead past Fiftieth Street; the miles of traffic signals, all green now; the lights of cars and street lamps; countless neon signs; and the moving black dots of people. And a violent instantaneous explosion of absolute terror roared through him. For a motionless instant he saw himself externally— bent practically double, balanced on this narrow ledge, nearly half his body projecting out above the street far below—and he began to tremble violently, panic flaring through his mind and muscles, and he felt the blood rush from the surface of his skin.

In the fractional moment before horror paralyzed him, as he stared between his legs at that terrible length of street far beneath him, a fragment of his mind raised his body in a spasmodic jerk to an upright position again, but so violently that his head scraped hard against the wall, bouncing off it, and his body swayed outward to the knife edge of balance, and he very nearly plunged backward and fell. Then he was leaning far into the corner again, squeezing and pushing into it, not only his face but his chest and stomach, his back arching; and his fingertips clung with all the pressure of his pulling arms to the shoulder-high half-inch indentation in the bricks.

He was more than trembling now; his whole body was racked with a violent shuddering beyond control, his eyes squeezed so tightly shut it was painful, though he was past awareness of that. His teeth were exposed in a frozen grimace, the strength draining like water from his knees and calves. It was extremely likely, he knew, that he would faint, slump down along the wall, his face scraping, and then drop backward, a limp weight, out into nothing. And to save his life he concentrated on holding on to consciousness, drawing deliberate deep breaths of cold air into his lungs, fighting to keep his senses aware.

Then he knew that he would not faint, but he could not stop shaking nor open his eyes. He stood where he was, breathing deeply, trying to hold back the terror of the glimpse he had had of what lay below him; and he knew he had made a mistake in not making himself stare down at the street, getting used to it and accepting it, when he had first stepped out onto the ledge.

It was impossible to walk back. He simply could not do it. He couldn't bring himself to make the slightest movement. The strength was gone from his legs; his shivering hands— numb, cold, and desperately rigid—had lost all deftness; his easy ability to move and balance was gone. Within a step or two, if he tried to move, he knew that he would stumble and fall.

Seconds passed, with the chill faint wind pressing the side of his face, and he could hear the toned-down volume of the street traffic far beneath him. Again and again it slowed and then stopped, almost to silence; then presently, even this high, he would hear the click of the traffic signals and the subdued roar of the cars starting up again. During a lull

in the street sounds, he called out. Then he was shouting "*Help!*" so loudly it rasped his throat. But he felt the steady pressure of the wind, moving between his face and the blank wall, snatch up his cries as he uttered them, and he knew they must sound directionless and distant. And he remembered how habitually, here in New York, he himself heard and ignored shouts in the night. If anyone heard him, there was no sign of it, and presently Tom Benecke knew he had to try moving; there was nothing else he could do.

Eyes squeezed shut, he watched scenes in his mind like scraps of motion-picture film— he could not stop them. He saw himself stumbling suddenly sideways as he crept along the ledge and saw his upper body arc outward, arms flailing. He saw a dangling shoestring caught between the ledge and the sole of his other shoe, saw a foot start to move, to be stopped with a jerk, and felt his balance leaving him. He saw himself falling with a terrible speed as his body revolved in the air, knees clutched tight to his chest, eyes squeezed shut, moaning softly.

Out of utter necessity, knowing that any of these thoughts might be reality in the very next seconds, he was slowly able to shut his mind against every thought but what he now began to do. With fear-soaked slowness, he slid his left foot an inch or two toward his own impossibly distant window. Then he slid the fingers of his shivering left hand a corresponding distance. For a moment he could not bring himself to lift his right foot from one ledge to the other; then he did it, and became aware of the harsh exhalation of air from his throat and realized that he was panting. As his right hand, then, began to slide along the brick edging, he was astonished to feel the yellow paper pressed to the bricks underneath his stiff fingers, and he uttered a terrible, abrupt bark that might have been a laugh or a moan. He opened his mouth and took the paper in his teeth, pulling it out from under his fingers.

By a kind of trick — by concentrating his entire mind on first his left foot, then his left hand, then the other foot, then the other hand — he was able to move, almost imperceptibly, trembling steadily, very nearly without thought. But he could feel the terrible strength of the pent-up horror on just the other side of the flimsy barrier he had erected in his mind; and he knew that if it broke through he would lose this thin artificial control of his body.

During one slow step he tried keeping his eyes closed; it made him feel safer, shutting him off a little from the fearful reality of where he was. Then a sudden rush of giddiness swept over him and he had to open his eyes wide, staring sideways at the cold rough brick and angled lines of mortar, his cheek tight against the building. He kept his eyes open then, knowing that if he once let them flick outward, to stare for an instant at the lighted windows across the street, he would be past help.

He didn't know how many dozens of tiny sidling steps he had taken, his chest, belly, and face pressed to the wall; but he knew the slender hold he was keeping on his mind and body was going to break. He had a sudden mental picture of his apartment on just the other side of this wall — warm, cheerful, incredibly spacious. And he saw himself striding through it, lying down on the floor on his back, arms spread wide, reveling in its unbelievable security. The impossible remoteness of this utter safety, the contrast between it and where he now stood, was more than he could bear. And the barrier broke then, and the fear of the awful height he stood on coursed through his nerves and muscles.

A fraction of his mind knew he was going to fall, and he began taking rapid blind steps with no feeling of what he was doing, sidling with a clumsy desperate swiftness, fingers scrabbling along the brick, almost hopelessly resigned to the sudden backward pull and swift motion outward and down. Then his moving left hand slid onto not brick but sheer emptiness, an impossible gap in the face of the wall, and he stumbled.

His right foot smashed into his left anklebone; he staggered sideways, began falling, and the claw of his hand cracked against glass and wood, slid down it, and his fingertips were pressed hard on the puttyless edging of his window. His right hand smacked gropingly beside it as he fell to his knees; and, under the full weight and direct downward pull of his sagging body, the open window dropped shudderingly in its frame till it closed and his wrists struck the sill and were jarred off.

For a single moment he knelt, knee bones against stone on the very edge of the ledge, body swaying and touching nowhere else, fighting for balance. Then he lost it, his shoulders plunging backward, and he flung his arms forward, his hands smashing against the window casing on either side; and — his body moving backward — his fingers clutched the narrow wood stripping of the upper pane.

For an instant he hung suspended between balance and falling, his fingertips pressed onto the quarter-inch wood strips. Then, with utmost delicacy, with a focused concentration of all his senses, he increased even further the strain on his fingertips hooked to these slim edgings of wood. Elbows slowly bending, he began to draw the full weight of his upper body forward, knowing that the instant his fingers slipped off these quarter-inch strips he'd plunge backward and be falling. Elbows imperceptibly bending, body shaking with the strain, the sweat starting from his forehead in great sudden drops, he pulled, his entire being and thought concentrated in his fingertips. Then suddenly, the strain slackened and ended, his chest touching the windowsill, and he was kneeling on the ledge, his forehead pressed to the glass of the closed window.

Dropping his palms to the sill, he stared into his living room — at the red-brown davenport across the room, and a magazine he had left there; at the pictures on the walls and the gray rug; the entrance to the hallway; and at his papers, typewriter, and desk, not two feet from his nose. A movement from his desk caught his eye and he saw that it was a thin curl of blue smoke; his cigarette, the ash long, was still burning in the ashtray where he'd left it — this was past all belief — only a few minutes before.

His head moved, and in faint reflection from the glass before him he saw the yellow paper clenched in his front teeth. Lifting a hand from the sill he took it from his mouth; the moistened corner parted from the paper, and he spat it out.

For a moment, in the light from the living room, he stared wonderingly at the yellow sheet in his hand and then crushed it into the side pocket of his jacket.

He couldn't open the window. It had been pulled not completely closed, but its lower edge was below the level of the outside sill; there was no room to get his fingers underneath it. Between the upper sash and the lower was a gap not wide enough — reaching up, he tried — to get his fingers into; he couldn't push it open. The upper window panel, he knew from long experience, was impossible to move, frozen tight with dried paint.

Very carefully observing his balance, the fingertips of his left hand again hooked to the narrow stripping of the window casing, he drew back his right hand, palm facing the glass, and then struck the glass with the heel of his hand.

His arm rebounded from the pane, his body tottering. He knew he didn't dare strike a harder blow.

But in the security and relief of his new position, he simply smiled; with only a sheet of glass between him and the room just before him, it was not possible that there wasn't a way past it. Eyes narrowing, he thought for a few moments about what to do. Then his eyes widened, for nothing occurred to him. But still he felt calm: the trembling, he realized, had stopped. At the back of his mind there still lay the thought that once he was again in his home, he could give release to his feelings. He actually *would* lie on the floor, rolling, clenching tufts of the rug in his hands. He would literally run across the room, free to move as he liked, jumping on the floor, testing and reveling in its absolute security, letting the relief flood through him, draining the fear from his mind and body. His yearning for this was astonishingly intense, and somehow he understood that he had better keep this feeling at bay.

He took a half-dollar from his pocket and struck it against the pane, but without any hope that the glass would break and with very little disappointment when it did not. After a few moments of thought he drew his leg onto the ledge and picked loose the knot of his shoelace. He slipped off the shoe and, holding it across the instep, drew back his arm as far as he dared and struck the leather heel against the glass. The pane rattled, but he knew he'd been a long way from breaking it. His foot was cold and he slipped the shoe back on. He shouted again, experimentally, and then once more, but there was no answer.

The realization suddenly struck him that he might have to wait here till Clare came home, and for a moment the thought was funny. He could see Clare opening the front door, withdrawing her key from the lock, closing the door behind her, and then glancing up to see him crouched on the other side of the window. He could see her rush across the room, face astounded and frightened, and hear himself shouting instructions: "Never mind how I got here! Just open the wind——" She couldn't open it, he remembered, she'd never been able to; she'd always had to call him. She'd have to get the building superintendent or a neighbor, and he pictured himself smiling, and answering their questions as he climbed in. "I just wanted to get a breath of fresh air, so——"

He couldn't possibly wait here till Clare came home. It was the second feature she'd wanted to see, and she'd left in time to see the first. She'd be another three hours or—— He glanced at his watch; Clare had been gone eight minutes. It wasn't possible, but only eight minutes ago he had kissed his wife goodbye. She wasn't even at the theater yet!

It would be four hours before she could possibly be home, and he tried to picture himself kneeling out here, fingertips hooked to these narrow strippings, while first one movie, preceded by a slow listing of credits, began, developed, reached its climax, and then finally ended. There'd be a newsreel next, maybe, and then an animated cartoon, and then interminable scenes from coming pictures. And then, once more, the beginning of a full-length picture—while all the time he hung out here in the night.

He might possibly get to his feet, but he was afraid to try. Already his legs were cramped, his thigh muscles tired; his knees hurt, his feet felt numb, and his hands were stiff. He couldn't possibly stay out here for four hours, or anywhere near it. Long before that his legs and arms would give out; he would be forced to try changing his position often—stiffly, clumsily, his coordination and strength gone—and he would fall. Quite realistically, he knew that he would fall; no one could stay out here on this ledge for four hours.

A dozen windows in the apartment building across the street were lighted. Looking over his shoulder, he could see the top of a man's head behind the newspaper he was reading; in another window he saw the blue-gray flicker of a television screen. No more than twenty-odd yards from his back were scores of people, and if just one of them would walk idly to his window and glance out. . . . For some moments he stared over his shoulder at the lighted rectangles, waiting. But no one appeared. The man reading his paper turned a page and then continued his reading. A figure passed another of the windows and was immediately gone.

In the inside pocket of his jacket he found a little sheaf of papers, and he pulled one out and looked at it in the light from the living room. It was an old letter, an advertisement of some sort; his name and address, in purple ink, were on a label pasted to the envelope. Gripping one end of the envelope in his teeth, he twisted it into a tight curl. From his shirt pocket he brought out a book of matches. He didn't dare let go the casing with both hands but, with the twist of paper in his teeth, he opened the matchbook with his free hand; then he bent one of the matches in two without tearing it from the folder, its red-tipped end now touching the striking surface. With his thumb, he rubbed the red tip across the striking area.

He did it again, then again, and still again, pressing harder each time, and the match suddenly flared, burning his thumb. But he kept it alight, cupping the matchbook in his hand and shielding it with his body. He held the flame to the paper in his mouth till it caught.

Then he snuffed out the match flame with his thumb and forefinger, careless of the burn, and replaced the book in his pocket. Taking the paper twist in his hand, he held it flame down, watching the flame crawl up the paper, till it flared bright. Then he held it behind him over the street, moving it from side to side, watching it over his shoulder, the flame flickering and guttering in the wind.

There were three letters in his pocket and he lighted each of them, holding each till the flame touched his hand and then dropping it to the street below. At one point, watching over his shoulder while the last of the letters burned, he saw the man across the street put down his paper and stand—even seeming to glance toward Tom's window. But when he moved, it was only to walk across the room and disappear from sight.

There were a dozen coins in Tom Benecke's pocket and he dropped them, three or four at a time. But if they struck anyone, or if anyone noticed their falling, no one connected them with their source.

His arms had begun to tremble from the steady strain of clinging to this narrow perch, and he did not know what to do now and was terribly frightened. Clinging to the window stripping with one hand, he again searched his pockets. But now—he had left his wallet on the dresser when he'd changed clothes—there was nothing left but the yellow sheet. It occurred to him irrelevantly that his death on the sidewalk below would be an eternal mystery; the window closed—why, how, and from where could he have fallen? No one would be able to identify his body for a time, either—the thought was somehow unbearable and increased his fear. All they'd find in his pockets would be the yellow sheet. *Contents of the dead man's pockets,* he thought, *one sheet of paper bearing penciled notations—incomprehensible.*

He understood fully that he might actually be going to die; his arms, maintaining his balance on the ledge, were trembling steadily now. And it occurred to him then with all the force of a revelation that, if he fell, all he was ever going to have out of life he would then, abruptly, have had. Nothing, then, could ever be changed; and nothing more—no least experience or pleasure—could ever be added to his life. He wished, then, that he had not allowed his wife to go off by herself tonight—and on similar nights. He thought of all the evenings he had spent away from her, working; and he regretted them. He thought wonderingly of his fierce ambition and of the direction his life had taken; he thought of the hours he'd spent by himself, filling the yellow sheet that had brought him out here. *Contents of the dead man's pockets,* he thought with sudden fierce anger, *a wasted life.*

He was simply not going to cling here till he slipped and fell; he told himself that now. There was one last thing he could try; he had been aware of it for some moments, refusing to think about it, but now he faced it. Kneeling here on the ledge, the fingertips of one hand pressed to the narrow strip of wood, he could, he knew, draw his other hand back a yard perhaps, fist clenched tight, doing it very slowly till he sensed the outer limit of balance, then, as hard as he was able from the distance, he could drive his fist forward against the glass. If it broke, his fist smashing through, he was safe; he might cut himself badly, and probably would, but with his arm inside the room, he would be secure. But if the glass did not break, the rebound, flinging his arm back, would topple him off the ledge. He was certain of that.

He tested his plan. The fingers of his left hand clawlike on the little stripping, he drew back his other fist until his body began teetering backward. But he had no leverage now—he could feel that there would be no force to his swing—and he moved his fist slowly forward till he rocked forward on his knees again and could sense that this swing would carry its greatest force. Glancing down, however, measuring the distance from his fist to the glass, he saw it was less than two feet.

It occurred to him that he could raise his arm over his head, to bring it down against the glass. But, experimenting in slow motion, he knew it would be an awkward blow without the force of a driving punch, and not nearly enough to break the glass.

Facing the window, he had to drive a blow from the shoulder, he knew now, at a distance of less than two feet; and he did not know whether it would break through the heavy glass. It might; he could picture it happening, he could feel it in the nerves of his arm. And it might not; he could feel that too—feel his fist striking this glass and being instantaneously flung back by the unbreaking pane, feel the fingers of his other hand breaking loose, nails scraping along the casing as he fell.

He waited, arm drawn back, fist balled, but in no hurry to strike; this pause, he knew, might be an extension of his life. And to live even a few seconds longer, he felt, even out here on this ledge in the night, was infinitely better than to die a moment earlier than he had to. His arm grew tired, and he brought it down.

Then he knew that it was time to make the attempt. He could not kneel here hesitating indefinitely till he lost all courage to act, waiting till he slipped off the ledge. Again he drew back his arm, knowing this time that he would not bring it down till he struck. His elbow protruding over Lexington Avenue far below, the fingers of his other hand pressed down bloodlessly tight against the narrow stripping, he waited, feeling the sick tenseness and terrible excitement building. It grew and swelled toward the moment of action, his nerves tautening. He thought of Clare—just a wordless, yearning thought—and then drew his arm back just a bit more, fist so tight his fingers pained him, and knowing he was going to do it. Then with full power, with every last scrap of strength he could bring to bear, he shot his arm forward toward the glass, and he said, "Clare!"

He heard the sound, felt the blow, felt himself falling forward, and his hand closed on the living-room curtains, the shards and fragments of glass showering onto the floor. And then, kneeling there on the ledge, an arm thrust into the room up to the shoulder, he began picking away the protruding slivers and great wedges of glass from the window frame, tossing them in onto the rug. And, as he grasped the edges of the empty window frame and climbed into his home, he was grinning in triumph.

He did not lie down on the floor or run through the apartment, as he had promised himself; even in the first few moments it seemed to him natural and normal that he should be where he was. He simply turned to his desk, pulled the crumpled yellow sheet from his pocket, and laid it down where it had been, smoothing it out; then he absently laid a pencil across it to weight it down. He shook his head wonderingly, and turned to walk toward the closet.

There he got out his topcoat and hat and, without waiting to put them on, opened the front door and stepped out, to go find his wife. He turned to pull the door closed and the warm air from the hall rushed through the narrow opening again. As he saw the yellow paper, the pencil flying, scooped off the desk and, unimpeded by the glassless window, sail out into the night and out of his life, Tom Benecke burst into laughter and then closed the door behind him.

FOR STUDY AND DISCUSSION

1. The main character of this story, Tom, makes a number of important choices that directly affect the story's plot. What choice has he already made when the story opens? Why does he risk his life to retrieve the paper?

2. The two settings — ledge and apartment — are important in this story. How does the author set up a contrast between them? How does he make you feel about each setting?

3. Describe four crises that hold us in suspense while Tom is on the ledge. Why does the last crisis seem the worst?

4. How does the title of this story help to intensify our feelings of suspense?

5. How do Tom's actions at the end of the story show that the experience has changed him? How would you describe this change?

6. What do you think this story says about work, ambition, and human relationships?

LANGUAGE AND VOCABULARY

Using Context Clues

The words and sentences surrounding a word are called its *context*. At times, you can determine the meaning of an unfamiliar word by looking closely at its context. Use context clues to determine the meanings of the italicized words below. Check your guesses in a dictionary.

The strength was gone from his legs; his shivering hands — numb, cold, and desperately rigid — had lost all *deftness*; his easy ability to move and balance was gone.

. . . he saw the yellow paper, the pencil flying, scooped off the desk and, *unimpeded* by the glassless window, sail out into the night and out of his life . . . .

FOR COMPOSITION

Using Specific Details

Much of the power of this story comes from the detailed narration of what happens during Tom's harrowing experience on the ledge. Look back at the paragraph on page 25 beginning "Seconds passed." Note the details the author provides as he narrates these events. What specific things does Tom do? What does he think? What sensations does he feel?

Write a paragraph narrating what happens to a character in a tight situation. Tell precisely what the character does for a few minutes of time. Include specific details about the person's sensations, actions, and thoughts.

ABOUT THE AUTHOR

Jack Finney (1911–   ) often writes about the strange and bizarre. In one of his stories, "The Love Letter," a young man finds a letter hidden in an old desk and begins a correspondence with a woman who has been dead for many years. In another story called "Of Missing Persons," he imagines that several famous missing persons have left for a utopian world called Verna. Some of Finney's short stories are in his collection called *The Third Level.* Two of his novels, *Five Against the House* and *The Body Snatchers,* have been made into movies. Finney was born in Milwaukee and lived for a time in New York City, where he worked in an advertising agency. He later moved to Mill Valley, California.

The Monkey's Paw
W. W. Jacobs

I

Without, the night was cold and wet, but in the small parlor of Lakesnam Villa the blinds were drawn and the fire burned brightly. Father and son were at chess, the former, who possessed ideas about the game involving radical changes, putting his king into such sharp and unnecessary perils that it even provoked comment from the white-haired old lady knitting placidly by the fire.

"Hark at the wind," said Mr. White, who, having seen a fatal mistake after it was too late, was amiably desirous of preventing his son from seeing it.

"I'm listening," said the latter, grimly surveying the board as he stretched out his hand. "Check."[1]

"I should hardly think that he'd come tonight," said his father, with his hand poised over the board.

"Mate," replied the son.

"That's the worst of living so far out," bawled Mr. White, with sudden and unlooked-for violence; "of all the beastly, slushy, out-of-the-way places to live in, this is the worst. Pathway's a bog, and the road's a torrent. I don't know what people are thinking about. I suppose because only two houses on the road are let, they think it doesn't matter."

"Never mind, dear," said his wife soothingly; "perhaps you'll win the next one."

Mr. White looked up sharply, just in time to intercept a knowing glance between mother and son. The words died away on his lips, and he hid a guilty grin in his thin gray beard.

"There he is," said Herbert White, as the gate banged to loudly and heavy footsteps came toward the door.

The old man rose with hospitable haste, and, opening the door, was heard condoling with the new arrival. The new arrival also condoled with himself, so that Mrs. White said, "Tut, tut!" and coughed gently as her husband entered the room, followed by a tall burly man, beady of eye and rubicund of visage.[2]

"Sergeant Major Morris," he said, introducing him.

The sergeant major shook hands, and, taking the proffered seat by the fire, watched contentedly while his host got out whiskey and tumblers and stood a small copper kettle on the fire.

At the third glass his eyes got brighter, and he began to talk, the little family circle regarding with eager interest this visitor from distant parts, as he squared his broad shoulders in the chair and spoke of strange scenes and doughty deeds, of wars and plagues and strange peoples.

"Twenty-one years of it," said Mr. White, nodding at his wife and son. "When he went away he was a slip of a youth in the warehouse. Now look at him."

---

1. **Check**: in chess, a move directly attacking the king. "Mate" (checkmate) means the end of the game, when the king is unable to move.

2. **rubicund** (rōō′bə-kənd) **of visage** (vĭz′ĭj): red-faced.

"He don't look to have taken much harm," said Mrs. White politely.

"I'd like to go to India myself," said the old man, "just to look around a bit, you know."

"Better where you are," said the sergeant major, shaking his head. He put down the empty glass and, sighing softly, shook it again.

"I should like to see those old temples and fakirs[3] and jugglers," said the old man. "What was that you started telling me the other day about a monkey's paw or something, Morris?"

"Nothing," said the soldier hastily. "Leastways, nothing worth hearing."

"Monkey's paw?" said Mrs. White curiously.

"Well, it's just a bit of what you might call

magic, perhaps," said the sergeant major offhandedly.

His three listeners leaned forward eagerly. The visitor absent-mindedly put his empty glass to his lips and then set it down again. His host filled it for him.

"To look at," said the sergeant major, fumbling in his pocket, "it's just an ordinary little paw, dried to a mummy."

He took something out of his pocket and proffered it. Mrs. White drew back with a grimace, but her son, taking it, examined it curiously.

"And what is there special about it?" inquired Mr. White as he took it from his son and, having examined it, placed it upon the table.

"It had a spell put on it by an old fakir," said the sergeant major, "a very holy man. He

3. **fakirs** (fə-kîrs′): Moslem or Hindu holy men, some of whom claim the ability to perform miracles.

wanted to show that fate ruled people's lives, and that those who interfered with it did so to their sorrow. He put a spell on it so that three separate men could each have three wishes from it."

His manner was so impressive that his hearers were conscious that their light laughter jarred somewhat.

"Well, why don't you have three, sir?" said Herbert White cleverly.

The soldier regarded him in the way that middle age is wont to regard presumptuous youth. "I have," he said quietly, and his blotchy face whitened.

"And did you really have the three wishes granted?" asked Mrs. White.

"I did," said the sergeant major, and his glass tapped against his strong teeth.

"And has anybody else wished?" inquired the old lady.

"The first man had his three wishes, yes," was the reply. "I don't know what the first two were, but the third was for death. That's how I got the paw."

His tones were so grave that a hush fell upon the group.

"If you've had your three wishes, it's no good to you now, then, Morris," said the old man at last. "What do you keep it for?"

The soldier shook his head. "Fancy, I suppose," he said slowly. "I did have some idea of selling it, but I don't think I will. It has caused enough mischief already. Besides, people won't buy. They think it's a fairy tale, some of them, and those who do think anything of it want to try it first and pay me afterward."

"If you could have another three wishes," said the old man, eyeing him keenly, "would you have them?"

"I don't know," said the other. "I don't know."

He took the paw, and dangling it between his front finger and thumb, suddenly threw it upon the fire. White, with a slight cry, stooped down and snatched it off.

"Better let it burn," said the soldier solemnly.

"If you don't want it, Morris," said the old man, "give it to me."

"I won't," said his friend doggedly. "I threw it on the fire. If you keep it, don't blame me for what happens. Pitch it on the fire again, like a sensible man."

The other shook his head and examined his new possession closely. "How do you do it?" he inquired.

"Hold it up in your right hand and wish aloud," said the sergeant major, "but I warn you of the consequences."

"Sounds like the *Arabian Nights*,"[4] said Mrs. White, as she rose and began to set the supper. "Don't you think you might wish for four pairs of hands for me?"

Her husband drew the talisman[5] from his pocket and then all three burst into laughter as the sergeant major, with a look of alarm on his face, caught him by the arm. "If you must wish," he said gruffly, "wish for something sensible."

Mr. White dropped it back into his pocket, and placing chairs, motioned his friend to the table. In the business of supper the talisman was partly forgotten, and afterward the three sat listening in an enthralled fashion to a second installment of the soldier's adventures in India.

"If the tale about the monkey paw is not more truthful than those he has been telling us," said Herbert, as the door closed behind their guest, just in time for him to catch the last train, "we shan't make much out of it."

---

4. *Arabian Nights:* a collection of tales from ancient India, Persia, and Arabia.
5. **talisman** (tăl′ĭs-mən): an object with magic powers, supposed to bring good luck.

"Did you give him anything for it, Father?" inquired Mrs. White, regarding her husband closely.

"A trifle," said he, coloring slightly. "He didn't want it, but I made him take it. And he pressed me again to throw it away."

"Likely," said Herbert, with pretended horror. "Why, we're going to be rich, and famous, and happy. Wish to be an emperor, Father, to begin with: then you can't be bossed around."

He darted round the table, pursued by the maligned Mrs. White armed with an antimacassar.[6]

Mr. White took the paw from his pocket and eyed it dubiously. "I don't know what to wish for, and that's a fact," he said slowly. "It seems to me I've got all I want."

"If you only cleared the house, you'd be quite happy, wouldn't you?" said Herbert, with his hand on his shoulder. "Well, wish for two hundred pounds,[7] then; that'll just do it."

His father, smiling shamefacedly at his own credulity, held up the talisman, as his son, with a solemn face somewhat marred by a wink at his mother, sat down at the piano and struck a few impressive chords.

"I wish for two hundred pounds," said the old man distinctly.

A fine crash from the piano greeted the words, interrupted by a shuddering cry from the old man. His wife and son ran toward him.

"It moved," he cried, with a glance of disgust at the object as it lay on the floor. "As I wished it twisted in my hands like a snake."

"Well, I don't see the money," said his son, as he picked it up and placed it on the table, "and I bet I never shall."

"It must have been your fancy, Father," said his wife, regarding him anxiously.

He shook his head. "Never mind, though; there's no harm done, but it gave me a shock all the same."

They sat down by the fire again while the two men finished their pipes. Outside, the wind was higher than ever, and the old man started nervously at the sound of a door banging upstairs. A silence unusual and depressing settled upon all three, which lasted until the old couple rose to retire for the night.

"I expect you'll find the cash tied up in a big bag in the middle of your bed," said Herbert, as he bade them good night, "and something horrible squatting up on top of the wardrobe watching you as you pocket your ill-gotten gains."

---

6. **antimacassar** (ăn'tĭ-mə-kăs'ər): a small covering to protect the back or arms of a chair.
7. **two hundred pounds:** English money equal to about a thousand dollars at the time of this story.

II

In the brightness of the wintry sun next morning as it streamed over the breakfast table Herbert laughed at his fears. There was an air of prosaic wholesomeness about the room which it had lacked on the previous night, and the dirty, shriveled little paw was pitched on the sideboard with a carelessness which betokened no great belief in its virtues.

"I suppose all old soldiers are the same," said Mrs. White. "The idea of our listening to such nonsense! How could wishes be granted in these days? And if they could, how could two hundred pounds hurt you, Father?"

"Might drop on his head from the sky," said the frivolous Herbert.

"Morris said the things happened so naturally," said his father, "that you might if you so wished attribute it to coincidence."

"Well, don't break into the money before I come back," said Herbert, as he rose from the table. "I'm afraid it'll turn you into a mean, avaricious man, and we shall have to disown you."

His mother laughed, and followed him to the door, watched him down the road, and, returning to the breakfast table, was very happy at the expense of her husband's credulity. All of which did not prevent her from scurrying to the door at the postman's knock, nor prevent her from referring somewhat shortly to retired sergeant majors of bibulous[8] habits when she found that the post brought a tailor's bill.

"Herbert will have some more of his funny remarks, I expect, when he comes home," she said, as they sat at dinner.

"I dare say," said Mr. White, pouring himself out some beer; "but for all that, the thing moved in my hand; that I'll swear to."

---

8. **bibulous** (bĭb′yə-ləs): drinking.

"You thought it did," said the old lady soothingly.

"I say it did," replied the other. "There was no thought about it. I had just— What's the matter?"

His wife made no reply. She was watching the mysterious movements of a man outside, who, peering in an undecided fashion at the house, appeared to be trying to make up his mind to enter. In mental connection with the two hundred pounds, she noticed that the stranger was well dressed and wore a silk hat of glossy newness. Three times he paused at the gate, and then walked on again. The fourth time he stood with his hand upon it, and then with sudden resolution flung it open and walked up the path. Mrs. White at the same moment placed her hands behind her, and hurriedly unfastening the strings of her apron, put that useful article of apparel beneath the cushion of her chair.

She brought the stranger, who seemed ill at ease, into the room. He gazed furtively at Mrs. White, and listened in a preoccupied fashion as the old lady apologized for the appearance of the room, and her husband's coat, a garment which he usually reserved for the garden. She then waited patiently for him to broach his business, but he was at first strangely silent.

"I—was asked to call," he said at last, and stooped and picked a piece of cotton from his trousers. "I came from Maw and Meggins."

The old lady started. "Is anything the matter?" she asked breathlessly. "Has anything happened to Herbert? What is it? What is it?"

Her husband interposed. "There, there, Mother," he said hastily. "Sit down and don't jump to conclusions. You've not brought bad news, I'm sure, sir," and he eyed the other wistfully.

"I'm sorry—" began the visitor.

"Is he hurt?" demanded the mother.

The visitor bowed in assent. "Badly hurt," he said quietly, "but he is not in any pain."

"Oh, thank God!" said the old woman, clasping her hands. "Thank God for that! Thank——"

She broke off suddenly as the sinister meaning of the assurance dawned upon her and she saw the awful confirmation of her fears in the other's averted face. She caught her breath, and turning to her husband, laid her trembling old hand upon his. There was a long silence.

"He was caught in the machinery," said the visitor at length, in a low voice.

"Caught in the machinery," repeated Mr. White, in a dazed fashion, "yes."

He sat staring blankly out at the window, and taking his wife's hand between his own, pressed it as he had been wont to do in their old courting days nearly forty years before.

"He was the only one left to us," he said, turning gently to the visitor. "It is hard."

The other coughed, and, rising, walked slowly to the window. "The firm wished me to convey their sincere sympathy with you in your great loss," he said, without looking around. "I beg that you will understand I am only their servant and merely obeying orders."

There was no reply; the old woman's face was white, her eyes staring, and her breath inaudible; on the husband's face was a look such as his friend the sergeant might have carried into his first action.

"I was to say that Maw and Meggins disclaim all responsibility," continued the other. "They admit no liability at all, but in consideration of your son's services they wish to present you with a certain sum as compensation."

Mr. White dropped his wife's hand, and rising to his feet, gazed with a look of horror at his visitor. His dry lips shaped the words, "How much?"

"Two hundred pounds," was the answer.

Unconscious of his wife's shriek, the old man smiled faintly, put out his hands like a sightless man, and dropped, a senseless heap, to the floor.

III

In the huge new cemetery, some two miles distant, the old people buried their dead, and came back to a house steeped in shadow and silence. It was all over so quickly that at first they could hardly realize it, and remained in a state of expectation as though of something else to happen—something else which was to lighten this load, too heavy for old hearts to bear. But the days passed, and expectations gave place to resignation—the hopeless resignation of the old, sometimes miscalled apathy. Sometimes they hardly exchanged a word, for now they had nothing to talk about, and their days were long to weariness.

It was about a week after that that the old man, waking suddenly in the night, stretched out his hand and found himself alone. The room was in darkness, and the sound of subdued weeping came from the window. He raised himself in bed and listened.

"Come back," he said tenderly. "You will be cold."

"It is colder for my son," said the old woman, and wept afresh.

The sound of her sobs died away on his ears. The bed was warm, and his eyes heavy with sleep. He dozed fitfully, and then slept until a sudden wild cry from his wife awoke him with a start.

"The monkey's paw!" she cried wildly. "The monkey's paw!"

He started up in alarm. "Where? Where is it? What's the matter?"

She came stumbling across the room toward him. "I want it," she said quietly. "You've not destroyed it?"

"It's in the parlor, on the bracket,"[9] he replied, marveling. "Why?"

She cried and laughed together, and bending over, kissed his cheek.

"I only just thought of it," she said hysterically. "Why didn't I think of it before? Why didn't you think of it?"

"Think of what?" he questioned.

"The other two wishes," she replied rapidly. "We've only had one."

"Was not that enough?" he demanded fiercely.

"No," she cried triumphantly; "we'll have one more. Go down and get it quickly, and wish our boy alive again."

The man sat up in bed and flung the bed-

---

9. **bracket:** shelf.

clothes from his quaking limbs. "You are mad!" he cried, aghast.

"Get it," she panted; "get it quickly, and wish—Oh, my boy, my boy!"

Her husband struck a match and lit the candle. "Get back to bed," he said unsteadily. "You don't know what you are saying."

"We had the first wish granted," said the old woman feverishly; "why not the second?"

"A coincidence," stammered the old man.

"Go and get it and wish," cried his wife, quivering with excitement.

The old man turned and regarded her, and his voice shook. "He has been dead ten days, and besides he—I would not tell you else, but—I could only recognize him by his clothing. If he was too terrible for you to see then, how now?"

"Bring him back," cried the old woman, and dragged him toward the door. "Do you think I fear the child I have nursed?"

He went down in the darkness, and felt his way to the parlor, and then to the mantelpiece. The talisman was in its place, and a horrible fear that the unspoken wish might bring his mutilated son before him ere he could escape from the room seized upon him, and he caught his breath as he found that he had lost the direction of the door. His brow cold with sweat, he felt his way round the table, and groped along the wall until he found himself in the small passage with the unwholesome thing in his hand.

Even his wife's face seemed changed as he entered the room. It was white and expectant, and to his fears seemed to have an unnatural look upon it. He was afraid of her.

"Wish!" she cried, in a strong voice.

"It is foolish and wicked," he faltered.

"Wish!" repeated his wife.

He raised his hand. "I wish my son alive again."

The talisman fell to the floor, and he

regarded it shudderingly. Then he sank trembling into a chair as the old woman, with burning eyes, walked to the window and raised the blind.

He sat until he was chilled with the cold, glancing occasionally at the figure of the old woman peering through the window. The candle end, which had burned below the rim of the china candlestick, was throwing pulsating shadows on the ceiling and walls, until, with a flicker larger than the rest, it expired. The old man, with an unspeakable sense of relief at the failure of the talisman, crept back to his bed, and a minute or two afterward the old woman came silently and apathetically beside him.

Neither spoke, but both lay silently listening to the ticking of the clock. A stair creaked, and a squeaky mouse scurried noisily through the wall. The darkness was oppressive, and after lying for some time screwing up his courage, the husband took the box of matches, and striking one, went downstairs for a candle.

At the foot of the stairs the match went out, and he paused to strike another, and at the same moment a knock, so quiet and stealthy as to be scarcely audible, sounded on the front door.

The matches fell from his hand. He stood motionless, his breath suspended until the knock was repeated. Then he turned and fled swiftly back to his room, and closed the door behind him. A third knock sounded through the house.

"*What's that?*" cried the old woman, starting up.

"A rat," said the old man, in shaking tones —"a rat. It passed me on the stairs."

His wife sat up in bed listening. A loud knock resounded through the house.

"It's Herbert!" she screamed. "It's Herbert!"

She ran to the door, but her husband was

before her, and catching her by the arm, held her tightly.

"What are you going to do?" he whispered hoarsely.

"It's my boy; it's Herbert!" she cried, struggling mechanically. "I forgot it was two miles away. What are you holding me for? Let's go. I must open the door."

"Don't let it in," cried the old man, trembling.

"You're afraid of your own son," she cried, struggling. "Let me go. I'm coming, Herbert; I'm coming."

There was another knock, and another. The old woman with a sudden wrench broke free and ran from the room. Her husband followed to the landing, and called after her appealingly as she hurried downstairs. He heard the chain rattle back and the bottom bolt drawn slowly and stiffly from the socket. Then the old woman's voice, strained and panting.

"The bolt," she cried loudly. "Come down. I can't reach it."

But her husband was on his hands and knees groping wildly on the floor in search of the paw. If he could only find it before the thing outside got in. A perfect fusillade of knocks reverberated through the house, and he heard the scraping of a chair as his wife put it down in the passage against the door. He heard the creaking of the bolt as it came slowly back, and at the same moment he found the monkey's paw, and frantically breathed his third and last wish.

The knocking ceased suddenly, although the echoes of it were still in the house. He heard the chair drawn back and the door opened. A cold wind rushed up the staircase, and a long loud wail of disappointment and misery from his wife gave him courage to run down to her side, and then to the gate beyond. The street lamp flickering opposite shone on a quiet and deserted road.

FOR STUDY AND DISCUSSION

1. The main action begins when Mr. White snatches the monkey's paw out of the fire. Everything up to this point is introduction and preparation. How is each member of the White family characterized in this introduction?

2. Setting is usually an important element in horror stories. How does the setting of the opening scene help to create a mood of mystery and uneasiness?

3. The sergeant major had told Mr. White that the wishes were granted so naturally that it could seem like coincidence. How is this shown to be true with the first wish?

4. Could the "granting" of the second and third wishes also be attributed to coincidence, and not to the supernatural? Why, or why not?

5. How does the monkey's paw change the relationship between the husband and wife?

6. What point in the story would you identify as the *climax*—that intense moment when you finally realize how the plot will turn out?

7. Do you think Mr. White could have rephrased his first and second wishes so that he could have gotten what he really wanted? Explain your answer.

8. How do the events of the story bear out the old fakir's belief about the danger of tampering with fate?

FORESHADOWING AND SUSPENSE

Foreshadowing is the use of clues that hint at what will happen later in a story. A skillful writer can provide such clues without giving the plot away, and sometimes a reader does not even recognize the foreshadowing until after the story is finished. Look back at the first part of "The Monkey's Paw." Where does the author foreshadow the fact that the monkey's paw will bring horror with it? Look at the game of chess that opens the story. How does the characterization of Mr. White foreshadow his later actions?

How can each of these statements be considered examples of foreshadowing?

> Mr. White says, "I don't know what to wish for, and that's a fact . . . It seems to me I've got all I want."
> Herbert says, "Well, I don't see the money . . . and I bet I never shall."
> Mrs. White says, "How could wishes be granted in these days? And if they could, how could two hundred pounds hurt you, Father?"

Every horror story depends on suspense for part of its effect. Suspense is usually greatest when we are curious or worried about a character whom we like or admire. How does the fact that the monkey's paw can grant *three* wishes keep you in suspense right up until the end of this story? Did your feelings for Herbert and for his parents increase your sense of anxiety? Explain.

The moment of greatest suspense probably comes between the making of the second wish and the making of the third. How do the setting and the dialogue heighten the suspense of this scene?

FOR RESEARCH

Comparing Plots

1. This story uses an old plot based on the granting of wishes to ordinary mortals. In many stories based on this plot, the wishes bring unhappiness or destruction to the characters. In a collection of the Grimms' fairy tales, find "The Fisherman and His Wife." In a short essay, tell how the two characters in the Grimms' story misuse the wishes. Are these characters at all like those in Jacobs' story? How would you state the "moral lesson" of the fairy tale?

2. Another famous story of a talisman is Robert Louis Stevenson's "The Bottle Imp." Read that story and compare it with "The Monkey's Paw." How does the bottle imp affect the lives of the mortals who own it? What do you think accounts for the popularity of this kind of story?

ABOUT THE AUTHOR

William Wymark Jacobs (1863–1943) was born and grew up near the shipping area on the Thames River in London, where his father worked on the docks. As a young man, Jacobs passed a Civil Service exam and worked for the government's Savings Bank Department and later for the General Post Office. Jacobs never enjoyed this work; storytelling was more to his liking.

Jacobs' experiences on the docks and his interest in the tales of seafarers are reflected in the titles of his books, such as *Many Cargoes, Deep Water, Captains All, More Cargoes,* and *Snug Harbor.* "The Monkey's Paw," his most famous story, has been dramatized as a one-act play.

Character

One of the greatest pleasures of reading fiction is getting acquainted with a wider range and variety of people than we could ever know in life. Often the characters in fiction seem more interesting than the people we meet in life because we can know them better. Fiction, for two reasons, allows us to see more deeply into the inner nature of a character than we usually can in life. First, fiction places characters in crucial situations, which test them and expose their natures. Second, fiction can take us inside a character's mind and let us experience inner thoughts and feelings that in life we could only guess at. Of course, fictional characters are imaginary people and have only imaginary existence. Yet, if their author has made them seem believable, they can help us to understand something about real people, including ourselves.

To be believable, characters cannot be either all good or all bad; we know that real people are not like that. To be believable, characters must also be consistent: they must not act one way on one occasion and an entirely different way on another, unless there is a clear reason for the change. Sudden changes of heart for no apparent reason should be no more common in literature than they are in life.

A writer may present characters ("characterize" them) directly or indirectly. In *direct characterization*, the writer explicitly tells us what a character is like (for example, stupid, silly, kind). In *indirect characterization*, the writer shows us what the character does or says or thinks or feels, and lets us draw our own conclusions about what the character is like. Most writers use both forms of characterization. What we are *told* about a character will have little force unless we are also *shown* the character in action.

Road to the Isles

Jessamyn West

It was the last Thursday in January, about nine in the evening, cold and raining. The three Delahantys sat close about the living-room fireplace – Mr. Delahanty at the built-in desk working on his schedule, Mrs. Delahanty on the sofa reading, and between them, crosswise in the wing chair, their daughter.

Cress was apparently studying the program of the folk-dance festival in which she was to appear the next evening. For the most part, however, she did not even see the program. She saw, instead, herself, infinitely graceful, moving through the figures of the dance that had been so difficult for her to master.

The high school folk-dancing class was made up of two kinds of performers – those with natural ability, who had themselves elected the class, and those who, in the language of the physical education department, were "remedials." The remedials had been

sent into the class willy-nilly in an effort to counteract in them defects ranging from antisocial attitudes to what Miss Ingols, the gym teacher, called "a general lack of grace." Cress had achieved the class under this final classification but now, at midterm, had so far outgrown it as to be the only remedial with a part in the festival.

The first five numbers on the program, "Tsiganotchka," "Ladies' Whim," "Meitschi Putz Di," "Hiawatha," and "Little Man in a Fix," Cress ignored. It was not only that she was not in these but that they were in no way as beautiful as "Road to the Isles," in which Mary Lou Hawkins, Chrystal O'Conor, Zelma Mayberry, Bernadine Deevers, and Crescent Delahanty took part. The mere sight of her name beside that of Bernadine Deevers, Tenant High School's most gifted dancer – most gifted *person*, really – instantly called up to Cress a vision of herself featly[1] footing it in laced kirtle[2] and starched skirts, a vision of herself dancing not only the outward steps of "Road to the Isles" but its inner meaning: what Miss Ingols had called "the achievement of the impossible."

Cress thought that she was particularly adapted to dancing that meaning because she had so recently come that way herself. If she had been given three wishes when school opened in September, two of them would have been that Bernadine be her friend and that she herself succeed in the folk-dancing class. Both had then seemed equally impossible. Now not only did she have a part in the festival but Bernadine was her dear friend and coming to spend the weekend with her. At the minute the evening reached what she considered its peak of mellowness, she intended to speak to her father and mother about the festival and Bernadine's visit. She was exceedingly uncertain about their performances on both these occasions.

The rain suddenly began to fall harder. Cress's father, hearing it on the roof, watched with gratification as the water streamed across the dark windowpanes. "Just what the oranges have been a-thirsting for," he said.

Mrs. Delahanty closed her book. "How's the schedule coming?" she asked her husband.

"OK, I guess," said Mr. Delahanty.

Cress looked up from the festival program with embarrassment. The schedule was one of the things she wanted to speak to her father about. She hoped he wouldn't mention it while Bernadine was visiting them. Every winter, as work on the ranch slackened, he drew up a schedule for the better ordering of his life. And every spring, as work picked up,

he abandoned it as easily as if it had never been. Last winter, he had made a plan called "A Schedule of Exercises to Ensure Absolute Fitness," which included not only the schedule of exercises and the hours at which he proposed to practice them but a list of the weaknesses they were to counteract. He had even gone so far, last winter, as to put on a pair of peculiar short pants and run six times around the orchard without stopping, arms flailing, chest pumping—a very embarrassing sight, and one that Cress could not possibly have explained to Bernadine.

This winter, the subject of her father's schedule-making was not in itself so unsuitable. He had bought a new encyclopedia set and was mapping out a reading program that would enable him, by a wise use of his spare time, to cover the entire field of human knowledge in a year. The name of the schedule, written at the top of a sheet of Cress's yellow graph paper, was, in fact, "Human Knowledge in a Year." There was nothing about this plan that would call for embarrassing public action, like running around the orchard in shorts, but it was so incredibly naive and dreamy that Cress hoped her father would not speak of it. Bernadine was far too sophisticated for schedules.

"Where are you now on your schedule, John?" Mrs. Delahanty asked.

Mr. Delahanty, who liked to talk about his plans almost as much as he liked to make them, put down his pen and picked up the sheet of paper on which he had been writing. "I've got all the subjects I want to read up about listed, and the times I'll have free *for* reading listed. Nothing left to do now but decide what's the best time for what. For instance, if you were me, Gertrude, would you spend the fifteen minutes before breakfast on art? Or on archaeology, say?"

"You don't even have fifteen minutes be-

---

1. **featly:** skillfully.
2. **kirtle** (kûrt'l): dress.

fore breakfast," Mrs. Delahanty said.

Mr. Delahanty picked up his pen. "I thought you wanted to discuss this."

"Oh, I do!" said Mrs. Delahanty. "Well, if I had fifteen minutes before breakfast, I'd read about archaeology."

"Why?" asked Mr. Delahanty.

"It's more orderly that way," Mrs. Delahanty said.

"Orderly?" asked Mr. Delahanty.

"A-r-c," Mrs. Delahanty spelled, "comes before a-r-t."

Mr. Delahanty made an impatient sound. "I'm not going at this alphabetically, Gertrude. Cut and dried. What I'm thinking about is what would make the most interesting morning reading. The most interesting and inspiring."

"Art is supposed to be more inspiring," Mrs. Delahanty told him. "If that's what you're after."

This seemed to decide Mr. Delahanty. "No, I think science should be the morning subject," he said, and wrote something at the top of a sheet—"Science," Cress supposed. "That's better," he said. "That leaves art for the evening, when I'll have time to read aloud to you."

"Don't change your schedule around for my sake, John," said Mrs. Delahanty, who hated being read to about anything.

"I'm not. All personal considerations aside, that's a more logical arrangement. Now the question is, which art?"

This seemed to Cress the moment for which she had been waiting. "Dancing is one of the earliest and most important of the arts," she said quickly.

"Oho!" said her father. "I thought you were in a coma."

"I've been rehearsing," said Cress.

"Rehearsing!" exclaimed Mr. Delahanty.

"In my mind," Cress said.

"So that's what was going on—'Ladies' Whim,' 'Tsiganotchka'——"

"Father," Cress interrupted, "I've told you and told you the t's silent. Why don't you take the program and practice the names? I'll help you." Cress got up and took the program across to her father.

"Practice them," said Mr. Delahanty with surprise, reading through the dances listed. "What do I care how they're pronounced? 'Korbushka,' 'Kohanotchka,' " he said, mispronouncing wildly. "I'm not going to Russia."

"But you're going to the folk-dance festival," Cress reminded him.

"I don't have to go. If you don't want——"

"I do, Father. You know I want you to go. Only I don't want you to mispronounce the names."

"Look, Cress," Mr. Delahanty said. "I promise you I'll keep my mouth shut the whole time I'm there. No one will know you have a father who can't pronounce. Mute I'll come and mute I'll go."

"I don't want you to be mute," Cress protested. "And even if I did, you couldn't very well be mute the whole time Bernadine's here. And Bernadine's the star of the program."

"To Bernadine," said Mr. Delahanty, referring to the program once again, "I shall speak of 'Badger,' and 'The Lumberman's Two Step.' I can pronounce them fine and they ought to hold Bernadine. She's not going to be here long, is she?"

"Friday to Monday," said Mrs. Delahanty.

"In that case," said Mr. Delahanty, "maybe I should find another one. How about 'The Irish Jollity,' Cress? Do I say that all right?"

"Now, John!" Mrs. Delahanty reproved her husband.

"It's all right for him to joke about it to me, Mother. But he mustn't before Bernadine. Bernadine's serious about dancing. She's going to be a great artist."

"A great dancer?" Mrs. Delahanty asked.

"She hasn't decided what kind of an artist yet," Cress said. "Only to be great in something."

"Well, well," said Mr. Delahanty. "I'm beginning to look forward to meeting Bernadine."

"You already have," Cress told him. "Bernadine was one of the girls who rode with us to the basketball game."

Mr. Delahanty squinted his eyes, as if trying to peer backward to the Friday two weeks before when he had provided Cress and four of her friends with transportation to an out-of-town game. He shook his head. "Can't recall any Bernadine," he said.

"She was the one in the front seat with us," Cress reminded him.

"That girl!" exclaimed Mr. Delahanty, remembering. "But her name wasn't Bernadine, was it?"

"No," Cress told him. "That's what I wanted to explain to you, because tomorrow's Friday, too."

Mr. Delahanty left desk and schedule and walked over in front of the fireplace. From this position, he could get a direct view of his daughter.

"What's this you're saying, Cress?" he asked. "Her name isn't Bernadine because tomorrow's Friday. Is that what you said?"

"Yes, it is," Cress told him, seriously. "Only it's not just tomorrow. Her name isn't Bernadine on any Friday."

Mr. Delahanty appealed to his wife. "Do you hear what I hear, Gertrude?"

"Mother," Cress protested, "this isn't anything funny. In fact, it's a complete tragedy."

"Well, Cress dear," her mother said reasonably, "I haven't said a word. And your father's just trying to get things straight."

"He's trying to be funny about a tragedy," Cress insisted obstinately.

"Now, Cress," Mr. Delahanty urged, "you're jumping to conclusions. Though I admit I think it's queer to have a name on Fridays you don't have the rest of the week. And I don't see anything tragic about it."

"That's what I'm trying to tell you, only you keep acting as if it's a joke."

"What is Bernadine's name on Fridays, Cress?" asked her mother.

"Nedra," said Cress solemnly.

Mr. Delahanty snapped his fingers. "Yes, sir," he said, "that's it! That's what they called her, all right."

"Of course," said Cress. "Everyone does on Fridays, out of respect for her sorrow."

"Just what is Bernadine's sorrow, Cress?" her mother asked.

"Bernadine never did say — out and out, that is. Once in a while she tries to. But she just can't. It overwhelms her. But we all know what, generally speaking, must have happened."

"What?" asked Mr. Delahanty. "Generally speaking?"

Cress looked at her father suspiciously, but his face was all sympathetic concern.

"On some Friday in the past," she said, "Nedra had to say no to someone. Someone she loved."

"How old is Berna — Nedra?" Mrs. Delahanty asked.

"Sixteen," Cress said. "Almost."

"Well, it couldn't have been too long ago then, could it?" her mother suggested.

"Was this person," Mr. Delahanty ventured, "this person Nedra said no to, a male?"

"Of course," said Cress. "I told you it was a complete tragedy, didn't I? His name was Ned. That much we know."

"Then the Nedra is in honor of — Ned?" asked her mother.

"In honor and loving memory," Cress told her. "On the very next Friday, Ned died."

Mr. Delahanty said nothing. Mrs. Delahanty said, "Poor boy!"

"I think he was probably more than a boy," Cress said. "He owned two drugstores."

After the elder Delahantys had thought about this for a while, Mr. Delahanty asked, "This 'no' Bernadine—Nedra—said, was it to a proposal of marriage?"

"We don't ever ask about that," Cress told her father disapprovingly. "It doesn't seem like good taste to us."

"No, I don't suppose it is," Mr. Delahanty admitted.

"Anyway," Cress said, "that's Bernadine's tragedy and we all respect it and her wish to be called Nedra on Fridays. And tomorrow is a Friday, and it would be pretty awful to have her upset before the festival."

Mr. Delahanty stepped briskly back to his desk. "Don't you worry for a second, Cress," he said. "As far as I'm concerned, the girl's name is Nedra."

"Thank you, Father," Cress said. "I knew you'd understand. Now I'd better go to bed." At the door to the hallway, she turned and spoke once again. "If I were you, Father, I wouldn't say anything about your schedule to Bernadine."

"I hadn't planned on talking to her about it. But what's wrong with it?" Mr. Delahanty sounded a little testy.

"Oh, nothing," Cress assured him. "I think it's dear and sweet of you to make schedules. Only," she explained, "it's so idealistic."

After Cress left the room, Mr. Delahanty said, "What's . . . wrong with being idealistic?"

Cress thought that her friend, in her costume for "Fado Blanquita," the Spanish dance in which she performed the solo part, looked like the queen of grace and beauty. And she said so.

"This does rather suit my type," Bernadine admitted. She was leaning out from the opened casement window of Cress's room into the shimmering, rain-washed air. She tautened her costume's already tight bodice, fluffed up its already bouffant skirt, and extended her hands in one of the appealing gestures of the dance toward the trees of the orange orchard upon which the window opened.

"Is your father a shy man?" she asked.

Mr. Delahanty, who had been working near the driveway to the house when the two girls got off the school bus an hour before, had, instead of lingering to greet them, quickly disappeared behind a row of trees. Now, in rubber boots, carrying a light spade that he was using to test the depth to which the night before's rain had penetrated the soil, he came briefly into sight, waved his spade, and once again disappeared.

"No," said Cress, who thought her father rather bold, if anything. "He's just busy. After the rain, you know."

"Rain, sunshine. Sunshine, rain," Bernadine said understandingly. She moved her hands about in the placid afternoon air as if scooping up samples. "Farming is an awfully elemental life, I expect. My father"—Bernadine's father, J. M. Deevers, was vice president of the Tenant First National Bank—"probably doesn't know one element from another. I expect your father's rather an elemental type, too, isn't he? Fundamentally, I mean?"

"I don't know, Nedra," Cress said humbly.

"He's black-haired," Bernadine said. "It's been my experience that black-haired men are very elemental." She brought her expressive hands slowly down to her curving red satin bodice. "You must have a good deal of confidence in your family to let them go to-night," she went on briskly.

"Let them!" Cress repeated, amazed at the word.

"Perhaps they're different from my family. Mine always keep me on pins and needles about what they're going to say and do next."

"Mine, too," Cress admitted, though loyalty to her father and mother would not permit her to say how greatly they worried her. She never went anyplace with them that she was not filled with a tremulous concern lest they do or say something that would discredit them all. She stayed with them. She attempted to guide them. She hearkened to every word said to them, so that she could prompt them with the right answers. But *let* them! "They always just take it for granted that where I go, they go," she said. "There's not much question of letting."

"Mine used to be that way," Bernadine confided. "But after what happened at the festival last year, I put my foot down. 'This year,' I told them, 'you're not going.' "

"What happened last year?" asked Cress, who had not then been a dancer.

"After the program was over last year, Miss Ingols asked for parent participation in the dancing. And my father participated. He danced the 'Hopak,' and pretty soon he was lifting Miss Ingols off the floor at every other jump."

"Oh, Nedra," Cress said. "How terrible! What did Ingols do?"

"Nothing," said Bernadine. "That was the disgusting part. As a matter of fact, she seemed to enjoy it. But you can imagine how I suffered."

Cress nodded. She could. She was thinking how she would suffer if her father, in addition to mispronouncing all the dances, went out on the gymnasium floor and, before all her friends, misdanced them.

"Are your parents the participating type?" Bernadine asked.

Cress nodded with sad conviction. "Father is. And Mother is if encouraged."

"You'd better warn them right away," Bernadine said. "Your father just came in the back door. You could warn him now."

Cress walked slowly down the hallway toward the kitchen. Before the evening was over, her father, too, would probably be jouncing Miss Ingols around, and even calling Bernadine Bernadine — then all would be ruined completely, all she had looked forward to for so long. In the kitchen, she noted signs of the special supper her mother was cooking because of Bernadine: the coleslaw salad had shreds of green peppers and red apples mixed through it tonight to make it festive; the party sherbet glasses, with their long icicle stems, awaited the lemon pudding. But her mother was out of the kitchen — on the back porch telling her father to hurry, because they would have to have dinner early if they were to get to the festival in time.

"Festival!" Cress heard her father say. "I wish I'd never heard of that festival. How did Cress ever come to get mixed up in this dancing business, anyway?" he asked. "She's no dancer. Why, the poor kid can hardly get through a room without knocking something over. Let alone dance!"

"That's *why* she's mixed up with it," her mother explained. "To overcome her awkwardness. And she *is* better."

"But is she good enough?" asked her father. "I'd hate to think of her making a spectacle of herself — to say nothing of having to sit and watch it."

"Now, John," Cress heard her mother say soothingly. "You're always too concerned about Cress. Will she do this right? Will she do that right? Stop worrying. Cress'll probably be fine."

"Maybe fall on her ear, too," her father said morosely. "They oughtn't to put so much responsibility on kids. Performing in public. Doesn't it worry you any?"

"Certainly it worries me. But all parents worry. And remember, we'll have the star of the performance with us. You can concentrate on Nedra if watching Cress is too much for you."

"That Nedra! The only dance I can imagine that girl doing is one in which she would carry somebody's head on a platter."[3]

Cress had started back down the hall before her father finished this sentence, but she had not gone so far as to miss its final word. She stopped in the bathroom to have a drink of water and to see how she looked in the mirror over the washbasin. She looked different. For the first time in her life, she saw herself through other eyes than her own. Through her parents' eyes. Did parents worry about the figures their *children* cut? Were they embarrassed for *them*, and did they wonder if they were behaving suitably, stylishly, well? Cress felt a vacant, hollow space beneath her heart, which another glass of water did nothing to fill. Why, *I'm* all right, Cress thought. *I* know how to behave. I'll get by. *They're* the ones . . . but she looked at her face again and it was wavering, doubtful—not the triumphant face she had imagined, smiling in sureness as she danced the come-and-go figures of "Road to the Isles."

She went back to her room full of thought. Bernadine was changing her costume, and her muffled voice came from under all her skirts. "Did you tell them?" this muffled voice asked.

"No," said Cress, "I didn't."

"Why not? Won't you be worried?"

"They're the ones who are worrying. About me."

"About you?"

"Father thinks I may fall on my ear."

Bernadine, clear of her skirts, nodded in smiling agreement. "It's a possibility that sometimes occurs to *me*, Cress dear."

Cress gazed at her friend speculatively. "They're worried about you, too," she said.

"Me?" asked Bernadine, her smile fading.

"Father said the only dance he could imagine you doing was one with a head on a platter."

"Salome!" Bernadine exclaimed with pleasure. "Your father's imaginative, isn't he? Sympathetically imaginative?"

"I guess so," Cress said, and in her confusion told everything. "He keeps schedules."

"Schedules?"

"For the better ordering of his life."

Bernadine laughed again. "How precious!" she said.

Then, as if remembering after too long a lapse the day and her bereavement, she said, "Neddy was like that, too."

"Neddy," repeated Cress, pain for the present making Bernadine's past seem not only past but silly. "Oh, shut up about Neddy, *Bernadine!*"

Bernadine gave a little gasp. "Have you forgotten it's Friday?"

"I don't care what day it is," Cress said. She walked over to her bed, picked up the pillow, and lay down. Then she put the pillow over her face.

---

3. **platter:** a reference to the Biblical character Salome (sə-lō'mē), who danced for King Herod and was granted the head of John the Baptist as a reward. (See Matthew 14:8.)

FOR STUDY AND DISCUSSION

1. At the beginning of this story, we are told that Cress sees herself as a graceful dancer. What evidence indicates that this is an illusion?

2. Cress idealizes Bernadine, whom she thinks of as the "most gifted person" in school and as a romantic heroine with a tragic past. What does she come to realize about Bernadine? Why does she change her attitude toward her friend?

3. What does Cress realize about her parents as a result of the overheard conversation? How is their concern about Cress like Cress's earlier concern about them?

4. What exactly does Cress "see" when she sees herself for the first time through eyes other than her own?

5. The author spends quite a bit of time describing Mr. Delahanty's idealistic schedule. What is the purpose of his schedule? Do you think the author intends us to see a similarity between the character of Mr. Delahanty and that of his daughter? Explain.

DIRECT AND INDIRECT CHARACTERIZATION

A writer can create characters in two ways: by direct presentation and by indirect presentation. When characters are presented directly, the writer tells us explicitly what they are like, or what motivates them. Jessamyn West, for example, uses direct characterization when she *tells* us explicitly how Cress feels about her parents: "loyalty to her father and mother would not permit her to say how greatly they worried her."

In indirect characterization, the writer *shows* us the characters in action, lets us *hear* them speaking, and lets us know how other characters feel about them, so that we have the pleasure of drawing our own conclusions about the kinds of people they are. We receive most of our knowledge of Cress in this story through indirect characterization. For example, though Jessamyn West tells us directly how Cress feels about her parents, she also lets us *watch* and *listen to* Cress as she instructs her father on how to behave during Bernadine's visit and at the recital. Look back at this scene, beginning on page 45. What do you learn about Cress and her parents from observing them in this scene?

Jessamyn West never tells us directly what kind of person Bernadine is or what her qualities are, but we form a very strong impression of Bernadine by observing her in action and by noticing how she affects other people. How would you characterize Bernadine directly?

The climax of this story occurs when Cress overhears her parents' conversation. We hear what Cress says, we watch her actions, and we know her thoughts, but we are never told explicitly *how* she has changed. If you were to characterize Cress directly, how would you explain what has happened to her at the end of the story? Would you describe this change as a necessary, good change, or is it a destructive one? Explain.

LANGUAGE AND VOCABULARY

Analyzing Words with *counter-* **and** *anti-*
If you didn't know the meanings of the italicized words in this sentence, you could find clues in their parts:

The remedials had been sent into the class willy-nilly in an effort to *counteract* in them defects ranging from *antisocial* attitudes to what Miss Ingols, the gym teacher, called "a general lack of grace."

Counteract is made up of two parts. The first part is a prefix, *counter-*, which means "opposite to" or "against," from the Latin word *contra*. *Counteract* means "to act against" or "to undo something." The purpose of the remedial class in this story is to act against, or undo, certain of the dancers' defects.

The word *antisocial* is also made up of two parts. The prefix *anti-*, from a Greek word, also means "against," but in the sense of "being hostile to," or of "operating against something," or of "neutralizing something," or of "reversing something." *Social* means "getting along with other people." What is an *antisocial* attitude? What does the prefix *anti-* mean in that word?

Write a definition of each of the following words, showing how they incorporate the meanings of *counter-* or *anti-*. Check your definitions in a dictionary.

anticlimax	counterbalance
antidote	counterclockwise
antihero	counterfeit
antiseptic	counterproductive

FOR DRAMATIZATION

Writing a Play

Turn "Road to the Isles" into a play with two scenes. What additional dialogue will you need to write? How will you make Cress's thoughts clear to the audience? What stage directions will you write to tell how the actors and actresses should move and how they should deliver their lines?

You might want to make up additional scenes based on the story. For example, imagine that the author had not ended the story as she did, but continued with the following scenes:

The dance recital

A conversation between Cress's parents and Bernadine

A conversation between Cress and Miss Ingols

ABOUT THE AUTHOR

When she was growing up in California, Jessamyn West (1907–1984) had a real friend named Bernadine, who told her, "If it's a life-and-death matter, you can do it." That was when Jessamyn, like Cress in "Road to the Isles," feared failure in performing in front of an audience. Jessamyn West began writing in her twenties when she was bedridden with tuberculosis. "I am not proud of the manner in which I came to writing," she once said, "unwilling, until I was backed into a corner by disease, and unable to do anything else except perhaps crochet, to pick up my pen. Talent is helpful in writing, but guts are absolutely necessary. Without the guts to try, the talent may never be discovered . . . ."

The Friendly Persuasion, Jessamyn West's first book, is a collection of stories about a Quaker family living in Indiana during the Civil War. She based the book on anecdotes of her own great-grandparents. Her stories about Cress were gathered into a book called *Cress Delahanty*.

The Sentimentality of William Tavener

Willa Cather

It takes a strong woman to make any sort of success of living in the West, and Hester undoubtedly was that. When people spoke of William Tavener as the most prosperous farmer in McPherson County, they usually added that his wife was a "good manager." She was an executive woman, quick of tongue and something of an imperatrix.[1] The only reason her husband did not consult her about his business was that she did not wait to be consulted.

It would have been quite impossible for one man, within the limited sphere of human action, to follow all Hester's advice, but in the end William usually acted upon some of her suggestions. When she incessantly denounced the "shiftlessness" of letting a new threshing machine stand unprotected in the open, he eventually built a shed for it. When she sniffed contemptuously at his notion of fencing a hog corral with sod walls, he made a spiritless beginning on the structure—merely to "show his temper," as she put it—but in the end he went off quietly to town and bought enough barbed wire to complete the fence. When the first heavy rains came on, and the pigs rooted down the sod wall and made little paths all over it to facilitate their ascent, he heard his wife relate with relish the story of the little pig that built a mud house, to the minister at the dinner table, and William's gravity never relaxed for an instant. Silence, indeed, was William's refuge and his strength.

William set his boys a wholesome example to respect their mother. People who knew him very well suspected that he even admired her. He was a hard man towards his neighbors, and even towards his sons: grasping, determined, and ambitious.

There was an occasional blue day about the house when William went over the store bills, but he never objected to items relating to his wife's gowns or bonnets. So it came about that many of the foolish, unnecessary little things that Hester bought for her boys, she had charged to her personal account.

One spring night Hester sat in a rocking chair by the sitting-room window, darning socks. She rocked violently and sent her long needle vigorously back and forth over her gourd,[2] and it took only a very casual glance to see that she was wrought up over something. William sat on the other side of the

---

1. **imperatrix** (ĭm'pĕ-rä'trĭx): In ancient Rome, the title of *imperator* was given to the supreme commander or emperor. An imperatrix is an emperor who is a woman.

2. **gourd** (gôrd): a fruit related to the pumpkin. Hester placed a dried, hollow gourd inside the sock she was mending.

table reading his farm paper. If he had noticed his wife's agitation, his calm, clean-shaven face betrayed no sign of concern. He must have noticed the sarcastic turn of her remarks at the supper table, and he must have noticed the moody silence of the older boys as they ate. When supper was but half over, little Billy, the youngest, had suddenly pushed back his plate and slipped away from the table, manfully trying to swallow a sob. But William Tavener never heeded ominous forecasts in the domestic horizon, and he never looked for a storm until it broke.

After supper the boys had gone to the pond under the willows in the big cattle corral, to get rid of the dust of plowing. Hester could hear an occasional splash and a laugh ringing clear through the stillness of the night, as she sat by the open window. She sat silent for almost an hour reviewing in her mind many plans of attack. But she was too vigorous a woman to be much of a strategist, and she usually came to her point with directness. At last she cut her thread and suddenly put her darning down, saying emphatically:

"William, I don't think it would hurt you to let the boys go to that circus in town tomorrow."

William continued to read his farm paper, but it was not Hester's custom to wait for an answer. She usually divined his arguments and assailed them one by one before he uttered them.

"You've been short of hands all summer, and you've worked the boys hard, and a man ought use his own flesh and blood as well as he does his hired hands. We're plenty able to afford it, and it's little enough our boys ever spend. I don't see how you can expect 'em to be steady and hard workin', unless you encourage 'em a little. I never could see much harm in circuses, and our boys have never been to one. Oh, I know Jim Howley's boys get drunk an' carry on when they go, but our boys ain't that sort, an' you know it, William. The animals are real instructive, an' our boys don't get to see much out here on the prairie. It was different where we were raised, but the boys have got no advantages here, an' if you don't take care, they'll grow up to be greenhorns."

Hester paused a moment, and William folded up his paper, but vouchsafed no remark. His sisters in Virginia had often said that only a quiet man like William could ever have lived with Hester Perkins. Secretly, William was rather proud of his wife's "gift of speech," and of the fact that she could talk in prayer meeting as fluently as a man. He confined his own efforts in that line to a brief prayer at Covenant meetings.

Hester shook out another sock and went on.

"Nobody was ever hurt by goin' to a circus. Why, law me! I remember I went to one myself once, when I was little. I had most forgot about it. It was over at Pewtown, an' I remember how I had set my heart on going. I don't think I'd ever forgiven my father if he hadn't taken me, though that red clay road was in a frightful way after the rain. I mind they had an elephant and six poll parrots, an' a Rocky Mountain lion, an' a cage of monkeys, an' two camels. My! but they were a sight to me then!"

Hester dropped the black sock and shook her head and smiled at the recollection. She was not expecting anything from William yet, and she was fairly startled when he said gravely, in much the same tone in which he announced the hymns in prayer meeting:

"No, there was only one camel. The other was a dromedary."

She peered around the lamp and looked at him keenly.

"Why, William, how come you to know?"

William folded his paper and answered with some hesitation, "I was there, too."

Hester's interest flashed up. "Well, I never, William! To think of my finding it out after all these years! Why, you couldn't have been much bigger'n our Billy then. It seems queer I never saw you when you was little, to remember about you. But then you Back Creek folks never have anything to do with us Gap people. But how come you to go? Your father was stricter with you than you are with your boys."

"I reckon I shouldn't 'a gone," he said slowly, "but boys will do foolish things. I had done a good deal of fox hunting the winter before, and Father let me keep the bounty money. I hired Tom Smith's Tap to weed the corn for me, an' I slipped off unbeknownst to Father an' went to the show."

Hester spoke up warmly: "Nonsense, William! It didn't do you no harm, I guess. You was always worked hard enough. It must have been a big sight for a little fellow. That clown must have just tickled you to death."

William crossed his knees and leaned back in his chair.

"I reckon I could tell all that fool's jokes now. Sometimes I can't help thinkin' about 'em in meetin' when the sermon's long. I mind I had on a pair of new boots that hurt me like the mischief, but I forgot all about 'em when that fellow rode the donkey. I recall I had to take them boots off as soon as I got out of sight o' town, and walked home in the mud barefoot."

"O poor little fellow!" Hester ejaculated, drawing her chair nearer and leaning her elbows on the table. "What cruel shoes they did use to make for children. I remember I went up to Back Creek to see the circus wagons go by. They came down from Romney, you know. The circus men stopped at the creek to water the animals, an' the elephant got stubborn an' broke a big limb off the yellow willow tree that grew there by the tollhouse porch, an' the Scribners were 'fraid as death he'd pull the house down. But this much I saw him do; he waded in the creek an' filled his trunk with water and squirted it in

at the window and nearly ruined Ellen Scribner's pink lawn dress that she had just ironed an' laid out on the bed ready to wear to the circus."

"I reckon that must have been a trial to Ellen," chuckled William, "for she was mighty prim in them days."

Hester drew her chair still nearer William's. Since the children had begun growing up, her conversation with her husband had been almost wholly confined to questions of economy and expense. Their relationship had become purely a business one, like that between landlord and tenant. In her desire to indulge her boys she had unconsciously assumed a defensive and almost hostile attitude towards her husband. No debtor ever haggled with his usurer more doggedly than did Hester with her husband in behalf of her sons. The strategic contest had gone on so long that it had almost crowded out the memory of a closer relationship. This exchange of confidences tonight, when common recollections took them unawares and opened their hearts, had all the miracle of romance. They talked on and on; of old neighbors, of old familiar faces in the valley where they had grown up, of long forgotten incidents of their youth — weddings, picnics, sleighing parties and baptizings. For years they had talked of nothing else but butter and eggs and the prices of things, and now they had as much to say to each other as people who meet after a long separation.

When the clock struck ten, William rose and went over to his walnut secretary and unlocked it. From his red leather wallet he took out a ten-dollar bill and laid it on the table beside Hester.

"Tell the boys not to stay late, an' not to drive the horses hard," he said quietly, and went off to bed.

Hester blew out the lamp and sat still in the dark a long time. She left the bill lying on the table where William had placed it. She had a painful sense of having missed something, or lost something; she felt that somehow the years had cheated her.

The little locust trees that grew by the fence were white with blossoms. Their heavy odor floated in to her on the night wind and recalled a night long ago, when the first whippoorwill of the spring was heard, and the rough, buxom girls of Hawkins Gap had held her laughing and struggling under the locust trees, and searched in her bosom for a lock of her sweetheart's hair, which is supposed to be on every girl's breast when the first whippoorwill sings. Two of those same girls had been her bridesmaids. Hester had been a very happy bride. She rose and went softly into the room where William lay. He was sleeping heavily, but occasionally moved his hand before his face to ward off the flies. Hester went into the parlor and took the piece of mosquito net from the basket of wax apples and pears that her sister had made before she died. One of the boys had brought it all the way from Virginia, packed in a tin pail, since Hester would not risk shipping so precious an ornament by freight. She went back to the bedroom and spread the net over William's head. Then she sat down by the bed and listened to his deep, regular breathing until she heard the boys returning. She went out to meet them and warn them not to waken their father.

"I'll be up early to get your breakfast, boys. Your father says you can go to the show." As she handed the money to the eldest, she felt a sudden throb of allegiance to her husband and said sharply, "And you be careful of that, an' don't waste it. Your father works hard for his money."

The boys looked at each other in astonishment and felt that they had lost a powerful ally.

FOR STUDY AND DISCUSSION

1. This story is a portrait of two characters and their relationship, which changes as the result of a conversation. What specific words are used to describe Hester and William as the story opens?

2. How do Hester and William act and speak "uncharacteristically" during their conversation? Find those details that indicate that Hester is beginning to feel much closer to her husband.

3. Why is it appropriate that images of a circus should bring romance back to William's and Hester's lives?

4. As she sits in the dark after William has gone to bed, what regrets does Hester have? How does she show her changed attitude toward her husband?

5. Cather tells us that Hester and William had waged a "strategic contest" over the years. Why had Hester fought this battle, which changed the basis of their relationship from "romance" to "business"? What does the last line of the story mean?

6. Look up the meanings of the word *sentimentality* in a dictionary. Which meaning applies to the use of the word in the title? Why do you think Cather did not use Hester's name in the title?

DYNAMIC AND STATIC CHARACTERS

In many stories, a crucial event will cause the main character to change in some important way. Usually the change is an inner change—a change in attitude toward self or others, a new confidence, a sudden awareness. A character who undergoes such a change is called a *dynamic character*. A character who stays the same throughout a story is called a *static character*.

Why can we call Hester a dynamic character? Do you feel you understand the reason for her change in attitude? Explain.

How about William? Do we know if he undergoes any real change in the story? Are we ever allowed to share William's inner thoughts and feelings, as we share Hester's? Cite passages to support your answer.

Is your own attitude toward these characters changed by the end of the story? Explain.

FOR COMPOSITION

Writing a Character Analysis
Write a brief essay in which you discuss the characterization of William and Hester Tavener. Do you feel that their characterizations are realistic, given your own experience of human behavior? Be specific, and, where appropriate, quote passages from the story to support your opinions. You might want to speculate on whether Hester's new awareness is temporary or permanent.

ABOUT THE AUTHOR

Willa Cather (1873–1947), who from the age of ten grew up on the frontier in Nebraska, admired people like the pioneers who lived in sod huts and plain frame farmhouses and who fought to preserve their traditional spiritual values. Some of Cather's most famous novels were inspired by her romantic memories of her Nebraska girlhood. *My Ántonia,* for example, is the story of a Bohemian immigrant girl who triumphs over hardships and disappointments because of her vibrant strength of character. In some stories—especially those that show the lonely world of farm women—Cather suggests a less idealistic attitude. She won the Pulitzer Prize for fiction in 1922.

The Beginning of Grief

L. Woiwode

From the way his five children gathered around him at the dinner table Stanion could tell something was wrong. He put his silverware down beside his plate, leaving untouched the food he had prepared and heaped there, and leaned his forehead on clasped hands as if to say grace. He was reaching his limit. Beneath his closed eyelids, inflamed by lime burns and bits of sand, he saw pulsing networks, as though his vessels were of neon, and then the substance and strength of his muscles and long limbs seemed to move upward, pulsing, and he felt weak, out of touch with the big bulk of his body, reduced to less than he was, less than he'd ever been, trapped within the small sphere of his eye. The size of his world now.

He would quit work late, drive from whatever part of the county his job, plastering, had taken him to that day, back to Minneapolis, and pick up the little ones, the two girls, at the baby sitter's, and then drive back home, to the outskirts of St. Paul, and cook dinner and call the three boys in to the table—now that it was summer, they spent the day at home alone—only to see in their attitudes that they were trying to conceal something. Then another circuit, familiar as the first, began. He would have to travel through the events of their day, prying his way into them, find out what the trouble was, find out who had caused it, and set right the one who was at fault, or, if there had been fighting, punish him. He hated it. It was difficult for him to pass judgment on anyone, much less his own

children, and even harder for him to see them hurt. His wife had always handled the discipline.

She was prudent and judicious, and had no patience with any kind of wrongdoing. For years she tried to persuade him to give up his job, because she felt his employers were taking advantage of him. They went on long vacations and left the business in his hands. They showed up for work irregularly, at their leisure, knowing that he would keep things in order, and never increased his wages. But they were well-meaning and young, and he stayed on with them, in spite of her disapproval, because he liked them and knew that without him they wouldn't have a business. The memory of it, along with a thousand other memories, tormented him now. A year ago she died. The torment was more than grief. It grew, linking one memory to another, linking networks of them together, and would not let her go.

"Dad? Are you all right?"

He let his arms drop beside his plate. "Yes. Just tired."

She was the periphery of everything, closing around his vision, his mind, his actions, like a second conscience. His ideas, before he could speak them, were observed by her and he gave them up. The sheen of her hair was in the hair of the older girl, who was only five, and to run his hand over the girl's hair was excruciating, almost a sin. Her indignation was in his voice when he began arguing bitterly with his employers and when, ten months ago, he gave them final notice. He mortgaged the house, sold the car, hired a laborer, and started a business of his own. *Wm. Stanion & Sons, Plastering,* he hand-painted on the doors and tailgate of an old pickup he bought.

All they had for transportation was the pickup. In winter and when it was raining, the six of them rode in the cab, the boys holding the girls on their laps, an acrid smell of rubber and gasoline enwrapping them, the bags of plaster color breaking and spilling and staining the floorboards, then merging into a muddy gray. In good weather the boys rode in the bed of the truck, and at first they liked it so much that they sang and shouted, they stood and made wings like birds, they held their arms like Superman, and he had to keep knocking on the rear window and signaling them to sit. But lately when they went anywhere the boys huddled down with their backs against the cab, and Stanion could see, as they climbed out over the tailgate at their destination, her gestures and her averted eyes when she was suffering silent humiliation.

He would have taken his life just to end the torment, just to be at peace, and maybe to be with her (who could say?), if it hadn't been for the children. And when they were bad or unhappy he felt there was no use. He looked across the table at his middle son, Kevin, aged ten, who sat with his elbows on the tabletop and his eyes lowered, forking food into his mouth as fast as he could. Kevin's large skull had a bluish tint to it. A few days ago, for some unaccountable reason, he had taken out the electric razor and shaved off all his hair.

"Well, what kind of trouble did you cause today?" Stanion asked, and his words made him feel weary and resentful. He was being unjust. He couldn't help it. It seemed Kevin was always the guilty one. He had a bad temper, a savage energy, and was unpredictable. When she was alive, she seemed to favor Kevin, yet he was the only one she lost her temper with. Once she caught him striking matches along the foundation of the house and came up behind him, grabbed him by the arm, grabbed up a bundle of the matches, set the matches ablaze, and held them under his hand until he understood what it felt like to be burned.

Kevin couldn't stand to lose. When the simplest game or argument didn't go in his favor, he started a fight, and if he was left alone with the younger ones he set up strict rules, such as no singing or talking, no TV, no dinner, or he made them march in unison around the room, and if they violated the rules or disobeyed his commands he hit them or shoved them into a closet and held the door shut.

Kevin looked up, gave an impatient scowl, and said, "What did I *do?* Nothing." His gray eyes looked even larger now that he had no hair, and his long eyelashes, catching the light of the bare bulb overhead, sparkled as he blinked several times. He was also a practiced liar.

"*Nothing?* Then what's the matter? Why do you act so guilty? Why are you all so quiet?"

"We're eating," Kevin said.

Stanion turned to his eldest son, who sat next to Kevin, and said in a restrained and altered tone, as though speaking to an arbiter, "Carl, what is this?" Carl was twelve but could be left alone with the girls, the youngest of whom was only three, in complete trust. He understood them, sensed their needs, anticipated their whims, was gentle, and so could care for them better than most adults. He was straightforward and truthful unless he was protecting one of the others, in which case, with his intelligence, he could make himself a blank.

"Carl," Stanion said, placing both fists, broad as saucers, on the tabletop. "I asked you a question. What's been going on here?"

"I don't know."

"You don't know?"

"I don't think I really saw it."

"Saw what?"

"Anything that happened."

"Then something did happen."

"I don't know."

"You just said it did."

"I didn't see it."

"Ach!"

It was futile. The two girls, sitting along the side of the table to his left, their wide eyes fastened on him, went pale at the sound of his voice. It angered him to keep at it this way, to give it such importance, but his interrogating and lecturing were becoming harder to control, obsessive, and more involved and emotional. He rarely lifted a hand against the children, as she sometimes had; he felt it was unnecessary and wrong, and, besides, he feared the strength of an adult against a child, especially his own strength. He stared for a long time at the open lime burns on his knuckles, clenching his fists, angered even more by his indecisiveness, and then reached for his fork. He stopped. His youngest son, Jim, who sat across from the girls, alone at that side of the table, looked anxiously at Stanion, then at his brothers, and then at his food, which he had hardly touched.

This boy, changed so by her death, had become Stanion's favorite. He was no longer exuberant and cheerful. He woke at night and wandered through the bedrooms trailing a blanket, saying her name, and if his wanderings and the sound of his voice didn't wake Stanion so that he could take the boy into bed with him, he searched through all the rooms of the house, went out the door into the backyard, went to the plot where she had had her garden, and lay down there and slept until morning. He was old enough to know his mother as his sisters would never know her, but too young to be a companion to his brothers, who became close after her death. When he approached them, shy and ill at ease, they sent him to play with the girls. For a while he had quietly accepted this. But since he started school he had been bringing home his own playmates — a procession of the most reticent, underfed, tattered, backward boys in his class. He invited them in for meals, offered them the pick of his toys, and attached himself to them, feeding off their presence, praising them, devoting himself to them, until they became bored with his passive reverence and worshipful stare and stopped coming to the house. Now the boy's eyes, light green, large and seductive, were traveling around the table with a harried look.

With his lime-burned hand, Stanion reached out and touched the boy's shoulder. "You didn't do anything, did you, Jim?" he asked, and the boy, shrugging off Stanion's hand, turned clear around and took hold of the back of his chair and broke into tears.

"Carl! What's this about? Answer me!"

"I don't know how to," Carl said, and looked aside at Kevin, who was still eating as fast as he could.

"Did he hurt Jim?" Stanion demanded. "Is Kevin the cause of this?"

Carl lowered his eyes.

"Jim, you can tell me," Stanion said. "You don't have to be afraid now."

"I'm done," Kevin said, and scraped back his chair. "I'm going out."

"You sit right where you are till I'm through with you."

Kevin sat, piled more food on his plate, and started eating again.

"And if we have to sit here all night till I find out what's been going on," Stanion said, "we will."

Jim shifted his weight restlessly, his eyes made an anxious circuit of the table, and then, shrinking back in his chair, he cried out, "He kicked Marvin!"

"Who did?"

"Kevin!"

"*Kicked* him?"

"Then Marvin went home! He was crying!" Marvin, a frail boy who had just moved up from Kentucky, was Jim's most recent and most enduring friend.

"What is this? Carl!"

Carl kept his eyes down, picking at his food, then murmured, "We were having a track meet over at the school and Marvin was on Kevin's side. Jim and I were on the other. Marvin got tired toward the end and didn't want to run, so maybe Kevin did something. I don't know. I didn't see it. I was running."

Realizing that Carl had said all he was going to say, Stanion moved his eyes to Kevin. "Is this true?"

"No."

"Don't lie to me."

"Marvin just started crying and wanted to go home, that's all. He's a baby."

"Quit eating and look at me when I speak to you. Now nobody just starts crying for no reason—I know that and you know it too."

"I told him to play right. He wasn't playing right."

"Wasn't playing 'right.' What's right?"

Sensing he had exposed himself, brought out something that had caused trouble in the past, Kevin's face lost its color and he seemed breathless, as though he were running again,

circling something dangerous. "We were way ahead in points," he said, "and then Marvin faked like he was tired. He wouldn't do anything any more. Then when we were all running the mile he just walked along. He could have got second or third, at least, and we score 5, 3, 1. He didn't care whether we got those last points. We needed them."

"You mean you hurt him just because you were worried about losing?"

"Who says I hurt him?"

"Jim said you kicked him."

"If I had to run every race, Marvin could run at least one. He was just in the field events."

"How could you do such a thing?"

"What?"

"Whatever you did."

"Well, what would you do if you were all tired out and came around the track about the third time and there your teammate was, just walking along just like an old lady."

"So you kicked him."

"I brushed against him. Maybe I nicked him with my foot."

"Can't you leave other people alone? Don't you realize he's one of the few friends Jim's got? Let him run or walk or crawl or sit on his can or do what he wants. You hear me!" Silverware jumped as Stanion hit the tabletop. "What's the matter with you? What makes you think you're a judge of others?"

"I know I was running and he wasn't."

"He's not you. He's——"

"He was on my side!"

"Will you *listen* to me!"

Stanion started to rise, and his belt caught on the edge of the table, upsetting his coffee and a carton of milk. Kevin pushed himself back from the table and tipped over his chair, and the slap that was meant for him carried past and struck the youngest girl. She went back off her stool neatly as a bundle and dropped to the floor. When she realized where she was, she started wailing, and her sister joined in.

"Now look! Look what you made me do," Stanion said, and started around the table with all the galling details—the girl on the floor, the puddle of coffee and milk beside her, Jim with his hands over his face—streaming along the edge of his vision, sharpening his outrage. Kevin hadn't got to his feet, and was maneuvering around among the chairs on his hands and knees, trying to make it to a safe spot, his rump raised. Stanion came up behind him and kicked hard and struck bone, and Kevin, his limbs splaying out, hit flat on his stomach. Stanion lifted him to his feet. "Now get upstairs," he said. "Get upstairs before something worse happens."

Kevin gave him a furious going over with his eyes before he turned and ran up the steps. And then, as Kevin disappeared around the corner, Stanion realized what he had done and started trembling. He sent Jim and Carl outside, took the girls, one in each arm, and carried them into the bedroom and tried to comfort them. Their eyes were wide with terror, and the youngest girl didn't want to be touched.

When they were calmed, he undressed them and put them to bed, hardly aware of what he was doing. The presence in the upstairs room demanded all his attention. He went into the kitchen and sat at the table, his broad workman's knees bending with effort. He ached from balancing on a springy scaffold the whole day, all the while carrying a hawk of heavy plaster and reaching overhead to skim a finish coat on the ceiling. He felt too old to go on with the work. Tonight brought it to an end. No. There was bookwork to do, orders to call in, material to get, his lunch to pack.

He wanted to go upstairs but wasn't sure it was the right thing to do. He didn't want his thoughts to focus. He was afraid of what he'd done. He started eating, but the food was chilly and he had no appetite.

He gathered up the dishes, carried them to the sink, shook detergent over them, adjusted the temperature of the water, and let it run while he took a rag from the S-trap under the sink and wiped off the table. Then he got down on his hands and knees, and as he was mopping up the milk and coffee his vision narrowed, the patch of linoleum he was staring at darkened, and he felt faint. He stood up and leaned against the table. An even, abrasive sound was traveling through his consciousness as though it meant to erode it. He hurried over to the sink and shut off the water. The sound stayed.

He dipped a plate in and out of the water, rinsing off the grease, and his sight fastened on the soapy rainbow sliding along the plate's rim. He let it slip beneath the suds. He had an image of her turning from the sink, inclining her head to one side and lifting the hair from her cheek with the back of her hand, her face flushed, her eyes traveling around the room restlessly, but with an abstract look, as though there was no name for what she was searching for.

He went up the steps. Kevin was lying face down on the unmade bed, his back heaving, his exclamations and sobs muted by a pillow he held clasped over his head. Stanion eased himself onto the edge of the bed and lifted the pillow away. "Listen. Listen, now. I've tried—"

The boy grabbed at the loose bedclothes and tucked them around his face.

"How many times have I told you—" Stanion began, then stopped. He couldn't stand being sanctimonious. He looked away and saw the bed—with Kevin's legs, Kevin's body half covered with a sheet stretched out on it—and part of his own shoulder enclosed in a mirror, and it was as though he were looking through to the past. The scene, scaled down, dimmer than in hospital light, was a scene he had lived through once, with her, and it was the same. Those close to you showed up well and were solid and understandable, were fixed for good in your mind—but only in your mind. Their real selves were at a distance, a part of the world, and the world opened up, took them without reason; was opening up just as before, the body beside him falling away, while he sat off to the side, his shoulder showing in the tilted mirror, helpless.

Then he felt himself being drawn down too. He searched for something outside him to hold to. Wadded socks lay on the floor, gathering tufts of dust. Tubes and coils of a dismantled radio were strewn in one corner along with a model pistol of plastic, model ships, and a Boy Scout neckerchief. Dirty clothes were spread over the top of the dresser, trailing down its front, and more clothes were draped over the back of a chair.

"If your mother—" Stanion stopped. The words only took him down deeper. He put his hands on the boy's shoulders and tried to lift him up, but Kevin struggled free and dropped back onto the mattress.

"Don't now," Stanion said. "Don't carry on so. Please. Sit up."

"I'm sorry!"

"I know. Now don't."

"I can't stop!"

"Try to look at it—"

"My head hurts! It feels like something wants to come out of it!"

Stanion passed his hand over Kevin's skull, and the sensation of stiff stubble rubbing across the palm of his hand—what led the boy to do this? what did this hark back to?—made him feel even more helpless and afraid. "Don't now," he said, and his being closed around the words. Father, mother, nurse, teacher, arbiter, guardian, judge—all the roles were too much. He no longer had the power to reach through to his children as the person he was, their father, the man who loved them, and let them know he loved them, and that inability, more than anything else, was the thing breaking him.

He heard a muffled sound, regular and tense, and at first he thought it was a summons, a last thing he would have to face up to, and when nothing came he believed it was the labored beating of his own heart. He turned. Kevin was lying in the same position, face down, but his hand was tapping over the covers in a widening arc, feeling its way toward Stanion; it touched him tentatively, backed away, and then came down, damp and hot with perspiration, on his thigh. Stanion took the hand in his and an order came over the room.

"I'm sorry," Kevin said in a muffled voice. "Forgive me."

"Did I hurt you?"

"No."

"Do you want to come downstairs?"

"No."

"Do you feel any better?"

"Yes."

"I've sent Jim and Carl outdoors. The girls are in bed. I'm sorry they had to see it."

"I didn't mean to do it. He wasn't playing right."

"I know. Here," he said, and raised Kevin and arranged him so they were sitting next to one another. "Let's go downstairs and do the dishes," Stanion said. "Then we'll both feel better." He put his arm around his son's waist. "Will you come downstairs and help me do the dishes?"

FOR STUDY AND DISCUSSION

1. The main characters in this story are William Stanion and his son Kevin. The father's character is well defined because we are able to share his inner thoughts and feelings. Using details from the story, tell what kind of person William Stanion is.

2. We can watch Kevin and listen to him, and we know how other people feel about him, but his inner thoughts and feelings are not directly revealed. From clues you are given, tell what kind of a person you think Kevin is.

3. Stanion's dead wife is an important presence in this story. How has her death affected the entire family? In what specific ways do memories of his wife "torment" Stanion?

4. Kevin, who has shaved his head, cries out, "My head hurts! It feels like something wants to come out of it!" What do you think Kevin is trying to release?

5. The climax of this story occurs when Stanion takes Kevin's outstretched hand. What comes "over the room" when this happens? What changes do you think are taking place in Kevin and his father?

COMPLEX CHARACTERIZATION

In simple forms of fiction—such as in some mystery and adventure stories—the characters are "all good" or "all bad." But in serious fiction, we find that characters cannot be so easily pigeonholed. These characters are complex. We find there is more than one side to them, just as there is more than one side to us all. At times, the central characters in such stories do things we admire a great deal, but they also do things that are not so admirable. It is important in such stories to understand the characters' *motivations*—the reasons they act as they do.

The character of William Stanion in this story is a complex one. We are told in the opening paragraph that Stanion is "reaching his limit," that he feels "weak" and "out of touch." When we learn that his wife has died, we feel great sympathy for him. But then he tangles with a difficult son. What other side of Stanion do we see when he strikes out at Kevin? What are his motives for acting so impulsively, even cruelly?

Kevin is also a complex character. How would you explain Kevin's cruelty to a younger child?

FOR COMPOSITION

Expressing an Opinion

Stories like "The Beginning of Grief," which trace the pattern of an internal conflict, are different in many ways from stories like "Leiningen Versus the Ants," which trace the pattern of an exciting external conflict. In a paragraph, tell which kind of story you prefer to read, and why. If you enjoy both kinds of stories, state your reasons and tell what effect each kind of story has on you.

ABOUT THE AUTHOR

Larry Woiwode (woi′wōōd-ē) (1941–   ) has worked as a professional writer since his graduation from the University of Illinois in 1964. Born in Carrington, North Dakota, Woiwode has translated his personal knowledge of Midwestern life into two novels and numerous short stories. Woiwode's first novel, *What I'm Going to Do (I Think)*, won the William Faulkner award for the best first novel in 1969. Woiwode has earned much critical praise for his second novel, *Beyond the Bedroom Wall*, published in 1975.

Setting

Edgar Allan Poe opens "The Fall of the House of Usher," one of his famous horror stories, with this scene:

> During the whole of a dull, dark, and soundless day in the autumn of the year, when the clouds hung oppressively low in the heavens, I had been passing alone, on horseback, through a singularly dreary tract of country, and at length found myself, as the shades of the evening drew on, within view of the melancholy House of Usher. I know not how it was—but, with the first glimpse of the building, a sense of insufferable gloom pervaded my spirit.

Clearly, the *setting* of this story—the time and place of its action—is significant. The author tells us what the day is like (dull, dark, and soundless), what time of year it is (autumn), what time of day it is (evening), and what the surroundings are like (dreary and melancholy). This description not only gives us a vivid picture of a setting, but it also creates an atmosphere, or emotional climate. It is hard to read about dull dark days in the autumn of the year at evening in a dreary country without feeling a sense of uneasiness and gloom.

In Poe's story, setting is used to create atmosphere. Setting can also have other functions in fiction. Setting may be a significant element in the plot. In Carl Stephenson's story "Leiningen Versus the Ants" (page 3), for example, a vast horde of ravenous ants, native to a South American setting, must be overcome by the main character. Setting can be used to reveal something about character. In "María Tepache" (page 76), the main character's home is described: "The window had burlap curtains, and Doña María explained why she put them up long ago. 'In a place where there aren't any curtains on the windows you can't expect children to turn out well.'" Details of this setting are used to reflect a woman's hopes for the future.

Chee's Daughter

Juanita Platero and
Siyowin Miller

The hat told the story, the big, black, drooping Stetson. It was not at the proper angle, the proper rakish angle for so young a Navajo. There was no song, and that was not in keeping either. There should have been at least a humming, a faint, all-to-himself "he he he heya," for it was a good horse he was riding, a slender-legged, high-stepping buckskin that would race the wind with light knee-urging. This was a day for singing, a warm winter day, when the touch of the sun upon the back belied the snow high on distant mountains.

Wind warmed by the sun touched his high-boned cheeks like flicker[1] feathers, and still he rode on silently, deeper into Little Canyon, until the red rock walls rose straight upward from the stream bed and only a narrow piece of blue sky hung above. Abruptly the sky widened where the canyon walls were pushed back to make a wide place, as though in ancient times an angry stream had tried to go all ways at once.

---

1. **flicker:** woodpecker.

This was home—this wide place in the canyon—levels of jagged rock and levels of rich red earth. This was home to Chee, the rider of the buckskin, as it had been to many generations before him.

He stopped his horse at the stream and sat looking across the narrow ribbon of water to the bare-branched peach trees. He was seeing them each springtime with their age-gnarled limbs transfigured beneath veils of blossom pink; he was seeing them in autumn laden with their yellow fruit, small and sweet. Then his eyes searched out the indistinct furrows of the fields beside the stream, where each year the corn and beans and squash drank thirstily of the overflow from summer rains. Chee was trying to outweigh today's bitter betrayal of hope by gathering to himself these reminders of the integrity of the land. Land did not cheat! His mind lingered deliberately on all the days spent here in the sun caring for the young plants, his songs to the earth and to the life springing from it— ". . . In the middle of the wide field . . . Yellow Corn Boy . . . He has started both ways . . ." then the harvest and repayment in full measure. Here was the old feeling of wholeness and of oneness with the sun and earth and growing things.

Chee urged the buckskin toward the family compound where, secure in a recess of overhanging rock, was his mother's dome-shaped hogan,[2] red rock and red adobe like the ground on which it nestled. Not far from the hogan was the half-circle of brush like a dark shadow against the canyon wall—corral for sheep and goats. Farther from the hogan, in full circle, stood the horse corral made of heavy cedar branches sternly interlocked. Chee's long thin lips curved into a smile as he passed his daughter's tiny hogan squatted like a round Pueblo oven beside the corral. He remembered the summer day when together they sat back on their heels and plastered wet adobe all about the circling wall of rock and the woven dome of piñon[3] twigs. How his family laughed when the Little One herded the bewildered chickens into her tiny hogan as the first snow fell.

Then the smile faded from Chee's lips and his eyes darkened as he tied his horse to a corral post and turned to the strangely empty compound. "Someone has told them," he thought, "and they are inside weeping." He passed his mother's deserted loom on the south side of the hogan and pulled the rude wooden door toward him, bowing his head, hunching his shoulders to get inside.

His mother sat sideways by the center fire, her feet drawn up under her full skirts. Her hands were busy kneading dough in the chipped white basin. With her head down, her voice was muffled when she said, "The meal will soon be ready, Son."

Chee passed his father sitting against the wall, hat over his eyes as though asleep. He passed his older sister, who sat turning mutton ribs on a crude wire grill over the coals, noticed tears dropping on her hands. "She cared more for my wife than I realized," he thought.

Then because something must be said sometime, he tossed the black Stetson upon a bulging sack of wool and said, "You have heard, then." He could not shut from his mind how confidently he had set the handsome new hat on his head that very morning, slanting the wide brim over one eye: he was going to see his wife, and today he would ask the doctors about bringing her home; last week she had looked so much better.

---

2. **hogan:** traditional Navajo house, usually made of earth walls supported by timber.

3. **piñon** (pĭn′yōn′): small pine tree.

His sister nodded but did not speak. His mother sniffled and passed her velveteen sleeve beneath her nose. Chee sat down, leaning against the wall. "I suppose I was a fool for hoping all the time. I should have expected this. Few of our people get well from the coughing sickness.[4] But *she* seemed to be getting better."

His mother was crying aloud now and blowing her nose noisily on her skirt. His father sat up, speaking gently to her.

Chee shifted his position and started a cigarette. His mind turned back to the Little One. At least she was too small to understand what had happened, the Little One who had been born three years before in the sanitarium where his wife was being treated for the coughing sickness, the Little One he had brought home to his mother's hogan to be nursed by his sister, whose baby was a few months older. As she grew fat-cheeked and sturdy-legged, she followed him about like a shadow; somehow her baby mind had grasped that of all those at the hogan who cared for her and played with her, he—Chee—belonged most to her. She sat cross-legged at his elbow when he worked silver at the forge; she rode before him in the saddle when he drove the horses to water; often she lay wakeful on her sheep pelts until he stretched out for the night in the darkened hogan and she could snuggle warm against him.

4. **coughing sickness:** tuberculosis.

Chee blew smoke slowly, and some of the sadness left his dark eyes as he said, "It is not as bad as it might be. It is not as though we are left with nothing."

Chee's sister arose, sobs catching in her throat, and rushed past him out the doorway. Chee sat upright, a terrible fear possessing him. For a moment his mouth could make no sound. Then: "The Little One! Mother, where is she?"

His mother turned her stricken face to him. "Your wife's people came after her this morning. They heard yesterday of their daughter's death through the trader at Red Sands."

Chee started to protest, but his mother shook her head slowly. "I didn't expect they would want the Little One either. But there is nothing you can do. She is a girl child and belongs to her mother's people; it is custom."

Frowning, Chee got to his feet, grinding his cigarette into the dirt floor. "Custom! When did my wife's parents begin thinking about custom? Why, the hogan where they live doesn't even face the east!"[5] He started toward the door. "Perhaps I can overtake them. Perhaps they don't realize how much we want her here with us. I'll ask them to give my daughter back to me. Surely, they won't refuse."

His mother stopped him gently with her outstretched hand. "You couldn't overtake them now. They were in the trader's car. Eat and rest, and think more about this."

"Have you forgotten how things have always been between you and your wife's people?" his father said.

That night, Chee's thoughts were troubled —half-forgotten incidents became disturbingly vivid—but early the next morning he saddled the buckskin and set out for the settlement of Red Sands. Even though his father-in-law, Old Man Fat, might laugh, Chee knew that he must talk to him. There were some things to which Old Man Fat might listen.

Chee rode the first part of the fifteen miles to Red Sands expectantly. The sight of sandstone buttes[6] near Cottonwood Spring reddening in the morning sun brought a song almost to his lips. He twirled his reins in salute to the small boy herding sheep toward many-colored Butterfly Mountain, watched with pleasure the feathers of smoke rising against tree-darkened western mesas from the hogans sheltered there. But as he approached the familiar settlement sprawled in mushroom growth along the highway, he began to feel as though a scene from a bad dream was becoming real.

Several cars were parked around the trading store, which was built like two log hogans side by side, with red gas pumps in front and a sign across the tar-paper roofs: *Red Sands Trading Post — Groceries   Gasoline   Cold Drinks   Sandwiches   Indian Curios.* Back of the trading post an unpainted frame house and outbuildings squatted on the drab, treeless land. Chee and the Little One's mother had lived there when they stayed with his wife's people. That was according to custom—living with one's wife's people— but Chee had never been convinced that it was custom alone which prompted Old Man Fat and his wife to insist that their daughter bring her husband to live at the trading post.

Beside the post was a large hogan of logs, with brightly painted pseudo-Navajo[7] designs

---

5. **east:** according to Navajo custom, the door of a hogan faces the east.

6. **buttes** (byo͞ots): steep, flat-topped hills rising above a plain.
7. **pseudo-Navajo** (so͞o′dō-năv′ə-hō′): fake or imitation Navajo.

A cold wind blowing down from the mountains began to whistle about Chee's ears. It flapped the gaudy Navajo rugs which were hung in one long bright line to attract tourists. It swayed the sign *Navajo Weaver at Work* beside the loom where Old Man Fat's wife sat hunched in her striped blanket, patting the colored thread of a design into place with a wooden comb. Tourists stood watching the weaver. More tourists stood in a knot before the hogan where the sign said: *See Inside a Real Navajo Home   25¢*.

Then the knot seemed to unravel as a few people returned to their cars; some had cameras; and there against the blue door Chee saw the Little One standing uncertainly. The wind was plucking at her new purple blouse and wide green skirt; it freed truant strands of soft dark hair from the meager queue[8] into which it had been tied with white yarn.

"Isn't she cunning!" one of the women tourists was saying as she turned away.

Chee's lips tightened as he began to look around for Old Man Fat. Finally he saw him passing among the tourists collecting coins.

Then the Little One saw Chee. The uncertainty left her face, and she darted through the crowd as her father swung down from his horse. Chee lifted her in his arms, hugging her tight. While he listened to her breathless chatter, he watched Old Man Fat bearing down on them, scowling.

As his father-in-law walked heavily across the graveled lot, Chee was reminded of a statement his mother sometimes made: "When you see a fat Navajo, you see one who hasn't worked for what he has."

Old Man Fat was fattest in the middle. There was indolence in his walk even though he seemed to hurry, indolence in his cheeks

on the roof—a hogan with smoke-smudged windows and a garish blue door which faced north to the highway. Old Man Fat had offered Chee a hogan like this one. The trader would build it if he and his wife would live there and Chee would work at his forge, making silver jewelry where tourists could watch him. But Chee had asked instead for a piece of land for a cornfield and help in building a hogan far back from the highway and a corral for the sheep he had brought to this marriage.

---

8. **queue** (kyoō): braid.

so plump they made his eyes squint, eyes now smoldering with anger.

Some of the tourists were getting into their cars and driving away. The old man said belligerently to Chee, "Why do you come here? To spoil our business? To drive people away?"

"I came to talk with you," Chee answered, trying to keep his voice steady as he faced the old man.

"We have nothing to talk about," Old Man Fat blustered and did not offer to touch Chee's extended hand.

"It's about the Little One." Chee settled his daughter more comfortably against his hip as he weighed carefully all the words he had planned to say. "We are going to miss her very much. It wouldn't be so bad if we knew that *part* of each year she could be with us. That might help you too. You and your wife are no longer young people and you have no young ones here to depend upon." Chee chose his next words remembering the thriftlessness of his wife's parents, and their greed. "Perhaps we could share the care of this little one. Things are good with us. So much snow this year will make lots of grass for the sheep. We have good land for corn and melons."

Chee's words did not have the expected effect. Old Man Fat was enraged. "Farmers, all of you! Long-haired farmers! Do you think everyone must bend his back over the short-handled hoe in order to have food to eat?" His tone changed as he began to brag a little. "We not only have all the things from cans at the trader's, but when the Pueblos come past here on their way to town, we buy their salty jerked[9] mutton, young corn for roasting, dried sweet peaches."

Chee's dark eyes surveyed the land along the highway as the old man continued to brag

about being "progressive." *He* no longer was tied to the land. He and his wife made money easily and could *buy* all the things they wanted. Chee realized too late that he had stumbled into the old argument between himself and his wife's parents. They had never understood his feeling about the land — that a man took care of his land and it in turn took care of him. Old Man Fat and his wife scoffed at him, called him a Pueblo farmer, all during that summer when he planted and weeded and harvested. Yet they ate the green corn in their mutton stews, and the chili paste from the fresh ripe chilis, and the tortillas from the cornmeal his wife ground. None of this working and sweating in the sun for Old Man Fat, who talked proudly of his easy way of living — collecting money from the trader who rented this strip of land beside the highway, collecting money from the tourists.

Yet Chee had once won that argument. His wife had shared his belief in the integrity of the earth, that jobs and people might fail one, but the earth never would. After that first year she had turned from her own people and gone with Chee to Little Canyon.

Old Man Fat was reaching for the Little One. "Don't be coming here with plans for my daughter's daughter," he warned. "If you try to make trouble, I'll take the case to the government man in town."

The impulse was strong in Chee to turn and ride off while he still had the Little One in his arms. But he knew his time of victory would be short. His own family would uphold the old custom of children, especially girl children, belonging to the mother's people. He would have to give his daughter up if the case were brought before the headman of Little Canyon, and certainly he would have no better chance before a strange white man in town.

9. **jerked:** preserved, by being cut into strips and dried in the sun.

He handed the bewildered Little One to her grandfather who stood watching every movement suspiciously. Chee asked, "If I brought you a few things for the Little One, would that be making trouble? Some velvet for a blouse, or some of the jerky she likes so well . . . this summer's melon?"

Old Man Fat backed away from him. "Well," he hesitated, as some of the anger disappeared from his face and beads of greed shone in his eyes. "Well," he repeated. Then as the Little One began to squirm in his arms and cry, he said, "No! No! Stay away from here, you and all your family."

The sense of his failure deepened as Chee rode back to Little Canyon. But it was not until he sat with his family that evening in the hogan, while the familiar bustle of meal preparing went on about him, that he began to doubt the wisdom of the things he'd always believed. He smelled the coffee boiling and the oily fragrance of chili powder dusted into the bubbling pot of stew; he watched his mother turning round crusty fried bread in the small black skillet. All around him was plenty—a half of mutton hanging near the door, bright strings of chili drying, corn hanging by the braided husks, cloth bags of dried peaches. Yet in his heart was nothing.

He heard the familiar sounds of the sheep outside the hogan, the splash of water as his father filled the long drinking trough from the water barrel. When his father came in, Chee could not bring himself to tell a second time of the day's happenings. He watched his wiry, soft-spoken father while his mother told the story, saw his father's queue of graying hair quiver as he nodded his head with sympathetic exclamations.

Chee's doubting, acrid thoughts kept forming: Was it wisdom his father had passed on to him, or was his inheritance only the stubbornness of a long-haired Navajo resisting change? Take care of the land and it will take care of you. True, the land had always given him food, but now food was not enough. Perhaps if he had gone to school, he would have learned a different kind of wisdom, something to help him now. A schoolboy might even be able to speak convincingly to this government man whom Old Man Fat threatened to call, instead of sitting here like a clod of earth itself—Pueblo farmer indeed. What had the land to give that would restore his daughter?

In the days that followed, Chee herded sheep. He got up in the half-light, drank the hot coffee his mother had ready, then started the flock moving. It was necessary to drive the sheep a long way from the hogan to find good winter forage. Sometimes Chee met friends or relatives who were on their way to town or to the road camp where they hoped to get work; then there was friendly banter and an exchange of news. But most of the days seemed endless; he could not walk far enough or fast enough from his memories of the Little One or from his bitter thoughts. Sometimes it seemed his daughter trudged beside him, so real he could almost hear her footsteps—the muffled pad-pad of little feet in deerhide. In the glare of a snowbank he would see her vivid face, brown eyes sparkling. Mingling with the tinkle of sheep bells he heard her laughter.

When, weary of following the small sharp hoof marks that crossed and recrossed in the snow, he sat down in the shelter of a rock, it was only to be reminded that in his thoughts he had forsaken his brotherhood with the earth and sun and growing things. If he remembered times when he had flung himself against the earth to rest, to lie there in the sun until he could no longer feel where he left off and the earth began, it was to remember also that now he sat like an alien against the same earth; the belonging together was gone. The earth was one thing and he was another.

It was during the days when he herded sheep that Chee decided he must leave Little Canyon. Perhaps he would take a job silversmithing for one of the traders in town. Perhaps, even though he spoke little English, he could get a job at the road camp with his cousins; he would ask them about it.

Springtime transformed the mesas. The peach trees in the canyon were shedding fragrance and pink blossoms on the gentled wind. The sheep no longer foraged for the yellow seeds of chamiso[10] but ranged near the hogan with the long-legged new lambs, eating tender young grass.

Chee was near the hogan on the day his cousins rode up with the message for which he waited. He had been watching with mixed emotions while his father and his sister's husband cleared the fields beside the stream.

"The boss at the camp says he needs an extra hand, but he wants to know if you'll be willing to go with the camp when they move it to the other side of the town?" The tall cousin shifted his weight in the saddle.

The other cousin took up the explanation. "The work near here will last only until the new cutoff beyond Red Sands is finished. After that, the work will be too far away for you to get back here often."

That was what Chee had wanted—to get away from Little Canyon—yet he found himself not so interested in the job beyond town as in this new cutoff which was almost finished. He pulled a blade of grass, split it thoughtfully down the center, as he asked questions of his cousins. Finally he said: "I

need to think more about this. If I decide on this job, I'll ride over."

Before his cousins were out of sight down the canyon, Chee was walking toward the fields, a bold plan shaping in his mind. As the plan began to flourish, wild and hardy as young tumbleweed, Chee added his own voice softly to the song his father was singing: ". . . In the middle of the wide field . . . Yellow Corn Boy . . . I wish to put in."

Chee walked slowly around the field, the rich red earth yielding to his footsteps. His plan depended upon this land and upon the things he remembered most about his wife's people.

Through planting time Chee worked zealously and tirelessly. He spoke little of the large new field he was planting, because he felt so strongly that just now this was something between himself and the land. The first days he was ever stooping, piercing the ground with the pointed stick, placing the corn kernels there, walking around the field and through it, singing, ". . . His track leads into the ground . . . Yellow Corn Boy . . . his track leads into the ground." After that, each day Chee walked through his field watching for the tips of green to break through; first a few spikes in the center and then more and more, until the corn in all parts of the field was above ground. Surely, Chee thought, if he sang the proper songs, if he cared for this land faithfully, it would not forsake him now, even though through the lonely days of winter he had betrayed the goodness of the earth in his thoughts.

Through the summer Chee worked long days, the sun hot upon his back, pulling weeds from around young corn plants; he planted squash and pumpkin; he terraced a small piece of land near his mother's hogan and planted carrots and onions and the moisture-loving chili. He was increasingly rest-

---

10. **chamiso** (chə-mē′sō): shrub that forms dense thickets.

less. Finally he told his family what he hoped the harvest from this land would bring him. Then the whole family waited with him, watching the corn: the slender graceful plants that waved green arms and bent to embrace each other as young winds wandered through the field, the maturing plants flaunting their pollen-laden tassels in the sun, the tall and sturdy parent corn with new-formed ears and a froth of purple, red, and yellow corn beards against the dusty emerald of broad leaves.

Summer was almost over when Chee slung the bulging packs across two pack ponies. His mother helped him tie the heavy rolled pack behind the saddle of the buckskin. Chee knotted the new yellow kerchief about his neck a little tighter, gave the broad black hat brim an extra tug, but these were only gestures of assurance and he knew it. The land had not failed him. That part was done. But this he was riding into? Who could tell?

When Chee arrived at Red Sands, it was as he had expected to find it—no cars on the highway. His cousins had told him that even the Pueblo farmers were using the new cutoff to town. The barren gravel around the Red Sands Trading Post was deserted. A sign banged against the dismantled gas pumps: *Closed until further notice.*

Old Man Fat came from the crude summer shelter built beside the log hogan from a few branches of scrub cedar and the sides of wooden crates. He seemed almost friendly when he saw Chee.

"Get down, my son," he said, eyeing the bulging packs. There was no bluster in his voice today, and his face sagged, looking somewhat saddened, perhaps because his cheeks were no longer quite full enough to push his eyes upward at the corners. "You are going on a journey?"

Chee shook his head. "Our fields gave us so much this year, I thought to sell or trade this

to the trader. I didn't know he was no longer here."

Old Man Fat sighed, his voice dropping to an injured tone. "He says he and his wife are going to rest this winter; then after that he'll build a place up on the new highway."

Chee moved as though to be traveling on, then jerked his head toward the pack ponies. "Anything you need?"

"I'll ask my wife," Old Man Fat said as he led the way to the shelter. "Maybe she has a little money. Things have not been too good with us since the trader closed. Only a few tourists come this way." He shrugged his shoulders. "And with the trader gone—no credit."

Chee was not deceived by his father-in-law's unexpected confidences. He recognized them as a hopeful bid for sympathy and, if possible, something for nothing. Chee made no answer. He was thinking that so far he had been right about his wife's parents: their thriftlessness had left them with no resources to last until Old Man Fat found another easy way of making a living.

Old Man Fat's wife was in the shelter working at her loom. She turned rather wearily when her husband asked with noticeable deference if she would give him money to buy supplies. Chee surmised that the only income here was from his mother-in-law's weaving.

She peered around the corner of the shelter at the laden ponies, and then she looked at Chee. "What do you have there, my son?"

Chee smiled to himself as he turned to pull the pack from one of the ponies, dragged it to the shelter where he untied the ropes. Pumpkins and hard-shelled squash tumbled out, and the ears of corn—pale yellow husks fitting firmly over plump ripe kernels, blue corn, red corn, yellow corn, many-colored corn, ears and ears of it—tumbled into every corner of the shelter.

"Yooooh," Old Man Fat's wife exclaimed as she took some of the ears in her hands. Then she glanced up at her son-in-law. "But we have no money for all this. We have sold almost everything we own—even the brass bed that stood in the hogan."

Old Man Fat's brass bed. Chee concealed his amusement as he started back for another pack. That must have been a hard parting. Then he stopped, for, coming from the cool darkness of the hogan was the Little One, rubbing her eyes as though she had been asleep. She stood for a moment in the doorway, and Chee saw that she was dirty, barefoot, her hair uncombed, her little blouse shorn of all its silver buttons. Then she ran toward Chee, her arms outstretched. Heedless of Old Man Fat and his wife, her father caught her in his arms, her hair falling in a dark cloud across his face, the sweetness of her laughter warm against his shoulder.

It was the haste within him to get this slow waiting game played through to the finish that made Chee speak unwisely. It was the desire to swing her before him in the saddle and ride fast to Little Canyon that prompted his words. "The money doesn't matter. You still have something. . . ."

Chee knew immediately that he had overspoken. The old woman looked from him to the corn spread before her. Unfriendliness began to harden in his father-in-law's face. All the old arguments between himself and his wife's people came pushing and crowding in between them now.

Old Man Fat began kicking the ears of corn back onto the canvas as he eyed Chee angrily. "And you rode all the way over here thinking that for a little food we would give up our daughter's daughter?"

Chee did not wait for the old man to reach for the Little One. He walked dazedly to the shelter, rubbing his cheek against her soft dark hair, and put her gently into her grandmother's lap. Then he turned back to the horses. He had failed. By his own haste he had failed. He swung into the saddle, his hand touching the roll behind it. Should he ride on into town?

Then he dismounted, scarcely glancing at Old Man Fat, who stood uncertainly at the corner of the shelter, listening to his wife. "Give me a hand with this other pack of corn, Grandfather," Chee said, carefully keeping the small bit of hope from his voice.

Puzzled, but willing, Old Man Fat helped carry the other pack to the shelter, opening it to find more corn as well as carrots and round, pale yellow onions. Chee went back for the roll behind the buckskin's saddle and carried it to the entrance of the shelter, where he cut the ropes and gave the canvas a nudge with his toe. Tins of coffee rolled out, small plump cloth bags; jerked meat from several butcherings spilled from a flour sack; and bright red chilis splashed like flames against the dust.

"I will leave all this anyhow," Chee told them. "I would not want my daughter nor even you old people to go hungry."

Old Man Fat picked up a shiny tin of coffee, then put it down. With trembling hands he began to untie one of the cloth bags—dried sweet peaches.

The Little One had wriggled from her grandmother's lap, unheeded, and was on her knees, digging her hands into the jerked meat.

"There is almost enough food here to last all winter." Old Man Fat's wife sought the eyes of her husband.

Chee said, "I meant it to be enough. But that was when I thought you might send the Little One back with me." He looked down at his daughter noisily sucking jerky. Her mouth, both fists, were full of it. "I am sorry that you feel you cannot bear to part with her."

Old Man Fat's wife brushed a straggly wisp of gray hair from her forehead as she turned to look at the Little One. Old Man Fat was looking too. And it was not a thing to see. For in that moment the Little One ceased to be their daughter's daughter and became just another mouth to feed.

"And why not?" the old woman asked wearily.

Chee was settled in the saddle, the barefooted Little One before him. He urged the buckskin faster, and his daughter clutched his shirtfront. The purpling mesas flung back the echo: ". . . My corn embrace each other. In the middle of the wide field . . . Yellow Corn Boy embrace each other."

FOR STUDY AND DISCUSSION

1. Find passages in this story that describe the traditional Navajo belief about the land and about people's relationship to it. Why does Chee begin to doubt his beliefs about the land?

2. Chee refers to "the old arguments" between himself and his wife's parents. What is the basis of this old conflict? What new conflict between Chee and his in-laws is the basis of this story?

3. How does the land itself finally help solve Chee's conflicts?

4. This story is basically about a clash between two cultures and two sets of values. How are the contrasting values represented by the contrasting settings: the trading post and Chee's home in Little Canyon? Which setting and set of values are sterile and destructive? Which are fruitful and supporting?

FOR COMPOSITION

Describing Contrasting Settings

In this story, we are given descriptions of two contrasting settings: the setting of the trading post and the setting of Chee's home in Little Canyon. In two paragraphs, describe two contrasting settings that you know well. Use specific details that will help your readers visualize the two settings. Try to communicate your feelings about the two different places.

ABOUT THE AUTHORS

Juanita Platero and Siyowin Miller have collaborated on several stories about the conflict in values between the old Navajo ways and the new ways of industrial society. Platero herself is a Navajo, who lived at one time on a reservation in New Mexico, the setting for "Chee's Daughter."

María Tepache

Amado Muro

In San Antonio, I got off a Southern Pacific freight train near the tracks that spidered out from the roundhouse turntable. When I quit the train it was almost five o'clock, and the sky was dark with the smoky pall of thunderheads. I was tired and chilled and hungry. I hoped to find something to eat and then get on to Houston.

Nearby was a small white-frame Mexican grocery with a corrugated tin porch held up by a few warped scantlings.[1] The window displayed lettuce heads and coffee in paper sacks, and near the door was a wire bin of oranges. A dog lay on the porch before the door. I went in and asked a buxom, gray-haired woman with a round face and untroubled eyes if she could spare some day-olds.

"Ay, Señora Madre de San Juan, I just fed four hoboes and I can't feed no more," she said.

I started out the door then, but she called me back. She stared at me, her dark eyes becoming very round. "Hijole, paisanito,[2] what spider has stung you—you look sad and burdened like the woodcutter's burro," she said. "Well, I don't blame you. When bread becomes scarce so do smiles."

The gray-haired woman wore a blue dress that was cut straight and came to her knees, and she had on huaraches. She told me her name was María Rodriguez, but she said people all called her María Tepache because she liked tepache[3] with big pineapple chunks in it so well. We talked of different things—about where she came from was one. She came from a Durango[4] village populated mostly, she said, by old men, old women, and goats.

"I was born in one of those homes where burros sleep with Christians," she said. "I can read and eat with a spoon, but I'm not one of those women meant to live in homes that would be like cathedrals if they had bells. In our adobe-hut village, we lived a primitive life with no more light than the sky gives and no more water than that of the river. But my fa-

---

1. **scantlings:** small pieces of wood.
2. **"Hijole, paisanito":** "Son of a gun, country boy."
3. **tepache:** a fermented drink made with pineapples and cloves.

4. **Durango:** state in northwest Mexico.

ther never stopped feeding me because he couldn't give me bonbons or clothing me because he couldn't dress me in silks."

She asked me where I was from, her face intent with strong interest. When I told her, she appeared surprised. "¡Válgame San Crispin! I'd never have guessed it," she said.

When I asked why, she smiled and said: "Most Chihuahua people don't talk so fast as we of Durango. But you talk fast, and with the accent of Santa María de todo el mundo."

After that she put on a cambaye[5] apron with a big bow in back, and led me to the back of the store where all the living was done. "This is your humble kitchen—come in," she invited.

The place was like all the homes of poor Mexicans that I'd seen in Texas. There was a broken-legged wood stove, a shuck-tick bed, a straight-back chair, a mirror with the quicksilver gone, and a table covered with oilcloth frayed and dark at the edges. Beyond the stove and to one side was an old cupboard with the doors standing open. The kitchen's bare floor was clean, and the walls were painted wood with only a calendar picture of Nicolás Bravo that hung crookedly from its nail as decoration. On a tiny shelf in a corner was a gilt-framed picture of María Guadalupana[6] and a crucified Christ.

The window had burlap curtains, and Doña María explained why she put them up long ago. "In a place where there aren't any curtains on the windows you can't expect children to turn out well," she said.

She lit a coal-oil lamp and set it on the table. Outside it was beginning to rain. Wind blew the rain in through the window and made the lamp burn unevenly and smoke the chimney. The chimney blackened until only a ring around the base gave off light. Doña María closed the window and afterward stood near the lamp and told me she was a widow. Standing there very still with heavy lashes lowered, she spoke of her husband and her voice was husky. The dog that had lain on the porch was curled on the floor by the bed, his head resting on his outspread paws and his eyes watching her.

"In our village my husband was an adobero, and he came here to earn dólarotes in the pecan mills," she said. "I wasn't one of those model Mexican wives who leave their wills in the church, but we were happy together and I never worried that he'd fall in love with another chancluda[7] prettier than me. He couldn't read or write, but I went through the fourth grade at the Justo Sierra School and I taught him about numbers so he could count the stars with our first son. When our centavos married and multiplied, he talked about going back to Mexico. '¡Ay Mariquita! If we can go back someday I swear I'll climb Popocatepetl[8] on my hands,' he told me. 'We could go to Puebla on the other side of the volcanoes, and buy land near the magueyes and milpas.[9] We'll buy three cows, and each will give her three litros. Our chilpayates will never dance the Jarabe Moreliano with hunger.' "

Her eyes softened in a reflection of faraway dreaminess. She said her husband made Puebla sound like Baghdad, and talked of singing to her with twenty mariachis.

"Now I live with no more company than my own sins," she said. "I pass my life tend-

---

5. **cambaye:** cotton.
6. **María Guadalupana:** Our Lady of Guadalupe, the patron saint of Mexico.

7. **chancluda:** a lower-class girl; a poor girl.
8. **Popocatepetl** (pō-pō-kăt′ə-pĕt′l): dormant volcano in Mexico.
9. **magueyes and milpas:** cactus plants and cornfields.

ing the store, and mending the clothes of my many grandchildren." She broke off and lowered her lids over her eyes, veiling them. Her mouth grew set, a thin, straight line; she passed her hands over her forehead as though awakening from sleep. Her gray hair was in a tangled cloud about her face, and she looked older than I'd thought at first seeing her. But when she looked up toward me, she was smiling again and her dark eyes were calm and reflective. "My grandchildren are less brutos than I," she said. "All of them know how to speak the gringo."

I hung my crumpled crush hat on a nail behind the kitchen door and went out in the backyard to split stovewood. The backyard was cluttered with piled-up packing boxes and crates, and the grass was yellow with sand. There was a stumpy cottonwood near the water tap, and a row of sweet peas clinging to a network of strings tacked on the fence. The cottonwood leaves had turned yellow, but they were still flat with green streaks showing in them. Every once in a while the wind would shake the branches and a flurry of dry leaves and dust funneled up near me.

I split wood, carried out ash buckets, and brought water in a zinc pail. While I worked, Doña María bent over a larded frying pan and told me about her father.

"He was a shepherd and a good man — never ambitious for the centavos," she said. "He was happy and contented with no more ambition than not to lose a lamb and go down to Santiago Papasquiaro two or three times a year to hear the mariachis play in the plaza and listen to the church bells."

When I finished the chores, night was coming and the rain was heavier. There was lightning, vivid flashes that scarred the sky, and I could see San Antonio's lights golden as oil lamps beyond the New Braunfels Bridge. The rain fell through the yellow lamplight streaming from the kitchen window and cars, their lamps wet gems, moved slowly across the high bridge. Their headlights seemed to draw the raindrops, like moths. I looked at them for a moment, rain spattering off my shoulders, then went inside.

Doña María had finished setting the table. She wiped sweat from her forehead with a fold of her apron, and began to fan herself. Then she motioned me to a plate filled with refried beans, rice, and blanquillos.

"Esa es mecha,"[10] she said. "It will make you feel like shouting, 'Yo soy Mexicano,' in the middle of a crowded street. Eat — one can think of nothing good when he's hungry."

I ate so fast I grew short of breath. Doña María watched me with her arms wrapped in her apron and crossed over her chest. She looked solemn except for a faint flicker of a smile at the corner of her mouth. The dog sat on his haunches beside her bare legs.

When I finished, she gave me an ixtle[11] shopping bag filled with tamales de dulce, nopalitos, a milk bottle of champurrado, and a tambache of flour tortillas[12] wrapped in a piece of newspaper. I tried halfheartedly to refuse it. But she insisted I take it.

"I have enough for today, perhaps tomorrow, and another day too," she said. "After that, God will say."

When I thanked her, she smiled her mild smile and told me to say the prayer of San Luisito every day.

"May the Indian Virgin who spoke with Juan Diego protect you and cover you with her mantle," she said when I went out the door, "and may you become rich enough to drink chocolate made with milk and eat gorditas fried in Guadalajara butter."

---

10. **"Esa es mecha"**: "This is dynamite."
11. **ixtle:** a kind of cactus fiber.
12. **a tambache of flour tortillas:** a bundle of flour tortillas wrapped in a moist cloth.

FOR STUDY AND DISCUSSION

1. What does María Tepache reveal about her values when she invites the young stranger to share a meal?
2. What details of the setting reveal that María Tepache doesn't have much money herself?
3. How do her husband's dreams contrast with the realities of María Tepache's present life? Do you think she is happy now? Explain.
4. María Tepache gives a religious blessing to the young stranger when he leaves. What else does she wish for him?
5. What do you think the young stranger learned from his evening with María Tepache?

LOCAL COLOR

Local color refers to details that describe the speech, dress, customs, and scenery associated with a particular setting. The purpose of local color is to give the reader the unique flavor of a certain locale.

This story is set in San Antonio, Texas. The main incident involves a meal, and much of the local color comes from the Mexican-Spanish terms that refer to food. Note, for example, the mention of *blanquillos* (eggs), *nopalitos* (fried cactus), and *champurrado* (a drink made with sweetened cornmeal). Notice also that María Tepache sprinkles her conversation with other Mexican-Spanish words and expressions. Refer to a Spanish-English dictionary and define some of these terms. Would you have had as vivid a picture of María Tepache and her locale if the story had been written entirely in English?

FOR COMPOSITION

Establishing Local Color
In the second paragraph, Amado Muro uses description to establish the local color of this particular section of San Antonio:

Nearby was a small white-frame Mexican grocery with a corrugated tin porch held up by a few warped scantlings. The window displayed lettuce heads and coffee in paper sacks, and near the door was a wire bin of oranges. A dog lay on the porch before the door. I went in and asked a buxom, gray-haired woman with a round face and untroubled eyes if she could spare some day-olds.

Notice the specific mention of "corrugated tin porch," "warped scantlings," "paper sacks," "wire bin," and even the presence of the dog on the porch. Write a brief essay in which you describe a setting you know very well. Use specific details to suggest the particular flavor of that locale. If you can, put a person in this setting and try to reproduce the person's characteristic way of speaking.

Point of View

When writers set out to tell their stories, they must immediately decide on a point of view. *Point of view* simply means the vantage point from which the story is told. The most familiar point of view is the *omniscient point of view*. The word *omniscient* means "all-knowing." In a story told from an omniscient point of view, there is no identifiable narrator. In such a story we tend to think of the writer—not any of the characters—as the storyteller. The omniscient point of view enables the writer to look into the hearts of all of the characters in the story and to reveal their thoughts and feelings to us. With an omniscient narrator, a writer can tell us as much or as little about the characters as he or she wants to. This is how the familiar story of Cinderella might begin if told from the omniscient point of view:

> Once upon a time there was a girl named Cinderella. Cinderella got her name because she was forced to work as a servant and sleep near the cinders. Cinderella was treated cruelly by her wicked stepmother, who was jealous of the girl's good looks and sweet temper because her own daughters were ugly and mean.

A story can also be told from a *limited third-person point of view*. This means that the story is narrated by someone who stands outside the story, but who sees everything from the limited vantage point of only one character. With such a point of view, we feel as if we are taken inside one character's head, for all of our attention is riveted on this one person. With this point of view, we usually do not know much of what the other characters are thinking and feeling. This is how Cinderella's story might begin if told from a limited third-person point of view:

> Once upon a time there was a girl named Cinderella, who was treated cruelly by her stepmother. Cinderella often wept bitterly in her ashy corner. Nightmares haunted her, and she feared the darkened scullery when the rats came out and played about her feet. At times, she wondered if her goodness would ever be rewarded.

Finally, a writer can use the *first-person point of view*. This simply means that the writer lets one of the characters tell the story. This narrator can be the hero or heroine of the story, or a minor character who is observing the action. This person speaks as "I," which is how the point of view got its name. In the first-person point of view, we might hear the story told in the diction of the narrator. When a story is told in the first person, by a character in the story, we know only what that character reports to us. The advantage of this point of view is that it creates immediacy and intimacy. If Cinderella's story were told in a first-person point of view, this is what we might get:

I had spent sixteen years sitting in the cinders of the kitchen. My stepmother must have hated me, because she made me do the dirty work. I could not understand the reasons for her feelings, for I had always treated her with respect. I slept in the ashes, and was tortured by nightmares and fear of rats.

It is important to remember that the narrator of a story is different from the author of the story. Sometimes, for example, women write stories that are narrated by men and vice versa. Sometimes stories are told by animals.

To analyze the point of view of a story, ask these questions: Who is the narrator of this story? Is this narrator a character in the story, or does the narrator stand outside the story? Does the narrator know about all the action and characters in the story, or is the narrator's view limited to one character only? How does the point of view affect my reaction to the story's characters and events?

The Quiet Man

Maurice Walsh

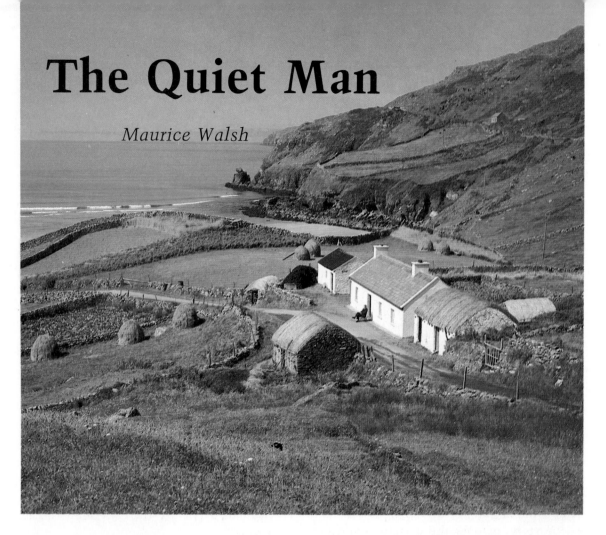

Shawn Kelvin, a blithe young lad of twenty, went to the States to seek his fortune. And fifteen years thereafter he returned to his native Kerry,[1] his blitheness sobered and his youth dried to the core, and whether he had made his fortune or whether he had not, no one could be knowing for certain. For he was a quiet man, not given to talking about himself and the things he had done. A quiet man, under middle size, with strong shoulders and deep-set blue eyes below brows darker than his dark hair—that was Shawn Kelvin. One

shoulder had a trick of hunching slightly higher than the other, and some folks said that came from a habit he had of shielding his eyes in the glare of an open-hearth furnace in a place called Pittsburgh, while others said it used to be a way he had of guarding his chin that time he was a sort of sparring-partner punching bag at a boxing camp.

Shawn Kelvin came home and found that he was the last of the Kelvins and that the farm of his forefathers had added its few acres to the ranch of Big Liam O'Grady of Moyvalla. Shawn took no action to recover his land, though O'Grady had got it meanly. He had had enough of fighting, and all he wanted now

---

1. **Kerry:** a county in southwestern Ireland.

was peace. He quietly went amongst the old and kindly friends and quietly looked about him for the place and peace he wanted; and when the time came, quietly produced the money for a neat, handy, small farm on the first warm shoulder of Knockanore Hill below the rolling curves of heather. It was not a big place but it was in good heart, and it got all the sun that was going; and, best of all, it suited Shawn to the tiptop notch of contentment; for it held the peace that tuned to his quietness, and it commanded the widest view in all Ireland — vale and mountain and the lifting green plain of the Atlantic Sea.

There, in a four-roomed, lime-washed, thatched cottage, Shawn made his life, and, though his friends hinted his needs and obligations, no thought came to him of bringing a wife into the place. Yet Fate had the thought and the dream in her loom for him. One middling imitation of a man he had to do chores for him, an ex-navy pensioner handy enough about house and byre,[2] but with no relish for the sustained work of the field — and, indeed, as long as he kept house and byre shipshape, he found Shawn an easy master.

Shawn himself was no drudge toiler. He knew all about drudgery and the way it wears out a man's soul. He plowed a little and sowed a little, and at the end of a furrow he would lean on the handles of the cultivator, wipe his brow, if it needed wiping, and lose himself for whole minutes in the great green curve of the sea out there beyond the high black portals of Shannon mouth. And sometimes of an evening he would see, under the glory of the sky, the faint smoke smudge of an American liner. Then he would smile to himself — a pitying smile — thinking of the poor devils, with dreams of fortune luring them, going out to sweat in Ironville or to stand in a breadline.[3] All these things were behind Shawn forever.

Market days he would go down and across to Listowel town, seven miles, to do his bartering; and in the long evenings, slowly slipping into the endless summer gloaming, his friends used to climb the winding lane to see him. Only the real friends came that long road, and they were welcome — fighting men who had been out in the "Sixteen";[4] Matt Tobin the thresher, the schoolmaster, the young curate — men like that. A stone jar of malt whiskey would appear on the table, and there would be a haze of smoke and a maze of warm, friendly disagreements.

"Shawn, old son," one of them might hint, "aren't you sometimes terrible lonely?"

"Never!" might retort Shawn derisively. "Why?"

"Nothing but the daylight and the wind and the sun setting with the wrath o' God."

"Just that! Well?"

"But after stirring times beyond in the States — "

"Ay! Tell me, fine man, have you ever seen a furnace in full blast?"

"A great sight."

"Great surely! But if I could jump you into a steel foundry this minute, you would be sure that God had judged you faithfully into the very hob[5] of hell."

And then they would laugh and have another small one from the stone jar.

---

2. **byre** (bīr): cow barn.

3. **breadline:** During the Great Depression in America in the 1930's, people waited in lines for free food.
4. **the "Sixteen":** the unsuccessful Irish rebellion against English rule in 1916.
5. **hob:** ledge inside a fireplace, used for keeping food warm.

And on Sundays Shawn used to go to church, three miles down to the gray chapel above the black cliffs of Doon Bay. There Fate laid her lure for him.

Sitting quietly on his wooden bench or kneeling on the dusty footboard, he would fix his steadfast, deep-set eyes on the vestmented celebrant and say his prayers slowly or go into that stranger trance, beyond dreams and visions, where the soul is almost at one with the unknowable.

But after a time, Shawn's eyes no longer fixed themselves on the celebrant. They went no farther than two seats ahead. A girl sat there, Sunday after Sunday she sat in front of him, and Sunday after Sunday his first casual admiration grew warmer.

She had a white nape to her neck and short red hair above it, and Shawn liked the color and wave of that flame. And he liked the set of her shoulders and the way the white neck had of leaning a little forward and she at her prayers—or her dreams. And the service over, Shawn used to stay in his seat so that he might get one quick but sure look at her face as she passed out. And he liked her face, too—the wide-set gray eyes, cheekbones firmly curved, clean-molded lips, austere yet sensitive. And he smiled pityingly at himself that one of her name should make his pulses stir—for she was an O'Grady.

One person, only, in the crowded chapel noted Shawn's look and the thought behind the look. Not the girl. Her brother, Big Liam O'Grady of Moyvalla, the very man who as good as stole the Kelvin acres. And that man smiled to himself, too—the ugly, contemptuous smile that was his by nature—and, after another habit he had, he tucked away his bit of knowledge in his mind corner against a day when it might come in useful for his own purposes.

The girl's name was Ellen—Ellen O'Grady.

But in truth she was no longer a girl. She was past her first youth into that second one that had no definite ending. She might be thirty—she was no less—but there was not a lad in the countryside would say she was past her prime. The poise of her and the firm set of her bones below clean skin saved her from the fading of mere prettiness. Though she had been sought in marriage more than once, she had accepted no one, or rather, had not been allowed to encourage anyone. Her brother saw to that.

Big Liam O'Grady was a great rawboned, sandy-haired man, with the strength of an ox and a heart no bigger than a sour apple. An overbearing man given to berserk rages. Though he was a churchgoer by habit, the true god of that man was Money—red gold, shining silver, dull copper—the trinity[6] that he worshiped in degree. He and his sister Ellen lived on the big ranch farm of Moyvalla, and Ellen was his housekeeper and maid of all work. She was a careful housekeeper, a good cook, a notable baker, and she demanded no wage. All that suited Big Liam splendidly, and so she remained single.

Big Liam himself was not a marrying man. There were not many spinsters with a dowry big enough to tempt him, and the few there had acquired expensive tastes—a convent education, the deplorable art of hitting jazz out of a piano, the damnable vice of cigarette smoking, the purse-emptying craze for motor cars—such things.

But in due time, the dowry and the place—with a woman tied to them—came under his nose, and Big Liam was no longer tardy. His neighbor, James Carey, died in March and left his fine farm and all on it to his widow, a

6. **trinity:** The author is comparing Big Liam's trinity of money to the Christian Trinity of Father, Son, and Holy Spirit.

youngish woman without children, a woman with a hard name for saving pennies. Big Liam looked once at Kathy Carey and looked many times at her broad acres. Both pleased him. He took the steps required by tradition. In the very first week of the following Shrovetide,[7] he sent an accredited emissary to open formal negotiations, and that emissary came back within the hour.

"My soul," said he, "but she is the quick one! I hadn't ten words out of me when she was down my throat. 'I am in no hurry,' says she, 'to come wife to a house with another woman at the fire corner. When Ellen is in a place of her own, I will listen to what Liam O'Grady has to say.'"

"She will, I say!" Big Liam stopped him. "She will so."

There, now, was the right time to recall Shawn Kelvin and the look in his eyes. Big Liam's mind corner promptly delivered up its memory. He smiled knowingly and contemptuously. Shawn Kelvin daring to cast sheep's eyes at an O'Grady! The undersized chicken heart, who took the loss of the Kelvin acres lying down! The little Yankee runt hidden away on the shelf of Knockanore! But what of it? The required dowry would be conveniently small, and the girl would never go hungry, anyway. There was Big Liam O'Grady, far descended from many chieftains.

The very next market day at Listowel he sought out Shawn Kelvin and placed a huge, sandy-haired hand on the shoulder that hunched to meet it.

"Shawn Kelvin, a word with you! Come and have a drink."

Shawn hesitated. "Very well," he said then. He did not care for O'Grady, but he would hurt no man's feelings.

---

7. **Shrovetide:** the three days before Ash Wednesday.

They went across to Sullivan's bar and had a drink, and Shawn paid for it. And Big Liam came directly to his subject—almost patronizingly, as if he were conferring a favor.

"I want to see Ellen settled in a place of her own," said he.

Shawn's heart lifted into his throat and stayed there. But that steadfast face with the steadfast eyes gave no sign and, moreover, he could not say a word with his heart where it was.

"Your place is small," went on the big man, "but it is handy, and no load of debt on it, as I hear. Not much of a dowry ever came to Knockanore, and not much of a dowry can I be giving with Ellen. Say two hundred pounds at the end of harvest, if prices improve. What do you say, Shawn Kelvin?"

Shawn swallowed his heart, and his voice came slow and cool: "What does Ellen say?"

"I haven't asked her," said Big Liam. "But what would she say, blast it?"

"Whatever she says, she will say it herself, not you, Big Liam."

But what could Ellen say? She looked within her own heart and found it empty; she looked at the granite crag of her brother's face and contemplated herself a slowly withering spinster at his fire corner; she looked up at the swell of Knockanore Hill and saw the white cottage among the green small fields below the warm brown of the heather. Oh, but the sun would shine up there in the lengthening spring day and pleasant breezes blow in sultry summer; and finally she looked at Shawn Kelvin, that firmly built, small man with the clean face and the lustrous eyes below steadfast brow. She said a prayer to her God and sank head and shoulders in a resignation more pitiful than tears, more proud than the pride of chieftains. Romance? Welladay!

Shawn was far from satisfied with that

A scene from *The Quiet Man*, with Maureen O'Hara as Ellen, Victor McLaglen as Big Liam, John Wayne as Shawn, and Barry Fitzgerald as the matchmaker (a part written for the movie). Directed by John Ford.
Republic Pictures, 1952.

resigned acceptance, but then was not the time to press for a warmer one. He knew the brother's wizened soul, guessed at the girl's clean one, and saw that she was doomed beyond hope to a fireside sordidly bought for her. Let it be his own fireside then. There were many worse ones—and God was good.

Ellen O'Grady married Shawn Kelvin. One small statement; and it holds the risk of tragedy, the chance of happiness, the probability of mere endurance—choices wide as the world.

But Big Liam O'Grady, for all his resolute promptness, did not win Kathy Carey to wife. She, foolishly enough, took to husband her own cattleman, a gay night rambler, who gave her the devil's own time and a share of happiness in the bygoing. For the first time, Big Liam discovered how mordant the wit of his

neighbors could be, and to contempt for Shawn Kelvin he now added an unreasoning dislike.

Shawn Kelvin had got his precious, red-haired woman under his own roof now. He had no illusions about her feelings for him. On himself, and on himself only, lay the task of molding her into a wife and lover. Darkly, deeply, subtly, away out of sight, with gentleness, with restraint, with a consideration beyond kenning,[8] that molding must be done, and she that was being molded must never know. He hardly knew himself.

First he turned his attention to material things. He hired a small servant maid to help

8. **kenning:** understanding.

her with the housework. Then he acquired a rubber-tired tub cart and half-bred gelding[9] with a reaching knee action. And on market days, husband and wife used to bowl down to Listowel, do their selling and their buying, and bowl smoothly home again, their groceries in the well of the cart and a bundle of secondhand American magazines on the seat at Ellen's side. And in the nights, before the year turned, with the wind from the plains of the Atlantic keening[10] above the chimney, they would sit at either side of the flaming peat fire, and he would read aloud strange and almost unbelievable things out of the high-colored magazines. Stories, sometimes, wholly unbelievable.

Ellen would sit and listen and smile and go on with her knitting or her sewing; and after a time it was sewing she was at mostly—small things. And when the reading was done, they would sit and talk quietly in their own quiet way. For they were both quiet. Woman though she was, she got Shawn to do most of the talking. It could be that she, too, was probing and seeking, unwrapping the man's soul to feel the texture thereof, surveying the marvel of his life as he spread it diffidently before her. He had a patient, slow, vivid way of picturing for her the things he had seen and felt. He made her see the glare of molten metal, lambent[11] yet searing, made her feel the sucking heat, made her hear the clang; she could see the roped square under the dazzle of the hooded arcs with the curling smoke layer above it, understand the explosive restraint of the game, thrill when he showed her how to stiffen wrist for the final devastating right hook. And often enough the stories were hu-

morous, and Ellen would chuckle, or stare, or throw back her red, lovely curls in laughter. It was grand to make her laugh.

Shawn's friends, in some hesitation at first, came in ones and twos up the slope to see them. But Ellen welcomed them with her smile that was shy and, at the same time, frank, and her table was loaded for them with scones and crumpets and cream cakes and heather honey; and at the right time it was she herself that brought forth the decanter of whiskey—no longer the half-empty stone jar —and the polished glasses. Shawn was proud as sin of her. She would sit then and listen to their discussions and be forever surprised at the knowledgeable man her husband was— the way he would discuss war and politics and making of songs, the turn of speech that summed up a man or a situation. And sometimes she would put in a word or two and he listened too, and they would look to see if her smile commended them, and be a little chastened by the wisdom of that smile—the age-old smile of the matriarch from whom they were all descended. In no time at all, Matt Tobin the thresher, who used to think, "Poor old Shawn! Lucky she was to get him," would whisper to the schoolmaster: "Herrin's alive! That fellow's luck would astonish nations."

Women, in the outside world, begin by loving their husbands; and then, if Fate is kind, they grow to admire them; and, if Fate is not unkind, may descend no lower than liking and enduring. And there is the end of lawful romance. Look now at Ellen O'Grady. She came up to the shelf of Knockanore and in her heart was only a nucleus of fear in a great emptiness, and that nucleus might grow into horror and disgust. But, glory of God, she, for reason piled on reason, presently found herself admiring Shawn Kelvin; and with or without reason, a quiet liking came to her for this quiet man who was so gentle and consid-

---

9. **gelding** (gĕl′dĭng): horse.
10. **keening:** moaning; wailing.
11. **lambent:** glowing.

erate; and then, one great heart-stirring dark o'night, she found herself fallen head and heels in love with her own husband. There is the sort of love that endures, but the road to it is a mighty chancy one.

A woman, loving her husband, may or may not be proud of him, but she will fight like a tiger if anyone, barring herself, belittles him. And there was one man that belittled Shawn Kelvin. Her brother, Big Liam O'Grady. At fair or market or chapel that dour giant deigned not to hide his contempt and dislike. Ellen knew why. He had lost a wife and farm; he had lost in herself a frugally cheap housekeeper; he had been made the butt of a sly humor; and for these mishaps, in some twisted way, he blamed Shawn. But—and there came in the contempt—the little Yankee runt, who dared say nothing about the lost Kelvin acres, would not now have the gall or guts to demand the dowry that was due. Lucky the hound to stean[12] an O'Grady to hungry Knockanore! Let him be satisfied with that luck!

One evening before a market day, Ellen spoke to her husband: "Has Big Liam paid you my dowry yet, Shawn?"

"Sure there's no hurry, girl," said Shawn.

"Have you ever asked him?"

"I have not. I am not looking for your dowry, Ellen."

"And Big Liam could never understand that." Her voice firmed. "You will ask him tomorrow."

"Very well so, agrah,"[13] agreed Shawn easily.

And the next day, in that quiet diffident way of his, he asked Big Liam. But Big Liam was brusque and blunt. He had no loose money and Kelvin would have to wait till he had. "Ask me again, Shawneen,"[14] he finished, his face in a mocking smile, and turning on his heel, he plowed his great shoulders through the crowded market.

His voice had been carelessly loud and people had heard. They laughed and talked amongst themselves. "Begogs! The devil's own boy. Big Liam! What a pup to sell! Stealing the land and keeping a grip on the fortune! Ay, and a dangerous fellow, mind you, the same Big Liam! He would smash little Shawn at the wind of a word. And devil the bit his Yankee sparring tricks would help him!"

A friend of Shawn's, Matt Tobin the thresher, heard that and lifted his voice: "I would like to be there the day Shawn Kelvin loses his temper."

"A bad day for poor Shawn!"

"It might then," said Matt Tobin, "but I would come from the other end of Kerry to see the badness that would be in it for someone."

Shawn had moved away with his wife, not heeding or not hearing.

"You see, Ellen?" he said in some discomfort. "The times are hard on the big ranchers, and we don't need the money, anyway."

"Do you think Big Liam does?" Her voice had a cut in it. "He could buy you and all Knockanore and be only on the fringe of his hoard. You will ask him again."

"But, girl dear, I never wanted a dowry with you."

She liked him to say that, but far better would she like to win for him the respect and admiration that was his due. She must do that now at all costs. Shawn, drawing back now, would be the butt of his fellow men.

---

12. **stean:** bring.
13. *agrah:* "my love," in Irish.

14. **Shawneen:** little Shawn; here, a term of mockery. The speaker may be making a pun on the word *shoneen,* "an upstart."

"You foolish lad! Big Liam would never understand your feelings, with money at stake." She smiled and a pang went through Shawn's breast. For the smile was the smile of an O'Grady, and he could not be sure whether the contempt in it was for himself or for her brother.

Shawn asked Big Liam again, unhappy in his asking, but also dimly comprehending his woman's object. And Shawn asked again a third time. The issue was become a famous one now. Men talked about it, and women too. Bets were made on it. At fair or market, if Shawn was seen approaching Big Liam, men edged closer and women edged away. Someday the big fellow would grow tired of being asked, and in one of his terrible rages half kill the little lad as he had half killed other men. A great shame! Here and there, a man advised Shawn to give up asking and put the matter in a lawyer's hands. "I couldn't do that," was Shawn's only answer. Strangely enough, none of these prudent advisers were amongst Shawn's close friends. His friends frowned and said little, but they were always about, and always amongst them was Matt Tobin.

The day at last came when Big Liam grew tired of being asked. That was the big October cattle fair at Listowel, and he had sold twenty head of fat Polled Angus beeves at a good price. He was a hard dealer and it was late in the day before he settled at his own figure, so that the banks were closed and he was not able to make a lodgment.[15] He had, then, a great roll of bills in an inner vest pocket when he saw Shawn and Ellen coming across to where he was bargaining with Matt Tobin for a week's threshing. Besides, the day being dank, he had had a drink or two more than was good for him and the whiskey had loos-

ened his tongue and whatever he had of discretion. By the powers!—it was time and past time to deal once and for all with this little gadfly of a fellow, to show him up before the whole market. He strode to meet Shawn, and people got out of his savage way and edged in behind to lose nothing of this dangerous game.

He caught Shawn by the hunched shoulder—a rending grip—and bent down to grin in his face.

"What is it, little fellow? Don't be ashamed to ask!"

Matt Tobin was probably the only one there to notice the ease with which Shawn wrenched his shoulder free, and Matt Tobin's eyes brightened. But Shawn did nothing further and said no word. His deep-set eyes gazed steadily at the big man.

The big man showed his teeth mockingly. "Go on, you whelp! What do you want?"

"You know, O'Grady."

"I do. Listen, Shawneen!" Again he brought his handclap on the little man's shoulder. "Listen, Shawneen! If I had a dowry to give my sister, 'tis not a little shrimp like you would get her!"

His great hand gripped and he flung Shawn backward as if he were only the image of a man filled with chaff.

Shawn went backward, but he did not fall. He gathered himself like a spring, feet under him, arms half raised, head forward into hunched shoulder. But as quickly as the spring coiled, as quickly it slackened, and he turned away to his wife. She was there facing him, tense and keen; her face pale and set, and a gleam of the race in her eyes.

"Woman, woman!" he said in his deep voice. "Why would you and I shame ourselves like this?"

"Shawn!" she cried. "Will you let him shame you now?"

---

15. **lodgment:** deposit.

"But your own brother, Ellen—before them all?"

"And he cheating you——"

"Glory of God!" His voice was distressed. "What is his dirty money to me? Are you an O'Grady, after all?"

That stung her and she stung him back in one final effort. She placed a hand below her breast and looked *close* into his face. Her voice was low and bitter, and only he heard: "I am an O'Grady. It is a great pity that the father of this my son is a Kelvin and a coward."

The bosses[16] of Shawn Kelvin's cheekbones were like hard marble, but his voice was as soft as a dove's.

"Is that the way of it? Let us be going home then, in the name of God!"

He took her arm, but she shook his hand off; nevertheless, she walked at his side, head up, through the people that made way for them. Her brother mocked them with his great, laughing bellow.

"That fixes the pair of them!" he cried, brushed a man who laughed with him out of his way, and strode off through the fair.

There was talk then—plenty of it. "Murder, but Shawn had a narrow squeak that time! Did you see the way he flung him? I wager he'll give Big Liam a wide road after this. And he by way of being a boxer! That's a pound you owe me, Matt Tobin."

"I'll pay it," said Matt Tobin, and that is all he said. He stood, wide-legged, looking at the ground, his hand ruefully rubbing the back of his head and dismay and gloom on his face. His friend had failed him in the face of the people.

Shawn and Ellen went home in their tub cart and had not a single word or glance for each other on the road. And all that evening,

at table or fireside, a heart-sickening silence held them in its grip. And all that night they lay side by side, still and mute. There was only one subject that possessed them and on that they dared speak no longer. They slept little. Ellen, her heart desolate, lay on her side, staring into the dark, grieving for what she had said and unable to unsay it. Shawn, on his back, contemplated things with a cold clarity. He realized that he was at the fork of life and that a finger pointed unmistakably. He must risk the very shattering of all happiness, he must do a thing so final and decisive that, once done, it could never again be questioned. Before morning he came to his decision, and it was bitter as gall. He cursed himself. "Oh, you fool! You might have known that you should never have taken an O'Grady without breaking the O'Gradys."

He got up early in the morning at his usual hour and went out, as usual, to his morning chores—rebedding and foddering the cattle, rubbing down the half-bred, helping the servant maid with the milk in the creaming pans—and, as usual, he came in to his breakfast, and ate it unhungrily and silently, which was not usual. But, thereafter he again went out to the stable, harnessed his gelding and hitched him to the tub cart. Then he returned to the kitchen and spoke for the first time.

"Ellen, will you come with me down to see your brother?"

She hesitated, her hands thrown wide in a helpless, hopeless gesture. "Little use you going to see my brother, Shawn. 'Tis I should go and—and not come back."

"Don't blame me now or later, Ellen. It has been put on me and the thing I am going to do is the only thing to be done. Will you come?"

"Very well," she agreed tonelessly. "I will be ready in a minute."

And they went the four miles down into the vale to the big farmhouse of Moyvalla. They

---

16. **bosses:** knobs.

drove into the great square of cobbled yard and found it empty.

On one side of the square was the long, low, lime-washed dwelling house; on the other, fifty yards away, the two-storied line of steadings[17] with a wide arch in the middle; and through the arch came the purr and zoom of a threshing machine. Shawn tied the half-bred to the wheel of a farm cart and, with Ellen, approached the house.

A slattern servant girl leaned over the kitchen half-door and pointed through the arch. The master was out beyond in the haggard[18] – the rickyard – and would she run across for him?

"Never mind, achara,"[19] said Shawn, "I'll get him. . . . Ellen, will you go in and wait?"

"No," said Ellen, "I'll come with you." She knew her brother.

As they went through the arch, the purr and zoom grew louder and, turning the corner, they walked into the midst of activity. A long double row of cone-pointed cornstacks stretched across the yard and, between them, Matt Tobin's portable threshing machine was busy. The smooth-flying, eight-foot driving wheel made a sleepy purr and the black driving belt ran with a sag and heave to the red-painted thresher. Up there on the platform, bare-armed men were feeding the flying drum with loosened sheaves, their hands moving in a rhythmic sway. As the toothed drum bit at the corn sheaves it made an angry snarl that changed and slowed into a satisfied zoom. The wide conveying belt was carrying the golden straw up a steep incline to where other men were building a long rick; still more men were attending to the corn shoots, shoulders bending under the weight of the sacks as they ambled across to the granary. Matt Tobin

himself bent at the face of his engine, feeding the fire box with sods of hard black peat. There were not less than two score men about the place, for, as was the custom, all Big Liam's friends and neighbors were giving him a hand with the threshing – "the day in harvest."

Big Liam came round the flank of the engine and swore. He was in his shirt sleeves, and his great forearms were covered with sandy hair.

"Look who's here!"

He was in the worst of tempers this morning. The stale dregs of yesterday's whiskey were still with him, and he was in the humor that, as they say, would make a dog bite its father. He took two slow strides and halted, feet apart and head truculently forward.

"What is it this time?" he shouted. That was the un-Irish welcome he gave his sister and her husband.

Shawn and Ellen came forward steadily, and, as they came, Matt Tobin slowly throttled down his engine. Big Liam heard the change of pitch and looked angrily over his shoulder.

"What do you mean, Tobin? Get on with the work!"

"Big Liam, this is my engine, and if you don't like it, you can leave it!" And at that he drove the throttle shut and the purr of the flywheel slowly sank.

"We will see in a minute," threatened Big Liam, and turned to the two now near at hand.

"What is it?" he growled.

"A private word with you. I won't keep you long." Shawn was calm and cold.

"You will not – on a busy morning," sneered the big man. "There is no need for private words between me and Shawn Kelvin."

"There is need," urged Shawn. "It will be

17. **steadings:** farm buildings.
18. **haggard** (hăg'ərd): hay yard. Ricks are stacks of hay.
19. *achara:* "dear friend," in Irish.

best for us all if you hear what I have to say in your own house."

"Or here on my own land. Out with it! I don't care who hears!"

Shawn looked round him. Up on the thresher, up on the straw rick, men leaned idle on fork handles and looked down at him; from here and there about the stackyard, men moved in to see, as it might be, what had caused the stoppage, but only really interested in the two brothers-in-law. He was in the midst of Clan O'Grady, for they were mostly O'Grady men—big, strong, blond men, rough, confident, proud of their breed. Matt Tobin was the only man he could call a friend. Many of the others were not unfriendly, but all had contempt in their eyes, or, what was worse, pity. Very well! Since he had to prove himself, it was fitting that he do it here amongst the O'Grady men.

Shawn brought his eyes back to Big Liam—deep, steadfast eyes that did not waver. "O'Grady," said he—and he no longer hid his contempt—"you set a great store by money."

"No harm in that. You do it yourself, Shawneen."

"Take it so! I will play that game with you as long as you like. You would bargain your sister and cheat; I will sell my soul. Listen, you big brute! You owe me two hundred pounds. Will you pay it?" There was an iron quality in his voice that was somehow awesome. The big man, about to start forward overbearingly, restrained himself to a brutal playfulness.

"I will pay it when I am ready."

"Today."

"No; nor tomorrow."

"Right. If you break your bargain, I break mine."

"What's that?" shouted Big Liam.

"If you keep your two hundred pounds, you keep your sister."

"What is it?" shouted Big Liam again, his voice breaking in astonishment. "What is that you say?"

"You heard me. Here is your sister Ellen! Keep her!"

He was completely astounded out of his truculence. "You can't do that!"

"It is done," said Shawn.

Ellen O'Grady had been quiet as a statue at Shawn's side, but now, slow like doom, she faced him. She leaned forward and looked into his eyes and saw the pain behind the strength.

"To the mother of your son, Shawn Kelvin?" she whispered that gently to him.

His voice came cold as a stone out of a stone face: "In the face of God. Let Him judge me."

"I know—I know!" That was all she said, and walked quietly across to where Matt Tobin stood at the face of his engine.

Matt Tobin placed a hand on her arm.

"Give him time, *acolleen*,"[20] he whispered urgently. "Give him his own time. He's slow but he's deadly as a tiger when he moves."

Big Liam was no fool. He knew exactly how far he could go. There was no use, at this juncture, in crushing the runt under a great fist. There was some force in the little fellow that defied dragooning.[21] Whatever people might think of Kelvin, public opinion would be dead against himself. Worse, his inward vision saw eyes leering in derision, mouths open in laughter. The scandal on his name would not be bounded by the four seas of Erin. He must change his stance while he had time. These thoughts passed through his mind while he thudded the ground three times with iron-shod heel. Now he threw up his head and bellowed his laugh.

---

20. *acolleen:* "dear girl," in Irish.
21. **dragooning:** forcing someone to do something.

"You fool! I was only making fun of you. What are your dirty few pounds to the likes of me? Stay where you are."

He turned, strode furiously away, and disappeared through the arch.

Shawn Kelvin was left alone in that wide ring of men. The hands had come down off the ricks and thresher to see closer. Now they moved back and aside, looked at one another, lifted eyebrows, looked at Shawn Kelvin, frowned, and shook their heads. They knew Big Liam. They knew that, yielding up the money, his savagery would break out into something little short of killing. They waited, most of them, to prevent that savagery going too far.

Shawn Kelvin did not look at anyone. He stood still as a rock, his hands deep in his pockets, one shoulder hunched forward, his eyes on the ground, and his face strangely calm. He seemed the least perturbed man there. Matt Tobin held Ellen's arm in a steadying grip and whispered in her ear: "God is good, I tell you."

Big Liam was back in two minutes. He strode straight to Shawn and halted within a pace of him.

"Look, Shawneen!" In his raised hand was a crumpled bundle of greasy bank notes. "Here is your money. Take it, and then see what will happen to you. Take it!" He thrust it into Shawn's hand. "Count it. Make sure you have it all—and then I will kick you out of this haggard—and look"—he thrust forward a hairy fist—"if ever I see your face again, I will drive that through it. Count it, you spawn."

Shawn did not count it. Instead he crumpled it into a ball in his strong fingers. Then he turned on his heel and walked, with surprising slowness, to the face of the engine. He gestured with one hand to Matt Tobin, but it was Ellen, quick as a flash, who obeyed the gesture. Though the hot bar scorched her hand, she jerked open the door of the firebox and the leaping peat flames whispered out at her. And forthwith, Shawn Kelvin, with one easy sweep, threw the crumpled ball of notes into the heart of the flame. The whisper lifted one tone and one scrap of burned paper floated out of the funnel top. That was all the fuss the fire made of its work.

But there was fuss enough outside.

Big Liam O'Grady gave one mighty shout. No, it was more an anguished scream than a shout:

"My money! My good money!"

He gave two furious bounds forward, his great arms raised to crush and kill. But his hands never touched the small man.

"You dumb ox!" said Shawn Kelvin between his teeth. That strong, hunched shoulder moved a little, but no one there could follow the terrific drive of that hooked right arm. The smack of bone on bone was sharp as whip crack, and Big Liam stopped dead, went back on his heel, swayed a moment, and staggered back three paces.

"Now and forever! Man of the Kelvins!" roared Matt Tobin.

But Big Liam was a man of iron. That blow should have laid him out on his back—blows like it had tied men to the ground for the full count. But Big Liam only shook his head, grunted like a boar, and drove in at the little man. And the little man, instead of circling away, drove in at him, compact of power.

The men of the O'Gradys saw then an exhibition that they had not knowledge enough to appreciate fully. Thousands had paid as much as ten dollars each to see the great Tiger Kelvin in action, his footwork, his timing, his hitting; and never was his action more devastating than now. He was a thunderbolt on two feet and the big man a glutton.

Big Liam never touched Shawn with clenched fist. He did not know how. Shawn,

A scene from *The Quiet Man*.
Republic Pictures, 1952.

actually forty pounds lighter, drove him by sheer hitting across the yard.

Men for the first time saw a two-hundred-pound man knocked clean off his feet by a body blow. They saw for the first time the deadly restraint and explosion of skill.

Shawn set out to demolish his enemy in the briefest space of time, and it took him five minutes to do it. Five, six, eight times he knocked the big man down, and the big man came again, staggering, slavering, raving, vainly trying to rend and smash. But at last he stood swaying and clawing helplessly, and Shawn finished him with his terrible double hit—left below the breastbone and right under the jaw.

Big Liam lifted on his toes and fell flat on his back. He did not even kick as he lay.

Shawn did not waste a glance at the fallen giant. He swung full circle on the O'Grady men and his voice of iron challenged them:

"I am Shawn Kelvin, of Knockanore Hill. Is there an O'Grady amongst you thinks himself a better man? Come then."

His face was deep-carved stone, his great chest lifted, the air whistled through his nostrils; his deep-set flashing eyes dared them.

No man came.

He swung around then and walked straight to his wife. He halted before her.

His face was still of stone, but his voice quivered and had in it all the dramatic force of the Celt:

"Mother of my son, will you come home with me?"

She lifted to the appeal, voice and eye:

"Is it so you ask me, Shawn Kelvin?"

His face of stone quivered at last, "As my wife only—Ellen Kelvin!"

"Very well, heart's treasure." She caught his arm in both of hers. "Let us be going home."

"In the name of God," he finished for her.

And she went with him, proud as the morning, out of that place. But a woman, she would have the last word.

"Mother of God!" she cried. "The trouble I had to make a man of him!"

"God Almighty did that for him before you were born," said Matt Tobin softly.

FOR STUDY AND DISCUSSION

1. It is obvious early in the story that the author is setting up a contrast between Shawn Kelvin and Big Liam. What does Shawn seem to value most? What does Big Liam value more than anything else?

2. Shawn Kelvin and Liam O'Grady differ in more than values. How does the author also contrast their appearances?

3. How does Ellen intensify the conflict between the two men? How does Ellen change after she marries Shawn Kelvin?

4. To Shawn, Ellen, and Big Liam, Ellen's unpaid dowry comes to mean something different. What is each character's attitude toward this money?

5. We are held in suspense by several conflicts in this story—there are external conflicts between Shawn and Big Liam and between Shawn and Ellen, and there is an inner conflict that Shawn himself must overcome. How would you describe each one of these conflicts?

6. What would you say is the *climax* of this story—that point of greatest emotional intensity when we finally know what will happen to the characters and their conflicts?

7. At the end of the story, Ellen states that *she* had made "a man" out of her quiet husband. Why is she mistaken?

OMNISCIENT POINT OF VIEW

Maurice Walsh tells his story from the *omniscient point of view*. He is the all-knowing narrator who allows us to share the private, unspoken thoughts and feelings of his three main characters: Shawn, Ellen, and Big Liam. For example, he tells us exactly what Ellen thinks and feels when she considers Shawn's proposal:

She looked within her own heart and found it empty; she looked at the granite crag of her brother's face and contemplated herself a slowly withering spinster at his fire corner . . . .

What does the narrator tell us about Shawn's private reactions to her acceptance? What are we told about Big Liam's motivations when he suggests that Shawn marry his sister?

In any point of view, the author may withhold information for effect. What important information does the author of "The Quiet Man" save until the end of the story? Where in the story does he foreshadow his surprising news about Shawn's background?

FIGURATIVE LANGUAGE

Big Liam thinks that Shawn Kelvin cast "sheep's eyes" at Ellen. Liam's face, in turn, is described as a "granite crag." We know that these expressions are not literally true. They are *figures of speech*, in which one thing is compared to some other, different thing. Such figures of speech can tell a great deal about a character. What does the first figure of speech reveal about the way Big Liam sees Shawn Kelvin? What does the second one reveal about Big Liam himself?

What are the figures of speech in each of the following sentences? What comparisons are being made in each one? What does each tell you about the character involved?

Big Liam O'Grady was a great rawboned, sandy-haired man, with the strength of an ox and a heart no bigger than a sour apple.

The bosses of Shawn Kelvin's cheekbones were like hard marble, but his voice was as soft as a dove's.

FOR COMPOSITION

Analyzing the Appeal of a Story
"The Quiet Man" is a story that has endured for many years and has been a favorite with readers of all ages. In an essay, analyze what you think is the basic appeal of the story. Is it the old conflict between the bully and the little guy? Is it the interesting characterizations of Big Liam, Ellen, and the Quiet Man? Or is it the appeal of the love story? Do you know other stories or films that have been popular because they have the same appeal? Be specific in your answers.

ABOUT THE AUTHOR

Maurice Walsh (1879–1964) described himself as "the son and the grandson and the great-great-grandson of farmers and rebels." He was born in Kerry, the southwestern Irish county that provides the setting for "The Quiet Man." Walsh said that his earliest stories were about "Australian bush-ranging, and Klondike gold-digging, and the Boer War, and other subjects with which I was closely acquainted at a distance." In his twenties he became an employee of the British Customs Excise Service and traveled throughout Ireland, Wales, and England, and often to Scotland, where he fell in love with and married a red-haired Scottish woman. In Dublin during the Irish Civil War, confined indoors at night because of sniping and separated from his family, Walsh resumed his writing. "Up to then," he said, "I had scarcely written a thing — too busy living."

Blues Ain't No Mockin Bird

Toni Cade Bambara

The puddle had frozen over, and me and Cathy went stompin in it. The twins from next door, Tyrone and Terry, were swingin so high out of sight we forgot we were waitin our turn on the tire. Cathy jumped up and came down hard on her heels and started tap-dancin. And the frozen patch splinterin every which way underneath kinda spooky. "Looks like a plastic spider web," she said. "A sort of weird spider, I guess, with many mental problems." But really it looked like the crystal paperweight Granny kept in the parlor. She was on the back porch, Granny was, making the cakes drunk. The old ladle dripping rum into the Christmas tins, like it used to drip maple syrup into the pails when we lived in the Judson's woods, like it poured cider into the vats when we were on the Cooper place, like it used to scoop buttermilk and soft cheese when we lived at the dairy.

"Go tell that man we ain't a bunch of trees."

"Ma'am?"

"I said to tell that man to get away from here with that camera." Me and Cathy look over toward the meadow where the men with the station wagon'd been roamin around all mornin. The tall man with a huge camera lassoed to his shoulder was buzzin our way.

"They're makin movie pictures," yelled Tyrone, stiffenin his legs and twistin so the tire'd come down slow so they could see.

"They're makin movie pictures," sang out Terry.

"That boy don't never have anything original to say," say Cathy grown-up.

By the time the man with the camera had cut across our neighbor's yard, the twins were out of the trees swingin low and Granny was onto the steps, the screen door bammin soft and scratchy against her palms. "We thought we'd get a shot or two of the house and everything and then—"

"Good mornin," Granny cut him off. And smiled that smile.

"Good mornin," he said, head all down the way Bingo does when you yell at him about the bones on the kitchen floor. "Nice place you got here, Aunty. We thought we'd take a—"

"Did you?" said Granny with her eyebrows. Cathy pulled up her socks and giggled.

"Nice things here," said the man, buzzin his camera over the yard. The pecan barrels, the sled, me and Cathy, the flowers, the printed stones along the driveway, the trees, the twins, the toolshed.

"I don't know about the thing, the it, and the stuff," said Granny, still talkin with her eyebrows. "Just people here is what I tend to consider."

Cameraman stopped buzzin. Cathy giggled into her collar.

"Mornin, ladies," a new man said. He had

come up behind us when we weren't lookin. "And gents," discoverin the twins givin him a nasty look. "We're filmin for the county," he said with a smile. "Mind if we shoot a bit around here?"

"I do indeed," said Granny with no smile. Smilin man was smiling up a storm. So was Cathy. But he didn't seem to have another word to say, so he and the cameraman backed on out the yard, but you could hear the camera buzzin still. "Suppose you just shut that machine off," said Granny real low through her teeth, and took a step down off the porch and then another.

"Now, Aunty," Camera said, pointin the thing straight at her.

"Your mama and I are not related."

Smilin man got his notebook out and a chewed-up pencil. "Listen," he said movin back into our yard, "we'd like to have a statement from you . . . for the film. We're filmin for the county, see. Part of the food-stamp campaign. You know about the food stamps?"

Granny said nuthin.

"Maybe there's somethin you want to say for the film. I see you grow your own vegetables," he smiled real nice. "If more folks did that, see, there'd be no need——"

Granny wasn't sayin nuthin. So they backed on out, buzzin at our clothesline and the twins' bicycles, then back on down to the meadow. The twins were danglin in the tire, lookin at Granny. Me and Cathy were waitin, too, cause Granny always got somethin to say. She teaches steady with no letup. "I was on this bridge one time," she started off. "Was a crowd cause this man was goin to jump, you understand. And a minister was there and the police and some other folks. His woman was there, too."

"What was they doin?" asked Tyrone.

"Tryin to talk him out of it was what they was doin. The minister talkin about how it was a mortal sin, suicide. His woman takin bites out of her own hand and not even knowin it, so nervous and cryin and talkin fast."

"So what happened?" asked Tyrone.

"So here comes . . . this person . . . with a camera, takin pictures of the man and the minister and the woman. Takin pictures of the man in his misery about to jump, cause life so bad and people been messin with him so bad. This person takin up the whole roll of film practically. But savin a few, of course."

"Of course," said Cathy, hatin the person. Me standin there wonderin how Cathy knew it was "of course" when I didn't and it was *my* grandmother.

After a while Tyrone say, "Did he jump?"

"Yeh, did he jump?" say Terry all eager.

And Granny just stared at the twins till their faces swallow up the eager and they don't even care any more about the man jumpin. Then she goes back onto the porch and lets the screen door go for itself. I'm lookin to Cathy to finish the story cause she knows Granny's whole story before me even. Like she knew how come we move so much and Cathy ain't but a third cousin we picked up on the way last Thanksgivin visitin. But she knew it was on account of people drivin Granny crazy till she'd get up in the night and start packin. Mumblin and packin and wakin everybody up sayin, "Let's get on away from here before I kill me somebody." Like people wouldn't pay her for things like they said they would. Or Mr. Judson bringin us boxes of old clothes and raggedy magazines. Or Mrs. Cooper comin in our kitchen and touchin everything and sayin how clean it all was. Granny goin crazy, and Granddaddy Cain pullin her off the people, sayin, "Now, now, Cora." But next day loadin up the truck, with rocks all in his jaw, madder than Granny in the first place.

"I read a story once," said Cathy soundin like Granny teacher. "About this lady Goldilocks who barged into a house that wasn't even hers. And not invited, you understand. Messed over the people's groceries and broke up the people's furniture. Had the nerve to sleep in the folks' bed."

"Then what happened?" asked Tyrone. "What they do, the folks, when they come in to all this mess?"

"Did they make her pay for it?" asked Terry, makin a fist. "I'd've made her pay me."

I didn't even ask. I could see Cathy actress was very likely to just walk away and leave us in mystery about this story which I heard was about some bears.

"Did they throw her out?" asked Tyrone, like his father sounds when he's bein extra nasty-plus to the washin-machine man.

"Woulda," said Terry. "I woulda gone upside her head with my fist and——"

"You woulda done whatcha always do—go cry to Mama, you big baby," said Tyrone. So naturally Terry starts hittin on Tyrone, and next thing you know they tumblin out the tire and rollin on the ground. But Granny didn't say a thing or send the twins home or step out on the steps to tell us about how we can't afford to be fightin amongst ourselves. She didn't say nuthin. So I get into the tire to take my turn. And I could see her leanin up against the pantry table, starin at the cakes she was puttin up for the Christmas sale, mumblin real low and grumpy and holdin her forehead like it wanted to fall off and mess up the rum cakes.

Behind me I hear before I can see Granddaddy Cain comin through the woods in his field boots. Then I twist around to see the shiny black oilskin cuttin through what little left there was of yellows, reds, and oranges. His great white head not quite round cause of this bloody thing high on his shoulder, like he was wearin a cap on sideways. He takes the shortcut through the pecan grove, and the sound of twigs snapping overhead and underfoot travels clear and cold all the way up to us. And here comes Smilin and Camera up behind him like they was goin to do somethin. Folks like to go for him sometimes. Cathy say it's because he's so tall and quiet and like a king. And people just can't stand it. But Smilin and Camera don't hit him in the head or nuthin. They just buzz on him as he stalks by with the chicken hawk slung over his shoulder, squawkin, drippin red down the back of the oilskin. He passes the porch and stops a second for Granny to see he's caught the hawk at last, but she's just starin and mumblin, and not at the hawk. So he nails the bird to the toolshed door, the hammerin crackin through the eardrums. And the bird flappin himself to death and droolin down the door to paint the gravel in the driveway red, then brown, then black. And the two men movin up on tiptoe like they was invisible or we were blind, one.

"Get them persons out of my flower bed, Mister Cain," say Granny moanin real low like at a funeral.

"How come your grandmother calls her husband 'Mister Cain' all the time?" Tyrone whispers all loud and noisy and from the city and don't know no better. Like his mama, Miss Myrtle, tell us never mind the formality as if we had no better breeding than to call her Myrtle, plain. And then this awful thing—a giant hawk—come wailin up over the meadow, flyin low and tilted and screamin, zigzaggin through the pecan grove, breakin branches and hollerin, snappin past the clothesline, flyin every which way, flyin into things reckless with crazy.

"He's come to claim his mate," say Cathy fast, and ducks down. We all fall quick and

flat into the gravel driveway, stones scrapin my face. I squinch my eyes open again at the hawk on the door, tryin to fly up out of her death like it was just a sack flown into by mistake. Her body holdin her there on that nail, though. The mate beatin the air over-head and clutchin for hair, for heads, for landin space.

The cameraman duckin and bendin and runnin and fallin, jigglin the camera and scared. And Smilin jumpin up and down swipin at the huge bird, tryin to bring the hawk down with just his raggedy ole cap. Granddaddy Cain straight up and silent, watchin the circles of the hawk, then aimin the hammer off his wrist. The giant bird fallin, silent and slow. Then here comes Cam-era and Smilin all big and bad now that the awful screechin thing is on its back and bro-ken, here they come. And Granddaddy Cain looks up at them like it was the first time noticin, but not payin them too much mind cause he's listenin, we all listenin, to that low groanin music comin from the porch. And we figure any minute, somethin in my back tells me any minute now, Granny gonna bust through that screen with somethin in her hand and murder on her mind. So Granddaddy say above the buzzin, but quiet, "Good day, gentlemen." Just like that. Like he'd invited them in to play cards and they'd stayed too long and all the sandwiches were gone and Reverend Webb was droppin by and it was time to go.

They didn't know what to do. But like Cathy say, folks can't stand Granddaddy tall and silent and like a king. They can't neither. The smile the men smilin is pullin the mouth back and showin the teeth. Lookin like the wolf man, both of them. Then Granddaddy holds his hand out—this huge hand I used to sit in when I was a baby and he'd carry me through the house to my mother like I was a gift on a tray. Like he used to on the trains. They called the other men just waiters. But they spoke of Granddaddy separate and said, The Waiter. And said he had engines in his feet and motors in his hands and couldn't no train throw him off and couldn't nobody turn him round. They were big enough for motors, his hands were. He held that one hand out all still and it gettin to be not at all a hand but a person in itself.

"He wants you to hand him the camera," Smilin whispers to Camera, tiltin his head to talk secret like they was in the jungle or somethin and come upon a native that don't speak the language. The men start untyin the straps, and they put the camera into that great hand speckled with the hawk's blood all black and crackly now. And the hand don't even drop with the weight, just the fingers move, curl up around the machine. But Granddaddy lookin straight at the men. They lookin at each other and everywhere but at Granddaddy's face.

"We filmin for the county, see," say Smilin. "We puttin together a movie for the food-stamp program . . . filmin all around these parts. Uhh, filmin for the county."

"Can I have my camera back?" say the tall man with no machine on his shoulder, but still keepin it high like the camera was still there or needed to be. "Please, sir."

Then Granddaddy's other hand flies up like a sudden and gentle bird, slaps down fast on top of the camera and lifts off half like it was a calabash cut for sharing.

"Hey," Camera jumps forward. He gathers up the parts into his chest and everything unrollin and fallin all over. "Whatcha tryin to do? You'll ruin the film." He looks down into his chest of metal reels and things like he's protectin a kitten from the cold.

"You standin in the misses' flower bed," say Granddaddy. "This is our own place."

The two men look at him, then at each other, then back at the mess in the cameraman's chest, and they just back off. One sayin over and over all the way down to the meadow, "Watch it, Bruno. Keep ya fingers off the film." Then Granddaddy picks up the hammer and jams it into the oilskin pocket, scrapes his boots, and goes into the house. And you can hear the squish of his boots headin through the house. And you can see the funny shadow he throws from the parlor window onto the ground by the string-bean patch. The hammer draggin the pocket of the oilskin out so Granddaddy looked even wider. Granny was hummin now—high, not low and grumbly. And she was doin the cakes again, you could smell the molasses from the rum.

"There's this story I'm goin to write one day," say Cathy dreamer. "About the proper use of the hammer."

"Can I be in it?" Tyrone say with his hand up like it was a matter of first come, first served.

"Perhaps," say Cathy, climbin onto the tire to pump us up. "If you there and ready."

1. The narrator of this story watches a conflict between her grandparents and two cameramen who intrude on their land. What do the cameramen want? What is their attitude?

2. The narrator says, "Granny always got somethin to say. She teaches steady with no letup." What story does the grandmother tell to explain her feelings about the cameramen?

3. Cathy seems to understand Granny better than the narrator does. What story does Cathy tell to support the grandmother's story? What is the main point of both of these "teaching stories"?

4. Cathy says that Granddaddy Cain is "like a king." How does the grandfather's way of dealing with the intruders seem "kingly" or majestic?

5. In the midst of this human conflict, the giant hawk comes to the rescue of his suffering mate. How could these great birds remind you of the older couple themselves?

6. The unusual title of this story seems to suggest that some people cannot understand the "blues." The "blues," of course, is a kind of slow, sad music that expresses suffering or unhappiness. Which characters in this story know what the "blues" really are?

FIRST-PERSON POINT OF VIEW

"Blues Ain't No Mockin Bird" is told from the *first-person point of view.* It is a story about a conflict between adults that is narrated by a young character who is an observer of the action. This first-person narrator has a sense of humor and a highly individual way of speaking. These qualities make her seem real to us and help to make her story enjoyable. What original way does the narrator have of describing Cathy, whom she seems to envy a

bit? What funny names does she give the cameramen? What other comical remarks does she make as she tells her story?

This young narrator makes humorous remarks that might make us smile, but she also makes it clear that this conflict is anything but comical to the older people. The narrator cannot tell us the unspoken thoughts and feelings of her grandparents, but she does report on what they say and do. She also helps us to see these two people through the eyes of a child who loves and admires them. Notice what she tells us about her grandfather—this man who is holding a bloodied hawk is remembered in a tender moment by his young granddaughter:

> Then Granddaddy holds his hand out—this huge hand I used to sit in when I was a baby and he'd carry me through the house to my mother like I was a gift on a tray.

What other details does the young narrator tell us about her grandparents as she knows and remembers them? How do these descriptions affect your feelings for these characters?

While the tense confrontation takes place between the adults, the children are playing in the yard. Where does the narrator make it clear that the children—all except Cathy—do not fully understand what is happening?

FOR COMPOSITION

Writing from Another Point of View

At the end of the story, Granddaddy Cain goes back into the house. In a paragraph, write what he might be thinking about the incident that has just occurred with the cameramen. Write from the first-person point of view, as if Granddaddy Cain himself is speaking. Before you write, review the characterization of the grandfather, especially the paragraph on page 100 beginning "They didn't know what to do." What would be the tone of this paragraph written from the grandfather's point of view —would he feel bitter, angry, sad, triumphant, compassionate?

ABOUT THE AUTHOR

Toni Cade Bambara took her last name from a signature on a sketchbook she found in her great-grandmother's trunk. (Bambara is the name of a people of northwest Africa who are noted for their delicate wood carvings.) Toni Cade is a New Yorker, who went to schools in New York City, in the South, in Paris, and in Florence, Italy. She has worked as a social investigator and as a recreation director, and has most recently taught English in college. She is the author of *The Black Woman, Tales and Stories for Black Folks,* and two collections of short stories: *Gorilla, My Love,* from which "Blues Ain't No Mockin Bird" is taken, and *The Sea Birds Are Still Alive.* Poet Lucille Clifton said of the stories in *Gorilla, My Love:* "She has captured it all, how we really talk, how we really are; and done it with love and respect. I laughed until I cried, then laughed again."

Shaving

Leslie Norris

Earlier, when Barry had left the house to go to the game, an overnight frost had still been thick on the roads, but the brisk April sun had soon dispersed it, and now he could feel the spring warmth on his back through the thick tweed of his coat. His left arm was beginning to stiffen up where he'd jarred it in a tackle, but it was nothing serious. He flexed his shoulders against the tightness of his jacket and was surprised again by the unexpected weight of his muscles, the thickening strength of his body. A few years back, he thought, he had been a small, unimportant boy, one of a swarming gang laughing and jostling to school, hardly aware that he pos-sessed an identity. But time had transformed him. He walked solidly now, and often alone. He was tall, strongly made, his hands and feet were adult and heavy, the rooms in which all his life he'd moved had grown too small for him. Sometimes a devouring restlessness drove him from the house to walk long dis-tances in the dark. He hardly understood how it had happened. Amused and quiet, he walked the High Street among the morning shoppers.

He saw Jackie Bevan across the road and remembered how, when they were both six years old, Jackie had swallowed a pin. The flustered teachers had clucked about Jackie as

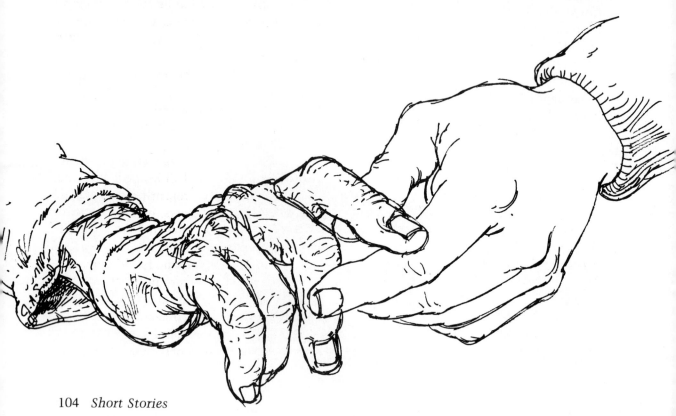

he stood there, bawling, cheeks awash with tears, his nose wet. But now Jackie was tall and suave, his thick, pale hair sleekly tailored, his gray suit enviable. He was talking to a girl as golden as a daffodil.

"Hey, hey!" called Jackie. "How's the athlete, how's Barry boy?"

He waved a graceful hand at Barry.

"Come and talk to Sue," he said.

Barry shifted his bag to his left hand and walked over, forming in his mind the answers he'd make to Jackie's questions.

"Did we win?" Jackie asked. "Was the old Barry Stanford magic in glittering evidence yet once more this morning? Were the invaders sent hunched and silent back to their hovels in the hills? What was the score? Give us an epic account, Barry, without modesty or delay. This is Sue, by the way."

"I've seen you about," the girl said.

"You could hardly miss him," said Jackie. "Four men, roped together, spent a week climbing him—they thought he was Everest. He ought to carry a warning beacon, he's a danger to aircraft."

"Silly," said the girl, smiling at Jackie. "He's not much taller than you are."

She had a nice voice too.

"We won," Barry said. "Seventeen points to three, and it was a good game. The ground was hard, though."

He could think of nothing else to say.

"Let's all go for a frivolous cup of coffee," Jackie said. "Let's celebrate your safe return from the rough fields of victory. We could pour libations[1] all over the floor for you."

"I don't think so," Barry said. "Thanks. I'll go straight home."

"Okay," said Jackie, rocking on his heels so that the sun could shine on his smile. "How's your father?"

"No better," Barry said. "He's not going to get better."

"Yes, well," said Jackie, serious and uncomfortable, "tell him my mother and father ask about him."

"I will," Barry promised. "He'll be pleased."

Barry dropped the bag in the front hall and moved into the room which had been the dining room until his father's illness. His father lay in the white bed, his long body gaunt, his still head scarcely denting the pillow. He seemed asleep, thin blue lids covering his eyes, but when Barry turned away he spoke.

"Hullo, Son," he said. "Did you win?"

His voice was a dry, light rustling, hardly louder than the breath which carried it. Its sound moved Barry to a compassion that almost unmanned him, but he stepped close to the bed and looked down at the dying man.

"Yes," he said. "We won fairly easily. It was a good game."

His father lay with his eyes closed, inert, his breath irregular and shallow.

"Did you score?" he asked.

"Twice," Barry said. "I had a try in each half."

He thought of the easy certainty with which he'd caught the ball before his second try; casually, almost arrogantly he had taken it on the tips of his fingers, on his full burst for the line, breaking the fullback's tackle. Nobody could have stopped him. But watching his father's weakness he felt humble and ashamed, as if the morning's game, its urgency and effort, was not worth talking about. His father's face, fine-skinned and pallid, carried a dark stubble of beard, almost a week's growth, and his obstinate, strong hair stuck out over his brow.

---

1. **pour libations** (lī-bā′shənz): When a warrior in ancient Greece returned home victorious, he would pour libations, or offerings of wine, onto the ground in thanksgiving to the gods.

"Good," said his father, after a long pause. "I'm glad it was a good game."

Barry's mother bustled about the kitchen, a tempest of orderly energy.

"Your father's not well," she said. "He's down today, feels depressed. He's a particular man, your father. He feels dirty with all that beard on him."

She slammed shut the stove door.

"Mr. Cleaver was supposed to come up and shave him," she said, "and that was three days ago. Little things have always worried your father, every detail must be perfect for him."

Barry filled a glass with milk from the refrigerator. He was very thirsty.

"I'll shave him," he said.

His mother stopped, her head on one side.

"Do you think you can?" she asked. "He'd like it if you can."

"I can do it," Barry said.

He washed his hands as carefully as a surgeon. His father's razor was in a blue leather case, hinged at the broad edge and with one hinge broken. Barry unfastened the clasp and took out the razor. It had not been properly cleaned after its last use and lather had stiffened into hard yellow rectangles between the teeth of the guard. There were water-shaped rust stains, brown as chocolate, on the surface of the blade. Barry removed it, throwing it in the wastebin. He washed the razor until it glistened, and dried it on a soft towel, polishing the thin handle, rubbing its metal head to a glittering shine. He took a new blade from its waxed envelope, the paper clinging to the thin metal. The blade was smooth and flexible to the touch, the little angles of its cutting clearly defined. Barry slotted it into the grip of the razor, making it snug and tight in the head.

The shaving soap, hard, white, richly aromatic, was kept in a wooden bowl. Its scent was immediately evocative and Barry could almost see his father in the days of his health, standing before his mirror, thick white lather on his face and neck. As a little boy Barry had loved the generous perfume of the soap, had waited for his father to lift the razor to his face, for one careful stroke to take away the white suds in a clean revelation of the skin. Then his father would renew the lather with a few sweeps of his brush, one with an ivory handle and the bristles worn, which he still used.

His father's shaving mug was a thick cup, plain and serviceable. A gold line ran outside the rim of the cup, another inside, just below the lip. Its handle was large and sturdy, and the face of the mug carried a portrait of the young Queen Elizabeth II, circled by a wreath of leaves, oak perhaps, or laurel. A lion and unicorn balanced precariously on a scroll above her crowned head, and the Union Jack, the Royal Standard, and other flags were furled each side of the portrait. And beneath it all, in small black letters, ran the legend: "Coronation June 2nd 1953." The cup was much older than Barry. A pattern of faint translucent cracks, fine as a web, had worked itself haphazardly, invisibly almost, through the white glaze. Inside, on the bottom, a few dark bristles were lying, loose and dry. Barry shook them out, then held the cup in his hand, feeling its solidness. Then he washed it ferociously, until it was clinically clean.

Methodically he set everything on a tray, razor, soap, brush, towels. Testing the hot water with a finger, he filled the mug and put that, too, on the tray. His care was absorbed, ritualistic. Satisfied that his preparations were complete, he went downstairs, carrying the tray with one hand.

His father was waiting for him. Barry set the tray on a bedside table and bent over his father, sliding an arm under the man's thin shoulders, lifting him without effort so that he sat against the high pillows.

"By God, you're strong," his father said. He was as breathless as if he'd been running.

"So are you," said Barry.

"I was," his father said. "I used to be strong once."

He sat exhausted against the pillows.

"We'll wait a bit," Barry said.

"You could have used your electric razor," his father said. "I expected that."

"You wouldn't like it," Barry said. "You'll get a closer shave this way."

He placed the large towel about his father's shoulders.

"Now," he said, smiling down.

The water was hot in the thick cup. Barry wet the brush and worked up the lather. Gently he built up a covering of soft foam on the man's chin, on his cheeks and his stark cheekbones.

"You're using a lot of soap," his father said.

"Not too much," Barry said. "You've got a lot of beard."

His father lay there quietly, his wasted arms at his sides.

"It's comforting," he said. "You'd be surprised how comforting it is."

Barry took up the razor, weighing it in his hand, rehearsing the angle at which he'd use it. He felt confident.

"If you have prayers to say . . ." he said.

"I've said a lot of prayers," his father answered.

Barry leaned over and placed the razor delicately against his father's face, setting the head accurately on the clean line near the ear where the long hair ended. He held the razor in the tips of his fingers and drew the blade sweetly through the lather. The new edge moved light as a touch over the hardness of the upper jaw and down to the angle of the chin, sliding away the bristles so easily that Barry could not feel their release. He sighed as he shook the razor in the hot water, washing away the soap.

"How's it going?" his father asked.

"No problem," Barry said. "You needn't worry."

It was as if he had never known what his father really looked like. He was discovering under his hands the clear bones of the face and head, they became sharp and recognizable under his fingers. When he moved his father's face a gentle inch to one side, he touched with his fingers the frail temples, the blue veins of his father's life. With infinite and meticulous care he took away the hair from his father's face.

"Now for your neck," he said. "We might as well do the job properly."

"You've got good hands," his father said. "You can trust those hands, they won't let you down."

Barry cradled his father's head in the crook of his left arm, so that the man could tilt back his head, exposing the throat. He brushed fresh lather under the chin and into the hollows alongside the stretched tendons. His father's throat was fleshless and vulnerable, his head was a hard weight on the boy's arm. Barry was filled with unreasoning protective love. He lifted the razor and began to shave.

"You don't have to worry," he said. "Not at all. Not about anything."

He held his father in the bend of his strong arm and they looked at each other. Their heads were very close.

"How old are you?" his father said.

"Seventeen," Barry said. "Near enough seventeen."

"You're young," his father said, "to have this happen."

"Not too young," Barry said. "I'm bigger than most men."

"I think you are," his father said.

He leaned his head tiredly against the boy's shoulder. He was without strength, his face was cold and smooth. He had let go all his authority, handed it over. He lay back on his pillow, knowing his weakness and his mortality, and looked at his son with wonder, with a curious humble pride.

"I won't worry then," he said. "About anything."

"There's no need," Barry said. "Why should you worry?"

He wiped his father's face clean of all soap with a damp towel. The smell of illness was everywhere, overpowering even the perfumed lather. Barry settled his father down and took away the shaving tools, putting them by with the same ceremonial precision with which he'd prepared them: the cleaned and glittering razor in its broken case; the soap, its bowl wiped and dried, on the shelf between the brush and the coronation mug; all free of taint. He washed his hands and scrubbed his nails. His hands were firm and broad, pink after their scrubbing. The fingers were short and strong, the little fingers slightly crooked, and soft dark hair grew on the backs of his hands and his fingers just above the knuckles. Not long ago they had been small bare hands, not very long ago.

Barry opened wide the bathroom window. Already, although it was not yet two o'clock, the sun was retreating and people were moving briskly, wrapped in their heavy coats against the cold that was to come. But now the window was full in the beam of the dying sunlight, and Barry stood there, illuminated in its golden warmth for a whole minute, knowing it would soon be gone.

FOR STUDY AND DISCUSSION

1. The two main characters in this story are at different stages of life. In what ways is Barry contrasted with his father? How does this contrast between the two characters make you feel about each of them?

2. The act of shaving is important because it is the act by which Barry "comes of age." During the shaving ritual, he takes on the authority and responsibilities once held by his father. Which passages indicate that Barry has taken up his father's authority? What passages make Barry seem like a parent, and his father like a trusting child?

3. At what point in this story do you realize that Barry's father accepts his own death? What details in the last two paragraphs indicate that Barry accepts the fact that someday his own youth will be gone?

4. "Shaving" is clearly concerned with more than shaving. How would you state the central idea or truth about life that the author expresses in this story?

LIMITED THIRD-PERSON POINT OF VIEW

"Shaving" is told from the *limited third-person point of view*. A story told from this point of view is narrated by someone who stands outside the action, but who sees almost everything from the vantage point of one character. In "Shaving" the narrator takes us inside the mind of the main character, Barry, and lets us see the world chiefly through his eyes. For example, we are told that "He [Barry] saw Jackie Bevan across the road and remembered how, when they were both six years old, Jackie had swallowed a pin." The narrator also reveals what Barry thinks and feels about himself: "Sometimes a devouring restlessness drove him from the house to walk long distances in the dark. He hardly understood how it had happened." Although other characters appear in the story, it is chiefly Barry's thoughts and feelings that we are allowed to share. By adopting the limited third-person point of view, the author rivets our attention to his main character.

The point of view a writer chooses does much to determine the kind of story he or she will tell. By telling this story in the third person, from Barry's vantage point, Leslie Norris naturally focuses on Barry's "coming of age." If Norris had told the same story from the vantage point of Barry's father, how do you think the focus of the story would have been different? How do you think the story would have changed if it had been told from an omniscient point of view? From a first-person point of view, with Barry himself narrating?

FOR COMPOSITION

Explaining the Tone of a Story

Tone is the attitude a writer takes toward a subject or an audience. A writer's tone can be lighthearted, cynical, affectionate, bitter, scornful, compassionate, detached, and so on. It is important to think about the tone of a piece of writing, for if you misinterpret the tone, you can misread the entire story or poem.

You might think that the tone of a story about a dying man would be depressing or bitter. But is this the case in "Shaving"? To sense the tone in this story, you have to look at how the writer describes the characters, what point of view he has chosen, and what he tells about the characters' feelings for each other. You have to look at the writer's descriptions of the setting—what mood or atmosphere do the passages evoke?

In a brief essay, discuss the tone in "Shaving." Tell how you think this writer feels about Barry and his father. Is his attitude toward youth and age cynical, bitter, sympathetic, compassionate, or something else? Use specific quotations from the story to support your opinion.

ABOUT THE AUTHOR

Leslie Norris (1921–   ), a poet and short-story writer, was born in a mining town in Wales at a time when birches and grasses still covered the industrial debris. He has said that he is glad he grew up when the world was innocent and golden, in a tiny country whose borders had been trampled over so often that they had become meaningless for centuries. Norris, who now lives and teaches in Sussex, England, has contributed to such American publications as *The New Yorker* and *The Atlantic Monthly.* In 1976 he published *Sliding,* a collection of his short stories. The setting for these stories is the countryside of Wales. Writer Joan Aiken has described these stories as dealing with "poignant human puzzles and predicaments against a radiant country background."

Symbol

A *symbol* is something that stands for itself and for something broader than itself as well. In literature, a symbol may be an object, a person, a situation, or an action that suggests or represents a wider meaning. A simple example is name symbolism. Usually a name simply identifies a person. But if a name also tells us something *about* the person, then the name also has a symbolic meaning. Mistress Slipslop, for example, is a comic character in Henry Fielding's novel *Joseph Andrews*. Her name is symbolic, because she uses words as sloppily as her name suggests.

In Jack Finney's story "Contents of the Dead Man's Pockets" (page 20), a sheet of yellow paper covered with facts and figures comes to symbolize an absurd and meaningless way of life. It does so when the hero imagines his dead body lying on the sidewalk eleven stories below:

> All they'd find in his pockets would be the yellow sheet. *Contents of the dead man's pockets*, he thought, *one sheet of paper bearing penciled notations — incomprehensible.*

Finney explains the symbolism for us a few sentences later:

> *Contents of the dead man's pockets*, he thought with sudden fierce anger, *a wasted life.*

Symbolism is an extraordinarily rich fictional device. It also places a large responsibility on the reader. We must be careful not to let our imaginations run away with us and see symbols everywhere. Symbols do not occur in all stories, and they cannot mean just anything.

The Masque° of the Red Death

Edgar Allan Poe

The "Red Death" had long devastated the country. No pestilence had ever been so fatal or so hideous. Blood was its Avatar[1] and its seal—the redness and the horror of blood. There were sharp pains, and sudden dizziness, and then profuse bleeding at the pores, with dissolution. The scarlet stains upon the body and especially upon the face of the victim were the pest ban which shut him out from the aid and from the sympathy of his fellow men. And the whole seizure, progress, and termination of the disease were the incidents of half an hour.

But the Prince Prospero was happy and dauntless and sagacious. When his dominions were half depopulated, he summoned to his presence a thousand hale and lighthearted friends from among the knights and dames of his court and with these retired to the deep seclusion of one of his castellated abbeys.[2] This was an extensive and magnificent structure, the creation of the prince's own eccentric yet august taste. A strong and lofty wall girdled it in. This wall had gates of iron. The courtiers, having entered, brought furnaces and massy hammers and welded the bolts. They resolved to leave means neither of ingress nor egress to the sudden impulses of despair or of frenzy from within. The abbey

---

° **Masque** (măsk): a masquerade; a masked ball.
1. **Avatar** (ăv′ə-tär′): a visible sign or embodiment of an invisible force.
2. **castellated** (kăs′tə-lā′tĭd) **abbeys:** convents or monasteries with towers like those of a castle.

was amply provisioned. With such precautions the courtiers might bid defiance to contagion. The external world could take care of itself. In the meantime it was folly to grieve or to think. The prince had provided all the appliances of pleasure. There were buffoons, there were improvisatori,[3] there were ballet dancers, there were musicians, there was Beauty, there was wine. All these and security were within. Without was the "Red Death."

It was toward the close of the fifth or sixth month of his seclusion, and while the pestilence raged most furiously abroad, that the Prince Prospero entertained his thousand friends at a masked ball of the most unusual magnificence.

It was a voluptuous scene, that masquerade. But first let me tell of the rooms in which it was held. There were seven—an imperial suite. In many palaces, however, such suites form a long and straight vista, while the folding doors slide back nearly to the walls on either hand, so that the view of the whole extent is scarcely impeded. Here the case was very different, as might have been expected from the duke's love of the bizarre. The apartments were so irregularly disposed that the vision embraced but little more than one at a time. There was a sharp turn at every twenty or thirty yards and at each turn a novel effect. To the right and left, in the middle of each wall, a tall and narrow Gothic window looked out upon a closed corridor which pursued the windings of the suite. These windows were of stained glass whose color varied in accordance with the prevailing hue of the decorations of the chamber into which it opened. That at the eastern extremity was hung, for example, in blue—and vividly blue were its windows. The second chamber was purple in its ornaments and tapestries, and here the panes were purple. The third was green throughout, and so were the casements. The fourth was furnished and lighted with orange—the fifth with white—the sixth with violet. The seventh apartment was closely shrouded in black velvet tapestries that hung all over the ceiling and down the walls, falling in heavy folds upon a carpet of the same material and hue. But in this chamber only, the color of the windows failed to correspond with the decorations. The panes here were scarlet—a deep blood color. Now in no one of the seven apartments was there any lamp or candelabrum amid the profusion of golden ornaments that lay scattered to and fro or depended from the roof. There was no light of any kind emanating from lamp or candle within the suite of chambers. But in the corridors that followed the suite, there stood, opposite to each window, a heavy tripod, bearing a brazier of fire, that projected its rays through the tinted glass and so glaringly illumined the room. And thus were produced a multitude of gaudy and fantastic appearances. But in the western or black chamber the effect of the firelight that streamed upon the dark hangings through the blood-tinted panes was ghastly in the extreme and produced so wild a look upon the countenances of those who entered that there were few of the company bold enough to set foot within its precincts at all.

It was in this apartment, also, that there stood against the western wall a gigantic clock of ebony. Its pendulum swung to and fro with a dull, heavy, monotonous clang; and when the minute hand made the circuit of the face and the hour was to be stricken, there came from the brazen lungs of the clock a sound which was clear and loud and deep and exceedingly musical, but of so peculiar a note and emphasis that, at each lapse of an hour, the musicians of the orchestra were con-

---

3. **improvisatori** (ĭm′prə-vē′zə-tôr′ē): poets who compose verses on the spur of the moment.

strained to pause, momentarily, in their performance, to hearken to the sound; and thus the waltzers perforce ceased their evolutions; and there was a brief disconcert of the whole gay company; and, while the chimes of the clock yet rang, it was observed that the giddiest grew pale and the more aged and sedate passed their hands over their brows as if in confused revery or meditation. But when the echoes had fully ceased, a light laughter at once pervaded the assembly; the musicians looked at each other and smiled as if at their own nervousness and folly and made whispering vows, each to the other, that the next chiming of the clock should produce in them no similar emotion; and then, after the lapse of sixty minutes (which embrace three thousand and six hundred seconds of the Time that flies), there came yet another chiming of the clock, and then were the same disconcert and tremulousness and meditation as before.

But, in spite of these things, it was a gay and magnificent revel. The tastes of the duke were peculiar. He had a fine eye for colors and effects. He disregarded the *decora* of mere fashion. His plans were bold and fiery, and his conceptions glowed with barbaric luster. There are some who would have thought him mad. His followers felt that he was not. It was necessary to hear and see and touch him to be *sure* that he was not.

He had directed, in great part, the movable embellishments of the seven chambers, upon occasion of this great fete; and it was his own guiding taste which had given character to the masqueraders. Be sure they were grotesque. There were much glare and glitter and piquancy and phantasm—much of what has been since seen in *Hernani*.[4] There were arabesque figures with unsuited limbs and ap-

pointments. There were delirious fancies such as the madman fashions. There were much of the beautiful, much of the wanton, much of the bizarre, something of the terrible, and not a little of that which might have excited disgust. To and fro in the seven chambers there stalked, in fact, a multitude of dreams. And these—the dreams—writhed in and about, taking hue from the rooms and causing the wild music of the orchestra to seem as the echo of their steps. And, anon, there strikes the ebony clock which stands in the hall of the velvet. And then, for a moment, all is still, and all is silent save the voice of the clock. The dreams are stiff-frozen as they stand. But the echoes of the chime die away—they have endured but an instant—and a light, half-subdued laughter floats after them as they depart. And now again the music swells, and the dreams live and writhe to and fro more merrily than ever, taking hue from the many-tinted windows through which stream the rays from the tripods. But to the chamber which lies most westwardly of the seven, there are now none of the maskers who venture; for the night is waning away; and there flows a ruddier light through the blood-colored panes; and the blackness of the sable drapery appalls; and to him whose foot falls upon the sable carpet, there comes from the near clock of ebony a muffled peal more solemnly emphatic than any which reaches *their* ears who indulge in the more remote gaieties of the other apartments.

But these other apartments were densely crowded, and in them beat feverishly the heart of life. And the revel went whirlingly on, until at length there commenced the sounding of midnight upon the clock. And then the music ceased, as I have told; and the evolutions of the waltzers were quieted; and there was an uneasy cessation of all things as before. But now there were twelve strokes to

4. *Hernani:* a romantic play by the French writer Victor Hugo.

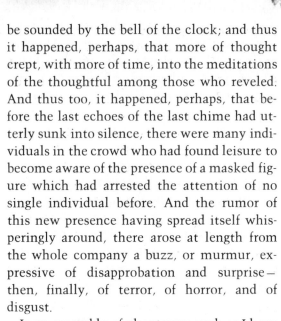

be sounded by the bell of the clock; and thus it happened, perhaps, that more of thought crept, with more of time, into the meditations of the thoughtful among those who reveled. And thus too, it happened, perhaps, that before the last echoes of the last chime had utterly sunk into silence, there were many individuals in the crowd who had found leisure to become aware of the presence of a masked figure which had arrested the attention of no single individual before. And the rumor of this new presence having spread itself whisperingly around, there arose at length from the whole company a buzz, or murmur, expressive of disapprobation and surprise — then, finally, of terror, of horror, and of disgust.

In an assembly of phantasms such as I have painted, it may well be supposed that no ordinary appearance could have excited such sensation. In truth the masquerade license of the night was nearly unlimited; but the figure in question had out-Heroded Herod[5] and gone beyond the bounds of even the prince's indefinite decorum. There are chords in the hearts of the most reckless which cannot be touched without emotion. Even with the utterly lost, to whom life and death are equally jests, there are matters of which no jest can be made. The whole company, indeed, seemed now deeply

5. **out-Heroded Herod:** overplayed his part. Herod was the king in the Bible who went so far as to massacre innocent babies in the hopes of killing the infant Jesus. Anyone who out-Herods Herod does something excessive, or goes too far.

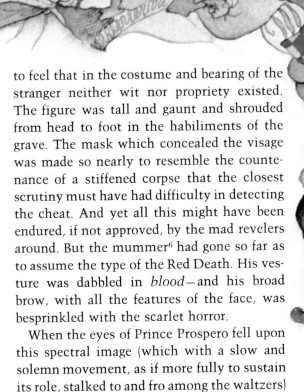

to feel that in the costume and bearing of the stranger neither wit nor propriety existed. The figure was tall and gaunt and shrouded from head to foot in the habiliments of the grave. The mask which concealed the visage was made so nearly to resemble the countenance of a stiffened corpse that the closest scrutiny must have had difficulty in detecting the cheat. And yet all this might have been endured, if not approved, by the mad revelers around. But the mummer[6] had gone so far as to assume the type of the Red Death. His vesture was dabbled in *blood*—and his broad brow, with all the features of the face, was besprinkled with the scarlet horror.

When the eyes of Prince Prospero fell upon this spectral image (which with a slow and solemn movement, as if more fully to sustain its role, stalked to and fro among the waltzers) he was seen to be convulsed, in the first moment with a strong shudder either of terror or distaste; but, in the next, his brow reddened with rage.

"Who dares"—he demanded hoarsely of the courtiers who stood near him—"who dares insult us with this blasphemous mockery? Seize him and unmask him—that we may know whom we have to hang, at sunrise, from the battlements!"

It was in the eastern or blue chamber in which stood the Prince Prospero as he uttered these words. They rang throughout the seven rooms loudly and clearly, for the prince was a

6. **mummer:** masked figure.

bold and robust man, and the music had become hushed at the waving of his hand.

It was in the blue room where stood the prince, with a group of pale courtiers by his side. At first, as he spoke, there was a slight rushing movement of this group in the direction of the intruder, who, at the moment, was also near at hand, and now, with deliberate and stately step, made closer approach to the speaker. But from a certain nameless awe with which the mad assumptions of the mummer had inspired the whole party, there were found none who put forth hand to seize him; so that, unimpeded, he passed within a yard of the prince's person; and, while the vast assembly, as if with one impulse, shrank from the centers of the rooms to the walls, he made his way uninterruptedly, but with the same solemn and measured step which had distinguished him from the first, through the blue chamber to the purple—through the purple to the green—through the green to the orange—through this again to the white—and even thence to the violet ere a decided movement had been made to arrest him. It was then, however, that the Prince Prospero, maddening with rage and the shame of his own momentary cowardice, rushed hurriedly through the six chambers, while none followed him on account of a deadly terror that had seized upon all. He bore aloft a drawn dagger and had approached, in rapid impetuosity, to within three or four feet of the retreating figure, when the latter, having attained the extremity of the velvet apartment, turned suddenly and confronted his pursuer. There was a sharp cry—and the dagger dropped gleaming upon the sable carpet, upon which, instantly afterward, fell prostrate in death the Prince Prospero. Then, summoning the wild courage of despair, a throng of the revelers at once threw themselves into the black apartment and, seizing the mummer, whose tall figure stood erect and motionless within the shadow of the ebony clock, gasped in unutterable horror at finding the grave cerements[7] and corpselike mask, which they handled with so violent a rudeness, untenanted by any tangible form.

And now was acknowledged the presence of the Red Death. He had come like a thief in the night. And one by one dropped the revelers in the blood-bedewed halls of their revel and died each in the despairing posture of his fall. And the life of the ebony clock went out with that of the last of the gay. And the flames of the tripods expired. And Darkness and Decay and the Red Death held illimitable dominion over all.

---

7. **cerements** (sîr'mənts): burial clothes; shroud.

FOR STUDY AND DISCUSSION

1. This story takes place in a country devastated by the plague. How do Prince Prospero and his friends try to escape? What kind of life do they lead in their world apart?
2. Describe the seven rooms of the prince's suite. What is significant about the number seven, about the colors of the rooms, and about their progression from east to west?
3. What do you think is symbolized by the seventh room—the black room with the blood-red windows? Why do the masqueraders avoid this room?
4. What does the ebony clock in the seventh room symbolize?
5. In the paragraph that describes the masquerade on page 113, find words and phrases that suggest nightmare or madness.
6. Who or what is the uninvited guest—the masked figure with the face of a corpse? What does his arrival in this incredibly rich, sealed-off world symbolize?

LANGUAGE AND VOCABULARY

Understanding Denotation and Connotation

All words have *denotations*, which are their strict dictionary meanings or definitions. The denotative meaning of *blood*, for example, is "a red fluid that circulates through the heart, veins, and arteries of vertebrates." Many words also have *connotations*, feelings and associations that have come to be attached to the words in addition to their strict, literal meanings. The word *blood*, for example, is especially rich in connotations. Blood is often associated with thoughts of death, wounds, and pain.

Poe, of course, was aware of these two aspects of the meanings of words. Reread the paragraph beginning "In an assembly of phantasms" on page 114. Explain the denotative and the connotative meanings of the following words:

phantasms	gaunt	corpse
license	shrouded	horror
jest		

How do words like these affect your feelings as you read this paragraph?

FOR COMPOSITION

Analyzing the Effect of a Story

Poe believed that every detail in a short story should contribute to a single emotional effect. In a brief essay, explain the "single emotional effect" you think is conveyed by this story. Cite words and passages from the story that you think contribute most forcefully to this effect.

ABOUT THE AUTHOR

Edgar Allan Poe (1809–1849) is one of America's most important writers. He is famous for his detective stories and tales of mystery and horror, and also for his poetry and literary criticism. The son of traveling actors, Poe was orphaned at the age of three and raised by John Allan, a wealthy businessman of Richmond, Virginia. Poe was an excellent athlete and a brilliant student, but his guardian disapproved of his literary ambitions and sent him to the University of Virginia on a very small allowance. Poe left the university because of gambling debts and joined the army, where he served honorably for two years. He entered West Point in an attempt to make peace with Allan, but deliberately got himself expelled from the military academy when he realized that a reconciliation was hopeless. Cast off by the wealthy Allans, Poe went to live with a poor aunt. He married her daughter, Virginia Clemm, before the girl was fourteen. In Richmond, New York, Baltimore, and Philadelphia, Poe eked out a living for his small household as a magazine editor and newspaper writer. The death of his young wife from tuberculosis intensified Poe's despair. By the time he died on a rainy Baltimore sidewalk a few years later, he was showing signs of insanity.

Among Poe's famous tales of horror and suspense — most of which depict violent inner experiences — are "The Black Cat," "The Tell-Tale Heart," "The Pit and the Pendulum," and "The Fall of the House of Usher." His poems include "The Raven" and "Annabel Lee."

Poe's detective stories set the pattern for most modern detective fiction. In stories such as "The Murders in the Rue Morgue" and "The Purloined Letter," his detective Dupin, a genius, unravels mysteries by his brilliant powers of intuition.

A White Heron
Sarah Orne Jewett

I

The woods were already filled with shadows one June evening, just before eight o'clock, though a bright sunset still glimmered faintly among the trunks of the trees. A little girl was driving home her cow, a plodding, dilatory, provoking creature in her behavior, but a valued companion for all that. They were going away from the western light, and striking deep into the dark woods, but their feet were familiar with the path, and it was no matter whether their eyes could see it or not.

There was hardly a night the summer through when the old cow could be found waiting at the pasture bars; on the contrary, it was her greatest pleasure to hide herself away among the high huckleberry bushes, and though she wore a loud bell, she had made the discovery that if one stood perfectly still it would not ring. So Sylvia had to hunt for her until she found her, and call "Co'! Co'!" with never an answering "Moo," until her childish patience was quite spent. If the creature had not given good milk and plenty of it, the case would have seemed very different to her owners. Besides, Sylvia had all the time there was, and very little use to make of it. Sometimes in pleasant weather it was a consolation to look upon the cow's pranks as an intelligent attempt to play hide-and-seek, and as the child had no playmates, she lent herself to this amusement with a good deal of zest. Though this chase had been so long that the wary animal herself had given an unusual signal of her whereabouts, Sylvia had only laughed when she came upon Mistress Moolly at the swamp side, and urged her affectionately homeward with a twig of birch leaves. The old cow was not inclined to wander farther, she even turned in the right direction for once as they left the pasture, and stepped along the road at a good pace. She was quite ready to be milked now and seldom stopped to browse. Sylvia wondered what her grandmother would say because they were so late. It was a great while since she had left home at half past five, but everybody knew the difficulty of making this errand a short one. Mrs. Tilley had chased the horned torment too many summer evenings herself to blame anyone else for lingering, and was only thankful as she waited that she had Sylvia, nowadays, to give such valuable assistance. The good woman suspected that Sylvia loitered occasionally on her own account; there never was such a child for straying about out of doors since the world was made! Everybody said that it was a good change for a little maid who had tried to grow for eight years in a crowded manufacturing town, but, as for Sylvia herself, it seemed as if she never had been alive at all before she came to live at the farm. She thought often with wistful compassion of a wretched dry geranium that belonged to a town neighbor.

" 'Afraid of folks,' " old Mrs. Tilley said to herself, with a smile, after she had made the unlikely choice of Sylvia from her daughter's houseful of children, and was returning to the farm. " 'Afraid of folks,' they said! I guess she won't be troubled no great with 'em up to the old place!'' When they reached the door of the lonely house and stopped to unlock it, and the cat came to purr loudly and rub against them, a deserted pussy, indeed, but fat with young robins, Sylvia whispered that this was a beautiful place to live in and she never should wish to go home.

The companions followed the shady wood road, the cow taking slow steps and the child very fast ones. The cow stopped long at the brook to drink, as if the pasture were not half a swamp, and Sylvia stood still and waited, letting her bare feet cool themselves in the shoal water, while the great twilight moths struck softly against her. She waded on through the brook as the cow moved away, and listened to the thrushes with a heart that beat fast with pleasure. There was a stirring in the great boughs overhead. They were full of little birds and beasts that seemed to be wide-awake and going about their world, or else saying good night to each other in sleepy twitters. Sylvia herself felt sleepy as she walked along. However, it was not much farther to the house, and the air was soft and sweet. She was not often in the woods so late as this, and it made her feel as if she were a part of the gray shadows and the moving leaves. She was just thinking how long it seemed since she first came to the farm a year ago and wondering if everything went on in the noisy town just the same as when she was there; the thought of the great red-faced boy who used to chase and frighten her made her hurry along the path to escape from the shadow of the trees.

Suddenly this little woods-girl is horror-stricken to hear a clear whistle not very far away. Not a bird's whistle, which would have a sort of friendliness, but a boy's whistle, determined and somewhat aggressive. Sylvia left the cow to whatever sad fate might await her and stepped discreetly aside into the bushes, but she was just too late. The enemy had discovered her and called out in a very cheerful and persuasive tone, ''Halloa, little girl, how far is it to the road?'' and trembling Sylvia answered almost inaudibly, ''A good ways.''

She did not dare to look boldly at the tall young man, who carried a gun over his shoulder, but she came out of her bush and again followed the cow, while he walked alongside.

''I have been hunting for some birds,'' the stranger said kindly, ''and I have lost my way and need a friend very much. Don't be afraid,'' he added gallantly. ''Speak up and tell me what your name is and whether you think I can spend the night at your house and go out gunning early in the morning.''

Sylvia was more alarmed than before. Would not her grandmother consider her much to blame? But who could have foreseen such an accident as this? It did not appear to be her fault, and she hung her head as if the stem of it were broken, but managed to answer, ''Sylvy,'' with much effort when her companion again asked her name.

Mrs. Tilley was standing in the doorway when the trio came into view. The cow gave a loud moo by way of explanation.

''Yes, you'd better speak up for yourself, you old trial! Where'd she tuck herself away this time, Sylvy?'' Sylvia kept an awed silence; she knew by instinct that her grandmother did not comprehend the gravity of the situation. She must be mistaking the stranger for one of the farmer lads of the region.

The young man stood his gun beside the door and dropped a heavy game bag beside it; then he bade Mrs. Tilley good evening and repeated his wayfarer's story and asked if he could have a night's lodging.

''Put me anywhere you like,'' he said. ''I

must be off early in the morning, before day; but I am very hungry, indeed. You can give me some milk at any rate, that's plain."

"Dear sakes, yes," responded the hostess, whose long slumbering hospitality seemed to be easily awakened. "You might fare better if you went out on the main road a mile or so, but you're welcome to what we've got. I'll milk right off, and you make yourself at home. You can sleep on husks or feathers," she proffered graciously. "I raised them all myself. There's good pasturing for geese just below here toward the ma'sh. Now step round and set a plate for the gentleman, Sylvy!" And Sylvia promptly stepped. She was glad to have something to do, and she was hungry herself.

It was a surprise to find so clean and comfortable a little dwelling in this New England wilderness. The young man had known the horrors of its most primitive housekeeping and the dreary squalor of that level of society which does not rebel at the companionship of hens. This was the best thrift of an old-fashioned farmstead, though on such a small scale that it seemed like a hermitage. He listened eagerly to the old woman's quaint talk, he watched Sylvia's pale face and shining gray eyes with ever growing enthusiasm, and insisted that this was the best supper he had eaten for a month; then, afterward, the new-made friends sat down in the doorway together while the moon came up.

Soon it would be berry time, and Sylvia was a great help at picking. The cow was a good milker, though a plaguy[1] thing to keep track of, the hostess gossiped frankly, adding presently that she had buried four children, so that Sylvia's mother and a son (who might be dead) in California were all the children she had left. "Dan, my boy, was a great hand to go gun-

A scene from *A White Heron*, dramatized for television, 1978.

ning," she explained sadly. "I never wanted for pa'tridges or gray squer'ls while he was to home. He's been a great wand'rer, I expect, and he's no hand to write letters. There, I don't blame him. I'd ha' seen the world myself if it had been so I could.

"Sylvia takes after him," the grandmother continued affectionately, after a minute's pause. "There ain't a foot o' ground she don't know her way over, and the wild creatur's counts her one o' themselves. Squer'ls she'll

---

1. **plaguy** (plā′gē): annoying; troublesome.

tame to come an' feed right out o' her hands, and all sorts o' birds. Last winter she got the jaybirds to bangeing[2] here, and I believe she'd 'a' scanted herself of her own meals to have plenty to throw out amongst 'em if I hadn't kep' watch. Anything but crows, I tell her, I'm willin' to help support—though Dan he went an' tamed one o' them that did seem to have reason same as folks. It was round here a good spell after he went away. Dan an' his father they didn't hitch[3]—but he never held up his head ag'in after Dan had dared him an' gone off."

The guest did not notice this hint of family sorrows in his eager interest in something else.

"So Sylvy knows all about birds, does she?" he exclaimed, as he looked round at the little girl who sat, very demure but increasingly sleepy, in the moonlight. "I am making a collection of birds myself. I have been at it ever since I was a boy." (Mrs. Tilley smiled.) "There are two or three very rare ones I have been hunting for these five years. I mean to get them on my own ground if they can be found."

"Do you cage 'em up?" asked Mrs. Tilley doubtfully, in response to this enthusiastic announcement.

"Oh, no, they're stuffed and preserved, dozens and dozens of them," said the ornithologist,[4] "and I have shot or snared every one myself. I caught a glimpse of a white heron three miles from here on Saturday, and I have followed it in this direction. They have never been found in this district at all. The little white heron, it is," and he turned again to look at Sylvia with the hope of discovering that the rare bird was one of her acquaintances.

But Sylvia was watching a hoptoad in the narrow footpath.

"You would know the heron if you saw it," the stranger continued eagerly. "A queer tall white bird with soft feathers and long thin legs. And it would have a nest perhaps in the top of a high tree, made of sticks, something like a hawk's nest."

Sylvia's heart gave a wild beat; she knew that strange white bird, and had once stolen softly near where it stood in some bright green swamp grass, away over at the other side of the woods. There was an open place where the sunshine always seemed strangely yellow and hot, where tall, nodding rushes grew, and her grandmother had warned her that she might sink in the soft black mud underneath and never be heard of more. Not far beyond were the salt marshes and beyond those was the sea, the sea which Sylvia wondered and dreamed about, but never had looked upon, though its great voice could often be heard above the noise of the woods on stormy nights.

"I can't think of anything I should like so much as to find that heron's nest," the handsome stranger was saying. "I would give ten dollars to anybody who could show it to me," he added desperately, "and I mean to spend my whole vacation hunting for it if need be. Perhaps it was only migrating, or had been chased out of its own region by some bird of prey."

Mrs. Tilley gave amazed attention to all this, but Sylvia still watched the toad, not divining, as she might have done at some calmer time, that the creature wished to get to its hole under the doorstep, and was much hindered by the unusual spectators at that hour of the evening. No amount of thought, that night, could decide how many wished-for

---

2. **bangeing** (băng'ĭng): loitering; gathering around.
3. **hitch:** get along.
4. **ornithologist** (ôr'nə-thŏl'ə-jĭst): person who studies birds.

treasures the ten dollars, so lightly spoken of, would buy.

The next day the young sportsman hovered about the woods, and Sylvia kept him company, having lost her first fear of the friendly lad, who proved to be most kind and sympathetic. He told her many things about the birds and what they knew and where they lived and what they did with themselves. And he gave her a jackknife, which she thought as great a treasure as if she were a desert islander. All day long he did not once make her troubled or afraid except when he brought down some unsuspecting singing creature from its bough. Sylvia would have liked him vastly better without his gun; she could not understand why he killed the very birds he seemed to like so much. But as the day waned, Sylvia still watched the young man with loving admiration. She had never seen anybody so charming and delightful: the woman's heart, asleep in the child, was vaguely thrilled by a dream of love. Some premonition of that great power stirred and swayed these young foresters who traversed the solemn woodlands with soft-footed silent care. They stopped to listen to a bird's song; they pressed forward again eagerly, parting the branches—speaking to each other rarely and in whispers; the young man going first and Sylvia following, fascinated, a few steps behind, with her gray eyes dark with excitement.

She grieved because the longed-for white heron was elusive, but she did not lead the guest, she only followed, and there was no such thing as speaking first. The sound of her own unquestioned voice would have terrified her—it was hard enough to answer yes or no when there was need of that. At last evening began to fall, and they drove the cow home together, and Sylvia smiled with pleasure when they came to the place where she heard the whistle and was afraid only the night before.

II

Half a mile from home, at the farther edge of the woods, where the land was highest, a great pine tree stood, the last of its generation. Whether it was left for a boundary mark, or for what reason, no one could say; the woodchoppers who had felled its mates were dead and gone long ago, and a whole forest of sturdy trees, pines, and oaks and maples had grown again. But the stately head of this old pine towered above them all and made a landmark for sea and shore miles and miles away. Sylvia knew it well. She had always believed that whoever climbed to the top of it could see the ocean; and the little girl had often laid her hand on the great rough trunk and looked up wistfully at those dark boughs that the wind always stirred, no matter how hot and still the air might be below. Now she thought of the tree with a new excitement, for why, if one climbed it at break of day, could not one see all the world, and easily discover whence the white heron flew, and mark the place, and find the hidden nest?

What a spirit of adventure, what wild ambition! What fancied triumph and delight and glory for the later morning when she could make known the secret! It was almost too real and too great for the childish heart to bear.

All night the door of the little house stood open, and the whippoorwills came and sang upon the very step. The young sportsman and his old hostess were sound asleep, but Sylvia's great design kept her broad awake and watching. She forgot to think of sleep. The short summer night seemed as long as the winter darkness, and at last when the whippoorwills ceased, and she was afraid the morning would after all come too soon, she stole out of the house and followed the pasture path through the woods, hastening toward the open ground beyond, listening with a sense of comfort and companionship to the drowsy twitter of a half-awakened bird, whose perch she had jarred in passing. Alas, if the great wave of human interest which flooded for the first time this dull little life should sweep away the satisfactions of an existence heart to heart with nature and the dumb life of the forest!

There was the huge tree asleep yet in the paling moonlight, and small and hopeful Sylvia began with utmost bravery to mount to the top of it, with tingling, eager blood coursing the channels of her whole frame, with her bare feet and fingers that pinched and held like bird's claws to the monstrous ladder reaching up, up, almost to the sky itself. First she must mount the white oak tree that grew alongside, where she was almost lost among the dark branches and green leaves heavy and wet with dew; a bird fluttered off its nest, and a red squirrel ran to and fro and scolded pettishly at the harmless housebreaker. Sylvia felt her way easily. She had often climbed there and knew that higher still one of the oak's upper branches chafed against the pine trunk, just where its lower boughs were set close together. There, when she made the dangerous pass from one tree to the other, the great enterprise would really begin.

She crept out along the swaying oak limb at last and took the daring step across into the old pine tree. The way was harder than she thought; she must reach far and hold fast, the sharp dry twigs caught and held her and scratched her like angry talons, the pitch made her thin little fingers clumsy and stiff as she went round and round the tree's great stem, higher and higher upward. The sparrows and robins in the woods below were beginning to wake and twitter to the dawn, yet it seemed much lighter there aloft in the pine tree, and the child knew that she must hurry if her project were to be of any use.

The tree seemed to lengthen itself out as she went up and to reach farther and farther upward. It was like a great mainmast to the voyaging earth; it must truly have been amazed that morning through all its ponderous frame as it felt this determined spark of human spirit creeping and climbing from higher branch to branch. Who knows how steadily the least twigs held themselves to advantage this light, weak creature on her way! The old pine must have loved his new dependent. More than all the hawks, and bats, and moths, and even the sweet-voiced thrushes, was the brave, beating heart of the solitary gray-eyed child. And the tree stood still and held away the winds that June morning while the dawn grew bright in the east.

Sylvia's face was like a pale star, if one had seen it from the ground, when the last thorny bough was past, and she stood trembling and tired but wholly triumphant high in the treetop. Yes, there was the sea with the dawning sun making a golden dazzle over it, and toward that glorious east flew two hawks with slow-moving pinions.[5] How low they looked in the air from that height when before one had only seen them far up and dark against the blue sky. Their gray feathers were as soft as moths; they seemed only a little way from the tree, and Sylvia felt as if she too could go flying away among the clouds. Westward, the woodlands and farms reached miles and miles into the distance; here and there were church steeples and white villages; truly it was a vast and awesome world.

The birds sang louder and louder. At last the sun came up bewilderingly bright. Sylvia could see the white sails of ships out at sea, and the clouds that were purple and rose-colored and yellow at first began to fade away. Where was the white heron's nest in the sea

---

5. **pinions** (pĭn′yənz): wings.

of green branches, and was this wonderful sight and pageant of the world the only reward for having climbed to such a giddy height? Now look down again, Sylvia, where the green marsh is set among the shining birches and dark hemlocks; there where you saw the white heron once you will see him again; look, look! a white spot of him like a single floating feather comes up from the dead hemlock and grows larger, and rises, and comes close at last, and goes by the landmark pine with steady sweep of wing and outstretched slender neck and crested head. And wait! do not move a foot or a finger, little girl, do not send an arrow of light and consciousness from your two eager eyes, for the heron has perched on a pine bough not far beyond yours, and cries back to his mate on the nest, and plumes his feathers for the new day!

The child gives a long sigh a minute later when a company of shouting catbirds comes also to the tree, and vexed by their fluttering and lawlessness the solemn heron goes away. She knows his secret now, the wild, light, slender bird that floats and wavers and goes back like an arrow presently to his home in the green world beneath. Then Sylvia, well satisfied, makes her perilous way down again, not daring to look far below the branch she stands on, ready to cry sometimes because her fingers ache and her lamed feet slip. Wondering over and over again what the stranger would say to her, and what he would think when she told him how to find his way straight to the heron's nest.

"Sylvy, Sylvy!" called the busy old grandmother again and again, but nobody answered, and the small husk bed was empty, and Sylvia had disappeared.

The guest waked from a dream, and remembering his day's pleasure hurried to dress himself that it might sooner begin. He was sure from the way the shy little girl looked once or twice yesterday that she had at least seen the white heron, and now she must really be persuaded to tell. Here she comes now, paler than ever, and her worn old frock is torn and tattered and smeared with pine pitch. The grandmother and the sportsman stand in the door together and question her, and the splendid moment has come to speak of the dead hemlock tree by the green marsh.

But Sylvia does not speak after all, though the old grandmother fretfully rebukes her, and the young man's kind appealing eyes are looking straight in her own. He can make them rich with money; he has promised it, and they are poor now. He is so well worth making happy, and he waits to hear the story she can tell.

No, she must keep silence! What is it that suddenly forbids her and makes her dumb? Has she been nine years growing, and now, when the great world for the first time puts out a hand to her, must she thrust it aside for a bird's sake? The murmur of the pine's green branches is in her ears, she remembers how the white heron came flying through the golden air and how they watched the sea and the morning together, and Sylvia cannot speak; she cannot tell the heron's secret and give its life away.

Dear loyalty that suffered a sharp pang as the guest went away disappointed later in the day, that could have served and followed him and loved him as a dog loves! Many a night Sylvia heard the echo of his whistle haunting the pasture path as she came home with the loitering cow. She forgot even her sorrow at the sharp report of his gun and the piteous sight of thrushes and sparrows dropping silent to the ground, their songs hushed and their pretty feathers stained and wet with blood. Were the birds better friends than their hunter might have been — who can tell? Whatever treasures were lost to her, woodlands and summertime, remember! Bring your gifts and graces and tell your secrets to this lonely country child!

1. Look up the name *Sylvia* or the word *sylvan,* in a dictionary. Why is *Sylvia* an appropriate name for this character?

2. What is Sylvia's central conflict? At what point do you know how her conflict is resolved?

3. In many stories the hero or heroine must undergo a dangerous and difficult journey or overcome fearful odds to achieve a desired goal. What episode represents Sylvia's "perilous journey"? What does she obtain or achieve at the end of her ordeal?

4. Several plants, birds, and animals are mentioned in the story. Most of them are used as details to describe the setting. A few of them, however, are used to symbolize something else. What do you think is symbolized by the "wretched dry geranium" (page 118) that belonged to Sylvia's town neighbor? How does it differ from the flowers in the woods?

5. The central symbol is the white heron. Why doesn't Sylvia reveal the bird's nesting place to her new friend? What does the heron symbolize?

6. This story suggests a conflict between two settings and two kinds of values. One setting is Sylvia's "green world"; the other is the world of the town. What different values are represented by each setting? How does the author want you to feel about these settings and values? Cite passages from the story to support your answer.

7. This author shifts her point of view several times. Sometimes she tells the story as an omniscient narrator, knowing the thoughts of all the characters. At times, she interrupts the story to state her own opinions. Once she uses the second-person pronoun and talks to Sylvia directly. Find examples of these shifts in point of view. Did they affect your reactions to the story? Explain.

LANGUAGE AND VOCABULARY

Recognizing Combining Forms

A combining form is a word part that combines with other words or word parts to form a new word. The combining form *-logy* comes from the Greek word *logos* ("word") and means "study of, science of, or theory of." A word that ends in *-ologist* refers to a person who studies a particular subject. The young man in "A White Heron" is an ornithologist and his field of study is ornithology.

Another commonly used combining form is *-sophy*, from the Greek word *sophia*, meaning "skill or wisdom." (The word *sophomore*, for example, combines the word *sophia* with the word *moros*, which means "foolish." What does *sophomore* literally mean?)

Use a college dictionary or unabridged dictionary to find out what other combining forms are used in each of these words.

archaeology	philosophy	theology
philology	psychology	theosophy

FOR COMPOSITION

Using Figures of Speech

This author uses several figures of speech to help you imagine Sylvia's difficulties and her feelings as she climbs the tall pine tree. Notice how the figures of speech in these sentences help you to share the experience of the climb by appealing to a few of your senses:

> . . . the sharp dry twigs caught and held her and scratched her like angry talons . . . .

> The tree . . . was like a great mainmast to the voyaging earth . . . .

Write a paragraph in which you describe some natural object you are familiar with. Use figures of speech that compare this object to something else. Try to include specific details that appeal to one or more of the senses.

ABOUT THE AUTHOR

On her forty-eighth birthday, Sarah Orne Jewett (1849–1909) remarked, "This is my birthday and I am always nine years old." In her writing, Jewett recorded the serenity and happiness of her childhood in South Berwick, Maine, where she spent her entire life. Because she was chronically ill as a child, she had little formal schooling. Her father, a country doctor, took her with him whenever he visited his patients, and her desire to write about these country people came early. "When I was, perhaps, fifteen, the first 'city boarders' began to make their appearance near Berwick; and the way they misconstrued the country people and made game of their peculiarities fired me with indignation. I determined to teach the world that country people were not the awkward, ignorant set those people seemed to think. I wanted the world to know their grand, simple lives . . . ." "A White Heron" comes from her short-story collection called *The Country of the Pointed Firs and Other Stories.*

Irony

All irony involves a difference, or discrepancy, between what appears to be and what really is—that is, between appearance and reality. The simplest kind of irony is *verbal irony*. In verbal irony, a speaker or writer says the opposite of what he or she means; such a person speaks "tongue in cheek," as we say. Verbal irony is common in everyday conversation. When someone describes a ten-course meal as a "light snack," the speaker is being ironic. When Frank O'Connor refers to two characters in his story (page 128) as "the duke's children," he is being ironic: they are children of working-class families and are anything but "duke's children."

Another, usually more important, kind of irony is *dramatic irony*. In dramatic irony, the discrepancy is between what a character says (or thinks) and what the reader knows is true. In dramatic irony, a character is not aware of something the reader is aware of. Maurice Walsh uses dramatic irony in his story "The Quiet Man" (page 82). If we read that story carefully, we find hints that Shawn Kelvin, the "quiet man," was really a prizefighter in the United States. Thus, we have guessed at something that Shawn's enemy, the bully Big Liam O'Grady, does not know.

A third kind of irony often used in fiction is *irony of situation*. Irony of situation occurs when a situation turns out to be different from what we had expected. A famous example of irony of situation occurs in O. Henry's story "The Gift of the Magi." In that story, a young husband and wife are nearly penniless, and it is Christmas. Out of love for her husband, the wife cuts off and sells her long hair to buy him a watch chain. At the end of the story, however, she discovers that her husband has sold his watch to buy her a set of combs for her long hair. This situation is ironic because the characters' actions bring about results that are the opposite of what they had expected.

Irony is an important element in fiction because it drives home the truth that human life itself is unpredictable. In fiction, just as in life, our words and our actions do not always have the meanings or results we expect them to have.

The Duke's Children

Frank O'Connor

I could never see precisely what was supposed to be exaggerated in the plots of novelists like Dickens. To this day I can still read about some mysterious street urchin, brought up to poverty and vice by a rag picker, who turns out to be the missing heir to an earldom, and see nothing peculiar about it. To me, it all seems the most natural thing in the world.

Having always been Mother's pet, I was comparatively grown-up when the truth about my own birth broke on me first. In fact, I was already at work as a messenger boy on the railway. Naturally, I had played with the idea as I had played with scores of other ideas, but suddenly, almost in a day, every other possibility disappeared, and I knew I had nothing whatever in common with the two commonplace creatures with whom my fate had become so strangely linked.

It wasn't only their poverty that repelled me, though that was bad enough, or the tiny terrace house we lived in, with its twelve-foot square of garden in front, its crumbling stumps of gateposts and low wall that had lost its railing. It was their utter commonness, their squabbles about money, their low friends and fatuous[1] conversations. You could see that no breath of fineness had ever touched them. They seemed like people who had been crippled from birth and never known what it was to walk or run or dance. Though I might be—for the moment, at least—only a messenger, I had those long spells when by some sort of instinct I knew who I really was, could stand aside and watch myself come up the road after my day's work with relaxed and measured steps, turning my head slowly to greet some neighbor and raising my cap with a grace and charm that came of centuries of breeding. Not only could I see myself like that; there were even times when I could hear an interior voice that preceded and dictated each movement as though it were a fragment of a storybook: "He raised his cap gracefully while his face broke into a thoughtful smile."

And then, as I turned the corner, I would see Father at the gate in his house clothes, a ragged trousers and vest, an old cap that came down over his eyes, and boots cut into something that resembled sandals and that he insisted on calling his "slippers." Father was a creature of habit. No sooner was he out of his working clothes than he was peppering[2] for his evening paper, and if the newsboy were five minutes late, Father muttered: "I don't know what's coming over that boy at all!" and drifted down to the main road to listen for him. When the newsboy did at last appear, Father would grab the paper from his hand and

almost run home, putting on his spectacles awkwardly as he ran and triumphantly surveying the promised treat of the headlines.

And suddenly everything would go black on me, and I would take the chair by the open back door while Father, sitting at the other end, uttered little exclamations of joy or rage and Mother asked anxiously how I had got on during the day. Most of the time I could reply only in monosyllables. How could I tell her that nothing had happened at work that was not as common as the things that happened at home: nothing but those moments of blinding illumination when I was alone in the station yard on a spring morning with sunlight striking the cliffs above the tunnel, and, picking my way between the rails and the trucks, I realized that it was not for long, that I was a duke or earl, lost, stolen, or strayed from my proper home, and that I had only to be discovered for everything to fall into its place? Illumination came only when I had escaped; most often when I crossed the yard on my way from work and dawdled in the passenger station before the bookstall, or watched a passenger train go out on its way to Queenstown or Dublin[3] and realized that one day some train like that would take me back to my true home and patrimony.

These gloomy silences used to make Father mad. He was a talkative man, and every little incident of his day turned into narrative and drama for him. He seemed forever to be meeting old comrades of his army days whom he had not met for fifteen years, and astounding changes had always taken place in them in the meantime. When one of his old friends called, or even when some woman from

---

1. **fatuous** (făch′o͞o-əs): silly; foolish.
2. **peppering**: impatient.

3. **Queenstown or Dublin:** Queenstown is the name the English gave to the seaport of Cobh, which is in southern Ireland. Dublin, a port on the eastern coast, is the capital of the Republic of Ireland.

The Duke's Children   129

across the square dropped in for a cup of tea, he would leave everything, even his newspaper, to talk. His corner by the window permitting him no room for drama, he would stamp about the tiny kitchen, pausing at the back door to glance up at the sky or by the other door into the little hallway to see who was passing outside in the square. It irritated him when I got up in the middle of all this, took my cap, and went quietly out. It irritated him even more if I read while he and the others talked, and, when some question was addressed to me, put down my book and gazed at him blankly. He was so coarse in grain that he regarded it as insolence. He had no experience of dukes, and had never heard that interior voice which dictated my movements and words. "Slowly the lad lowered the book in which he had been immersed and gazed wonderingly at the man who called himself his father."

One evening I was coming home from work when a girl spoke to me. She was a girl called Nancy Harding whose elder brother I knew slightly. I had never spoken to her—indeed, there were not many girls I did speak to. I was too conscious of the fact that, though my jacket was good enough, my trousers were an old blue pair of Father's, cut down and with a big patch in the seat. But Nancy, emerging from a house near the quarry, hailed me as if we were old friends and walked with me up the road. She was slim and dark-haired with an eager and inconsequent[4] manner, and her chatter bewildered and charmed me. My own conversation was of a rather portentous[5] sort.

"I was down with Madge Regan, getting the answers for my homework," she explained. "I don't know what's wrong with me, but I can't do those blooming old sums. Where were you?"

"Oh, I was at work," I answered.

"At work?" she exclaimed in astonishment. "Till this hour?"

"I have to work from eight to seven," I said modestly.

"But aren't they terrible hours?" she said.

"Ah, I'm only filling in time," I explained lightly. "I don't expect to be there long."

This was prophetic, because I was sacked a couple of months later, but at the same time I just wanted to make it clear if there was any exploitation being done, it was I and not the railway company that was doing it. We walked slowly, and she stood under the gas lamp at the end of the square with me. Darkness or day, it was funny how people made a rendezvous of gas lamps. They were our playrooms when we were kids and our clubs as we became older. And then, for the first time, I heard the words running through my head as though they were dictating to someone else behind myself. "Pleased with his quiet conversation and well-bred voice, she wondered if he could really be the son of the Delaneys at all." Up to this, the voice had paid no attention to other people; now that it had begun to expand its activities it took on a new reality, and I longed to repeat the experience.

I had several opportunities, because we met like that a couple of times when I was coming home from work. I was not observant, and it wasn't until years after that it struck me that she might have been waiting for me at the same house at the same time. And one evening, when we were standing under our gas lamp, I talked a little too enthusiastically about some storybook, and Nancy asked for the loan of it. I was pleased with her attention but alarmed at the thought of her seeing where I lived.

4. **inconsequent** (ĭn-kŏn'sə-kwənt): not logical.
5. **portentous** (pôr-tĕn'təs): pompous; self-important.

"I'll bring it with me tomorrow," I said.

"Ah, come on and get it for me now," she said coaxingly, and I glanced over my shoulder and saw Father at the gate, his head cocked, listening for the newsboy. I felt suddenly sick. I knew such a nice girl couldn't possibly want to meet Father, but I didn't see how I was to get the book without introducing them. We went up the little uneven avenue together.

"This is Nancy Harding, Dad," I said in an offhand tone. "I just want to get a book for her."

"Oh, come in, girl, come in," he said, smiling amiably. "Sit down, can't you, while you're waiting?" Father's sociability almost caused him to forget the newsboy. "Min," he called to Mother, "you keep an eye on the paper," and he set a chair in the middle of the kitchen floor. As I searched in the front room for the book, which in my desperation I could not find, I heard Mother go for the paper and Father talking away like mad to Nancy, and when I went into the kitchen, there he was in his favorite chair, the paper lying unopened on the table beside him while he told an endless, pointless story about old times in the neighborhood. Father had been born in the neighborhood, which he seemed to think a matter for pride, but if there was one of Father's favorite subjects I could not stand, it was the still wilder and more sordid life people had lived there when he was growing up. This story was about a wake[6] — all his juiciest stories were about wakes — and a tired woman getting jealous of the corpse in the bed. He was so pleased with Nancy's attention that he was dramatizing even more than usual, and I stood silent in the kitchen door for several minutes with a ducal air of scorn before he

even noticed me. As I saw Nancy to the road I felt humiliated to the depths of my being. I noticed that the hallway was streaming with damp, that our gate was only a pair of brick stumps from which the cement had fallen away, and that the square, which had never been adopted by the council, was full of washing. There were two washerwomen on the terrace, each with a line of her own.

But that wasn't the worst. One evening when I came home, Mother said joyously:

"Oh, your dad ran into that nice little Harding girl on his way home."

"Oh, did he?" I asked indifferently, though feeling I had been kicked hard in the stomach.

"Oh, my goodness!" Father exclaimed, letting down his paper for a moment and crowing. "The way that one talks! Spatter! spatter! spatter! And, by the way," he added, looking at me over his glasses, "her Aunt Lil used to be a great friend of your mother's at one time. Her mother was a Clancy. I knew there was something familiar about her face."

"I'd never have recognized it," Mother said gravely. "Such a quiet little woman as Miss Clancy used to be."

"Oh, begor,[7] there's nothing quiet about that niece," chortled Father, but he did not sound disapproving. Father liked young people with something to say for themselves — not like me.

I was mortified. It was bad enough not seeing Nancy myself, but to have her meet Father like that, in his working clothes coming from the manure factory down the glen, and hear him — as I had no doubt she did hear him — talk in his ignorant way about me was too much. I could not help contrasting Father with Mr. Harding, whom I occasionally met coming from work and whom I looked at with

---

6. **wake:** watch or vigil over a body before its burial.

7. **begor:** a mild Irish oath.

a respect that bordered on reverence. He was a small man with a face like a clenched fist, always very neatly dressed, and he usually carried his newspaper rolled up like a baton and sometimes hit his thigh with it as he strode briskly home.

One evening when I glanced shyly at him, he nodded in his brusque way. Everything about him was brusque, keen, and soldierly, and when I saw that he recognized me, I swung into step beside him. He was like a military procession with a brass band, the way he always set the pace for anyone who accompanied him.

"Where are you working now?" he asked sharply with a side glance at me.

"Oh, on the railway still," I said. "Just for a few months, anyway."

"And what are you doing there?"

"Oh, just helping in the office," I replied lightly. I knew this was not exactly true, but I hated to tell anybody that I was only a messenger boy. "Of course, I study in my spare time," I added hastily. It was remarkable how the speeding up of my pace seemed to speed up my romancing as well. There was something breathless about the man that left me breathless, too. "I thought of taking the Indian Civil Service exam[8] or something of the sort. There's no future in railways."

"Isn't there?" he asked with some surprise.

"Not really," I answered indifferently. "Another few years and it will all be trucks. I really do it only as a stopgap. I wouldn't like to take any permanent job unless I could travel. Outside Ireland, I mean. You see, languages are my major interest."

"Are they?" he asked in the same tone. "How many do you know?"

"Oh, only French and German at the moment—I mean, enough to get round with," I said. The pace was telling on me. I felt I wasn't making the right impression. Maybe to be a proper linguist you needed to know a dozen languages. I mended my hand as best I could. "I'm going to do Italian and Spanish this winter if I get time. You can't get anywhere in the modern world without Spanish. After English it's the most spoken of them all."

"Go on!" he said.

I wasn't altogether pleased with the results of this conversation. The moment I had left him, I slowed down to a gentle stroll, and this made me realize that the quick march had committed me farther than I liked to go. All I really knew of foreign languages was a few odd words and phrases, like echoes of some dream of my lost fatherland, which I learned and repeated to myself with a strange, dreamy pleasure. It was not prudent to pretend that I knew the languages thoroughly. After all, Mr. Harding had three daughters, all well educated. People were always being asked to his house, and I had even been encouraging myself with the prospect of being asked as well. But now, if I were invited, it would be mainly because of my supposed knowledge of foreign languages, and when Nancy or one of her sisters burst into fluent French or German, my few poetic phrases would not be much help. I needed something more practical, something to do with railways, for preference. I had an old French phrase book, which I had borrowed from somebody, and I determined to learn as much as I could of this by heart.

I worked hard, spurred on by an unexpected meeting with Nancy's eldest sister, Rita, who suddenly stopped and spoke to me on the road, though to my astonishment and relief she spoke in English.

Then, one evening when I was on my usual

---

8. **Indian Civil Service exam:** a test given to persons applying for jobs in government service in India. (Britain ruled India at this time.)

walk, which in those days nearly always brought me somewhere near Nancy's house, I ran into her going in, and we stood at the street corner near her home. I was pleased with this because Rita came out soon afterward and said in a conspiratorial tone: "Why don't ye grab the sofa before Kitty gets it?" which made Nancy blush, and then her father passed and nodded to us. I waved back to him, but Nancy had turned her back as he appeared so that she did not see him. I drew her attention to him striding down the road, but somehow this only put her in mind of my father.

"I saw him again the other day," she said with a smile that hurt me.

"Did you?" I asked with a sniff. "What was he talking about? His soldiering days?"

"No," she said with interest. "Does he talk about them?"

"Does he ever talk about anything else?" I replied wearily. "I have that last war off by heart. It seems to have been the only thing that ever happened to him."

"He knows a terrible lot, though, doesn't he?" she asked.

"He's concealed it pretty well," I replied. "The man is an out-and-out failure, and he's managed to turn Mother into one as well. I suppose she had whatever brains there were between them—which wasn't much, I'm afraid."

"Go on!" said Nancy with a bewildered air. "Then why did she marry him?"

" 'Echo answers why,' "[9] I said with a laugh at being able to get in a phrase that had delighted me in some storybook. "Oh, I suppose it was the usual thing."

Nancy blushed again and made to leave.

---

9. **"Echo answers why"**: a reference to a Greek myth about a nymph named Echo. Echo always repeated the last words spoken to her.

"Well, it's well to be you," she said, "knowing what's wrong with him. God alone knows what's wrong with mine."

I was sorry she had to go in such a hurry, but pleased with the impression of culture and sophistication I had managed to convey, and I looked forward to showing off a bit more when I went to one of their Sunday evening parties. With that, and some really practical French, I could probably get anywhere.

At the same time it struck me that they were very slow about asking me, and my evening walks past their house took on a sort of stubborn defiance. At least, I wouldn't let them ignore me. It wasn't until weeks later that the bitter truth dawned on me—that I was not being invited because nobody wanted me there. Nancy had seen my home and talked to my parents; her sisters and father had seen me; and all of them had seen my cut-down trousers with the patch on the seat. It mattered nothing to them even if I spoke French and German like an angel, even if I were liable to be sent off to India in the next few months. They did not think I was their class.

Those were the bitterest weeks of my life. With a sort of despair I took my evening walk in the early winter days past their house, but never saw anybody, and as I turned up the muddy lane behind it and heard the wind moaning in the branches, and looked down across the sloping field to their house, nestling in the hollow with the light shining brilliantly in the kitchen, where the girls did their homework, it seemed to be full of all the beauty I would never know. Sometimes, when I was leaning over the lane wall and watching it, it even seemed possible that I was what they thought, not the son of a duke but the son of a laborer in the manure factory; but at other times, as I was walking home by myself, tired and dispirited, the truth blazed up angrily in me again, and I knew that when it became known, the Hardings would be the first to regret their blindness. At such times I was always making brilliant loveless matches and then revealing coldly to Nancy that I had never cared for anyone but her.

It was at the lowest depth of my misery that I was introduced to a girl called May Dwyer, and somehow, from the first moment, I found that there was no need for me to indulge in invention. Invention and May would never have gone together. She had a directness of approach I had never met with before in a girl. The very first evening I saw her home she asked me if I could afford the tram fare. That shocked me, but afterwards I was grateful. Then she asked me in to see her parents, which scared me stiff, but I promised to come in another night when it wasn't so late, and at once she told me which evenings she was free. It was not forwardness or lightness in her; it was all part of a directness that made her immediately both a companion and a sweetheart. I owe her a lot, for without her I might still be airing my French and German to any woman who attracted me.

Even when I did go in with her for a cup of tea, I felt at home after the first few minutes. Her father was a long, sad Civil Servant,[10] and her mother a bright, direct little woman not unlike May herself, and whatever he said, the pair of them argued with and jeered him unmercifully. This only made him hang his head lower, but suddenly, after I had been talking for a while, he began to argue with me about the state of the country, which seemed to cause him a lot of concern. In those days I was very optimistic on the subject, and I put my hands deep in my trousers pockets and answered him back politely but firmly. Then he caught me out on a matter of fact, and sud-

denly he gave a great crow of delight and went out to bring in two bottles of Guinness.[11] By this time I was so much in my element that I accepted the Guinness: I always have loved a good argument.

May said when I was leaving, "Do you ever stop once you start?"

"It's not so often I meet an intelligent talker," I said loftily.

"When you've heard as much of my old fellow as I have, maybe you won't think he's so intelligent," she said, but she did not sound indignant, and I had an impression that she was really quite pleased at having brought home a young fellow who could entertain her father. It gave her the feeling that she was really all the time an intellectual, but had met the wrong sort of boy. In the years I was courting her we quarreled often, but between her father and me it was a case of love at first sight. After I was fired from the railway, it was he who got me another job and insisted on my looking after it. The poor devil had always been pining for a man in the house.

Then one evening I ran into Nancy Harding, whom I had not seen for months. It was an embarrassing moment because I realized at once that my fantasy had all come true. If I had not actually made a brilliant match, I had as good as done so, and yet she was my first and purest love.

"I hear you and May Dwyer are very great these days," she said, and something in her tone struck me as peculiar. Afterward I realized that it was the tone I was supposed to adopt when I broke the news to her.

"I've seen quite a lot of her," I admitted.

"You weren't long getting hooked," she went on with a smile that somehow did not come off.

"I don't know about being 'hooked,' as you

---

10. **Civil Servant:** government employee.

11. **Guinness:** a brand of dark-brown ale.

call it," I said, getting on my dignity at once. "She asked me to her house and I went, that's all."

"Oh, we know all about it," said Nancy, and this time there was no mistaking the malice in her tone. "You don't have to tell me anything."

"Well, there isn't so much to tell," I replied with a bland smile.

"And I suppose she talks French and German like a native?" asked Nancy.

This reference to the falsehoods I had told did hurt me. I had known they were indiscreet, but it hadn't occurred to me that they would become a joke in the Harding family.

"I don't honestly know what you're talking about, Nancy," I said weakly. "May asked me to her house and I went, just as I'd have gone to yours if you'd asked me. That's all there is to it."

"Oh, is that all?" she asked in her commonest tone, and suddenly, to my astonishment, I saw tears in her eyes. "And if you had a house like mine you wouldn't mind asking people there either, would you? And sisters like mine! And a father like mine! It's all very

well for you to grouse[12] about your old fellow, but if you had one like mine you'd have something to talk about. Blooming old pig, wouldn't open his mouth to you. 'Tis easy for you to talk, Larry Delaney!"

And then she shot away from me to conceal her tears, and I was left standing there on the pavement, stunned. Too stunned really to have done anything about it. It had all happened too suddenly, and been too great an intrusion on my fantasy for me to grasp it at all. I was so astonished and upset that, though I was to have met May that night, I didn't go. Instead I went for a lonely walk by myself, over the hills to the river, to think what I should do about it. In the end, of course, I did nothing at all; I had no experience to indicate to me what I could do; and it was not until years later that I ever realized that the reason I had cared so much for Nancy was that she, like myself, was one of the duke's children, one of those outcasts of a lost fatherland who go through life living above and beyond themselves like some image of man's original aspiration.

---

12. **grouse:** complain.

FOR STUDY AND DISCUSSION

1. The most important character in this story is the narrator, Larry Delaney. When does Larry realize what he calls "the truth" about his birth? What do you think the change from "Mother's pet" to "messenger boy" has to do with the onset of this illusion?

2. At several points Larry hears an interior voice describing him as if he were a character in a story: "He raised his cap gracefully while his face broke into a thoughtful smile." How is Larry different from the confident character in his illusion?

3. One conflict in this story revolves around Larry and Nancy. Larry longs to be invited to Nancy's home. What does he *think* is the reason he isn't invited? What is ironic about the *real* reason Nancy never asks him?

4. Another conflict takes place between children and their fathers. How are Larry's and Nancy's attitudes toward their fathers similar? How is May's attitude different?

5. Given what Larry dislikes about his own father, what is ironic about the fact that he takes to May's father so enthusiastically?

6. Larry tells us it was years later that he realized Nancy was also one of the "duke's children." How does this add an ironic twist to the fact that they never got together?

THREE TYPES OF IRONY

When Larry Delaney says he learned "the truth" about his birth, he is using *verbal irony*—that is, he says one thing (he learned "the truth") but he means the opposite (he invented a story).

Larry behaves as if he is the lost son of a duke or earl. We, of course, know that Larry is fooling himself and Nancy with his airs. This creates *dramatic irony*—we, the readers, are aware of something that the characters are not aware of.

This whole story is built around an *ironic situation*. Larry believes his pretensions will win Nancy over. The result is just the reverse: his pretensions really cause the misunderstanding that separates them forever.

The ironic reversal in a story is usually most powerful when the hero or heroine recognizes that things are not what they seem to be. Does this narrator come to such a recognition at the end of the story? How would you describe his feelings at this moment? How did the ending affect you?

FOR COMPOSITION

Writing a Character Analysis
In "The Duke's Children," Nancy, Larry, and May have remarkably different views of one another's fathers. Using one paragraph for each character, analyze the characters of Mr. Delaney, Mr. Harding, and Mr. Dwyer. Write objective descriptions based on the story.

ABOUT THE AUTHOR

Frank O'Connor (1903–1966) is the pen name of Michael O'Donovan, born in the city of Cork in Ireland. As a boy, he wrote in Irish, which he learned chiefly from his grandmother. Because he came from a poor family, and because times were hard in Ireland when he was a boy, O'Connor was unable to receive any formal education beyond the fourth grade. Nevertheless, he became a master of the modern short story. Several of his humorous stories, like "The Duke's Children," are narrated by a young boy or young man. For others, read "First Confession" and "My Oedipus Complex."

The Bet
Anton Chekhov
Translated from the Russian by Constance Garnett

It was a dark autumn night. The old banker was walking up and down his study and remembering how, fifteen years before, he had given a party one autumn evening. There had been many clever men there, and there had been interesting conversations. Among other things, they had talked of capital punishment. The majority of the guests, among whom were many journalists and intellectual men, disapproved of the death penalty. They considered that form of punishment out of date, immoral, and unsuitable for Christian states. In the opinion of some of them the death penalty ought to be replaced everywhere by imprisonment for life.

"I don't agree with you," said their host the banker. "I have not tried either the death penalty or imprisonment for life, but if one may judge *a priori*,[1] the death penalty is more moral and more humane than imprisonment for life. Capital punishment kills a man at once, but lifelong imprisonment kills him slowly. Which executioner is the more hu-

---

1. *a priori* (ä prē-ōr′ē): based on theory, not experience.

mane, he who kills you in a few minutes or he who drags the life out of you in the course of many years?"

"Both are equally immoral," observed one of the guests, "for they both have the same object—to take away life. The state is not God. It has not the right to take away what it cannot restore when it wants to."

Among the guests was a young lawyer, a young man of five-and-twenty. When he was asked his opinion, he said:

"The death sentence and the life sentence are equally immoral, but if I had to choose between the death penalty and imprisonment for life, I would certainly choose the second. To live anyhow is better than not at all."

A lively discussion arose. The banker, who was younger and more nervous in those days, was suddenly carried away by excitement; he struck the table with his fist and shouted at the young man:

"It's not true! I'll bet you two millions you wouldn't stay in solitary confinement for five years."

"If you mean that in earnest," said the young man, "I'll take the bet, but I would stay not five but fifteen years."

"Fifteen? Done!" cried the banker. "Gentlemen, I stake two millions!"

"Agreed! You stake your millions and I stake my freedom!" said the young man.

And this wild, senseless bet was carried out! The banker, spoiled and frivolous, with millions beyond his reckoning, was delighted at the bet. At supper he made fun of the young man, and said:

"Think better of it, young man, while there is still time. To me two millions are a trifle, but you are losing three or four of the best years of your life. I say three or four, because you won't stay longer. Don't forget either, you unhappy man, that voluntary confinement is a great deal harder to bear than compulsory. The thought that you have the right to step out in liberty at any moment will poison your whole existence in prison. I am sorry for you."

And now the banker, walking to and fro, remembered all this, and asked himself: "What was the object of that bet? What is the good of that man's losing fifteen years of his life and my throwing away two millions? Can it prove that the death penalty is better or worse than imprisonment for life? No, no. It was all nonsensical and meaningless. On my part it was the caprice of a pampered man, and on his part simple greed for money. . . ."

Then he remembered what followed that evening. It was decided that the young man should spend the years of his captivity under the strictest supervision in one of the lodges in the banker's garden. It was agreed that for fifteen years he should not be free to cross the threshold of the lodge, to see human beings, to hear the human voice, or to receive letters and newspapers. He was allowed to have a musical instrument and books, and was allowed to write letters, to drink wine, and to smoke. By the terms of the agreement, the only relations he could have with the outer world were by a little window made purposely for that object. He might have anything he wanted—books, music, wine, and so on—in any quantity he desired, by writing an order, but could receive them only through the window. The agreement provided for every detail and every trifle that would make his imprisonment strictly solitary, and bound the young man to stay there *exactly* fifteen years, beginning from twelve o'clock of November 14, 1870, and ending at twelve o'clock of November 14, 1885. The slightest attempt on his part to break the conditions, if only two minutes before the end, released the banker from the obligation to pay him two millions.

For the first year of his confinement, as far as one could judge from his brief notes, the prisoner suffered severely from loneliness and depression. The sounds of the piano could be heard continually day and night from his lodge. He refused wine and tobacco. Wine, he wrote, excites the desires, and desires are the worst foes of the prisoner; and besides, nothing could be more dreary than drinking good wine and seeing no one. And tobacco spoiled the air of his room. In the first year the books he sent for were principally of a light character; novels with a complicated love plot, sensational and fantastic stories, and so on.

In the second year the piano was silent in the lodge, and the prisoner asked only for the classics. In the fifth year music was audible again, and the prisoner asked for wine. Those who watched him through the window said that all that year he spent doing nothing but eating and drinking and lying on his bed, frequently yawning and talking angrily to himself. He did not read books. Sometimes at night he would sit down to write; he would spend hours writing, and in the morning tear up all that he had written. More than once he could be heard crying.

In the second half of the sixth year the prisoner began zealously studying languages, philosophy, and history. He threw himself eagerly into these studies—so much so that the banker had enough to do to get him the books he ordered. In the course of four years some six hundred volumes were procured at his request. It was during this period that the banker received the following letter from his prisoner:

"My dear Jailer, I write you these lines in six languages. Show them to people who know the languages. Let them read them. If they find not one mistake, I implore you to fire a shot in the garden. That shot will show me that my efforts have not been thrown away. The geniuses of all ages and of all lands speak different languages, but the same flame burns in them all. Oh, if you only knew what unearthly happiness my soul feels now from being able to understand them!" The prisoner's desire was fulfilled. The banker ordered two shots to be fired in the garden.

Then, after the tenth year, the prisoner sat immovably at the table and read nothing but the Gospel. It seemed strange to the banker that a man who in four years had mastered six hundred learned volumes should waste nearly a year over one thin book easy of comprehension. Theology and histories of religion followed the Gospels.

In the last two years of his confinement the prisoner read an immense quantity of books quite indiscriminately. At one time he was busy with the natural sciences, then he would ask for Byron[2] or Shakespeare. There were notes in which he demanded at the same time books on chemistry, and a manual of medicine, and a novel, and some treatise on philosophy or theology. His reading suggested a man swimming in the sea among the wreckage of his ship, and trying to save his life by greedily clutching first at one spar and then at another.

The old banker remembered all this, and thought:

"Tomorrow at twelve o'clock he will regain his freedom. By our agreement I ought to pay him two millions. If I do pay him, it is all over with me: I shall be utterly ruined."

Fifteen years before, his millions had been beyond his reckoning; now he was afraid to ask himself which were greater, his debts or his assets. Desperate gambling on the Stock

---

2. **Byron:** George Gordon, Lord Byron (1788–1824), English Romantic poet.

Exchange, wild speculation, and the excitability which he could not get over even in advancing years, had by degrees led to the decline of his fortune, and the proud, fearless, self-confident millionaire had become a banker of middling rank, trembling at every rise and fall in his investments. "Cursed bet!" muttered the old man, clutching his head in despair. "Why didn't the man die? He is only forty now. He will take my last penny from me, he will marry, will enjoy life, will gamble on the Exchange; while I shall look at him with envy like a beggar, and hear from him every day the same sentence: 'I am indebted to you for the happiness of my life, let me help you!' No, it is too much! The one means of being saved from bankruptcy and disgrace is the death of that man!"

It struck three o'clock. The banker listened; everyone was asleep in the house, and nothing could be heard outside but the rustling of the chilled trees. Trying to make no noise, he took from a fireproof safe the key of the door which had not been opened for fifteen years, put on his overcoat, and went out of the house.

It was dark and cold in the garden. Rain was falling. A damp, cutting wind was racing about the garden, howling and giving the trees no rest. The banker strained his eyes, but could see neither the earth nor the white statues, nor the lodge, nor the trees. Going to the spot where the lodge stood, he twice called the watchman. No answer followed. Evidently the watchman had sought shelter from the weather, and was now asleep somewhere either in the kitchen or in the greenhouse.

"If I had the pluck to carry out my intention," thought the old man, "suspicion would fall first upon the watchman."

He felt in the darkness for the steps and the door, and went into the entry of the lodge. Then he groped his way into a little passage and lighted a match. There was not a soul there. There was a bedstead with no bedding on it, and in the corner there was a dark cast-iron stove. The seals on the door leading to the prisoner's rooms were intact.

When the match went out the old man, trembling with emotion, peeped through the little window. A candle was burning dimly in the prisoner's room. He was sitting at the table. Nothing could be seen but his back, the hair on his head, and his hands. Open books were lying on the table, on the two easy chairs, and on the carpet near the table.

Five minutes passed and the prisoner did not once stir. Fifteen years' imprisonment had taught him to sit still. The banker tapped at the window with his finger, and the prisoner made no movement whatever in response. Then the banker cautiously broke the seals off the door and put the key in the keyhole. The rusty lock gave a grating sound

and the door creaked. The banker expected to hear at once footsteps and a cry of astonishment, but three minutes passed and it was as quiet as ever in the room. He made up his mind to go in.

At the table a man unlike ordinary people was sitting motionless. He was a skeleton with the skin drawn tight over his bones, with long curls like a woman's, and a shaggy beard. His face was yellow with an earthy tint in it, his cheeks were hollow, his back long and narrow, and the hand on which his shaggy head was propped was so thin and delicate that it was dreadful to look at it. His hair was already streaked with silver, and seeing his emaciated, aged-looking face, no one would have believed that he was only forty. He was asleep. . . . In front of his bowed head there lay on the table a sheet of paper, on which there was something written in fine handwriting.

"Poor creature!" thought the banker, "he is asleep and most likely dreaming of the millions. And I have only to take this half-dead man, throw him on the bed, stifle him a little with the pillow, and the most conscientious expert would find no sign of a violent death. But let us first read what he has written here. . . ."

The banker took the page from the table and read as follows:

"Tomorrow at twelve o'clock I regain my freedom and the right to associate with other men, but before I leave this room and see the sunshine, I think it necessary to say a few words to you. With a clear conscience I tell you, as before God, who beholds me, that I despise freedom and life and health, and all that your books call the good things of the world.

"For fifteen years I have been intently studying earthly life. It is true I have not seen the earth nor men, but in your books I have drunk fragrant wine, I have sung songs, I have hunted stags and wild boars in the forests, have loved women. . . . Beauties as ethereal as clouds, created by the magic of your poets and geniuses, have visited me at night, and have whispered in my ears wonderful tales that have set my brain in a whirl. In your books I have climbed to the peaks of Elburz and Mont Blanc,[3] and from there I have seen the sun rise and have watched it at evening flood the sky, the ocean, and the mountaintops with gold and crimson. I have watched from there the lightning flashing over my head and cleaving the storm clouds. I have seen green forests, fields, rivers, lakes, towns. I have heard the singing of the sirens,[4] and the strains of the

---

3. **Elburz** (ĕl-bŏŏrz′) **and Mont Blanc** (môɴ bläɴ′): Elburz is a mountain range in northern Iran; Mont Blanc, in France, is the highest peak in the Alps.
4. **sirens:** in Greek mythology, sea nymphs who had beautiful unearthly voices.

shepherds' pipes; I have touched the wings of comely devils who flew down to converse with me of God. . . . In your books I have flung myself into the bottomless pit, performed miracles, slain, burned towns, preached new religions, conquered whole kingdoms. . . .

"Your books have given me wisdom. All that the unresting thought of man has created in the ages is compressed into a small compass in my brain. I know that I am wiser than all of you.

"And I despise your books, I despise wisdom and the blessings of this world. It is all worthless, fleeting, illusory, and deceptive, like a mirage. You may be proud, wise, and fine, but death will wipe you off the face of the earth as though you were no more than mice burrowing under the floor, and your posterity, your history, your immortal geniuses will burn or freeze together with the earthly globe.

"You have lost your reason and taken the wrong path. You have taken lies for truth, and hideousness for beauty. You would marvel if, owing to strange events of some sort, frogs and lizards suddenly grew on apple and orange trees instead of fruit, or if roses began to smell like a sweating horse; so I marvel at you who

exchange heaven for earth. I don't want to understand you.

"To prove to you in action how I despise all that you live by, I renounce the two millions of which I once dreamed as of paradise and which now I despise. To deprive myself of the right to the money I shall go out from here five minutes before the time fixed, and so break the compact. . . ."

When the banker had read this he laid the page on the table, kissed the strange man on the head, and went out of the lodge, weeping. At no other time, even when he had lost heavily on the Stock Exchange, had he felt so great a contempt for himself. When he got home he lay on his bed, but his tears and emotion kept him for hours from sleeping.

Next morning the watchmen ran in with pale faces, and told him they had seen the man who lived in the lodge climb out of the window into the garden, go to the gate, and disappear. The banker went at once with the servants to the lodge and made sure of the flight of his prisoner. To avoid arousing unnecessary talk, he took from the table the writing in which the millions were renounced, and when he got home locked it up in the fireproof safe.

FOR STUDY AND DISCUSSION

1. A *flashback* is a narrative device in which past events and conversations are recalled. What essential information is provided by the two flashbacks at the beginning of this story?

2. What is about to happen in the present?

3. During the fifteen years, the banker and the lawyer have changed in important ways. How has the banker changed?

4. This story is told from the limited point of view of one character, the banker. How does the narrator reveal the prisoner's state of mind?

5. Why does the prisoner deliberately forfeit the money? How would you describe his view of human life?

6. Has the prisoner's letter changed the banker's view of himself? Explain. Why does the banker put the letter in the safe?

7. The bet was made to test certain views about human life. Whose viewpoint was proved valid—the prisoner's or the banker's?

IRONY OF SITUATION

In "The Bet" Chekhov uses *irony of situation,* the kind of irony in which what happens is the opposite of what we expect will happen. The basis of the bet itself provides part of the irony in this story. Look back at the conversation at the opening of the story in which the banker talks of such things as morality and humaneness. Why is it ironic that this particular bet should lead the banker to decide to murder his prisoner?

Because we have not had a chance to know the prisoner's thoughts, we are as much surprised as the banker is by the letter. Like the banker, we expect that the prisoner would, after fifteen years, look forward to his release and the two million which would help him

achieve his "life's happiness." Ironically, the bet has proved something different to the prisoner. What did he expect it to prove? What has it actually proved to him?

FOR COMPOSITION

Explaining the Tone of a Story

Tone is the attitude a writer takes toward a subject or an audience. Two writers can write on the same subject and convey entirely different tones: one might view a topic with great sympathy and compassion, whereas the other might take a cynical and pessimistic approach. In a brief essay, discuss the tone revealed in "The Bet." What attitude toward life, happiness, wealth, wisdom, and death does the author convey? Support your opinion by quoting passages from the story.

ABOUT THE AUTHOR

Anton Chekhov (1860–1904), a Russian, was the grandson of a serf and the son of a shopkeeper. While a medical student, he supported himself and his family by writing short stories for comic magazines. After the publication of his first book, he gave up medicine to become a writer. A master of the short-story form, Chekhov is also one of the most important modern dramatists, known for such plays as *The Cherry Orchard, Uncle Vanya, The Three Sisters,* and *The Sea Gull.* In a letter written in 1889, Chekhov said of his work: "I weave in the life of good people, their fate, deeds, words, ideas, and hopes. My goal is to kill two birds with one stone: to paint life in its true aspects, and to show how far this life falls short of the ideal life. I don't know what this ideal life is, just as it is unknown to all of us."

The Storyteller *Saki*

It was a hot afternoon, and the railway carriage was correspondingly sultry, and the next stop was at Templecombe, nearly an hour ahead. The occupants of the carriage were a small girl, and a smaller girl, and a small boy. An aunt belonging to the children occupied one corner seat, and the further corner seat on the opposite side was occupied by a bachelor who was a stranger to their party, but the small girls and the small boy emphatically occupied the compartment. Both the aunt and the children were conversational in a limited, persistent way, reminding one of the attentions of a housefly that refused to be discouraged. Most of the aunt's remarks seemed to begin with "Don't," and nearly all of the children's remarks began with "Why?" The bachelor said nothing out loud.

"Don't, Cyril, don't," exclaimed the aunt, as the small boy began smacking the cushions of the seat, producing a cloud of dust at each blow.

"Come and look out of the window," she added.

The child moved reluctantly to the window. "Why are those sheep being driven out of that field?" he asked.

"I expect they are being driven to another field where there is more grass," said the aunt weakly.

"But there is lots of grass in that field," protested the boy; "there's nothing else but grass there. Aunt, there's lots of grass in that field."

"Perhaps the grass in the other field is better," suggested the aunt fatuously.

"Why is it better?" came the swift, inevitable question.

"Oh, look at those cows!" exclaimed the aunt. Nearly every field along the line had contained cows or bullocks, but she spoke as though she were drawing attention to a rarity.

"Why is the grass in the other field better?" persisted Cyril.

The frown on the bachelor's face was deepening to a scowl. He was a hard, unsympathetic man, the aunt decided in her mind. She was utterly unable to come to any satisfactory decision about the grass in the other field.

The smaller girl created a diversion by beginning to recite "On the Road to Mandalay."[1] She only knew the first line, but she put her limited knowledge to the fullest possible use. She repeated the line over and over again in a dreamy but resolute and very audible voice; it seemed to the bachelor as though someone had had a bet with her that she could not repeat the line aloud two thousand times without stopping. Whoever it was who had made the wager was likely to lose his bet.

"Come over here and listen to a story," said the aunt, when the bachelor had looked twice at her and once at the communication cord.[2]

The children moved listlessly toward the aunt's end of the carriage. Evidently her reputation as a storyteller did not rank high in their estimation.

In a low, confidential voice, interrupted at frequent intervals by loud, petulant ques-

---

1. **"On the Road to Mandalay":** a rousing poem by Rudyard Kipling. The first line is: "By the old Moulmein Pagoda, lookin' eastward to the sea . . . ."
2. **communication cord:** emergency signal used to summon the conductor.

tions from her listeners, she began an unenterprising and deplorably uninteresting story about a little girl who was 'good, and made friends with everyone on account of her goodness, and was finally saved from a mad bull by a number of rescuers who admired her moral character.

"Wouldn't they have saved her if she hadn't been good?" demanded the bigger of the small girls. It was exactly the question that the bachelor had wanted to ask.

"Well, yes," admitted the aunt lamely, "but I don't think they would have run quite so fast to her help if they had not liked her so much."

"It's the stupidest story I've ever heard," said the bigger of the small girls, with immense conviction.

"I didn't listen after the first bit, it was so stupid," said Cyril.

The smaller girl made no actual comment on the story, but she had long ago recommenced a murmured repetition of her favorite line.

"You don't seem to be a success as a storyteller," said the bachelor suddenly from his corner.

The aunt bristled in instant defense at this unexpected attack.

"It's a very difficult thing to tell stories that children can both understand and appreciate," she said stiffly.

"I don't agree with you," said the bachelor.

"Perhaps *you* would like to tell them a story," was the aunt's retort.

"Tell us a story," demanded the bigger of the small girls.

"Once upon a time," began the bachelor, "there was a little girl called Bertha, who was extraordinarily good."

The children's momentarily aroused interest began at once to flicker; all stories seemed dreadfully alike, no matter who told them.

"She did all that she was told, she was always truthful, she kept her clothes clean, ate milk puddings as though they were jam tarts, learned her lessons perfectly, and was polite in her manners."

"Was she pretty?" asked the bigger of the small girls.

"Not as pretty as any of you," said the bachelor, "but she was horribly good."

There was a wave of reaction in favor of the story; the word horrible in connection with goodness was a novelty that commended itself. It seemed to introduce a ring of truth that was absent from the aunt's tales of infant life.

"She was so good," continued the bachelor, "that she won several medals for goodness, which she always wore, pinned on to her dress. There was a medal for obedience, another medal for punctuality, and a third for good behavior. They were large metal medals, and they clinked against one another as she walked. No other child in the town where she lived had as many as three medals, so everybody knew that she must be an extra good child."

"Horribly good," quoted Cyril.

"Everybody talked about her goodness, and the Prince of the country got to hear about it, and he said that as she was so very good she might be allowed once a week to walk in his park, which was just outside the town. It was a beautiful park, and no children were ever allowed in it, so it was a great honor for Bertha to be allowed to go there."

"Were there any sheep in the park?" demanded Cyril.

"No," said the bachelor, "there were no sheep."

"Why weren't there any sheep?" came the inevitable question arising out of that answer.

The aunt permitted herself a smile, which might almost have been described as a grin.

"There were no sheep in the park," said the bachelor, "because the Prince's mother had once had a dream that her son would either be killed by a sheep or else by a clock falling on him. For that reason the Prince never kept a sheep in his park or a clock in his palace."

The aunt suppressed a gasp of admiration.

"Was the Prince killed by a sheep or by a clock?" asked Cyril.

"He is still alive, so we can't tell whether the dream will come true," said the bachelor unconcernedly; "anyway, there were no sheep in the park, but there were lots of little pigs running all over the place."

"What color were they?"

"Black with white faces, white with black spots, black all over, gray with white patches, and some were white all over."

The storyteller paused to let a full idea of the park's treasures sink into the children's imaginations; then he resumed:

"Bertha was rather sorry to find that there were no flowers in the park. She had promised her aunts, with tears in her eyes, that she would not pick any of the kind Prince's flowers, and she had meant to keep her promise, so of course it made her feel silly to find that there were no flowers to pick."

"Why weren't there any flowers?"

"Because the pigs had eaten them all," said the bachelor promptly. "The gardeners had told the Prince that you couldn't have pigs and flowers, so he decided to have pigs and no flowers."

There was a murmur of approval at the excellence of the Prince's decision; so many people would have decided the other way.

"There were lots of other delightful things in the park. There were ponds with gold and blue and green fish in them, and trees with beautiful parrots that said clever things at a moment's notice, and hummingbirds that hummed all the popular tunes of the day. Bertha walked up and down and enjoyed herself immensely, and thought to herself: 'If I were not so extraordinarily good, I should not have been allowed to come into this beautiful park and enjoy all there is to be seen in it,' and her three medals clinked against one another as she walked and helped to remind her how very good she really was. Just then an enormous wolf came prowling into the park to see if it could catch a fat little pig for its supper."

"What color was it?" asked the children, amid an immediate quickening of interest.

"Mud color all over, with a black tongue and pale gray eyes that gleamed with unspeakable ferocity. The first thing that it saw in the park was Bertha; her pinafore was so spotlessly white and clean that it could be seen from a great distance. Bertha saw the wolf and saw that it was stealing toward her, and she began to wish that she had never been allowed to come into the park. She ran as hard as she could, and the wolf came after her with huge leaps and bounds. She managed to reach a shrubbery of myrtle bushes, and she hid herself in one of the thickest of the bushes. The wolf came sniffing among the branches, its black tongue lolling out of its mouth and its pale gray eyes glaring with rage. Bertha was terribly frightened, and thought to herself: 'If I had not been so extraordinarily good, I should have been safe in the town at this moment.' However, the scent of the myrtle was so strong that the wolf could not sniff out where Bertha was hiding, and the bushes were so thick that he might have hunted about in them for a long time without catching sight of her; so he thought he might as well go off and catch a little pig instead. Bertha was trembling very much at having the wolf prowling and sniffing so near her, and as she trembled the medal for obedience clinked against the

medals for good conduct and punctuality. The wolf was just moving away when he heard the sound of the medals clinking and stopped to listen; they clinked again in a bush quite near him. He dashed into the bush, his pale gray eyes gleaming with ferocity and triumph, and dragged Bertha out and devoured her to the last morsel. All that was left of her were her shoes, bits of clothing, and the three medals for goodness."

"Were any of the little pigs killed?"

"No, they all escaped."

"The story began badly," said the smaller of the two girls, "but it had a beautiful ending."

"It is the most beautiful story that I ever heard," said the bigger of the small girls, with immense decision.

"It is the *only* beautiful story I have ever heard," said Cyril.

A dissentient[3] opinion came from the aunt.

"A most improper story to tell to young children! You have undermined the effect of years of careful teaching."

"At any rate," said the bachelor, collecting his belongings preparatory to leaving the carriage, "I kept them quiet for ten minutes, which was more than you were able to do."

"Unhappy woman!" he observed to himself as he walked down the platform of Templecombe station; "for the next six months or so those children will assail her in public with demands for an improper story!"

---

3. **dissentient** (dĭ-sĕn′shənt): dissenting; not agreeing.

FOR STUDY AND DISCUSSION

1. What is the obvious "moral" of the aunt's story? What would you say is the main point of the bachelor's story?

2. How is the aunt like Bertha, the "horribly good" heroine of the bachelor's story?

3. Did the bachelor's story satisfy you as it satisfied the children? Why, or why not?

4. What would you say is the conflict in this episode on a train? Who or what wins the struggle?

5. The children seem to recognize "a ring of truth" in the bachelor's story, and they pronounce its ending as "beautiful." What do you think these reactions are meant to reveal about children?

6. What is ironic about the fact that the storyteller favored by the children is a bachelor?

FOR COMPOSITION

Reversing a Familiar Story

Write an ironic reversal of some well-known children's story: "Sleeping Beauty," "Cinderella," and "The Three Pigs" are possibilities. Be sure to use irony and reverse the story's setting, characters, and ending. Strive for a humorous tone.

ABOUT THE AUTHOR

Hector Hugh Munro (1870–1916), a Scottish novelist, playwright, and short-story writer, was born in Burma, the son of an inspector general of the Burma police. When his mother died shortly before he was two, he was sent to England to live with two aunts, who brought him up with rigid strictness. (The aunt in "The Storyteller" is supposed to be modeled after his Aunt Charlotte.) Munro left school at fifteen to travel throughout Europe with his father. In his early twenties, he served a year with the Burma police but left to try a writing career in London. As a journalist, Munro published news stories and political sketches while, in his spare time, he wrote a serious history of Russia, two novels, and several books of short stories. At the beginning of World War I, Munro enlisted in the British army. He was sent to France as a corporal and was killed in action in a shallow trench the following year.

Munro is best known for his brief short stories, which are often humorous, ironic, and, beneath the surface, sinister. "The Open Window," "The Interlopers," and "Sredni Vashtar" are three of his best-known stories. His pen name, Saki, comes from *The Rubáiyát of Omar Khayyám*, in which a wine bearer named Saki goes "among the guests star-scattered on the grass."

Theme

The *theme* of a story is its controlling idea—the central insight that the story gives us about human life.

A theme is not necessarily an idea that a writer consciously decides to focus on before beginning a story. Writers do not, as a rule, tell a story in order to illustrate a particular idea. Rather, they try to write truthfully about life, and their particular way of looking at people and events gives their stories a central focus. We must not expect to find a theme stated outright in a story. Sometimes it may be, but more often we must state it for ourselves after we have thought about the characters and what has happened to them.

The theme of a story is not the same as a "moral." A moral is a practical bit of advice about how to conduct our lives. Morals usually instruct us to "do" something or "not to do" something: "A stitch in time saves nine," or "There's no use crying over spilt milk," or "Waste not, want not." Stories are not sermons, and most short-story writers are not interested in "preaching" to their readers. In attempting to determine the theme of a story, we should ask not what it *teaches*, but what it *reveals* about human experience.

There is no single "right" way to state the theme of a story. We should simply be sure that our statement of theme truly expresses the story's underlying idea. The theme of Jessamyn West's story "Road to the Isles" (page 43) might be stated in several ways: "We often are so deceived by our illusions that we cannot see life realistically. It may be painful to have our illusions destroyed and to realize that other people have recognized failings that we have been blind to." Or, "As young people, we often fail to see ourselves, our parents, or our friends in a realistic light. When we suddenly are forced to look at things as they really are, the shock of recognition can hurt." Notice, by the way, that a statement of theme is not very exciting. A statement of theme merely sums up dryly to our conscious mind what the story makes us deeply feel.

Through the Tunnel

Doris Lessing

Going to the shore on the first morning of the vacation, the young English boy stopped at a turning of the path and looked down at a wild and rocky bay, and then over to the crowded beach he knew so well from other years. His mother walked on in front of him, carrying a bright striped bag in one hand. Her other arm, swinging loose, was very white in the sun. The boy watched that white, naked arm, and turned his eyes, which had a frown behind them, toward the bay and back again to his mother. When she felt he was not with her, she swung around. "Oh, there you are, Jerry!" she said. She looked impatient, then smiled. "Why, darling, would you rather not come with me? Would you rather — " She frowned, conscientiously worrying over what amusements he might secretly be longing for, which she had been too busy or too careless to imagine. He was very familiar with that anxious, apologetic smile. Contrition sent him running after her. And yet, as he ran, he looked back over his shoulder at the wild bay; and all morning, as he played on the safe beach, he was thinking of it.

Next morning, when it was time for the routine of swimming and sunbathing, his mother said, "Are you tired of the usual beach, Jerry? Would you like to go somewhere else?"

"Oh, no!" he said quickly, smiling at her out of that unfailing impulse of contrition—a sort of chivalry. Yet, walking down the path with her, he blurted out, "I'd like to go and have a look at those rocks down there."

She gave the idea her attention. It was a wild-looking place, and there was no one there; but she said, "Of course, Jerry. When you've had enough, come to the big beach. Or just go straight back to the villa, if you like." She walked away, that bare arm, now slightly reddened from yesterday's sun, swinging. And he almost ran after her again, feeling it unbearable that she should go by herself, but he did not.

She was thinking. Of course he's old enough to be safe without me. Have I been keeping him too close? He mustn't feel he ought to be with me. I must be careful.

He was an only child, eleven years old. She was a widow. She was determined to be neither possessive nor lacking in devotion. She went worrying off to her beach.

As for Jerry, once he saw that his mother had gained her beach, he began the steep descent to the bay. From where he was, high up among red-brown rocks, it was a scoop of moving bluish green fringed with white. As he went lower, he saw that it spread among small promontories and inlets of rough, sharp rock, and the crisping, lapping surface showed stains of purple and darker blue. Finally, as he ran sliding and scraping down the last few yards, he saw an edge of white surf and the shallow, luminous movement of water over white sand, and, beyond that, a solid, heavy blue.

He ran straight into the water and began swimming. He was a good swimmer. He went out fast over the gleaming sand, over a middle region where rocks lay like discolored monsters under the surface, and then he was in the real sea—a warm sea where irregular cold currents from the deep water shocked his limbs.

When he was so far out that he could look back not only on the little bay but past the promontory that was between it and the big beach, he floated on the buoyant surface and looked for his mother. There she was, a speck of yellow under an umbrella that looked like a slice of orange peel. He swam back to shore, relieved at being sure she was there, but all at once very lonely.

On the edge of a small cape that marked the side of the bay away from the promontory was a loose scatter of rocks. Above them, some boys were stripping off their clothes. They came running, naked, down to the rocks. The English boy swam toward them, but kept his distance at a stone's throw. They were of that coast; all of them were burned smooth dark brown and speaking a language he did not understand. To be with them, of them, was a craving that filled his whole body. He swam a little closer; they turned and watched him with narrowed, alert dark eyes. Then one smiled and waved. It was enough. In a minute, he had swum in and was on the rocks beside them, smiling with a desperate, nervous supplication. They shouted cheerful greetings at him; and then, as he preserved his nervous, uncomprehending smile, they understood that he was a foreigner strayed from his own beach, and they proceeded to forget him. But he was happy. He was with them.

They began diving again and again from a high point into a well of blue sea between rough, pointed rocks. After they had dived and come up, they swam around, hauled themselves up, and waited their turn to dive again. They were big boys—men, to Jerry. He dived, and they watched him; and when he swam around to take his place, they made

way for him. He felt he was accepted and he dived again, carefully, proud of himself.

Soon the biggest of the boys poised himself, shot down into the water, and did not come up. The others stood about, watching. Jerry, after waiting for the sleek brown head to appear, let out a yell of warning; they looked at him idly and turned their eyes back toward the water. After a long time, the boy came up on the other side of a big dark rock, letting the air out of his lungs in a spluttering gasp and a shout of triumph. Immediately the rest of them dived in. One moment, the morning seemed full of clattering boys; the next, the air and the surface of the water were empty. But through the heavy blue, dark shapes could be seen moving and groping.

Jerry dived, shot past the school of underwater swimmers, saw a black wall of rock looming at him, touched it, and bobbed up at once to the surface, where the wall was a low barrier he could see across. There was no one visible; under him, in the water, the dim shapes of the swimmers had disappeared. Then one, and then another of the boys came up on the far side of the barrier of rock, and he understood that they had swum through some gap or hole in it. He plunged down again. He could see nothing through the stinging salt water but the blank rock. When he came up, the boys were all on the diving rock, preparing to attempt the feat again. And now, in a panic of failure, he yelled up, in English, "Look at me! Look!" and he began splashing and kicking in the water like a foolish dog.

They looked down gravely, frowning. He knew the frown. At moments of failure, when he clowned to claim his mother's attention, it was with just this grave, embarrassed inspection that she rewarded him. Through his hot shame, feeling the pleading grin on his face like a scar that he could never remove, he looked up at the group of big brown boys on the rock and shouted, *"Bonjour! Merci! Au revoir! Monsieur, monsieur!"* while he hooked his fingers round his ears and waggled them.

Water surged into his mouth; he choked, sank, came up. The rock, lately weighted with boys, seemed to rear up out of the water as their weight was removed. They were flying down past him, now, into the water; the air was full of falling bodies. Then the rock was empty in the hot sunlight. He counted one, two, three. . . .

At fifty, he was terrified. They must all be drowning beneath him, in the watery caves of the rock! At a hundred, he stared around him at the empty hillside, wondering if he should yell for help. He counted faster, faster, to hurry them up, to bring them to the surface quickly, to drown them quickly—anything rather than the terror of counting on and on into the blue emptiness of the morning. And then, at a hundred and sixty, the water beyond the rock was full of boys blowing like brown whales. They swam back to the shore without a look at him.

He climbed back to the diving rock and sat down, feeling the hot roughness of it under his thighs. The boys were gathering up their bits of clothing and running off along the shore to another promontory. They were leaving to get away from him. He cried openly, fists in his eyes. There was no one to see him, and he cried himself out.

It seemed to him that a long time had passed, and he swam out to where he could see his mother. Yes, she was still there, a yellow spot under an orange umbrella. He swam back to the big rock, climbed up, and dived into the blue pool among the fanged and angry boulders. Down he went, until he touched the wall of rock again. But the salt was so painful in his eyes that he could not see.

He came to the surface, swam to shore, and went back to the villa to wait for his mother. Soon she walked slowly up the path, swinging her striped bag, the flushed, naked arm dangling beside her. "I want some swimming goggles," he panted, defiant and beseeching.

She gave him a patient, inquisitive look as she said casually, "Well, of course, darling."

But now, now, now! He must have them this minute, and no other time. He nagged and pestered until she went with him to a shop. As soon as she had bought the goggles, he grabbed them from her hand as if she were going to claim them for herself, and was off, running down the steep path to the bay.

Jerry swam out to the big barrier rock, adjusted the goggles, and dived. The impact of the water broke the rubber-enclosed vacuum, and the goggles came loose. He understood that he must swim down to the base of the rock from the surface of the water. He fixed the goggles tight and firm, filled his lungs, and floated, face down on the water. Now he

could see. It was as if he had eyes of a different kind—fish eyes that showed everything clear and delicate and wavering in the bright water.

Under him, six or seven feet down, was a floor of perfectly clean, shining white sand, rippled firm and hard by 'the tides. Two grayish shapes steered there, like long, rounded pieces of wood or slate. They were fish. He saw them nose toward each other, poise motionless, make a dart forward, swerve off, and come around again. It was like a water dance. A few inches above them the water sparkled as if sequins were dropping through it. Fish again—myriads of minute fish, the length of his fingernail, were drifting through the water, and in a moment he could feel the innumerable tiny touches of them against his limbs. It was like swimming in flaked silver. The great rock the big boys had swum through rose sheer out of the white sand—black, tufted lightly with greenish weed. He could see no gap in it. He swam down to its base.

Again and again he rose, took a big chestful of air, and went down. Again and again he groped over the surface of the rock, feeling it, almost hugging it in the desperate need to find the entrance. And then, once, while he was clinging to the black wall, his knees came up and he shot his feet out forward and they met no obstacle. He had found the hole.

He gained the surface, clambered about the stones that littered the barrier rock until he found a big one, and, with this in his arms, let himself down over the side of the rock. He dropped, with the weight, straight to the sandy floor. Clinging tight to the anchor of stone, he lay on his side and looked in under the dark shelf at the place where his feet had gone. He could see the hole. It was an irregular, dark gap; but he could not see deep into it. He let go of his anchor, clung with his hands to the edges of the hole, and tried to push himself in.

He got his head in, found his shoulders jammed, moved them in sidewise, and was inside as far as his waist. He could see nothing ahead. Something soft and clammy touched his mouth; he saw a dark frond moving against the grayish rock, and panic filled him. He thought of octopuses, of clinging weed. He pushed himself out backward and caught a glimpse, as he retreated, of a harmless tentacle of seaweed drifting in the mouth of the tunnel. But it was enough. He reached the sunlight, swam to shore, and lay on the diving rock. He looked down into the blue well of water. He knew he must find his way through that cave, or hole, or tunnel, and out the other side.

First, he thought, he must learn to control his breathing. He let himself down into the water with another big stone in his arms, so that he could lie effortlessly on the bottom of the sea. He counted. One, two, three. He counted steadily. He could hear the movement of blood in his chest. Fifty-one, fifty-two. . . . His chest was hurting. He let go of the rock and went up into the air. He saw that the sun was low. He rushed to the villa and found his mother at her supper. She said only, "Did you enjoy yourself?" and he said, "Yes."

All night the boy dreamed of the water-filled cave in the rock, and as soon as breakfast was over he went to the bay.

That night, his nose bled badly. For hours he had been underwater, learning to hold his breath, and now he felt weak and dizzy. His mother said, "I shouldn't overdo things, darling, if I were you."

That day and the next, Jerry exercised his lungs as if everything, the whole of his life, all that he would become, depended upon it. Again his nose bled at night, and his mother insisted on his coming with her the next day. It was a torment to him to waste a day of his careful self-training, but he stayed with her on that other beach, which now seemed a place for small children, a place where his mother might lie safe in the sun. It was not his beach.

He did not ask for permission, on the following day, to go to his beach. He went before his mother could consider the complicated rights and wrongs of the matter. A day's rest, he discovered, had improved his count by ten. The big boys had made the passage while he counted a hundred and sixty. He had been counting fast, in his fright. Probably now, if he tried, he could get through that long tunnel, but he was not going to try yet. A curious, most unchildlike persistence, a controlled impatience, made him wait. In the meantime, he lay underwater on the white sand, littered now by stones he had brought down from the upper air, and studied the entrance to the tunnel. He knew every jut and corner of it, as far as it was possible to see. It was as if he already felt its sharpness about his shoulders.

He sat by the clock in the villa when his mother was not near, and checked his time. He was incredulous and then proud to find he could hold his breath without strain for two minutes. The words *two minutes*, authorized by the clock, brought close the adventure that was so necessary to him.

In another four days, his mother said casually one morning, they must go home. On the day before they left, he would do it. He would do it if it killed him, he said defiantly to himself. But two days before they were to leave—a day of triumph when he increased his count by fifteen—his nose bled so badly that he turned dizzy and had to lie limply over the big rock like a bit of seaweed, watching the thick red blood flow onto the rock and trickle slowly down to the sea. He was frightened. Supposing he turned dizzy in the tunnel? Supposing he died there, trapped? Supposing—his head went around in the hot sun, and he almost gave up. He thought he would return to the house and lie down, and next summer, perhaps, when he had another year's growth in him — *then* he would go through the hole.

But even after he had made the decision, or thought he had, he found himself sitting up on the rock and looking down into the water; and he knew that now, this moment, when his nose had only just stopped bleeding, when his head was still sore and throbbing — this was the moment when he would try. If he did not do it now, he never would. He was trembling with fear that he would not go; and he was trembling with horror at that long, long tunnel under the rock, under the sea. Even in the open sunlight, the barrier rock seemed very wide and very heavy; tons of rock pressed down on where he would go. If he died there, he would lie until one day — perhaps not before next year — those big boys would swim into it and find it blocked.

He put on his goggles, fitted them tight, tested the vacuum. His hands were shaking. Then he chose the biggest stone he could carry and slipped over the edge of the rock until half of him was in the cool, enclosing water and half in the hot sun. He looked up once at the empty sky, filled his lungs once, twice, and then sank fast to the bottom with the stone. He let it go and began to count. He took the edges of the hole in his hands and drew himself into it, wriggling his shoulders in sidewise as he remembered he must, kicking himself along with his feet.

Soon he was clear inside. He was in a small rockbound hole filled with yellowish-gray water. The water was pushing him up against the roof. The roof was sharp and pained his back. He pulled himself along with his hands — fast, fast — and used his legs as levers. His head knocked against something; a sharp pain dizzied him. Fifty, fifty-one, fifty-two. . . . He was without light, and the water seemed to press upon him with the weight of rock.

Seventy-one, seventy-two. . . . There was no strain on his lungs. He felt like an inflated balloon, his lungs were so light and easy, but his head was pulsing.

He was being continually pressed against the sharp roof, which felt slimy as well as sharp. Again he thought of octopuses, and wondered if the tunnel might be filled with weed that could tangle him. He gave himself a panicky, convulsive kick forward, ducked his head, and swam. His feet and hands moved freely, as if in open water. The hole must have widened out. He thought he must be swimming fast, and he was frightened of banging his head if the tunnel narrowed.

A hundred, a hundred and one. . . . The water paled. Victory filled him. His lungs were beginning to hurt. A few more strokes and he would be out. He was counting wildly; he said a hundred and fifteen, and then, a long time later, a hundred and fifteen again. The water was a clear jewel-green all around him. Then he saw, above his head, a crack running up through the rock. Sunlight was falling through it, showing the clean, dark rock of the tunnel, a single mussel shell, and darkness ahead.

He was at the end of what he could do. He looked up at the crack as if it were filled with air and not water, as if he could put his mouth to it to draw in air. A hundred and fifteen, he heard himself say inside his head — but he had said that long ago. He must go on into the blackness ahead, or he would drown. His head was swelling, his lungs cracking. A hundred and fifteen, a hundred and fifteen pounded through his head, and he feebly clutched at rocks in the dark, pulling himself forward, leaving the brief space of sunlit water behind. He felt he was dying. He was no longer quite conscious. He struggled on in the darkness between lapses into unconsciousness. An immense, swelling pain filled his head, and then the darkness cracked with an explosion of green light. His hands, groping forward, met nothing; and his feet, kicking back, propelled him out into the open sea.

He drifted to the surface, his face turned up to the air. He was gasping like a fish. He felt he would sink now and drown; he could not swim the few feet back to the rock. Then he was clutching it and pulling himself up onto it. He lay face down, gasping. He could see nothing but a red-veined, clotted dark. His eyes must have burst, he thought; they were full of blood. He tore off his goggles and a gout of blood went into the sea. His nose was bleeding, and the blood had filled the goggles.

He scooped up handfuls of water from the cool, salty sea, to splash on his face, and did not know whether it was blood or salt water he tasted. After a time, his heart quieted, his eyes cleared, and he sat up. He could see the local boys diving and playing half a mile away. He did not want them. He wanted nothing but to get back home and lie down.

In a short while, Jerry swam to shore and climbed slowly up the path to the villa. He flung himself on his bed and slept, waking at the sound of feet on the path outside. His mother was coming back. He rushed to the bathroom, thinking she must not see his face with bloodstains, or tearstains, on it. He came out of the bathroom and met her as she walked into the villa, smiling, her eyes lighting up.

"Have a nice morning?" she asked, laying her hand on his warm brown shoulder a moment.

"Oh, yes, thank you," he said.

"You look a bit pale." And then, sharp and anxious, "How did you bang your head?"

"Oh, just banged it," he told her.

She looked at him closely. He was strained; his eyes were glazed-looking. She was worried. And then she said to herself, Oh, don't fuss! Nothing can happen. He can swim like a fish.

They sat down to lunch together.

"Mummy," he said, "I can stay under water for two minutes—three minutes, at least." It came bursting out of him.

"Can you, darling?" she said. "Well, I shouldn't overdo it. I don't think you ought to swim any more today."

She was ready for a battle of wills, but he gave in at once. It was no longer of the least importance to go to the bay.

FOR STUDY AND DISCUSSION

1. Near the beginning of this story, the author writes of Jerry's feelings about the boys on the rocks: "To be with them, of them, was a craving that filled his whole body." Why do you think Jerry felt it was so important to join the group of divers?

2. Why does swimming through the tunnel become important to Jerry? What details in the description of his preparations suggest that he is undergoing some change?

3. Describe Jerry's passage through the tunnel. What physical and mental conflicts must Jerry face during his ordeal?

4. At the end of the story, we are told that Jerry felt it was "no longer of the least importance" to go to the bay with the older boys. What accounts for this change in Jerry's attitude? What details show that his attitude toward his mother has also changed?

5. The author suggests that passage through the tunnel was more than just a test of physical stamina for Jerry. What do you think his passage through the tunnel could represent?

THEME

The *theme* of a story is its controlling idea, the central insight that it makes about life or human behavior. Theme is usually implied, though in some stories it is directly stated. Not every story will have a theme. The purpose of many mystery stories, for example, is simply to pose a problem for the reader to solve. Theme exists only in those stories that attempt to make a serious statement about life.

Discovering and stating the theme of a story is sometimes a difficult task. The best way to begin looking for theme in many stories is to focus on the story's main character. Ask yourself what conflicts this character has faced. Determine what changes he or she has undergone and what is the significance of these changes. The answers to these questions should help you understand what is most important in the story and what it says about life or about human behavior.

Here are two statements about "Through the Tunnel." Which do you think is the better statement of the theme, and why?

1. Young people sometimes feel the need to perform daring stunts, just to experience the thrill of danger.

2. By overcoming great obstacles and facing danger alone, a young person may acquire greater maturity and independence.

FOR COMPOSITION

Analyzing a Setting

This story has two settings: the "safe beach" and the "wild bay." The setting of the wild bay is where the boy undergoes the ordeal that changes him. In a brief essay, explain how Lessing uses imagery and figures of speech to make the bay seem fearful and threatening. What details make the underwater tunnel seem like a place of entombment or burial? Use specific quotations from the story in your discussion.

ABOUT THE AUTHOR

Doris Lessing (1919–   ), who was born to British parents living in Persia, grew up on a plantation in Southern Rhodesia. She started writing when she was eighteen but destroyed her first six novels. When she was thirty, she moved to England, where she continued to write while supporting herself with a variety of odd jobs. Now she is considered one of the foremost writers of fiction in this century. Africa provides the setting for many of her early stories and novels. She has said that writers brought up on that continent have many advantages, "being at the center of a modern battlefield, part of a society in rapid, dramatic change." Her most famous novel, *The Golden Notebook,* is a long experimental work that examines the life of a woman struggling to find self-fulfillment.

"Through the Tunnel," which was written in 1957, is from her collection of stories called *The Habit of Loving.* Though many writers have given up writing short stories because of a dwindling market, Doris Lessing says she would go on writing stories even if there were no home for them but a private drawer.

Harrison Bergeron
Kurt Vonnegut

The year was 2081, and everybody was finally equal. They weren't only equal before God and the law. They were equal every which way. Nobody was smarter than anybody else. Nobody was better looking than anybody else. Nobody was stronger or quicker than anybody else. All this equality was due to the 211th, 212th, and 213th Amendments to the Constitution, and to the unceasing vigilance of agents of the United States Handicapper General.

Some things about living still weren't quite right, though. April, for instance, still drove people crazy by not being springtime. And it was in that clammy month that the H-G men took George and Hazel Bergeron's fourteen-year-old son, Harrison, away.

It was tragic, all right, but George and Hazel couldn't think about it very hard. Hazel had a perfectly average intelligence, which meant she couldn't think about anything except in short bursts. And George, while his intelligence was way above normal, had a little mental-handicap radio in his ear. He was required by law to wear it at all times. It was tuned to a government transmitter. Every twenty seconds or so, the transmitter would send out some sharp noise to keep people like George from taking unfair advantage of their brains.

George and Hazel were watching television. There were tears on Hazel's cheeks, but she'd forgotten for the moment what they were about.

On the television screen were ballerinas.

A buzzer sounded in George's head. His thoughts fled in panic, like bandits from a burglar alarm.

"That was a real pretty dance, that dance they just did," said Hazel.

"Huh?" said George.

"That dance—it was nice," said Hazel.

"Yup," said George. He tried to think a little about the ballerinas. They weren't really very good—no better than anybody else would have been, anyway. They were burdened with sash weights and bags of birdshot, and their faces were masked, so that no one, seeing a free and graceful gesture or a pretty face, would feel like something the cat drug in. George was toying with the vague notion that maybe dancers shouldn't be handicapped. But he didn't get very far with it before another noise in his ear radio scattered his thoughts.

George winced. So did two out of the eight ballerinas.

Hazel saw him wince. Having no mental handicap herself, she had to ask George what the latest sound had been.

"Sounded like somebody hitting a milk bottle with a ball-peen hammer," said George.

"I'd think it would be real interesting, hearing all the different sounds," said Hazel, a little envious. "All the things they think up."

"Um," said George.

"Only, if I was Handicapper General, you know what I would do?" said Hazel. Hazel, as a matter of fact, bore a strong resemblance to the Handicapper General, a woman named Diana Moon Glampers. "If I was Diana Moon Glampers," said Hazel, "I'd have chimes on Sunday—just chimes. Kind of in honor of religion."

"I could think, if it was just chimes," said George.

"Well—maybe make 'em real loud," said Hazel. "I think I'd make a good Handicapper General."

"Good as anybody else," said George.

"Who knows better'n I do what normal is?" said Hazel.

"Right," said George. He began to think glimmeringly about his abnormal son who was now in jail, about Harrison, but a twenty-one-gun salute in his head stopped that.

"Boy!" said Hazel, "that was a doozy, wasn't it?"

It was such a doozy that George was white and trembling, and tears stood on the rims of his red eyes. Two of the eight ballerinas had collapsed to the studio floor, were holding their temples.

"All of a sudden you look so tired," said Hazel. "Why don't you stretch out on the sofa, so's you can rest your handicap bag on the pillows, honeybunch." She was referring to the forty-seven pounds of birdshot in a canvas bag, which was padlocked around George's neck. "Go on and rest the bag for a little while," she said. "I don't care if you're not equal to me for a while."

George weighed the bag with his hands. "I don't mind it," he said. "I don't notice it any more. It's just a part of me."

"You been so tired lately—kind of wore out," said Hazel. "If there was just some way we could make a little hole in the bottom of the bag, and just take out a few of them lead balls. Just a few."

"Two years in prison and two thousand dollars fine for every ball I took out," said George. "I don't call that a bargain."

"If you could just take a few out when you came home from work," said Hazel. "I mean—you don't compete with anybody around here. You just set around."

"If I tried to get away with it," said George, "then other people'd get away with it—and pretty soon we'd be right back to the dark ages again, with everybody competing against everybody else. You wouldn't like that, would you?"

"I'd hate it," said Hazel.

"There you are," said George. "The minute people start cheating on laws, what do you think happens to society?"

If Hazel hadn't been able to come up with an answer to this question, George couldn't have supplied one. A siren was going off in his head.

"Reckon it'd fall all apart," said Hazel.

"What would?" said George blankly.

"Society," said Hazel uncertainly. "Wasn't that what you just said?"

"Who knows?" said George.

The television program was suddenly interrupted for a news bulletin. It wasn't clear at first as to what the bulletin was about, since the announcer, like all announcers, had a serious speech impediment. For about half a minute, and in a state of high excitement, the announcer tried to say, "Ladies and gentlemen —"

He finally gave up, handed the bulletin to a ballerina to read.

"That's all right —" Hazel said of the announcer, "he tried. That's the big thing. He tried to do the best he could with what God gave him. He should get a nice raise for trying so hard."

"Ladies and gentlemen —" said the ballerina, reading the bulletin. She must have been extraordinarily beautiful, because the mask she wore was hideous. And it was easy to see that she was the strongest and most graceful of all the dancers, for her handicap bags were as big as those worn by two-hundred-pound men.

And she had to apologize at once for her voice, which was a very unfair voice for a woman to use. Her voice was a warm, luminous, timeless melody. "Excuse me —" she said, and she began again, making her voice absolutely uncompetitive.

"Harrison Bergeron, age fourteen," she said in a grackle squawk, "has just escaped from jail, where he was held on suspicion of plotting to overthrow the government. He is a genius and an athlete, is underhandicapped, and should be regarded as extremely dangerous."

A police photograph of Harrison Bergeron was flashed on the screen — upside down, then sideways, upside down again, then right side up. The picture showed the full length of Harrison against a background calibrated in feet and inches. He was exactly seven feet tall.

The rest of Harrison's appearance was Halloween and hardware. Nobody had ever borne heavier handicaps. He had outgrown hindrances faster than the H-G men could think them up. Instead of a little ear radio for a mental handicap, he wore a tremendous pair of earphones, and spectacles with thick wavy lenses. The spectacles were intended to make him not only half blind, but to give him whanging headaches besides.

Scrap metal was hung all over him. Ordinarily, there was a certain symmetry, a military neatness to the handicaps issued to strong people, but Harrison looked like a walking junkyard. In the race of life, Harrison carried three hundred pounds.

And to offset his good looks, the H-G men required that he wear at all times a red rubber ball for a nose, keep his eyebrows shaved off, and cover his even white teeth with black caps at snaggle-tooth random.

"If you see this boy," said the ballerina, "do not — I repeat, do not — try to reason with him."

There was the shriek of a door being torn from its hinges.

Screams and barking cries of consternation came from the television set. The photograph of Harrison Bergeron on the screen jumped again and again, as though dancing to the tune of an earthquake.

George Bergeron correctly identified the earthquake, and well he might have — for many was the time his own home had danced to the same crashing tune. "That must be Harrison!"

The realization was blasted from his mind instantly by the sound of an automobile collision in his head.

When George could open his eyes again, the

photograph of Harrison was gone. A living, breathing Harrison filled the screen.

Clanking, clownish, and huge, Harrison stood in the center of the studio. The knob of the uprooted studio door was still in his hand. Ballerinas, technicians, musicians, and announcers cowered on their knees before him, expecting to die.

"I am the Emperor!" cried Harrison. "Do you hear? I am the Emperor! Everybody must do what I say at once!" He stamped his foot and the studio shook.

"Even as I stand here—" he bellowed, "crippled, hobbled, sickened—I am a greater ruler than any man who ever lived! Now watch me become what I *can* become!"

Harrison tore the straps of his handicap harness like wet tissue paper, tore straps guaranteed to support five thousand pounds.

Harrison's scrap-iron handicaps crashed to the floor.

Harrison thrust his thumbs under the bar of the padlock that secured his head harness. The bar snapped like celery. Harrison smashed his headphones and spectacles against the wall.

He flung away his rubber-ball nose, revealed a man that would have awed Thor, the god of thunder.

"I shall now select my Empress!" he said, looking down on the cowering people. "Let the first woman who dares rise to her feet claim her mate and her throne!"

A moment passed, and then a ballerina arose, swaying like a willow.

Harrison plucked the mental handicap from her ear, snapped off her physical handicaps with marvelous delicacy. Last of all, he removed her mask.

She was blindingly beautiful.

"Now—" said Harrison, taking her hand, "shall we show the people the meaning of the word *dance?* Music!" he commanded.

The musicians scrambled back into their chairs, and Harrison stripped them of their handicaps, too. "Play your best," he told them, "and I'll make you barons and dukes and earls."

The music began. It was normal at first—cheap, silly, false. But Harrison snatched two musicians from their chairs, waved them like batons as he sang the music as he wanted it played. He slammed them back into their chairs.

The music began again and was much improved.

Harrison and his Empress merely listened to the music for a while—listened gravely, as though synchronizing their heartbeats with it.

They shifted their weights to their toes.

Harrison placed his big hands on the girl's tiny waist, letting her sense the weightlessness that would soon be hers.

And then, in an explosion of joy and grace, into the air they sprang!

Not only were the laws of the land abandoned, but the law of gravity and the laws of motion as well.

They reeled, whirled, swiveled, flounced, capered, gamboled, and spun.

They leaped like deer on the moon.

The studio ceiling was thirty feet high, but each leap brought the dancers nearer to it.

It became their obvious intention to kiss the ceiling.

They kissed it.

And then, neutralizing gravity with love and pure will, they remained suspended in air inches below the ceiling, and they kissed each other for a long, long time.

It was then that Diana Moon Glampers, the Handicapper General, came into the studio with a double-barreled ten-gauge shotgun. She fired twice, and the Emperor and the Empress were dead before they hit the floor.

Diana Moon Glampers loaded the gun again. She aimed it at the musicians and told them they had ten seconds to get their handicaps back on.

It was then that the Bergerons' television tube burned out.

Hazel turned to comment about the blackout to George. But George had gone out into the kitchen for a can of beer.

George came back in with the beer, paused while a handicap signal shook him up. And then he sat down again. "You been crying?" he said to Hazel.

"Yup," she said.

"What about?" he said.

"I forget," she said. "Something real sad on television."

"What was it?" he said.

"It's all kind of mixed up in my mind," said Hazel.

"Forget sad things," said George.

"I always do," said Hazel.

"That's my girl," said George. He winced. There was the sound of a riveting gun in his head.

"Gee—I could tell that one was a doozy," said Hazel.

"You can say that again," said George.

"Gee—" said Hazel, "I could tell that one was a doozy."

FOR STUDY AND DISCUSSION

1. "Harrison Bergeron" is a *satire*, a form of writing that attacks and ridicules some social evil or human weakness. On what principle is the society in this satire based? What aspects of actual societies is the author mocking?
2. In traditional stories, the hero is a superhuman figure, superior to ordinary people. Usually this hero "saves" the people from an enemy. In what passages of the story does Harrison Bergeron remind you of this superhuman kind of hero? How is the result of Harrison's efforts an ironic reversal of what happens in the traditional heroic stories?
3. What would you say is the conflict in this story? Did the climax surprise you? Why, or why not?
4. Like all satires, this one has a serious point to make. What do you think Vonnegut is saying about equality in this story?

FOR COMPOSITION

Expressing an Opinion

In a paragraph, explain your response to Vonnegut's satiric story. Tell what you think the theme of the story is, and then tell whether you agree with this theme. Tell if you enjoyed reading the story, and why. What did you think of the ending—would you have preferred a different ending? Why, or why not?

ABOUT THE AUTHOR

Kurt Vonnegut (1922–   ) turned to writing full time after working as a police reporter, a public-relations man, and a teacher. Vonnegut was once known primarily as a science-fiction writer, but is now recognized chiefly for his social satire. In much of his work, including the story "Harrison Bergeron," Vonnegut uses the techniques of science fiction and social satire to take a moral stand. One of Vonnegut's best-known novels, *Slaughterhouse-Five*, is based partly upon his experiences as a German prisoner of war during World War II. Vonnegut was being held in an abandoned slaughterhouse in Dresden in eastern Germany at the time the city was fire-bombed by the Allies. Vonnegut's description of this experience is woven into a story that carries a strong message against all war.

In ancient Egyptian mythology, the phoenix was a bird connected with worship of the sun. It was about the size of an eagle, with beautiful red and golden feathers, and it lived in the Arabian desert. Only one phoenix existed at any time. After five hundred years or more, when it was about to die, the phoenix built itself a pyre, set fire to it, and died in the flames. From its ashes, a new phoenix arose. Sylvia Townsend Warner uses this mythical bird in a modern story with a surprising twist.

The Phoenix

Sylvia Townsend Warner

Lord Strawberry, a nobleman, collected birds. He had the finest aviary[1] in Europe, so large that eagles did not find it uncomfortable, so well laid out that both hummingbirds and snow buntings had a climate that suited them perfectly. But for many years the finest set of apartments remained empty, with just a label saying: "PHOENIX. *Habitat: Arabia.*"

Many authorities on bird life had assured Lord Strawberry that the phoenix is a fabulous[2] bird, or that the breed was long extinct. Lord Strawberry was unconvinced: his family had always believed in phoenixes. At intervals he received from his agents (together with statements of their expenses) birds which they declared were the phoenix but which turned out to be orioles, macaws, turkey buzzards dyed orange, etc., or stuffed crossbreeds, ingeniously assembled from various plumages. Finally Lord Strawberry went himself to Arabia, where, after some months, he found a phoenix, won its confidence, caught it, and brought it home in perfect condition.

It was a remarkably fine phoenix, with a charming character—affable to the other birds in the aviary and much attached to Lord Strawberry. On its arrival in England it made a great stir among ornithologists, journalists, poets, and milliners, and was constantly visited. But it was not puffed up by these attentions, and when it was no longer in the news, and the visits fell off, it showed no pique or rancor. It ate well, and seemed perfectly contented.

It costs a great deal of money to keep up an aviary. When Lord Strawberry died, he died penniless. The aviary came on the market. In normal times the rarer birds, and certainly the phoenix, would have been bid for by the trustees of Europe's great zoological societies, or by private persons in the U.S.A.; but as it hap-

1. **aviary** (ā′vē-ĕr′ē): a building or large cage where birds are kept.
2. **fabulous:** here, imaginary; existing only in stories.

pened Lord Strawberry died just after a world war, when both money and birdseed were hard to come by (indeed the cost of birdseed was one of the things which had ruined Lord Strawberry). The London *Times* urged in a leader[3] that the phoenix be bought for the London Zoo, saying that a nation of bird lovers had a moral right to own such a rarity; and a fund, called the Strawberry Phoenix Fund, was opened. Students, naturalists, and schoolchildren contributed according to their means; but their means were small, and there were no large donations. So Lord Strawberry's executors (who had the death duties[4] to consider) closed with the higher offer of Mr. Tancred Poldero, owner and proprietor of Poldero's Wizard Wonderworld.

For quite a while Mr. Poldero considered his phoenix a bargain. It was a civil and obliging bird, and adapted itself readily to its new surroundings. It did not cost much to feed; it did not mind children; and though it had no tricks, Mr. Poldero supposed it would soon pick up some. The publicity of the Strawberry Phoenix Fund was now most helpful. Almost every contributor now saved up another half-crown in order to see the phoenix. Others, who had not contributed to the fund, even paid double to look at it on the five-shilling days.

But then business slackened. The phoenix was as handsome as ever, and as amiable; but, as Mr. Poldero said, it hadn't got Udge. Even at popular prices the phoenix was not really popular. It was too quiet, too classical. So people went instead to watch the antics of the baboons, or to admire the crocodile who had eaten the woman.

One day Mr. Poldero said to his manager, Mr. Ramkin:

---

3. **leader:** a leading article.
4. **death duties:** inheritance taxes in Britain.

"How long since any fool paid to look at the phoenix?"

"Matter of three weeks," replied Mr. Ramkin.

"Eating his head off," said Mr. Poldero. "Let alone the insurance. Seven shillings a week it costs me to insure that bird, and I might as well insure the Archbishop of Canterbury."

"The public don't like him. He's too quiet for them, that's the trouble. Won't mate nor nothing. And I've tried him with no end of pretty pollies, ospreys, and Cochin Chinas, and the Lord knows what. But he won't look at them."

"Wonder if we could swap him for a livelier one," said Mr. Poldero.

"Impossible. There's only one of him at a time."

"Go on!"

"I mean it. Haven't you ever read what it says on the label?"

They went to the phoenix's cage. It flapped its wings politely, but they paid no attention. They read:

"PANSY. *Phoenix phoenixissima formosissima arabiana.* This rare and fabulous bird is UNIQUE. The World's Old Bachelor. Has no mate and doesn't want one. When old, sets fire to itself and emerges miraculously reborn. Specially imported from the East."

"I've got an idea," said Mr. Poldero. "How old do you suppose that bird is?"

"Looks in its prime to me," said Mr. Ramkin.

"Suppose," continued Mr. Poldero, "we could somehow get him alight? We'd advertise it beforehand, of course, work up interest. Then we'd have a new bird, and a bird with some romance about it, a bird with a life story. We could sell a bird like that."

Mr. Ramkin nodded.

"I've read about it in a book," he said. "You've got to give them scented woods and what not, and they build a nest and sit down on it and catch fire spontaneous. But they won't do it till they're old. That's the snag."

"Leave that to me," said Mr. Poldero. "You get those scented woods, and I'll do the aging."

It was not easy to age the phoenix. Its allowance of food was halved, and halved again, but though it grew thinner, its eyes were undimmed and its plumage glossy as ever. The heating was turned off; but it puffed out its feathers against the cold, and seemed none the worse. Other birds were put into its cage, birds of a peevish and quarrelsome nature. They pecked and chivied[5] it; but the phoenix was so civil and amiable that after a day or two they lost their animosity. Then Mr. Poldero tried alley cats. These could not be won by good manners, but the phoenix darted above their heads and flapped its golden wings in their faces, and daunted them.

Mr. Poldero turned to a book on Arabia, and read that the climate was dry. "Aha!" said he. The phoenix was moved to a small cage that had a sprinkler in the ceiling. Every night the sprinkler was turned on. The phoenix began to cough. Mr. Poldero had another good idea. Daily he stationed himself in front of the cage to jeer at the bird and abuse it.

When spring was come, Mr. Poldero felt justified in beginning a publicity campaign about the aging phoenix. The old public favorite, he said, was nearing its end. Meanwhile he tested the bird's reactions every few days by putting a few tufts of foul-smelling straw and some strands of rusty barbed wire into the cage, to see if it were interested in nesting yet. One day the phoenix began turning over the straw. Mr. Poldero signed a contract for the film rights. At last the hour seemed ripe. It was a fine Saturday evening in May. For some

weeks the public interest in the aging phoenix had been working up, and the admission charge had risen to five shillings. The enclosure was thronged. The lights and the cameras were trained on the cage, and a loudspeaker proclaimed to the audience the rarity of what was about to take place.

"The phoenix," said the loudspeaker, "is the aristocrat of bird life. Only the rarest and most expensive specimens of oriental wood, drenched in exotic perfumes, will tempt him to construct his strange love nest."

Now a neat assortment of twigs and shavings, strongly scented, was shoved into the cage.

"The phoenix," the loudspeaker continued, "is as capricious as Cleopatra, as luxurious as

___

5. **chivied** (chĭv′ēd): bothered; nagged.

la du Barry,[6] as heady as a strain of wild gypsy music. All the fantastic pomp and passion of the ancient East, its languorous magic, its subtle cruelties . . ."

"Lawks!" cried a woman in the crowd. "He's at it!"

A quiver stirred the dulled plumage. The phoenix turned its head from side to side. It descended, staggering, from its perch. Then wearily it began to pull about the twigs and shavings.

The cameras clicked, the lights blazed full on the cage. Rushing to the loudspeaker Mr. Poldero exclaimed:

"Ladies and gentlemen, this is the thrilling moment the world has breathlessly awaited. The legend of centuries is materializing before our modern eyes. The phoenix . . ."

The phoenix settled on its pyre and appeared to fall asleep.

The film director said:

"Well, if it doesn't evaluate more than this, mark it instructional."

At that moment the phoenix and the pyre burst into flames. The flames streamed upwards, leaped out on every side. In a minute or two everything was burned to ashes, and some thousand people, including Mr. Poldero, perished in the blaze.

---

6. **Cleopatra . . . la du Barry:** Cleopatra was a queen of ancient Egypt, and Madame du Barry was a woman kept in splendor by Louis XV, an eighteenth-century king of France.

FOR STUDY AND DISCUSSION

1. This story is a fantasy set in a world where the mythical phoenix exists alongside other characters who are so ordinary that we recognize them immediately. What details are used to characterize the phoenix? How is Mr. Poldero characterized?

2. What happens to the phoenix in the hands of the profit-minded Mr. Poldero? How does the phoenix bear up under Mr. Poldero's indignities?

3. Mr. Poldero soon learns that myths cannot be tampered with. How does he learn this lesson? How did you feel when this story reached its surprising climax?

4. The author is clearly mocking, or satirizing, certain human failings in this story. The public, for example, loses interest in the phoenix because it is "too quiet, too classical." They go off instead to admire the baboons and the crocodile who had eaten the woman. Which of our preferences in entertainment is the author mocking here? What is she mocking in the final scene, where the phoenix's last minutes are being filmed for publicity?

LANGUAGE AND VOCABULARY

Recognizing Slang

Slang is an informal or a nonstandard use of language that develops from the attempt to say something in a new, humorous, or forceful way. Sylvia Townsend Warner seems to have coined the word *Udge* as humorous slang meaning "appeal" or "the ability to attract attention":

The phoenix was as handsome as ever, and as amiable; but, as Mr. Poldero said, it hadn't got Udge.

Many slang words eventually move into standard usage, though some go out of style quickly and are soon forgotten. The word *sham*, for example, meaning "pretense, trick, or fraud," was coined in New England from the word *shame* and was once considered slang. Use a dictionary to find out which of the following words are used as slang, or once were considered slang. What does each word mean?

banter	mob	rap
hoopla	pizazz	spiel

FOR COMPOSITION

Writing a Fantasy

In this story, ordinary people acquire a fabulous bird and misuse it because they do not really understand what they possess. Write a brief fantasy of your own, telling what happens when ordinary people suddenly acquire or discover something that is believed to exist only in the world of story and myth. In your story, describe the "thing" acquired, tell how the people acquire it, and then tell what they do with it. Here are some things and characters from the world of story and myth you might use. (If you don't know what these are, a dictionary or an encyclopedia will help.)

centaur	magic carpet
Cupid	Pegasus
El Dorado	siren or mermaid
Fountain of Youth	unicorn

ABOUT THE AUTHOR

Sylvia Townsend Warner (1893–1978), a native of Middlesex, England, began her writing career over half a century ago. Her first novel, *Lolly Willowes*, was published in 1926 and became the first book ever chosen by the Book-of-the-Month Club. After that she published in nearly every literary form, including books of poetry and a biography of Jane Austen. Warner also published an edition of Tudor church music. Warner was much interested in the mythical as well as in the ordinary. Her last book, *Kingdoms of Elfin*, is a collection of short stories about a race of elves inhabiting Europe. Sharing the qualities of both angels and people, these characters are at once enchanting mythical creatures and familiar and comical human types.

Practice in Reading and Writing

DESCRIPTION AND NARRATION

Reading Description

Descriptive writing uses sensory details to "re-create" a person, a place, or an object. Description usually tells how something looks, but it might also describe how it sounds, tastes, smells, or feels to the touch. The details in some descriptive passages work together to produce a strong impression: perhaps of evil or innocence, or of horror, tidiness, danger, comfort. The following passage from Carl Stephenson's story "Leiningen Versus the Ants" describes a scene that meets the hero's eyes one morning:

> He rose with the sun and went out on the flat roof of his house. And a scene like one from Dante lay around him; for miles in every direction there was nothing but a black, glittering multitude, a multitude of rested, sated, but nonetheless voracious ants: yes, look as far as one might, one could see nothing but that rustling black throng, except in the north, where the great river drew a boundary they could not hope to pass. But even the high stone breakwater, along the bank of the river, which Leiningen had built as a defense against inundations, was, like the paths, the shorn trees and shrubs, the ground itself, black with ants.

1. What specific details help you visualize this scene?
2. What word describes the sound that Leiningen hears?

3. What words would you use to describe the main impression created by this passage? What details in particular contribute to this impression?

Reading Narration

Narrative writing relates a series of connected events or actions. Most writers organize the events of a narrative in chronological order, though occasionally we find the chronological order interrupted for a flashback to a past event. Few storytellers use paragraphs of pure narration alone. More often, writers will also include descriptive details to help the action come alive. The following paragraphs from "Leiningen Versus the Ants" tell what happens as the hero races through the army of flesh-eating ants.

Leiningen ran. He ran in long equal strides, with only one thought, one sensation, in his being—he *must* get through. He dodged all trees and shrubs; except for the split seconds his soles touched the ground, the ants should have no opportunity to alight on him. That they would get to him soon, despite the salve on his boots, the petrol in his clothes, he realized only too well, but he knew even more surely that he must, and that he would, get to the weir.

Apparently the salve was some use after all; not until he had reached halfway did he feel ants under his clothes, and a few on his face. Mechanically, in his stride, he struck at them, scarcely conscious of their bites. He saw he was drawing appreciably near the weir—the distance grew less and less—sank to five hundred—three—two—one hundred yards.

Then he was at the weir and gripping the ant-hulled wheel. Hardly had he seized it when a horde of infuriated ants flowed over his hands, arms, and shoulders. He started the wheel—before it turned once on its axis the swarm covered his face. Leiningen strained like a madman, his lips pressed tight; if he opened them to draw breath. . . .

He turned and turned; slowly the dam lowered until it reached the bed of the river. Already the water was overflowing the ditch. Another minute, and the river was pouring through the nearby gap in the breakwater. The flooding of the plantation had begun.

---

1. List the key events in this passage.
2. Although narratives relate many events, they usually are concerned with one *main event*. What would you say is the main event of this passage? (A good way to discover the main event is to try to rewrite the passage in just ten words.)
3. Narratives usually include descriptive details that make the action come alive. The second sentence here, for example, helps us visualize how Leiningen ran: in "long equal strides." What other details help make this action vivid and real?
4. What descriptive details create an impression of horror?
5. These events are told in *chronological order*—the order in which they occur in time. What words help you to follow the order of the events? (Look for words such as *then*, *next*, or *a minute later*.)

Reading Dialogue

In addition to descriptive details, stories usually use *dialogue* — the direct quotation of the characters' speech. Dialogue serves many purposes: it moves the story forward, it interprets character, and it breaks up long passages of solid prose. Dialogue also helps us *hear* the story, as if it is actually taking place in front of us. Here is a passage of dialogue from Toni Cade Bambara's "Blues Ain't No Mockin Bird." The speakers are an old woman and a cameraman who is trespassing on her property. The cameraman speaks first:

"We thought we'd get a shot or two of the house and everything and then —"

"Good mornin," Granny cut him off. And smiled that smile.

"Good mornin," he said, head all down the way Bingo does when you yell at him about the bones on the kitchen floor. "Nice place you got here, Aunty. We thought we'd take a —"

"Did you?" said Granny with her eyebrows. Cathy pulled up her socks and giggled.

"Nice things here," said the man, buzzin his camera over the yard. The pecan barrels, the sled, me and Cathy, the flowers, the printed stones along the driveway, the trees, the twins, the toolshed.

"I don't know about the thing, the it, and the stuff," said Granny, still talkin with her eyebrows. "Just people here is what I tend to consider."

---

1. What clues tell how the characters feel?
2. What *actions* are part of the dialogue — that is, what do you visualize these people doing?

3. Rewrite this scene as a straight narrative, omitting all dialogue. Do you think a dramatic effect has been lost?

Writing a Story

Narrate a series of related events that hold some interest for you — either events that actually took place or events that you imagine. Choose events in which "something happens" — in which a character does accomplish something, or fails to. In other words, by the end of your story, something must have changed. Include description to make your characters and action come alive. To dramatize your action, use some dialogue.

For Further Reading

Buck, Pearl, *Fourteen Stories* (paperback, Pocket Books, 1976)
> These stories are written by one of America's Nobel Prize winners, a gifted storyteller who is the author of *The Good Earth.*

Cather, Willa, *Five Stories* (Random House, 1956; paperback, Vintage)
> The fiction of this famous American writer is often set on the Midwest prairies. This collection includes "Paul's Case" and "Neighbor Rosicky."

Chekhov, Anton, *Great Stories by Chekhov,* edited by David H. Greene (paperback, Dell)
> Here are brief stories of irony and tragedy by one of the masters of modern psychological fiction.

Gold, Robert S., editor, *Point of Departure, 19 Stories of Youth and Discovery* (paperback, Dell, 1967)
> All of these stories deal with the conflicts of adolescence—including "The First Death of Her Life" by Elizabeth Taylor, "Sucker" by Carson McCullers, and "A Summer's Reading" by Bernard Malamud.

Jewett, Sarah Orne, *The Country of the Pointed Firs and Other Stories* (paperback, Anchor, 1954)
> Jewett's stories confront time and change. They are all set in rural Maine at the end of the last century.

Johnson, Dorothy M., *A Man Called Horse* (paperback, Ballantine, 1953)
> One of the great American writers of the Western frontier tells of white settlements and displaced Indian tribes. The collection includes "Scars of Honor" and "A Man Called Horse."

Lessing, Doris, *African Stories* (paperback, Popular Library, 1975)
> These stories are set in the villages and plains of Africa, and include "A Sunrise on the Veld" and "No Witchcraft for Sale."

O'Connor, Frank, *Stories by Frank O'Connor* (Knopf, 1952; paperback, Vintage)
> Eighteen of the Irish writer's own humorous favorites are here, including "Judas," "The Idealist," and "My Oedipus Complex."

Poe, Edgar Allan, *Great Tales and Poems* (paperback, Washington Square Press)
> These tales of horror by the inventor of the modern detective story include such thrillers as "Murders in the Rue Morgue," "The Cask of Amontillado," and "The Pit and the Pendulum."

Saki, *Incredible Tales* (paperback, Dell, 1966)
> These thirty-one brief stories by Saki are marked by horror, humor, and irony. They include "The Open Window," "The Interlopers," and "Tobermory" (about a cat of superior intellect).

Vonnegut, Kurt, *Welcome to the Monkey House* (Delacorte, 1968; paperback, Dell)
> This grab bag contains some of Vonnegut's best fiction—funny, sad, wild, memorable. It includes "Tom Edison's Shaggy Dog," "EPICAC," and "Tomorrow and Tomorrow and Tomorrow."

West, Jessamyn, *Cress Delahanty* (Harcourt Brace Jovanovich, 1954)
> West's now-classic stories tell of a teen-aged girl whose adolescent years are marked by heartache, humor, and comedy. The stories trace Cress's experiences from her twelfth year through her sixteenth.

NONFICTION
Essays

The word *essay* dates back to a sixteenth-century French writer named Montaigne. Montaigne liked to jot down his thoughts on a wide variety of subjects—from the joys of the countryside to the evils of government. When he decided to publish his informal compositions, he called them *Essais,* the French word for "attempts." Since Montaigne's time, essays have been written by countless writers on nearly every conceivable subject. Essays have been written to entertain, to inform, to explain, and to persuade, and have made use of all four major forms of discourse: *description,* which presents a picture or an impression of a subject; *narration,* which relates a series of events; *exposition,* which explains a subject; and *argument* or *persuasion,* which attempts to influence people's ideas or actions. Whatever its form, the essay has remained essentially what it was for Montaigne: a play of the mind on a subject, an "attempt" to say something about a subject, but not everything. Whenever you read a feature article, a sports column, a movie review, or an editorial, you are reading an essay.

All of the essays included here show the play of the writer's mind on a subject—whether it be E. B. White's humorous reflections on the Model T Ford or Harry Crews's serious thoughts about birds of prey. Through each of these essays we see the writer's personality, the individual mind that selects the subject of the essay, shapes its organization, and selects those details that this particular writer has noticed and wants to report. The essays you will read here, and probably most of the ones you read every day, are *informal* or *familiar* essays: they have an informal tone, as if the author were speaking directly to you. Other essays are classified as *formal.* They are serious in tone and subject, and more objective in point of view. One of the rewards of reading any kind of essay is meeting people—the essayists—through the ideas that interest them.

Harry Crews (1935–   ) is an American novelist who teaches writing at the University of Florida. As one critic has said, Crews writes with a hand that is sure, tough, and trained. In this essay, he tells, in precise detail, how he cared for a wounded hawk. Crews has written a novel called *The Hawk Is Dying*, in which a man's interest in training hawks becomes an obsession. In *A Childhood: The Biography of a Place*, Crews tells of his earliest years, growing up on a sharecropper's farm in Georgia.

The Hawk Is Flying

Harry Crews

I was jogging between Lake Swan and Lake Rosa on a ridge full of blackjack oak when I saw the hawk, tail feathers fanned and wings half spread, beside a dump of palmetto[1] about twenty yards off the dim path. From the attitude of her wings and tail I first thought she was sitting on a kill, maybe a rabbit or a rat, but then she turned her wild dandelion eyes toward me and I knew that she was there in the sand not because of something she had killed but because she herself had almost been killed. Blood was dark and clotted on the trailing edge of her right wing. Someone had brought her down with a gun and then not had the decency to find where she fell.

I stood there in the path for a long time, deciding whether or not to kill her. I knew the chances of keeping her alive were slim after she'd been hurt. But leaving her wing-shot in the dirt like that would take more meanness than I thought I could manage. At the same time, though, I knew the right thing to do would be to step quickly across the sand and kick her to death. I watched her where she sat quietly, feathers ruffled now and unafraid, and I knew I was not going to find it in myself either to leave her or kill her. There was nothing to do but take her up and try to save her.

Because the direct stare of a man is terrifying to a hawk, I kept my eyes averted and slowly circled to the edge of the palmetto, where I knelt in the sand. Her sharp, hooked beak was open from heat and exhaustion and her peach-colored tongue beat like a pulse with her rapid breathing. From her size and plumage she was obviously a red-tailed hawk, less than two years old and in her prime, but even so she would have a nervous system as fine and as delicate as a Swiss watch and be subject to death by heart attack or apoplexy if she was not handled carefully. I would need not only whatever skill I might have but also enormous luck, since she would rather die than submit to me. Moving very slowly so as not to disturb her any more than was absolutely necessary, I took off one of my Adidas shoes and rolled down a long one-size-fits-all sweat sock I was wearing. Then, moving the hand that held the sock out in front of her so that she would follow it with her eyes, I eased my other hand over her back and pinned her wings down so she could not beat them against the ground. Her shallow, rapid heart trembled under the fine bright feathers of her breast. I tore the toe out of the sock and put it around her neck like a collar and rolled it down until she was encased in a tight tube of elastic cotton. All that was visible was her head at one end of the sock and talons at the other.

On the long slow walk back home, the only sound she made was a soft clucking very much like that of a chicken. I held her as loosely as I could because I was worried about the heat of my hands and the way she was wrapped. I really expected her to die, but apparently she was not hurt as badly as I thought. By the time I put her on my bed, her breathing had slowed and she had grown calm under the tight sock.

I sat down and opened my desk and there, nearly filling the bottom drawer, was leather from all the years I had kept and trained and flown hawks. On top was a pair of leather welder's gloves, the right one bloodstained between the thumb and forefinger. And under the gloves were several pairs of eighteen-inch jesses[2] and two four-foot leashes and fifteen hoods, each one with the size and date it was

---

1. **palmetto:** a palm tree with fan-shaped leaves. The action of this narrative takes place in southern Georgia.

2. **jesses:** straps that are fastened around a hawk's leg, with a ring at one end for attaching a leash.

made cut into the top of it, and finally four tiny brass falcon bells and as many shark swivels, used to join the jesses to the leashes.

I took the hoods out of the drawer and arbitrarily selected number seven to fit to the hawk's head to see if it was lighttight. It was too big so I tried the next one down, number six, which was nearly right. When I went to number five the fit was perfect, so I drew the leather hood strings, and the hawk, in total darkness now, lay utterly still. With a pair of scissors I carefully cut away the sock. I put on the leather gloves and with my right hand under her breast lifted her to stand on the floor. In the darkness and confusion of the lighttight hood, she stood without moving while I looped the leather jesses around her legs and attached one of the bells to a tail feather. I then attached the ends of the two jesses to the shark swivel and hooked the other end of the swivel to a leash. Her blood-clotted wing hung half spread from her body. I ran my fingers gently along the leading edge to see whether or not the bone was broken. It was not. The flesh was torn, but not badly and I was able to remove four tiny birdshot from the wound with a pair of tweezers without cutting away any of her feathers. With the leather glove covering my wrist I touched her legs from behind, and as all hawks will do, she immediately stepped up and back, her talons gripping my arm tightly enough to hurt through the quarter-inch leather.

It has always seemed an awesome mystery to me that any hooded hawk anywhere in the world will step in precisely the same way if the backs of its legs are touched. It was true when Attila the Hun[3] carried hawks on his wrist and it is still true. Presumably it is something that will be true forever. It is part of the reason men have been fascinated with the art of falconry through all the centuries of recorded history.

The hood was the only way I could possibly keep her while her wing healed because without the hood she would beat herself to death at the end of the jesses. A hood makes a hawk's movements and reactions predictable, but there is something about it that is disgusting, too. To make a hawk as docile as a kitten, to reduce even the biggest and most magnificent raptor[4] in the world to something any child can carry, has always caused a sour ball of shame to settle solid as bone inside me.

I made a perch for her out of a broomstick attached to the top of a ladder-back chair and put her on it. She gripped the perch and sat as still as if she had been killed and stuffed. Eventually she would move, but only a little. She would lower her head and rake at the hood with her talons, but not for long, and the period of quietness would give her some chance of staying alive until she healed. I drew the blinds on the windows and stood watching her in the darkened room, thinking again of the perverse pleasure and unreasonable joy, dating all the way back to my childhood, that I have found in meat-eating birds.

One of my most vivid memories is of riding bareback on a mule in the pinewoods of south Georgia and seeing a buzzard walk out of the stomach of a dead and bloated cow, a piece of putrid flesh caught in its stinking beak. And right behind that memory is a hawk swinging into our farmyard and driving its talons into the back of a screaming chicken and flying toward the darkened tree line on the horizon. And necessarily linked to that memory is my

---

3. **Attila the Hun:** barbarian chieftain (406?–453) whose armies overran most of central Europe in the fifth century.

4. **raptor:** a bird, such as the eagle, hawk, or owl, that captures and feeds upon other animals.

FOR STUDY AND DISCUSSION

1. What specific details in this essay show that Crews is knowledgeable about hawks and is skilled in handling them?

2. This essay tells a great deal about hawks, but it also reveals something about Crews himself. For example, Crews must make a decision when he finds the hawk lying wounded in the dump of palmetto. What do you think his decision reveals about Crews? What else does the essay reveal about him?

3. Why does Crews find the process of hooding a hawk disgusting? Why must he hood this hawk?

4. Crews says that he finds birds of prey "abhorrently beautiful." What do you think this means? What other aspects of nature could also be seen in this way?

5. Why do you think Crews feels bad at the end of the essay?

LANGUAGE AND VOCABULARY

Recognizing Specific Words

Crews, like all good writers, usually chooses a specific word rather than a general one. For example, he says *jogging* rather than *running*, *clotted* rather than *dried*, *trembled* rather than *moved*. Find three examples of specific words in the paragraph on page 176 beginning "One of my most vivid memories." Discuss how they help you visualize the scene Crews is describing.

FOR COMPOSITION

Explaining a Process

Crews's essay is primarily a narrative, but it also contains passages of *exposition*, the form of writing that explains something or that

gives information about something. Crews's explanation of how to care for a wounded hawk is so precise and his descriptions are so vivid that most readers find themselves as interested in the process as Crews is. Crews describes the process step by step: he starts with an explanation of how he managed to get the hawk home, and he concludes with a detailed explanation of how he got the hawk to eat and to fly to a lure.

Write an essay of your own explaining some process you are familiar with. Describe each step of the process in detail. Use specific words that will help your reader visualize the actions that must be performed. Try to include one paragraph explaining why this particular process interests you.

John Steinbeck (1902–1968) is a Nobel Prize winner and the author of such classic American novels as *The Grapes of Wrath* and *Of Mice and Men*. Late in his life, Steinbeck decided to make a trip throughout the United States to rediscover his native land. Steinbeck had a special truck built for his trip, with a small house riding on its back, and for company he took along his large blue-colored French poodle named Charley. Steinbeck wrote an account of his long and eventful trip in *Travels with Charley*, a best-selling book filled with personal reflections on America, on Steinbeck, and on Charley. In the following essay from that book, Steinbeck describes their visit to Yellowstone National Park.

Travels with Charley

John Steinbeck

I must confess to a laxness in the matter of National Parks. I haven't visited many of them. Perhaps this is because they enclose the unique, the spectacular, the astounding— the greatest waterfall, the deepest canyon, the highest cliff, the most stupendous works of man or nature. And I would rather see a good Brady[1] photograph than Mount Rushmore. For it is my opinion that we enclose and celebrate the freaks of our nation and of our civilization. Yellowstone National Park is no more representative of America than is Disneyland.

This being my natural attitude, I don't know what made me turn sharply south and cross a state line to take a look at Yellowstone. Perhaps it was a fear of my neighbors. I could hear them say, "You mean you were that near to Yellowstone and didn't go? You must be crazy." Again it might have been the American tendency in travel. One goes, not so much to see but to tell afterward. Whatever my purpose in going to Yellowstone, I'm glad I went because I discovered something about Charley I might never have known.

A pleasant-looking National Park man checked me in and then he said, "How about that dog? They aren't permitted in except on leash."

"Why?" I asked.

"Because of the bears."

"Sir," I said, "this is an unique dog. He does not live by tooth or fang. He respects the rights of cats to be cats although he doesn't admire them. He turns his steps rather than disturb an earnest caterpillar. His greatest fear is that someone will point out a rabbit and suggest that he chase it. This is a dog of peace and tranquillity. I suggest that the greatest danger to your bears will be pique at being ignored by Charley."

The young man laughed. "I wasn't so much worried about the bears," he said. "But our bears have developed an intolerance for dogs. One of them might demonstrate his prejudice with a clip on the chin, and then—no dog."

"I'll lock him in the back, sir. I promise you Charley will cause no ripple in the bear world, and as an old bear-looker, neither will I."

"I just have to warn you," he said. "I have no doubt your dog has the best of intentions. On the other hand, our bears have the worst. Don't leave food about. Not only do they steal but they are critical of anyone who tries to reform them. In a word, don't believe their sweet faces or you might get clobbered. And don't let the dog wander. Bears don't argue."

We went on our way into the wonderland of nature gone nuts, and you will have to believe what happened. The only way I can prove it would be to get a bear.

---

1. **Brady:** Mathew B. Brady (1823?–1896) was a famous photographer of American scenes and people.

Less than a mile from the entrance I saw a bear beside the road, and it ambled out as though to flag me down. Instantly a change came over Charley. He shrieked with rage. His lips flared, showing wicked teeth that have some trouble with a dog biscuit. He screeched insults at the bear, which hearing, the bear reared up and seemed to me to over-top Rocinante.[2] Frantically I rolled the windows shut and, swinging quickly to the left, grazed the animal, then scuttled on while Charley raved and ranted beside me, describing in detail what he would do to that bear if he could get at him. I was never so astonished in my life. To the best of my knowledge Charley had never seen a bear, and in his whole history had showed great tolerance for every living thing. Besides all this, Charley is a coward, so deep-seated a coward that he has developed a technique for concealing it. And yet he showed every evidence of wanting to get out and murder a bear that outweighed him a thousand to one. I don't understand it.

A little farther along two bears showed up, and the effect was doubled. Charley became a maniac. He leaped all over me, he cursed and growled, snarled and screamed. I didn't know he had the ability to snarl. Where did he learn it? Bears were in good supply, and the road became a nightmare. For the first time in his life Charley resisted reason, even resisted a cuff on the ear. He became a primitive killer lusting for the blood of his enemy, and up to this moment he had had no enemies. In a bearless stretch, I opened the cab, took Charley by the collar, and locked him in the house. But that did no good. When we passed other bears he leaped on the table and scratched at the windows trying to get out at them. I could hear canned goods crashing as he struggled in his mania. Bears simply brought out the Hyde in my Jekyll-headed dog. What could have caused it? Was it a prebreed memory of a time when the wolf was in him? I know him well. Once in a while he tries a bluff, but it is a palpable lie. I swear that this was no lie. I am certain that if he were released, he would have charged every bear we passed and found victory or death.

It was too nerve-racking, a shocking spectacle, like seeing an old, calm friend go insane. No amount of natural wonders, of rigid cliffs and belching waters, of smoking springs could even engage my attention while that pandemonium went on. After about the fifth encounter I gave up, turned Rocinante about, and retraced my way. If I had stopped the night and bears had gathered to my cooking, I dare not think what would have happened.

At the gate the park guard checked me out. "You didn't stay long. Where's the dog?"

"Locked up back there. And I owe you an apology. That dog has the heart and soul of a bear killer and I didn't know it. Heretofore he has been a little tenderhearted toward an underdone steak."

"Yeah!" he said. "That happens sometimes. That's why I warned you. A bear dog would know his chances, but I've seen a Pomeranian go up like a puff of smoke. You know, a well-favored bear can bat a dog like a tennis ball."

I moved fast, back the way I had come, and I was reluctant to camp for fear there might be some unofficial nongovernment bears about. That night I spent in a pretty auto court near Livingston. I had my dinner in a restaurant, and when I had settled in with a drink and a comfortable chair and my bathed bare feet on a carpet with red roses, I inspected Charley. He was dazed. His eyes held a faraway look and he was totally exhausted, emotionally no

---

2. **Rocinante** (rō′sē-nän′tä): the name Steinbeck has given his truck. In the great Spanish novel *Don Quixote*, Rocinante is the horse that carries the hero on all his luckless quests.

doubt. Mostly he reminded me of a man coming out of a long, hard drunk—worn out, depleted, collapsed. He couldn't eat his dinner, he refused the evening walk, and once we were in he collapsed on the floor and went to sleep. In the night I heard him whining and yapping, and when I turned on the light his feet were making running gestures and his body jerked and his eyes were wide open, but it was only a night bear. I awakened him and gave him some water. This time he went to sleep and didn't stir all night. In the morning he was still tired. I wonder why we think the thoughts and emotions of animals are simple.

FOR STUDY AND DISCUSSION

1. John Steinbeck's account of his visit to Yellowstone National Park resembles a short story. Identify the beginning, middle, and end of the "story." What is the conflict and how is it resolved?

2. Steinbeck develops humor by describing Charley's reaction to the bears as if the dog were a person having a fit of anger. What words and phrases describe Charley's "rage"? What humorous pun, or play on words, describes Charley's dream at the end of the story?

3. Steinbeck expresses the theme of his essay in the sentence "I wonder why we think the thoughts and emotions of animals are simple." How does his essay support this observation?

FOR COMPOSITION

Comparing Points of View
Harry Crews (page 174) and John Steinbeck both express personal opinions and feelings about the animal world in their essays. In a short essay of your own, explain the point of view expressed by each of these writers. Tell where you think they agree and where you think they disagree in their feelings and opinions about animals.

The American humorist James Thurber (1894–1961) was born and raised in Columbus, Ohio. Thurber later used Columbus as the setting for comic stories about his eccentric family. Thurber's association with *The New Yorker* began in 1927, and most of his stories, sketches, and fables first appeared in that magazine.

A *fable* is a brief story that teaches a moral or practical lesson. For centuries, fables have been a favorite form for preserving and sharing wisdom. Like many other writers of fables, Thurber uses animal characters to make his points about human behavior. Because their essential purpose is to teach, not just to tell a story, fables are sometimes categorized as story-essays. They are among the oldest of all literary forms; Thurber calls *his* "fables for our time."

The Scotty Who Knew Too Much
James Thurber

Several summers ago there was a Scotty who went to the country for a visit. He decided that all the farm dogs were cowards, because they were afraid of a certain animal that had a white stripe down its back. "You are a pussycat and I can lick you," the Scotty said to the farm dog who lived in the house where the Scotty was visiting. "I can lick the little animal with the white stripe, too. Show him to me."

"Don't you want to ask any questions about him?" said the farm dog.

"Nah," said the Scotty. "*You* ask the questions."

So the farm dog took the Scotty into the woods and showed him the white-striped animal and the Scotty closed in on him, growling and slashing. It was all over in a moment and the Scotty lay on his back. When he came to, the farm dog said, "What happened?"

"He threw vitriol,"[1] said the Scotty, "but he never laid a glove on me."

A few days later the farm dog told the Scotty there was another animal all the farm dogs were afraid of. "Lead me to him," said the Scotty. "I can lick anything that doesn't wear horseshoes."

"Don't you want to ask any questions about him?" said the farm dog.

"Nah," said the Scotty. "Just show me where he hangs out." So the farm dog led him to a place in the woods and pointed out the little animal when he came along. "A clown,"

---

1. **vitriol** (vĭt′rē-ōl′): literally, sulfuric acid.

said the Scotty, "a pushover," and he closed in, leading with his left and exhibiting some mighty fancy footwork. In less than a second the Scotty was flat on his back, and when he woke up the farm dog was pulling quills out of him.

"What happened?" said the farm dog.

"He pulled a knife on me," said the Scotty, "but at least I have learned how you fight out here in the country, and now I am going to beat you up." So he closed in on the farm dog, holding his nose with one front paw to ward off the vitriol and covering his eyes with the other front paw to keep out the knives. The Scotty couldn't see his opponent and he couldn't smell his opponent and he was so badly beaten that he had to be taken back to the city and put in a nursing home.

Moral: It is better to ask some of the questions than to know all the answers.

FOR STUDY AND DISCUSSION

1. What human qualities do you recognize in the Scotty? How does Thurber *satirize,* or poke fun at, certain comic types—for example, the braggart—in the way the Scotty talks?

2. What does the moral have to do with the story? Do you think Thurber is using this fable to make a serious point? Explain.

FOR COMPOSITION

Writing a Fable

Write a fable of your own, inventing a situation in which an animal who represents some kind of person learns about life. Choose the animal carefully; a quick-tempered Scotty is perfect for Thurber's story—an even-tempered collie or sheepdog would not have done. State your moral at the end of your story, as Thurber does. You might write a fable to illustrate one of these famous moral lessons, or you might twist the moral to suit your own humorous purpose:

> Absence makes the heart grow fonder.
> Out of sight, out of mind.
> Don't burn your bridges until they're crossed.
> Too many cooks spoil the broth.
> Many hands make light work.

R. J. Heathorn (1914–   ) is an Englishman who writes for British and American periodicals. In this essay, the voice we hear is an ironic one. It says to us: "I mean more than I am saying." Though we know by the end of the first paragraph that Heathorn is writing satirically, his targets may not be immediately evident. The fun of reading the essay is discovering what they are.

Learn with BOOK

R. J. Heathorn

A new aid to rapid—almost magical—learning has made its appearance. Indications are that if it catches on, all the electronic gadgets will be so much junk. The new device is known as Built-in Orderly Organized Knowledge. The makers generally call it by its initials, BOOK.

Many advantages are claimed over the old-style learning and teaching aids on which most people are brought up nowadays. It has no wires, no electric circuits to break down. No connection is needed to an electricity power point. It is made entirely without mechanical parts to go wrong or need replacement.

Anyone can use BOOK, even children, and it fits comfortably into the hands. It can be conveniently used sitting in an armchair by the fire.

How does this revolutionary, unbelievably easy invention work? Basically BOOK consists only of a large number of paper sheets. These may run to hundreds where BOOK covers a lengthy program of information. Each sheet bears a number in sequence, so that the sheets cannot be used in the wrong order. To make it even easier for the user to keep the sheets in the proper order, they are held firmly in place by a special locking device called a "binding."

Each sheet of paper presents the user with an information sequence in the form of symbols, which he absorbs optically for automatic registration on the brain. When one sheet has been assimilated, a flick of the finger turns it over and further information is found on the other side. By using both sides of each sheet in this way a great economy is effected, thus reducing both the size and cost of BOOK. No buttons need to be pressed to move from one sheet to another, to open or close BOOK, or to start it working.

BOOK may be taken up at any time and used by merely opening it. Instantly it is ready for use. Nothing has to be connected up or switched on. The user may turn at will to any sheet, going backwards or forwards as he pleases. A sheet is provided near the beginning as a location finder for any required information sequence.

A small accessory, available at trifling extra cost, is the BOOKmark. This enables the user to pick up his program where he left off on the previous learning session. BOOKmark is versatile and may be used in any BOOK.

The initial cost varies with the size and subject matter. Already a vast range of BOOKs is available, covering every conceivable subject and adjusted to different levels of aptitude. One BOOK, small enough to be held in the hands, may contain an entire learning schedule. Once purchased, BOOK requires no further cost; no batteries or wires are needed, since the motive power, thanks to the ingenious device patented by the makers, is supplied by the brain of the user.

BOOKs may be stored on handy shelves, and for ease of reference the program schedule is normally indicated on the back of the binding.

Altogether the Built-in Orderly Organized Knowledge seems to have great advantages with no drawbacks. We predict a big future for it.

FOR STUDY AND DISCUSSION

1. In this essay, the writer seems to be saying: if books were introduced today, into a society addicted to electronic gadgets, this is how they would be advertised. Although he is talking about books, Heathorn is really poking fun at our addiction to electronic gadgets. What are some of the gadgets that are the targets of Heathorn's satire? How is BOOK superior to them?

2. By describing BOOK in mechanical terms, Heathorn is also making fun of a kind of *jargon*—in this case, the specialized vocabulary used to describe electronic gadgets. How does he describe binding, table of contents, and title? What words does he use when he's talking about the contents of BOOK?

SATIRE

Any kind of writing that pokes fun at some aspect of human behavior is called *satire*. The ridicule in satire can be bitter, or it can be gentle and humorous. "Learn with BOOK" is an example of genial satire. Its mockery is meant not to insult or hurt, but to point out the foolishness of some of our attitudes and practices.

One of the tools of the satirist is the absurd comparison. Throughout his essay Heathorn compares books to electronic gadgets. The absurdity of this comparison dramatizes our addiction to gadgets. It makes us realize how much simpler it is to read a book than it is to plug ourselves into a computer.

Satirists criticize society in the hope of bringing about some change. In your opinion, what changes would Heathorn like to bring about in our society?

Not everyone agrees with a satirist, of course. How would you respond to Heathorn?

FOR COMPOSITION

Writing a Satire
Heathorn takes something that is familiar (a book) and describes it as if it is a great new invention. Think of some other thing or activity that has been around for a long time, and write a brief announcement of it, as if it is a brand new invention. (You might try an ordinary activity like walking or talking.) Describe several "advantages" that this "new invention" has over other gadgets or activities. Before you write, decide what the target of your satire will be.

In her highly acclaimed novels and essays, Joan Didion (1934–   ) has been a perceptive observer of contemporary American life. She pays special attention to Los Angeles, a city she has lived in for many years. In this excerpt from her essay "Los Angeles Notebook," Didion discusses the hot, dry wind known as the Santa Ana and how it affects human behavior. This selection comes from Didion's collection of essays called *Slouching Towards Bethlehem*.

Los Angeles Notebook

Joan Didion

There is something uneasy in the Los Angeles air this afternoon, some unnatural stillness, some tension. What it means is that tonight a Santa Ana will begin to blow, a hot wind from the northeast whining down through the Cajon and San Gorgonio Passes, blowing up sandstorms out along Route 66, drying the hills and the nerves to the flash point.[1] For a few days now we will see smoke back in the canyons, and hear sirens in the night. I have neither heard nor read that a Santa Ana is due, but I know it, and almost everyone I have seen today knows it too. We know it because we feel it. The baby frets. The maid sulks. I rekindle a waning argument with the telephone company, then cut my losses and lie down, given over to whatever it is in the air. To live with the Santa Ana is to accept, consciously or unconsciously, a deeply mechanistic view of human behavior.[2]

I recall being told, when I first moved to Los Angeles and was living on an isolated beach,

---

1. **flash point:** temperature at which a volatile substance will ignite with a flash.

2. **mechanistic . . . behavior:** the theory that human behavior can be explained in terms of physical and chemical influences.

189

that the Indians would throw themselves into the sea when the bad wind blew. I could see why. The Pacific turned ominously glossy during a Santa Ana period, and one woke in the night troubled not only by the peacocks screaming in the olive trees but by the eerie absence of surf. The heat was surreal.[3] The sky had a yellow cast, the kind of light sometimes called "earthquake weather." My only neighbor would not come out of her house for days, and there were no lights at night, and her husband roamed the place with a machete. One day he would tell me that he had heard a trespasser, the next a rattlesnake.

"On nights like that," Raymond Chandler[4] once wrote about the Santa Ana, "every booze party ends in a fight. Meek little wives feel the edge of the carving knife and study their husbands' necks. Anything can happen." That was the kind of wind it was. I did not know then that there was any basis for the effect it had on all of us, but it turns out to be another of those cases in which science bears out folk wisdom. The Santa Ana, which is named for one of the canyons it rushes through, is a *foehn*[5] wind, like the *foehn* of Austria and Switzerland and the *hamsin* of Israel. There are a number of persistent malevolent winds, perhaps the best known of which are the mistral of France and the Mediterranean sirocco, but a *foehn* wind has distinct characteristics: it occurs on the leeward slope of a mountain range and, although the air begins as a cold mass, it is warmed as it comes down the mountain and appears finally as a hot dry wind. Whenever and wherever a *foehn* blows, doctors hear about headaches and nausea and allergies, about "nervousness," about "depression." In Los Angeles

some teachers do not attempt to conduct formal classes during a Santa Ana, because the children become unmanageable. In Switzerland, the suicide rate goes up during the *foehn*, and in the courts of some Swiss cantons[6] the wind is considered a mitigating[7] circumstance for crime. Surgeons are said to watch the wind, because blood does not clot normally during a *foehn*. A few years ago an Israeli physicist discovered that not only during such winds, but for the ten or twelve hours which precede them, the air carries an unusually high ratio of positive to negative ions. No one seems to know exactly why that should be; some talk about friction and others suggest solar disturbances. In any case the positive ions are there, and what an excess of positive ions does, in the simplest terms, is make people unhappy. One cannot get much more mechanistic than that.

Easterners commonly complain that there is no "weather" at all in southern California, that the days and the seasons slip by relentlessly, numbingly bland. That is quite misleading. In fact the climate is characterized by infrequent but violent extremes: two periods of torrential subtropical rains which continue for weeks and wash out the hills and send subdivisions[8] sliding toward the sea; about twenty scattered days a year of the Santa Ana, which, with its incendiary dryness, invariably means fire. At the first prediction of a Santa Ana, the Forest Service flies men and equipment from northern California into the southern forests, and the Los Angeles Fire Department cancels its ordinary nonfirefighting routines. The Santa Ana caused Malibu to burn the way it did in 1956, and Bel Air in 1961, and Santa Barbara in 1964. In the winter

---

3. **surreal:** dreamlike; unnatural.
4. **Raymond Chandler:** American writer (1888–1959), author of detective novels set in Los Angeles.
5. *foehn* (fān).

6. **cantons:** states of the Swiss Republic.
7. **mitigating:** leading toward a softening or reduction of punishment.
8. **subdivisions:** housing developments.

of 1966–67 eleven men were killed fighting a Santa Ana fire that spread through the San Gabriel Mountains.

Just to watch the front-page news out of Los Angeles during a Santa Ana is to get very close to what it is about the place. The longest single Santa Ana period in recent years was in 1957, and it lasted not the usual three or four days but fourteen days, from November 21 until December 4. On the first day 25,000 acres of the San Gabriel Mountains were burning, with gusts reaching 100 miles an hour. In town, the wind reached Force 12, or hurricane force, on the Beaufort Scale; oil derricks were toppled and people ordered off the downtown streets to avoid injury from flying objects. On November 22 the fire in the San Gabriels was out of control. On November 24 six people were killed in automobile accidents, and by the end of the week the Los Angeles *Times* was keeping a box score of traffic deaths. On November 26 a prominent Pasadena attorney, depressed about money, shot and killed his wife, their two sons, and himself. On November 27 a South Gate divorcée, twenty-two, was murdered and thrown from a moving car. On November 30 the San Gabriel fire was still out of control, and the wind in town was blowing eighty miles an hour. On the first day of December four people died violently, and on the third the wind began to break.

It is hard for people who have not lived in Los Angeles to realize how radically the Santa Ana figures in the local imagination. The city burning is Los Angeles' deepest image of itself: Nathanael West perceived that, in *The Day of the Locust*,[9] and at the time of the 1965 Watts riots what struck the imagination most indelibly were the fires. For days one could drive the Harbor Freeway and see the city on fire, just as we had always known it would be in the end. Los Angeles weather is the weather of catastrophe, of apocalypse, and, just as the reliably long and bitter winters of New England determine the way life is lived there, so the violence and the unpredictability of the Santa Ana affect the entire quality of life in Los Angeles, accentuate its impermanence, its unreliability. The wind shows us how close to the edge we are.

---

9. *The Day of the Locust:* novel by Nathanael West (1903–1940) about a group of people living in Los Angeles in the 1930's. At the end of the novel, an artist imagines a raging fire consuming the city.

FOR STUDY AND DISCUSSION

1. How does living with a Santa Ana convince Didion of a "mechanistic view of human behavior"? What scientific evidence does Didion use to show that weather can influence human behavior?
2. What does Didion conclude about the weather's effect on life in Los Angeles? What do you think she means by saying: "The wind shows us how close to the edge we are"?
3. What do you think of Didion's opinions?

FOR COMPOSITION

Describing a Place
Joan Didion's essay is a fine example of an essay about a place. She is successful in describing one aspect of Los Angeles because she knows her subject well and can select details that best characterize it. Write a short essay describing a place you know well. Concentrate on a few specific details. Try to conclude your essay by explaining how your subject is special in some way.

For over fifty years, E. (Elwyn) B. (Brooks) White (1899–1985) entertained and informed readers with his essays, many of which first appeared in *The New Yorker* magazine. One of the pleasures of reading essays comes from discovering something about another personality. E. B. White's readers came to know him through his essays as a person of wisdom and abiding good humor. White had the unusual distinction of excelling in two literary areas. He was also the E. B. White who wrote the famous children's classics *Stuart Little* and *Charlotte's Web*.

In 1936 White wrote this essay about the Model T Ford. For almost three decades the immensely popular, practical, and unpredictable Model T had played a major role in American life. Now it was about to vanish from American roads and White wished to bid it a warm and thoughtful farewell. In the clear, crisp, and graceful style for which he is known, White re-creates the Model T and an earlier America it helped to shape.

Farewell, My Lovely!

Lee Strout White°

(An aging male kisses an old flame goodbye, circa 1936)

I see by the new Sears Roebuck catalogue that it is still possible to buy an axle for a 1909 Model T Ford, but I am not deceived. The great days have faded, the end is in sight. Only one page in the current catalogue is devoted to parts and accessories for the Model T; yet everyone remembers springtimes when the Ford gadget section was larger than men's clothing, almost as large as household furnishings. The last Model T was built in 1927, and the car is fading from what scholars call the American scene — which is an understatement, because to a few million people who grew up with it, the old Ford practically *was* the American scene.

It was the miracle God had wrought. And it was patently the sort of thing that could only happen once. Mechanically uncanny, it was like nothing that had ever come to the world

---

°This essay originally appeared in *The New Yorker* over the pseudonym Lee Strout White. It was suggested by a manuscript submitted to the magazine by Richard Lee Strout and was written by E. B. White. Reprinted by permission. Copr. © 1936, 1964 The New Yorker Magazine, Inc.; published in book form by G. P. Putnam under the title "Farewell to Model T" in 1936. Reprinted under its original title in *Essays of E. B. White*, Harper & Row, 1977.

Model T about to enter a covered bridge.

Model T Sedan, 1915-1916, price $750.00

Family outing, 1914, in a Model T.

Home demonstration agent with her Model T, after 1914.

Tinkering with the Model T's

before. Flourishing industries rose and fell with it. As a vehicle, it was hard-working, commonplace, heroic; and it often seemed to transmit those qualities to the persons who rode in it. My own generation identifies it with Youth, with its gaudy, irretrievable excitements; before it fades into the mist, I would like to pay it the tribute of the sigh that is not a sob, and set down random entries in a shape somewhat less cumbersome than a Sears Roebuck catalogue.

The Model T was distinguished from all other makes of cars by the fact that its transmission was of a type known as planetary—which was half metaphysics,[1] half sheer friction. Engineers accepted the word *planetary* in its epicyclic[2] sense, but I was always conscious that it also meant "wandering," "erratic." Because of the peculiar nature of this planetary element, there was always, in Model T, a certain dull rapport between engine and wheels, and even when the car was in a state known as neutral, it trembled with a deep imperative and tended to inch forward. There was never a moment when the bands[3] were not faintly egging the machine on. In this respect it was like a horse, rolling the bit on its tongue, and country people brought to it the same technique they used with draft animals.[4]

Its most remarkable quality was its rate of acceleration. In its palmy days the Model T could take off faster than anything on the road. The reason was simple. To get under way, you simply hooked the third finger of the right hand around a lever on the steering column, pulled down hard, and shoved your left foot forcibly against the low-speed pedal. These were simple, positive motions; the car responded by lunging forward with a roar. After a few seconds of this turmoil, you took your toe off the pedal, eased up a mite on the throttle, and the car, possessed of only two forward speeds, catapulted directly into high with a series of ugly jerks and was off on its glorious errand. The abruptness of this departure was never equaled in other cars of the period. The human leg was (and still is) incapable of letting in a clutch[5] with anything like the forthright abandon that used to send Model T on its way. Letting in a clutch is a negative, hesitant motion, depending on delicate nervous control; pushing down the Ford pedal was a simple, country motion—an expansive act, which came as natural as kicking an old door to make it budge.

The driver of the old Model T was a man enthroned. The car, with top up, stood seven feet high. The driver sat on top of the gas tank, brooding it with his own body. When he wanted gasoline, he alighted, along with everything else in the front seat; the seat was pulled off, the metal cap unscrewed, and a wooden stick thrust down to sound the liquid in the well. There were always a couple of these sounding sticks kicking around in the ratty subcushion regions of a flivver.[6] Refueling was more of a social function then, because the driver had to unbend, whether he wanted to or not. Directly in front of the driver was the windshield—high, uncompromisingly erect. Nobody talked about

---

1. **metaphysics:** a branch of highly speculative philosophy; popularly, any deep or mysterious reasoning.
2. **epicyclic** (ep′ə-sī′klĭk): based on a geometric principle involving rotating circles, adopted for use in simple transmissions.
3. **bands:** belts that drive the wheels.
4. **draft animals:** work animals.

5. **clutch:** a mechanical device in an automobile for engaging and disengaging the engine.
6. **flivver:** slang for a small, cheap, usually old car.

air resistance, and the four cylinders pushed the car through the atmosphere with a simple disregard of physical law.

There was this about a Model T: the purchaser never regarded his purchase as a complete, finished product. When you bought a Ford, you figured you had a start—a vibrant, spirited framework to which could be screwed an almost limitless assortment of decorative and functional hardware. Driving away from the agency, hugging the new wheel between your knees, you were already full of creative worry. A Ford was born naked as a baby, and a flourishing industry grew up out of correcting its rare deficiencies and combating its fascinating diseases. Those were the great days of lily-painting. I have been looking at some old Sears Roebuck catalogues, and they bring everything back so clear.

First you bought a Ruby Safety Reflector for the rear, so that your posterior would glow in another's car's brilliance. Then you invested thirty-nine cents in some radiator Moto Wings, a popular ornament which gave the Pegasus[7] touch to the machine and did something godlike to the owner. For nine cents you bought a fan-belt guide to keep the belt from slipping off the pulley.

You bought a radiator compound to stop leaks. This was as much a part of everybody's equipment as aspirin tablets are of a medicine cabinet. You bought special oil to prevent chattering, a clamp-on dash light, a patching outfit, a toolbox which you bolted to the running board, a sun visor, a steering-column brace to keep the column rigid, and a set of emergency containers for gas, oil, and water— three thin, disklike cans which reposed in a case on the running board during long, impor-

tant journeys—red for gas, gray for water, green for oil. It was only a beginning. After the car was about a year old, steps were taken to check the alarming disintegration. (Model T was full of tumors, but they were benign.) A set of antirattlers (ninety-eight cents) was a popular panacea. You hooked them onto the gas and spark rods, to the brake pull rod, and to the steering-rod connections. Hood silencers, of black rubber, were applied to the fluttering hood. Shock absorbers and snubbers gave "complete relaxation." Some people bought rubber pedal pads, to fit over the standard metal pedals. (I didn't like these, I remember.) Persons of a suspicious or pugnacious turn of mind bought a rear-view mirror; but most Model T owners weren't worried by what was coming from behind because they would soon enough see it out in front. They rode in a state of cheerful catalepsy.[8] Quite a large mutinous clique among Ford owners went over to a foot accelerator (you could buy one and screw it to the floorboard), but there was a certain madness in these people, because the Model T, just as she stood, had a choice of three foot pedals to push, and there were plenty of moments when both feet were occupied in the routine performance of duty and when the only way to speed up the engine was with the hand throttle.

Gadget bred gadget. Owners not only bought ready-made gadgets, they invented gadgets to meet special needs. I myself drove my car directly from the agency to the blacksmith's, and had the smith affix two enormous iron brackets to the port running board to support an army trunk.

People who owned closed models builded

---

7. **Pegasus:** winged horse of Greek mythology.

8. **catalepsy:** condition in which feeling and consciousness are temporarily lost and the muscles become rigid.

along different lines: they bought ball-grip handles for opening doors, window anti-rattlers, and delux flower vases of the cut-glass antisplash type. People with delicate sensibilities garnished their car with a device called the Donna Lee Automobile Dissemi-nator—a porous vase guaranteed, according to Sears, to fill the car with a "faint clean odor of lavender." The gap between open cars and closed cars was not as great then as it is now: for $11.95, Sears Roebuck converted your touring car into a sedan and you went forth re-newed. One agreeable quality of the old Fords was that they had no bumpers, and their fend-ers softened and wilted with the years and permitted the driver to squeeze in and out of tight places.

Tires were 30 × 3½, cost about $12, and punctured readily. Everybody carried a Jiffy patching set, with nutmeg grater to roughen the tube before the goo was spread on. Every-body was capable of putting on a patch, ex-pected to have to, and did have to.

During my association with Model T's, self-starters were not a prevalent accessory. They were expensive and under suspicion. Your car came equipped with a serviceable crank, and the first thing you learned was how to Get Results. It was a special trick, and until you learned it (usually from another Ford owner, but sometimes by a period of ap-palling experimentation) you might as well have been winding up an awning. The trick was to leave the ignition switch off, proceed to the animal's head, pull the choke[9] (which was a little wire protruding through the radia-tor) and give the crank two or three noncha-lant upward lifts. Then, whistling as though thinking about something else, you would

saunter back to the driver's cabin, turn the ig-nition on, return to the crank, and this time, catching it on the down stroke, give it a quick spin with plenty of that. If this procedure was followed, the engine almost always responded —first with a few scattered explosions, then with a tumultuous gunfire, which you checked by racing around to the driver's seat and retarding the throttle. Often, if the emergency brake hadn't been pulled all the way back, the car advanced on you the instant the first explosion occurred and you would hold it back by leaning your weight against it. I can still feel my old Ford nuzzling me at the curb, as though looking for an apple in my pocket.

In zero weather, ordinary cranking became an impossibility, except for giants. The oil thickened, and it became necessary to jack up the rear wheels, which, for some planetary reason, eased the throw.

The lore and legend that governed the Ford were boundless. Owners had their own theories about everything; they discussed mu-tual problems in that wise, infinitely re-sourceful way old women discuss rheuma-tism. Exact knowledge was pretty scarce, and often proved less effective than superstition. Dropping a camphor ball into the gas tank was a popular expedient; it seemed to have a tonic effect on both man and machine. There wasn't much to base exact knowledge on. The Ford driver flew blind. He didn't know the temperature of his engine, the speed of his car, the amount of his fuel, or the pressure of his oil (the old Ford lubricated itself by what was amiably described as the "splash sys-tem"). A speedometer cost money and was an extra, like a windshield wiper. The dashboard of the early models was bare save for an igni-tion key; later models, grown effete, boasted an ammeter which pulsated alarmingly with

---

9. **choke:** the valve that cuts off air to the carburetor, providing a richer mixture of gasoline for the engine.

the throbbing of the car. Under the dash was a box of coils, with vibrators which you adjusted, or thought you adjusted. Whatever the driver learned of his motor, he learned not through instruments but through sudden developments. I remember that the timer was one of the vital organs about which there was ample doctrine. When everything else had been checked, you "had a look" at the timer. It was an extravagantly odd little device, simple in construction, mysterious in function. It contained a roller, held by a spring, and there were four contact points on the inside of the case against which, many people believed, the roller rolled. I have had a timer apart on a sick Ford many times. But I never really knew what I was up to—I was just showing off before God. There were almost as many schools of thought as there were timers. Some people, when things went wrong, just clenched their teeth and gave the timer a smart crack with a wrench. Other people opened it up and blew on it. There was a school that held that the timer needed large amounts of oil; they fixed it by frequent baptism. And there was a school that was positive it was meant to run dry as a bone; these people were continually taking it off and wiping it. I remember once spitting into a timer; not in anger, but in a spirit of research. You see, the Model T driver moved in the realm of metaphysics. He believed his car could be hexed.

One reason the Ford anatomy was never reduced to an exact science was that, having "fixed" it, the owner couldn't honestly claim that the treatment had brought about the cure. There were too many authenticated cases of Fords fixing themselves—restored naturally to health after a short rest. Farmers soon discovered this, and it fitted nicely with their draft-horse philosophy: "Let 'er cool off and she'll snap into it again."

A Ford owner had Number One Bearing[10] constantly in mind. This bearing, being at the front end of the motor, was the one that always burned out, because the oil didn't reach it when the car was climbing hills. (That's what I was always told, anyway.) The oil used to recede and leave Number One dry as a clam flat; you had to watch that bearing like a hawk. It was like a weak heart—you could hear it start knocking, and that was when you stopped to let her cool off. Try as you would to keep the oil supply right, in the end Number One always went out. "Number One Bearing burned out on me and I had to have her replaced," you would say, wisely; and your companions always had a lot to tell about how to protect and pamper Number One to keep her alive.

Sprinkled not too liberally among the millions of amateur witch doctors who drove Fords and applied their own abominable cures were the heaven-sent mechanics who could really make the car talk. These professionals turned up in undreamed-of spots. One time, on the banks of the Columbia River in Washington, I heard the rear end[11] go out of my Model T when I was trying to whip it up a steep incline onto the deck of a ferry. Something snapped; the car slid backward into the mud. It seemed to me like the end of the trail. But the captain of the ferry, observing the withered remnant, spoke up.

"What's got her?" he asked.

"I guess it's the rear end," I replied, listlessly. The captain leaned over the rail and stared. Then I saw that there was a hunger in his eyes that set him off from other men.

"Tell you what," he said, carelessly, trying

---

10. **Bearing:** any part of a machine on which another part revolves or slides.
11. **rear end:** set of gears that is part of the rear axle; also known as the differential.

to cover up his eagerness, "Let's pull her up onto the boat, and I'll help you fix her while we're going back and forth on the river."

We did just this. All that day I plied between the towns of Pasco and Kennewick, while the skipper (who had once worked in a Ford garage) directed the amazing work of resetting the bones of my car.

Springtime in the heyday of the Model T was a delirious season. Owning a car was still a major excitement, roads were still wonderful and bad. The Fords were obviously conceived in madness: any car which was capable of going from forward into reverse without any perceptible mechanical hiatus[12] was bound to be a mighty challenging thing to the human imagination. Boys used to veer them off the highway into a level pasture and run wild with them, as though they were cutting up with a girl. Most everybody used the reverse pedal quite as much as the regular foot brake — it distributed the wear over the bands and wore them all down evenly. That was the big trick, to wear all the bands down evenly, so that the final chattering would be total and the whole unit scream for renewal.

The days were golden, the nights were dim and strange. I still recall with trembling those loud, nocturnal crises when you drew up to a signpost and raced the engine so the lights would be bright enough to read destinations by. I have never been really planetary since. I suppose it's time to say goodbye. Farewell, my lovely!

---

12. **hiatus** (hī-ā′təs): pause.

FOR STUDY AND DISCUSSION

1. E. B. White characterizes the Model T as "hard-working, commonplace, heroic," much like the horse, which, for many people, it replaced. Where in the essay does White describe the Model T as if it were a horse?

2. Another way that White characterizes the Model T and expresses his affection for it is by personifying it—by describing the car as if it were a person. For example, White says "A Ford was born naked as a baby . . . ." What human qualities does White give to a faulty Number One Bearing (page 197)? To his broken-down Model T (page 198)? How does White personify the Model T in his title and subtitle?

3. White admires the Model T for its metaphysical qualities—mysterious qualities that go beyond predictable physical reality. What were some of the mysteries that the Ford owner had to deal with?

4. At the beginning of the essay, White says that his generation identifies the Model T with youth and excitement. How does White illustrate the vanished era of his youth in the last two paragraphs? What is his tone in these paragraphs?

METAPHORS

E. B. White's metaphors make his descriptions especially imaginative and at times add humor to the essay. White uses a metaphor when he says of the Model T: "before it fades into the mist, I would like to pay it the tribute of the sigh that is not a sob. . . ." Literally, he is saying that the car is about to be lost in fog. But White means, of course, that the car is about to vanish from the American scene. The metaphor is effective because it puts a humorous picture in our minds. White also creates the following metaphorical descriptions of the Model T:

> The driver of the old Model T was *a man enthroned.*

> . . . a flourishing industry grew up out of correcting its rare deficiencies and combating its fascinating *diseases.*

> Model T was *full of tumors,* but they were benign.

> The Ford driver *flew blind.*

> I have had a timer apart on a *sick Ford* many times.

> There was a school that held that the timer needed large amounts of oil; they fixed it by frequent *baptism.*

What does each statement say literally? What is White really saying? Which of these metaphors show that White looks on the Model T as if it were a person?

FOR COMPOSITION

Writing a Personal Essay
1. Americans are fascinated by mechanical wonders. Write a brief essay describing some other invention that has captured people's imaginations the way the Model T did. Tell if this invention gave rise to accessories and if any lore or legends grew up around it.

2. E. B. White's essay is an affectionate description of a vanished part of his youth. In a short essay, describe something from your own past that is no longer a part of your life. Tell what made the now-vanished object important to your generation.

A journalist and artist, Tom Wolfe (1931–   ) has been a reporter and writer for *New York* magazine and other periodicals. Wolfe is interested in the American scene: the way Americans think and feel about themselves, the sources of American social values, the different worlds and perceptions of American youths and adults. Wolfe is known as much for his lively style as for the content of his social criticism. His freewheeling use of language is shown in the title of the book this essay comes from: *The Kandy-Kolored Tangerine Flake Streamline Baby.* The title refers to a car that has been personally customized.

In this description of the demolition derby, Wolfe is concerned with a subculture of American society. He invites the reader to make a judgment with him about the values of participants and spectators. This essay is to be enjoyed for Wolfe's keen observations and acute ear for language. In recalling the sights and sounds of the derby, Wolfe evokes the volatile world of the early 1960's.

Clean Fun at Riverhead

Tom Wolfe

The inspiration for the demolition derby came to Lawrence Mendelsohn one night in 1958 when he was nothing but a spareribbed twenty-eight-year-old stock-car driver halfway through his tenth lap around the Islip, L.I., Speedway and taking a curve too wide. A lubbery young man with a Chicago boxcar haircut came up on the inside in a 1949 Ford and caromed him twelve rows up into the grandstand, but Lawrence Mendelsohn and his entire car did not hit one spectator.

"That was what got me," he said. "I remember I was hanging upside down from my seat belt like a side of Jersey bacon and wondering why no one was sitting where I hit. 'Lousy promotion,' I said to myself.

"Not only that, but everybody who *was* in the stands forgot about the race and came running over to look at me gift-wrapped upside down in a fresh pile of junk."

At that moment occurred the transformation of Lawrence Mendelsohn, racing driver, into Lawrence Mendelsohn, promoter, and, a few transactions later, owner of the Islip Speedway, where he kept seeing more of this same underside of stock-car racing that everyone in the industry avoids putting into words. Namely, that for every purist who comes to see the fine points of the race, such as who is going to win, there are probably five waiting for the wrecks to which stock-car racing is so gloriously prone.

The pack will be going into a curve when suddenly two cars, three cars, four cars tangle, spinning and splattering all over each other and the retaining walls, upside down, right side up, inside out and in pieces, with the seams bursting open and disks, rods, wires, and gasoline spewing out and yards of sheet metal shearing off like Reynolds Wrap and crumpling into the most baroque shapes, after which an ash-blue smoke starts seeping up from the ruins and a thrill begins to spread over the stands like Newburg sauce.[1]

So why put up with the monotony between crashes?

Such, in brief, is the early history of what is culturally the most important sport ever originated in the United States, a sport that ranks with the gladiatorial games of Rome as a piece of national symbolism. Lawrence Mendelsohn had a vision of an automobile sport that would be all crashes. Not two cars, not three cars, not four cars, but 100 cars would be out in an arena doing nothing but smashing each other into shrapnel. The car that outrammed and outdodged all the rest, the last car that could still move amid the smoking heap, would take the prize money.

So at 8:15 at night at the Riverhead Raceway, just west of Riverhead, L.I., on Route 25, amid the quaint tranquillity of the duck and turkey farm flatlands of eastern Long Island, Lawrence Mendelsohn stood up on the back of a flat truck in his red neon warm-up jacket and lectured his 100 drivers on the rules and niceties of the new game, the "demolition derby." And so at 8:30 the first 25 cars moved out onto the raceway's quarter-mile stock-car track. There was not enough room for 100 cars to mangle each other. Lawrence Mendelsohn's dream would require four heats. Now the 25 cars were placed at intervals all about the circumference of the track, making flatulent revving noises, all headed not around the track but toward a point in the center of the infield.

Then the entire crowd, about 4,000, started chanting a countdown, "Ten, nine, eight, seven, six, five, four, three, two," but it was impossible to hear the rest, because right after "two" half the crowd went into a strange whinnying wail. The starter's flag went up, and the 25 cars took off, roaring into second gear with no mufflers, all headed toward that same point in the center of the infield, converging nose on nose.

The effect was exactly what one expects that many simultaneous crashes to produce: the unmistakable tympany of automobiles colliding and cheap-gauge sheet metal buckling; front ends folding together at the same cockeyed angles police photographs of night-time wreck scenes capture so well on grainy paper; smoke pouring from under the hoods and hanging over the infield like a howitzer cloud; a few of the surviving cars lurching eccentrically on bent axles. At last, after four heats, there were only two cars moving through the junk, a 1953 Chrysler and a 1958 Cadillac. In the Chrysler a small fascia[2] of muscles named Spider Ligon, who smoked a cigar while he drove, had the Cadillac cornered up against a guard rail in front of the main grandstand. He dispatched it by swinging around and backing full throttle through the left side of its grille and radiator.

By now the crowd was quite beside itself. Spectators broke through a gate in the retaining screen. Some rushed to Spider Ligon's car, hoisted him to their shoulders and marched off the field, howling. Others clambered over

---

1. **Newburg sauce:** a rich, creamy sauce.

2. **fascia** (făsh′ē-ə): a layer of connective tissue that covers muscles.

the stricken cars of the defeated, enjoying the details of their ruin, and howling. The good, full cry of triumph and annihilation rose from Riverhead Raceway, and the demolition derby was over.

That was the 154th demolition derby in two years. Since Lawrence Mendelsohn staged the first one at Islip Speedway in 1961, they have been held throughout the United States at the rate of one every five days, resulting in the destruction of about 15,000 cars. The figures alone indicate a gluttonous appetite for the sport. Sportswriters, of course, have managed to ignore demolition derbies even more successfully than they have ignored stock-car racing and drag racing. All in

all, the new automobile sports have shown that the sports pages, which on the surface appear to hum with life and earthiness, are at bottom pillars of gentility. This drag racing and demolition derbies and things, well, there are too many kids in it with sideburns, tight Levis, and winkle-picker boots.[3]

Yet the demolition derbies keep growing on word-of-mouth publicity. The "nationals" were held last month at Langhorne, Pa., with 50 cars in the finals, and demolition-derby fans everywhere know that Don McTavish, of Dover, Mass., is the new world's champion.

---

3. **winkle-picker boots:** boots with narrow, sharply pointed toes.

About 1,250,000 spectators have come to the 154 contests held so far. More than 75 percent of the derbies have drawn full houses.

The nature of their appeal is clear enough. Since the onset of the Christian era, i.e., since about A.D. 500, no game has come along to fill the gap left by the abolition of the purest of all sports, gladiatorial combat. As late as A.D. 300 these bloody duels, usually between men but sometimes between women and dwarfs, were enormously popular not only in Rome but throughout the Roman Empire. Since then no game, not even boxing, has successfully acted out the underlying motifs of most sport, that is, aggression and destruction.

Boxing, of course, is an aggressive sport, but one contestant has actually destroyed the other in a relatively small percentage of matches. Other games are progressively more sublimated[4] forms of sport. Often, as in the case of football, they are encrusted with oddments of passive theology and metaphysics[5] to the effect that the real purpose of the game is to foster character, teamwork, stamina, physical fitness, and the ability to "give-and-take."

But not even those wonderful clergymen who pray in behalf of Congress, expressway ribbon-cuttings, urban renewal projects, and testimonial dinners for ethnic aldermen would pray for a demolition derby. The demolition derby is, pure and simple, a form of gladiatorial combat for our times.

As hand-to-hand combat has gradually disappeared from our civilization, even in wartime, and competition has become more and more sophisticated and abstract, Americans have turned to the automobile to satisfy their love of direct aggression. The mild-mannered man who turns into a bear behind the wheel of a car—i.e., who finds in the power of the automobile a vehicle for the release of his inhibitions—is part of American folklore. Among teen-agers the automobile has become the symbol, and in part the physical means, of triumph over family and community restrictions. Seventy-five percent of all car thefts in the United States are by teen-agers out for "joy rides."

The symbolic meaning of the automobile tones down but by no means vanishes in adulthood. Police traffic investigators have long been convinced that far more accidents are purposeful crashes by belligerent drivers than they could ever prove. One of the heroes of the era was the Middle Eastern diplomat who rammed a magazine writer's car from behind in the Kalorama embassy district of Washington two years ago. When the American bellowed out the window at him, he backed up and smashed his car again. When the fellow leaped out of his car to pick a fight, he backed up and smashed his car a third time, then drove off. He was recalled home for having "gone native."

The unabashed, undisguised, quite purposeful sense of destruction of the demolition derby is its unique contribution. The aggression, the battering, the ruination are there to be enjoyed. The crowd at a demolition derby seldom gasps and often laughs. It enjoys the same full-throated participation as Romans at the Colosseum. After each trial or heat at a demolition derby, two drivers go into the finals. One is the driver whose car was still going at the end. The other is the driver the crowd selects from among the 24 vanquished on the basis of his courage, showmanship, or simply the awesomeness of his crashes. The numbers of the cars are read over loudspeakers, and the crowd chooses one with its

---

4. **sublimated:** containing a hidden impulse—usually one that is socially unacceptable.
5. **metaphysics:** a branch of highly speculative philosophy; popularly, any deep or mysterious reasoning.

cheers. By the same token, the crowd may force a driver out of competition if he appears cowardly or merely cunning. This is the sort of driver who drifts around the edge of the battle avoiding crashes with the hope that the other cars will eliminate one another. The umpire waves a yellow flag at him and he must crash into someone within 30 seconds or run the risk of being booed off the field in dishonor and disgrace.

The frank relish of the crowd is nothing, however, compared to the kick the contestants get out of the game. It costs a man an average of $50 to retrieve a car from a junkyard and get it running for a derby. He will only get his money back—$50—for winning a heat. The chance of being smashed up in the madhouse first 30 seconds of a round are so great, even the best of drivers faces long odds in his shot at the $500 first prize. None of that matters to them.

Tommy Fox, who is nineteen, said he entered the demolition derby because, "You know, it's fun. I like it. You know what I mean?" What was fun about it? Tommy Fox had a way of speaking that was much like the early Marlon Brando. Much of what he had to say came from the trapezii,[6] which he rolled quite a bit, and the forehead, which he cocked, and the eyebrows, which he could bring together expressively from time to time. "Well," he said, "you know, like when you hit 'em, and all that. It's fun."

Tommy Fox had a lot of fun in the first heat. Nobody was bashing around quite like he was in his old green Hudson. He did not win, chiefly because he took too many chances, but the crowd voted him into the finals as the best showman.

"I got my brother," said Tommy. "I came in from the side and he didn't even see me."

His brother is Don Fox, thirty-two, who owns the junkyard where they both got their cars. Don likes to hit them, too, only he likes it almost too much. Don drives with such abandon, smashing into the first car he can get a shot at and leaving himself wide open, he does not stand much chance of finishing the first three minutes.

For years now sociologists have been calling upon one another to undertake a serious study of America's "car culture." No small part of it is the way the automobile has, for one very large segment of the population, become the focus of the same sort of quasi-religious dedication as art is currently for another large segment of a higher social order. Tommy Fox is unemployed, Don Fox runs a junkyard, Spider Ligon is a maintenance man for Brookhaven Naval Laboratory, but to categorize them as such is getting no closer to the truth than to have categorized William Faulkner in 1926 as a clerk at Lord & Taylor, although he was.

Tommy Fox, Don Fox, and Spider Ligon are acolytes[7] of the car culture, an often esoteric world of arts and sciences that came into its own after World War II and now has believers of two generations. Charlie Turbush, thirty-five, and his son, Buddy, seventeen, were two more contestants, and by no stretch of the imagination can they be characterized as bizarre figures or cultists of the death wish. As for the dangers of driving in a demolition derby, they are quite real by all physical laws. The drivers are protected only by crash helmets, seat belts, and the fact that all glass, interior handles, knobs, and fixtures have been

---

6. **trapezii** (trā-pē′zē-ī): muscles of the upper back. Rolling them would involve hunching the shoulders.

7. **acolytes** (ăk′ə-līts′): attendants; followers; helpers.

removed. Yet Lawrence Mendelsohn claims that there have been no serious injuries in 154 demolition derbies and now gets his insurance at a rate below that of stock-car racing.

The sport's future may depend in part on word getting around about its relative safety. Already it is beginning to draw contestants here and there from social levels that could give the demolition derby the cachet[8] of respectability. In Eastern derbies so far two doctors and three young men of more than passable connections in Eastern society have entered under whimsical *noms de combat*[9] and emerged neither scarred nor victorious. Bullfighting had to win the same social combat.

All of which brings to mind that fine afternoon when some highborn Roman women were out in Nero's box at the Colosseum watching this Thracian carve an ugly little Samnite up into prime cuts, and one said, darling, she had an inspiration, and Nero, needless to say, was all for it. Thus began the new vogue of Roman socialites fighting as gladiators themselves, for kicks. By the second century A.D. even the Emperor Commodus was out there with a tiger's head as a helmet hacking away at some poor dazed fall guy. He did a lot for the sport. Arenas sprang up all over the empire like shopping-center bowling alleys.

The future of the demolition derby, then, stretches out over the face of America. The sport draws no lines of gender, and post-debs[10] may reach Lawrence Mendelsohn at his office in Deer Park.

---

8. **cachet** (kă-shā'): a sign of official approval.
9. *noms de combat* (nōm' də kŏm'bä): French for "fighting names."
10. **post-debs:** young women who have made their debuts, or entrances into high society.

FOR STUDY AND DISCUSSION

1. Tom Wolfe's essays have made him well known as a social critic. In your opinion, is Wolfe's attitude throughout this essay critical of the demolition derby and of certain aspects of society? Support your answer with quotations from the essay.
2. Does Wolfe intend the title of his essay to be taken seriously, or is the title ironic — that is, does Wolfe say one thing but mean something else? Explain.
3. Wolfe compares the demolition derby to the gladiatorial games of Rome. What similarities does Wolfe see between the derby and the Roman games? The crowd at the Roman games often decided whether the gladiator lived or died. What role does the crowd play in deciding the outcome of the derby?
4. Wolfe calls the derby "the most important sport ever originated in the United States, a sport that ranks with the gladiatorial games of Rome as a piece of national symbolism." Do you agree with this statement, or do you think Wolfe is exaggerating? Are there other places in this essay where you think Wolfe exaggerates to make his points?
5. On page 204 Wolfe mentions America's "car culture." What do you think he means by this? Do you think E. B. White's essay on the Model T (page 192) reflects this "car culture"? Tell why, or why not.

STYLE AND PURPOSE

Tom Wolfe is known for his fast-paced, freewheeling style, which is often characterized by a piling up of metaphors and whatever colloquial vocabulary is suited to his subject. A good example is found in the paragraph beginning "All of which brings to mind" on this page. Wolfe is talking here about the gladiatorial games of Rome, but he describes them in lively, colloquial language: the Thracian "carves up" an opponent into "prime cuts." One woman says "darling." Nero is "all for it." The socialites are fighting "for kicks." The emperor is "hacking away" at some "fall guy." The arenas spring up over the empire "like shopping-center bowling alleys."

Look at the paragraph on page 201 beginning "The pack will be going into a curve." How many sentences are in this fast-moving passage? What strongly visual similes are used here? What verbs create a sense of rapid, often violent action?

A writer as skilled as Wolfe knows how to suit his style to his subject matter. Wolfe's style, for example, would hardly be appropriate in E. B. White's affectionate portrait of the Model T, nor in Harry Crews's thoughtful essay on hawks. Look at how the founder of the derby speaks (page 200). How does Wolfe's style match the speech of Lawrence Mendelsohn?

Underneath Wolfe's seemingly casual style is a serious intent. Wolfe always tries to answer the question: "What does it all mean?" What meaning do you think he sees in the demolition derby?

FOR COMPOSITION

Supporting an Opinion

Wolfe's essay definitely presents a point of view: aggression and destruction are basic to the demolition derby and to most sports. Write a brief essay in which you explain whether you agree or disagree with Wolfe's point of view. Cite precisely which statements you agree with or disagree with. Explain your own position clearly. Then cite facts to support your views.

Biography
and
Autobiography

Biography and autobiography try to capture the qualities of character that define a person's life. All sorts of people have been the subjects of biography and autobiography—from men and women who have changed the world, to ordinary people whose lives may be like our own. The approaches to biography and autobiography are many. Some biographers present the facts and documents objectively and let us interpret for ourselves the life and personality of the individual. Most biographers, however, and all autobiographers, make subjective connections for us. These writers interpret and sort out the evidence themselves, as Hermann Hagedorn does here in his portrait of Socrates (page 274).

Biographical and autobiographical articles may be organized around one or two major episodes to which other experiences and impressions are linked, or they may present a series of events and episodes without making any single one the focus of interest. Writers may use one part of a life to say something about the whole, or they may give us an overview, a sense of a life from the beginning to the end, as Van Wyck Brooks does here in his portrait of Emily Dickinson (page 242).

Biography and autobiography are like history: in them we discover a point of view, a philosophy of people and life. This is one important interest of biography—to understand the meaning of human life and perhaps the secret of success and failure in living.

Dylan Thomas (1914–1953) was born in Swansea, a seaport town in southern Wales. Here he spent a happy childhood, and here, at the local grammar school, he received all his formal education. Upon leaving school, he worked for a while as a newspaper reporter, but soon turned to writing poetry full time. The brilliance of Thomas' poetry, which is full of vigor and unusual imagery, was recognized with the publication of his first book, which appeared when he was only twenty. His prose, however, was not widely read until after his death in New York at the age of thirty-nine. Thomas' reputation had grown enormously through his poetry readings for British and American audiences. By the time of his death, he had become a celebrated figure. Many consider him one of the greatest poets of his age.

"A Child's Christmas in Wales" quickly reveals Thomas' poetic gift and bears out the comment of the American poet Conrad Aiken, who referred to Thomas as "a born language-lover and language-juggler" with "a genuine and outrageous gift of gab." This autobiographical sketch, fantastic and realistic at the same time, is full of the joy of living.

© Rollie McKenna.

A Child's Christmas in Wales

Dylan Thomas

One Christmas was so much like another, in those years around the sea-town corner now and out of all sound except the distant speaking of the voices I sometimes hear a moment before sleep, that I can never remember whether it snowed for six days and six nights when I was twelve or whether it snowed for twelve days and twelve nights when I was six. All the Christmases roll down toward the two-tongued sea, like a cold and headlong moon bundling down the sky that was our street; and they stop at the rim of the ice-edged, fish-freezing waves, and I plunge my hands in the snow and bring out whatever I can find. In goes my hand into that wool-white bell-tongued ball of holidays resting at the rim of the carol-singing sea, and out come Mrs. Prothero and the firemen.

It was on the afternoon of the day of Christmas Eve, and I was in Mrs. Prothero's garden, waiting for cats, with her son Jim. It was snowing. It was always snowing at Christmas. December, in my memory, is white as Lapland, though there were no reindeer. But there were cats. Patient, cold, and callous, our hands wrapped in socks, we waited to snowball the cats. Sleek and long as jaguars and horrible-whiskered, spitting and snarling, they would slink and sidle over the white back-garden walls, and the lynx-eyed hunters, Jim and I, fur-capped and moccasined trappers from Hudson Bay, off Mumbles Road, would hurl our deadly snowballs at the green of their eyes. The wise cats never appeared. We were so still, Eskimo-footed arctic marksmen in the muffling silence of the eternal snows—eternal, ever since Wednesday—that we never heard Mrs. Prothero's first cry from her igloo at the bottom of the garden. Or, if we heard it at all, it was, to us, like the far-off challenge of our enemy and prey, the neighbor's polar cat. But soon the voice grew louder.

"Fire!" cried Mrs. Prothero, and she beat the dinner gong.

And we ran down the garden, with the snowballs in our arms, toward the house; and smoke, indeed, was pouring out of the dining room, and the gong was bombilating,[1] and Mrs. Prothero was announcing ruin like a town crier in Pompeii.[2] This was better than all the cats in Wales standing on the wall in a row. We bounded into the house, laden with snowballs, and stopped at the open door of the smoke-filled room. Something was burning all right; perhaps it was Mr. Prothero, who always slept there after midday dinner with a newspaper over his face. But he was standing in the middle of the room, saying, "A fine Christmas!" and smacking at the smoke with a slipper.

---

1. **bombilating:** This word means "buzzing" or "humming," but Thomas has invented a new meaning for it, something like "clanging."
2. **Pompeii** (pŏm-pā′): an ancient Italian city buried by an eruption of Mount Vesuvius in A.D. 79.

"Call the fire brigade," cried Mrs. Prothero as she beat the gong.

"They won't be there," said Mr. Prothero, "it's Christmas."

There was no fire to be seen, only clouds of smoke and Mr. Prothero standing in the middle of them, waving his slipper as though he were conducting.

"Do something," he said.

And we threw all our snowballs into the smoke—I think we missed Mr. Prothero—and ran out of the house to the telephone box.

"Let's call the police as well," Jim said.

"And the ambulance."

"And Ernie Jenkins, he likes fires."

But we only called the fire brigade, and soon the fire engine came and three tall men in helmets brought a hose into the house and Mr. Prothero got out just in time before they turned it on. Nobody could have had a noisier Christmas Eve. And when the firemen turned off the hose and were standing in the wet, smoky room, Jim's aunt, Miss Prothero, came downstairs and peered in at them. Jim and I waited, very quietly, to hear what she would say to them. She said the right thing, always. She looked at the three tall firemen in their shining helmets, standing among the smoke and cinders and dissolving snowballs, and she said: "Would you like anything to read?"

Years and years and years ago, when I was a boy, when there were wolves in Wales, and birds the color of red-flannel petticoats whisked past the harp-shaped hills, when we sang and wallowed all night and day in caves that smelt like Sunday afternoons in damp front farmhouse parlors, and we chased, with the jawbones of deacons, the English and the bears, before the motor car, before the wheel, before the duchess-faced horse, when we rode the daft and happy hills bareback, it snowed and it snowed. But here a small boy says: "It snowed last year, too. I made a snowman and

© Rollie McKenna.

Dylan Thomas' son Colm in Laugharne, Wales, 1953.

my brother knocked it down and I knocked my brother down and then we had tea."

"But that was not the same snow," I say. "Our snow was not only shaken from whitewash buckets down the sky, it came shawling[3] out of the ground and swam and drifted out of the arms and hands and bodies of the trees; snow grew overnight on the roofs of the houses like a pure and grandfather moss, mi-

---

3. **shawling:** a word that Thomas invented. The snow acts like a shawl, blanketing the ground.

nutely white-ivied the walls and settled on the postman, opening the gate, like a dumb, numb thunderstorm of white, torn Christmas cards."

"Were there postmen then, too?"

"With sprinkling eyes and wind-cherried noses, on spread, frozen feet they crunched up to the doors and mittened on them manfully. But all that the children could hear was a ringing of bells."

"You mean that the postman went rat-a-tat-tat and the doors rang?"

"I mean that the bells that the children could hear were inside them."

"I only hear thunder sometimes, never bells."

"There were church bells, too."

"Inside them?"

"No, no, no, in the bat-black, snow-white belfries, tugged by bishops and storks. And they rang their tidings over the bandaged town, over the frozen foam of the powder and ice-cream hills, over the crackling sea. It seemed that all the churches boomed for joy under my window; and the weathercocks crew for Christmas, on our fence."

"Get back to the postmen."

"They were just ordinary postmen, fond of walking and dogs and Christmas and the snow. They knocked on the doors with blue knuckles. . . ."

"Ours has got a black knocker. . . ."

"And then they stood on the white Welcome mat in the little, drifted porches and huffed and puffed, making ghosts with their breath, and jogged from foot to foot like small boys wanting to go out."

"And then the Presents?"

"And then the Presents, after the Christmas box. And the cold postman, with a rose on his button nose, tingled down the tea-tray-slithered run of the chilly glinting hill. He went in his icebound boots like a man on fishmonger's slabs. He wagged his bag like a frozen camel's hump, dizzily turned the corner on one foot, and was gone."

"Get back to the Presents."

"There were the Useful Presents: engulfing mufflers of the old coach days, and mittens made for giant sloths; zebra scarfs of a substance like silky gum that could be tug-o'-warred down to the galoshes; blinding tam-o'-shanters like patchwork tea cozies[4] and bunny-suited busbies[5] and balaclavas[6] for victims of headshrinking tribes; from aunts who always wore wool next to the skin there were mustached and rasping vests that made you wonder why the aunts had any skin left at all; and once I had a little crocheted nose bag from an aunt now, alas, no longer whinnying with us. And pictureless books in which small boys, though warned with quotations not to, *would* skate on Farmer Giles's pond and did and drowned; and books that told me everything about the wasp, except why."

"Go on to the Useless Presents."

"Bags of moist and many-colored jelly babies and a folded flag and a false nose and a tram conductor's cap and a machine that punched tickets and rang a bell; never a catapult;[7] once, by mistake that no one could explain, a little hatchet; and a celluloid duck that made, when you pressed it, a most unducklike sound, a mewing moo that an ambitious cat might make who wished to be a cow; and a painting book in which I could make the grass, the trees, the sea and the animals any color I pleased, and still the dazzling sky-blue sheep are grazing in the red field under the rainbow-billed and pea-green birds. Hard-

---

4. **tea cozies:** padded covers used to keep teapots hot.
5. **busbies:** tall fur hats.
6. **balaclavas:** knitted caps that cover the head and most of the face.
7. **catapult:** a toy model of an ancient weapon that hurls stones or toy spears.

Estuary of the River Taf, Wales, a view from Thomas' study.

boileds, toffee, fudge and all-sorts, crunches, cracknels, humbugs, glaciers, marzipan, and butterwelsh[8] for the Welsh. And troops of bright tin soldiers who, if they could not fight, could always run. And Snakes-and-Families and Happy Ladders. And Easy Hobbi-Games for Little Engineers, complete with instructions. Oh, easy for Leonardo![9] And a whistle to make the dogs bark to wake up the old man next door to make him beat on the wall with his stick to shake our picture off the wall. And a packet of cigarettes: you put one in your mouth and you stood at the corner of the street and you waited for hours, in vain, for an old lady to scold you for smoking a cigarette, and then with a smirk you ate it. And then it was breakfast under the balloons.''

"Were there uncles, like in our house?"

"There are always uncles at Christmas. The same uncles. And on Christmas mornings, with dog-disturbing whistle and sugar fags,[10] I would scour the swatched town for the news of the little world, and find always a dead bird by the white post office or by the deserted swings; perhaps a robin, all but one of his fires out. Men and women wading or scooping back from chapel, with taproom noses[11] and wind-bussed cheeks, all albinos, huddled their stiff black jarring feathers against the irreligious snow. Mistletoe hung from the gas brackets in all the front parlors; there was sherry and walnuts and bottled beer and crackers by the dessertspoons; and cats in their furabouts watched the fires; and the

8. **Hard-boileds . . . butterwelsh:** kinds of candy.
9. **Leonardo:** Leonardo da Vinci, the famous fifteenth-century Italian painter, architect, and sculptor, who was also an engineer.

10. **sugar fags:** candy cigarettes.
11. **taproom noses:** A taproom is a barroom. Thomas means that their noses were red as if they'd been drinking too much.

© Rollie McKenna.

high-heaped fire spat, all ready for the chestnuts and the mulling pokers. Some few large men sat in the front parlors, without their collars, uncles almost certainly, trying their new cigars, holding them out judiciously at arms' length, returning them to their mouths, coughing, then holding them out again as though waiting for the explosion; and some few small aunts, not wanted in the kitchen, nor anywhere else for that matter, sat on the very edges of their chairs, poised and brittle, afraid to break, like faded cups and saucers."

Not many those mornings trod the piling streets: an old man always, fawn-bowlered,[12] yellow-gloved and, at this time of year, with spats of snow, would take his constitutional to the white bowling green and back, as he would take it wet or fire on Christmas Day or Doomsday; sometimes two hale young men, with big pipes blazing, no overcoats and wind-blown scarfs, would trudge, unspeaking, down to the forlorn sea, to work up an appetite, to blow away the fumes, who knows, to walk into the waves until nothing of them was left but the two curling smoke clouds of their inextinguishable briars.[13] Then I would be slapdashing home, the gravy smell of the dinners of others, the bird smell, the brandy, the pudding and mince, coiling up to my nostrils, when out of a snow-clogged side lane would come a boy the spit of myself, with a pink-tipped cigarette and the violet past of a black eye, cocky as a bullfinch, leering all to himself. I hated him on sight and sound, and would be about to put my dog whistle to my lips and blow him off the face of Christmas

---

12. **fawn-bowlered:** wearing a bowler, or derby hat, of fawn color—a pale, yellowish brown.

13. **briars:** tobacco pipes made of briarroot.

A Child's Christmas in Wales 213

when suddenly he, with a violet wink, put *his* whistle to *his* lips and blew so stridently, so high, so exquisitely loud that gobbling faces, their cheeks bulged with goose, would press against their tinseled windows, the whole length of the white echoing street. For dinner we had turkey and blazing pudding, and after dinner the uncles sat in front of the fire, loosened all buttons, put their large moist hands over their watch chains, groaned a little, and slept. Mothers, aunts, and sisters scuttled to and fro, bearing tureens. Auntie Bessie, who had already been frightened, twice, by a clockwork mouse, whimpered at the sideboard and had some elderberry wine. The dog was sick. Auntie Dosie had to have three aspirins, but Auntie Hannah, who liked port,[14] stood in the middle of the snowbound backyard, singing like a big-bosomed thrush. I would blow up balloons to see how big they would blow up to; and, when they burst, which they all did, the uncles jumped and rumbled. In the rich and heavy afternoon, the uncles breathing like dolphins and the snow descending, I would sit among festoons and Chinese lanterns and nibble dates and try to make a model man-o'-war, following the Instructions for Little Engineers, and produce what might be mistaken for a seagoing tramcar. Or I would go out, my bright new boots squeaking, into the white world, onto the seaward hill, to call on Jim and Dan and Jack and to pad through the still streets, leaving huge deep footprints on the hidden pavements.

"I bet people will think there's been hippos."

"What would you do if you saw a hippo coming down our street?"

"I'd go like this, bang! I'd throw him over the railings and roll him down the hill and then I'd tickle him under the ear and he'd wag his tail."

"What would you do if you saw *two* hippos?"

Iron-flanked and bellowing he-hippos clanked and battered through the scudding snow toward us as we passed Mr. Daniel's house.

"Let's post Mr. Daniel a snowball through his letter box."

"Let's write things in the snow."

"Let's write, 'Mr. Daniel looks like a spaniel' all over his lawn."

Or we walked on the white shore. "Can the fishes see it's snowing?"

The silent one-clouded heavens drifted on to the sea. Now we were snow-blind travelers lost on the north hills, and vast dewlapped dogs, with flasks round their necks, ambled and shambled up to us, baying "Excelsior."[15] We returned home through the poor streets where only a few children fumbled with bare red fingers in the wheel-rutted snow and cat-called after us, their voices fading away, as we trudged uphill, into the cries of the dock birds and the hooting of ships out in the whirling bay. And then, at tea the recovered uncles would be jolly; and the ice cake loomed in the center of the table like a marble grave. Auntie Hannah laced her tea with rum, because it was only once a year.

Bring out the tall tales now that we told by the fire as the gaslight bubbled like a diver. Ghosts whooed like owls in the long nights when I dared not look over my shoulder; animals lurked in the cubbyhole under the stairs where the gas meter ticked. And I re-

---

14. **port:** a sweet, dark-red wine, originally made only in Portugal.

15. **"Excelsior"** (ĕk-sĕl′sē-ər): "higher, always upward." The imagined dogs (St. Bernards) are urging them to keep on going.

Street in Laugharne, Wales.   © Rollie McKenna.

One, two, three, and we began to sing, our voices high and seemingly distant in the snow-felted darkness round the house that was occupied by nobody we knew. We stood close together, near the dark door.

"Good King Wenceslas looked out
On the Feast of Stephen . . ."

And then a small, dry voice, like the voice of someone who has not spoken for a long time, joined our singing: a small, dry, eggshell voice from the other side of the door: a small dry voice through the keyhole. And when we stopped running we were outside *our* house; the front room was lovely; balloons floated under the hot-water-bottle-gulping gas; everything was good again and shone over the town.

"Perhaps it was a ghost," Jim said.

"Perhaps it was trolls," Dan said, who was always reading.

"Let's go in and see if there's any jelly left," Jack said. And we did that.

Always on Christmas night there was music. An uncle played the fiddle, a cousin sang "Cherry Ripe," and another uncle sang "Drake's Drum." It was very warm in the little house. Auntie Hannah, who had got on to the parsnip wine, sang a song about Bleeding Hearts and Death, and then another in which she said her heart was like a Bird's Nest; and then everybody laughed again; and then I went to bed. Looking through my bedroom window, out into the moonlight and the unending smoke-colored snow, I could see the lights in the windows of all the other houses on our hill and hear the music rising from them up the long, steadily falling night. I turned the gas down, I got into bed. I said some words to the close and holy darkness, and then I slept.

member that we went singing carols once, when there wasn't the shaving of a moon to light the flying streets. At the end of a long road was a drive that led to a large house, and we stumbled up the darkness of the drive that night, each one of us afraid, each one holding a stone in his hand in case, and all of us too brave to say a word. The wind through the trees made noises as of old and unpleasant and maybe webfooted men wheezing in caves. We reached the black bulk of the house.

"What shall we give them? Hark the Herald?"

"No," Jack said, "Good King Wenceslas. I'll count three."

A Child's Christmas in Wales   215

FOR STUDY AND DISCUSSION

1. An autobiographical essay sometimes tries to give an objective account of the writer's own life, a straightforward report of events and people. Thomas is not interested in objective truth; he wants to evoke the world of the past, to re-create it in concrete detail and image. How does Thomas indicate in the first paragraph that his essay will not be a straightforward, objective account, but rather something very subjective and personal?

2. How does Thomas establish the point of view of a child at the beginning of the essay? What is gained by introducing another child on page 210, who asks the grown man about his childhood?

3. Find two points in the essay where the boy passes from the real world into an imaginary one.

4. Children are often amused by events and behavior that adults miss. What in the adult world does Thomas as a boy find amusing or comic?

5. What are some of the differences between the child's and the adult's Christmas? What in Christmas do child and adult share?

6. Why do you think Thomas calls the darkness "holy" in his last sentence? What does this word tell about Thomas' attitude toward his childhood?

7. What impression do you get of Thomas as a man from the way he tells about Christmas in Wales?

STYLE AND PURPOSE

Thomas is a poet, and like all poets he uses figures of speech, in which one thing is compared to some other, different thing. Figures of speech are not literally true, but they help us to see similarities between things that

© Rollie McKenna.

Thomas in his study, Laugharne, Wales.

seem to be completely different. For example, here is how Thomas describes the ringing of the church bells over the snowy town:

> . . . in the bat-black, snow-white belfries, tugged by bishops and storks. And they rang their tidings over the bandaged town,

over the frozen foam of the powder and ice-cream hills, over the crackling sea. It seemed that all the churches boomed for joy under my window; and the weathercocks crew for Christmas on our fence.

Thomas uses figures of speech in saying that the bells are pulled by bishops "and storks," that the snowy town is "bandaged," that the snowy hills are "powder" and "ice cream," that the icy sea is "crackling," that the churches are booming "for joy" (churches are inanimate objects and cannot feel anything).

Notice how Thomas also creates a musical quality, especially by using alliteration (the repetition of consonant sounds, usually at the beginning of words): "bat-black," "frozen foam," "weathercocks crew for Christmas."

Find the figurative language in the following passages from this essay. Look also for the use of alliteration to create musical effects. How do these passages give you the sense that you are seeing the world through the eyes of an imaginative child?

In goes my hand into that wool-white bell-tongued ball of holidays resting at the rim of the carol-singing sea, and out come Mrs. Prothero and the firemen.

We were so still, Eskimo-footed arctic marksmen in the muffling silence of the eternal snows—eternal, ever since Wednesday—that we never heard Mrs. Prothero's first cry from her igloo at the bottom of the garden.

And then, at tea the recovered uncles would be jolly; and the ice cake loomed in the center of the table like a marble grave.

And then a small, dry voice, like the voice of someone who has not spoken for a long time, joined our singing: a small, dry, egg-shell voice from the other side of the door: a small dry voice through the keyhole.

LANGUAGE AND VOCABULARY

Defining Hyphenated Adjectives

Following an old tradition in English poetry, Thomas frequently creates original and sometimes elaborate hyphenated adjectives. For instance, "fish-freezing waves" is a vivid and original way of saying "waves so cold they would freeze even the fish." Below are more of Thomas' hyphenated adjectives. Locate each one in its context, and write out what you think it means:

horrible-whiskered (page 209)
wind-cherried (page 211)
tea-tray-slithered (page 211)
rainbow-billed (page 211)
dog-disturbing (page 212)
one-clouded (page 214)
snow-felted (page 215)
hot-water-bottle-gulping (page 215)

FOR ORAL RECITATION

Those who have had the pleasure of hearing Dylan Thomas' own recording of "A Child's Christmas in Wales" can never read the essay again without hearing the cadences of Thomas' voice. Select a passage of the essay and prepare it for your own oral reading. Watch for Thomas' chantlike rhythms. Note also where his memories speed up (as in the tongue-twisting "wool-white bell-tongued ball of holidays resting at the rim of the carol-singing sea"), and where they take on a slower pace (as in "and out come Mrs. Prothero and the firemen").

Mark Twain (1835–1910), or—to call him by the name his parents gave him—Samuel Langhorne Clemens, is perhaps America's most widely read writer. He grew up near the Mississippi, a river that dominated the lives of the people who lived along its banks. Twain worked on the river as a young man and wrote about it for years afterward. He took his pen name, Mark Twain, from the cry of the leadsman who measured the depth of the river waters. "By the mark, twain!" indicated a depth of two fathoms. This depth made a river pilot feel comfortable, Clemens once said, which is why he chose Mark Twain for his pen name.

Twain first received popular recognition as a writer in 1869 with the publication of *The Innocents Abroad,* a humorous travelogue based on his experiences as a tourist in Europe, Egypt, and the Near East. After the success of *The Innocents Abroad,* Twain published many more works of fiction and nonfiction, including *Life on the Mississippi, The Adventures of Tom Sawyer,* and his masterpiece, *The Adventures of Huckleberry Finn.* These books depict America in its exuberant youth, and develop themes that are typically American: the small-town childhood; the search for identity; the lure of the frontier; the struggle between freedom and bondage. Twain's fresh humor is also typically American in its irreverence toward stuffiness of all kinds.

The following selection is from *Roughing It* (1872), a collection of humorous anecdotes describing Twain's adventures in the Far West and Hawaii. In this particular adventure, Twain is in the Nevada Territory, in search of silver. Comical as it is, this narrative reflects dreams and values that the young Twain shared with a generation of Americans.

I Find Fool Gold   *Mark Twain*

After leaving the Sink,[1] we traveled along the Humboldt River a little way. People accustomed to the monster milewide Mississippi grow accustomed to associating the term *river* with a high degree of watery grandeur. Consequently, such people feel rather disappointed when they stand on the shores of the Humboldt or the Carson and find that a "river" in Nevada is a sickly rivulet which is just the counterpart of the Erie Canal in all respects save that the canal is twice as long and four times as deep. One of the pleasantest and most invigorating exercises one can contrive is to run and jump across the Humboldt River till he is overheated, and then drink it dry.

On the fifteenth day we completed our march of two hundred miles and entered Unionville, Humboldt County, in the midst of a driving snowstorm. Unionville consisted of eleven cabins and a liberty pole. Six of the cabins were strung along one side of a deep canyon, and the other five faced them. The rest of the landscape was made up of bleak mountain walls that rose so high into the sky from both sides of the canyon that the village

California News. Oil painting by William Sidney Mount (1807–1868).

---

1. **the Sink:** a basin, or small lake, of the Humboldt River in Nevada.

Mining scene near Nevada City, California, 1852.

was left, as it were, far down in the bottom of a crevice. It was always daylight on the mountaintops a long time before the darkness lifted and revealed Unionville.

We built a small, rude cabin in the side of the crevice and roofed it with canvas, leaving a corner open to serve as a chimney, through which the cattle used to tumble occasionally, at night, and mash our furniture and interrupt our sleep. It was very cold weather and fuel was scarce. Indians brought brush and bushes several miles on their backs; and when we could catch a laden Indian, it was well—and when we could not (which was the rule, not the exception), we shivered and bore it.

I confess, without shame, that I expected to find masses of silver lying all about the ground. I expected to see it glittering in the sun on the mountain summits. I said nothing about this, for some instinct told me that I might possibly have an exaggerated idea about it, and so, if I betrayed my thought, I might bring derision upon myself. Yet I was

as perfectly satisfied in my own mind as I could be of anything that I was going to gather up, in a day or two, or at furthest a week or two, silver enough to make me satisfactorily wealthy—and so my fancy was already busy with plans for spending this money. The first opportunity that offered, I sauntered carelessly away from the cabin, keeping an eye on the other boys, and stopping and contemplating the sky when they seemed to be observing me; but as soon as the coast was manifestly clear, I fled away as guiltily as a thief might have done and never halted till I was far beyond sight and call. Then I began my search with a feverish excitement that was brimful of expectation—almost, of certainty.

I crawled about the ground, seizing and examining bits of stone, blowing the dust from them or rubbing them on my clothes, and then peering at them with anxious hope. Presently I found a bright fragment and my heart bounded! I hid behind a boulder and polished it and scrutinized it with a nervous eagerness and a delight that was more pronounced than absolute certainty itself could have afforded. The more I examined the fragment the more I was convinced that I had found the door to fortune. I marked the spot and carried away my specimen. Up and down the rugged mountainside I searched, with always increasing interest and always augmenting gratitude that I had come to Humboldt and come in time. Of all the experiences of my life, this secret search among the hidden treasures of silverland was the nearest to unmarred ecstasy. It was a delirious revel. By and by, in the bed of a shallow rivulet, I found a deposit of shining yellow scales, and my breath almost forsook me! A gold mine, and in my simplicity I had been content with vulgar silver! I was so excited that I half believed my overwrought imagination was deceiving me. Then a fear came upon me that people might be observing me and would guess my secret. Moved by this thought, I made a circuit of the place, and ascended a knoll to reconnoiter. Solitude. No creature was near. Then I returned to my mine, fortifying myself against possible disappointment, but my fears were groundless—the shining scales were still there. I set about scooping them out, and for an hour I toiled down the windings of the stream and robbed its bed. But at last the descending sun warned me to give up the quest, and I turned homeward laden with wealth. As I walked along I could not help smiling at the thought of my being so excited over my fragment of silver when a nobler metal was almost under my nose. In this little time the former had so fallen in my estimation that once or twice I was on the point of throwing it away.

The boys were as hungry as usual, but I could eat nothing. Neither could I talk. I was full of dreams and far away. Their conversation interrupted the flow of my fancy somewhat, and annoyed me a little, too. I despised the sordid and commonplace things they talked about. But as they proceeded, it began to amuse me. It grew to be rare fun to hear them planning their poor little economies and sighing over possible privations and distresses when a gold mine, all our own, lay within sight of the cabin, and I could point it out at any moment. Smothered hilarity began to oppress me, presently. It was hard to resist the impulse to burst out with exultation and reveal everything; but I did resist. I said within myself that I would filter the great news through my lips calmly and be serene as a summer morning while I watched its effect in their faces. I said:

California gold miner, around 1850.

FOR
CALIFORNIA
AND THE
GOLD REGION DIRECT!

The Magnificent, Fast Sailing and favorite packet Ship,

JOSEPHINE,

BURTHEN 400 TONS, CAPT.

Built in the most *superb* manner of Live Oak, White Oak and Locust, for a New York and Liverpool Packet; thoroughly Copper-fastened and Coppered. She is a very fast sailer, having crossed the Atlantic from Liverpool to New-York in 14 days, the shortest passage ever made by a *Sailing Ship.*
Has superior accommodations for Passengers, can take Gentlemen with their Ladies and families. Will probably reach SAN FRANCISCO THIRTY DAYS ahead of any Ship sailing at the same time. Will sail about the

10th November Next.

For Freight or Passage apply to the subscriber,

RODNEY FRENCH,
No. 103 North Water Street, Rodman's Wharf.

"Where have you all been?"

"Prospecting."

"What did you find?"

"Nothing."

"Nothing? What do you think of the country?"

"Can't tell, yet," said Mr. Ballou, who was an old gold miner, and had likewise had considerable experience among the silver mines.

"Well, haven't you formed any sort of opinion?"

"Yes, a sort of a one. It's fair enough here, maybe, but overrated. Seven-thousand-dollar ledges are scarce, though. That Sheba may be rich enough, but we don't own it; and, besides, the rock is so full of base metals that all the science in the world can't work it. We'll not starve here, but we'll not get rich, I'm afraid."

"So you think the prospect is pretty poor?"

"No name for it!"

"Well, we'd better go back, hadn't we?"

"Oh, not yet—of course not. We'll try it a riffle² first."

"Suppose, now—this is merely a supposition, you know—suppose you could find a ledge that would yield, say, a hundred and fifty dollars a ton—would that satisfy you?"

"Try us once!" from the whole party.

"Or suppose—merely a supposition, of course—suppose you were to find a ledge that would yield two thousand dollars a ton—would *that* satisfy you?"

"Here—what do you mean? What are you coming at? Is there some mystery behind all this?"

"Never mind. I am not saying anything. You know perfectly well there are no rich mines here—of course you do. Because you have been around and examined for yourselves. Anybody would know that, that had been around. But just for the sake of argument, suppose—in a kind of general way—suppose some person were to tell you that two-thousand-dollar ledges were simply contemptible—contemptible, understand—and that right yonder, in sight of this very cabin, there were piles of pure gold and pure silver—oceans of it—enough to make you all rich in twenty-four hours! Come!"

"I should say he was as crazy as a loon!" said old Ballou, but wild with excitement, nevertheless.

"Gentlemen," said I, "I don't say anything—I haven't been around, you know, and of course don't know anything—but all I ask of you is to cast your eye on *that*, for instance, and tell me what you think of it!" and I tossed my treasure before them.

There was an eager scrabble for it, and a closing of heads together over it under the candlelight. Then old Ballou said:

"Think of it? I think it is nothing but a lot of granite rubbish and nasty glittering mica that isn't worth ten cents an acre!"

So vanished my dreams. So melted my wealth away. So toppled my airy castle to the earth and left me stricken and forlorn.

Moralizing, I observed, then, that "all that glitters is not gold."

Mr. Ballou said I could go further than that, and lay it up among my treasures of knowledge that *nothing* that glitters is gold. So I learned then, once for all, that gold in its native state is but dull, unornamental stuff, and that only lowborn metals excite the admiration of the ignorant with an ostentatious glitter. However, like the rest of the world, I still go on underrating men of gold and glorifying men of mica. Commonplace human nature cannot rise above that.

---

2. **try it a riffle:** to search for gold or silver with a riffle —a sievelike device for extracting precious metals from a stream.

FOR STUDY AND DISCUSSION

1. Mark Twain describes himself here as an inexperienced young man led astray by youthful enthusiasm and overblown expectations. What does Twain expect to find when he begins prospecting? How do his dreams lead him into an embarrassing mistake?

2. Twain has the yarn spinner's love of humor. What exaggeration do you find in his opening description of the Humboldt River? What humorous description does he give of Unionville and the cabins?

3. *Dramatic irony* is a form of irony in which the reader perceives something that a character in the story does not know. Does Twain's narrative contain dramatic irony? (Did you catch on before Twain did?)

4. Bernard De Voto, a distinguished biographer of Mark Twain, said of Twain's books: "They are the first American literature of the highest rank which portrays the ordinary bulk of Americans, expresses them, accepts their values, and delineates their hopes . . . ." What American hopes and values do you think Twain portrays in this story?

5. What personal view of human nature does Twain present at the conclusion of this narrative?

LANGUAGE AND VOCABULARY

Explaining Different Shades of Meaning
In the following paragraphs Twain uses seven different words or phrases to name seven different ways of "seeing" or "looking."

. . . I sauntered carelessly away from the cabin, *keeping an eye on* the other boys, and stopping and *contemplating* the sky when they seemed to be *observing* me; but as soon as the coast was manifestly clear, I fled away as guiltily as a thief might have done and never halted till I was far beyond sight and call. Then I began my *search* with a feverish excitement that was brimful of expectation—almost, of certainty.

I crawled about the ground, seizing and *examining* bits of stone, blowing the dust from them or rubbing them on my clothes, and then *peering* at them with anxious hope. Presently I found a bright fragment and my heart bounded! I hid behind a boulder and polished it and *scrutinized* it with a nervous eagerness and a delight that was more pronounced than absolute certainty itself could have afforded.

Define each of the italicized words in this passage, consulting the dictionary if you need to. Explain the different shades of meaning they convey. Does your dictionary list any synonyms for the verbs *see* or *look?* Could any of these words be used in place of Twain's words and convey the same meaning? Give reasons for your answer.

FOR COMPOSITION

Writing an Anecdote
"I Find Fool Gold" is an *anecdote,* a brief, entertaining story about some happening. Unlike a short story, an anecdote does not have a complicated plot or well-developed characters, but it can, as you see, make a point. Twain uses anecdotes frequently.

Write a short, humorous anecdote of your own. Make your anecdote illustrate a point, perhaps the same point illustrated by Twain's narrative.

Ralph Ellison (1914–   ) was born in Oklahoma City and was educated at Tuskegee Institute in Alabama. His famous novel about black American life, *Invisible Man*, was published in 1952 and received the National Book Award that year. His collection of essays, *Shadow and Act*, was published in 1964. Ellison has taught literature and writing at a number of universities and has received numerous honors for his writing.

As a writer, Ellison is deeply interested in how we discover who we are, and how we acquire the values we live by. That is one of the themes of *Invisible Man*. In an essay called "Hidden Name and Complex Fate," Ellison discusses the influence of his name on his career as a writer and considers the question of his identity as a man and writer. A portion of that essay is reprinted here.

Living with a Name

Ralph Ellison

In the dim beginnings, before I ever thought consciously of writing, there was my own name, and there was, doubtless, a certain magic in it. From the start I was uncomfortable with it, and in my earliest years it caused me much puzzlement. Neither could I understand what a poet was, nor why, exactly, my father had chosen to name me after one. Perhaps I could have understood it perfectly well had he named me after his own father, but that name had been given to an older brother who died and thus was out of the question. But why hadn't he named me after a hero, such as Jack Johnson, or a soldier like Colonel Charles Young, or a great seaman like Admiral Dewey, or an educator like Booker T. Washington, or a great orator and abolitionist like Frederick Douglass? Or again, why hadn't he named me (as so many Negro parents had done) after President Teddy Roosevelt?

Instead, he named me after someone called Ralph Waldo Emerson, and then, when I was three, he died. It was too early for me to have understood his choice, although I'm sure he must have explained it many times, and it was also too soon for me to have made the connection between my name and my father's love for reading. Much later, after I began to write and work with words, I came to suspect that he was aware of the suggestive powers of names and of the magic involved in naming.

I recall an odd conversation with my mother during my early teens in which she mentioned their interest in, of all things, prenatal culture![1] But for a long time I actually knew only that my father read a lot, and that he admired this remote Mr. Emerson, who was something called a "poet and philosopher"—so much so that he named his second son after him.

I knew, also, that whatever his motives, the combination of names he'd given me caused me no end of trouble from the moment when I could talk well enough to respond to the ritualized question which grown-ups put to very young children. Emerson's name was quite familiar to Negroes in Oklahoma during those days when World War I was brewing, and adults, eager to show off their knowledge of literary figures, and obviously amused by the joke implicit in such a small brown nubbin of a boy carrying around such a heavy moniker, would invariably repeat my first two names and then to my great annoyance, they'd add "Emerson."

And I, in my confusion, would reply, "No, no, I'm not Emerson; he's the little boy who lives next door." Which only made them laugh all the louder. "Oh, no," they'd say, "you're Ralph Waldo Emerson," while I had fantasies of blue murder.

For a while the presence next door of my little friend, Emerson, made it unnecessary for me to puzzle too often over this peculiar adult confusion. And since there were other Negro boys named Ralph in the city, I came to suspect that there was something about the combination of names which produced their laughter. Even today I know of only one other Ralph who had as much comedy made out of his name, a campus politician and deep-voiced orator whom I knew at Tuskegee, who was called in friendly ribbing, *Ralph Waldo Emerson Edgar Allan Poe*, spelled "Powe."

This must have been quite a trial for him, but I had been initiated much earlier.

During my early school years the name continued to puzzle me, for it constantly evoked in the faces of others some secret. It was as though I possessed some treasure or some defect, which was invisible to my own eyes and ears; something which I had but did not *possess*, like a piece of property in South Carolina, which was mine but which I could not have until some future time. I recall finding, about this time, while seeking adventure in back alleys—which possess for boys a superiority over playgrounds like that which kitchen utensils possess over toys designed for infants—a large photographic lens. I remember nothing of its optical qualities, of its speed or color correction, but it gleamed with crystal mystery and it was beautiful.

Mounted handsomely in a tube of shiny brass, it spoke to me of distant worlds of possibility. I played with it, looking through it with squinted eyes, holding it in shafts of sunlight, and tried to use it for a magic lantern.[2] But most of this was as unrewarding as my attempts to make the music come from a phonograph record by holding the needle in my fingers.

I could burn holes through newspapers with it, or I could pretend that it was a telescope, the barrel of a cannon, or the third eye of a monster—*I* being the monster—but I could do nothing at all about its proper function of making images; nothing to make it yield its secret. But I could not discard it.

Older boys sought to get it away from me by offering knives or tops, agate marbles or whole zoos of grass snakes and horned toads in trade, but I held on to it. No one, not even the white boys I knew, had such a lens, and it

---

1. **prenatal culture:** the development of a child, especially in character or intellect, while in the womb.

2. **magic lantern:** an old-fashioned projector that shows still pictures from transparent slides.

was my own good luck to have found it. Thus I would hold on to it until such time as I could acquire the parts needed to make it function. Finally I put it aside and it remained buried in my box of treasures, dusty and dull, to be lost and forgotten as I grew older and became interested in music.

I had reached by now the grades where it was necessary to learn something about Mr. Emerson and what he had written, such as the "Concord Hymn" and the essay "Self-Reliance," and in following his advice, I reduced the "Waldo" to a simple and, I hoped, mysterious "W," and in my own reading I avoided his works like the plague. I could no more deal with my name—I shall never really master it—than I could find a creative use for my lens.

FOR STUDY AND DISCUSSION

1. How did Ellison's name influence the way others treated him as a boy? How did his name create confusion for the young Ellison?
2. Ellison makes an *analogy* between the photographic lens and his name. An analogy is a comparison made between two different things to show the similarities between them. What similar problems did Ellison have in using his photographic lens and in dealing with his name? What similar feelings did Ellison have for these two things?
3. Early in this selection, Ellison mentions the "suggestive powers of names" and "the magic involved in naming." How can names have "suggestive powers" and "magic"? Do you know of any names that could have such powers—either for good or for ill?
4. How do advertisers make use of the "suggestive powers of names"?

FOR COMPOSITION

Writing a Report
Ellison alludes, or refers, to a number of famous people in this selection. Look up the following names in biographical dictionaries in your library. You will find some of them in reference books devoted to prominent black Americans. Write a brief report explaining why these people would have been important to Ellison as a boy.

Jack Johnson
Colonel Charles Young
Admiral George Dewey
Booker T. Washington
Frederick Douglass
President Theodore Roosevelt

In 1970 playwright Lillian Hellman (1906–1984) won a National Book Award for *An Unfinished Woman*, her first book of memoirs. This book was followed by two sequel volumes, *Pentimento* (1974) and *Scoundrel Time* (1977). Lillian Hellman was born in New Orleans and educated at New York University and Columbia University. She spent many years in New York working for a theatrical producer before she began writing her own plays. Among her many highly acclaimed plays are *The Children's Hour* (1934), *The Little Foxes* (1939), and *Watch on the Rhine* (1941). The following selection is from her best-selling book of memoirs, *Pentimento*.

Julia   *Lillian Hellman*

Childhood is less clear to me than to many people: when it ended I turned my face away from it for no reason that I know about, certainly without the usual reason of unhappy memories. For many years that worried me, but then I discovered that the tales of former children are seldom to be trusted. Some people supply too many past victories or pleasures with which to comfort themselves, and other people cling to pains, real and imagined, to excuse what they have become.

I think I have always known about my memory: I know when it is to be trusted and when some dream or fantasy entered on the life, and the dream, the need of dream, led to distortion of what happened. And so I knew early that the rampage angers of an only child were distorted nightmares of reality. But I trust absolutely what I remember about Julia.

Now, so many years later, I could climb the steps without a light, move in the night through the crowded rooms of her grandparents' great Fifth Avenue house with the endless chic-shabby rooms, their walls covered with pictures, their tables crowded with objects whose value I didn't know. True, I cannot remember anything said or done in that house except for the first night I was allowed to sleep there. Julia and I were both twelve years old that New Year's Eve night, sitting at a late dinner, with courses of fish and meats, and sherbets in between to change the tastes, "clear the palate" is what her grandmother said, with watered wine for us, and red and white wine and champagne for the two old people. (Were they old? I don't know: they were her grandparents.) I cannot remember any talk at the table, but after dinner we were allowed to go with them to the music room. A servant had already set the phonograph for "So Sheep May Safely Graze," and all four of us listened until Julia rose, kissed the hand of her grandmother, the brow of her grandfather, and left the room, motioning for me to follow. It was an odd ritual, the whole thing, I thought, the life of the very rich, and beyond my understanding.

Each New Year's Eve of my life has brought back the memory of that night. Julia and I lay in twin beds and she recited odds and ends of poetry—every once in a while she would stop and ask me to recite, but I didn't know anything—Dante[1] in Italian, Heine[2] in German, and even though I could not understand either language, the sounds were so lovely that I felt a sweet sadness as if much was ahead in the world, much that was going to be fine and fulfilling if I could ever find my way. I did recite Mother Goose and she did Donne's[3] "Julia," and laughed with pleasure "at his tribute to me." I was ashamed to ask if it was a joke.

Very late she turned her head away for sleep, but I said, "More, Julia, please. Do you know more?" And she turned on the light again and recited from Ovid and Catullus,[4] names to me without countries.

I don't know when I stopped listening to look at the lovely face propped against the pillow—the lamp throwing fine lights on the thick dark hair. I cannot say now that I knew or had ever used the words gentle or delicate or strong, but I did think that night that it was the most beautiful face I had ever seen. . . .

---

1. **Dante:** Dante Alighieri (dän'tä ä'lē-gyä'rē), Italian poet (1265–1321) author of *The Divine Comedy*.
2. **Heine:** Heinrich Heine (hī'nə), German poet and essayist (1797–1856).
3. **Donne:** John Donne, English poet (1573–1631).
4. **Ovid and Catullus:** Roman poets of the first century B.C.

FOR STUDY AND DISCUSSION

1. Visiting Julia's Fifth Avenue house was, for Hellman, like entering a new and fascinating world. Which events of her first night there seemed to make the whole thing "an odd ritual"?
2. Why do you think that Hellman, who was later to become a writer, remembered these particular experiences of that New Year's Eve?
3. What is your opinion of Hellman's opening remarks about "the tales of former children"?

FOR COMPOSITION

Writing a Memoir

The word *memoir* comes from a French word for "memory," and in this brief excerpt, a writer remembers a particular evening of her childhood. Notice the specific details that describe a few precise memories: the grandparents' house, the meal, the music, the recitation of poems. Write a brief memoir in which you recall an incident of the past—either from your own experience or from someone else's. Use specific details to help your reader share a few precise memories of this experience.

Julius Caesar.

Plutarch (46?–120?) was the first modern biographer and the greatest biographer of the ancient world. He was born in central Greece about a hundred years after the death of Julius Caesar. Plutarch's main interest was the characters of famous men and how these men shaped history. He was particularly interested in the story of the collapse of the Roman Republic, between about 100 and 30 B.C. After much reading and research, he wrote biographies of ten important Romans who lived during the decline of Rome. Among them are Pompey, Caesar, Cicero, Brutus, and Antony, all of whom figure, in one way or another, in Shakespeare's play, *The Tragedy of Julius Caesar*. Shakespeare, in fact, read Plutarch in a translation that was published in England in 1579, and he based his play on Plutarch's biography. The selection that follows is a modern translation of the last part of Plutarch's *Life of Caesar*.

Julius Caesar (102?–44 B.C.) was born to a noble Roman family. His career was full of dramatic events: wars throughout the Mediterranean world, intrigue and undercover politics at home, civil war, dictatorship, government reforms. The last five years of Caesar's life were a particularly complex period in Roman history. Caesar's military victories in the Gallic Wars and the victories of Pompey (who was his son-in-law as well as his principal opponent in the government) brought Roman power to a new height. But Rome's republican form of government was weakening. In 49 B.C., Caesar's rivalry with Pompey flared into civil war. Caesar, then in the north of Italy, attacked the forces of Pompey and defeated them. Pompey fled to Egypt where he was eventually murdered, and Caesar was elected consul, or ruling magistrate of the republic. After defeating other opposing elements in the civil war, Caesar was named dictator for ten years by the Roman senate. He then sailed to Spain, defeated Pompey's sons, and returned to Rome. This selection from Plutarch opens with Caesar's victorious return to Rome. However, as Caesar enters the city in triumph, a conspiracy to overthrow him is already under way.

The Life of Caesar

Plutarch

Translated from the Greek by Rex Warner

The ruins of the Roman Forum.

What made Caesar most openly and mortally hated was his passion to be made King. It was this which made the common people hate him for the first time, and it served as a most useful pretext for those others who had long hated him but had up to now disguised their feelings. Yet those who were trying to get this honor conferred on Caesar actually spread the story among the people that it was foretold in the Sibylline books[1] that Parthia[2] could only be conquered by the Romans if the Roman army was led by a king; and as Caesar was coming down from Alba to Rome, they ventured to salute him as "King," which caused a disturbance among the people. Caesar, upset by this himself, said that his name was not King but Caesar. These words were received in total silence, and he went on his way looking far from pleased. Then there was an occasion when a number of extravagant honors had been voted for him in the senate, and Caesar happened to be sitting above the rostra. Here he was approached by the consuls and the praetors[3] with the whole senate following behind; but instead of rising to receive them, he behaved to them as though they were merely private individuals and, after receiving their message, told them that his honors ought to be cut down rather than increased. This conduct of his offended not only the senate but the people as well, who felt that his treatment of the senators was an insult to the whole state. There was a general air of the deepest dejection, and everyone who was in a position to do so went away at once. Caesar

himself realized what he had done and immediately turned to go home. He drew back his toga and, uncovering his throat, cried out in a loud voice to his friends that he was ready to receive the blow from anyone who liked to give it to him. Later, however, he excused his behavior on account of his illness,[4] saying that those who suffer from it are apt to lose control of their senses if they address a large crowd while standing; in these circumstances they are very subject to fits of giddiness and may fall into convulsions and insensibility. This excuse, however, was not true. Caesar himself was perfectly willing to rise to receive the senate; but, so they say, one of his friends, or rather his flatterers, Cornelius Balbus, restrained him from doing so. "Remember," he said, "that you are Caesar. You are their superior and ought to let them treat you as such."

Another thing which caused offense was his insulting treatment of the tribunes.[5] The feast of the Lupercalia[6] was being celebrated. Caesar, sitting on a golden throne above the rostra and wearing a triumphal robe, was watching this ceremony; and Antony, who was consul at the time, was one of those taking part in the sacred running. When he came running into the forum, the crowd made way for him. He was carrying a diadem[7] with a wreath of laurel tied round it, and he held this out to Caesar. His action was followed by some applause, but it was not much and it was not spontaneous. But when Caesar pushed the diadem away from him, there was a general shout of applause. Antony then of-

---

1. **Sibylline books:** nine ancient prophetic books, supposed to reveal the destiny of Rome.
2. **Parthia:** ancient country southeast of the Caspian Sea, in what is now part of Iran and the U.S.S.R.
3. **praetors** (prē′tərz): A praetor was a magistrate with judicial duties, ranking just below consul.

4. **illness:** Caesar suffered from epilepsy.
5. **tribunes:** in ancient Rome, city officials with the special responsibility of guarding the interests of the common people.
6. **Lupercalia** (loo′pər-kā′lē-ə): a Roman religious festival held on February 15, during which priests, magistrates, and young noblemen held races through the streets of Rome.
7. **diadem:** a crown, the symbol of royalty.

fered him the diadem for the second time, and again only a few applauded, though, when Caesar again rejected it, there was applause from everyone. Caesar, finding that the experiment had proved a failure, rose from his seat and ordered the wreath to be carried to the Capitol. It was then discovered that his statues had been decorated with royal diadems, and two of the tribunes, Flavius and Marullus, went round the statues and tore down the decorations. They then found out who had been the first to salute Caesar as King, and led them off to prison. The people followed the tribunes and were loud in their applause, calling them Brutuses—because it was Brutus[8] who first put an end to the line of Kings in Rome and gave to the senate and the people the power that had previously been in the hands of one man. This made Caesar angry. He deprived Marullus and Flavius of their tribuneship and in speaking against them he insulted the people at the same time.

It was in these circumstances that people began to turn their thoughts toward Marcus Brutus. He was thought to be, on his father's side, a descendant of the Brutus who had abolished the monarchy; on his mother's side he came from another famous family, the Servilii; and he was a son-in-law and a nephew of Cato.[9] But his own zeal for destroying the new monarchy was blunted by the honors and favors which he had received from Caesar. It was not only that at Pharsalus[10] after Pompey's flight his own life had been spared and the lives of many of his friends at his request; he was also a person in whom Caesar had particular trust. He had been given the most important of the praetorships for this very year and was to be consul three years later. For this post he had been preferred to Cassius, who had been the rival candidate. Caesar, indeed, is said to have admitted that Cassius had the better claims of the two for the office. "But," he added, "I cannot pass over Brutus." And once, when the conspiracy was already formed and some people were actually accusing Brutus to Caesar of being involved in it, Caesar laid his hand on his body and said to the accusers: "Brutus will wait for this skin of mine"—implying that Brutus certainly had the qualities which would entitle him to power, but that he would not, for the sake of power, behave basely and ungratefully.

However, those who were eager for the change and who looked to Brutus as the only, or at least the most likely, man to bring it about, used, without venturing to approach him personally, to come by night and leave papers all over the platform and the chair where he sat to do his work as praetor. Most of the messages were of this kind: "You are asleep, Brutus" or "You are no real Brutus." And when Cassius observed that they were having at least something of an effect on Brutus' personal pride, he redoubled his own efforts to incite him further. Cassius, as I have mentioned in my *Life of Brutus,* had reasons of his own for hating Caesar; moreover, Caesar was suspicious of him, and once said to his friends: "What do you think Cassius is aiming at? Personally I am not too fond of him; he is much too pale." And on another occasion it is said that, when Antony and Dolabella were accused to him of plotting a revolution, Caesar said: "I'm not much afraid of these fat, long-haired people. It's the other type I'm more frightened of, the pale thin ones"—by which he meant Brutus and Cassius.

8. **Brutus:** an earlier Brutus who was thought to be an ancestor of Caesar's friend Marcus Brutus.

9. **Cato:** Marcus Porcius Cato (95–46 B.C.), famous for his courage and honor. He supported Pompey against Caesar.

10. **Pharsalus:** a city in Greece, near which Caesar defeated Pompey in 48 B.C.

Fate however, seems to be not so much unexpected as unavoidable. Certainly, before this event, they say that strange signs were shown and strange apparitions were seen. As for the lights in the sky, the crashing sounds heard in all sorts of directions by night, the solitary specimens of birds coming down into the forum, all these, perhaps, are scarcely worth mentioning in connection with so great an event as this. But the philosopher Strabo says that a great crowd of men all on fire were seen making a charge; also that from the hand of a soldier's slave a great flame sprang out so that the hand seemed to the spectators to be burning away; but when the flame died out, the man was uninjured. He also says that when Caesar himself was making a sacrifice, the heart of the animal being sacrificed was missing—a very bad omen indeed, since in the ordinary course of nature no animal can exist without a heart. There is plenty of authority too for the following story:

A soothsayer[11] warned Caesar to be on his guard against a great danger on the day of the month of March which the Romans call the Ides;[12] and when this day had come, Caesar, on his way to the senate house, met the soothsayer and greeted him jestingly with the words: "Well, the Ides of March have come," to which the soothsayer replied in a soft voice: "Yes, but they have not yet gone." And on the previous day Marcus Lepidus was entertaining Caesar at supper and Caesar, according to his usual practice, happened to be signing letters as he reclined at table. Mean-

while the conversation turned to the question of what sort of death was the best, and, before anyone else could express a view on the subject, Caesar cried out: "The kind that comes unexpectedly." After this, when he was sleeping as usual by the side of his wife, all the doors and windows of the bedroom flew open at once; Caesar, startled by the noise and by the light of the moon shining down on him, noticed that Calpurnia was fast asleep, but she was saying something in her sleep which he could not make out and was groaning in an inarticulate way. In fact she was dreaming at that time that she was holding his murdered body in her arms and was weeping over it. Though some say that it was a different dream which she had. They say that she dreamed that she saw the gable ornament[13] of the house torn down and for this reason fancied that she was weeping and lamenting. In any case, when it was day, she implored Caesar, if it was possible, not to go out and begged him to postpone the meeting of the senate; or if, she said, he had no confidence in her dreams, then he ought to inquire about the future by sacrifices and other methods of divination.[14] Caesar himself, it seems, was affected and by no means easy in his mind; for he had never before noticed any superstition in Calpurnia and now he could see that she was in very great distress. And when the prophets, after making many sacrifices, told him that the omens were unfavorable, he decided to send for Antony and to dismiss the senate.

At this point Decimus Brutus, surnamed Albinus, intervened. Caesar had such confidence in him that he had made him the sec-

---

11. **soothsayer:** literally, truth-sayer, one who claims to be able to foretell events.
12. **Ides:** the 15th of March in the ancient Roman calendar. The Romans called the day that fell in the middle of the month "the Ides."

13. **gable ornament:** This ornament was put up by decree of the senate as a mark of honor and distinction.
14. **divination:** the act of trying to foretell the future or penetrate the unknown, using magic or other special rites.

ond heir in his will, yet he was in the conspiracy with the other Brutus and Cassius. Now, fearing that if Caesar escaped this day the whole plot would come to light, he spoke derisively of the prophets and told Caesar that he ought not to give the senate such a good opportunity for thinking that they were being treated discourteously; they had met, he said, on Caesar's instructions, and they were ready to vote unanimously that Caesar should be declared King of all the provinces outside Italy with the right of wearing a diadem in any other place except Italy, whether on sea or land; but if, when they were already in session, someone were to come and tell them that they must go away for the time being and come back again when Calpurnia had better dreams, it would be easy to imagine what Caesar's enemies would have to say themselves and what sort of a reception they would give to Caesar's friends when they tried to prove that Caesar was not a slave master or a tyrant. If, however, he had really made up his mind to treat this day as inauspicious, then, Decimus Brutus said, it would be better for him to go himself to the senate, speak personally to the senators, and adjourn the meeting.

While he was speaking, Brutus took Caesar by the hand and began to lead him toward the door. And before he had gone far from the door a slave belonging to someone else tried to approach him, but being unable to get near him because of the crowds who pressed round him, forced his way into the house and put himself into the hands of Calpurnia, asking her to keep him safe until Caesar came back, since he had some very important information to give him.

Then there was Artemidorus, a Cnidian by birth, and a teacher of Greek philosophy, who, for that reason, had become acquainted with Brutus and his friends. He had thus acquired a very full knowledge of the conspiracy and he came to Caesar with a small document in which he had written down the information which he intended to reveal to him. But when he saw that Caesar took each document that was given to him and then handed it to one of his attendants, he came close up to him and said: "Read this one, Caesar, and read it quickly and by yourself. I assure you that it is important and that it concerns you personally." Caesar then took the document and was several times on the point of reading it, but was prevented from doing so by the numbers of people who came to speak to him. It was the only document which he did keep with him and he was still holding it in his hand when he went on into the senate.

It may be said that all these things could have happened as it were by chance. But the place where the senate was meeting that day and which was to be the scene of the final struggle and of the assassination made it perfectly clear that some heavenly power was at work, guiding the action and directing that it should take place just here. For here stood a statue of Pompey, and the building had been erected and dedicated by Pompey as one of the extra amenities attached to his theater. Indeed it is said that, just before the attack was made on him, Caesar turned his eyes toward the statue of Pompey and silently prayed for its good will. This was in spite of the fact that Caesar was a follower of the doctrines of Epicurus;[15] yet the moment of crisis, so it would seem, and the very imminence of the dreadful deed made him forget his former rationalistic views and filled him with an emo-

---

15. **Epicurus:** a Greek philosopher who taught that happiness is achieved through the pursuit of honor, prudence, and peace of mind. The Epicureans did not believe in an afterlife, nor in divine intervention in human affairs.

tion that was intuitive or divinely inspired.

Now Antony, who was a true friend of Caesar's and also a strong man physically, was detained outside the senate house by Brutus Albinus, who deliberately engaged him in a long conversation. Caesar himself went in and the senate rose in his honor. Some of Brutus' party took their places behind his chair and others went to meet him as though they wished to support the petition being made by Tillius Cimber on behalf of his brother who was in exile. So, all joining in with him in his entreaties, they accompanied Caesar to his chair. Caesar took his seat and continued to reject their request; as they pressed him more and more urgently, he began to grow angry with them. Tillius then took hold of his toga with both hands and pulled it down from his neck. This was the signal for the attack. The first blow was struck by Casca, who wounded Caesar in the neck with his dagger. The wound was not mortal and not even a deep one, coming as it did from a man who was no doubt much disturbed in mind at the beginning of such a daring venture. Caesar, therefore, was able to turn round and grasp the knife and hold on to it. At almost the same moment the striker of the blow and he who was struck cried out together—Caesar, in Latin, "Casca, you villain, what are you doing?" while Casca called to his brother in Greek: "Help, brother."

So it began, and those who were not in the conspiracy were so horror-struck and amazed at what was being done that they were afraid to run away and afraid to come to Caesar's help; they were too afraid even to utter a word. But those who had come prepared for the murder all bared their daggers and hemmed Caesar in on every side. Whichever way he turned he met the blows of daggers and saw the cold steel aimed at his face and at his eyes. So he was driven this way and that,

and, like a wild beast in the toils,[16] had to suffer from the hands of each one of them; for it had been agreed that they must all take part in this sacrifice and all flesh themselves with his blood. Because of this compact Brutus also gave him one wound in the groin. Some say that Caesar fought back against all the rest, darting this way and that to avoid the blows and crying out for help, but when he saw that Brutus had drawn his dagger, he covered his head with his toga and sank down to the ground. Either by chance or because he was pushed there by his murderers, he fell down against the pedestal on which the statue of Pompey stood, and the pedestal was drenched with his blood, so that one might have thought that Pompey himself was presiding over this act of vengeance against his enemy, who lay there at his feet struggling convulsively under so many wounds.[17]

So Caesar was done to death and, when it was over, Brutus stepped forward with the intention of making a speech to explain what had been done. The senators, however, would not wait to hear him. They rushed out through the doors of the building and fled to their homes, thus producing a state of confusion, terror, and bewilderment amongst the people. Some bolted their doors; others left their counters and shops and could be observed either running to see the place where Caesar had been killed or, once they had seen it, running back again. Antony and Lepidus, who were Caesar's chief friends, stole away and hid in houses belonging to other people. Brutus and his party, on the other hand, just as they were, still hot and eager from the murder, marched all together in one body from

---

16. **in the toils:** at bay, in a net or trap.
17. Caesar is said to have received twenty-three wounds, and many of his assailants were wounded by one another in the confusion.

The assassination scene from William Shakespeare's
Julius Caesar. BBC-TV.

the senate house to the Capitol, holding up
their naked daggers in front of them and, far
from giving the impression that they wanted
to escape, looking glad and confident. They
called out to the people that liberty had been
restored, and they invited the more distinguished persons whom they met to join in
with them. Some of these did join in the
procession and go up with them to the Capitol, pretending that they had taken part in the
deed and thus claiming their share in the
glory of it. Among these were Caius Octavius
and Lentulus Spinther who suffered later for
their imposture. They were put to death by
Antony and young Caesar, and did not even
have the satisfaction of enjoying the fame
which caused their death, since no one believed that they had taken part in the action.
Even those who inflicted the death penalty on
them were punishing them not for what they
did but for what they would have liked to
have done.

Next day Brutus and his party came down
from the Capitol and Brutus made a speech.
The people listened to what he said without
expressing either pleasure or resentment at
what had been done. Their complete silence
indicated that they both pitied Caesar and
respected Brutus. The senate passed a decree
of amnesty[18] and tried to reconcile all parties.
It was voted that Caesar should be worshiped
as a god and that there should be no alteration
made, however small, in any of the measures
passed by him while he was in power. On
the other hand, provinces and appropriate
honors were given to Brutus and his friends.
Everyone thought, therefore, that things

18. **amnesty:** general pardon.

were not only settled but settled in the best possible way.

But when Caesar's will was opened and it was discovered that he had left a considerable legacy to each Roman citizen, and when the people saw his body, all disfigured with its wounds, being carried through the forum, they broke through all bounds of discipline and order. They made a great pile of benches, railings, and tables from the forum and, placing the body upon this, burned it there. Then, carrying blazing brands, they ran to set fire to the houses of the murderers, while others went up and down through the city trying to find the men themselves to tear them to pieces. They, however, were well barricaded and not one of them came in the way of the mob. But there was a man called Cinna, one of Caesar's friends, who, they say, happened to have had a strange dream during the previous night. He dreamed that Caesar invited

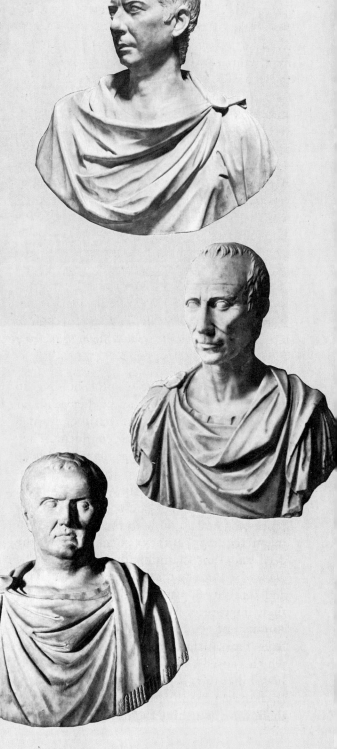

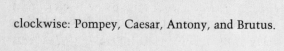

clockwise: Pompey, Caesar, Antony, and Brutus.

him to supper and he declined the invitation; Caesar then led him along by the hand, though he did not want to go and was pulling in the opposite direction. Now when Cinna heard that they were burning Caesar's body in the forum he got up and went there out of respect for his memory, though he felt a certain amount of misgiving as a result of his dream and was also suffering from a fever. One of the crowd who saw him there asked who he was and, when he had learned the name, told it to another. So the name was passed on and it was quickly accepted by everyone that here was one of the men who had murdered Caesar, since among the conspirators there was in fact a man with this same name of Cinna. The crowd, thinking that this was he, rushed on him and tore him limb from limb on the spot. It was this more than anything else which frightened Brutus and Cassius, and within a few days they withdrew from the city. What they did and what happened to them before they died has been related in my *Life of Brutus*.

Caesar was fifty-six years old when he died.[19] He had survived Pompey by not much more than four years. As for the supreme power which he had pursued during the whole course of his life throughout such dangers and which at last and with such difficulty he had achieved, the only fruit he reaped from it was an empty name and a glory which made him envied by his fellow citizens. But that great divine power or genius, which had watched over him and helped him in his life, even after his death remained active as an avenger of his murder, pursuing and tracking down the murderers over every land and sea until not one of them was left

and visiting with retribution all, without exception, who were in any way concerned either with the death itself or with the planning of it.

So far as human coincidences are concerned, the most remarkable was that which concerned Cassius. After his defeat at Philippi he killed himself with the very same dagger which he had used against Caesar. And of supernatural events there was, first, the great comet, which shone very brightly for seven nights after Caesar's murder and then disappeared; and also the dimming of the sun. For the whole of that year the sun's orb rose dull and pale; the heat which came down from it was feeble and ineffective, so that the atmosphere, with insufficient warmth to penetrate it, lay dark and heavy on the earth and fruits and vegetables never properly ripened, withering away and falling off before they were mature because of the coldness of the air.

But, more than anything else, the phantom which appeared to Brutus made it clear that the murder of Caesar was not pleasing to the gods. The story is as follows: Brutus was about to take his army across from Abydos[20] to the mainland on the other side of the straits, and one night was lying down, as usual, in his tent, not asleep, but thinking about the future. He fancied that he heard a noise at the entrance to the tent and, looking toward the light of the lamp which was almost out, he saw a terrible figure, like a man, though unnaturally large and with a very severe expression. He was frightened at first, but, finding that this apparition just stood silently by his bed without doing or saying anything, he said: "Who are you?" Then the phantom replied: "Brutus, I am your evil ge-

---

19. According to Plutarch, Caesar was born in 100 B.C., but modern scholars believe that he was actually born in 102 B.C. Thus he was fifty-eight, not fifty-six, when he died.

20. **Abydos:** an ancient town on the Dardanelles, in Asia Minor.

nius. You shall see me at Philippi." On this occasion Brutus answered courageously: "Then I shall see you," and the supernatural visitor at once went away. Time passed and he drew up his army against Antony and Caesar[21] near Philippi. In the first battle he conquered the enemy divisions that were op-

posed to him, and, after routing them, broke through and sacked Caesar's camp. But in the night before the second battle the same phantom visited him again. It spoke no word, but Brutus realized that his fate was upon him and exposed himself to every danger in the battle. He did not die, however, in the fighting. It was after his troops had been routed that he retired to a steep rocky place, put his naked sword to his breast and with the help of a friend, so they say, who assisted him in driving the blow home, killed himself.

---

21. **Caesar:** Gaius Octavius (63 B.C.–A.D. 14), the nephew of Julius Caesar, who, in 27 B.C., under the title of Augustus Caesar, became the first Roman emperor.

FOR STUDY AND DISCUSSION

1. Historians often do more than report the events of a person's life: they also may state or imply explanations for those events. One historian might show that people shape their own lives. Another historian might show that a force outside the control of a person—upbringing, environment, "fate"—is the shaping influence. Do you think Plutarch shows that Caesar was in control of his destiny? Does he suggest that if Caesar had been a different kind of man, he might have avoided being killed? Cite passages from the text to support your answers.

2. Plutarch implies certain truths—lessons to be drawn from Caesar's life and death. Where, for example, does he imply that a divine justice punishes the guilty? What lesson about the use of power does he want you to draw from Caesar's assassination?

3. Plutarch was inclined toward mysticism in religion and he served as a priest in the Temple of Apollo in Greece. Look back at his nar-

rative of the events that followed Caesar's death. What details show that Plutarch believed that supernatural forces caused the natural world to respond to human events?

4. Has Plutarch presented a favorable portrayal of Caesar, or is he neutral in his feelings about him? Explain.

5. Does Plutarch present Brutus in a more positive light than the other conspirators? Explain. What do you think is Plutarch's attitude toward Brutus?

FOR COMPOSITION

Writing a Report

Read an account of the public life of a great American leader—Washington, Lincoln, Wilson, Franklin Delano Roosevelt, Martin Luther King, Jr.—to find out what one historian believes were the major causes of the leader's successes and failures. Try to single out the causes that are most emphasized. Write a report of your findings.

Two Portraits

Emily Dickinson

Though Emily Dickinson is today considered one of the greatest poets America has produced, only a few of her poems were published while she lived. The bulk of her poetry was published after her death in 1886. Born in 1830 in Amherst, Massachusetts, she lived almost her whole life in the home of her parents in close companionship with them and with her sister Lavinia and her brother Austin, who lived nearby. Her father, Edward Dickinson, was a man of independent character and mind, qualities he encouraged in his children. The family lived, Lavinia is quoted as saying, "like friendly and absolute monarchs, each in his own domain."

After completing her education at Amherst Academy, Emily attended Mount Holyoke Female Seminary (now Mount Holyoke College) for a short time. Returning home, she gave more and more time to writing poetry. Her first known poem was written as a valentine in 1850. Increasingly, she wrote poems into her letters to the occasional amazement of their receivers. Emily Dickinson wrote 1,775 poems in her lifetime. More than two thirds of these were written in a seven-year period; 366 poems were written in 1862 alone, certainly one of the most important years of her life.

On April 15 of 1862, Dickinson wrote to the critic Thomas Wentworth Higginson. "Are you too deeply occupied to say if my Verse is alive?" she asked. Had Higginson been a more perceptive reader of poetry, and had he encouraged the publication of the poems, the course of Dickinson's life might have been different. But Higginson did not encourage publication. The two met in 1870, when Higginson visited Amherst College. "I never was with anyone who drained my nerve power so much," he wrote his wife. "Without touching her, she drew from me. I am glad not to live near her."

Higginson's unsympathetic treatment of her poetry was perhaps one of many experiences that forced Emily Dickinson into seclusion. We cannot be sure why she never left the area of the family house after 1865. In 1884 her health broke down. In May of 1886 she wrote to her cousins: "Called back," and a few days later she was dead.

Van Wyck Brooks (1886–1963) was one of America's most distinguished literary historians. Born in Plainfield, New Jersey, he was educated at Harvard, taught at Stanford University for a short time, and traveled widely before he began writing a history of American literature. The first volume of that history, *The Flowering of New England*, published in 1936, won the Pulitzer Prize and was a best seller for fifty-nine weeks—a rare achievement for a scholarly work. Many volumes followed, forming a large work that Brooks titled *Makers and Finders*.

In his essay on Emily Dickinson, Brooks looks at the eccentricities that formed a legend after the poet's death, and he places her in the setting of family and small-town life in a remote part of New England in the middle of the nineteenth century. Brooks also raises a question that has long fascinated —and baffled—her biographers: Why did she retire into seclusion? Like all of Dickinson's biographers, Brooks can only guess at the answer to this question.

Emily Dickinson   *Van Wyck Brooks*

The Dickinsons lived in the principal house in Amherst. A large, square, red-brick mansion that stood behind a hemlock hedge, with three gates accurately closed, it was a symbol of rural propriety and all the substantialities of western New England. Edward Dickinson, the lawyer, had always had his office in the village, and four times a day, in his broadcloth coat and beaver hat, with a gold-headed cane in his hand, he had passed through one of the gates, going or coming. A thin severe punctilious man who had once been a member of Congress, a friend of Daniel Webster[1] in his youth, a Calvinist[2] of the strictest persuasion, he was a pillar of Amherst College until his death in 1874. The college had been founded, largely by his father, to check the sort of errors that were spreading from Harvard, and he never abated his rigor in the interests of pleasure. He was said to have laughed on one occasion, but usually he was as cold and still as the white marble mantel in his parlor. The story was told in Amherst, however, that once he had rung the church bell, as if to summon the people to a fire. The whole town came running, for he rang the bell excitedly.

---

1. **Daniel Webster:** American statesman and orator (1782–1852).

2. **Calvinist:** a believer in the religious doctrines of the theologian John Calvin (1509–1564). Calvinists emphasize God's sternness and believe in a strict moral code.

The Dickinson home in Amherst, Massachusetts, as seen from the back garden.

He wished to call attention to the sunset.

Next door, behind the hemlock hedge, another ample dwelling stood, suggesting in its style an Italian villa. Here lived the Squire's son Austin, once his partner, who kept open house for the college. While the Dickinson mansion was somewhat forbidding, with the stamp of the Squire's grim ways and his invalid wife, the villa was a center of Hampshire hospitality that shared its rolling lawns and charming garden. Olmsted[3] had visited there, when he was planning Central Park, to examine the shrubs and trees, the plants and flowers; and distinguished guests at the college commencements and lecturers during the winter season were received and welcomed there as nowhere else. Emerson,[4] Wendell Phillips,[5] and Beecher[6] had stayed in this house next door, and Samuel Bowles of the *Springfield Republican* was an intimate friend of all the Dickinsons. The *Republican* was a school for journalists, known far and

3. **Olmsted:** Frederick Law Olmsted (1822–1903), American landscape architect. He designed New York's Central Park.

4. **Emerson:** Ralph Waldo Emerson (1803–1882), American writer and philosopher.
5. **Wendell Phillips:** American abolitionist and social reformer (1811–1884).
6. **Beecher:** Henry Ward Beecher (1813–1887), American clergyman famous for his powerful sermons.

wide, and travelers—Dickens and Kingsley[7] among them—constantly stopped at Springfield in order to have a chat with Samuel Bowles. His paper was a sovereign authority in Amherst, and he often drove over for a call at the villa or the mansion, sometimes bringing manuscripts by well-known authors to show the Dickinson daughters before they were published. His favorite was Emily, who was older than Lavinia, but Emily usually "elfed it" when visitors came. She was always in the act of disappearing. Through the blinds of her western windows, overlooking the garden, she observed the hospitalities of the villa, and snatches of whatever was current in the books and talk of a college town, in the politics and thought of the moment, reached her when the guests had gone away. But even her oldest friends seldom saw her. While sometimes, in the evening, she flitted across the garden, she never left the place by day or night. To have caught a fleeting glimpse of her was something to boast of, and a young girl across the way who watched at night for a light at her window was thrilled if Miss Emily's shadow appeared for a moment. There were nursemaids who thought she was a witch. They frightened the children by uttering her name, as if there were something malign in Miss Dickinson's queerness.

While her friends seldom saw her, and almost never face to face—for she spoke from the shadows of the hallway, as they sat in the parlor, or sometimes down the stairs—they were used to receiving little letters from her. These letters were also peculiar. Miss Dickinson rarely addressed the envelopes. Some other hand, perhaps her sister's, performed this office for her. More often the names of the person and town had been clipped from a printed paper and pasted together, as if it were a sort of violation to expose the strokes of her pen to the touch of the postman. The letters themselves were brief and cryptic, usually only a line or two: "Do you look out tonight?" for example. "The moon rides like a girl through a topaz town." Or "The frogs sing sweet today—they have such pretty, lazy times—how nice to be a frog." Or "Tonight the crimson children are playing in the West." Or "The lawn is full of south and the odors tangle, and I hear today for the first the river in the tree." Now and again, some fine phrase emerged from the silvery spray of words—"Not what the stars have done, but what they are to do, is what detains the sky." Sometimes her notes had a humorous touch: "Father steps like Cromwell[8] when he gets the kindlings," or "Mrs. S. gets bigger, and rolls down the lane to church like a reverend marble." But her messages often contained no words at all. She would lower baskets of goodies out of the window to children waiting below. At times, instead of a letter, she sent a poem, an odd little fragment of three or four lines, with a box of chocolate caramels or frosted cakes and a flower or a sprig of pine on top, heliotrope, perhaps, or an oleander blossom or a dandelion tied with a scarlet ribbon. Her letters were rhythmical, they scanned like the poems, and they were congested with images—every phrase was an image; while the poems themselves suggested nursery rhymes or Dr. Watts's[9] hymns, broken up and

---

7. **Kingsley:** Charles Kingsley (1819–1875), English novelist.

8. **Cromwell:** Oliver Cromwell (1599–1658), English general who led the Puritan revolt against King Charles I. Cromwell's name is associated with formidable power.
9. **Watts:** Isaac Watts (1674–1748) was an English hymn writer.

filled with a strange new content. They might have struck unsympathetic readers as a sort of transcendental baby talk. It was evident that Miss Dickinson had lost the art of communication, as the circle of her school friends understood it. She vibrated toward them, she put forth shy, impalpable tentacles, she instantly signalized with a verse or a note every event in their lives. But she did not speak the language of the world outside her, and one gathered that she did not wish to touch it. She was rapt in a private world of sensations and thoughts. It was even observed that her handwriting went through three distinct phases and that toward the end the letters never touched. Each character, separately formed, stood quite alone.

She had been a recluse since the early sixties, and her family surmised the reason. She had fallen in love with a married man, a Philadelphia clergyman, and had buried herself at home by way of refuge. When her supposed lover supposedly pursued her there, her sister dashed across to the house next door and exclaimed to their brother Austin's wife, "Sue, come! That man is here. Father and Mother are away, and I am afraid Emily will go away with him." Such was the family legend, which may have been apocryphal.[10] Undoubtedly, the clergyman came to see her, but probably only to call. Was he in love with Emily? Probably not. In any case, she did not go away. She withdrew from all activities outside the household, and her mind turned in upon itself. She had hitherto been eminently social, or as much so as her little world permitted. Born in 1830, in the red-brick mansion, she had grown up a lively girl who was always a center of attention. She was a capital mimic. She travestied the young-lady pieces, the "Battle of Prague" and others, which she

played on the mahogany piano, and her odd and funny stories enthralled her friends. Later they remembered that she placed bouquets of flowers in the pews of those she liked best, at church. Dancing and cardplaying were not allowed in Amherst, but Noah Webster's granddaughter, who lived there, evaded the prohibition on behalf of her circle. She held "P.O.M." meetings for the Poetry of Motion, and Emily Dickinson excelled in this branch of learning. She joined in picnics and walks over the Amherst hills with groups of boys and girls from the town and the college. They had "sugaring-off" parties and valentine parties, and they often climbed Mount Norwottuck where they found ferns and lady's-slippers; and sometimes they met at a brookside in the woods, where the boys went fishing and the girls made chowder. Emily was an ardent botanist. She knew the haunts of all the wild flowers in the region, and sometimes she scrambled along through the forest, perhaps with her big dog Carlo. She was an expert cook. At home she baked the bread and boiled her father's puddings, but her father was difficult to please. He read "lonely and rigorous books," she said, on Sunday afternoons, fearing that anything else might "joggle the mind"; and Shakespeare, the Bible, and Dr. Watts's hymns were the reading that he chose for his daughter. He did not like her to work in the garden, or to make visits without him, and when she was too witty he left the table. At fifteen she could not tell the time: her father supposed he had taught her, but she had not understood him, and she did not dare to ask him again or ask anyone else who might have told her. Now and again, she rebelled. She smashed a plate or a teacup, and her friends and her brother found ways to provide her with books, hiding them in the box-bush that stood beside the front door or on the parlor piano, under the cover. In one way or

---

10. **apocryphal** (ə-pŏk′rə-fəl): fictitious; not true.

another, she contrived to read most of the current authors, especially the Brontës and the Brownings, with Hawthorne, Coleridge, Irving, Keats, and Ruskin. One of her special favorites was Sir Thomas Browne, and she loved the drollery of Dickens. For the rest, she read Heine in German and Emerson's poems, and Frank B. Sanborn's letters in the *Springfield Republican* kept her in the literary current. She was by no means passive in this house of duty. Once, at a funeral in Hadley, whither she had gone with her father in the family barouche,[11] she ran away for several hours with a young cousin from Worcester and drove back to Amherst in his buggy. At school, she declared her independence. She had been sent as a boarding pupil to Mary Lyon's seminary, where she had written her themes on the nature of sin. She had listened to lectures on total depravity as if, like most of the other girls, she had meant to be a missionary's wife; but when, one day, Miss Lyon asked all the girls to rise, all who wished to be Christians, Emily alone refused to do so. She had found that she could not share the orthodox faith. Otherwise her life went on, with a few journeys here and there, like that of any country lawyer's daughter. As a young girl, she had visited Boston. She remembered the concerts and Bunker Hill, the Chinese Museum and Mount Auburn; and later, on two occasions, she stayed in Cambridge to receive some treatment for her eyes. When her father was serving his term in Congress, in 1854, she spent seven weeks in Washington with him. Her father's friends were struck by her charm and her wit. It was on her way home that she stopped at Philadelphia and received the sudden shock that had changed her life.

This was the whole of Miss Dickinson's story, so far as outward events were concerned, when Thomas Wentworth Higginson[12] entered the picture. Higginson had written an appeal in *The Atlantic*, addressed to the rising generation. Remembering the days of *The Dial*, when the hazel wand, waved over New England, had indicated hidden springs of talent in many a country town, he said that to find a "new genius" was an editor's greatest privilege. If any such existed who read *The Atlantic*, let him court the editor—"draw near him with soft approaches and mild persuasions." Higginson added a number of admonitions: "Charge your style with life . . . Tolerate no superfluities. . . . There may be years of crowded passion in a word, and half a life in a sentence." This appeal was anonymous, but many of the Amherst people knew who wrote the articles in *The Atlantic*, for Sanborn's literary gossip kept them posted; and presently Colonel Higginson, who was living in Worcester, received an odd little letter. The letter was unsigned, but the writer sent four poems, and she placed in a separate envelope the signature "Emily Dickinson." She begged this distant friend to be her "master." The poems puzzled Higginson. While he felt a curious power in them, he was not prepared for a "new genius" who broke so many rules as this lady in Amherst, who punctuated with dashes only and seemed to have small use for rhyme and merely wished to know if she was "clear." She did not ask him to publish the poems, and he did not pass them on to the editor, but he wrote her a sympathetic letter that was followed by a long correspondence. She continued to send him poems at intervals, signing her notes "your gnome" and "your

---

11. **barouche:** four-wheeled carriage with a folding top.

12. **Thomas Wentworth Higginson** (1823–1911): See page 241.

scholar," but, although she asked him again if he would be her "preceptor,"[13] and he offered her a number of suggestions, she never changed a line or a word to please him. In one note she said, "If I read a book and it makes my whole body so cold no fire can ever warm me, I know that is poetry. If I feel physically as if the top of my head were taken off, I know that is poetry. These are the only ways I know it. Is there any other way?" And once she replied, when he asked her for a photograph, "I had no portrait now, but am small, like the wren; and my hair is bold, like the chestnut burr; and my eyes like the sherry in the glass that the guest leaves." This feminine mystification piqued[14] the colonel. He wrote, "You enshroud yourself in this fiery mist and I cannot reach you, but only rejoice in the rare sparkles of light." When she told him that her companions were the hills and the sundown, he replied that she ought to come to Boston: she would find herself at home at Mrs. Sargent's. At last, in 1870, he went to Amherst. After a brief delay, while he waited in the parlor, he heard a faint footstep in the hallway and a shy, little childlike creature glided in. She carried two daylilies, which she placed in his hand, saying, in a soft, breathless voice, "These are my introduction," adding in a whisper, "Forgive me if I am frightened. I never see strangers and hardly know what to say." She spoke of her household occupations and said that "people must have puddings," and she added a few detached enigmatic remarks. She seemed to the amiable Higginson as unique and remote as Undine or Mignon or Thekla.[15] But he was disturbed by the tension

in the air and was glad he did not live too near this lady. There was something abnormal about her, he felt. He had never met anyone before who drained his nerve power so much.

At that time, Miss Dickinson was forty years old and had long since withdrawn from the world; and the friends who came to see her sister were used to the "hurrying whiteness" that was always just going through a door. She sometimes swept into the parlor, bowed and touched a hand or two, poised over the flowered Brussels carpet, and vanished like a ghost or an exhalation; but even these appearances had grown rarer and rarer. Only the neighbors' children really saw her. She had given up wearing colors and was always dressed in diaphanous white, with a cameo pin that held the ruching[16] together. She was decisive in manner, anything but frail. Her complexion was velvety white, her lips were red. Her hair was bound with a chestnut-colored snood, and when it was chilly she wore a little shoulder cape crocheted with soft white worsted run through with a ribbon. She often had a flower in her hand. She moved about in a sort of reverie, flitting "as quick as a trout" when she was disturbed. (This was one of her sister Lavinia's phrases.) The children knew her "high, surprised voice." They knew her dramatic way of throwing up her hands as she ended one of the stories she liked to tell them. She made them her fellow conspirators. They followed her upstairs and heard her comments on the guests she had left in the parlor. She would say, with finger on lip, as feminine callers left, "Listen! Hear them kiss, the traitors!" Or, peeping down the

---

13. **preceptor:** teacher.
14. **piqued** (pēkt): offended.
15. **Undine . . . Thekla:** various mysterious women. Undine is a legendary water sprite. Mignon is a mysterious Italian girl in a story by Goethe. Thekla is a saint about whom little is known.

16. **ruching** (roo'shĭng): pleats of lace or ribbon.

stairs, she would say of some man, "Look, dear, his face is as pretty as a cloth pink," or "His face is as handsome and meaningless as the full moon." She remarked, apropos of some scholarly person, "He has the facts, but not the phosphorescence of learning." She said that her own ideal caller was always just going out of sight, and that it made her shiver to hear people talk as if they were "taking all the clothes off their souls." She called herself the "cow lily," because of the orange lights in her hair and her eyes, and she observed that the housemaid moved about "in a calico sarcophagus."[17] Once she said to her little niece, who was puzzled by her shy ways, "No one could ever punish a Dickinson by shutting her up alone." Meanwhile, her life went on with her flowers and her sister. She had a small conservatory, opening out of the dining room, a diminutive glass chamber with shelves around it; and there she grouped the ferns and the jasmine, the lilies and the heliotrope and the oxalis plants in their hanging baskets. She had a little watering pot, with a long slender spout that was like the antenna of an insect, and she sat up all night at times in winter to keep her flowers from freezing. The garden was her special care, and occasionally one saw her at dusk through the gate, fluttering about the porch like a moth in the moonlight. When it was damp, she knelt on an old red army blanket that she had thrown on the ground, to reach the flowers. Usually, on summer evenings, she sat for a while with Lavinia on the side piazza, overlooking the flagged path that led to the villa. There stood the giant daphne odora,[18] moved out from the conservatory, and the two small oleanders in their tubs.

The front door of the Dickinson home.

Meanwhile, since 1862, Miss Dickinson had been writing poems, although there were very few of her friends who knew it. They all knew the little rhymes she sent them with arbutus buds, but they did not know how seriously she pursued her writing, at night, beside the Franklin stove in the upstairs corner bedroom, in the light that often glimmered over the snow. From her window she had caught suggestions that gave her a pic-

---

17. **sarcophagus** (sär-kŏf′ə-gəs): tomb; coffin.
18. **daphne odora**: a fragrant plant.

ture, a fancy, an image. Perhaps a boy passed whistling, or a neighbor on her way to church, or a dog with feet "like intermittent plush"; or perhaps she knew that a traveling circus was going to pass in the early morning, and she sat up to watch the "Algerian procession." A dead fly on the windowpane stirred her imagination, and once in the glare of a fire at night she saw a caterpillar measuring a leaf far down in the orchard. She saw the bluebirds darting round "with little dodging feet,"

"The motions of the dipping birds,
The lightning's joined road;"

and all these observations went into her verses. She wrote on sheets of notepaper, which she sewed together, rolling and tying the bundles with a thread or a ribbon and tucking them away in the drawers of her bureau; although sometimes the back of an envelope served her as well. But, casual in this, she was anything but casual—she was a cunning workman—in her composition. Poetry was her solitaire and, so to speak, her journal, for, like Thoreau[19] in Concord, she watched the motions of her mind, recording its ebbs and flows and the gleams that shot through it; and she labored over her phrases to make them right. Were they all her own? Were there echoes in them, or anything of the conventional, the rhetorical, the fat? Were they clear, were they exact, were they compact? She liked the common hymn meters, and the meters of nursery jingles, which had been deeply ingrained in her mind as a child, and she seemed to take a rebellious joy in violating all their rules, fulfilling the traditional patterns while she also broke them.

She was always experimenting with her rhymes and her rhythms, sometimes adding extra syllables to break up their monotony, sometimes deliberately twisting a rhyme, as Emerson did, for the sake of harshness, to escape the mellifluous[20] effect of conventional poems. Many of her pieces were like parodies of hymns, whose gentle glow in her mind had become heat lightning. For Emily Dickinson's light was quick. It was sudden, sharp and evanescent; and this light was the dry light that is closest to fire.

The visible setting of these poems was the New England countryside, the village, the garden, the household that she knew so well, a scene, the only scene she knew, that she invested with magic, so that the familiar objects become portents and symbols. Here were the hills, the changing seasons, the winter light, the light of spring, the bee, the mouse, the hummingbird, the cricket, the lonely houses off the road, the village inn, the lamppost that became, in the play of her fancy, sublime or droll; and with what gifts of observation she caught the traits of her birds and insects, of everything that crept or ran or flew—the snake "unbraiding in the sun," the robin's eyes, "like frightened beads," the umbrella of the bat that was "quaintly halved." She often seemed a little girl, amusing herself with childish whimsies, and, in fact, as the ward of her father, she remained in some ways adolescent; and, as she dressed to the end in the fashion of her early youth, so she retained the imagery of the child in the household. But her whimsies sometimes turned into bold ideas. She saw the mountain, like her father, sitting "in his eternal chair"; her ocean had a "basement," like the house in Amherst, and her

---

19. **Thoreau:** Henry David Thoreau (1817–1862), American naturalist and writer. In his book *Walden*, Thoreau describes a time he lived alone in the woods near Concord, Massachusetts.

20. **mellifluous** (mə-lĭf′lōō-əs): sweet and smooth (like honey).

wind and snow swept the road like the brooms that she had been taught to use—the brooms of the breeze swept vale and tree and hill. A journey to the Day of Judgment struck her as a "buggy ride," and she saw a "schoolroom" in the sky. She domesticated the universe and read her own experience into the motions of nature and the world she observed. The sun rose in the east for her "a ribbon at a time," and the "housewife in the evening West" came back to "dust the pond." Clouds for her were "millinery," mountains wore bonnets, shawls, and sandals, eternity "rambled" with her, like her dog Carlo; the wind had fingers and combed the sky, and March walked boldly up and knocked like a neighbor. Volcanoes purred for her like cats, and she saw the planets "frisking about," her Providence kept a store on the village street, and she thought of death as coming with a broom and a dustpan. The moon slid down the stairs for her "to see who's there," and the grave for her was a little cottage where she could "lay the marble tea." One could not "fold a flood," she said, and "put it in a drawer," but she rolled up the months in mothballs and laid them away, as she had swept up the heart and put away love; and she saw hope, fear, time, future, and past as persons to rally, welcome, play with, flee, or tease.

The turns of fancy[21] that marked these poems were sharp and unpredictable, and yet they were singularly natural—nothing was forced. Miss Dickinson lived in a world of paradox, for, while her eye was microscopic, her imagination dwelt with mysteries and grandeurs. Ribbons and immortality were mingled in her mind, which passed from one to the other with the speed of lightning,

though she sometimes took a mischievous pleasure in extravagant combinations of thought, uniting the droll and the sublime, the trivial and the grand. There was in this an element of the characteristic American humor that liked to play with incongruities, and Miss Dickinson maintained in the poems of her later years the fun-loving spirit she had shown as a schoolgirl. To juxtapose the great and the small, in unexpected ways, had been one of her prime amusements as the wit of her circle, and this, like the laconic speech that also marked the Yankee, had remained an essential note of her style as a poet. "Shorter than a snake's delay," her poems were packed with meaning; and, swiftly as her images changed, they were scarcely able to keep the pace with which her mind veered from mood to mood, from faith to mockery, from mysticism to rationalism, through ecstasy, disillusion, anguish, joy. These poems were fairylike in their shimmer and lightness, they moved like bees upon a raft of air; and yet one felt behind them an energy of mind and spirit that only the rarest poets ever possessed. Was not Emily Dickinson's idiom the final proof that she possessed it? Her style, her stamp, her form were completely her own.

Such were the games of solitaire that Miss Dickinson played in the silent room, as lonely as Jane Eyre,[22] in her red-curtained alcove, dreaming over the book with its pictures of the arctic wastes and the rock that stood up in the sea of billow and spray. Miss Dickinson had only this "acre of a rock," and yet what a harvest it yielded of grape and maize. Having but a crumb, she was sovereign of them all, as she said quite truly; for her constant theme was deprivation, the "banquet of abstemious-

---

21. **fancy:** here, imagination.

22. **Jane Eyre:** heroine of Charlotte Brontë's novel of the same name, published in 1847.

ness," and this sharpened as nothing else her perception of values. When the well's dry, we know the worth of water, and she felt that she knew victory because she knew defeat, she felt that she knew love because she had lost it. Certainly for all she missed she made up in intensity: where others merely glowed, she was incandescent.

FOR STUDY AND DISCUSSION

1. On page 245 Van Wyck Brooks gives one possible explanation of why Dickinson became a recluse. According to her family, why did she withdraw from the outside world? What had her life been like before this?

2. Brooks says that Thomas Wentworth Higginson was not prepared for Dickinson's "new genius." Why was Higginson disturbed by Emily Dickinson? What technical aspects of her poetry was he unprepared to accept?

3. Brooks says that Dickinson's poetry "domesticated the universe." In other words, she used everyday objects and experiences to evoke spiritual or universal ideas. What examples from Dickinson's poetry does Brooks use to illustrate this? Can you see how this tendency might have resulted from the kind of life the poet led? Explain.

4. Dickinson's constant poetic theme, says Brooks, was *deprivation*, which means "loss," or "being kept away from something." According to Brooks, how did Dickinson benefit from her "deprived" life?

5. Several times Brooks describes Dickinson in terms of fire and light. On page 249 he says that her "light was quick . . . this light was the dry light that is closest to fire." What image does he use to describe Dickinson in the last sentences of the essay? How would you explain this comparison in your own words?

FOR COMPOSITION

Analyzing a Poem

Van Wyck Brooks identifies several qualities that distinguish Emily Dickinson's poetry:

1. Settings familiar to the poet
2. Rhymes and rhythms that are varied to avoid a singsong effect
3. Phrases that are clear, exact, and compact
4. Use of familiar objects and experiences to suggest spiritual or universal ideas

Write a short analysis of the following poem by Dickinson. Use one paragraph to explain whether it reflects any of the above characteristics. Use another paragraph to tell what meaning the poem has for you.

> The saddest noise, the sweetest noise,
>   The maddest noise that grows—
> The birds, they make it in the spring,
>   At night's delicious close.
>
> Between the March and April line—
>   That magical frontier
> Beyond which summer hesitates,
>   Almost too heavenly near.
>
> It makes us think of all the dead
>   That sauntered with us here,
> By separation's sorcery
>   Made cruelly more dear.
>
> It makes us think of what we had,
>   And what we now deplore.
> We almost wish those siren throats
>   Would go and sing no more.
>
> An ear can break a human heart
>   As quickly as a spear,
> We wish the ear had not a heart
>   So dangerously near.

Another view of Emily Dickinson's life is provided by the play *The Belle of Amherst* by William Luce (1931–   ). Luce first read Dickinson when he was a boy "in sophomore English." The experience kindled in him a lifelong affection for the poet and her works. When he finally decided to write a play about Dickinson, he spent two years reading and rereading the biographical studies done of her, all of her collected letters, and, of course, all of her poems. As he read, Luce collected excerpts from the letters and poems as well as comments reported by her biographers. Luce found that when he wove these excerpts together in a conversational style, blending his own words in as smoothly as possible, a story emerged. What resulted was *The Belle of Amherst,* a play in which the character Emily Dickinson appears alone onstage to tell the story of her life, as Luce imagines the poet herself might actually have told it.

The Belle of Amherst is a rather uncommon form of biography—the dramatized biography. It is also a rather uncommon form of drama—the one-person play. But in Luce's opinion the marriage of these two uncommon forms is well suited to Dickinson's story. She was a seclusive person who spoke to the world through poems that are extremely dramatic. Luce decided that Dickinson alone should tell her story.

The Belle of Amherst was produced on Broadway in 1976, with Julie Harris playing the role of Emily Dickinson. What follows are excerpts from that play, three scenes from Act One and two scenes from Act Two.

The Belle of Amherst

William Luce

Act One

Scene 1

The curtain is always up.

The stage suggests two rooms. The backdrop depicts the silhouettes of seven trees against the sky.

Stage right is Emily Dickinson's *bedroom. It contains a narrow iron bed with railings at the head and foot. At the end of the bed is a trunk. By a window seat a doll sits on the floor. Downstage are a small square table and chair at which* Emily *does her writing. A kerosene lamp is on the table. On the floor beside the table is a carved box or chest containing* Emily's *finished poems.*

Stage left is the Dickinson parlor. It has a square piano of the 1850 period, settee, chair, books, table, pictures, low chest, tea cart, and hall tree.

Emily Dickinson *is a delicate, sensitive, and quaint woman, but with an inner strength. Her manner ranges from the childlike and whimsical to the deeply poignant.*

Emily *enters from stage left. It is 1883. She is fifty-three years old, which in her case is not too relevant, since she appears younger than she is. Her hair is auburn, parted in the center, and pulled back. She is dressed in a simple full-length white dress with an apron over it.*

Emily (*enters, carrying the teapot. She calls back over her shoulder*). Yes, Vinnie, I have the tea, dear!

[*She places the tea on the tea cart, then looks up wide-eyed at the audience. Slowly she picks up a plate with slices of dark cake on it, walks shyly downstage, and extends it to the audience.*]

This is my introduction. Black cake. My own special recipe.

Forgive me if I'm frightened. I never see strangers and hardly know what I say. My sister, Lavinia—she's younger than I—she says I tend to wander back and forth in time. So you must bear with me. I was born December tenth, eighteen thirty, which makes me—*fifty-three?*

Welcome to Amherst. My name is Emily Elizabeth Dickinson. Elizabeth is for my Aunt Elisabeth Currier. She's Father's sister. Oh, how the trees stand up straight when they hear Aunt Libbie's little boots come thumping into Amherst! She's the only male relative on the female side.

Dear Aunt Libbie.

But I don't use my middle name any more—since I became a *poet.*

Professor Higginson, the literary critic, doesn't think my poems are—no matter. I've had seven poems published—anonymously, to be sure. So you see why I prefer to introduce myself to you as a poet.

Here in Amherst, I'm known as Squire Edward Dickinson's half-cracked daughter. Well, I am! The neighbors can't figure me out. I don't cross my father's ground to any house or town. I haven't left the house for years.

> The soul selects her own society—
> then—shuts the door—

Why should I socialize with village gossips?

[Emily *turns to the window, still holding the cake.*]

There goes one of them now—Henrietta Sweetser—everyone knows Henny. She'd even intimidate the anti-Christ. Look at her! She's strolling by the house, trying to catch a glimpse of me. Would *you* like that?

So I give them something to talk about. I dress in white all year round, even in winter. "Bridal white," Henny calls it.

[*She mimics back-fence gossips.*]

"Dear, dear! Dresses in bridal white, she does, every day of the blessed year. Year in, year out. Disappointed in love as a girl, so I hear. Poor creature. All so very sad. And her sister, Lavinia, a spinster too. Didn't you know? Oh, yes. Stayed unmarried just to be at home and take care of Miss Emily. Two old maids in that big house. What a lonely life, to shut yourself away from good people like us."

Indeed!

You should see them come to the door bearing gifts, craning their necks, trying to see over Vinnie's shoulder. But I'm too fast for them. I've already run upstairs two steps at a time. And I hide there until they leave. You can imagine what they make of that!

One old lady came to the door the other day to get a peek inside. I surprised her by answering the door myself. She stammered something about looking for a house to buy.

[*Mischievously*]

To spare the expense of moving, I directed her to the cemetery.

[Emily *suddenly realizes that she is still holding the cake.*]

Oh! The cake!

I do all the baking here at Homestead. I even banged the spice for this cake. My father always raved about my baking. He would eat no cake or bread but mine.

[*She samples a piece of cake.*]

Mm. Lovely.

No, no—it's easy to make. The recipe? Of course. It's really very simple. Now, I'll go slowly.

[*She places the cake on the tea cart.*]

BLACK CAKE: two pounds of flour, two pounds of sugar, two pounds of butter, nineteen eggs, five pounds of raisins, one and a half pounds of currants, one and a half pounds of citron, one half-pint of brandy—I never use Father's best—one half-pint of molasses, two nutmegs, five teaspoons of cloves, mace, and cinnamon, and—oh, yes, two teaspoons of soda, and one and a half teaspoons of salt.

[Emily *has removed her apron.*]

Just beat the butter and sugar together, add the nineteen eggs, one at a time—now this is very important—*without beating*. Then, beat the mixture again, adding the brandy alternately with the flour, soda, spices, and salt that you've sifted together. Then the molasses. Now, take your five pounds of raisins, and three pounds of currants and citron, and gently sprinkle in all eight pounds—slowly now—as you stir. Bake it for three hours if you use cake pans. If you use a milk pan, as I do, you'd better leave it in the oven six or seven hours.

Everybody *loves* it. I hope you will too. Thank you.

[*She hangs her apron on the back of the chair. Then she sits down and pours tea.*]

Sometimes I bake one for a neighbor and I enclose a short note that is usually so obscure . . .

[*Gleefully*]

. . . no one can understand it! I hear my little notes are becoming collectors' items in the village. People compare them to see who has the strangest one.

Excuse me . . .

[*She writes a note.*]

"We must be careful what we say. No bird resumes its egg."

That'll keep them guessing! Oh, that reminds me—I must send a note to Mrs. Hills. She's just been admitted to the Maplewood Infirmary . . .

[Emily *reads aloud as she writes*.]

> Surgeons must be very careful
> When they take the knife!
> Underneath their fine incisions
> Stirs the Culprit—*Life!*

That'll cheer her up.

I'm told one woman in Amherst is imitating me now. Probably Clarissa Cartwright. Just what Amherst needs—another eccentric.

Oh, I do have fun with them! My menagerie.

I guess people in small towns must have their local characters. And for Amherst, that's what I am. But do you know something?

[*Confidentially*]

I enjoy the game. I've never said this to anyone before, but I'll tell *you*. I do it on purpose. The white dress, the seclusion. It's all—deliberate.

[*She moves downstage and sits on the low chest*.]

But my brother, Austin—he knows. He says, "Emily! Stop your posing!"

Austin knows me through and through, as no one else does. Father and Mother never understood me. And Vinnie—Vinnie doesn't know me either. Austin and I are unlike most everyone, and are therefore more dependent on each other for delight. But—I do think—sometimes—the stories about me distress him.

In a way, the stories are true. Oh, I believe in truth. But I think it can be *slanted* just a little. Do you know what I'm saying?

> Tell all the Truth but tell it slant—
> Success in Circuit lies
> Too bright for our infirm Delight
> The Truth's superb surprise
>
> As Lightning to the Children eased
> With explanation kind
> The Truth must dazzle gradually
> Or every man be blind—

[Emily *moves to the parlor chair*.]

Words are my life. I look at words as if they were entities, sacred beings. There are words to which I lift my hat when I see them sitting on a page. Sometimes I write one . . .

[Emily *writes "circumference" on a paper and holds it up to be seen.*]

"Circumference" . . .

. . . and I look at its outlines until it starts to glow brighter than any sapphire. I hesitate which word to take when I write a poem. A poet can choose but a few words, and they have to be the chiefest words, the best words.

> A word is dead
> When it is said,
> Some say.
> I say it just
> Begins to live
> That day.

If I read Keats, Shelley, Shakespeare, Mrs. Browning, Emily Brontë—oh, what an after-noon for heaven, when Brontë entered there! —and they make my whole body so cold, no fire can ever warm me, I know that is poetry. Have you ever felt that way?

If I feel physically as if the top of my head were taken off, I know *that* is poetry. These are the only ways I know it. Is there any other way?

My friend Helen Jackson—oh, you'd love her—she's moved to Colorado—Helen is a fine scholar of words and a well-known writer. She has the facts, but not the phospho-rescence.

Oh. *Phosphorescence.*

[*She writes it down.*]

Now, there's a word to lift your hat to. Can you spell it?

To find that phosphorescence, that light within, that's the genius behind poetry.

Scene 2

Emily (*comes downstage*). People find it hard to believe that I had a normal childhood. They visualize instead a miniature version of me as I am now, a pint-sized little Emily, dressed all in white, lisping riddles and aphorisms in baby talk—and of course, hiding from the family.

I guess I'm to blame for that false impres-sion.

Actually, at fifteen, I was a very typical Amherst girl. I went to dances. I giggled my way through classes, quilting bees, and scores of parties. I was trying very hard to believe I was a ravishing beauty. I was infatuated with one dashing young man after another. Unfor-tunately, they didn't know it. If they did, they were smarter than I gave them credit for.

And I sent valentines.

[Emily *sits at her desk and converses with Austin.*]

Austin.
  Austin!
  How many valentines has my handsome brother received?
  Eleven?

[*Annoyed*]

I haven't received any! Vinnie's received some beautiful ones, but I've almost lost hope. Austin! Come in here.

[*She holds up two valentines.*]

Which do you prefer? Do you think the heart's too big?
  The cupids?
  Austin. Do you think you could—tell Thomas that I'm simply pining away for a valentine? Well, surely he hasn't lost his former affection for me.

[*Plaintively*]

Well, why can't you?
  Well, there you stand with eleven valentines, eleven! And your highly accomplished and gifted sister has been entirely overlooked!
  Oh, why can't you? Please?

[*She rises from the desk.*]

Austin, come back! What are brothers for?

[Emily *returns to her desk and proceeds to write.*]

"Oh, Abiah! My dearest girlfriend! Will *you* be my valentine? I would love to send you a bouquet if I had an opportunity, and you could press it and write under it, 'The Last Flowers of Summer.' Wouldn't it be poetical? And you know, that is what young ladies aim to be nowadays—poetical.
  "I am growing handsome very fast, indeed.

[Emily *picks up a fan and poses with it.*]

"I expect I shall be the Belle of Amherst when I reach my seventeenth year. I don't doubt that I shall have perfect crowds of admirers at that age. Then, at dances, how I shall delight to make them await my bidding, and with what delight shall I witness their suspense while I make my *final decision!*"
  Why, James Francis Billings! Excuse me, Mother.

[Emily *sweeps into the parlor.*]

What handsome whiskers! How have you been?
  Isn't this a wonderful party?
  Oh, thank you! It's a *Godey's Lady's Book*[1] pattern.
  I'm well, thank you!

[*She sits at his invitation.*]

Oh, thank you!
  Yes, isn't it? July is such a *glorious* month!

[*She flutters her fan.*]

Oh, yes, delicious refreshments. Did you sample the rhubarb cupcakes? I baked them myself.
  Oh. You don't like rhubarb. Well, a lot of people don't like rhubarb, I guess.
  Oh my, yes! I *adore* cooking. I can't get

---

1. *Godey's Lady's Book:* a magazine popular at the time.

enough of cooking. Mother says any man I marry will . . .

My sister? Oh—Lavinia is well.

Yes, I'll tell her.

[*She rises and moves downstage center, as if trying to detain him.*]

Uh, Mr. Billings. How do you like going to school at Ipswich Seminary? Mr. Billings . . .

[*To herself*]

It seems Mr. Billings found the pretty girl in yellow.

[Emily *returns to the parlor and puts on her shawl.*]

Father's house and my garden—this is my world. And for my companions I have the hills and the sundown and my dog, Carlo, large as myself, that my father bought me. They're better than beings, because *they know*, but don't tell. And the noise in the pool at noon excels my piano.

You see, I've never had to go anywhere to find my paradise. I found it all right here—the only world I wanted—here in Amherst, Massachusetts.

Massachusetts.

Now there's a word to lift your hat to!

[*She is now downstage center.*]

Paradise is no journey, because it's within. But for that very cause, it's the most arduous of journeys. I travel the road into my soul all the time.

I dwell in Possibility—
A fairer House than Prose—
More numerous of Windows—
Superior—for Doors—

Of Chambers as the Cedars—
Impregnable of Eye—
And for an Everlasting Roof
The Gables of the Sky—

Of Visitors—the fairest—
For Occupation—This—
The spreading wide my narrow Hands
To gather Paradise—

Scene 3

Emily *(rises).* Father never kissed us good night in his life. I know he loved us, but oh, he was so—austere. Why, he hardly ever smiled!

[Emily *has gotten the picture of her father.*]

I remember the day we went to the photographer to have his picture taken.

[*She shows it to the audience.*]

That poor photographer, trying to be cordial and put Father at ease!

He said, "Er—Squire Dickinson. Could you smile a little? Please?"

Father said, "I am smiling!"

You see? He looks like a bear. He didn't approve of Santa Claus and all such prowling gentlemen.

[*She replaces the picture.*]

Father forbade many things. When my sister, Vinnie, was a girl, she enjoyed showing off her pretty white shoulders by wearing her summer frocks quite low . . .

[*She demonstrates to the audience.*]

. . . about here. It was the fashion. And then she'd languish about the house looking dreamy-eyed, primping in front of the mirror, running to the window every time a boy walked by the house.

[Emily *imitates her sister.*]

Hello, Benjamin!
Father could take only so much of this. Then he'd bark at her, "Lavinia! Don't be so affected! Put on a shawl!" And poor Vin would flounce dramatically out of the room and stomp up the steps to her room and slam the door. Bang! She pouted the rest of the day. Trouble was, she was even prettier when she pouted.
But Father was—oh, so proper. Very de-manding. Inflexible. That's why any show of leniency or understanding on his part would disarm us completely. I remember when he discovered I was writing till two or three o'clock in the morning.

[*She goes to the bedroom and sits at her desk, becoming absorbed in writing. Then she looks up, startled.*]

But Father—I thought you were asleep.
No, I didn't notice the time.
Two o'clock? Is it that late?
But this is the only time the house is quiet, Father. Except for Vinnie—she snores like a poker and shovel and pair of tongs.
Yes, Father. I know you have a rule about early rising. But I haven't missed one morn-ing, have I?

Tired? I do?
Well, I was—writing.
Yes. Good night, Father.

[*She turns back.*]

Just a—poem—Father.
  Now?
  Out loud?

[*She clears her throat.*]

To make a prairie—a *prairie*, Father . . .

  To make a prairie it takes a
    clover and one bee,
  One clover, and a bee,
  And revery.
  The revery alone will do,
  If bees are few.

Another one? Yes, Father, I do.

[*She stoops down beside the box of poems.*]

Excuse me. I keep my finished ones in here.

[Emily *removes a poem and sits at her desk again.*]

  I'll tell you how the Sun rose—
  A Ribbon at a time—
  The Steeples swam in Amethyst—
  The news, like Squirrels, ran—
  The Hills untied their Bonnets—
  The Bobolinks—begun—
  Then I said softly to myself—
  "That must have been the Sun"!
  But how he set—I know not—
  There seemed a purple stile
  That little Yellow boys and girls
  Were climbing all the while—
  Till when they reached the other side,

A Dominie[2] in Gray—
Put gently up the evening Bars—
And led the flock away—

Cancel the rule for me? Then I can sleep late in the morning. Oh, *thank you,* Father!

[*To the audience*]

See what I mean?

At the end of Act One, Emily Dickinson remembers how she and her sister-in-law, Sue, gathered together just the right poems to send to Thomas Wentworth Higginson. He had written an article in the April 1862 issue of The Atlantic, *inviting young writers to submit their work. Higginson did not publish any of Emily's poems, but he did correspond with her for eight years. And then, as Emily Dickinson tells it in the play, "the incredible happens. Thomas Wentworth Higginson is coming to Amherst!" As Act Two opens, Emily Dickinson is anxiously awaiting Higginson's arrival.*

Act Two

Scene 1

The stage is the same. The ensuing scene is a continuation of the conclusion of Act One.
  Emily *runs in from stage left and goes directly to her bedroom.*

Emily. Maggie![1] Watch for the coach. I'll be upstairs.

---

2. **Dominie:** a pastor, or member of the clergy.
1. **Maggie:** the family's maid.

[*She moves downstage, where she briefly sews together a booklet of poems as she talks.*]

Oh, surely, *this is the day.*

[*Shouting downstairs to Maggie*]

Maggie! When he comes, ask him to wait in the hall.

[*She looks at her watch.*]

Oh, it's almost time. I wonder how long he'll stay? Oh—what to say?

[*Practicing her introduction*]

Oh, Mr. Higginson. How is *dear* Mrs. Higginson? Good noon, Professor Higginson. How is Mrs. Higginson?

[*She picks up a fan.*]

Enchanted, Mr. Higginson. How is sweet Mrs. Higginson? . . . Another confinement?[2] . . . Sherry? It's Father's best. . . . Yes, August *is* a glorious month.

[*She gestures to a chair.*]

Please.

[*Much laughter and fanning*]

Oh, Mr. Higginson! How droll! I wish I'd thought of that. Oh, how witty! . . . My favorite books? Oh, let me see. *Jane Eyre*[3] I loved.

And *The Mill on the Floss.*[4] And of course— *your* inspired novel . . .

[*She produces the book from her desk drawer.*]

. . . *Malbone.* How *did* you do it? . . . Oh, Shakespeare is my lexicon. I owe *that* to Tutor Crowell. He made us read *everything.* He was . . .

[*She hears the coach.*]

Oh, a coach.

---

2. **confinement:** childbirth.
3. *Jane Eyre:* novel by Charlotte Brontë (1816–1855).

4. *The Mill on the Floss:* novel by George Eliot, the pen name of Mary Ann Evans (1819–1880).

[*She runs to the window.*]

It's stopping—oh, he's taller than I thought. And so imposing. Maggie! The door!

[Emily *runs to her desk, puts on her shawl. She then makes several attempts to select poems to take downstairs with her, finally deciding upon the box of poems itself.*]

Courage, Emily.

[*She goes to the parlor.*]

Mr. Higginson.

[*Breathless and tense*]

And *I* to meet *you.* Uh, how long are you going to stay? Oh, what I mean is—why has it taken eight years? Oh, I know you've been so busy. And then, you *were* away in the—the war—the *Civil* War, wasn't it?
    War to me is so—oblique. I can't grasp it. *My* wars are laid away in books.

[*She sits on the low chest, very excited. Her mind is running on one track only—publication.*]

But now, to the real purpose of your visit! I've been waiting to hear from your own lips— what you are planning for my poems. I have them right here—all the ones I've sent you.

[*She has them at hand.*]

These are the first four. And here . . .

[Emily *shuffles through many more papers, spilling some on the floor and scrambling to pick them up.*]

. . . are the later ones. I've bound them together. Oh, *this* one . . .

    I'll tell you how the Sun rose . . .

. . . *this* was Sue's choice. Sue is my sister-in-law. That's her house over there. It wasn't what I would have chosen. But perhaps for publication, it's more appropriate—more appealing to the reading public.

[*Her words tumble over each other.*]

But you will be the best judge of that, Mr. Higginson. Now, I have many more that you might feel would be better in a printed collection. Many, oh—well over a thousand you've never even read! Enough for several volumes, I should think. Oh, and I would prefer morocco-bound.[5]

[*She looks for his reaction.*]

Oh, dear, I must apologize, Mr. Higginson. I'm not giving you a chance to say anything. But could you tell me how to grow, or is it unconveyed, like melody or witchcraft?
    Well—no matter—please feel free to choose the poems you think are best for a book. And as for publishers, I'll rely solely upon your judgment. After all, you *are* my Preceptor.[6]

[Emily *finally sits back. Then slowly, she leans forward. What she is hearing from Higginson is shocking. Her mouth falls open.*]

But . . .

[*She clutches the arms of the chair.*]

---

5. **morocco-bound:** leather-bound.
6. **Preceptor:** teacher.

But—my meter is new—experimental. Not spasmodic!

Bad rhymes? Oh, no. You don't understand what I'm trying to—if I could only explain . . .

Uncontrolled? But, Mr. Higginson, when I try to organize, my little force explodes.

[She picks up a handful of poems.]

But surely a publisher will recognize . . .

[Emily *stops, her hand in midair. She is crushed.*]

Surely . . .

[*To the audience*]

> A great Hope fell
> You heard no noise
> The Ruin was within
> Oh cunning wreck that told no tale
> And let no Witness in
>
> A not admitting of the wound
> Until it grew so wide
> That all my Life had entered it
> And there were troughs beside
>
> A closing of the simple lid
> That opened to the sun
> Until the tender Carpenter
> Perpetual nail it down—

[She walks to the bedroom.]

I still send him poems. But always—from his polite replies, I get the uneasy feeling that they end up in some dusty drawer in his office.

[She reclines on the bed.]

I can talk about this now. But oh, when I heard Mr. Higginson's words—I became ill.

I understand another poet met with the same disappointing reception from Mr. Higginson. But *he* didn't give up as I did. Here . . .

[*She holds up a book.*]

. . . he got his poems published somehow. And his book has gone through nine editions already. Mr. Higginson says his poems are absolutely scandalous! His name?—(*Pause*)—Walt Whitman!

> Success is counted sweetest
> By those who ne'er succeed.
> To comprehend a nectar
> Requires sorest need.
>
> Not one of all the purple Host
> Who took the Flag today
> Can tell the definition
> So clear of Victory
>
> As he defeated—dying—
> On whose forbidden ear
> The distant strains of triumph
> Burst agonized and clear!

Perhaps no one will ever read my poems. They seem to me like an undelivered letter lost in transit. Destiny is strange.

[*Under her breath, deriding herself*]

Going to be famous!

Squire Dickinson and his wife have died. The house in Amherst is quiet now. Only Emily and Lavinia are there.

Scene 2

Emily (*to the audience*). Since Father's death, I've worried about Vinnie. She says the strangest things. She treats me as if I were a child and she my nursemaid.

[*She goes to the bedroom.*]

We had a terrible fire in Amherst on the Fourth of July, at night—and Vinnie tried to make me believe it was only the holiday fireworks!

She kept saying, "Emily, it's only the Fourth of July!" Well, I know a fire when I see one! And what a night that was for Mr. Frink and his noble fire brigade! It was lighter than day for a while. People running up and down Main Street, shouting. It was like a *theater night in London.* And Mother slept through it all. Vinnie's "only the Fourth of July"—I shall always remember. I think she'll tell me that when I die, to keep me from being afraid!

[Emily *sits at her desk.*]

A year after Father died, Mother had a stroke, in her room. She never walked again.

I suspect Mother was afraid of dying. She always avoided talking about it. One night, Austin and I were talking about the extension of consciousness after death, and Mother told Vinnie afterward—she thought it was "very improper."

Mother's dying almost stunned my spirit. She slipped from our fingers like a flake gathered by the wind, and is now part of the drift called "the infinite" . . .

. . . this was the way she died.

The Belle of Amherst 265

And when her breath was done
Took up her simple wardrobe
And started for the sun.
Her little figure at the gate
The Angels must have spied,
Since I could never find her
Upon the mortal side.

You see, we were never intimate, as mother and children, while she was our mother. But mines in the same ground meet by tunneling, and when she became our child, the affection came. Hold your parents tenderly, for the world will seem a strange and lonely place when they're gone.

[Emily's *vitality springs back, like one who is tired of serious subjects.*]

Oh, I wish I were just a—blade of grass! Then all these problems of the dust wouldn't terrify me. Why do we cling to the body, to this little frame? Why are we afraid to let go? Or sad when others do? If my own machinery should get slightly out of gear . . .

[*Imploringly*]

. . . please! Someone stop the wheel! For I know that with belts and bands of gold, I shall whiz triumphant on the new streams!

"Hope" is the thing with feathers—
That perches in the soul—
And sings the tune without the words—
And never stops—at all—

And sweetest—in the Gale—is heard—
And sore must be the storm—
That could abash the little Bird
That kept so many warm—

I've heard it in the chillest land—
And on the strangest Sea—
Yet, never, in Extremity,
It asked a crumb—of Me.

[*Pause*]

I just heard from Helen. She's in California now. A seaside village called Santa Monica. Helen says the sun shines there all the time, and there is bougainvillea[7] everywhere. And Abby Bliss and her husband have just founded the Syrian Protestant College in Beirut.

I've just had a lovely letter from Samuel Bowles and his wife, Mary. They're in Europe now, Paris, and they enclosed these stereopticon[8] pictures.

[*She holds up the viewer.*]

Isn't this a lovely thing?

[*She looks into it.*]

The Scottish moors!
    Vinnie gave it to me last Christmas. They're all the rage.

[*She inserts another card.*]

Oh, this is the *Mona Lisa.*

[*A long pause as she looks*]

I don't see what all the excitement is about.

[*Another card*]

---

7. **bougainvillea** (bōō′gən-vĭl′ē-ə): a flowering vine.
8. **stereopticon:** an old-fashioned instrument for viewing pictures.

This one is the Blue Grotto at Capri. Mary wrote they had to row out from the island to see it.

[*She continues looking at cards in the viewer.*]

Everyone is somewhere, but Emily. Emily is here. *Always here.*

    I never saw a Moor—
    I never saw the Sea—
    Yet know I how the Heather looks
    And what a Billow—
No, wave—
    And what a wave must be.

[*She puts down the viewer and begins writing.*]

    I never spoke with God
    Nor visited in Heaven—
    Yet certain am I of the spot
    As if the Chart were given—

Vinnie says a little boy ran away from Amherst a few days ago. When asked where he was going, he replied, "Vermont or Asia."
    What a smart little boy. I told Vinnie I wanted to run away too.
    I think I frightened her.

[Emily *rises and goes to the parlor.*]

I sit here with my little whip, cracking the time away. I rise, because the sun shines and sleep is over with. And I brush my hair, and dress myself, and wonder what I am and who has made me so.

The Belle of Amherst 267

I tie my Hat—I crease my Shawl—
Life's little duties do—precisely—
As the very least
Were infinite—to me—
I put new Blossoms in the Glass
And throw the old—away—
I push a petal from my Gown
That anchored there—I weigh
The time 'twill be till six o'clock
I have so much to do—
And yet—Existence—some way back—
Stopped—struck—my ticking—through—
Therefore—we do life's labor—
Though life's Reward—be done—
With scrupulous exactness—
To hold our Senses—on—

[*She sits in the parlor.*]

But there *are* the children. Thank God for that! They keep my imagination keen and alive. Austin and Sue gave me a niece and two nephews. Ned and Martha are the oldest. Little Gilbert was born when Ned was fourteen.

Once, when he was stung on the arm by a wasp, he begged Sue through his tears to read the Bible to the wasps.

[*She moves downstage.*]

When he was six, he and a little friend gave an animal show in a tent on the lawn. We asked him what he was going to do with the pennies they had gathered for admission.

He said, "We're going to give half to the college and half to the cat!"

When Sue tried to teach him to sing "There's No Place Like Home," he broke in, "Yes, *there is too!* Over at Aunt Emily's! Over at Aunt Emily's!"

October is a mighty month, for in it, little Gilbert died at eight years. Typhoid.

Not my little Gib!

I see him in the star, and meet his sweet velocity in everything that flies. The little boy we laid away never fluctuates, and his dim society is companion still.

His last cry in delirium was "Open the door, open the door! They're waiting for me!" Quite used to his commandment, his little aunt obeyed.

Who were waiting for him?

All we possess we would give to know. All this and more, though *is* there more, dear friends? More than Love and Death? *Tell me its name!*

I reason, Earth is short—
And Anguish—absolute—
And many hurt,
But, what of that?

I reason, we could die—
The best Vitality
Cannot excel Decay,
But, what of that?

[*She sits, a robe over her legs.*]

I reason, that in Heaven—
Somehow, it will be even—
Some new Equation, given—
But, what of that?

[*She pours tea.*]

I've had a curious winter, very swift, sometimes sober. I haven't felt well, much—and March amazes me! I didn't think of it, that's all. I hayed a little for the horse two Sundays ago, but it snowed since. Now—the full circle of seasons—spring has come, though delayed. But I would eat evanescence[9] slowly. The lawn is full of south and the odors tangle, and did you hear today for the first the river in the tree? Spring is a happiness so beautiful, so unique, so unexpected, that I don't know what to do with my heart.

[*Intimately, to the audience*]

I dare not take it. I dare not leave it. What do you advise?

Eight Saturday noons ago, I was making my black cake with Maggie—dear Maggie—when I saw a great darkness coming, and knew no more until late at night. I woke to find Austin and Vinnie and a strange physician, a Dr. Bigelow, bending over me, and supposed I was dying, or had died, all was so kind and hallowed.[10] I had fainted and lain unconscious for the first time in my life.

[*To herself*]

What flower did Austin plant on Gilbert's grave? Oh, yes, lilies of the valley. On Father's and Mother's it was—damson-hawthorn. I remember. When it shall come *my* turn, I want a buttercup. Surely the grass will give me *one.* I told Vinnie I want to be carried in a small white coffin out the back door of Homestead, into the blue, beloved air, through my garden and Father's barn, and out over the meadows of Amherst to the burial ground. And for my requiem[11]—

---

9. **evanescence:** a temporariness; a vanishing quality.
10. **hallowed:** sanctified; holy.

11. **requiem:** a hymn or musical piece played at a funeral.

That phraseless Melody —
The Wind does.

Oh, I can hear Vinnie say, "Don't talk like that, Emily." But *I* say, "Don't be afraid, dear Vinnie, it's only the Fourth of July."

My earliest friend wrote me the week before he died, "If I live, I will go to Amherst; if I die, I certainly will."

Ah, democratic Death!

Life is short, isn't it? When *one* is done, I wonder — is there not another? And then, if God is willing, perhaps we are neighbors again.

I wonder if I ever dreamed — or if I'm dreaming *now.* I cannot tell how Eternity seems. It sweeps around me like a sea. And this world is such a little place, just the red in the sky, before the sun rises. So let us keep fast hold of hands, please, that when the birds begin, none of us be missing!

The name They dropped upon my face
With water, in the country church —
Emily Elizabeth —
Is finished using, now,
And They can put it with my Dolls,
My childhood, and the string of spools
I've finished threading.

. . .

Because I could not stop for Death —
He kindly stopped for me —
The Carriage held but just Ourselves —
And Immortality.

We slowly drove — He knew no haste
And I had put away
My labor and my leisure too,
For His Civility —

We passed the School, where Children played
Their lessons scarcely done —

We passed the Fields of Gazing Grain —
We passed the Setting Sun —

We paused before a House that seemed
A Swelling of the Ground —
The Roof was scarcely visible —
The Cornice — but a Mound —

Since then — 'tis Centuries — but each
Feels shorter than the Day
I first surmised the Horses' Heads
Were toward Eternity —

[*She gets up.*]

Oh, it's six o'clock! And I promised Vinnie I'd peel the apples. You know, our visit was easier than I thought it would be. We very seldom have guests any more. *Coming, Vinnie!* But one more thing . . .

[*She carries the box of poems downstage center.*]

This is my letter to the World
That never wrote to Me —
The simple News that Nature told —
With tender Majesty

Her Message is committed
To Hands I cannot see —
For love of Her — Sweet — countrymen —
Judge tenderly — of Me

Oh, and when you make my cake, please tell me how you like it. And when next we meet — I'll give you my recipe for gingerbread!

[*She places the box on the floor.*]

Gingerbread! Now there's a word to lift your hat to!
Vinnie, I'm here!

[Emily *exits stage left.*]

FOR STUDY AND DISCUSSION

1. The dramatist imagines how Emily Dickinson would explain why she led such a secluded, private life. What speeches explain why the poet lived as she did? How does Luce's explanation differ from the one given by Dickinson's family, as reported on page 245 by Van Wyck Brooks?

2. Luce's primary aim in this play is to show us the poet as a real, living person. How would you characterize the Emily Dickinson you meet in this play? What did you think of her?

3. Luce takes several of Dickinson's poems and blends them naturally into the monologue. How does the poem on page 259, "I dwell in Possibility," relate to the lines that come before it? How does the poem on page 264, "A great Hope fell," relate to the passage that comes before it?

4. The mood of the scenes from Act One is lively and humorous, perhaps reflecting the poet's outlook up to the time of Higginson's visit. How does the mood change in the last scene of the play? What events in her life would account for Dickinson's mood in this last scene?

5. After reading the excerpts from this play, you have probably formed an impression of Emily Dickinson as a person. Is your impression different from the impression you received from the essay by Van Wyck Brooks? Explain your answer.

6. Where does the title of the play come from? In what ways is the title of the play ironic—in other words, did Dickinson become the "belle" of Amherst in the way she once thought she would? In what other way *has* she become the "belle of Amherst"?

ARTISTIC LICENSE

In writing this dramatization of Emily Dickinson's life, William Luce pulled together material from various sources. He used details from biographical studies of the poet, statements from her letters, and many of her poems. None of this material in itself would tell a dramatic story, so Luce adapted it for the stage. He arranged all the details he had gathered in chronological order and began shaping a drama. He added details of his own to flesh out the story—things that he imagined might have happened, but which may never have occurred at all. He also gave Emily Dickinson words to say she probably never said. In making all of these adaptations, Luce used what is called *artistic license*.

What speeches in the play correspond to details found in Brooks's article (page 242)? How has Luce used artistic license in his account of the scene between Dickinson and Higginson?

Artistic license permits a writer freedom to depart from the facts to create a new, cohesive story. The device has been used by writers down through the ages. For example, William Shakespeare used it to dramatize the tragedy of Julius Caesar. In our own time, artistic license has been used in many biographical dramas: for example, William Gibson's *The Miracle Worker* (the life of Helen Keller); Dore Schary's *Sunrise at Campobello* (the life of Franklin D. Roosevelt); and Frances Goodrich and Albert Hackett's *The Diary of Anne Frank*.

Normally, we do not go to literature for historical facts. We read literature because it brings characters to life; it moves us; it gives us insights into human nature. Has William Luce brought a character called "Emily Dickinson" to life? Did his play move you at all? Did it give you any insights into human life?

To find out more about the actual Emily Dickinson, read some of her letters and poems and compare them with Luce's play.

FOR COMPOSITION

Writing a Scene for a One-Person Play

In a one-person play, the audience listens and watches an actor alone onstage. Because two hours of unrelieved monologue would be boring, the playwright introduces "invisible" characters into the scene. Emily Dickinson speaks to an invisible Mr. Billings on page 258, an invisible father on page 260, and an invisible Mr. Higginson on page 263. Notice what words and responses of Dickinson's clue us in to what these invisible characters are saying and doing.

Choose one of the above scenes and write the lines that you think the imaginary character is saying to Dickinson. Compare your rewritten scene with those written by other students.

You might also rewrite the scene from the point of view of the invisible character. Have the character's lines expressed and Dickinson's lines only suggested.

Socrates

The Athenian philosopher Socrates, who was born in about 470 B.C., was put to death seventy years later for "neglecting the gods" and "corrupting the youth." Socrates was a wise man who preached moderation, self-control, and independent thinking. His life was dedicated to a search for knowledge. Socrates was also a devoted patriot. The combination of these qualities led to his death. He insisted on speaking out against what he considered wrong; and, although he had an opportunity to withdraw into exile before his trial and to escape during his imprisonment, his sense of civic duty prevented him from doing either. He treated with contempt the accusations made against him, but he freely accepted the court's death penalty on the ground that it was enacted by a legitimate court and therefore had to be obeyed.

Socrates' fame does not rest on his writings. Socrates was a philosopher and a teacher who wrote nothing. What we know of his character and his teachings is derived chiefly from the writings of Plato and Xenophon, two of his pupils.

In the following pages we have two glimpses of Socrates from the pens of two men separated in time by more than 2,300 years: Hermann Hagedorn (1892–1964), a contemporary American biographer; and Plato (427?–347? B.C.), who was Socrates' pupil and a great philosopher himself.

Socrates — His Life

Hermann Hagedorn

If your Greek toga had a buttonhole, Socrates' thumb would be through it, holding you pinned in your place while the goggle-eyed and delightful old gentleman asked you exactly how clever you think you are and what in the world, in the first place, makes you think you are clever anyway.

He is the first and greatest of all buttonholers. It makes no difference where you are or how busy you are. If Socrates fixes his eyes on you, he will come lumbering across the athletic field or the marketplace, and, smiling most courteously, he will engage you in conversation. Socrates is a glutton for conversation. Money means nothing to him. Fame, power, influence mean nothing. He never knows exactly where the next meal is coming from; but he must have conversation.

It is not that he wishes to hear himself talk; but he does want to hear what you have to say. He does not seek gossip, tips on the races or the discus throwers, or stories of the dancing girls, or wails on the political situation and the state of the war between Athens and Sparta. But he loves talk of fundamental things, of justice and virtue and wisdom and love and death and immortality. He can talk on these matters as no one else in his city — and it is a city of great talkers — and he can make you talk as you have never talked before.

Who is he, this man Socrates? What is his profession, his job? He is the son of a stonemason. For a while he was a stonemason himself. Yes, and he has been a soldier, not from choice, but because Athens needed all her able-bodied men in her wars with Sparta, the physical examination taking no account of height, or of eyes somewhat off center. At thirty-seven he is at the siege of Potidaea,[1] at great risk saving the life of a brilliant young fellow townsman, Alcibiades,[2] who proves, in the end, not to have been worth saving. At forty-five he is in the disastrous defeat at Delium, carrying Xenophon,[3] a young friend of his, who is to make his mark as a historian, off to safety on his broad shoulders. "He stalked along like a pelican," Alcibiades subsequently reports, "glaring around with his projecting crab's eyes, so that none of the enemy dared molest him."

But soldiering is the least important activity of this extraordinary person's life. It is as a conversationalist that Athens knows him — as the man who asks questions. If you enjoy con-

---

1. **Potidaea** (pŏt'ĭ-dē'ə): The revolt of this city from the Athenian League was the immediate cause of a war between Athens and Sparta.
2. **Alcibiades** (ăl'sĭ-bī'ə-dēz'): a disciple of Socrates and for many years his devoted friend. Political ambition proved his ruination and he became a traitor to Athens.
3. **Xenophon** (zĕn'ə-fən): another disciple of Socrates. His fame as a historian is based largely on his account of the *March of the Ten Thousand* — an expedition of conquest in which he took part as general.

versation and can answer Socrates' questions with intelligence, you love him and gratefully accept his invitations to walk under the olive trees with him or to spend the night with a few other sympathetic souls, talking about courage or happiness or the ideal republic. But if you don't enjoy high talk, if you think yourself wise and are really dull and Socrates shows you up by a keen question or two, you hate him and talk of him as a public nuisance and go around growling that if the government had any sand in its gizzard it would shut him up.

He is a queer customer, unquestionably. But he has a wise mind, a humble spirit, and a voice within him which he calls his daemon,[4] which lays a check on him, he says, when he is tempted to do wrong or stupid things. His clothes are always shabby. He goes about with bare feet. How he lives no one knows. The truth is that he has a small income, much too small to keep a family on in any style which Athens would approve. But he refuses to increase it, preferring to adjust his needs to his income rather than his income to his supposed needs. His wife, a sharp-tongued lady named Xantippe,[5] rails at him as an irresponsible loafer and gadabout. At home there are arguments in which, it is rumored, all of the questioning and most of the talking is for once done by the other party.

But Socrates is not a philosopher for nothing. When a friend asks him how he happened to marry Xantippe, of all women, he replies, "Those who want to learn to ride well choose restive horses, because, if they can handle these, they can manage any others. I want to learn to associate with all mankind, and I chose Xantippe, knowing that if I could bear her society, I should be able to get along with anyone!" Perhaps he is joking; but it would not be safe to be too sure.

He is not what would be called an established citizen, with a pleasant house to live in and taxes to growl about. He is something rarer, an institution. Everybody knows him. He has nothing to do all day except to ask questions and to talk, and as he does these things invariably in public places, he is as familiar a figure as the town constable. Even the comic writers poke fun at him in their plays. His questions always have point; that is one reason why people find them disturbing.

The oracle at Delphi, consulted by all the Greeks, has told Socrates that he is "the wisest of men." Socrates laughs at the idea. He isn't wise, he knows he isn't; that is all, in fact, that he does know. There are countless men wiser than himself, he is certain, in Athens alone. He sets about to prove it, and that is how the questioning begins. He goes to a statesman with a great reputation and asks for light on the nature of wisdom or happiness, and is most astonished to find that the statesman is as much in the dark as he is, though he thinks that he really knows.

"Well," says Socrates to himself, "I am wiser than this fellow anyway. He thinks that he knows, when he doesn't, and at least I know that I don't know."

Thereupon he calls on a great soldier, a great artist, a great philosopher. In every case his experience is the same. They all think they are wise, but when he pins them down, they do not really know anything at all, not even that they are ignorant. Men of vision, whom he thus questions, gratefully accept the light he throws into their darkness. But the men who are vain and self-important are indignant.

Young men crowd about him, however, fascinated and thrilled. It is a period of change in Athens. Thinking people find it difficult to

---

4. **daemon** (dē′mən): guardian spirit.
5: **Xantippe** (zăn-tĭp′ē).

believe in the old gods as their fathers did. When they look coolly at the stories of Jupiter and his adventures, of Venus and Juno, of Mars and Mercury[6] and the rest, the gods look rather shabby, a little too human in their frailties to be regarded as divine.

The young men are asking, "What is this earth made of; how did it come to be? What are we human beings here for? How can we be happy? What happens when we die?" The old myths give no answers that satisfy these eager questioners.

Socrates says to them, "Do not bother your heads overmuch with problems regarding creation or the substance of things. Here you are, a man, living for a while in the world with other men. What you must do is to think how you can live and help others to live most nobly and wisely."

They listen, and come day after day to hear his keen questioning and to answer as intelligently as they can. Those are congenial gatherings, for Socrates loves these young men as much as they love him.

"Some men," he has a way of saying, "have a fancy for a fine horse, or a dog, or a bird. What I fancy, and take delight in, is friends of a superior kind. If I know anything, I teach it to them. In common with them I turn over and explore the treasures of the wise men of old which have been left written in books. If we find anything good, we pick it out, and we think it a great gain if we can be beneficial to one another."

Majestic themes are discussed at those gatherings—fundamental questions of right and wrong, of the meaning of justice, the meaning of love. Questions of government are threshed through. Socrates is outspoken and spares no one. The government of Athens, splendid under the great Pericles,[7] has come to troublous times now that the leader is dead. There are wars without and revolutions within; and now the mob rules, and now a small group of powerful and wealthy citizens. The mob and the oligarchy,[8] as this small group is called, are equally unjust and despotic,[9] and in his quiet way Socrates strikes at them both.

When the Thirty Tyrants,[10] who are now ruling, send for Socrates in anger and forbid him to "discourse with the young," he merely asks them most humbly what they mean by "discourse," and whom exactly would they call "the young"? Can't he even ask directions or buy meat of anyone, say, under thirty? The Tyrants rage and threaten him with death. But Socrates pays no attention whatsoever to their orders, teaching as before.

But the old philosopher does not love a stupid mob any more than a stupid committee of tyrants. He says that democracy, if it is stupid and unjust, is as evil as stupid and cruel tyranny. Forms are comparatively unimportant; the essential thing is that government, whatever form it takes, shall be enlightened and just. It is a dangerous doctrine to preach, for it sets the stupid on both sides

---

6. **Jupiter . . . Mercury:** Hagedorn uses the Roman names for the gods. The Greek names for the gods cited here are Zeus, Aphrodite, Hera, Ares, and Hermes.

7. **Pericles** (pĕr′ə-klēz′): the Greek statesman under whom Athens rose to its greatest height in the fifth century B.C.
8. **oligarchy** (ŏl′ə-gär′kē): a small group that rules the government.
9. **despotic** (dĭ-spŏt′ĭk): tyrannical.
10. **Thirty Tyrants:** a committee of aristocrats who governed Athens at the close of the war with Sparta. After a reign of terror, they were overthrown and a democratic government was resumed.

against him. When the Thirty Tyrants are overthrown and the popular party comes into control, Socrates is a marked man.

Slowly the feeling against him in Athens takes definite form. The men he has shown up to themselves with his straightforward questions, the ruling classes he has made fun of, the blundering mob he has refused to praise and to bow down to, begin to ask themselves why they have borne with this gadfly[11] so long. He is teaching the young men of the city that in government, majorities are not enough. You must have intelligence also. Dangerous doctrine! He is corrupting the youth!

Socrates smiles and goes quietly on, not teaching any philosophy of his own so much as stimulating his pupils to think out an intelligent way of living for themselves. And then one day, a notice is posted in Athens:

Meletus,[12] son of Meletus, accuses Socrates, son of Sophroniscus,[13] as is underwritten. Socrates is guilty of crime — first, for neglecting the gods whom the city acknowledges, and setting forth other strange gods; next, for corrupting the youth. Penalty — death.

Meletus is a poet (or thinks he is), but there are other accusers, notably a democratic politician named Anytus[14] whose son Socrates has persuaded to give up his father's leather trade and devote himself to learning. Anytus feels strongly that to persuade any young man to give up the leather business for the shadowy rewards of scholarship is clear corruption.

Socrates seems to be the only individual in Athens who is not disturbed by the approaching trial. He does not even make any preparations for his speech of defense. All his life has been a preparation for it, he says, having been spent in learning what was right and trying to do it.

The trial is held before a jury of five hundred fifty-seven[15] citizens of Athens. Eloquently, Socrates speaks in his own behalf. He states his case as only he can state it, but his speech is not really a defense, but a lecture. If the jurymen are expecting him to back down in any respect, or to plead for his life, they are doomed to disappointment. On the contrary, he will not accept acquittal if it means that he shall stop his teaching. When he was a soldier and his commander placed him in a post of danger, there he was bound in honor to stay. It is the same now.

"Strange indeed would be my conduct, men of Athens," he insists, "if, now when God orders me, as I believe, to fulfill the philosopher's mission of searching into myself and other men, I were to desert my post through fear of death, or any other fear. Men of Athens, I honor and love you; but I shall obey God rather than you, and while I have life and strength, I shall never cease from the practice and teaching of philosophy."

The court declares him guilty, but only by a majority of five or six. According to ancient custom, he is asked what punishment he would regard as just. Fearlessly he replies that if it is required of him to say how the public in justice ought to treat him, he can only say that he should be recognized as a public bene-

---

11. **gadfly:** an irritating, bothersome fly that bites cattle and horses. Socrates believed that a teacher should be a gadfly to the state, criticizing it to bring about reforms.
12. **Meletus** (mǐ-lē′təs).
13. **Sophroniscus** (sō-frə-nĭs′kəs).
14. **Anytus** (ă-nī′təs).

15. Some authorities say five hundred one.

factor and given a pension for life; but, as an alternative, he proposes a small fine. The court regards his proposal as an insult, and he is condemned to death.

He takes the sentence with perfect calmness. Instead of pleading for mercy or sympathy, in fact, he turns about and encourages the court, as though he suspected that their consciences were pricking them for condemning him, and felt sorry for them.

"O Judges, be of good cheer about death," he says, "and know of a certainty that no evil can happen to a good man, either in life or after. I am not angry with my accusers, or with you, my condemners. The hour of departure is at hand, and we go our ways, I to die, and you to live. Which is better, God alone knows."

For a month he is in prison, with fetters on his ankles, surrounded by his friends; talking, questioning as always; refusing to escape, regretting nothing, fearing nothing. Then, one evening as the sun is setting, the young men gather around him for the last time.

One of them, Apollodorus, is loud in his lamentations. "I grieve most for this, Socrates," he cries, "that I see you about to die undeservedly."

But the old gentleman's sense of humor is as active as ever. With a smile he strokes his pupil's hair. "My dearest Apollodorus," he says, "would you rather see me die deservedly?"

The last scene has all the sad beauty of autumn, or dying day. Minute by minute the shadows deepen. Xantippe, Socrates' wife, is there, wailing. For all that she abused her philosopher these many years, she loves him, and he has to send her away at last because he will have no lamentations when the end comes.

The jailer, in tears, brings him the hemlock, the poison which he is to drink. Holding the cup to his lips, he drains it and begins to walk about as the jailer has told him to do. His friends try hard to keep back the tears, but when young Apollodorus gives a sudden exclamation of grief, they lose their grip of themselves for a moment.

Socrates alone remains calm. "What is this strange outcry?" he says. "I sent away the women mainly in order that they might not offend in this way, for I have heard that a man should die in peace. Be quiet then, and have patience."

The poison is working. He can no longer walk; he lies down. They all know the end is near. But once more he uncovers his face, remembering a debt he owes to the temple of the god of medicine. "Crito," he says, turning to one of the young men, "I owe a cock to Aesculapius.[16] Will you remember to pay the debt?"

"The debt shall be paid," Crito answers in low tones. "Is there anything else?"

There is nothing else, no word more. And his friends have, to comfort them, only the words which he spoke in answer to their question what they should do with his body: "You may do with it what you like, provided you do not imagine it to be me."

No, that quiet shape is not Socrates. He is elsewhere, questioning the eternities. And still he halts men in the churches and schools and marketplaces and on the buzzing highways of the world, asking them what they mean by the words they fling about so lightly; and what do they know—and are they really as wise as they imagine?

Magnificent old questioner that he was! Wisest and noblest of all the Greeks!

---

16. **Aesculapius** (ĕs'kyoo-lā'pē-əs) (or Asclepius): the Greek god of medicine.

1. What details does Hagedorn use to characterize Socrates as a great conversationalist, who was also honest, humorous, and courageous?
2. How does Hagedorn show that Socrates was a nonconformist—that is, someone who shows indifference to or contempt for accepted customs and ways of thinking?
3. What does the life of Socrates indicate about the problems of nonconformity?
4. In the next-to-last paragraph, what does Hagedorn mean when he says that Socrates still "halts men . . ."?
5. What do you think Hagedorn accomplishes by his use of colloquial English ("Socrates is a glutton for conversation") and by his use of the present tense?

THE BIOGRAPHER'S METHOD

A biographer may write objectively or subjectively. In an objective approach, which is often difficult to maintain, the biographer stands at a distance from an individual and reports on what happens in his or her life without giving personal opinions or evaluations. In a subjective approach, the biographer seems more personally involved with the individual, giving opinions on the person and on what happens to him or her. A biographer who takes a subjective approach can easily influence the way we think and feel.

Hagedorn takes a subjective approach. This is clear from the first paragraph when he calls Socrates a "delightful old gentleman." What other subjective evaluations does he make of Socrates? Where does he make subjective evaluations of Socrates' enemies?

How did Hagedorn make you feel about Socrates and about the men who condemned him?

FOR COMPOSITION

Writing a Biographical Essay
Hagedorn has divided his essay into three parts. First, he introduces Socrates and tells something about his background and convictions. Next, he narrates the events that lead up to a crucial time in Socrates' life (the trial). Finally, he describes how Socrates died and sums up the effect he has had on the world.

Following the outline of Hagedorn's portrait, write a brief biographical essay on another historical figure. Use an encyclopedia or history textbook to do research on your subject. If you think it will serve your purpose, imitate Hagedorn's conversational style and use of the present tense.

We remember Plato (427?–347? B.C.) not only as a student and devoted friend of Socrates, but also as a great philosopher in his own right. Plato founded in Athens the Academy, the school of philosophy where he taught for many years. Aristotle, another philosopher, was one of Plato's students.

Plato was not present at the death of Socrates, but he heard the story from those who witnessed the scene. Writing about it afterward in *Phaedo*, he told the story in the form of a dialogue: Phaedo, who was there, is telling the story to Echecrates (ē-kĕ′krə-tēz), who was not. This account of how Socrates prepared for his death is the last part of Phaedo's narrative.

The Death of Socrates   *Plato*

Translated from the Greek by Hugh Tredennick

Socrates said, "It is about time that I took my bath. I prefer to have a bath before drinking the poison rather than give the women the trouble of washing me when I am dead."

When he had finished speaking, Crito said, "Very well, Socrates. But have you no directions for the others or myself about your children or anything else? What can we do to please you best?"

"Nothing new, Crito," said Socrates; "just what I am always telling you. If you look after yourselves, whatever you do will please me and mine and you too, even if you don't agree with me now. On the other hand, if you neglect yourselves and fail to follow the line of life as I have laid it down both now and in the past, however fervently you agree with me now, it will do no good at all."

"We shall try our best to do as you say," said Crito. "But how shall we bury you?"

"Any way you like," replied Socrates, "that is, if you can catch me and I don't slip through your fingers." He laughed gently as he spoke, and turning to us went on: "I can't persuade Crito that I am this Socrates here who is talking to you now and marshaling all the arguments; he thinks that I am the one whom he will see presently lying dead; and he asks how he is to bury me! As for my long and elaborate explanation that when I have drunk the poison I shall remain with you no longer, but depart to a state of heavenly happiness, this attempt to console both you and myself seems to be wasted on him. You must give an assurance to Crito for me—the opposite of the one which he gave to the court which tried

The Death of Socrates. Oil painting by Jacques Louis David (1748–1825).
The Metropolitan Museum of Art, New York. Wolfe Fund.

me. He undertook that I should stay; but you must assure him that when I am dead I shall not stay, but depart and be gone. That will help Crito to bear it more easily and keep him from being distressed on my account when he sees my body being burned or buried, as if something dreadful were happening to me; or from saying at the funeral that it is Socrates whom he is laying out or carrying to the grave or burying. Believe me, my dear friend Crito: misstatements are not merely jarring in their immediate context; they also have a bad effect upon the soul. No, you must keep up your spirits and say that it is only my body that you are burying; and you can bury it as you please, in whatever way you think is most proper."

With these words he got up and went into another room to bathe; and Crito went after him, but told us to wait. So we waited, discussing and reviewing what had been said or else dwelling upon the greatness of the calamity which had befallen us; for we felt just as though we were losing a father and should be orphans for the rest of our lives. Meanwhile, when Socrates had taken his bath, his children were brought to see him—he had two little sons and one big boy—and the women of his household—you know—arrived. He talked to them in Crito's presence and gave them directions about carrying out his wishes; then he told the women and children to go away and came back himself to join us.

It was now nearly sunset, because he had

spent a long time inside. He came and sat down, fresh from the bath; and he had only been talking for a few minutes when the prison officer came in and walked up to him. "Socrates," he said, "at any rate I shall not have to find fault with you, as I do with others, for getting angry with me and cursing when I tell them to drink the poison—carrying out Government orders. I have come to know during this time that you are the noblest and the gentlest and the bravest of all the men that have ever come here, and now especially I am sure that you are not angry with me, but with them; because you know who are responsible. So now—you know what I have come to say—goodbye, and try to bear what must be as easily as you can." As he spoke he burst into tears, and turning round, went away.

Socrates looked up at him and said, "Goodbye to you, too; we will do as you say." Then addressing us, he went on, "What a charming person! All the time I have been here he has visited me and sometimes had discussions with me and shown me the greatest kindness; and how generous of him now to shed tears for me at parting! But come, Crito, let us do as he says. Someone had better bring in the poison, if it is ready prepared; if not, tell the man to prepare it."

"But surely, Socrates," said Crito, "the sun is still upon the mountains; it has not gone down yet. Besides, I know that in other cases people have dinner and enjoy their wine, and sometimes the company of those whom they love, long after they receive the warning; and only drink the poison quite late at night. No need to hurry; there is still plenty of time."

"It is natural that these people whom you speak of should act in that way, Crito," said Socrates, "because they think that they gain by it. And it is also natural that I should not; because I believe that I should gain nothing by

drinking the poison a little later—I should only make myself ridiculous in my own eyes if I clung to life and hugged it when it has no more to offer. Come, do as I say and don't make difficulties."

At this Crito made a sign to his servant, who was standing nearby. The servant went out and after spending a considerable time, returned with the man who was to administer the poison; he was carrying it ready prepared in a cup. When Socrates saw him he said, "Well, my good fellow, you understand these things; what ought I to do?"

"Just drink it," he said, "and then walk about until you feel a weight in your legs, and then lie down. Then it will act of its own accord."

As he spoke, he handed the cup to Socrates, who received it quite cheerfully, Echecrates, without a tremor, without any change of color or expression, and said, looking up under his brows with his usual steady gaze, "What do you say about pouring a libation[1] from this drink? Is it permitted, or not?"

"We only prepare what we regard as the normal dose, Socrates," he replied.

"I see," said Socrates. "But I suppose I am allowed, or rather bound, to pray the gods that my removal from this world to the other may be prosperous. This is my prayer, then; and I hope that it may be granted." With these words, quite calmly and with no sign of distaste, he drained the cup in one breath.

Up till this time most of us had beeen fairly successful in keeping back our tears; but when we saw that he was drinking, that he had actually drunk it, we could do so no longer; in spite of myself the tears came pouring out so that I covered my face and wept brokenheartedly—not for him, but for my own calamity in losing such a friend. Crito

---

1. **libation:** liquid poured out in honor of a deity.

had given up even before me and had gone out when he could not restrain his tears. But Apollodorus, who had never stopped crying even before, now broke out into such a storm of passionate weeping that he made everyone in the room break down, except Socrates himself, who said:

"Really, my friends, what a way to behave! Why, that was my main reason for sending away the women, to prevent this sort of disturbance; because I am told that one should make one's end in a tranquil frame of mind. Calm yourselves and try to be brave."

This made us feel ashamed, and we controlled our tears. Socrates walked about, and presently, saying that his legs were heavy, lay down on his back—that was what the man recommended. The man (he was the same one who had administered the poison) kept his hand upon Socrates and after a little while examined his feet and legs; then pinched his foot hard and asked if he felt it. Socrates said no. Then he did the same to his legs; and moving gradually upward in this way, let us see that he was getting cold and numb. Presently he felt him again and said that when it reached the heart, Socrates would be gone.

The coldness was spreading about as far as his waist when Socrates uncovered his face— for he had covered it up—and said (they were his last words): "Crito, we ought to offer a cock to Asclepius.[2] See to it, and don't forget."

"No, it shall be done," said Crito. "Are you sure that there is nothing else?"

Socrates made no reply to this question, but after a little while he stirred; and when the

---

2. **a cock to Asclepius** (ăs-klē′pē-əs): Asclepius (or Aesculapius) was the god of medicine. The sacrifice was made to the god by sick persons, either in the hope of waking up cured or in thanks for having been cured. In any event, Socrates here perhaps makes an almost humorous remark about the fact that his death is the cure for his life.

man uncovered him, his eyes were fixed. When Crito saw this, he closed the mouth and eyes.

Such, Echecrates, was the end of our comrade, who was, we may fairly say, of all those whom we knew in our time, the bravest and also the wisest and most upright man.

FOR STUDY AND DISCUSSION

1. In his speech before his judges, Socrates said that they should "be of good cheer about death, and know of a certainty that no evil can happen to a good man, either in life or after" (see page 279). How do Socrates' words and actions before his death bear out this belief? What is your opinion on this statement to the judges?

2. What qualities of Socrates' character are stressed in this narrative of his death?

3. How does Plato contrast Socrates with the other persons in this scene?

4. Does Socrates regard his death as a tragedy to his friends and family only, or does he find in it a larger significance? Cite passages from the text to support your answer.

FOR COMPOSITION

Comparing Essays

Hermann Hagedorn has also described the death of Socrates in his biographical account on page 274. Write a brief essay in which you compare Hagedorn's account with Plato's. Do the facts differ in any way? Do the writers approach their subject subjectively or objectively, or do they use both objective and subjective methods? How do the styles of the essays differ? Conclude by telling which account you found more moving, and explain why you feel this way.

Practice in Reading and Writing

EXPOSITION

Reading Essays of Opinion

Essays of opinion are examples of *exposition*, the kind of writing that sets forth ideas, that gives information, or that explains something. When writers use a personal opinion as the main topic of an essay, they develop this topic with what they hope will be forceful supporting evidence. The aim of such essays is to explain the writer's point of view, often with an eye toward convincing readers to adopt it as their own. In "Clean Fun at Riverhead," Tom Wolfe presents a controversial opinion about automobiles and aggression. Wolfe states his opinion in his first sentence: he believes that Americans have turned to automobiles to satisfy their love of direct aggression.

As hand-to-hand combat has gradually disappeared from our civilization, even in wartime, and competition has become more and more sophisticated and abstract, Americans have turned to the automobile to satisfy their love of direct aggression. The mild-mannered man who turns into a bear behind the wheel of a car—i.e., who finds in the power of the automobile a vehicle for the release of his inhibitions—is part of American folklore. Among teen-agers the automobile has become the symbol, and in part the physical means, of triumph over family and community restrictions. Seventy-five percent of all car thefts in the United States are by teen-agers out for "joy rides."

The symbolic meaning of the automobile tones down but by no means vanishes in adulthood. Police traffic investigators have long been convinced that far more accidents are purposeful crashes by belligerent drivers than they could ever prove. One of the heroes of the era was the Middle Eastern diplomat who rammed a magazine writer's car from behind in the Kalorama embassy district of Washington two years ago. When the American bellowed out the window at him, he backed up and smashed his car again. When the fellow leaped out of his car to pick a fight, he backed up and smashed his car a third time, then drove off. He was recalled home for having "gone native."

---

1. What examples does Wolfe use to support his opinion?

2. What statistic does he cite? What is the point of the statistic?

3. How does he use an anecdote to make his point more forceful?

4. Does Wolfe make any statements here that could be questioned? What personal conviction about our need for aggression, for example, lies behind his main point?

5. Did Wolfe convince you to accept his opinion? Why, or why not?

Writing an Essay of Opinion

Write a brief essay in which you present convincing details to support your own point of view about a topic. You might write an answer to Wolfe's essay: present examples, statistics, or anecdotes to support his point of view, or to disagree with him. In your essay, state your topic and your opinion on it in your opening or closing sentence.

For Further Reading

Bontemps, Arna, *The Harlem Renaissance Remembered* (Dodd, Mead, 1972)

A famous poet recollects the people who took part in the great flowering of black literature in New York City in the 1920's. Illustrated.

Durrell, Gerald, *A Zoo in My Luggage* (paperback, Penguin, 1976)

A best-selling writer tells of his expedition to the Cameroons to start a private zoo. The comedy ends when the animals arrive in England and Durrell has to keep them in his suburban home.

Elder, Lauren, with Shirley Streshnisky, *And I Alone Survived* (Dutton, 1978; paperback, Fawcett)

A small plane crashes in the High Sierras, and one passenger lives to tell her story.

Hamilton, Edith, *The Greek Way* and *The Roman Way* (Norton; paperback, Avon)

A famous classical scholar brings the ancient Greeks and Romans to vivid life.

Herriot, James, *All Creatures Great and Small* (St. Martin's, 1972; paperback, Bantam)

Entertaining and touching anecdotes focus on the experiences of a rural vet, whose patients include horses, goats, and an overweight dog.

Hersey, John, *Hiroshima* (Knopf, 1946; paperback, Bantam)

A prize-winning reporter wrote this compassionate account of the event that ushered in the Atomic Age — the bombing of Hiroshima on August 6, 1945.

Huberman, Elizabeth and Edward, editors, *Fifty Great Essays* (paperback, Bantam)

Here are some of the world's greatest essays, ranging from Joseph Addison's eighteenth-century essay on witches and witchcraft, to Abraham Lincoln's Second Inaugural Address, to Virginia Woolf's "The Death of the Moth."

Maynard, Joyce, *Looking Back: A Chronicle of Growing Old in the Sixties* (Doubleday, 1973; paperback, Avon)

By "growing old" the writer means "growing up." In this often-humorous book, a young newspaper columnist tells about her generation — the first to be "brought up on television."

Newman, Edwin, *Strictly Speaking: Will America Be the Death of English?* (Bobbs-Merrill, 1974; paperback, Warner Books)

This best seller takes a witty, deadpan look at the decline of our language. As one critic said, this book holds out the hope that if the end of English is near, at least it will go out laughing.

Rawlings, Marjorie Kinnan, *Cross Creek* (Scribner's; paperback, Ballantine)

These sketches about the people, scenery, and wildlife of the Florida back country are written by the Pulitzer Prize-winning author of *The Yearling.*

Thurber, James, *My Life and Hard Times* (paperback, Harper & Row)

The eccentric Thurber family has highly unusual (and hilarious) experiences in Columbus, Ohio. This collection includes "The Night the Bed Fell," "The Day the Dam Broke," and "The Dog That Bit People."

Van Lawick-Goodall, Jane, *In the Shadow of Man* (Houghton Mifflin, 1971; paperback, Dell)

A young woman kept this record of her months alone in a dense African forest, observing the habits of a family of chimpanzees.

White, E. B., *Essays of E. B. White* (Harper & Row, 1977)

White's reflections on the farm, the city, and the planet include the famous essay "Death of a Pig," featuring White's self-important dachshund named Fred.

In the nineteenth century, which often took itself very seriously, people were fond of defining poetry in terms such as "Lofty thoughts expressed in noble language" or "Beauty dressed out in melodious words." Anyone who has read much poetry knows better. There is nothing lofty about the thoughts of the speaker in Dorothy Parker's "One Perfect Rose" (page 332), who wishes her admirer would send her a limousine every once in a while. The subject matter of poetry is all of life, just as it is in other forms of literature.

If we do not limit the subject matter of poetry to the lofty and the beautiful, we need not put any such limitations on its language. There is nothing noble, or even melodious, about the language in Ted Hughes's "The Lake" (page 316).

> [It] Snuffles at my feet for what I might drop or kick up,
> Sucks and slobbers the stones, snorts through its lips

POETRY

What kind of language, then, is used in poetry? The answer is that a poet seeks the most meaningful words—those that are most expressive, most suggestive, and most precise for the poet's purpose.

And what is the poet's purpose? Like many simple questions, this one is hard to answer, though it's an important question to ask. Poetry, like other forms of literature, communicates feelings and experiences rather than objective facts. Poetry "says more and talks less" than other forms of expression, and it does this mainly by using a number of language resources not ordinarily used in strictly factual prose. These language "resources" include imagery, figurative language, rhythm, and, sometimes, rhyme.

Consider the differences between a factual inning-by-inning summary of a baseball game and an account written by a good sportswriter. (Sportswriters resemble poets: they want to give us the facts of the game, but they also want to make us feel as if we were watching it.) The factual summary might run like this: "Johnson hit a single to left. Calvetti hit a double to right, allowing Johnson to score." But the sportswriter writes: "Johnson smoked a grass-cutter between short and third. Calvetti, after taking two strikes, drove a screaming double off the right-field wall. Johnson took off like a frightened rabbit at the crack of the bat, rounded third with a full head of steam, and slid home in a cloud of dust." The sportswriter's account differs from the factual summary in a number of ways. First, it appeals to our senses; it allows us to *hear* "the crack of the bat" and *see* "a cloud of dust." Second, it uses figurative language: "smoked a grass-cutter," "screaming double," "like a frightened rabbit," "with a full head of steam." Third, its sentences are more rhythmical than those of the factual summary, and the rhythm helps suggest the speed and excitement of the play. Like this sports story, poetry communicates vividly through the deliberate use of certain language "resources."

As many poets have done, William Stafford has written a poem about his craft. "Report from a Far Place" is about poetry—about the power of words. Notice how the poet calls his products "word things" and compares them to "snowshoes" that help carry us over the "cold" of the world. Notice also the way he describes in the last lines what words can do for us. See if you agree that "Report from a Far Place" says more about poetry, and talks less about it, than this entire essay has done.

Report from a Far Place

Making these word things to
step on across the world, I
could call them snowshoes.

They creak, sag, bend, but
hold, over the great deep cold,
and they turn up at the toes.

In war or city or camp
they could save your life;
you can muse them by the fire.

Be careful, though: they
burn, or don't burn, in their own
strange way, when you say them.

William Stafford

Imagery

To help us participate in certain experiences, poets will create *images* — that is, they use words that put our senses to work. Images are chiefly visual, but some images can also help us hear something, smell it, taste it, even feel its texture or temperature. In these lines from his poem called "Give Me the Splendid Silent Sun," Walt Whitman uses a series of images so that we can imaginatively share certain sensations:

> Give me the splendid silent sun with all his beams full-dazzling,
> Give me juicy autumnal fruit ripe and red from the orchard,
> Give me a field where the unmowed grass grows,
> Give me an arbor, give me the trellised grape,
> Give me fresh corn and wheat, give me serene-moving animals teaching content,
> Give me nights perfectly quiet as on high plateaus west of the Mississippi, and I looking up at the stars . . .

*Innisfree is an island in Lough (Lake) Gill in western
Ireland (pictured at the left). Yeats was inspired to write
this poem while he was walking along a crowded street in
London. He thought of Innisfree when he heard the sound
of water falling from a small fountain that was part of a
window display.*

The Lake Isle of Innisfree

William Butler Yeats

I will arise and go now, and go to Innisfree,
And a small cabin build there, of clay and wattles° made:
Nine bean-rows will I have there, a hive for the honeybee,
And live alone in the bee-loud glade.

2. **wattles:** poles intertwined with twigs.

And I shall have some peace there, for peace comes drop-
     ping slow,   5
Dropping from the veils of the morning to where the
     cricket sings;
There midnight's all a glimmer, and noon a purple glow,
And evening full of the linnet's° wings.

8. **linnet's:** songbird's.

I will arise and go now, for always night and day
I hear lake water lapping with low sounds by the shore;   10
While I stand on the roadway, or on the pavements gray,
I hear it in the deep heart's core.

FOR STUDY AND DISCUSSION

1. What specific images help you visualize what this speaker is longing for? The next-to-last line describes the speaker's present surroundings. How do these images contrast with the others in the poem?

2. What images help you hear the sounds the speaker longs to hear?

3. The speaker says that he wants peace. In which line does the poet compare the coming of peace to the dropping of dew? What other images in the poem suggest peacefulness?

STANZAS

A *stanza* is any group of related lines that forms a division of a poem. Stanzas are usually used to mark divisions of thought in a poem, and so they function something as paragraphs do.

What is the main idea of each stanza in "The Lake Isle of Innisfree"? Which stanza is most dreamlike? Which stanza brings the speaker back to reality?

The middle stanza does not open with the same words that open the first and last stanzas. Notice that the middle stanza also has longer lines and slower movement. Why is it appropriate that this stanza be leisurely and serene in its movement?

FOR COMPOSITION

Describing an Ideal World

In this poem, Yeats describes an ideal world—one in which he could find peace and beauty. Yeats pictures his world as being on an island, where he can hear the lapping of lake water, the humming of bees, and the songs of crickets. He would like to live alone there in a simple cabin and tend his nine bean-rows. Write a paragraph in which you use specific images to describe the ideal world as you imagine it.

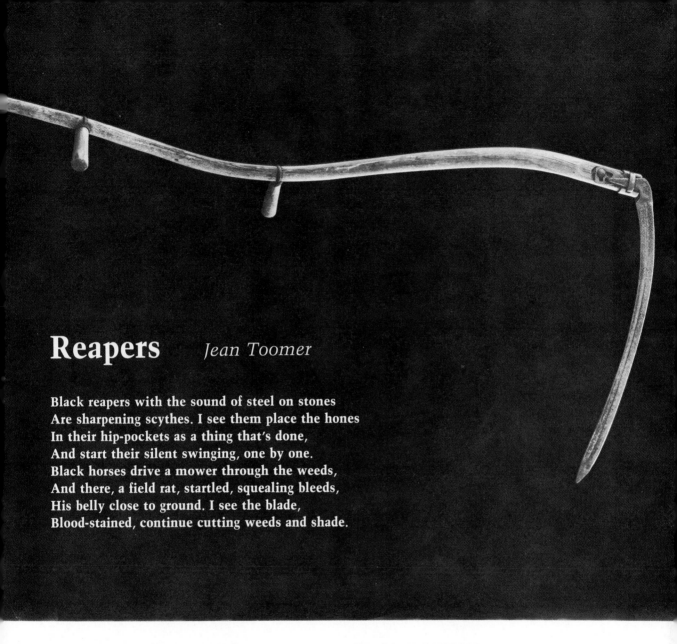

Reapers   *Jean Toomer*

Black reapers with the sound of steel on stones
Are sharpening scythes. I see them place the hones
In their hip-pockets as a thing that's done,
And start their silent swinging, one by one.
Black horses drive a mower through the weeds,
And there, a field rat, startled, squealing bleeds,
His belly close to ground. I see the blade,
Blood-stained, continue cutting weeds and shade.

FOR STUDY AND DISCUSSION

1. What images in this poem help you see and hear what the reapers and mower are doing?
2. What details suggest that the mower is impersonal—with no feeling for the life around it?
3. What other images in the poem help create a sense of menace?

FOR COMPOSITION

Describing Action
This poem uses specific images to describe actions that the speaker is observing. Describe some action you have observed carefully. Use a series of images that tell what movements and colors you see and what noise you hear. You might open with "I see . . ."

Above Pate Valley *Gary Snyder*

We finished clearing the last
Section of trail by noon,
High on the ridge-side
Two thousand feet above the creek—
Reached the pass, went on   5
Beyond the white pine groves,
Granite shoulders, to a small
Green meadow watered by the snow,
Edged with Aspen—sun
Straight high and blazing   10
But the air was cool.
Ate a cold fried trout in the
Trembling shadows. I spied
A glitter, and found a flake
Black volcanic glass—obsidian—   15
By a flower. Hands and knees
Pushing the Bear grass, thousands
Of arrowhead leavings over a
Hundred yards. Not one good
Head, just razor flakes   20
On a hill snowed all but summer,
A land of fat summer deer,
They came to camp. On their
Own trails. I followed my own
Trail here. Picked up the cold-drill,   25
Pick, singlejack, and sack
Of dynamite.
Ten thousand years.

FOR STUDY AND DISCUSSION

1. What specific images help you experience the setting of "Above Pate Valley"? How do the images make you feel about this setting?
2. How do you suppose the speaker's trails contrast with "their" trails?
3. The speaker talks about his tools in lines 25–27. How do these tools contrast with the remains he finds in the Bear grass?
4. The poet emphasizes *dynamite* by putting it on a separate line. What does dynamite suggest to you? How could dynamite and the speaker's other tools affect this valley that has remained the same for ten thousand years?

FOR COMPOSITION

Creating a Setting

Gary Snyder creates a setting—the mountain meadow above Pate Valley—with a series of concrete details. Most of Snyder's details give us visual images of the area, but some appeal to other senses too—our sense of heat and cold and our sense of taste, for example. In a short paragraph or simple poem, create a setting through the use of concrete details that appeal to one or more of the senses. If you choose to write a poem, use a conversational style, as Snyder does. Try to convey to your readers the look and the "feel" of the place you are describing.

Recuerdo   *Edna St. Vincent Millay*

We were very tired, we were very merry—
We had gone back and forth all night on the ferry.
It was bare and bright, and smelled like a stable—
But we looked into a fire, we leaned across a table,
We lay on the hill-top underneath the moon;   5
And the whistles kept blowing, and the dawn came
        soon.

We were very tired, we were very merry—
We had gone back and forth all night on the ferry;
And you ate an apple, and I ate a pear,
From a dozen of each we had bought somewhere;   10
And the sky went wan, and the wind came cold,
And the sun rose dripping, a bucketful of gold.

We were very tired, we were very merry—
We had gone back and forth all night on the ferry.
We hailed, "Good morrow, mother!" to a shawl-covered
        head,   15
And bought a morning paper, which neither of us read;
And she wept, "God bless you!" for the apples and the
        pears,
And we gave her all our money but our subway fares.

The Ferry Boat. Photograph by
Alfred Stieglitz (1864–1946).
Philadelphia Museum of Art. Given by Carl Zigrosser.

FOR STUDY AND DISCUSSION

1. *Recuerdo* means "memory" or "remembrance" in Spanish. What images in this poem help create a sense of romance and enchantment? Does the use of the past tense lend an edge of sadness to the poem? Explain.

2. This poet helps us to share her experience by using images that appeal to all the senses. What specific images appeal to your senses of taste, touch, smell, sight, and hearing?

3. Line 15 contains an example of a figure of speech called *synecdoche* (sĭ-nĕk′də-kē). In a synecdoche, a part of something is used to refer to or imply a whole. What does the "shawl-covered head" refer to? How does the shawl-covered head contrast with the other people in the poem?

4. Why do you think the speaker and her friend gave away their fruit and money?

FOR COMPOSITION

Using Specific Details

We can remember only a fraction of the things we experience, yet certain episodes remain especially vivid in our minds. In "Recuerdo" the poet captures in specific images a past experience. Think of some experience that is vivid in your own memory, and write a poem or a prose paragraph in which you use images to communicate what you saw, heard, smelled, tasted, or touched. Try to select images that create the mood you associate with the experience: joy, sadness, excitement, peace, or some other feeling.

To the Thawing Wind

Robert Frost

Come with rain, O loud Southwester!
Bring the singer, bring the nester;
Give the buried flower a dream;
Make the settled snowbank steam;
Find the brown beneath the white;   5
But whate'er you do tonight,
Bathe my window, make it flow,
Melt it as the ice will go;
Melt the glass and leave the sticks
Like a hermit's crucifix;   10
Burst into my narrow stall;
Swing the picture on the wall;
Run the rattling pages o'er;
Scatter poems on the floor;
Turn the poet out of door.   15

FOR STUDY AND DISCUSSION

1. The "loud Southwester" is a New England wind that sweeps in with the beginning of spring. What images of nature does the poet use to indicate the coming of the new season? How does he picture his window after the thaw?

2. What images in lines 11–15 help you sense the motion of the wind?

3. With the words "hermit" and "narrow stall" the poet suggests that he has lived quietly and closed in, just as nature has been "buried" and "settled." How is the wind's effect on the poet similar to its effect on nature?

FOR COMPOSITION

Contrasting Poems

Both Robert Frost and William Butler Yeats (page 293) have written poems that picture natural settings. The two poems are alike in that they both use a few vivid images that help us experience the beauty of nature, but the two poems are very different in mood. Write a paragraph in which you contrast the moods or feelings revealed in these two poems. Tell specifically what you think the mood of each poem is, and use details from the poems to support your opinion.

Ornamental Sketch with Verbs

May Swenson

Sunset runs in a seam
over the brows of buildings
    dropping west to the river,
turns the street to a gilded stagger,
makes the girl on skates,   5
    the man with the block of ice,
    the basement landlady calling her cat
    creatures in a dream,

scales with salamander-red
    the window-pitted walls,   10
hairs the gutters with brindled° light,
helmets cars and boys on bikes
and double-dazzles
    the policeman's portly coat,
halos the coal truck where   15
    nuggets race from a golden sled,

festoons lampposts to fantastic trees,
lacquers sooty roofs and pavements,
floats in every puddle
    pinks of cloud,   20
flamingos all the pigeons,
grands all dogs to chows,
enchants the ash cans into urns°
    and fire-escapes to Orleans balconies.

11. **brindled:** spotted and streaked.

23. **urns:** decorative vases.

FOR STUDY AND DISCUSSION

1. This poet piles up images that show how a sunset transforms an ordinary city street into something beautiful, even fabulous. The street itself, for example, becomes a "gilded stagger," an image that makes us see the light creating a zigzag pattern along the street. What happens to the people in the first stanza?

2. A seam can be a line or crease in a forehead. What image do you see in lines 1–2?

3. The poet announces in her title that this will be a sketch with "verbs." Note that from line 4 to the end of the poem, most lines begin with a verb. But in this poem, words that are normally nouns function as the verbs. How would you explain the meaning of *scales* (line 9), *hairs* (line 11), *helmets* (line 12), *halos* (line 15), and *flamingos* (line 21)?

4. Which images add a humorous tone to this "sketch"?

LANGUAGE AND VOCABULARY

Understanding Connotations

All words have *denotations*—that is, explicit meanings you find listed in a dictionary. Many words also have *connotations*—that is, suggestive meanings and associations that go beyond their strict dictionary definitions. For example, we read in "Recuerdo" (page 298) that the sun rose "dripping, a bucketful of gold." Strictly speaking, gold is a heavy, yellow, inert metallic chemical element with a high degree of ductility and malleability. But, of course, the word *gold* connotes, or suggests, much more than this. The poet relies on our recognizing that gold suggests something very precious—perhaps perfection, richness, happiness, beauty. Imagine how different the effect would have been if the poet had compared the sun to a bucketful of yellow paint.

In line 22 of "Ornamental Sketch with Verbs," the poet says that the sun "grands" all the dogs to "chows." This image makes us see dogs, probably mongrels, being magically transformed into chows, valuable members of a pure breed. But the word *chow* has certain connotations, too. Chows are of ancient lineage and were originally bred in China. They also have extraordinary blue-black tongues, and are often associated with fierceness. Thus the word *chow* not only puts a specific picture in our minds, but it also suggests, or connotes, something exotic. (How would the effect differ if the dogs had been turned into "Labrador retrievers"?)

What does each of the following words mean? Do any of them have connotations—that is, do they call forth associations or feelings?

salamander	lacquers	flamingos
festoons	kinks	urns

FOR COMPOSITION

Using Nouns as Verbs

This poet announces in her title that she will create an ornamental sketch with *verbs*. Create your own sketch with verbs. Imagine how a few specific objects in a scene might be transformed into other things. Imitate Swenson's technique and use a series of phrases in which nouns function as verbs, as in the phrase "flamingos all the pigeons." A description of a snowstorm, for example, might start with "cottons all the streets."

Boy with His Hair Cut Short

Muriel Rukeyser

Sunday shuts down on this twentieth-century evening.
The L° passes. Twilight and bulb define
the brown room, the overstuffed plum sofa,
the boy, and the girl's thin hands above his head.
A neighbor's radio sings stocks, news, serenade.   5

He sits at the table, head down, the young clear neck
    exposed,
watching the drugstore sign from the tail of his eye;
tattoo, neon, until the eye blears, while his
solicitous tall sister, simple in blue, bending
behind him, cuts his hair with her cheap shears.   10

The arrow's electric red always reaches its mark,
successful neon! He coughs, impressed by that
    precision.
His child's forehead, forever protected by his cap,
is bleached against the lamplight as he turns head
and steadies to let the snippets drop.   15

Erasing the failure of weeks with level fingers,
she sleeks the fine hair, combing: "You'll look fine
    tomorrow!
You'll surely find something, they can't keep turning
    you down;
the finest gentleman's not so trim as you!" Smiling, he
   raises
the adolescent forehead wrinkling ironic now.   20

He sees his decent suit laid out, new-pressed,
his carfare on the shelf. He lets his head fall, meeting
her earnest hopeless look, seeing the sharp blades
    splitting,
the darkened room, the impersonal sign, her motion,
the blue vein, bright on her temple, pitifully beating.   25

2. **L**: elevated train.

Manhattan Bridge Loop (1928). Oil painting by Edward Hopper (1882–1967).
Addison Gallery of American Art, Phillips Academy, Andover, Massachusetts.

FOR STUDY AND DISCUSSION

1. This poem was written during the Great Depression, when millions of people could not find work. What details reveal that this boy is looking for work? What details suggest that the boy and his sister do not have much money?

2. The sister speaks cheerfully in stanza 4. What words in stanza 5 reveal that she does not believe what she says?

3. How does the poet make you aware that the boy is feeling hopeless and despairing?

4. The poet puts the characters in a specific setting. What details suggest that the setting is impersonal and even ugly? How do the images describing the boy and his sister contrast with those describing the setting?

5. What specific words and images reveal that the poet sympathizes with these people and wants us to see their dignity?

FOR COMPOSITION

Comparing a Poem and a Painting
Note the painting by American artist Edward Hopper which accompanies this poem. Write a paragraph in which you compare the painting with Rukeyser's poem. What similarity do you see between the mood created by Hopper and the mood created by Rukeyser? What specific details does each artist use to establish the mood?

ABOUT THE AUTHORS

William Stafford (1914–   ) often writes of the vast, open spaces that characterize the landscape of his Kansas boyhood. Stafford's poems usually present a moral view of nature, of the family, and of home. "My poetry seems to me direct and communicative," he says, "with some oddity and variety. It is usually not formal. It is much like talk, with some enchantment." Stafford has served as the poetry consultant at the Library of Congress.

William Butler Yeats (1865–1939) was, more than any other individual, responsible for the revival of Irish literature at the turn of the century. Born in Ireland, the son of a well-known painter, Yeats divided his time between Dublin, London, and Sligo, a county in the west of Ireland where his grandparents lived. Poet, playwright, and editor, Yeats is regarded as one of the greatest poets writing in the English language in this century. This reputation was built on such poems as "Easter 1916," "The Second Coming," and "Among School Children." In 1923 Yeats received the Nobel Prize for literature.

Jean Toomer (1894–1967) grew up in the home of his grandfather, who had been acting governor of Louisiana during the Reconstruction period following the Civil War. After high school, Toomer restlessly wandered from one city and one college to another. He settled for a time in Georgia, where he was superintendent of a rural black school. With the publication of *Cane* (1923)—a collection of stories, sketches, and poems about Southern black life—Toomer became one of the leaders of the Harlem Renaissance of the 1920's.

Gary Snyder (1930–   ) writes poetry based on his rich and diverse experiences. He has worked as a seaman on a tanker, as a logger, and as a Forest Service crew member in the Pacific Northwest. He is also a serious follower of Zen Buddhism and a student of Oriental languages. Snyder has said of his poetry: "I try to hold both history and wilderness in mind, that my poems may approach the true measure of things and stand against the unbalance and ignorance of our times." In 1975 Snyder won the Pulitzer Prize for his book of poems called *Turtle Island*.

Edna St. Vincent Millay (1892–1950) began writing poetry as a child and had her first poems published in the "club page" of *St. Nicholas*, a children's magazine. "Renascence," a long poem written when she was nineteen, established her as an important American poet, and in 1923 she won the Pulitzer Prize for a collection called *The Harp-Weaver*. The themes that dominate Millay's most famous poems are a romantic celebration of youth and a concern with love, death, and the self.

Robert Frost (1878–1963) wrote of the birch trees, the stone walls, the white churches, the mountains, and the snowfalls of New England, and of the region's farmers, wanderers, and hired men. Frost moved to New England when he was a child, and as a young man he attempted farming and poetry writing. Neither venture met with much success. Discouraged, Frost moved with his family to England, and there published his first two books of poetry: *A Boy's Will* (1913) and *North of Boston* (1914). The books were immediate successes and Frost was soon one of America's most revered poets. He eventually won four Pulitzer Prizes and numerous other awards. Though he is beloved for his simple language and familiar country settings, Frost also reveals images of the tragic and disturbing side of human life. In one of his poems, Frost said that if an epitaph were to sum up his story, he had one ready: "I had a lover's quarrel with the world."

May Swenson (1919–   ), born in Utah, came to New York City at the age of thirty to write poetry. She has worked as an editor at New Directions Publishers in New York and has lectured at many colleges. The poet Elizabeth Bishop said that Swenson "looks, and sees, and rejoices in what she sees. Her poems are varied, energetic, and full of directness and optimism that are unusual in these days. . . ." Swenson has experimented with various forms of poetry, including riddle poems and concrete poems—poems that create shapes on the page.

Muriel Rukeyser (1913–1980) wrote poetry that reflects her deep emotional involvement in the social and political events of our times. She believed that our modern world is characterized by a widespread alienation and a loss of personal direction, and her poems illustrate these concerns. She was born in New York City and worked as a reporter for a time, often covering controversial events.

Figurative Language

At the heart of poetry is *figurative language* — the use of language to describe one thing in terms of something else. Poets can make us see lips as cherries, the sun as the eye of heaven, the world as a stage, or a lake as a slurping monster. Figurative language is not literally true, but it contains a kind of imaginative truth. Robert Burns tells us, "my Luve's like a red, red rose." We're fairly certain that his love does not have thorns, a green stem, and petals. But his figure of speech makes us think of all the ways the girl might be like a flower: fresh, soft, sweet, and maybe just as rosy.

People who study such things have categorized over a hundred different figures of speech. In this unit, we'll look at four: simile, metaphor, personification, and symbol.

The main thing to remember about figurative language is that it is always helping us to see comparisons and relationships. A *simile*, for example, is a straightforward comparison of two unlike things, using a word such as *like* or *as*. Burns uses a simile in saying his love is "like" a rose.

A *metaphor* is a more powerful figure of speech: it omits the specific word of comparison and directly identifies the two unlike things. If Burns had been in a metaphorical frame of mind, he could have said "my Luve *is* a red, red rose."

Personification is a special form of metaphor. In personification, an inanimate thing or an animal is given human qualities. Homer, writing centuries ago, described "rosy-fingered dawn," making us think of a woman with rosy fingers.

A *symbol* is an object, a person, an action, or an event that stands for itself and for something more than itself as well. A common symbol in literature is night, which often stands for death. Another is spring, which often symbolizes rebirth.

Figurative language comes as naturally to us as breathing. If you doubt it, look at your newspaper. You will probably find at least fifty figures of speech that are used every day.

Autumn   *T. E. Hulme*

A touch of cold in the Autumn night
I walked abroad,
And saw the ruddy moon lean over a hedge
Like a red-faced farmer.
I did not stop to speak, but nodded;
And round about were the wistful stars
With white faces like town children.

FOR STUDY AND DISCUSSION

1. What simile does the poet use to describe the moon?

2. What simile describes the stars?

3. What words in the poem suggest that the moon is familiar and friendly? What words suggest that the stars are outsiders, looking on the earth with longing?

FOR COMPOSITION

Creating Similes

T. E. Hulme's poem is based on two striking similes. Make up a list of similes of your own, in which you compare the moon and the stars to something else. You may also want to add to the list some similes from other poems you have read; if you do this, be sure to give credit to the authors. Remember that similes are created by the use of specific words of comparison, such as *like, as, than, resembles, similar to,* or *seems.*

The Base Stealer   *Robert Francis*

Poised between going on and back, pulled
Both ways taut like a tightrope-walker,
Fingertips pointing the opposites,
Now bouncing tiptoe like a dropped ball
Or a kid skipping rope, come on, come on,   5
Running a scattering of steps sidewise,
How he teeters, skitters, tingles, teases,
Taunts them, hovers like an ecstatic bird,
He's only flirting, crowd him, crowd him,
Delicate, delicate, delicate, delicate—now!   10

FOR STUDY AND DISCUSSION

1. The simile in lines 1–3 says the base stealer is like a tightrope walker. Why is this an appropriate comparison?

2. Find three other similes in the poem— comparisons between two unlike things using words such as *like* or *as*. In each of these, what is the movement of the base stealer compared to?

3. Stealing bases involves complicated and unusual kinds of movement. What verbs does the poet use to create vivid images of motion?

4. Even the rhythm of the poem suggests motion. Why is *delicate* repeated four times in the last line? What action is signaled by the word *now?*

A Pretty Woman   *Simon J. Ortiz*

We came to the edge
of the mesa
and looked below.

We could see
the shallow wash   5
snaking down
from the cut
between two mesas,
all the way from Black Mountain;

and the cottonwoods   10
from that distance
looked like a string of turquoise,

and the land was a pretty woman
smiling at us
looking at her.   15

FOR STUDY AND DISCUSSION

1. A simile compares two unlike things, using a specific word such as *like* or *as.* A metaphor, on the other hand, does not use *like* or *as,* but makes its comparison directly. There is one simile and one metaphor in the last two stanzas of this poem. How are the two figures of speech related? Is the poet comparing the trees to the color of turquoise, or to the shape of a string of beads? Explain.

2. In cultures all over the world, the earth has been personified as a woman—as Mother Nature or as a great Earth Mother. What human qualities does this poet give the earth?

3. What does the figurative language reveal about this poet's feelings for the land?

FOR COMPOSITION

Creating Metaphors

This poet uses a metaphor to describe the land as a "pretty woman" who is smiling. Create at least four other metaphors in which you describe a piece of land by comparing it vividly with something else. You might think of comparisons that suggest what a given area of land reminds you of in different kinds of weather, such as fog, shimmering heat, and snow.

Snake Hunt   *David Wagoner*

On sloping, shattered granite, the snake man
From the zoo bent over the half-shaded crannies
Where rattlesnakes take turns out of the sun,
Stared hard, nodded at me, then lunged
With his thick gloves and yanked one up like a root.   5

And the whole hillside sprang to death with a hissing
Metallic chattering rattle: they came out writhing
In his fists, uncoiling from daydreams,
Pale bellies looping out of darker diamonds
In the shredded sunlight, dropping into his sack.   10

As I knelt on rocks, my blood went cold as theirs.
One snake coughed up a mouse. I saw what a mouse
Knows, as well as anyone: there, beside me,
In a cleft a foot away from my braced fingers,
Still in its coils, a rattler stirred from sleep.   15

It moved the wedge of its head back into shadow
And stared at me, harder than I could answer,
Till the gloves came down between us. In the sack,
Like the disembodied muscles of a torso,
It and the others searched among themselves   20

For the lost good place. I saw them later
Behind plate-glass, wearing their last skins.
They held their venom behind wide-open eyes.

FOR STUDY AND DISCUSSION

1. What images in the first stanza help you see the place where the snakes live? What images in the second stanza help you see and hear what happens when the first snake is yanked out of the cranny?

2. The speaker says that his blood went as cold as the snakes' blood. Saying that your blood runs cold is a figurative way of saying that you are afraid. Why did the speaker feel fear as he knelt on the rocks?

3. The poet uses a simile to describe the snakes in the bag. How is the simile appropriate? How does it make you feel?

4. How does the image of the "lost good place" in the last stanza suggest a note of sadness, even of pity? How does this "lost good place" contrast with where the snakes are now?

5. The snakes were sleeping when the hunt started. What are they doing now? What details in this last stanza suggest that the speaker continues to feel a sense of danger?

LANGUAGE AND VOCABULARY

Understanding Connotations
Look at how each of the following words is used in this poem. What does each word literally mean? How does each one suggest, or connote, a sense of violence or destruction?

shattered	yanked	shredded
lunged	writhing	

FOR COMPOSITION

Writing an Explanation
In line 4, Wagoner says that the snake man "stared hard" at him before lunging to capture a snake. In line 17, he says that the snake "stared at me, harder than I could answer." In a paragraph, discuss the stare of the man and the stare of the snake. Explain the significance of each stare. Tell what you think Wagoner means by saying that the snake stared at him harder than he could answer.

Dreams *Langston Hughes*

Hold fast to dreams
For if dreams die
Life is a broken-winged bird
That cannot fly.

Hold fast to dreams
For when dreams go
Life is a barren field
Frozen with snow.

FOR STUDY AND DISCUSSION

1. What is life compared to in the two metaphors in this poem? How do the metaphors suggest a life that is not free, or that is empty and dead?
2. Explain what you think this poet means by the word *dreams*.

METAPHORS

A metaphor lets us see certain specific ways in which two unlike things are similar. When the poet says that life is "a broken-winged bird," he does not want us to think of life as having feathers and eating worms. He wants us to think of how life can be free, as a bird is when it's flying. What specific points of comparison does Hughes want us to see with his second metaphor?

Suppose Hughes had wanted to describe life *with* dreams. What metaphors might be used to express this idea?

Look at Edna St. Vincent Millay's poem "Recuerdo" on page 298. What metaphor does she use in line 12 to describe the rising sun? What specific points of comparison does she want us to see in this metaphor?

Metaphors can arouse strong feelings. What feelings would you say are aroused by Hughes's metaphors? What feelings do you think Millay wants to arouse with her description of the sun?

The Lake   *Ted Hughes*

Better disguised than the leaf insect,

A sort of subtler armadillo,
The lake turns with me as I walk,

Snuffles at my feet for what I might drop or kick up,
Sucks and slobbers the stones, snorts through its lips   5

Into broken glass, smacks its chops.
It has eaten several my size

Without developing a preference—
Prompt, with a splash, to whatever I offer.

It ruffles in its wallow, or lies sunning,   10
Digesting old, senseless bicycles

And a few shoes. The fish down there
Do not know they have been swallowed,

Any more than the girl out there, who over the stern of a
    rowboat
Tests its depth with her reflection.   15

How the outlet fears it—dragging it out,
Black and yellow, a maniac eel,

Battering it to death with sticks and stones!

FOR STUDY AND DISCUSSION

1. Throughout this poem, the speaker describes the lake as if it were a hungry creature. We get this impression through a series of metaphors. How do the verbs in lines 4–11 make you think of the lake as a living, hungry creature?

2. The poet says that the lake has eaten several of his size. How has it "swallowed" the girl in lines 14–15? What else has it eaten?

3. An outlet is a stream or river that flows out from a lake. What happens in lines 16–18 when this "creature" reaches the outlet?

4. Consider carefully the words used to describe the lake, and then tell how you think the speaker feels about it. Does he look at it with affection, fear, loathing, dislike, humor, fascination?

IMPLIED METAPHORS

Many metaphors are *implied*—that is, they are not directly stated. In this poem, Hughes uses a string of verbs in lines 4–11 to *imply*, or suggest, comparisons between a lake and some living creature. Notice that he never once directly says that the lake *is* a creature; his words imply the comparison. Lakes, for example, do not do things like "smack their chops," but animals do.

What metaphor does Hughes employ to describe the lake in line 17? Why is this metaphor an appropriate way to describe the lake as it reaches the outlet?

In "A Pretty Woman" on page 311, the poet describes the wash as "snaking down" between two mesas. What metaphor is implied in this verb? What picture does it put in your mind?

DEAD METAPHORS

Many metaphors have been part of our common speech for so long that they have lost their force. We call these *dead metaphors*. There are hundreds of examples: the leg of the chair, the head of the bed, and the foot of the table are a few that apply to furniture alone. What dead metaphor can you spot in the title of the poem "The Base Stealer" (page 310)?

Here are some other commonly used expressions that contain dead metaphors. What comparisons are being made in each one? Perhaps you can add to the list.

a cold shoulder	hounded by fear
a toadstool	consumed by jealousy
a fishy story	plagued with bad luck

FOR COMPOSITION

Paraphrasing a Poem

A *paraphrase* is a retelling of a piece of literature in simpler words. A good paraphrase of a poem will do the following: restate all metaphors in literal language, replace difficult words with simpler ones, and make clear what the poet suggests but does not actually state. A paraphrase of a poem will usually run longer than the poem itself. Here is a paraphrase of the first four lines of "The Lake." Using this paragraph as a beginning, paraphrase the rest of the poem, making clear all the poet is trying to say.

This lake hides its true nature as if it were disguised. It is better disguised than a leaf insect. It is more subtle in its disguise than an armadillo. As I walk around the lake, it seems to turn with me. It is like a snuffling beast, waiting at my feet for me to drop or kick up something for it to devour.

She Sweeps with Many-Colored Brooms
Emily Dickinson

She sweeps with many-colored brooms,
And leaves the shreds behind;
Oh, housewife in the evening west,
Come back, and dust the pond!

You dropped a purple raveling in,   5
You dropped an amber thread;
And now you've littered all the East
With duds° of emerald!   8. **duds**: clothes or belongings.

And still she plies her spotted brooms,
And still the aprons fly,   10
Till brooms fade softly into stars—
And then I come away.

FOR STUDY AND DISCUSSION

1. This poet uses a metaphor and talks about the sun as if it were a housewife. What words reveal that the subject is the setting sun? What do you think the "brooms" are?

2. Look at what the speaker says to the "housewife." Is this a careful housekeeper, or is she somewhat untidy? Explain.

3. Which metaphors here are based on the ordinary details of domestic life?

EXTENDED METAPHOR

Many times a poet will extend a metaphor throughout several lines of a poem or even throughout an entire poem. Dickinson extends her metaphor comparing the sunset to a housewife throughout the whole poem, and she finds many points of comparison between the two. For example, the streaks of light in the sky become raveled threads and bits of cloth, and the flying clouds become her aprons, which fly about as she works.

Look back at Ted Hughes's poem "The Lake" (page 316). Hughes extends a metaphor throughout his poem. How many points of comparison does he find between the lake and a hungry creature?

FOR COMPOSITION

Comparing Poems

Another poet describes a sunset on page 302. Look back at May Swenson's "Ornamental Sketch with Verbs" and write a paragraph comparing that poem with Dickinson's. How does each poet use images of color? What is the effect of the sunset in each poem? What is each poet's attitude toward the sunset?

Big Wind   *Theodore Roethke*

Where were the greenhouses going,
Lunging into the lashing
Wind, driving water
So far down the river
All the faucets stopped?— 5
So we drained the manure-machine
For the steam plant,
Pumping the stale mixture
Into the rusty boilers,
Watching the pressure gauge 10
Waver over to red,
As the seams hissed
And the live steam
Drove to the far
End of the rose-house, 15
Where the worst wind was,
Creaking the cypress window-frames,
Cracking so much thin glass
We stayed all night,
Stuffing the holes with burlap; 20
But she rode it out,
That old rose-house,
She hove into the teeth of it,
The core and pith of that ugly storm,
Ploughing with her stiff prow, 25
Bucking into the wind-waves
That broke over the whole of her,
Flailing her sides with spray,
Flinging long strings of wet across the roof-top,
Finally veering, wearing themselves out, merely 30
Whistling thinly under the wind-vents;
She sailed until the calm morning,
Carrying her full cargo of roses.

FOR STUDY AND DISCUSSION

1. What images does the poet use to help you see the storm? What images help you hear it?
2. This poem contains an extended metaphor. To what are the greenhouses compared throughout the poem? What verbs does the poet use to make this comparison?
3. What wider meaning can you see in the fact that this "cargo" of roses conquers an "ugly" storm?
4. How would you describe the poet's feeling for the rose-house?

FOR COMPOSITION

Creating Images

Write a poem or a prose paragraph that creates images of some kind of movement. Use precise verbs that will give your reader an impression of what you see and feel, perhaps even of what you hear. Try to use figurative language — perhaps an extended metaphor — to let your reader know what the action reminds you of and how you feel about it.

Mirror   *Sylvia Plath*

I am silver and exact. I have no preconceptions.°
Whatever I see I swallow immediately
Just as it is, unmisted by love or dislike.
I am not cruel, only truthful —
The eye of a little god, four-cornered.   5
Most of the time I meditate on the opposite wall.
It is pink, with speckles. I have looked at it so long
I think it is a part of my heart. But it flickers.
Faces and darkness separate us over and over.

1. **preconceptions:** prejudices; ideas or opinions formed in advance.

The Mirror (1900).
Oil painting by
William Merritt Chase
(1849–1916).
The Cincinnati Art Museum.

Now I am a lake. A woman bends over me,   10
Searching my reaches for what she really is.
Then she turns to those liars, the candles or the moon.
I see her back, and reflect it faithfully.
She rewards me with tears and an agitation of hands.
I am important to her. She comes and goes.   15
Each morning it is her face that replaces the darkness.
In me she has drowned a young girl, and in me an old
    woman
Rises toward her day after day, like a terrible fish.

FOR STUDY AND DISCUSSION

1. If this poem had no title, what clues would reveal that the speaker is a mirror?

2. In the first stanza, the mirror is personified, or given human qualities. What specific human characteristics does it have? In what ways is the mirror *not* fully human?

3. What does the mirror mean when it says it is not cruel, only truthful?

4. In the second stanza, the mirror-speaker opens with a metaphor. What words in this stanza extend the comparison of the mirror to a lake?

5. Why does the mirror call the moon and candles "liars"?

6. How would you explain what is happening in the last two lines? What emotional impact is created by the images in these lines?

THE SPEAKER OF A POEM

One of the first things you should do when you read a poem is look for clues that identify its speaker. Sometimes the speaker will seem to be the poet, but at other times the speaker will be someone or something altogether different. Speakers in poems have been rivers, ghosts, children, imaginary characters, and so on. Some poems have more than one speaker. In this poem, the speaker is a mirror, and what the mirror says reveals something about its particular character. How would you describe the kind of "person" this mirror is?

FOR COMPOSITION

Using Personification

Choose a familiar inanimate object and write a paragraph or a poem telling what it might say if it could speak. Here are some ideas:

a telephone booth	a television set
a schoolroom clock	a church
a worn-out dollar bill	a kitchen table

The Long Hill   *Sara Teasdale*

I must have passed the crest a while ago
  And now I am going down—
Strange to have crossed the crest and not to know,
  But the brambles were always catching the hem of my
    gown.

All the morning I thought how proud I should be   5
  To stand there straight as a queen,
Wrapped in the wind and the sun with the world under
    me—
  But the air was dull, there was little I could have seen.

It was nearly level along the beaten track
  And the brambles caught in my gown—   10
But it's no use now to think of turning back,
  The rest of the way will be only going down.

FOR STUDY AND DISCUSSION

1. What three reasons does the speaker give for not noticing when she reached the crest of the hill?
2. How was crossing the crest different from what she thought it would be?
3. This poem can be read on a simple literal level as being about a walk over a long hill. But usually people are not as serious and melancholy about a mere walk as this poet is. Thus, we can guess that the poem should also be read on another, deeper level. How can the "long hill" in the poem be seen as a symbol of life itself?
4. What is symbolized by the "crest" of the hill and by the "brambles" that catch in the speaker's gown?
5. What details in the poem suggest that the speaker is disappointed and regretful about her experience?

First Lesson

Philip Booth

Lie back, daughter, let your head
be tipped back in the cup of my hand.
Gently, and I will hold you. Spread
your arms wide, lie out on the stream
and look high at the gulls. A dead-   5
man's-float is face down. You will dive
and swim soon enough where this tidewater
ebbs to the sea. Daughter, believe
me, when you tire on the long thrash
to your island, lie up, and survive.   10
As you float now, where I held you
and let go, remember when fear
cramps your heart what I told you:
lie gently and wide to the light-year
stars, lie back, and the sea will hold you.   15

FOR STUDY AND DISCUSSION

1. On a literal level, this father is giving his daughter advice about floating, but the poem can also be interpreted on another, symbolic level. Everything that the father says can be understood as advice about becoming an adult. With this interpretation in mind, explain the following phrases: "the long thrash to your island," "lie up, and survive," "when fear cramps your heart."

2. When people take swimming lessons, often the first thing they learn is how to float. How would you explain the "first lesson" that this father is teaching his daughter?

3. How is "floating" a good symbol for the lesson the girl is learning?

SYMBOLS

On one level, Teasdale's poem is about a climb up a hill. On a deeper level, it is about a journey toward a crucial event. Symbols do not exist in every poem, and it would be a mistake to look for them all the time. But when you suspect that a poem is about more than appears on the surface, you can be fairly certain that the poem is also operating on a deeper, symbolic level.

Some symbols are common in literature and are used over and over again. Many writers, however, invent their own symbols, as Booth does in his poem. Booth teaches his daughter to float in the tidewater before she goes out to the sea. What would the tidewater symbolize, as opposed to the sea itself? What symbolic meaning can you find in the poet's use of the words "dead-man's-float" (lines 5–6) and "dive and swim" (lines 6–7)?

A Black Man Talks of Reaping

Arna Bontemps

A Crow Flew By (1949–1950).
Tempera painting by
Andrew Wyeth (1917–   ).
The Metropolitan Museum of Art,
New York.

I have sown beside all waters in my day.
I planted deep, within my heart the fear
That wind or fowl would take the grain away.
I planted safe against this stark, lean year.

I scattered seed enough to plant the land   5
In rows from Canada to Mexico
But for my reaping only what the hand
Can hold at once is all that I can show.

Yet what I sowed and what the orchard yields
My brother's sons are gathering stalk and root,   10
Small wonder then my children glean in fields
They have not sown, and feed on bitter fruit.

FOR STUDY AND DISCUSSION

1. This poem is best understood if we realize that it is a comment on a line from the Bible: "whatsoever a man soweth, that shall he also reap." (Galatians 6:7) In lines 1-6, the speaker describes what he has sown, or planted. According to lines 7-8, what is he allowed to reap, or harvest?

2. How is this situation different from what is stated in the Biblical passage?

3. What do you think the speaker means in lines 9-10 when he says that his "brother's sons" gather what he has sown?

4. What do you think the "bitter fruit" stands for in the final line?

5. This poem seems to be about sowing and reaping, but it is about much more than that. What is the real subject of the poem?

6. What words reveal the speaker's bitter tone? How does the poem suggest a sense of *irony*—that is, that a situation is entirely different from what was expected, or what seemed appropriate?

ALLUSIONS

An *allusion* is a reference to a person, a place, an event, or a literary work that the writer expects the reader to recognize and respond to. An allusion can call to the reader's mind a whole series of associations and feelings. Bontemps, for example, bases his poem on an allusion to the Bible.

Because of the central place they occupy in Western literature, the Bible and the myths of Greece and Rome are alluded to frequently. Each of the following excerpts contains one or more allusions to Greek or Roman mythology. Find and explain each allusion. If you can't recognize the allusion, look up the unfamiliar name in a good dictionary or en-cyclopedia. Better yet, read about the character in a mythology book.

So might I, standing on this pleasant lea,
Have glimpses that would make me less
　forlorn;
Have sight of Proteus rising from the sea;
Or hear old Triton blow his wreathèd
　horn.

William Wordsworth
from "The World Is Too Much with Us"

Earth outgrows the mythic fancies
Sung beside her in her youth;
And those debonair romances
Sound but dull beside the truth.
Phoebus' chariot is run!
Look up, poets, to the sun!
　Pan, Pan is dead.

Elizabeth Barrett Browning
from "The Dead Pan"

Sacred Goddess, Mother Earth,
　Thou from whose immortal bosom,
Gods, and men, and beasts have birth,
　Leaf and blade, and bud and blossom,
Breathe thine influence most divine
On thine own child Proserpine.

Percy Bysshe Shelley
from "Hymn to Proserpine"

ABOUT THE AUTHORS

T. E. Hulme (1883–1917) was an English philosopher and poet who was killed in action during World War I. Hulme advocated the use of "hard dry images" in poetry.

Robert Francis (1901–   ) was born in Pennsylvania, grew up in Massachusetts, and graduated from Harvard University. His books include *Collected Poems: 1936–1976* and an autobiography, *The Trouble with Francis.*

Simon J. Ortiz (1904–   ) was born in the Acoma Pueblo in New Mexico. He traces his interest in words and language to an old relative who used to visit Ortiz' childhood home and tell stories. Ortiz has published both fiction and poetry, drawing inspiration from the people and landscape of his native Southwest.

David Wagoner (1926–   ) was born in Massillon, Ohio. He served in the navy for two years during World War II, and then earned degrees from the Pennsylvania State University and Indiana University. His poetry has earned him Guggenheim and Ford fellowships. He is currently a professor of English at the University of Washington in Seattle. "Snake Hunt" is from his book of poetry called *Sleeping in the Woods* (1974).

Langston Hughes (1902–1967), born in Joplin, Missouri, was one of the key figures of the Harlem Renaissance of the 1920's, a cultural awakening that expressed the diversity and vitality of the black experience in America. Hughes got his start as a poet through a stroke of luck. When he was working in a Washington hotel, he left some of his poems beside the plate of poet Vachel Lindsay. Lindsay recognized the young poet's talent and introduced Hughes to the literary world. Hughes's poems were among the first to express the spirit of the blues in words.

Ted Hughes (1930–   ) grew up in a half-rural, half-industrial area of Yorkshire, England. Many of Hughes's poems, such as "The Lake," depict nature as wild and brutal, but this poet has a lyrical side, too, as seen in his books for children. Hughes is one of the outstanding poets of his generation.

Emily Dickinson (1830–1886) was born in Amherst, Massachusetts, where she lived her entire life. Though she wrote more than 1,700 poems—on bits of wrapping paper, envelopes, and old grocery bills—not more than seven of her poems were published during her lifetime. As critic Van Wyck Brooks says, Dickinson "domesticated the universe," often drawing metaphors from the details of ordinary life.

Theodore Roethke (rĕt'kē) (1908–1963) grew up "in and around a beautiful greenhouse" owned by his father and uncle in Saginaw, Michigan. "Big Wind" is one of several poems Roethke wrote about the greenhouse, which, he said, had a profound effect on his childhood. Roethke once wrote that "Big Wind" shows how a poet writing in free verse can use a formal device—in this case, repetition of participial and verbal forms—to keep the action going and give energy to the poem. Roethke sold his first poems when he was a graduate student at Harvard University. His collection called *The Waking* earned him the Pulitzer Prize in 1954. At the time of his death, Roethke was poet-in-residence at the University of Washington in Seattle.

Sylvia Plath (1932–1963) was born in Boston and graduated from Smith College. Her first volume of poetry was published when she was still in her twenties. *The Bell Jar* (1963), an autobiographical novel about a young girl's breakdown, appeared under a pseudonym, partly because Plath didn't consider it a serious work and partly because she felt too many people would be hurt by its details. The novelist Joyce Carol Oates has called Sylvia Plath "our acknowledged Queen of Sorrows, the spokeswoman for our most private, most helpless nightmares. . . ."

Sara Teasdale (1884–1933) was born in St. Louis and lived most of her adult life there and in New York City. Though wooed by the poet Vachel Lindsay, she married a St. Louis businessman instead. She was a victim of ill health and often withdrew into her own private world. She is remembered chiefly for a few graceful, simple lyrics.

Philip Booth (1925–   ), who was born in Hanover, New Hampshire, has been called the poet of Maine's coast, which is now his home. His poems often put humans on the edge of land, at the brink of the sea. Booth taught writing and literature at several colleges before becoming a professor of English at Syracuse University.

Arna Bontemps (bäwn'tämp) (1902–1973) was born in Alexandria, Louisiana, and educated at Pacific Union College and at the University of Chicago. As a young writer, Bontemps was a leader of the Harlem Renaissance, a literary movement of the 1920's. With Langston Hughes he compiled *The Poetry of the Negro*, an anthology that covers two hundred years of black poetry.

Tone

Think of all the ways "Good morning" can be spoken. A person may say it cheerfully or sullenly, cordially or grudgingly, stiffly or warmly, courteously or contemptuously, proudly or eagerly, with stiff politeness or with boisterous good will. In short, the words "Good morning" can be uttered so as to mean almost anything from "I love you" to "I don't really care to speak to you." The tone in which the words are spoken is as important as their dictionary definition.

Poets, too, communicate meaning through *tone*—that is, through the attitudes they take toward their subject matter or audience. Three poets can write on the same topic: one might be serious, one might be sarcastic, and one might be light and humorous. Thus, it is important to recognize a poet's tone, because if we misread the tone, we might badly misread the entire work.

Unlike vocal communications, poems cannot express tone through inflection, volume, and pitch. Tone is indicated in a poem by other methods: by the particular words chosen, by the arrangement of the words, by rhythm, sound, images, and figures of speech.

Miss Rosie *Lucille Clifton*

When I watch you
wrapped up like garbage
sitting, surrounded by the smell
of too old potato peels
or   5
when I watch you
in your old man's shoes
with the little toe cut out
sitting, waiting for your mind
like next week's grocery   10
I say
when I watch you
you wet brown bag of a woman
who used to be the best looking gal in Georgia
used to be called the Georgia Rose   15
I stand up
through your destruction
I stand up

FOR STUDY AND DISCUSSION

1. The "smell of too old potato peels" in lines 3–4 is an image that arouses unpleasant associations. What unpleasant metaphors and similes are used to describe Miss Rosie?

2. The poem shifts suddenly at line 14. How do the details in lines 14–15 change your perception of Miss Rosie?

3. Why do you suppose the speaker would "stand up" for this "wet brown bag of a woman"? What does this reveal about the poet's tone—the way she feels toward Miss Rosie?

4. How does repetition create rhythm here? What ideas are emphasized by the repetition?

FOR COMPOSITION

Writing a Poem

Imitate the conversational style of this poem and write a poem in which you describe someone or something that you would "stand up" for. Open with the words "When I" and close with the words "I stand up." Do not attempt rhyme or a regular rhythm. Make your poem sound as if you were speaking naturally.

One Perfect Rose   *Dorothy Parker*

A single flow'r he sent me, since we met.
  All tenderly his messenger he chose;
Deep-hearted, pure, with scented dew still wet—
  One perfect rose.

I knew the language of the floweret;   5
  "My fragile leaves," it said, "his heart enclose."
Love long has taken for his amulet
  One perfect rose.

Why is it no one ever sent me yet
  One perfect limousine, do you suppose?   10
Ah no, it's always just my luck to get
  One perfect rose.

FOR STUDY AND DISCUSSION

1. In the first two stanzas, this poet's *diction* — or choice of words — is the standard diction of romantic old-fashioned poetry. The shortened form of the word *flower* clues us in to this right away. What other words and phrases in these stanzas strike you as "poetic" or "romantic"?

2. How does the speaker's diction change in the third stanza?

3. The speaker says she'd prefer a limousine to a rose. What is the meaning of the word *limousine?* What associations does the word have?

4. How would you read this poem aloud to convey the speaker's change of tone from romantic tenderness to cynical humor?

POETIC INVERSION

At times, poets *invert*, or reverse, standard English word order. Sometimes this is done for emphasis, sometimes to make rhythms or rhymes work out. In the past, inversion was more common because poets worked under stricter metrical rules. Excessive inversion is often what makes those older poems sound artificial and old-fashioned today.

Dorothy Parker deliberately uses inversion in the first two stanzas to suggest an old-fashioned artificial style. For example, in the first line she says:

A single flow'r he sent me

In standard English we'd get rid of the poetic *flow'r* and say:

He sent me a single flower.

What words are inverted in lines 2, 3, and 6? Rephrase these lines in standard English word order. What happens to the tone of the poem when this is done?

A Blessing   *James Wright*

Just off the highway to Rochester, Minnesota,
Twilight bounds softly forth on the grass.
And the eyes of those two Indian ponies
Darken with kindness.
They have come gladly out of the willows   5
To welcome my friend and me.
We step over the barbed wire into the pasture
Where they have been grazing all day, alone.
They ripple tensely, they can hardly contain their
    happiness
That we have come.   10
They bow shyly as wet swans. They love each other.
There is no loneliness like theirs.
At home once more,
They began munching the young tufts of spring in
    the darkness.
I would like to hold the slenderer one in my arms,   15
For she has walked over to me
And nuzzled my left hand.
She is black and white,
Her mane falls wild on her forehead,
And the light breeze moves me to caress her long ear   20
That is delicate as the skin over a girl's wrist.
Suddenly I realize
That if I stepped out of my body I would break
Into blossom.

FOR STUDY AND DISCUSSION

1. What images describe the setting and the horses? What experience is central to the poem?
2. What metaphor at the end of the poem tells how the speaker feels about the experience?
3. The tone of this poem is joyful. It expresses the pleasure that comes from springtime and love. What images in the poem help to suggest this tone?

LANGUAGE AND VOCABULARY

Recognizing the Multiple Meanings of Words

Dictionaries list more than one meaning for most words, and some words, such as *call* and *light,* have more than ten different meanings. Poets often use a word to suggest more than one meaning, as an anonymous poet did in this humorous epitaph:

> This famous painter met his death
> Because he could not draw his breath.

How many definitions are listed for *blessing* in your dictionary? By choosing "A Blessing" as the title for his poem, James Wright implies that the blessing is the incident the poem describes. Which meanings of *blessing*—and there may be more than one—do you think the poet intends?

How many meanings does the dictionary list for the word *blossom?* Which meanings are suggested in line 24?

We say we "break into a sweat," or "break into song," or "break into a run." We also say we "break" a leg, or "break" a record. What does *break* mean in line 23? What picture do the words "break into blossom" give you?

Kindly Unhitch That Star, Buddy
Ogden Nash

I hardly suppose I know anybody who wouldn't rather be
    a success than a failure,
Just as I suppose every piece of crabgrass in the garden
    would much rather be an azalea,
And in celestial circles all the run-of-the-mill angels
    would rather be archangels or at least cherubim and
    seraphim,°
And in the legal world all the little process-servers hope
    to grow up into great big bailiffim and sheriffim.
Indeed, everybody wants to be a wow,   5
But not everybody knows exactly how.
Some people think they will eventually wear diamonds
    instead of rhinestones
Only by everlastingly keeping their noses to their ghrine-
    stones,
And other people think they will be able to put in more
    time at Palm Beach and the Ritz
By not paying too much attention to attendance at the of-
    fice but rather in being brilliant by starts and fits.   10
Some people after a full day's work sit up all night get-
    ting a college education by correspondence,
While others seem to think they'll get just as far by
    devoting their evenings to the study of the dif-
    ference in temperament between brunettance and
    blondance.
In short, the world is filled with people trying to achieve
    success,
And half of them think they'll get it by saying No and
    half of them by saying Yes,
And if all the ones who say No said Yes, and vice versa,
    such is the fate of humanity that ninety-nine per
    cent of them still wouldn't be any better off than
    they were before,   15

3. **cherubim** (chĕr′ə-bĭm′) and **seraphim** (sĕr′ə-fĭm′): ranks of angels.

Which perhaps is just as well because if everybody was a
  success nobody could be contemptuous of anybody
  else and everybody would start in all over again trying to be a bigger success than everybody else so
  they would have somebody to be contemptuous of
  and so on forevermore,
Because when people start hitching their wagons to a
  star,
That's the way they are.

FOR STUDY AND DISCUSSION

1. Nash's poem alludes to a saying by Ralph Waldo Emerson. In order to succeed, according to Emerson, "Hitch your wagon to a star." This is a figurative way of saying you should have a high goal in life. How does the title suggest that the speaker will take a humorous view of that old saying?

2. Although Nash's poem seems to be a rambling monologue, it can be divided into three sections. The first section opens with the idea that everybody wants to be a success, and lines 2–4 provide examples to support that idea. What is the main idea in lines 5–12 and lines 13–18?

3. Some of the humor is achieved through the rhyming *couplets*—pairs of rhyming lines. For example, Nash invents the words *bailiffim* and *sheriffim* to rhyme with *cherubim* and *seraphim*. Find two other examples of invented words used as rhymes.

4. A poem written in couplets usually has a regular meter, but Nash uses lines of enormously varying lengths. Find examples in the poem. How does the varying line length create humor and surprise?

FOR COMPOSITION

Adding to a Poem
Nash says that people would rather be successes than failures. Beginning with line 2, he gives examples of some "minor" things or people that would rather be more "important." For example, he says that every piece of crabgrass in the garden would rather be an azalea. Add more examples to Nash's poem: cite at least three other small, insignificant things that would rather be something more important. Think of extreme contrasts and be as absurd as you wish.

Embassy   *W. H. Auden*

As evening fell the day's oppression° lifted;
Far peaks came into focus; it had rained:
Across wide lawns and cultured flowers drifted
The conversation of the highly trained.

Two gardeners watched them pass and priced their shoes: 5
A chauffeur waited, reading in the drive,
For them to finish their exchange of views;
It seemed a picture of the private life.

Far off, no matter what good they intended,
The armies waited for a verbal error   10
With all the instruments for causing pain:

And on the issue of their charm depended
A land laid waste, with all its young men slain,
Its women weeping, and its towns in terror.

1. **day's oppression:** heavy atmosphere.

FOR STUDY AND DISCUSSION

1. An embassy is the official residence of an ambassador in a foreign country. What seems to be the purpose of the conversations being held at this embassy? What will happen if the diplomats commit a "verbal error"?
2. What images in the first two stanzas make the scene seem like "a picture of the private life"? In the last stanza, the poet describes a very different scene, a tragic one that might be brought about by what goes on at the embassy. How do the images in the last stanza contrast with those depicting the embassy?
3. What do you think is the speaker's attitude toward the embassy? What is the tone of the poem as a whole?

IRONY

The speaker in the poem describes the embassy as a beautiful place, a "picture of the private life." Yet the conversations taking place in this embassy may lead to tragic public events. When events or situations lead to consequences that are the opposite of what we expect, we have an example of *irony*. Why is it ironic, or inappropriate, that so much should depend on the diplomats' "charm"?

FOR COMPOSITION

Writing a Response
In a paragraph, give your response to Auden's poem. Did his use of ironic contrasts force you to think more deeply about these ideas? Refer to details in "Embassy" in your essay.

To an Athlete Dying Young

A. E. Housman

The time you won your town the race
We chaired you through the market-place;
Man and boy stood cheering by,
And home we brought you shoulder-high.

Today, the road all runners come,   5
Shoulder-high we bring you home,
And set you at your threshold down,
Townsman of a stiller town.

Smart lad, to slip betimes away
From fields where glory does not stay,   10
And early though the laurel grows
It withers quicker than the rose.

Eyes the shady night has shut
Cannot see the record cut,
And silence sounds no worse than cheers   15
After earth has stopped the ears:

Now you will not swell the rout
Of lads that wore their honors out,
Runners whom renown outran
And the name died before the man.   20

So set, before its echoes fade,
The fleet foot on the sill of shade,
And hold to the low lintel up
The still-defended challenge-cup.

And round that early-laureled head   25
Will flock to gaze the strengthless dead,
And find unwithered on its curls
The garland briefer than a girl's.

FOR STUDY AND DISCUSSION

1. To most people, the death of a young person is tragic. How does this poet feel about the young athlete's death?

2. Explain the contrasts set up in the first two stanzas. What is meant by the metaphor in line 5: "the road all runners come"? What is the "stiller town" in line 8?

3. The speaker calls the dead athlete a "smart lad" in line 9. What reasons does he give in stanzas 3–5 to explain why the young man is "smart" to have died young?

4. In stanzas 1–5, the speaker addresses the young athlete who is dead. Whom is he addressing in stanza 6? What scene in the land of the dead does he describe in the last stanza?

PARADOX

A *paradox* is a statement that reveals a kind of truth, though it seems to be self-contradictory. Paradox is a form of figurative language. Shakespeare created a famous paradox in his play *Julius Caesar* when he said, "Cowards die many times before their deaths." This makes us see cowardice as a moral death, which can happen over and over again.

Housman's poem contains a paradox in the sixth stanza. The poet says the dead athlete has a "fleet" foot and that he can hold up the cup in triumph. This seems to contradict other evidence in the poem. We know the boy is dead and can do none of these things. But if we think about this as a figure of speech, we can see that the poet wants us to imagine that somewhere, in some place, the athlete is still alive, even if only in memory. It is something like another popular paradox: "Though he is dead, he lives on."

The whole theme of the poem is a paradox. Why is it a paradox to see death as a victory?

FOR COMPOSITION

Paraphrasing a Poem

The purpose of a paraphrase is clarification. Because a poem packs a great deal of meaning into a few words, a paraphrase of a poem is usually longer than the poem itself. When you paraphrase a poem, be sure to explain the figures of speech as literally as you can and rephrase the difficult words.

A paraphrase of the first stanza of "To an Athlete Dying Young" might go like this:

The time you won the race for your town, we carried you through the marketplace on a chair. Men and boys stood by cheering, and when we brought you back home, we lifted you as high as our shoulders.

Continue paraphrasing the poem. When you're finished, compare your paraphrase with the poem itself. You'll see that the paraphrase fulfills an important function, but that it has none of the beauty and imaginative power of the original.

Ex-Basketball Player   *John Updike*

Pearl Avenue runs past the high-school lot,
Bends with the trolley tracks, and stops, cut off
Before it has a chance to go two blocks,
At Colonel McComsky Plaza. Berth's Garage
Is on the corner facing west, and there,   5
Most days, you'll find Flick Webb, who helps Berth out.

Flick stands tall among the idiot pumps —
Five on a side, the old bubble-head style,
Their rubber elbows hanging loose and low.
One's nostrils are two S's, and his eyes   10
An E and O. And one is squat, without
A head at all — more of a football type.

Once Flick played for the high-school team, the Wizards.
He was good: in fact, the best. In '46
He bucketed three hundred ninety points,   15
A county record still. The ball loved Flick.
I saw him rack up thirty-eight or forty
In one home game. His hands were like wild birds.

He never learned a trade, he just sells gas,
Checks oil, and changes flats. Once in a while,   20
As a gag, he dribbles an inner tube,
But most of us remember anyway.
His hands are fine and nervous on the lug wrench.
It makes no difference to the lug wrench, though.

Off work, he hangs around Mae's Luncheonette,   25
Grease-grey and kind of coiled, he plays pinball,
Sips lemon cokes, and smokes those thin cigars;
Flick seldom speaks to Mae, just sits and nods
Beyond her face towards bright applauding tiers
Of Necco Wafers, Nibs, and Juju Beads.   30

4. How would you describe the tone of the poem: that is, what is the speaker's attitude toward the ex-basketball player? How does the title itself suggest an attitude toward Flick? (Suppose, for example, the title were "Flick Webb" or "Gas-Station Attendant." What attitudes would these titles suggest?)

5. Both "Ex-Basketball Player" and "To an Athlete Dying Young" are about athletes. Are the poems alike in any other way? How would you describe the differences in their tones?

6. Ogden Nash's poem on page 336 is also about success and failure. How does Updike's tone differ from Nash's?

FOR COMPOSITION

Analyzing a Poem

In a brief essay, write an analysis of this poem. First, summarize what the poem says, paying attention to details in each stanza. Second, state what you think the poem's theme is—that is, what insight into life does it reveal? Third, explain the poem's effect on you. Do you think that the poem brings the "ex-basketball player" to life? How do you think the poet wants you to feel about Flick Webb—about the life he once led and the life he lives now?

FOR STUDY AND DISCUSSION

1. The poem is a character study. It contrasts Flick Webb's past glories with his present life. What specific lines and images present this contrast?

2. How does Flick himself contrast with his present setting, as described in the second stanza?

3. Except for the last lines, Flick is described from the outside, from the point of view of the speaker. Yet at the end of the poem we are given a glimpse into Flick's mind. Why does this image make such a powerful comment on Flick's life?

ABOUT THE AUTHORS

Lucille Clifton (1936–   ) says of her work, "I am a black woman poet, and I sound like one." She was born in Depew, New York, and educated at Howard University and Fredonia State Teachers' College. One of her books of poetry is called *An Ordinary Woman* (1974).

Dorothy Parker (1893–1967), a famous wit, said that she was "one of those awful children who write verse." At nineteen she was a member of *Vogue*'s editorial board, then a writer for *Vanity Fair* magazine and *The New Yorker*. During the Spanish Civil War, she served as an American correspondent in Spain. She also spent many years in Hollywood, where she wrote screenplays.

James Wright (1927–1980) said: "I have written about things I am deeply concerned with — crickets outside my window, cold and hungry old men, ghosts in the twilight, horses in a field, a red-haired child in her mother's arms, a feeling of desolation in the fall, some cities I have known." He was born in Martin's Ferry, Ohio, and lived in New York City. Like many poets, Wright earned his living as a college professor. In 1972 he was awarded the Pulitzer Prize for his *Collected Poems*.

Ogden Nash (1902–1971), who once described himself as a "worsifier," was born in Rye, New York. He worked in advertising and publishing until he was able to support himself and his family by writing humorous and satiric verse. Nash is now regarded as America's foremost humorous poet. He once remarked that he could say things in verse which he'd be tarred and feathered for saying in prose.

W. H. (Wystan Hugh) Auden (1907–1973), who was born in England, became an American citizen in 1946. Auden is ranked as one of the greatest twentieth-century poets writing in English. A critic has called him "the poet of conscience, of moral sensitivity." Auden's early poetry deals with the problems of modern society. It was he who labeled our time "the age of anxiety," in a book that won him the Pulitzer Prize in 1948. Auden's later poems focus on the eternal realities of love, art, religion, and the search for meaning. He once said that "what moves [the poet] to write are his encounters with the sacred in nature, in human beings, nothing else."

A. E. Housman (1859–1936) gained fame with his first book of poems, *A Shropshire Lad*, although he was born and grew up not in Shropshire but in the neighboring county of Worcestershire. Housman was a severe critic of his own work. He destroyed what didn't meet his own high standards and left behind him a small body of unquestionably excellent poems. Housman was a professor of Latin, and many of his themes — particularly those about the transitory nature of youth, life, and happiness — have their roots in classical Greek and Latin literature.

John Updike (1932–   ) is best known as a novelist and short-story writer, although he has published several books of poetry. "I began as a writer of light verse," he said, "and have tried to carry over into my serious or lyric verse something of the strictness and liveliness of the lesser form." Updike, who was born and raised in the small Pennsylvania town of Shillington, won highest honors at Harvard. One of his best-known novels is *Rabbit Run*, the story of a young man who has some things in common with Flick Webb, the ex-basketball player.

Musical Devices

One of the chief characteristics of poetry is its use of language to create musical effects. Some of the earliest known poems, the Greek *lyrikoi* and the Hebrew psalms, were, in fact, written to be accompanied by music, which was usually produced by a lyre or other stringed instrument. In choosing their words, poets always consider musical quality as well as meaning, and they often use sound to reinforce meaning. Edgar Allan Poe described poetry as "music . . . combined with a pleasurable idea." You can hear Poe's "music" in this first stanza of his poem "Annabel Lee":

> It was many and many a year ago,
>   In a kingdom by the sea,
> That a maiden there lived whom you may know
>   By the name of Annabel Lee;
> And this maiden she lived with no other thought
>   Than to love and be loved by me.

The principal device that Poe employs to make this stanza musical is *rhyme*—the repetition of accented vowel sounds and all succeeding sounds in words that appear close to each other. The words *ago/know* and *sea/Lee/me* are *end rhymes* —rhyming words that occur at the end of a poetic line. They are also *exact rhymes*—words that exactly repeat a sound. Other forms of rhyme that you will encounter in this section are *internal rhyme*—rhyme occurring within a line, and *approximate rhyme*—rhyme in which the final sounds of words are similar but not identical.

Poets make use of other forms of repetition besides rhyme. *Alliteration* is the repetition of consonant sounds, usually at the beginnings of words. *Assonance* is the repetition of vowel sounds. Another common form of repetition is the *refrain*, which is the recurring use of a phrase, an entire line, or a stanza. Refrains are especially popular in ballads, which are story poems that are often meant to be sung.

Onomatopoeia (ŏn'ə-măt'ə-pē'ə) is another musical device often used by poets. Onomatopoeia occurs when the sound of a word imitates or suggests its meaning. In this quotation from *The Princess* by Alfred, Lord Tennyson, the musical quality of the lines is enhanced by the onomatopoetic words *moan* and *murmuring*:

> The moan of doves in immemorial elms,
> And murmuring of innumerable bees.

In the poems to come, you will see how musical devices are used by many different poets to achieve widely different effects. If you look closely enough, you should be able to find music in all poetry. Beautiful or harsh, flowing or staccato, each poem plays a distinct tune.

Musical scene on an early Greek vase.

The Tuft of Flowers

Robert Frost

I went to turn the grass once after one
Who mowed it in the dew before the sun.

The dew was gone that made his blade so keen
Before I came to view the leveled scene.

I looked for him behind an isle of trees;   5
I listened for his whetstone° on the breeze.

6. **whetstone:** stone used to
sharpen tools.

But he had gone his way, the grass all mown,
And I must be, as he had been—alone,

"As all must be," I said within my heart,
"Whether they work together or apart."   10

But as I said it, swift there passed me by
On noiseless wing a bewildered butterfly,

Seeking with memories grown dim o'er night
Some resting flower of yesterday's delight.

And once I marked his flight go round and round,   15
As where some flower lay withering on the ground.

And then he flew as far as eye could see,
And then on tremulous wing came back to me.

I thought of questions that have no reply,
And would have turned to toss the grass to dry;   20

But he turned first, and led my eye to look
At a tall tuft of flowers beside a brook,

A leaping tongue of bloom the scythe had spared
Beside a reedy brook the scythe had bared.

The mower in the dew had loved them thus,   25
By leaving them to flourish, not for us,

Nor yet to draw one thought of ours to him,
But from sheer morning gladness at the brim.

The butterfly and I had lit upon,
Nevertheless, a message from the dawn,   30

That made me hear the wakening birds around,
And hear his long scythe whispering to the ground,

And feel a spirit kindred to my own;
So that henceforth I worked no more alone;

But glad with him, I worked as with his aid,   35
And weary, sought at noon with him the shade;

And dreaming, as it were, held brotherly speech
With one whose thought I had not hoped to reach.

"Men work together," I told him from the heart,
"Whether they work together or apart."   40

1. What details in the first part of the poem reveal the speaker's feeling of isolation and loneliness? How does the butterfly's bewilderment intensify this feeling?

2. Why did the early mower spare the tuft of flowers? What wordless "message" did this tuft of flowers pass on to the speaker?

3. The speaker's statements in lines 8–10 and 39–40 are paradoxes—statements that seem to contradict themselves, but which nevertheless express some truth. How do the two statements also contradict each other? What causes the speaker to change from one point of view to the other?

4. Many details in this poem suggest that communication can be carried on without speech. Why is it appropriate that the tuft of flowers be compared to a "leaping tongue"? What other details in the poem suggest that communication can be wordless? (Consider the role played by the butterfly.)

Rhyme is the repetition of accented vowel sounds and all succeeding sounds in words that appear close to each other. Rhyme is one of the chief ways by which a poet creates verbal music. Most rhymes are *end rhymes;* they occur at the ends of lines. Poets also can use *internal rhymes,* rhymes which occur within a line.

This poem is written in pairs of rhyming lines called *couplets.* If you look at the poem, you'll see that the last words in each pair of lines rhyme. Nearly all of the rhymes are *exact rhymes.* This means that the sounds of the accented vowels correspond exactly: *one/sun, keen/scene, trees/breeze.* One verse uses only *approximate rhyme.* This means that the sounds are similar but not exact. Which rhyme in the poem is not exact?

Notice that spelling has nothing to do with rhyme; it is the sound of the words that counts. *One* and *sun* are spelled differently, yet they are exact rhymes. What other words in the poem are spelled differently but rhyme exactly?

It is difficult to write an entire poem in couplets and not have it become monotonous. Frost has skillfully constructed this poem so that the rhymes contribute to the music but do not interfere with the meaning. To prevent a singsong effect, he has often used punctuation to force us to pause in unexpected places. We would not make a full pause at the end of the first line, for example. Instead, we must keep on reading until we come to the period at the end of line 2. Where are we forced to make pauses in reading lines 7–10 and 21–24?

In 1848, when Tennyson visited the lakes of Killarney in Ireland, he heard the echoes of the boatsman's bugle over the water. The experience inspired this famous poem, which is sometimes called "The Bugle Song." When Tennyson visited Killarney much later, another boatsman said, "So you're the gentleman that brought the money to the place" — suggesting that this poem had bolstered the tourist trade.

The Splendor Falls   *Alfred, Lord Tennyson*

The splendor falls on castle walls
   And snowy summits old in story;
The long light shakes across the lakes,
   And the wild cataract° leaps in glory.
Blow, bugle, blow, set the wild echoes flying,   5
Blow, bugle; answer, echoes, dying, dying, dying.

   O, hark, O, hear! how thin and clear,
      And thinner, clearer, farther going!
   O, sweet and far from cliff and scar°
      The horns of Elfland faintly blowing!   10
Blow, let us hear the purple glens replying,
Blow, bugle; answer, echoes, dying, dying, dying.

   O love, they die in yon rich sky,
      They faint on hill or field or river;
Our echoes roll from soul to soul,   15
      And grow for ever and for ever.
Blow, bugle, blow, set the wild echoes flying,
And answer, echoes, answer, dying, dying, dying.

4. **cataract:** waterfall.

9. **scar:** rocky place.

FOR STUDY AND DISCUSSION

1. What images in the first stanza help you see what the speaker sees? What images in the second stanza help you hear what he hears?

2. What images in the first two stanzas suggest that the speaker sees this setting as romantic, like something in a fairy tale?

3. How do the last two lines of each stanza help you hear the echoes of the bugle? What line makes the bugle and its echoes seem farther and farther away?

4. In the last stanza, Tennyson uses the echoes to make a point. Here the speaker addresses his love. What does the speaker say their "echoes" will do that the bugle's echoes do not do? What do you think he means by "echoes" in line 15?

RHYME

The music in this poem is achieved in two ways: the poet repeats words that help us hear the sound of the bugle and its dying echoes; and he uses end rhyme and internal rhyme.

Rhyme not only lends musical quality to a poem, but also gives it structure. End rhymes are often arranged in a certain pattern, called a *rhyme scheme*. Here is the rhyme scheme of the first stanza of "The Splendor Falls." Notice that a new letter of the alphabet is used to indicate each new end rhyme:

The splendor falls on castle walls	*a*
And snowy summits old in story;	*b*
The long light shakes across the lakes,	*c*
And the wild cataract leaps in glory.	*b*
Blow, bugle, blow, set the wild echoes flying,	*d*
Blow, bugle; answer, echoes, dying, dying, dying.	*d*

What is the rhyme scheme of the other stanzas? Is the pattern of end rhymes the same in each stanza?

This poem is famous for its internal rhymes. The first example is in line 1:

The splendor *falls* on castle *walls*

What lines in each stanza contain internal rhymes? Is there a pattern to these internal rhymes?

I Years Had Been from Home

Emily Dickinson

I years had been from home,
And now, before the door,
I dared not open, lest a face
I never saw before

Stare vacant into mine   5
And ask my business there..
My business—just a life I left,
Was such still dwelling there?

I fumbled at my nerve,
I scanned the windows o'er;   10
The silence like an ocean rolled,
And broke against my ear.

I laughed a wooden laugh
That I could fear a door,
Who danger and the dead had faced,   15
But never shook before.

I fitted to the latch
My hand, with trembling care,
Lest back the awful door should spring,
And leave me in the floor.   20

I moved my fingers off
As cautiously as glass,
And held my ears, and like a thief
Stole gasping from the house.

FOR STUDY AND DISCUSSION

1. This speaker stands before a door and is afraid to open it. The intensity of the speaker's feelings reveals that this poem is about more than just an effort to open a real door to some house. What does the speaker fear she'll find behind the door? What is the speaker looking for?

2. Why does the speaker steal away from the house "gasping," without opening the door?

3. The poet uses several vivid figures of speech to communicate feelings and sensations. Look at lines 11-12, 13, 21-22, and 23-24. How do the figures of speech in these lines suggest terror or rigidity?

4. This poem describes the feelings of someone who wants to know something, but is afraid of what she might find. To what situations in life could the experience in this poem apply?

APPROXIMATE RHYME

Approximate rhyme is rhyme in which the final vowel sounds are similar but not identical. The words *o'er/ear* in lines 10 and 12 are approximate rhymes. Modern poets make extensive use of approximate rhymes, but during her lifetime, Emily Dickinson was criticized for her imperfect rhymes. She maintained, however, that they were effective variations on standard rhymes. Find two more examples of approximate rhymes in the poem. What effect do these rhymes have on the way you read the poem?

Summer Remembered
Isabella Gardner

Sounds sum and summon the remembering of summers.
The humming of the sun
The mumbling in the honey-suckle vine
The whirring in the clovered grass
The pizzicato° plinkle of ice in an auburn   5
uncle's amber glass.
The whing of father's racquet and the whack
of brother's bat on cousin's ball
and calling voices call-
ing voices spilling voices . . .   10
The munching of saltwater at the splintered dock
The slap and slop of waves on little sloops
The quarreling of oarlocks hours across the bay
The canvas sails that bleat as they
are blown. The heaving buoy bell-   15
ing HERE I am
HERE you are HEAR HEAR

listen listen listen
The gramophone is wound
the music goes round and around   20
BYE BYE BLUES LINDY'S COMING
voices calling calling calling
"Children! Children! Time's Up
Time's Up"
Merrily sturdily wantonly the familial voices   25
cheerily chidingly call to the children TIME'S UP
and the mute children's unvoiced clamor sacks° the
     summer air
crying Mother Mother are you there?

5. **pizzicato:** the sound made by plucking a string on a violin or other stringed instrument.

27. **sacks:** ravages or destroys.

Detail from
Oyster Gatherers of Cancale
(1878). Oil painting by John
Singer Sargent (1856–1925).
The Corcoran Gallery of Art,
Washington, D.C.

FOR STUDY AND DISCUSSION

1. Line 1 of this poem introduces its subject, just as a topic sentence introduces the subject of a paragraph. What is the poem's subject? What is the function of lines 2–26?

2. Many of the sounds in this poem are described by means of metaphors. For example, in line 3 the sound of the wind in the honeysuckle is compared to the sound made by a person mumbling. What metaphors are used to describe sounds in lines 11, 13, and 14?

3. The images in the last two lines provide a sharp contrast to those in the rest of the poem. What images in lines 1–26 suggest a mood of peace, innocence, and fun? What images in lines 27–28 suggest anxiety and a threat of some kind?

ONOMATOPOEIA, ALLITERATION, AND ASSONANCE

The speaker of this poem recalls the "sounds" of summer, so it is appropriate that the poem uses a number of sound effects. To be appreciated fully, the poem should really be read aloud. The most obvious sound device used in the poem is *onomatopoeia*, the use of a word whose sound imitates or suggests its meaning. The word *humming* in line 2 is a good example of onomatopoeia. What onomatopoetic words are used to describe the sounds of bees in the grass, of the ice, of the games, and of the waves?

Another sound device used in the poem is *alliteration*, the repetition of consonant sounds, usually at the beginning of words. Alliteration seems to have a special appeal for the ear and is found in many familiar expressions: "a dime a dozen," "bigger and better," and "jump for joy." Alliteration is often used to reinforce meaning or to create a mood. In line 1, for example, the repeated "s" sounds suggest a quiet, hushed mood, as if someone is saying "Sh-h-h, listen." But often alliteration is simply used for pleasure. Where is alliteration used in lines 5, 7, 8, 12, 15, and 26? Is alliteration used to reinforce the meaning of any of these lines?

Related to alliteration is *assonance*—the repetition of vowel sounds in words. Lines 1–3 provide an example of assonance. How many times is the vowel sound "u" repeated in these lines? What vowel sound is repeated in line 5?

FOR COMPOSITION

Creating Sound Effects
Write a brief poem of your own in which you describe the sounds you associate with a particular season of the year, or with a particular place. Wherever possible, use onomatopoeia to echo these sounds. (Some onomatopoetic words that you might use are hiss, tap, hush, brush, patter, drip, buzz, tweet, sizzle, growl, grumble, roar, whisper, moan, bang.)

Splinter

Carl Sandburg

The voice of the last cricket
across the first frost
is one kind of goodbye.
It is so thin a splinter of singing.

FOR STUDY AND DISCUSSION

1. What season of the year is described in the poem?

2. Why is the cricket's song only *one* kind of goodbye?

3. What details suggest a sense of loss and sadness?

4. How would you explain the metaphor in the last line?

5. Sometimes a short "i" sound is used to suggest smallness or fragility, as in the words *inch, imp, flimsy,* and *thin.* Where does Sandburg use assonance and repeat the short "i" sound in this poem? Why is the repetition of this sound appropriate?

Fifteen   *William Stafford*

South of the Bridge on Seventeenth
I found back of the willows one summer
day a motorcycle with engine running
as it lay on its side, ticking over
slowly in the high grass. I was fifteen.   5

I admired all that pulsing gleam, the
shiny flanks, the demure headlights
fringed where it lay; I led it gently
to the road and stood with that
companion, ready and friendly. I was fifteen.   10

We could find the end of a road, meet
the sky on out Seventeenth. I thought about
hills, and patting the handle got back a
confident opinion. On the bridge we indulged
a forward feeling, a tremble. I was fifteen.   15

Thinking, back farther in the grass I found
the owner, just coming to, where he had flipped
over the rail. He had blood on his hand, was pale —
I helped him walk to his machine. He ran his hand
over it, called me good man, roared away.   20

I stood there, fifteen.

FOR STUDY AND DISCUSSION

1. What details in the second and third stanzas personify the motorcycle—that is, describe it as if it were a person? What kind of person does the boy think the machine is?

2. The word *thinking* in the last stanza marks a turning point in the poem. What word in this stanza indicates that the boy no longer sees the motorcycle as a person, but sees it for what it is? What accounts for the change in his thinking?

3. In your opinion, what does this poem have to say about youthful fantasies and adult realities?

REFRAIN

One form of repetition often used by poets is the *refrain*—a line or group of lines repeated throughout a poem. What is the refrain in this poem? What does the poet want to emphasize with this refrain?

In line 20, the owner of the motorcycle calls the boy a "good man." How does the final refrain show that the poet sees irony in this remark—that is, that he wants us to realize that the opposite is actually true?

FOR COMPOSITION

Using a Refrain

Write a brief poem of your own in which you use a refrain for emphasis and for setting a mood. You might imitate Stafford's poem and narrate an incident from your life. Your refrain might then begin with the words "I was____" and give the age at which the incident took place. Do not attempt to use rhyme and rhythm; try to imitate the conversational style of Stafford's poem.

ABOUT THE AUTHORS

Alfred, Lord Tennyson (1809–1892) was England's chief poetic spokesman during the age of Queen Victoria. Tennyson attended Cambridge University, but he was not an exceptional student and never received a degree. He read widely, though, and devoted his life to poetry. Tennyson is famous for such long poems as *Idylls of the King*, *In Memoriam*, and "The Lady of Shalott." He is also known for numerous short lyrics, many of which are found in a long collection called *The Princess*. Tennyson was England's poet laureate for over forty years.

Isabella Gardner (1915–1981) was born in Newton, Massachusetts, and for a time was a professional actress. From 1952 to 1956 she was an editor, with the poet Karl Shapiro, of the influential literary magazine *Poetry*. She gave poetry readings in many parts of the world. Her books include *Birthday from the Ocean* (1955) and *The Looking Glass* (1961).

Carl Sandburg (1878–1967) defined poetry as "the opening and closing of a door, leaving those who look through to guess what is seen during a moment." In 1914 Sandburg began to make a name for himself with poems that were published in *Poetry* magazine, rough yet tender verse about Chicago and its working people. His first book, *Chicago Poems* (1916), earned him praise for being one of the most energetic and original poets of the time. Sandburg is also the author of a celebrated biography of Abraham Lincoln.

Rhythm and Meter

Closely associated with the "music" of poetry is rhythm. The term *rhythm* refers to any regularly recurrent flow of motion or sound. In music, we recognize rhythm as the regular "beat" of a song. If we look closely, we can also observe a regular pattern in the way we breathe, or walk, or swim, or plow our fields. There is also rhythm in the way we talk.

In speech, rhythm is the natural rise and fall of language — the alternation between the stressed and unstressed syllables of words. Poets plot these alternations consciously, using rhythm, as they do musical devices, to enhance the meaning of what they write. When a line of poetry has a regularized rhythmic pattern, we say it has a *meter*. Poetry in meter is poetry in which we can detect a more or less regular "beat."

Poets writing in English have long recognized that writing with a "beat" makes an emotional impact on readers and listeners. In the poems to come, you will explore one of the most popular metrical forms in English — *iambic pentameter*. In the past century, many poets have experimented with an important departure from meter — *free verse*. This poetry, an example of which you will also read, is not controlled by any regular metrical pattern. Nevertheless, it uses strong rhythms, much as we use them in our natural speech.

Like musical devices, rhythm is best appreciated when you hear a poem read aloud. Try reading the following poems aloud as you study them, and discover for yourself the pleasure of rhythm in language.

Sea Fever   *John Masefield*

I must go down to the seas again, to the lonely sea and the
    sky,
And all I ask is a tall ship and a star to steer her by;
And the wheel's kick and the wind's song and the white
    sail's shaking,
And a gray mist on the sea's face and a gray dawn break-
    ing.

I must go down to the seas again, for the call of the run-
    ning tide   5
Is a wild call and a clear call that may not be denied;
And all I ask is a windy day with the white clouds flying,
And the flung spray and the brown spume,° and the sea   8. **spume** (spyo͞om): foam.
    gulls crying.

I must go down to the seas again, to the vagrant gypsy
    life,
To the gull's way and the whale's way where the wind's
    like a whetted knife;   10
And all I ask is a merry yarn from a laughing fellow-rover,
And quiet sleep and a sweet dream when the long trick's°   12. **trick:** sailor's turn of duty.
    over.

On a Lee Shore (1900). Oil painting by Winslow Homer (1836–1910).
Museum of Art, Rhode Island School of Design.

FOR STUDY AND DISCUSSION

1. We use the term *spring fever* to refer to a feeling of laziness and dreaminess. How would you define what Masefield means by "sea fever"?

2. What specific images help you see, hear, and feel what life on the sea is like?

3. How does Masefield use repetition to suggest the urgency of the sea's call and of the speaker's needs?

4. Masefield has used words that suggest certain sounds. What repeated consonant sound in lines 3, 7, and 10 might suggest the sound of wind?

5. Details in the last stanza suggest that Masefield is talking not only about life at sea, but about something broader as well. Suppose he has used the words "long trick" to mean life itself. What images in the last line could refer to death and to life after death? What sort of life does the speaker look for after his exciting "sea life" is over?

RHYTHM AND METER

If you read Masefield's poem aloud, you will notice its steady beat. The poem has a lilt and a kick to it, like the roll and toss of waves at sea. We call this the poem's *rhythm*. When rhythm follows a certain pattern, we call it *meter*. Meter is a regularized pattern of stressed and unstressed syllables. Poets vary the meter of a poem from time to time, usually for emphasis. This is how the metrical pattern of "Sea Fever" works out. The stressed syllables are marked (´) and the unstressed syllables (˘).

> Ĭ must́ gŏ dówn tŏ thĕ seás agái̇n, tŏ thĕ
> lónely̆ séa ănd thĕ sky̆,
> Ănd all Ĭ aśk iŝ ă táll shi̇p ănd ă star̆ tŏ steér
> hĕr by̆;
> Ănd thĕ wheél's ki̇ck ănd thĕ wind́'s sonğ
> ănd thĕ white sai̇l's shákin̆g,
> Ănd ă gráy mi̇st ŏn thĕ sea's face ănd ă gráy
> dăwn breákin̆g.

Masefield groups the stressed syllables together in line 3. Does he do this in any other lines?

Notice that there are seven heavily accented syllables in each line of the first stanza of the poem. Is this pattern followed throughout the other stanzas as well?

Birches   *Robert Frost*

When I see birches bend to left and right
Across the lines of straighter darker trees,
I like to think some boy's been swinging them.
But swinging doesn't bend them down to stay
As ice storms do. Often you must have seen them   5
Loaded with ice a sunny winter morning
After a rain. They click upon themselves
As the breeze rises, and turn many-colored
As the stir cracks and crazes° their enamel.
Soon the sun's warmth makes them shed crystal shells   10
Shattering and avalanching on the snow crust—
Such heaps of broken glass to sweep away
You'd think the inner dome of heaven had fallen.
They are dragged to the withered bracken° by the load,
And they seem not to break; though once they are
      bowed   15
So low for long, they never right themselves:

9. **crazes:** cracks into networks of tiny lines.

14. **bracken:** large coarse ferns.

You may see their trunks arching in the woods
Years afterwards, trailing their leaves on the ground
Like girls on hands and knees that throw their hair
Before them over their heads to dry in the sun.   20
But I was going to say when Truth broke in
With all her matter of fact about the ice storm,
I should prefer to have some boy bend them
As he went out and in to fetch the cows —
Some boy too far from town to learn baseball,   25
Whose only play was what he found himself,
Summer or winter, and could play alone.
One by one he subdued his father's trees
By riding them down over and over again
Until he took the stiffness out of them,   30
And not one but hung limp, not one was left
For him to conquer. He learned all there was
To learn about not launching out too soon
And so not carrying the tree away
Clear to the ground. He always kept his poise   35
To the top branches, climbing carefully
With the same pains you use to fill a cup
Up to the brim, and even above the brim.
Then he flung outward, feet first, with a swish,
Kicking his way down through the air to the ground.   40
So was I once myself a swinger of birches.
And so I dream of going back to be.
It's when I'm weary of considerations,
And life is too much like a pathless wood
Where your face burns and tickles with the cobwebs   45
Broken across it, and one eye is weeping
From a twig's having lashed across it open.
I'd like to get away from earth awhile
And then come back to it and begin over.
May no fate willfully misunderstand me   50
And half grant what I wish and snatch me away
Not to return. Earth's the right place for love:
I don't know where it's likely to go better.
I'd like to go by climbing a birch tree,
And climb black branches up a snow-white trunk   55
Toward heaven, till the tree could bear no more,
But dipped its top and set me down again.
That would be good both going and coming back.
One could do worse than be a swinger of birches.

Here, each iamb is marked off by the double lines. Each line has five unstressed syllables alternating with five stressed syllables.

"What we have in English is mostly iambic," Frost once said, and others have agreed that iambic rhythm comes closest to the ordinary rhythm of spoken English. "Birches" provides a good example of Frost's use of blank verse and of his occasional variations on that meter. This is how the meter of the first two lines of "Birches" works out:

Whĕn Í sĕe bírchĕs bénd tŏ léft ănd ríght
Ăcróss thĕ línes ŏf straíghtĕr dárkĕr treés

Continue marking the stressed and unstressed syllables in the first nine lines. Where does Frost depart from strict iambic pentameter? Does he ever depart from having five stressed syllables per line? How does the variation make the lines sound more natural?

FOR STUDY AND DISCUSSION

1. This poem can be divided into three nearly equal parts. In lines 1–20 the speaker describes the birches and tells how ice storms must have bent them. He calls this the Truth. What images and figures of speech does he use to help you experience this scene?

2. In lines 21–40, what does the speaker say he likes to imagine has bent the birches?

3. In lines 41–59, the speaker says he dreams of going back one day to be "a swinger of birches" again. Look at the way he describes the boy's climb up a birch in lines 28–38. How could climbing a birch, swinging, and coming down again symbolize the ways young people learn about life?

4. What simile in lines 44–47 describes the times when the speaker would "like to get away from earth awhile," then "come back to it and begin over"? Where does the speaker show that he does not want us to misunderstand what he means by getting away from earth? What do you think he does mean by the word *earth* here?

5. The speaker says he'd like to climb *"toward* heaven, till the tree could bear no more." What do you think he means by the word *heaven*? What kind of experience do you think he is talking about in lines 54–59?

BLANK VERSE

Blank verse is unrhymed iambic pentameter, which means that each line has five iambs. An *iamb* is an unaccented syllable followed by an accented syllable. *Blank* verse is so called because the ends of the lines are "blank" of rhyme. Some of the greatest English poetry is written in blank verse, including much of the poetry in Shakespeare's plays, as in these lines from *Julius Caesar:*

FOR COMPOSITION

Analyzing a Poem

Robert Frost first makes an observation, then tells about an incident, and finally applies the incident to some universal truth about life. Write a paragraph in which you explain clearly what the observation is, what the incident is, and what truth about life concludes the poem. Frost once said that a poem "begins in delight and ends in wisdom." In a second paragraph, discuss whether this poem begins in "delight" and ends in "wisdom."

Cavalry Crossing a Ford *Walt Whitman*

A line in long array where they wind betwixt green
  islands,
They take a serpentine course, their arms flash in the sun
    —hark to the musical clank,
Behold the silvery river, in it the splashing horses loiter-
  ing stop to drink,
Behold the brown-faced men, each group, each person a
  picture, the negligent rest on the saddles,
Some emerge on the opposite bank, others are just enter-
  ing the ford—while,
Scarlet and blue and snowy white,
The guidon° flags flutter gaily in the wind.

The Sixth Pennsylvania Cavalry.
Winslow Homer (1836–1910).
Gift of Charles Savage Homer,
1912–12–137.
Courtesy of the Cooper
Hewitt Museum, The
Smithsonian Institution's
National Museum of Design.

7. **guidon** (gī′dŏn′): small flag.

FOR STUDY AND DISCUSSION

1. What images does the poet use to help you see and hear the cavalry as it crosses a ford in the river? How many colors are used in this poem?
2. How are the images in the poem arranged to help you see the far-off line of cavalry move nearer and nearer?
3. Though Whitman describes a military scene, the effect is peaceful. What images help create a sense of peacefulness?

FREE VERSE

Walt Whitman was the first American poet to break free from the notion that iambic pentameter was the proper and greatest meter for verse written in English. In doing this, Whitman declared a second American "independence" from England—this time, a literary one.

The form of verse that Whitman used is called *free verse*. Free verse is so called because it is not controlled by any definite metrical pattern, nor by any definite pattern of rhyme, though it makes use of various rhythms and it often uses rhymes. Many of the poems in this book, in addition to Whitman's, are written in free verse. For other examples, look at Muriel Rukeyser's "Boy with His Hair Cut Short" (page 304) and Isabella Gardner's "Summer Remembered" (page 354). Notice how the loosely organized rhythms of these poems contrast with the meters and rhymes of A. E. Housman's "To an Athlete Dying Young" (page 339) and Alfred, Lord Tennyson's "The Splendor Falls" (page 349).

Free verse looks easy to write, but it isn't. Read Whitman's poem aloud and note how the poet has used many strong beats in each line. Notice also that the poem gains force because Whitman has ended many of its lines with strongly accented syllables.

Whitman also deliberately varies the length of his lines, which is a characteristic of free verse. Why are the long lines appropriate to describe the "serpentine" course of the army?

Where does Whitman repeat words and sentence patterns to create rhythm? What consonant sounds are alliterated in the first line to slow down the line and to suggest the length of the cavalry line? What two consonant sounds are alliterated in the last line, perhaps to suggest movement?

FOR COMPOSITION

Describing an Approaching Object

Imitate Whitman's pattern in this poem and write a paragraph (or a poem in free verse) describing something that at first is far away, and then moves closer and closer to where you are standing. Describe what you see and hear at different stages of the approach. Possibilities are an oncoming train; the ground as seen from a plane about to land; a dog running toward you.

ABOUT THE AUTHORS

John Masefield (1878–1967) was poet laureate of England for thirty-seven years. Orphaned at an early age, Masefield went off to sea at fifteen as an apprentice on a sailing ship. He jumped ship in New York City, and worked for three years in America before returning to England. He became a journalist, and eventually began writing poetry. His first collection of poems, *Salt-Water Ballads* (1902), launched his career as a poet. Another of his popular lyrics is "Cargoes."

Walt Whitman (1819–1892) was born on Long Island, New York, and worked for years as a printer, reporter, and newspaper editor. Not until he was thirty-six did he publish his revolutionary and controversial *Leaves of Grass*, the collection of poems he revised and added to for the rest of his life. During the American Civil War, Whitman served as a volunteer nurse. Some of his most famous poems deal with his wartime experiences.

Narrative Poetry

A *narrative poem* tells a story. Early storytellers, who entertained people in a time when hardly anyone could read or write, found that regular meter and rhyme helped them to remember the story and to hold their listeners' attention. Recitations of stories in verse took the place now held by books, radio, and television, and were a principal form of entertainment.

One kind of narrative poem is the *epic*—a long poem celebrating the deeds of a society's hero. Most epics are lofty poems, concerned with heroes and heroines who are larger-than-life, and told in stately and dignified language. The most famous epics are the *Iliad* and *Odyssey* by the Greek poet Homer, the *Aeneid* by the Roman poet Virgil, and *The Divine Comedy* by the Italian poet Dante. The greatest epic in English is *Paradise Lost* by John Milton.

An entirely different kind of narrative poem is the *ballad*—a relatively short poem originally meant for singing. The oldest ballads, known as *folk* or *popular ballads,* arose among the common people and were passed on by word of mouth for generations. Most ballads are tragic in mood and are concerned largely with sensational stories of murder, love, treachery, and the supernatural.

Literary ballads, unlike folk ballads, are written by known writers. Literary ballads sometimes try to imitate the style of folk ballads, but in general they tend to be more elaborate, both in language and in form.

Page of a ballad called "The Nut Brown Maid," from Richard Arnold's *Chronicles* (around 1503).

This folk ballad comes from the Border country, the region between Scotland and England that was once wild and lawless. Like all true Border ballads, this one celebrates an outlaw. It is based on an actual incident that took place about 1530. The Armstrongs were a powerful clan who made so many armed raids against the English that the Scottish king was forced to take action. The ballad would originally have been sung in a Scottish dialect.

Johnny Armstrong

There dwelt a man in fair Westmorland,
   Johnny Armstrong men did him call,
He had neither lands nor rents coming in,
   Yet he kept eight score men in his hall.

He had horse and harness for them all,   5
   Goodly steeds were all milk-white;
O the golden bands about their necks,
   And their weapons, they were all alike.

News then was brought unto the king
   That there was such a one as he,   10
That lived like a bold outlaw,
   And robbed all the north country.

The king he wrote out a letter then,
   A letter which was large and long;
He signed it with his own hand,   15
   And he promised to do him no wrong.

When this letter came Johnny unto,
   His heart it was as blithe as birds on the tree.
"Never was I sent for before any king,
   My father, my grandfather, nor none but me.   20

"And if we go the king before,
   I would we went most orderly;
Every man of you shall have his scarlet cloak,
   Laced with silver laces three.

"Every one of you shall have his velvet coat,
   Laced with silver lace so white;
O the golden bands about your necks,
   Black hats, white feathers, all alike."   25

By the morrow morning at ten of the clock,
   Toward Edinborough gone was he,   30
And with him all his eight score men;
   Good Lord, it was a goodly sight for to see!

When Johnny came before the king,
   He fell down on his knee,
"O pardon, my sovereign liege,"° he said,   35   **35. liege** (lēj): lord.
   "O pardon my eight score men and me!"

"Thou shalt have no pardon, thou traitor strong,
   For thy eight score men nor thee;
For tomorrow morning by ten of the clock,
   Both thou and them shall hang on the gallows tree."   40

But Johnny looked over his left shoulder,
   Good Lord, what a grievous look looked he!
Saying, "Asking grace of a graceless face—
   Why there is none for you nor me."

But Johnny had a bright sword by his side,   45
   And it was made of the metal so free,°   **46. free:** here, pure.
That had not the king stepped his foot aside,
   He had smitten his head from his fair body.

Saying, "Fight on, my merry men all,
   And see that none of you be ta'en;   50
For rather than men shall say we were hanged,
   Let them report how we were slain."

Then, God wot,° fair Edinborough rose,   **53. wot:** knows.
   And so beset poor Johnny round,
That fourscore and ten of Johnny's best men   55
   Lay gasping all upon the ground.

Then like a mad man Johnny laid about,
   And like a mad man then fought he,
Until a false Scot came Johnny behind,
   And run him through the fair body.   60

Saying, "Fight on, my merry men all,
  And see that none of you be ta'en;
For I will stand by and bleed but awhile,
  And then I will come and fight again."

News then was brought to young Johnny Armstrong,   65
  As he stood by his nurse's knee,
Who vowed if e'er he lived for to be a man,
  On the treacherous Scots revenged he'd be.

FOR STUDY AND DISCUSSION

1. Although Johnny is an outlaw, the ballad singer shows him to be more honorable and more likable than the king. What promise does the king break? What details in this song glorify Johnny?

2. *Irony of situation* occurs when what happens is the opposite of what is expected. What ironic situation is the basis of the tragedy in this ballad?

3. Folk ballads generally take their subject matter from sensational happenings. The most popular subjects of ballads are disappointed love, jealousy, betrayal, revenge, and sudden death. Which of these do you find in "Johnny Armstrong"? Which specific subject is introduced in the last stanza?

FOR COMPOSITION

Analyzing a Ballad

Folk ballads often use certain *conventions*, or widely accepted techniques and ways of saying things. Here are some of these conventions:

1. Ballads usually dramatize their action quickly, omitting unnecessary scenes or details.

2. Ballads often heighten the drama by using dialogue.

3. Suspense is often created in ballads by giving out information a little at a time.

4. Folk ballads have their favorite colors: we often find milk-white steeds, lily-white skin, golden hair, or ruby lips. Often the colors suggest certain things. White and gold, for example, usually suggest purity and perfection, and red can suggest blood.

5. Folk ballads often use stock phrases. The singers, relying only on their memories, could resort to a whole repertoire of stock phrases.

6. In structure, ballads usually use what we call the *ballad stanza*, a four-line stanza with the second and fourth lines rhyming. Usually the first and third lines contain four heavily accented syllables, and the second and fourth lines contain three.

Write an essay in which you analyze "Johnny Armstrong," noting which of these conventions are followed in that ballad. Cite lines from the poem to illustrate your findings.

This poem is based on an older ballad called "True
Thomas," which tells of a knight who was lured away by the
Queen of Elfland and forced to serve her for seven years.
Keats's poem takes up the story after the knight has
reappeared in the world of mortals. The poem's title means
"the beautiful lady without pity." The story is told as a
dialogue between the returned knight and a passer-by.

La Belle Dame sans Merci   *John Keats*

"O, what can ail thee, knight-at-arms,
  Alone and palely loitering?
The sedge° has withered from the lake,   **3. sedge** (sĕj): marsh grass.
  And no birds sing.

"O, what can ail thee, knight-at-arms,   5
  So haggard and so woebegone?
The squirrel's granary is full,
  And the harvest's done.

"I see a lily on thy brow,
  With anguish moist and fever dew,   10
And on thy cheeks a fading rose
  Fast withereth too."

"I met a lady in the meads,°   **13. meads** (mēdz): meadows.
  Full beautiful—a faery's child,
Her hair was long, her foot was light,   15
  And her eyes were wild.

"I made a garland for her head,
  And bracelets too, and fragrant zone;°   **18. fragrant zone:** belt of flowers.
She looked at me as she did love,
  And made sweet moan.   20

"I set her on my pacing steed,
  And nothing else saw all day long,
For sidelong would she bend and sing
  A faery's song.

"She found me roots of relish sweet,   25
    And honey wild, and manna dew,°
And sure in language strange she said
    'I love thee true.'

"She took me to her elfin grot,°
    And there she wept and sighed full sore,   30
And there I shut her wild wild eyes
    With kisses four.

"And there she lulled me asleep,
    And there I dreamed—Ah! woe betide!
The latest dream I ever dreamed   35
    On the cold hill side.

"I saw pale kings and princes too,
    Pale warriors, death-pale were they all;
They cried, 'La Belle Dame sans Merci
    Hath thee in thrall!'°   40

"I saw their starved lips in the gloam,°
    With horrid warning gaped wide,
And I awoke, and found me here,
    On the cold hill's side.

"And this is why I sojourn here,   45
    Alone and palely loitering,
Though the sedge is withered from the lake,
    And no birds sing."

26. **manna dew:** moist (dewy) substance in the stems of plants.

29. **grot:** cave.

40. **in thrall** (thrôl): enslaved.

41. **gloam:** twilight.

Drawing by Brian Froud.
© 1978, Rufus Publications, Inc.

FOR STUDY AND DISCUSSION

1. This poem tells a story entirely through dialogue. What question does the passer-by ask the knight? What images help you visualize the knight's sickly appearance?

2. What images help you visualize the setting? How does the setting help create a mood of gloom and loss?

3. Beginning with line 13, the knight speaks. What images in lines 13–32 create an atmosphere of romance and enchantment? What images in lines 35–44 help you experience the horror of the knight's dream?

4. La Belle Dame is a supernatural figure with whom the knight, a mortal, has fallen hopelessly in love. Is La Belle Dame totally sinister? Explain. Do you know of other stories of mortals who suffer when they love unattainable supernatural figures or figures from another world?

God Creating the Animals (early fourteenth century).
English miniature, from *The Illuminated French Bible of Holkam Hall.*
Courtesy, The British Library.

The Creation

James Weldon Johnson

And God stepped out on space,
And he looked around and said:
I'm lonely—
I'll make me a world.

And far as the eye of God could see   5
Darkness covered everything,
Blacker than a hundred midnights
Down in a cypress swamp.

Then God smiled,
And the light broke,   10
And the darkness rolled up on one side,
And the light stood shining on the other,
And God said: That's good!

Then God reached out and took the light in his hands,
And God rolled the light around in his hands   15
Until he made the sun;
And he set that sun a-blazing in the heavens.
And the light that was left from making the sun
God gathered it up in a shining ball
And flung it against the darkness,   20
Spangling the night with the moon and stars.
Then down between
The darkness and the light
He hurled the world;
And God said: That's good!   25

Then God himself stepped down—
And the sun was on his right hand,
And the moon was on his left;
The stars were clustered about his head,
And the earth was under his feet.   30
And God walked, and where he trod
His footsteps hollowed the valleys out
And bulged the mountains up.

Then he stopped and looked and saw
That the earth was hot and barren.   35
So God stepped over to the edge of the world
And he spat out the seven seas—
He batted his eyes, and the lightnings flashed—
He clapped his hands, and the thunders rolled—
And the waters above the earth came down,   40
The cooling waters came down.

Then the green grass sprouted,
And the little red flowers blossomed,
The pine tree pointed his finger to the sky,
And the oak spread out his arms,   45
The lakes cuddled down in the hollows of the ground,
And the rivers ran down to the sea;
And God smiled again,
And the rainbow appeared,
And curled itself around his shoulder.   50

Then God raised his arm and he waved his hand
Over the sea and over the land,
And he said: Bring forth! Bring forth!
And quicker than God could drop his hand,
Fishes and fowls   55
And beasts and birds
Swam the rivers and the seas,
Roamed the forests and the woods,
And split the air with their wings.
And God said: That's good!   60

Then God walked around,
And God looked around
On all that he had made.
He looked at his sun,
And he looked at his moon,   65
And he looked at his little stars;
He looked on his world
With all its living things,
And God said: I'm lonely still.

Then God sat down—   70
On the side of a hill where he could think;
By a deep, wide river he sat down;

With his head in his hands,
God thought and thought,
Till he thought: I'll make me a man!   75

Up from the bed of the river
God scooped the clay;
And by the bank of the river
He kneeled him down;
And there the great God Almighty   80
Who lit the sun and fixed it in the sky,
Who flung the stars to the most far corner of the night,
Who rounded the earth in the middle of his hand;
This Great God,
Like a mammy bending over her baby,   85
Kneeled down in the dust
Toiling over a lump of clay
Till he shaped it in his own image;

Then into it he blew the breath of life,
And man became a living soul.   90
Amen.   Amen.

FOR STUDY AND DISCUSSION

1. This poem retells the Biblical account of Creation given in Genesis 1 and 2. What vivid images and figures of speech help you visualize the Creation, particularly the creation of light, the sun, the moon and the stars, the world, and human beings?

2. How does the poet emphasize that God's creation is "good"?

3. According to the poem, why does God create "man," or the human race? The poet says that God created man "in his own image." What specific details reveal that this poet has given the Creator very human characteristics?

FOR ORAL READING

Prepare this poem for an oral reading. Note that the poem is written in free verse. It does not use rhyme but it uses strong rhythms, which are often created by repetition. Which words, phrases, and sentence structures are repeated over and over again as the poet tells the account of Creation? This poem evokes many feelings, which you should note. For example, where would you use your voice to convey feelings of power, action, and strength? Where would you change your tone to suggest tenderness, love, and awe?

ABOUT THE AUTHORS

John Keats (1795–1821), who saw his mother and brother die of tuberculosis, knew when he was only twenty-four years old that he was also dying of the disease. Keats's anguish over his illness was made more acute by the fact that he had fallen deeply in love with a young woman named Fanny Brawne, whom he knew he would never live to marry. Keats, who had studied medicine, also knew that he would never live to write the poetry he dreamed of writing. At the age of twenty-five, Keats died in Rome, where he had gone for the warmer climate. Keats's own sad epitaph was "Here lies one whose name is writ on water." His prediction proved untrue. In his few years, Keats produced some of the finest poems ever written in the English language.

James Weldon Johnson (1871–1938), American poet and essayist, received his B.A. and M.A. from Atlanta University and studied for three years at Columbia University. Johnson had an exceptionally versatile career, being at various times a high-school principal, an attorney, a songwriter, a United States consul in Venezuela and Nicaragua, secretary of the N.A.A.C.P., and a professor of literature. "The Creation" is one of seven old-time "sermons" that Johnson published in a book called *God's Trombones* (1927).

Dramatic Poetry

A *dramatic poem* presents one or more characters speaking, usually to each other, but sometimes to themselves or directly to the reader. A dramatic poem has many of the characteristics of a play: a definite setting, a dramatic situation, emotional conflict, vigorous speech, and natural language rhythms. The more dramatic a poem becomes, the more it reminds us of a play. In fact, the purest example of dramatic poetry is in verse plays, such as those written by William Shakespeare.

The *dramatic monologue* is a special kind of dramatic poem. In a dramatic monologue one character speaks to one or more other characters, whose replies are not given in the poem. The speaker, in a moment of great personal crisis, reveals his or her deepest thoughts and feelings. Reading a dramatic monologue is like listening to one end of a telephone conversation: from what is said at your end you must imagine what is said at the other.

The most famous dramatic monologue in English is "My Last Duchess," by Robert Browning. "The Laboratory," also by Browning, is another excellent example of this intensely dramatic kind of poem.

A scene from a film version of William Shakespeare's play *Hamlet*, with Laurence Olivier as Hamlet.

The phrase Ancien Régime *("the old order" in French) places this poem in France during the century or so before the French Revolution, when aristocrats involved in the whirl of court life had very little on their minds besides gossip, rivalries, and intrigue.*

The Laboratory   *Robert Browning*

Ancien Régime

Now that I, tying thy glass mask° tightly,
May gaze through these faint smokes curling whitely,
As thou pliest thy trade in this devil's smithy—
Which is the poison to poison her, prithee?°

He is with her; and they know that I know   5
Where they are, what they do. They believe my tears
    flow
While they laugh, laugh at me, at me fled to the drear
Empty church, to pray God in, for them!—I am here.

Grind away, moisten and mash up thy paste,
Pound at thy powder—I am not in haste!   10
Better sit thus, and observe thy strange things,
Than go where men wait me and dance at the King's.

That in the mortar°—you call it a gum?
Ah, the brave tree whence such gold oozings come!
And yonder soft phial,° the exquisite blue,   15
Sure to taste sweetly—is that poison too?

Had I but all of them, thee and thy treasures,
What a wild crowd of invisible pleasures!
To carry pure death in an earring, a casket,°
A signet,° a fan mount, a filigree basket.   20

1. **glass mask:** a face mask worn for protection against poisonous fumes.

4. **prithee:** I pray thee.

13. **mortar:** a hard bowl for grinding substances to a powder.

15. **phial** (fī′əl): small glass bottle.

19. **casket:** jewelry box.

20. **signet:** seal, probably on a ring.

Soon, at the King's, a mere lozenge° to give,
And Pauline° should have just thirty minutes to live!
But to light a pastille,° and Elise, with her head
And her breast and her arms and her hands, should drop
    dead!

Quick – is it finished? The color's too grim!   25
Why not soft like the phial's, enticing and dim?
Let it brighten her drink, let her turn it and stir,
And try it and taste, ere she fix and prefer!

What, a drop? She's not little, no minion° like me!
That's why she ensnared him; this never will free   30
The soul from those masculine eyes – say, "no!"
To that pulse's magnificent come and go.

For only last night, as they whispered, I brought
My own eyes to bear on her so, that I thought
Could I keep them one half minute fixed, she would
    fall,   35
Shriveled; she fell not; yet this does it all!

Not that I bid you spare her the pain!
Let death be felt and the proof remain;
Brand, burn up, bite into its grace –
He is sure to remember her dying face!   40

Is it done? Take my mask off! Nay, be not morose;
It kills her, and this prevents seeing it close:
The delicate droplet, my whole fortune's fee!
If it hurts her, beside, can it ever hurt me?

Now, take all my jewels, gorge gold to your fill,   45
You may kiss me, old man, on my mouth if you will!
But brush this dust off me, lest horror it brings
Ere I know it – next moment I dance at the King's!

21. **lozenge** (lŏz′ĭnj): piece of candy.
22. **Pauline:** The speaker would like to murder two other women as well: Pauline and Elise (line 23).
23. **pastille:** small candle used to perfume a room.

29. **minion:** here, a small person.

1. Which lines in this dramatic poem reveal that the speaker is a woman? To whom is she speaking?

2. What is the speaker planning to do with the poison?

3. How would you describe the passions that are driving this woman to commit murder? Which lines reveal that she is gloating over the murder, rather than feeling remorse about it?

4. What morbid fantasies about the poison does the speaker reveal in lines 17–24? What anxieties does she express in lines 25–32?

5. In the final stanza, the speaker pays for the poison. What has it cost her? What do you think her offer in line 46 reveals about her character?

6. There is great irony in this poem—a contrast between what seems to be true on the surface of things, and what actually *is* true. For example, this speaker probably is beautifully dressed, as she is on her way to a ball; she is certainly rich and bejeweled. How is her heart exactly the opposite of her beautiful appearance? At the end of the poem, the speaker asks that the dust of the chemist's shop be brushed from her clothing. What "horror" can she never "brush" from her heart?

FOR COMPOSITION

Analyzing a Poem

In the best dramatic monologues, we have a speaker, an audience, a setting, an interplay or a conflict between characters, action, and revelation of character. In a brief essay, analyze "The Laboratory" in terms of these characteristics. Use specific details from the poem to illustrate your analysis.

ABOUT THE AUTHOR

The name Robert Browning (1812–1889) is practically synonymous with the dramatic monologue, a form which he brought to a peak of perfection. Browning's poems shocked many readers with their objective treatment of the relationships between men and women, and some of Browning's contemporaries disapproved of his common, everyday language—he put into his verse such unpoetic things as vials of poison and aching corns. Browning eloped with Elizabeth Barrett, who at the time was a much more respected poet than he was. His "rescue" of the poet from her tyrannical father was one of the great love stories of the age.

Lyric Poetry

At times, poets wish to tell a story in poetic form, and they write what we call narrative poems. You have already seen how John Keats told a story in "La Belle Dame sans Merci," and James Weldon Johnson in "The Creation." At other times, a poet's principal aim is not to tell a story, but to express personal thoughts or emotions—about the serenity of an autumn day, for example, or the grace of a beautiful woman, or the remorse that follows the death of a friend. We call such poems *lyric* poems.

The word *lyric* is derived from the ancient Greek *lyrikos*, a short poem that was sung to the accompaniment of a lyre, a stringed instrument. Over the centuries, the lyric has lost its musical accompaniment, but it still is concerned with expressing personal thoughts and emotions. A lyric may reveal a moment of beauty or horror, joy or grief; it may present a rosy reminiscence of the past or a gloomy prediction for the future.

Over the centuries, certain forms of lyric poems have become particularly popular. Among these are the sonnet and the elegy. Most lyrics, however, do not fall easily into categories. The forms of the lyric are as varied as its infinite subjects and treatments.

A Red, Red Rose *Robert Burns*

O my Luve's like a red, red rose,
  That's newly sprung in June:
O my Luve's like the melodie
  That's sweetly played in tune.

As fair art thou, my bonnie lass,   5
  So deep in luve am I;
And I will luve thee still, my dear,
  Till a' the seas gang° dry.   8. **gang:** go.

Till a' the seas gang dry, my dear,
  And the rocks melt wi' the sun: 10
O I will luve thee still, my dear,
  While the sands o' life shall run.

And fare thee weel, my only Luve!
  And fare thee weel, a while!
And I will come again, my Luve,   15
  Though it ware ten thousand mile!

FOR STUDY AND DISCUSSION

1. Lines 1–2 of this love song contain one of the most famous similes in English poetry. Try to express in literal language the ideas and feelings suggested by this figure of speech. Would the effect have been different if Burns had written, "O my Luve's like a *violet*"?

2. What does the simile in lines 3–4 add to the characterization of the woman?

3. *Hyperbole* (hī-pûr'bə-lē) is a figure of speech that uses exaggeration for special effect. Where does the speaker use hyperboles to express the duration of his love? What images do these hyperboles create?

4. What details in the last stanza reveal that the speaker and his love are parting? Would you say that the mood of the poem is sad or happy? Explain.

LANGUAGE AND VOCABULARY

Recognizing Dialect and Archaic Words

If you have traveled from one part of the United States to another, you know that names for objects may differ regionally. A milkshake, for example, means one kind of drink in Cleveland and another in Boston. People talk about Southern accents and Western drawls when they want to point out that the same word may be pronounced differently in various parts of the country. *Dialect* is the term language experts use to describe a regional vocabulary and a regional way of speaking.

"A Red, Red Rose" is written in a Scottish dialect. Which words in the poem are different from words you would use?

Other words in the song are *archaic*—that is, they are not in common use today. Which words are these?

Try translating the poem into standard modern English. What is lost? How do the dialect and archaic usage affect the musical qualities of the poem?

Blue Girls   *John Crowe Ransom*

Twirling your blue skirts, traveling the sward°
Under the towers of your seminary,°
Go listen to your teachers old and contrary
Without believing a word.

Tie the white fillets° then about your hair   5
And think no more of what will come to pass
Than bluebirds that go walking on the grass
And chattering on the air.

Practice your beauty, blue girls, before it fail;
And I will cry with my loud lips and publish   10
Beauty which all our power shall never establish,
It is so frail.

For I could tell you a story which is true;
I know a lady with a terrible tongue,
Blear eyes fallen from blue,   15
All her perfections tarnished—yet it is not long
Since she was lovelier than any of you.

---

1. **sward:** grass.   2. **seminary:** private school.   5. **fillets:** ribbons.

The Orchard (1902). Platinum print photograph by Clarence H. White (1871–1925). The Museum of Modern Art, New York.

FOR STUDY AND DISCUSSION

1. How do you know that the speaker is older and wiser than the girls being addressed? What does the speaker notice about the girls?

2. To what are the girls compared in lines 6–8? What is the speaker emphasizing with this comparison?

3. Stanzas 1–3 consist of a series of directions, which the speaker gives to the girls. What does he advise them to do? According to stanzas 3 and 4, why is he telling them to do these things?

4. How does the image of "blear" blue eyes in the last stanza contrast with the images of blue in the rest of the poem?

5. How would you describe the tone in the first two stanzas? How does the tone change in the last two stanzas? What specific words and images establish the change in tone?

Shall I Compare Thee to a Summer's Day?
William Shakespeare

Shall I compare thee to a summer's day?
Thou art more lovely and more temperate.
Rough winds do shake the darling buds of May,
And summer's lease hath all too short a date.
Sometime too hot the eye of heaven shines,   5
And often is his gold complexion dimmed.
And every fair from fair sometime declines,
By chance or nature's changing course untrimmed.°   **8. untrimmed:** shorn (of its beauty).
But thy eternal summer shall not fade,
Nor lose possession of that fair thou owest,°   10 **10. owest:** ownest; possesses.
Nor shall Death brag thou wander'st in his shade
When in eternal lines to time thou grow'st.
  So long as men can breathe, or eyes can see,
  So long lives this, and this gives life to thee.

FOR STUDY AND DISCUSSION

1. In the first line of this poem, the speaker asks if he should compare a person to a summer's day. According to the next line, why is this person superior to summer? What details in lines 3–8 support the speaker's opinion?

2. In line 9, the speaker says this person's "eternal summer" shall not fade. What details in lines 12–14 reveal that the speaker hopes his poem will keep this person's "summer" alive? What line indicates that the speaker thinks his poem can conquer even death?

3. The concluding couplet sums up the poem. What is the main subject of the poem—love, nature, or the immortality of poetry? Explain.

4. In line 4, Shakespeare personifies summer by saying that it has a "lease," just as a tenant does. What metaphors create vivid pictures of the sun? How is death personified in line 11?

THE SONNET

The sonnet is a poetic form often used for serious topics like love, death, and religion. A sonnet has fourteen lines, and the lines are usually written in iambic pentameter (that is, each line has ten syllables with every second syllable accented).

There are two traditional rhyme schemes of a sonnet—the English (or Shakespearean) and the Italian (or Petrarchan). "Shall I Compare Thee . . ." is an English sonnet and so has three *quatrains* (groups of four lines) followed by a concluding *couplet* (two rhyming lines).

The rhyme scheme of a poem can be indicated by assigning a letter of the alphabet to each new rhyme sound. Thus, the rhyme scheme of the first quatrain of this sonnet is *abab*; the second, *cdcd*. What is the rhyme scheme of the whole poem?

The Sonnet-Ballad

Gwendolyn Brooks

Oh mother, mother, where is happiness?
They took my lover's tallness off to war,
Left me lamenting. Now I cannot guess
What I can use an empty heart-cup for.
He won't be coming back here any more.   5
Some day the war will end, but, oh, I knew
When he went walking grandly out that door
That my sweet love would have to be untrue.
Would have to be untrue. Would have to court
Coquettish death, whose impudent and strange   10
Possessive arms and beauty (of a sort)
Can make a hard man hesitate — and change.
And he will be the one to stammer, "Yes."
Oh mother, mother, where is happiness?

FOR STUDY AND DISCUSSION

1. What has happened to make the speaker ask, "where is happiness"? What does the speaker predict will happen to her lover?
2. What metaphor does the speaker use in line 4 to help you visualize her feeling of loss?
3. According to lines 9–12, how does the speaker know her lover will be "untrue"? In what unusual way does the speaker personify her rival, death? What do you think the speaker means by death's "beauty (of a sort)"?
4. How would you describe the emotion expressed in this lyric?

FOR COMPOSITION

Analyzing a Poem
Brooks calls her poem "The Sonnet-Ballad." In a brief essay, discuss how the poem meets the requirements of both a sonnet and a ballad. Is it a fourteen-line poem written in iambic pentameter? Does each group of rhyming lines develop the thought of the poem? How does the poem use repetition as a ballad does? Be specific, and use lines from the poem to illustrate your analysis.

Oh, Oh, You Will Be Sorry for That Word

Edna St. Vincent Millay

Oh, oh, you will be sorry for that word!
Give back my book and take my kiss instead.
Was it my enemy or my friend I heard,
"What a big book for such a little head!"
Come, I will show you now my newest hat,   5
And you may watch me purse my mouth and prink!
Oh, I shall love you still, and all of that.
I never again shall tell you what I think.
I shall be sweet and crafty, soft and sly;
You will not catch me reading any more: 10
I shall be called a wife to pattern by;
And some day when you knock and push the door,
Some sane day, not too bright and not too stormy,
I shall be gone, and you may whistle for me.

FOR STUDY AND DISCUSSION

1. How does the speaker let you know in lines 1–4 what has happened between herself and a man? What was "that word" that started the trouble?

2. This poem is heavy with irony—words and situations which the woman does not intend to be taken at face value. What is ironic about the kiss she offers the man in line 2? What is ironic about her statement in line 11?

3. How is the final statement an ironic reversal of what the man has been led to expect would happen? What does the word *whistle* imply about the way she feels the man thinks of her?

4. Edna St. Vincent Millay is noted for her mastery of the sonnet form. This is an English sonnet, consisting of three quatrains and a concluding couplet (see page 391). What is the rhyme scheme of the poem? How does each quatrain develop the dramatic situation?

Fear   *Hart Crane*

The host, he says that all is well
And the firewood glow is bright;
The food has a warm and tempting smell—
But on the window licks the night.

Pile on the logs. . . . Give me your hands,
Friends! No—it is not fright. . . .
But hold me . . . somewhere I heard demands. . . .
And on the window licks the night.

FOR STUDY AND DISCUSSION

1. What images in this poem suggest comfort, security, and companionship? What images suggest fear, loneliness, and foreboding?
2. To what is the poet comparing night when he says night "licks" the window? How would the emotional impact differ if the speaker had merely said "it is growing dark"?
3. When the speaker says he heard "de- mands," we begin to guess that this situation might symbolize something broader than it- self. What could the bright, warm, well- provisioned room symbolize? What could the night symbolize?
4. Like the poems by Brooks (page 392) and Millay (page 393), this is a dramatic poem. What action does the poet help you visualize in the second stanza?

Little Elegy   *X. J. Kennedy*

for a child who skipped rope

Here lies resting, out of breath,
Out of turns, Elizabeth
Whose quicksilver toes not quite
Cleared the whirring edge of night.

Earth whose circles round us skim
Till they catch the lightest limb,
Shelter now Elizabeth
And for her sake trip up Death.

FOR STUDY AND DISCUSSION

1. An *elegy* is a poem of mourning for a person who has died. What reasons would the poet have for calling this a "little" elegy?

2. Remember that Elizabeth skipped rope. What phrases in the poem are associated with skipping rope? What does the poet suggest about the timing of Elizabeth's death with the phrase "out of turns" in line 2?

3. Where does the poet use *night* as a metaphor for death?

4. The second verse is a prayer. What two things does the speaker ask Earth to do? What might the poet mean by the "circles" of Earth in line 5?

The Solitary Reaper

William Wordsworth

Behold her, single in the field,
Yon solitary Highland lass!
Reaping and singing by herself;
Stop here, or gently pass!
Alone she cuts and binds the grain,   5
And sings a melancholy strain;
O listen! for the vale profound
Is overflowing with the sound.

No nightingale did ever chaunt
More welcome notes to weary bands   10
Of travelers in some shady haunt,
Among Arabian sands:
A voice so thrilling ne'er was heard
In springtime from the cuckoo-bird,
Breaking the silence of the seas   15
Among the farthest Hebrides.°

Will no one tell me what she sings?—
Perhaps the plaintive numbers° flow
For old, unhappy, far-off things,
And battles long ago: 20
Or is it some more humble lay,°
Familiar matter of today?
Some natural sorrow, loss, or pain,
That has been, and may be again?

Whate'er the theme, the maiden sang   25
As if her song could have no ending;
I saw her singing at her work,
And o'er the sickle bending;—
I listened, motionless and still;
And, as I mounted up the hill,   30
The music in my heart I bore,
Long after it was heard no more.

16. **Hebrides:** islands off the north-west tip of Scotland.

18. **numbers:** measures (of the song).

21. **lay:** song.

FOR STUDY AND DISCUSSION

1. What images in the first stanza help you hear and see what the speaker is observing?
2. How does the second stanza show that the speaker's imagination has extended far beyond this particular Highland scene?
3. Though the speaker cannot understand the words to the song (the girl is singing in Erse, or Scots Gaelic), he knows that the music is melancholy. What does he imagine the song might be about? Why might he feel that a melancholy song is beautiful?
4. Why do you think the girl's song has such a strong effect on the speaker?

FOR COMPOSITION

Analyzing a Poem
This poem is about a song, so it is appropriate that it contains beautiful verbal music of its own. In a paragraph, describe the rhyme scheme of this lyric. Does the poet use alliteration to stress certain sounds? Is there a regular meter to the poem, or is it written in free verse? In a final sentence or two, tell what emotion you think is dominant in this lyric.

ABOUT THE AUTHORS

Robert Burns (1759–1796), born in Scotland, spent much of his life as a farmer. At the age of twenty-six, in order to earn enough money to marry the woman he loved and leave the country, he published his first book of poetry, *Poems: Chiefly in Scottish Dialect.* The book was an immediate success, Burns married his love, and he decided to remain in Scotland. Burns's last years were marked by poverty, yet when he died at thirty-seven, he was hailed as the national poet of Scotland. Many of his lyrics have been set to music. "Auld Lang Syne" and "Flow Gently, Sweet Afton" are two examples.

John Crowe Ransom (1888–1974) was an eminent poet, a teacher of eminent poets, and a leading figure in American literary criticism. Born in Pulaski, Tennessee, he was educated at Vanderbilt University, and, as a Rhodes scholar, at Oxford University. Ransom was a principal member of the Southern Agrarians, a group who wanted to preserve certain values and traditions of the old South. In 1937 he founded the important literary magazine *The Kenyon Review.* Ransom's poetry explores with wit and irony the traditional themes of love, death, and change. In 1964 he won a National Book Award for his *Selected Poems.*

For over three hundred and fifty years, William Shakespeare (1564–1616) has been regarded as the greatest writer in the English language. He was born in Stratford-on-Avon, then a small English market town of less than two thousand people. After a grammar-school education and an early marriage to Anne Hathaway, Shakespeare went to London and became, by 1592, a renowned playwright. His tragedies include *Macbeth, Hamlet, Julius Caesar,* and *Othello;* his comedies include *The Taming of the Shrew, A Midsummer Night's Dream,* and *As You Like It.* In addition to his plays, Shakespeare also wrote a brilliant series of sonnets. Around 1610 he left London and spent the rest of his life in Stratford as a respected citizen and country gentleman.

Gwendolyn Brooks (1917–   ) was born in Topeka, Kansas, but has lived most of her life in Chicago. Many of her poems are set in the South Side of Chicago, in a black community named Bronzeville. Against the background of Bronzeville, Brooks works out her favorite themes: the testing of personal and social experiences and the discovery of the joys and trials of being human. Brooks's first collection of poems is called *A Street in Bronzeville* (1945); her second book, *Annie Allen,* won a Pulitzer Prize in 1950. Brooks has also published a novel, *Maud Martha,* about a young girl growing up in Chicago.

Hart Crane (1899–1932), who had a troubled and unhappy childhood, left his home in Ohio at sixteen to wander about the country and write poetry. He turned down a chance to go to college, worked at various jobs, and ended up in New York where he spent ten furious years on his best-known work, *The Bridge*, a long poem about America. Finally, worn down by work and the feeling that his best years were behind him, Crane threw himself off a ship that was bringing him back to New York from Mexico.

X. J. (Joseph) Kennedy (1929–   ), a native of New Jersey, studied at Seton Hall University, Columbia University, the University of Paris, and the University of Michigan, and has been a professor of English at several colleges. Kennedy's poetry has been praised for its satiric wit and its ability to challenge and entertain. Supposedly, the X in his name was put there to distinguish him from the "better-known" Kennedys.

William Wordsworth (1770–1850), one of the leaders of the Romantic movement in English poetry, wrote poetry that exalted imagination, intuition, and feeling. Wordsworth rejected the artificial, high-flown diction that many poets had used before him, and tried to write in the language actually used by men and women. Wordsworth felt that one should go to nature for the deepest truths. In one of his poems he wrote:

> One impulse from a vernal wood
> May teach you more of man,
> Of moral evil and of good
> Than all the sages can.

Some of Wordsworth's other famous poems are "Lucy Gray," "I Wandered Lonely as a Cloud," "The World Is Too Much with Us" and "Composed upon Westminster Bridge."

Themes in Poetry

Down through the ages, certain themes — or basic ideas — have appeared over and over again in literature. No one can be sure why these particular themes keep reappearing in poems and stories; perhaps they endure because they reflect deep and universal human concerns. Three of these recurring themes are the subjects of the poems that follow: memories of childhood, the faces of nature, and the power of love.

Poets see the same things we all see, but they see them differently. Perhaps these poems will help you recognize things you have always been looking at but have never really "seen."

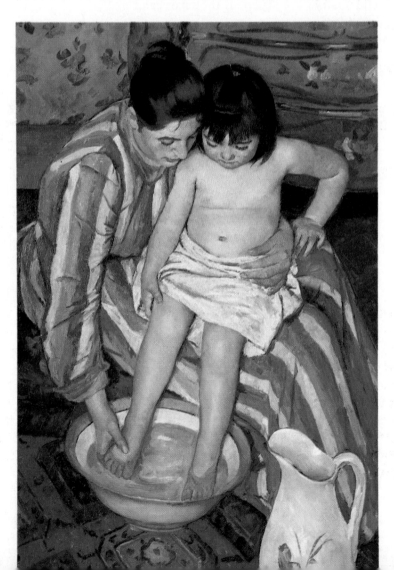

The Bath. Oil painting by Mary Cassatt (1845–1926). Collection of The Art Institute, Chicago.

Childhood Remembered

Running *Richard Wilbur*

1933
(North Caldwell, New Jersey)

What were we playing? Was it prisoner's base?
I ran with whacking keds
Down the cart-road past Rickard's place,
And where it dropped beside the tractor-sheds

Leapt out into the air above a blurred   5
Terrain, through jolted light,
Took two hard lopes, and at the third
Spanked off a hummock-side exactly right,

And made the turn, and with delighted strain
Sprinted across the flat   10
By the bull-pen, and up the lane.
Thinking of happiness, I think of that.

FOR STUDY AND DISCUSSION

1. This poet uses many images that help you share his experience. What words and phrases create images of motion? What physical setting do you see? What sounds do you hear?
2. Why do you think this particular run makes the speaker think of happiness? What reasons can you give for the fact that people often think of happiness in connection with childhood?

FOR COMPOSITION

Describing an Experience
Write a poem or a paragraph which begins, "Thinking of happiness, I think of . . ." Then describe a single experience that has made a strong impression on you. Follow Richard Wilbur's example and use specific images to help your reader share your experience.

*The title of this poem refers to creatures from Greek myth-
ology who were half human, half beast. The centaur had
the head, arms, and torso of a man and the body and legs
of a horse.*

The Centaur   *May Swenson*

The summer that I was ten—
Can it be there was only one
summer that I was ten? It must

have been a long one then—
each day I'd go out to choose   5
a fresh horse from my stable

which was a willow grove
down by the old canal.
I'd go on my two bare feet.

But when, with my brother's jack-knife,   10
I had cut me a long limber horse
with a good thick knob for a head,

and peeled him slick and clean
except a few leaves for the tail,
and cinched my brother's belt   15

around his head for a rein,
I'd straddle and canter him fast
up the grass bank to the path,

trot along in the lovely dust
that talcumed over his hoofs,   20
hiding my toes, and turning

his feet to swift half-moons.
The willow knob with the strap
jouncing between my thighs

was the pommel and yet the poll   25
of my nickering pony's head.
My head and my neck were mine,

yet they were shaped like a horse.
My hair flopped to the side
like the mane of a horse in the wind.   30

My forelock swung in my eyes,
my neck arched and I snorted.
I shied and skittered and reared,

stopped and raised my knees,
pawed at the ground and quivered.   35
My teeth bared as we wheeled

and swished through the dust again.
I was the horse and the rider,
and the leather I slapped to his rump

spanked my own behind.   40
Doubled, my two hoofs beat
a gallop along the bank,

the wind twanged in my mane,
my mouth squared to the bit.
And yet I sat on my steed   45

quiet, negligent riding,
my toes standing the stirrups,
my thighs hugging his ribs.

At a walk we drew up to the porch.
I tethered him to a paling.
Dismounting, I smoothed my skirt

and entered the dusky hall.
My feet on the clean linoleum
left ghostly toes in the hall.

Where have you been? said my mother.
Been riding, I said from the sink,
and filled me a glass of water.

What's that in your pocket? she said.
Just my knife. It weighted my pocket
and stretched my dress awry.

Go tie back your hair, said my mother,
and *Why is your mouth all green?*
*Rob Roy, he pulled some clover
as we crossed the field,* I told her.

50

55

60

FOR STUDY AND DISCUSSION

1. What specific childhood experience does this poet describe? How is the experience both real and imaginary?

2. What metamorphosis, or marvelous transformation, does this girl imagine she undergoes? What specific details in the poem describe the transformation?

3. The girl's mother asks her why her mouth is "all green." What does her answer reveal?

FOR COMPOSITION

Explaining a Title

This poem would have had a different effect if it had simply been about a child pretending that a willow branch was her horse. But the poem is entitled "The Centaur"; this title is important, since the word *centaur* is never mentioned in the poem itself. Look up *centaur* in a book about mythology or an encyclopedia. In one paragraph tell what you think the title is meant to suggest about the power of a child's imagination.

Eleven   *Archibald MacLeish*

And summer mornings the mute child, rebellious,
Stupid, hating the words, the meanings, hating
The Think now, Think, the O but Think! would leave
On tiptoe the three chairs on the verandah
And crossing tree by tree the empty lawn   5
Push back the shed door and upon the sill
Stand pressing out the sunlight from his eyes
And enter and with outstretched fingers feel
The grindstone and behind it the bare wall
And turn and in the corner on the cool   10
Hard earth sit listening. And one by one,
Out of the dazzled shadow in the room,
The shapes would gather, the brown plowshare, spades,
Mattocks, the polished helves of picks, a scythe
Hung from the rafters, shovels, slender tines   15
Glinting across the curve of sickles—shapes
Older than men were, the wise tools, the iron
Friendly with earth. And sit there, quiet, breathing
The harsh dry smell of withered bulbs, the faint
Odor of dung, the silence. And outside   20
Beyond the half-shut door the blind leaves
And the corn moving. And at noon would come,
Up from the garden, his hard crooked hands
Gentle with earth, his knees still earth-stained, smelling
Of sun, of summer, the old gardener, like   25
A priest, like an interpreter, and bend
Over his baskets.
            And they would not speak:
They would say nothing. And the child would sit there
Happy as though he had no name, as though
He had been no one: like a leaf, a stem,   30
Like a root growing—

Woodshed Interior. Watercolor
by Samuel Green (1909–   ).
Smith College Museum of Art,
Northampton, Massachusetts.

FOR STUDY AND DISCUSSION

1. In the first line the boy is described as
"mute." What clues let you know that he
remains silent by choice? Is his silence a part
of his rebellion? Explain.

2. The shed is a kind of sanctuary for the boy.
What sights and smells does he find there?
Why do these things make him happy?

3. The old gardener is like a priest or an interpreter. Why do you think the boy views
him in this way? Why is it appropriate that
the boy is compared to the other growing
things that the gardener cares for?

FOR COMPOSITION

Contrasting Poems

Each of these three poems has something different to say about childhood. In a short essay,
compare and contrast the images of childhood
developed by these poets. You may wish to
begin by briefly summarizing the actions described. Then describe the tone of each poem.
What does each poem say about the imagination of children? Conclude by explaining how
each poem dramatizes a different aspect of
childhood experience. Support your ideas
with quotations from the poems.

Nature the Gentlest Mother Is

Emily Dickinson

Nature the gentlest mother is,
Impatient of no child,
The feeblest or the waywardest.
Her admonition mild

In forest and the hill   5
By traveler be heard,
Restraining rampant squirrel
Or too impetuous bird.

How fair her conversation
A summer afternoon,   10
Her household her assembly,
And when the sun go down

Her voice among the aisles
Incite the timid prayer
Of the minutest cricket,   15
The most unworthy flower

When all the children sleep,
She turns as long away
As will suffice to light her lamps,
Then bending from the sky   20

With infinite affection
And infiniter care,
Her golden finger on her lip,
Wills silence everywhere.

FOR STUDY AND DISCUSSION

1. What details in this poem personify nature as a gentle and affectionate parent? What words and images show nature leading her children in evening prayers?

2. What image does the poet make you "see" in the last two stanzas and what feelings does it convey? What are the "lamps" referred to in line 19?

FOR COMPOSITION

Using Personification

Personification is a favorite device of poets, especially when the theme is nature. Many of us, at times, feel so close to nature we can almost think of it as a person. Emily Dickinson has portrayed nature as a gentle mother. In a paragraph or poem of your own, describe some aspect of nature as if it were a person. Begin your composition with the statement "Nature is a . . ." Try to describe, as Dickinson does, ways in which nature seems to imitate the specific actions of a person.

End of Summer

Stanley Kunitz

An agitation of the air,
A perturbation of the light
Admonished me the unloved year
Would turn on its hinge that night.

I stood in the disenchanted field   5
Amid the stubble and the stones,
Amazed, while a small worm lisped to me
The song of my marrow-bones.

Blue poured into summer blue,
A hawk broke from his cloudless tower,   10
The roof of the silo blazed, and I knew
That part of my life was over.

Already the iron door of the north
Clangs open: birds, leaves, snows
Order their populations forth,   15
And a cruel wind blows.

FOR STUDY AND DISCUSSION

1. Writers sometimes use the worm as a symbol of death or decay. How does Kunitz use the worm to indicate that the end of summer reminds him of his own mortality?

2. What do the images in the third stanza make you "see"? How does this last blaze of summer glory intensify the poet's feelings of loss?

3. Explain the metaphor developed in the first and last stanzas. What emotional effect is created by the image of an *iron* door clanging open?

4. Dickinson presents nature as a gentle mother. What contrasting image of nature is suggested in this poem?

FOR COMPOSITION

Analyzing a Poem

William Wordsworth once said that he wrote about the rustic life — a life close to nature — because "in that condition of life our elementary feelings coexist in a state of greater simplicity, and, consequently, may be more accurately contemplated, and more forcibly communicated." In a short essay, tell whether you think Kunitz's poem illustrates Wordsworth's statement. What "elementary" feelings does Kunitz express? What images from nature help him to express these feelings accurately and forcibly? Is Kunitz's poem a good illustration of Wordsworth's idea? Tell why or why not.

Once by the Pacific   *Robert Frost*

The shattered water made a misty din.
Great waves looked over others coming in,
And thought of doing something to the shore
That water never did to land before.
The clouds were low and hairy in the skies,   5
Like locks blown forward in the gleam of eyes.
You could not tell, and yet it looked as if
The shore was lucky in being backed by cliff,
The cliff in being backed by continent;
It looked as if a night of dark intent   10
Was coming, and not only a night, an age.
Someone had better be prepared for rage.
There would be more than ocean-water broken
Before God's last *Put out the Light* was spoken.

FOR STUDY AND DISCUSSION

1. How does the poet personify the clouds and waves? What details in the first six lines suggest violence and destruction?

2. From this specific natural scene, the poet goes on to talk about a much broader scene or situation. What does this setting make him think of? Whose "rage" is he talking about in line 12?

3. In Genesis, the Creator uses the words "Let there be light." How does Frost picture the end of the world in the last two lines?

FOR COMPOSITION

Comparing Poems

In a short essay, compare the three nature poems you have just read. In one paragraph, contrast the natural settings described in the poems, and discuss the tone of each poem. In your second paragraph, discuss what the poems have in common, if anything. Consider here whether the poems show any similarity in their use of imagery or figures of speech.

The Power of Love

A Birthday   *Christina Rossetti*

My heart is like a singing bird
  Whose nest is in a watered shoot;
My heart is like an apple tree
  Whose boughs are bent with thickset fruit;
My heart is like a rainbow shell   5
  That paddles in a halcyon sea;
My heart is gladder than all these
  Because my love is come to me.

Raise me a dais of silk and down;
  Hang it with vair and purple dyes;   10
Carve it in doves and pomegranates,
  And peacocks with a hundred eyes;
Work it in gold and silver grapes,
  In leaves and silver fleurs-de-lys;
Because the birthday of my life   15
  Is come, my love is come to me.

FOR STUDY AND DISCUSSION

1. In the first stanza, how are the images appropriate to describe the gladness of the speaker's heart? What words would you use to describe the way she is feeling?

2. In the second stanza, the speaker imagines that she will be elevated to a throne (*dais* is a platform, often for a throne). Look up the words in this stanza that are unfamiliar to you. What images here suggest a sense of royalty and of splendor?

3. This speaker is expressing all of these feelings because her love has come. What is suggested by the fact that she sees this event as "the birthday" of her life?

FOR COMPOSITION

Creating Similes

This poem is famous for the series of similes in the first stanza. Write a series of similes of your own, in which you describe some human feeling—love, contentment, joy, peace, anger, sadness, or some other feeling. Think of comparisons that create strong visual images, like these of Rossetti's. You might open your similes with the words "My feeling is like . . ."

Thy fingers make early flowers of

E. E. Cummings

Thy fingers make early flowers of
all things.
thy hair mostly the hours love:
a smoothness which
sings, saying   5
(though love be a day)
do not fear, we will go amaying.°

thy whitest feet crisply are straying.
Always
thy moist eyes are at kisses playing,   10
whose strangeness much
says; singing
(though love be a day)
for which girl art thou flowers bringing?

To be thy lips is a sweet thing   15
and small.
Death, Thee i call rich beyond wishing
if this thou catch,
else missing.
(though love be a day   20
and life be nothing, it shall not stop kissing).

---

7. **amaying:** gathering flowers and dancing, as if at a May Day celebration.

FOR STUDY AND DISCUSSION

1. What does the speaker mean when he says his love's fingers make "early," or new, flowers of all things? What kind of hair would you say has a "smoothness which sings"?
2. In the second verse, what playful question do the girl's eyes ask the speaker?
3. The refrain "though love be a day" is repeated in each stanza. What does this refrain make us remember? What is the poet's final response to this refrain?
4. What would you say is the poet's attitude toward love and its power?

Sonnet   *Countee Cullen*

Some for a little while do love, and some for long;
And some rare few forever and for aye;
Some for the measure of a poet's song,
And some the ribbon width of a summer's day.
Some on a golden crucifix do swear,   5
And some in blood do plight a fickle troth;
Some struck divinely mad may only stare,
And out of silence weave an iron oath.

So many ways love has none may appear
The bitter best, and none the sweetest worst;   10
Strange food the hungry have been known to bear,
And brackish° water slakes an utter thirst.   12. **brackish:** salty.
It is a rare and tantalizing fruit
Our hands reach for, but nothing absolute.

FOR STUDY AND DISCUSSION

1. What metaphors in lines 3 and 4 dramatize the poet's ideas about how long love lasts? What point about love is made in lines 5–8?
2. What analogies does the poet make in lines 11–12? What metaphor describes love in line 13? How does the final couplet sum up the idea of this poem?

FOR COMPOSITION

Discussing a Theme
Each of these three poems on love takes a different approach to the theme. In a short essay, discuss what you think each of the poems has to say about love. What is the tone of each poem? Do any of the poems use similar figures of speech or imagery? How does each poem give a different view of love's power? After you have discussed these questions, tell which poem you responded to most strongly and why.

ABOUT THE AUTHORS

Richard Wilbur (1921–   ), the son of a portrait painter, grew up in New Jersey. While serving in the army during World War II, Wilbur began writing poetry and published his first book, *The Beautiful Changes,* in 1947. Since 1957 Wilbur has been Professor of English at Wesleyan University in Middletown, Connecticut. *Things of This World* (1957), his third book of poetry, won three prizes in one year, including the Pulitzer Prize and the National Book Award.

Archibald MacLeish (1892–1982) wrote some deeply personal poems, and he also wrote poems expressing the dreams and aspirations of the nation. MacLeish was born in Illinois. He served as an ambulance driver and artillery captain in World War I, and was, at different times in his life, a lawyer, a Librarian of Congress, an Assistant Secretary of State, and an adviser to President Franklin D. Roosevelt. MacLeish won the Pulitzer Prize in 1933 for *Conquistador,* a long poem about Cortes' conquest of Mexico, and in 1953 for *Collected Poems: 1917–1952.* MacLeish was also a dramatist, and in 1959 he won his third Pulitzer Prize—for *J.B.,* his modernization of the Book of Job.

Stanley Kunitz (1905–   ), a native of Massachusetts, began publishing poetry as a young man, served in the army during World War II, and then became a teacher. His work had always been praised by fellow poets but was generally neglected by others until 1959. In that year, he won a Pulitzer Prize for his *Selected Poems: 1928–1958,* a book that had been turned down by five publishers. Even after his success, Kunitz remained modest, declining even to put himself in *Twentieth Century Authors,* a reference book he edited.

Christina Rossetti (1830–1894) was born in London, the daughter of an Italian political exile. Her brother was the equally famous poet and painter Dante Gabriel Rossetti. Many of Rossetti's finest poems reflect her feelings about love; she was deeply religious, however, and twice for religious reasons she broke off plans to marry. One of her famous love songs begins: "When I am dead, my dearest, / Sing no sad songs for me." Rossetti also wrote *Sing Song,* poems for children.

E. E. Cummings (1894–1962) once said that "poetry and every other art was and is and forever will be strictly and distinctly a question of individuality." Before the United States entered World War I, Cummings volunteered as an ambulance driver in the French army. A letter expressing disenchantment with the war landed him in a French detention camp, an experience he described in his first book, *The Enormous Room* (1922). Cummings is famous for his poetic experiments with punctuation, sentence structure, and the arrangement of words on the page.

Countee Cullen (1903–1946) was born in New York City, the son of a minister. He began writing poetry while in his teens and published his first book of poems, *Color,* when he was in college. In a brief writing career, Cullen published several volumes of verse, a translation of the classical Greek play *Medea,* and an original play written in collaboration with Arna Bontemps. His poems are largely traditional in form and concerned with universal themes—death, love, and human relationships. Along with Bontemps, Jean Toomer, and Langston Hughes, Cullen was a leader of the Harlem Renaissance of the 1920's.

Practice in Reading and Writing

Reading Poetry

Poetry is a compressed form of expression that asks for attention. You may find these suggestions useful in getting at the meaning of a poem. Apply them to the poem that follows.

1. What does the title reveal about the subject of the poem, or about its theme?

2. Pay attention to punctuation and read the poem in complete phrases or sentences, not in lines. Read the poem aloud.

3. If the meaning of a phrase or sentence is not clear, study its syntax (structure) and its punctuation. To be sure you understand the meaning of each difficult phrase or difficult sentence, try to rephrase it in your own words.

4. Make sure you know the meanings of all the words in the poem. Poets often make use of unusual word meanings. At times, they coin new words.

5. Identify the speaker of the poem.

6. Look for the figures of speech in the poem —particularly its metaphors. What do they reveal about the poet's feelings?

7. Does the poet repeat any words or phrases? What ideas are reinforced by the repetition?

Spellbound

The night is darkening round me,
The wild winds coldly blow;
But a tyrant spell has bound me
And I cannot, cannot go.

The giant trees are bending   5
Their bare boughs weighed with snow.
And the storm is fast descending,
And yet I cannot go.

Clouds beyond clouds above me,
Wastes beyond wastes below;   10
But nothing drear can move me;
I will not, cannot go.

Emily Brontë

Paraphrasing a Poem

Here is a poem about another kind of "spell." This is one of several poems that Maxine Kumin has written about a horse named Amanda, which she owned as a child. You should know that some people believe that pieces of hair or fingernails can ward off evil spells.

Amanda Is Shod

The way the cooked shoes sizzle
dropped in a pail of cold water
the way the coals in the portable forge
die out like hungry eyes
the way the nails go in aslant   5
each one the tip of a snake's tongue

and the look of the parings
after the farrier's knife
has sliced through.

I collect them   10
four marbled white C's
as refined as petrified wood
and dry them to circles of bone
and hang them away on my closet hook

lest anyone cast a spell on Amanda.   15

Maxine Kumin

One way to be sure you understand a difficult poem is to try to paraphrase it—that is, to restate it in your own words. Write a simple paraphrase of "Amanda Is Shod." The first two lines (which make up a phrase, not a full sentence) might be restated like this:

The way the horseshoes that are hot from the fire sizzle when they are dropped into the pail of cold water . . .

Writing About a Poem

Write a brief essay on "Amanda Is Shod," taking into consideration the suggestions on page 417. Tell what you see happening in the poem, specifically what is taking place in stanza 3. Conclude by giving your reaction to the poem.

For Further Reading

Bierhorst, John, editor, *In the Trail of the Wind: American Indian Poems and Ritual Orations* (Farrar, Straus and Giroux, 1971; paperback, Dell)

Translated from over forty languages, this collection includes battle songs, love lyrics, prayers, and dreams, from people as far-ranging as the Sioux, the Aztecs, and the ancient Maya.

Cole, William, editor, *The Birds and the Beasts Were There* (Collins, 1963); *A Book of Love Poems* (Viking, 1965); *Fireside Book of Humorous Poetry* (Simon and Schuster, 1959); *Pick Me Up: A Book of Short, Short Poems* (Macmillan, 1972).

Cole is an expert anthologist, as these sprightly collections prove. *Pick Me Up* is an excellent introduction to the pleasures of poetry. It includes groupings of poems under such headings as "The Wit of Poets," "The Poetry of Wit," "Flyers and Leapers," and "Ends."

Eliot, T. S., *Old Possum's Book of Practical Cats* (Harcourt Brace Jovanovich, 1968; paperback)

One of the most distinguished of contemporary poets, Eliot also had a good sense of humor and a fondness for cats. His comic feline portraits include "The Old Gumbie Cat," "Growltiger's Last Stand," "Gus the Theatre Cat," and "Shimbleshanks: the Railway Cat." Illustrated.

Frost, Robert, *Selected Poems* (Holt, Rinehart and Winston, 1963; paperback)

This collection of some of the Pulitzer Prize-winning poet's work is especially recommended for young adults.

Hayden, Robert, editor, *Kaleidoscope: Poems by American Negro Poets* (Harcourt Brace Jovanovich, 1967)

This collection gives an overview of the major black poets writing in America, from Phyllis Wheatley in the eighteenth century to Mari Evans and Gwendolyn Brooks in the twentieth.

Henderson, Harold, editor, *Introduction to Haiku* (Doubleday, 1958; paperback, Anchor)

Haiku is a very brief and very popular Japanese verse form. Most haiku create quick, unusual "pictures." This collection is illustrated.

Jones, Theodoric, *Great Story Poems* (paperback, Lion Press, 1972)

An illustrated collection of famous narrative poems, especially compiled for young adults.

Marquis, Don, *archy and mehitabel* (Doubleday; paperback, Anchor, 1973)

archy is a cockroach and mehitabel is a cat. archy is also a free-verse poet who records their songs and observations on the boss's typewriter at night. archy can type fairly well but he can't make capital letters. Illustrated.

McGinley, Phyllis, *Love Letters of Phyllis McGinley* (Viking, 1954; paperback)

This witty poet writes "love letters" to such unusual things as a factory, a playwright, a museum, and the city of New York.

Millay, Edna St. Vincent, *Collected Poems* (paperback, Harper & Row, 1975)

These lyrics were collected by the poet's daughter. The book is recommended for a young adult audience.

Untermeyer, Louis, editor, *Story Poems: An Anthology of Narrative Verse* (paperback, Washington Square Press); *Treasury of Great Poems*, two volumes (paperback, Simon and Schuster, 1964)

These last two books, in particular, would be good starters for a personal poetry library. The first volume begins with Geoffrey Chaucer's robust *Canterbury Tales* and ends with Robert Burns's lyrics. The second volume ranges from the Romantic poems of William Wordsworth to the contemporary poems of Dylan Thomas.

Tapestry by Edward Burne-Jones (1833-1898) and
William Morris (1834-1896). Detail
Birmingham Museums and Art Gallery.

> It befell in the days of the noble UTherpendragon, when he was King of England, that there was born to him a son who in time was King Arthur.°

So begins one version of the legend of King Arthur, a cycle of stories that has been shaped and passed down through over fourteen hundred years of English history. The Arthur legend tells of the adventures of an early king of Britain and the knights and ladies who made up his royal court at Camelot. It recalls a world of mounted warriors armed with lance, sword, and coat of mail. It tells of jousts, tournaments, and falconry, of wizards, enchantresses, and damsels in distress, of wars, quests, and the medieval code of chivalry. It tells of a great king who came to the throne from obscurity and of a noble idea that came to a tragic end. It is a legend that has fascinated readers throughout the world and inspired great writers to retell it.

THE LEGEND OF KING ARTHUR

"Did King Arthur actually live?" This question cannot be answered with a simple yes or no. It is unlikely that Arthur was ever a real king. Modern historians believe that he was a *dux bellorum* (war chief) of the Welsh. Arthur was trained in war by the Romans, and in 517 he led his cavalry to a great victory against Saxon invaders from Germany. It is thought that Arthur fought more battles against the Saxons but met with less success. His people were eventually driven back into Wales and Scotland. Medieval historians reported that Arthur was killed in the battle of Glastonbury in southwestern England and secretly buried there by his knights.

Stories of Arthur's exploits soon sprang up among his comrades in arms, and were passed from generation to generation by word of mouth. These early storytellers spoke a Celtic language, far different from the English language that was to develop centuries later. As the Celts told and retold the stories of Arthur, they began to shape a legend. Semiprofessional storytellers—singers, bards, or minstrels, as they were called—mingled their own imaginations with their memories to make the tale satisfy the hopes and dreams of their listeners. The Celts were a defeated people. Arthur had

---

° From Sidney Lanier's stories of King Arthur.

Ruins of Glastonbury Abbey.

Manuscript page from
Sir Gawain and the Green Knight
(fourteenth century).
Ms. Cotton Nero AX,
The British Library.

brought them momentary glory. He was not dead, they sang. He would return someday to drive out the Saxons. Hope was fading for the Celts, however, and Arthur's tale seemed destined to die with their dreams.

In 817, however, a monk named Nennius, who was educated in Latin, wrote a chronicle of the life of Arthur that was a mixture of history and legend. In this account Arthur was revealed as a hero who had almost singlehandedly turned back the invaders. Perhaps more than any other, this account put Arthur on his way to everlasting fame. During the next three hundred years, chiefly through the skill of the minstrels who entertained in the manor halls of the nobles, the legend began to take shape. The familiar characters appeared: Kay, Gawain, Bedivere, Gareth, and Gwynevere. Nennius' chronicle was retold in the everyday language of the people, and the Arthur stories gradually came to the attention of the whole of England.

The twelfth-century writer Geoffrey of Monmouth, who also wrote in Latin, became the first famous shaper of the Arthur legend. Geoffrey was writing a history of British kings. Geoffrey's history was actually not a history at all but an attempt to give England, now composed of many peoples—Normans,

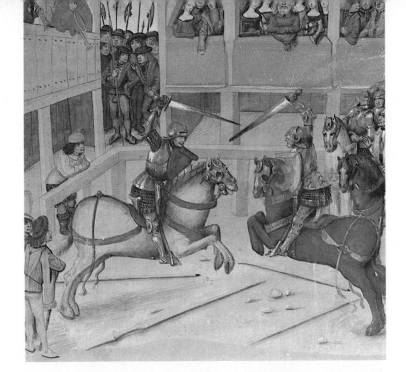

Joust before King Arthur.
Manuscript illumination.
Douce Ms. 383, f. 16, r., The
Bodleian Library, Oxford, England.

Saxons, Angles, Celts, and others—a beginning which would link it to ancient civilizations. Geoffrey made Arthur a descendant of Aeneas, the legendary founder of Rome. In this account Arthur began to lose some of the rough ways of the Celtic hero. Geoffrey wrote of him as a Norman king, modeled after Charlemagne, the great emperor of ninth-century Europe. Geoffrey was also the first to describe Arthur as a fifteen-year-old boy king and to tell about Arthur's magician-tutor, Merlyn. Geoffrey, too, told of Arthur's marriage to Gwynevere and of the betrayal of Arthur by the knight Modred.

Wace, a Norman who wrote in French, also retold the legend of Arthur, and he based his account on Geoffrey's. Wace added the famous Round Table, "ordained by Arthur that, when his fair fellowship sat to meat, their chairs should be alike, their service equal, and none before or after his fellow."

For the next two centuries, Arthur's story changed and spread. What had been a purely British legend found its way into France, Spain, Germany, and Italy. Courtly romances and knightly adventures added a new cast of characters, among them Launcelot, Tristram, Mark, Isolde, Galahad, Percivale, and many others.

A knight's tomb
in an English chuch.

Thomas Malory

The King Arthur legend belonged to England, however, and in 1470 one of the most important shapers of the legend, Sir Thomas Malory, a knight himself, made it forever English. Malory, writing in English, gathered together and retold many of the French romances dealing with Arthur and the knights. A printer, William Caxton, gave these stories an order and unified the whole in one work which he called *Morte d' Arthur* (*The Death of Arthur*).

By Malory's time, feudalism and knighthood were dying out. People were flocking to live in the cities, gunpowder was putting the knights out of work, and a wealthy merchant class was replacing the knights and nobles as the most influential group in England. Perhaps Malory was like the old warrior, trying to recapture the grandeur of the good old days. Or perhaps he was trying to give the institution of knighthood an order and virtue that it never had. Although the Church and the powerful kings and nobles had set down a code of conduct for knights, many disregarded it. Most knights were trained for fighting, and not much else. Unless they were kept busy, they could be a menace. Malory himself was a good example of a knight who took the law into his own hands. In fact, he wrote his stories about Arthur while serving time in prison.

Alfred, Lord Tennyson

Since Malory's time, scores of writers have used the Arthurian legends to please readers and to express their own views of what society should be like. The most prominent of these writers is Alfred, Lord Tennyson, the nineteenth-century English poet. Tennyson selected several popular Arthurian tales, changed them to suit his purpose, and retold them as poetry. He called this work the *Idylls of the King*. An idyll is characterized by its rural setting, and in Camelot, Arthur's fabled court and countryside, Tennyson found a peaceful background against which a high-minded Arthur and his knights played out a tragic story. Tennyson made his Arthur a great moral leader. Tennyson's Arthur conquers his enemies when he must, but his greatness is not in war but in moral superiority, specifically in the gathering of knights who serve him by bringing order and justice to the world.

T. H. White

In our own time, the English writer T. H. White found the Arthur legend a proper setting in which to search for new hope for a world wracked by war. White's own telling of the Arthur story, in four short novels, is humorous and human. Though he shows his appreciation for the past, White's viewpoint is modern. His portrayal of Arthur as a boy shows us a boy much like those we may know. With the help of Merlyn, who introduces him to wisdom, White's Arthur grows up to be a wise, judgelike king who gropes for a solution to his world's problems. His great idea is to use the skill and valor of his knights for good—for the high ideal of a peaceful, ordered, and just world. White's four novels about King Arthur are combined in one volume with the title *The Once and Future King*.

Why have writers continued to tell the story of King Arthur? Is it the romance and adventure, the classic struggle between good and evil, or the appeal of the story of the good king who will return to save his people? Perhaps we go to the story of King Arthur, as we do to all great legends, not to find historical facts, but to find what kind of dreams people dream; not, as the critic Northrop Frye has said, "to find out what a king *is*, or even what a king *could be*, but what we *would like* a king to be." In this sense, the King Arthur legend belongs to us all.

Drawing by
Aubrey Beardsley (1872–1898)
for the 1909 edition of
Malory's *Morte d' Arthur*.

According to T. H. White's lively retelling of the legend, Arthur is an orphan of unknown parentage, who lives with his guardian, Sir Ector. Sir Ector has a son named Kay, a disagreeable boy, who gives Arthur the nickname "Wart" because it more or less rhymes with "Art." Kay soon becomes a knight, but Arthur must be Kay's servant — his squire.

Although Arthur seems very ordinary, the magician Merlyn knows who he really is: the trueborn king of England. Merlyn thus takes the boy's education in hand and prepares him for the future Arthur knows nothing about. Under Merlyn's guidance, Arthur even learns the secret language of the animals and is given the chance to fly as a bird.

When Arthur is fifteen, England's king dies with no heir to succeed him. All of England's knights and barons journey to London to compete in a great jousting tournament on New Year's Day, each hoping to be acclaimed king. But at this time, a mysterious object appears in London: a sword stuck hilt-deep in an anvil on a slab of stone. On the sword are these words: "Whoso Pulleth Out This Sword of this Stone and Anvil, is Rightwise King Born of All England."

As this part of the story opens, Sir Ector, Sir Kay, Arthur (the Wart), and two old friends, Sir Grummore and Sir Pellinore, are setting out for London. Sir Kay can hardly wait to show off at the tournament — and maybe have a try at the sword.

Arthur Becomes King

T. H. White

Perhaps, if you happen not to have lived in the Old England of the twelfth century, or whenever it was, and in a remote castle on the borders of the Marches[1] at that, you will find it difficult to imagine the wonders of their journey.

The road, or track, ran most of the time along the high ridges of the hills or downs, and they could look down on either side of them upon the desolate marshes where the snowy reeds sighed, and the ice crackled, and the duck in the red sunsets quacked loud on the winter air. The whole country was like that. Perhaps there would be a moory marsh on one side of the ridge, and a forest of a hundred thousand acres on the other, with all the great branches weighted in white. They could sometimes see a wisp of smoke among the trees, or a huddle of buildings far out

---

1. **Marches:** boundaries that are in dispute.

Battle scene from a fourteenth-century manuscript.
Ms. 806, f. 262, The Pierpont Morgan Library, New York.

among the impassable roads, and twice they came to quite respectable towns which had several inns to boast of, but on the whole it was an England without civilization. The better roads were cleared of cover for a bowshot on either side of them, lest the traveler should be slain by hidden thieves.

They slept where they could, sometimes in the hut of some cottager who was prepared to welcome them, sometimes in the castle of a brother knight who invited them to refresh themselves, sometimes in the firelight and fleas of a dirty little hovel with a bush tied to a pole outside it—this was the sign board used at that time by inns—and once or twice on the open ground, all huddled together for warmth between their grazing chargers. Wherever they went and wherever they slept, the east wind whistled in the reeds, and the geese went over high in the starlight, honking at the stars.

London was full to the brim. If Sir Ector had not been lucky enough to own a little land in Pie Street, on which there stood a respectable

inn, they would have been hard put to it to find a lodging. But he did own it, and as a matter of fact drew most of his dividends[2] from that source, so they were able to get three beds among the five of them. They thought themselves fortunate.

On the first day of the tournament, Sir Kay managed to get them on the way to the lists[3] at least an hour before the jousts could possibly begin. He had lain awake all night, imagining how he was going to beat the best barons in England, and he had not been able to eat his breakfast. Now he rode at the front of the cavalcade, with pale cheeks, and Wart wished there was something he could do to calm him down.

For country people, who only knew the dismantled tilting ground[4] of Sir Ector's castle, the scene which met their eyes was ravishing.

2. **dividends:** White is having fun with history. Today, of course, a dividend is paid to stockholders in a corporation. Sir Ector would have received feudal tithes.
3. **lists:** fields where the tournament is held.
4. **tilting ground:** grounds where the knights practice tilting, or charging with lances. Tilts are the same as jousts.

It was a huge green pit in the earth, about as big as the arena at a football match. It lay ten feet lower than the surrounding country, with sloping banks, and the snow had been swept off it. It had been kept warm with straw, which had been cleared off that morning, and now the close-worn grass sparkled green in the white landscape. Round the arena there was a world of color so dazzling and moving and twinkling as to make one blink one's eyes. The wooden grandstands were painted in scarlet and white. The silk pavilions[5] of famous people, pitched on every side, were azure and green and saffron and checkered. The pennons and pennoncels[6] which floated everywhere in the sharp wind were flapping with every color of the rainbow, as they strained and slapped at their flagpoles, and the barrier down the middle of the arena itself was done in chessboard squares of black and white. Most of the combatants and their friends had not yet arrived, but one could see from those few who had come how the very people would turn the scene into a bank of flowers, and how the armor would flash, and the scalloped sleeves of the heralds jig in the wind, as they raised their brazen trumpets to their lips to shake the fleecy clouds of winter with joyances and fanfares.

"Good heavens!" cried Sir Kay. "I have left my sword at home."

"Can't joust without a sword," said Sir Grummore. "Quite irregular."

"Better go and fetch it," said Sir Ector. "You have time."

"My squire will do," said Sir Kay. "What a mistake to make! Here, squire, ride hard back to the inn and fetch my sword. You shall have a shilling if you fetch it in time."

The Wart went as pale as Sir Kay was, and looked as if he were going to strike him. Then he said, "It shall be done, master," and turned his ambling palfrey[7] against the stream of newcomers. He began to push his way toward their hostelry as best he might.

"To offer me money!" cried the Wart to himself. "To look down at this beastly little donkey-affair off his great charger and to call me squire! Oh, Merlyn, give me patience with the brute, and stop me from throwing his filthy shilling in his face."

When he got to the inn it was closed. Everybody had thronged to see the famous tournament, and the entire household had followed after the mob. Those were lawless days and it was not safe to leave your house—or even to go to sleep in it—unless you were certain that it was impregnable. The wooden shutters bolted over the downstairs windows were two inches thick, and the doors were double-barred.

"Now what do I do," asked the Wart, "to earn my shilling?"

He looked ruefully at the blind little inn, and began to laugh.

"Poor Kay," he said. "All that shilling stuff was only because he was scared and miserable, and now he has good cause to be. Well, he shall have a sword of some sort if I have to break into the Tower of London.

"How does one get hold of a sword?" he continued. "Where can I steal one? Could I waylay some knight even if I am mounted on an ambling pad, and take his weapons by force? There must be some swordsmith or armorer in a great town like this, whose shop would be still open."

He turned his mount and cantered off along

---

5. **pavilions:** tents.
6. **pennons and pennoncels:** flags bearing the knights' emblems. A pennoncel is smaller than a pennon.

7. **palfrey:** saddle horse, usually a small and gentle one.

How Arthur drew forth ÿ Sword.

the street. There was a quiet churchyard at the end of it, with a kind of square in front of the church door. In the middle of the square there was a heavy stone with an anvil on it, and a fine new sword was stuck through the anvil.

"Well," said the Wart, "I suppose it is some sort of war memorial, but it will have to do. I am sure nobody would grudge Kay a war memorial, if they knew his desperate straits."

He tied his reins round a post of the lych gate,[8] strode up the gravel path, and took hold of the sword.

"Come, sword," he said. "I must cry your mercy and take you for a better cause.

"This is extraordinary," said the Wart. "I feel strange when I have hold of this sword, and I notice everything much more clearly. Look at the beautiful gargoyles of the church, and of the monastery which it belongs to. See how splendidly all the famous banners in the aisle are waving. How nobly that yew[9] holds up the red flakes of its timbers to worship God. How clean the snow is. I can smell something like fetherfew and sweet briar— and is it music that I hear?"

It was music, whether of panpipes or of recorders, and the light in the churchyard was so clear, without being dazzling, that one could have picked a pin out twenty yards away.

"There is something in this place," said the Wart. "There are people. Oh, people, what do you want?"

Nobody answered him, but the music was loud and the light beautiful.

"People," cried the Wart, "I must take this sword. It is not for me, but for Kay. I will bring it back."

There was still no answer, and Wart turned back to the anvil. He saw the golden letters, which he did not read, and the jewels on the pommel,[10] flashing in the lovely light.

"Come, sword," said the Wart.

He took hold of the handles with both hands, and strained against the stone. There was a melodious consort[11] on the recorders, but nothing moved.

The Wart let go of the handles, when they were beginning to bite into the palms of his hands, and stepped back, seeing stars.

"It is well fixed," he said.

He took hold of it again and pulled with all his might. The music played more strongly, and the light all about the churchyard glowed like amethysts; but the sword still stuck.

"Oh, Merlyn," cried the Wart, "help me to get this weapon."

There was a kind of rushing noise, and a long chord played along with it. All round the churchyard there were hundreds of old friends. They rose over the church wall all together, like the Punch and Judy ghosts of remembered days, and there were badgers and nightingales and vulgar crows and hares and wild geese and falcons and fishes and dogs and dainty unicorns and solitary wasps and corkindrills[12] and hedgehogs and griffins[13] and the thousand other animals he had met. They loomed round the church wall, the lovers and helpers of the Wart, and they all spoke solemnly in turn. Some of them had come from

---

8. **lych gate:** roofed gate leading into a churchyard.
9. **yew:** evergreen tree with wide-spreading limbs.

10. **pommel:** the rounded, ornamental knob on the handle of the sword.
11. **consort:** harmony.
12. **corkindrills:** beasts feared in medieval times, now identified as crocodiles.
13. **griffins:** huge, mythical animals, half lion and half eagle.

the banners in the church, where they were painted in heraldry, some from the waters and the sky and the fields about—but all, down to the smallest shrew mouse, had come to help on account of love. Wart felt his power grow.

"Put your back into it," said a Luce (or pike) off one of the heraldic banners, "as you once did when I was going to snap you up. Remember that power springs from the nape of the neck."

"What about those forearms," asked a Badger gravely, "that are held together by a chest? Come along, my dear embryo, and find your tool."

A Merlin[14] sitting at the top of the yew tree cried out, "Now then, Captain Wart, what is the first law of the foot? I thought I once heard something about never letting go?"

"Don't work like a stalling woodpecker," urged a Tawny Owl affectionately. "Keep up a steady effort, my duck, and you will have it yet."

A White-front said, "Now, Wart, if you were once able to fly the great North Sea, surely you can coordinate a few little wing muscles here and there? Fold your powers together, with the spirit of your mind, and it will come out like butter. Come along, Homo sapiens, for all we humble friends of yours are waiting here to cheer."

The Wart walked up to the great sword for the third time. He put out his right hand softly and drew it out as gently as from a scabbard.

There was a lot of cheering, a noise like a hurdy-gurdy which went on and on. In the middle of this noise, after a long time, he saw Kay and gave him the sword. The people at the tournament were making a frightful row.

"But this is not my sword," said Sir Kay.

"It was the only one I could get," said the Wart. "The inn was locked."

"It is a nice-looking sword. Where did you get it?"

"I found it stuck in a stone, outside a church."

Sir Kay had been watching the tilting nervously, waiting for his turn. He had not paid much attention to his squire.

"That is a funny place to find one," he said.

"Yes, it was stuck through an anvil."

"What?" cried Sir Kay, suddenly rounding upon him. "Did you just say this sword was stuck in a stone?"

"It was," said the Wart. "It was a sort of war memorial."

Sir Kay stared at him for several seconds in amazement, opened his mouth, shut it again, licked his lips, then turned his back and plunged through the crowd. He was looking for Sir Ector, and the Wart followed after him.

"Father," cried Sir Kay, "come here a moment."

"Yes, my boy," said Sir Ector. "Splendid falls these professional chaps do manage. Why, what's the matter, Kay? You look as white as a sheet."

"Do you remember that sword which the King of England would pull out?"

"Yes."

"Well, here it is. I have it. It is in my hand. I pulled it out."

Sir Ector did not say anything silly. He looked at Kay and he looked at the Wart. Then he stared at Kay again, long and lovingly, and said, "We will go back to the church."

"Now then, Kay," he said, when they were at the church door. He looked at his firstborn kindly, but straight between the eyes. "Here is the stone, and you have the sword. It will make you the King of England. You are my son that I am proud of, and always will be,

---

14. **Merlin:** European falcon.

whatever you do. Will you promise me that you took it out by your own might?"

Kay looked at his father. He also looked at the Wart and at the sword.

Then he handed the sword to the Wart quite quietly.

He said, "I am a liar. Wart pulled it out."

As far as the Wart was concerned, there was a time after this in which Sir Ector kept telling him to put the sword back into the stone — which he did — and in which Sir Ector and Kay then vainly tried to take it out. The Wart took it out for them, and stuck it back again once or twice. After this, there was another time which was more painful.

He saw that his dear guardian was looking quite old and powerless, and that he was kneeling down with difficulty on a gouty[15] knee.

"Sir," said Sir Ector, without looking up, although he was speaking to his own boy.

"Please do not do this, Father," said the Wart, kneeling down also. "Let me help you up, Sir Ector, because you are making me unhappy."

"Nay, nay, my lord," said Sir Ector, with some very feeble old tears. "I was never your father nor of your blood, but I wote well ye are of an higher blood than I wend ye were."

"Plenty of people have told me you are not my father," said the Wart, "but it does not matter a bit."

"Sir," said Sir Ector humbly, "will ye be my good and gracious lord when ye are king?"

"Don't!" said the Wart.

"Sir," said Sir Ector, "I will ask no more of you but that you will make my son, your foster brother, Sir Kay, seneschal[16] of all your lands?"

Kay was kneeling down too, and it was more than the Wart could bear.

"Oh, do stop," he cried. "Of course he can be seneschal, if I have got to be this king, and, oh, Father, don't kneel down like that, because it breaks my heart. Please get up, Sir Ector, and don't make everything so horrible. Oh, dear, oh, dear, I wish I had never seen that filthy sword at all."

And the Wart also burst into tears.

After Arthur becomes king, he is plunged into war with a number of local rulers of England and Scotland who do not accept his right to rule them. England in the Middle Ages, like most of Europe, was governed according to the feudal system. This meant that the King of England did not rule the whole land directly. He ruled it through local leaders, each of whom was all-powerful in his own territory but was also bound to the king by an oath of obedience. Lot, mentioned in this selection, is the leader of those who are fighting against Arthur.

In the following selection we see Arthur as the King of England. He is preparing to unite his kingdom and establish a new order — one that will emphasize peace and good deeds.

The King of England painfully climbed the two hundred and eight steps which led to Merlyn's tower room, and knocked on the door. The magician was inside, with Archimedes[17] sitting on the back of his chair, busily trying to find the square root of minus one. He had forgotten how to do it.

"Merlyn," said the king, panting, "I want to talk to you."

He closed his book with a bang, leaped to

---

15. **gouty:** afflicted with gout, a disease that causes a painful swelling of the joints.
16. **seneschal** (sĕn'ə-shəl): chief administrator of a medieval noble's estate.

17. **Archimedes:** Merlyn's owl.

his feet, seized his wand of lignum vitae,[18] and rushed at Arthur as if he were trying to shoo away a stray chicken.

"Go away!" he shouted. "What are you doing here? What do you mean by it? Aren't you the King of England? Go away and send for me! Get out of my room! I never heard of such a thing! Go away at once and send for me!"

"But I am here."

"No, you're not," retorted the old man resourcefully. And he pushed the king out of the door, slamming it in his face.

"Well!" said Arthur, and he went off sadly down the two hundred and eight stairs.

An hour later, Merlyn presented himself in the Royal Chamber, in answer to a summons which had been delivered by a page.

"That's better," he said, and sat down comfortably on a carpet chest.

"Stand up," said Arthur, and he clapped his hands for a page to take away the seat.

Merlyn stood up, boiling with indignation. The whites of his knuckles blanched as he clenched them.

"About our conversation on the subject of chivalry," began the king in an airy tone. . . .

"I don't recollect such a conversation."

"No?"

"I have never been so insulted in my life!"

"But I am the king," said Arthur. "You can't sit down in front of the king."

"Rubbish!"

Arthur began to laugh more than was seemly, and his foster brother, Sir Kay, and his old guardian, Sir Ector, came out from behind the throne, where they had been hiding. Kay took off Merlyn's hat and put it on Sir Ector, and Sir Ector said, "Well, bless my soul, now I am a necromancer.[19] Hocus-Pocus." Then everybody began laughing, including Merlyn eventually, and seats were sent for so that they could sit down, and bottles of wine were opened so that it should not be a dry meeting.

"You see," he said proudly, "I have summoned a council."

There was a pause, for it was the first time that Arthur had made a speech, and he wanted to collect his wits for it.

"Well," said the king. "It is about chivalry. I want to talk about that."

Merlyn was immediately watching him with a sharp eye. His knobbed fingers fluttered among the stars and secret signs of his gown, but he would not help the speaker. You might say that this moment was the critical one in his career — the moment towards which he had been living backward for heaven knows how many centuries, and now he was to see for certain whether he had lived in vain.

"I have been thinking," said Arthur, "about Might and Right. I don't think things ought to be done because you are *able* to do them. I think they should be done because you *ought* to do them. After all, a penny is a penny in any case, however much Might is exerted on either side, to prove that it is or is not. Is that plain?"

Nobody answered.

"Well, I was talking to Merlyn on the battlements one day, and he mentioned that the last battle we had — in which seven hundred kerns[20] were killed — was not so much fun as I had thought it was. Of course, battles are not fun when you come to think about them. I mean, people ought not to be killed, ought they? It is better to be alive.

"Very well. But the funny thing is that Merlyn was helping me to win battles. He is

---

18. **lignum vitae:** the name of a tree, in Latin ("wood of life").

19. **necromancer:** magician.

20. **kerns:** lowborn foot soldiers.

The Enchanter Merlin.

still helping me, for that matter, and we hope to win the battle of Bedegraine together, when it comes off."

"We will," said Sir Ector, who was in the secret.[21]

"That seems to me to be inconsistent. Why does he help me to fight wars, if they are bad things?"

There was no answer from anybody, and the king began to speak with agitation.

"I could only think," said he, beginning to blush, "I could only think that I—that we—that he—that he wanted me to win them for a reason."

He paused and looked at Merlyn, who turned his head away.

"The reason was—was it?—the reason was that if I could be the master of my kingdom by winning these two battles, I could stop them afterwards and then do something about the business of Might. Have I guessed? Was I right?"

The magician did not turn his head, and his hands lay still in his lap.

"I was!" exclaimed Arthur.

And he began talking so quickly that he could hardly keep up with himself.

"You see," he said, "Might is not Right. But there is a lot of Might knocking about in this world, and something has to be done about it. It is as if People were half horrible and half nice. Perhaps they are even more than half horrible, and when they are left to themselves they run wild. You get the average baron that we see nowadays, people like Sir Bruce Sans Pitié, who simply go clod-hopping round the country dressed in steel, and doing exactly what they please, for sport. It is our Norman idea about the upper classes having a monopoly of power, without reference to justice.

Then the horrible side gets uppermost, and there is thieving and plunder and torture. The people become beasts.

"But, you see, Merlyn is helping me to win my two battles so that I can stop this. He wants me to put things right.

"Lot and Uriens and Anguish[22] and those—they are the old world, the old-fashioned order who want to have their private will. I have got to vanquish them with their own weapons—they force it upon me, because they live by force—and then the real work will begin. This battle at Bedegraine is the preliminary, you see. It is *after* the battle that Merlyn is wanting me to think about."

Arthur paused again for comment or encouragement, but the magician's face was turned away. It was only Sir Ector, sitting next to him, who could see his eyes.

"Now what I have thought," said Arthur, "is this. Why can't you harness Might so that it works for Right? I know it sounds nonsense, but, I mean, you can't just say there is no such thing. The Might is there, in the bad half of people, and you can't neglect it. You can't cut it out, but you might be able to direct it, if you see what I mean, so that it was useful instead of bad."

The audience was interested. They leaned forward to listen, except Merlyn.

"My idea is that if we can win this battle in front of us, and get a firm hold of the country, then I will institute a sort of order of chivalry. I will not punish the bad knights, or hang Lot, but I will try to get them into our Order. We shall have to make it a great honor, you see, and make it fashionable and all that. Everybody must want to be in. And then I shall make the oath of the order that Might is only to be used for Right. Do you follow? The

---

21. **in the secret:** Merlyn has devised a secret plan to win the battle.

22. **Lot and Uriens and Anguish:** local rulers in Britain before Arthur.

knights in my order will ride all over the world, still dressed in steel and whacking away with their swords—that will give an outlet for wanting to whack, you understand, an outlet for what Merlyn calls the foxhunting spirit—but they will be bound to strike only on behalf of what is good, to restore what has been done wrong in the past and to help the oppressed and so forth. Do you see the idea? It will be using the Might instead of fighting against it, and turning a bad thing into a good. There, Merlyn, that is all I can think of. I have thought as hard as I could, and I suppose I am wrong, as usual. But I did think. I can't do any better. Please say something!''

The magician stood up as straight as a pillar, stretched out his arms in both directions, looked at the ceiling and said the first few words of the Nunc Dimittis.[23]

---

23. **Nunc Dimittis:** the title of the Song of Simeon (Luke 2: 29–32), from its first words in Latin. The Nunc Dimittis begins: ''Lord, now lettest thou thy servant depart in peace . . . For mine eyes have seen thy salvation.'' According to the Biblical account, Simeon was an old man who had been allowed by God to live long enough to see the Messiah. When the child Jesus was brought to him, he uttered these words and was ready to die.

FOR STUDY AND DISCUSSION

1. In this episode, how does White show us that Arthur was not a very likely person to become the King of England?
2. White's main source for his novel was Thomas Malory's *Morte d' Arthur.* But Malory tells us very little about the thoughts or feelings of the main characters. White, on the other hand, makes his characters seem like real people, so that we can identify with them. What thoughts and feelings does Arthur express after Sir Kay has rather rudely ordered him to find his sword? In this incident, what kind of person does White show the young Arthur to be?
3. How does the character of Kay contrast with the character of Arthur? What are you supposed to think of Kay?
4. What details in the account of Arthur's ''trial'' with the sword show that he has extraordinary abilities that set him apart from others?
5. In the last part of this story, Arthur is changing and becoming ''kingly.'' What is Arthur's vision of the future? What do you think he means by ''the foxhunting spirit''?
6. Merlyn has been a key figure in Arthur's early life. Why do you think the old magician remains silent during Arthur's speech about Might and Right? Why does Merlyn finally react to the speech the way he does?

ANACHRONISMS

An *anachronism* is an object, an event, a person, or a thing that is chronologically out of place, usually something appropriate to an earlier period of time. For example, White refers to football in this selection. The sport of football was not known in medieval England, so football is an anachronism in this story. Writers sometimes create anachronisms as a result of carelessness or poor research. White, however, uses anachronisms intentionally, as a way of modernizing an old story and as a means of creating humor.

See if you can find other anachronisms in this selection. Which ones make the story humorous?

FOR COMPOSITION

Modernizing a Legend
The story you have just read is an example of an ancient legend that has been modernized. Choose a part of White's story to modernize in your own way. Provide thoughts and feelings for your Arthur that reflect the boys you have known and have grown up with. If you wish, claim artistic license and make Arthur a girl. You may want to use anachronisms for humor. Give your story a recognizable modern setting.

Comparing Stories
Write a brief essay in which you compare this part of Arthur's story with some other story, or movie, in which an unlikely person turns out to be someone very special. In your essay, cite the specific ways in which the plots and characters in the stories are alike, and specific ways in which they are different.

ABOUT THE AUTHOR

Terence Hansbury (T. H.) White (1906–1964) was born in Bombay, India, but went to England for his education. His first book, a collection of poems, was published when he was only nineteen. Later he wrote a number of detective stories. White was tremendously interested in a wide variety of subjects, including flying, movie-making, sailing, and falconry (a medieval sport still practiced by some people today). His novels about Arthur, combined in *The Once and Future King,* took almost twenty years to write. White visited America for the first time in 1960 when *Camelot,* a musical comedy based on *The Once and Future King,* opened on Broadway.

Arthur subdues the feudal lords of Britain and establishes his court at Camelot. Once peace is established, Arthur marries the beautiful Gwynevere, daughter of King Lodegreaunce. As a wedding present, King Lodegreaunce gives Arthur the Round Table.

The bravest and most skillful of all King Arthur's knights is Launcelot. He has come from France (as chivalry itself had come to England from France), and represents chivalry at its height. But there is another reason why Launcelot is so well known. Launcelot, who is Arthur's closest friend, eventually falls in love with Arthur's queen, Gwynevere, and she falls in love with him. For years Launcelot is torn between an undying friendship for Arthur and an undying love for Gwynevere. Eventually, this love breaks out into the open and helps to bring Arthur's brilliant court to ruin.

But here you will read about Launcelot at the height of his career, at a time when all is well at Camelot.

The Tale of Sir Launcelot du Lake

Sir Thomas Malory
Retold by Keith Baines

Sir Tarquine Captures Sir Lyonel

When King Arthur returned from Rome,[1] he settled his court at Camelot, and there gathered about him his knights of the Round Table, who diverted themselves with jousting and tournaments. Of all his knights one was supreme, both in prowess at arms and in nobility of bearing, and this was Sir Launcelot,

who was also the favorite of Queen Gwynevere, to whom he had sworn oaths of fidelity.

One day Sir Launcelot, feeling weary of his life at the court, and of only playing at arms, decided to set forth in search of adventure. He asked his nephew Sir Lyonel to accompany him, and when both were suitably armed and mounted, they rode off together through the forest.

At noon they started across a plain, but the intensity of the sun made Sir Launcelot feel sleepy, so Sir Lyonel suggested that they should rest beneath the shade of an apple tree

---

1. **Rome:** According to legend, when the Roman Emperor Lucius demanded his annual tribute from Britain, King Arthur refused to pay. Instead, he led his armies into Italy, defeated the Roman army, and killed Lucius.

Sir Launcelot of the Lake.

that grew by a hedge not far from the road. They dismounted, tethered their horses, and settled down.

"Not for seven years have I felt so sleepy," said Sir Launcelot, and with that fell fast asleep, while Sir Lyonel watched over him.

Soon three knights came galloping past, and Sir Lyonel noticed that they were being pursued by a fourth knight, who was one of the most powerful he had yet seen. The pursuing knight overtook each of the others in turn, and, as he did so, knocked each off his horse with a thrust of his spear. When all three lay stunned he dismounted, bound them securely to their horses with the reins, and led them away.

Without waking Sir Launcelot, Sir Lyonel mounted his horse and rode after the knight, and, as soon as he had drawn close enough, shouted his challenge. The knight turned about and they charged at each other, with the result that Sir Lyonel was likewise flung from his horse, bound, and led away a prisoner.

The victorious knight, whose name was Sir Tarquine, led his prisoners to his castle, and there threw them on the ground, stripped them naked, and beat them with thorn twigs. After that he locked them in a dungeon where many other prisoners, who had received like treatment, were complaining dismally.

Meanwhile, Sir Ector de Marys,[2] who liked to accompany Sir Launcelot on his adventures, and finding him gone, decided to ride

---

2. **Sir Ector de Marys:** Sir Launcelot's younger brother, not to be confused with the Sir Ector who was Arthur's foster father.

after him. Before long he came upon a forester.

"My good fellow, if you know the forest hereabouts, could you tell me in which direction I am most likely to meet with adventure?"

"Sir, I can tell you: Less than a mile from here stands a well-moated castle. On the left of the entrance you will find a ford where you can water your horse, and across from the ford a large tree from which hang the shields of many famous knights. Below the shields hangs a caldron of copper and brass: strike it three times with your spear, and then surely you will meet with adventure—such, indeed, that if you survive it, you will prove yourself the foremost knight in these parts for many years."

"May God reward you!" Sir Ector replied.

The castle was exactly as the forester had described it, and among the shields Sir Ector recognized several as belonging to knights of the Round Table. After watering his horse, he knocked on the caldron and Sir Tarquine, whose castle it was, appeared.

They jousted, and at the first encounter Sir Ector sent his opponent's horse spinning twice about before he could recover.

"That was a fine stroke; now let us try again," said Sir Tarquine.

This time Sir Tarquine caught Sir Ector just below the right arm and, having impaled him on his spear, lifted him clean out of the saddle, and rode with him into the castle, where he threw him on the ground.

"Sir," said Sir Tarquine, "you have fought better than any knight I have encountered in the last twelve years; therefore, if you wish, I will demand no more of you than your parole as my prisoner."

"Sir, that I will never give."

"Then I am sorry for you," said Sir Tarquine, and with that he stripped and beat him

and locked him in the dungeon with the other prisoners. There Sir Ector saw Sir Lyonel.

"Alas, Sir Lyonel, we are in a sorry plight. But tell me, what has happened to Sir Launcelot? for he surely is the one knight who could save us."

"I left him sleeping beneath an apple tree, and what has befallen him since I do not know," Sir Lyonel replied; and then all the unhappy prisoners once more bewailed their lot.

While Sir Launcelot still slept beneath the apple tree, four queens started across the plain. They were riding white mules and accompanied by four knights who held above them, at the tips of their spears, a green silk canopy to protect them from the sun. The party was startled by the neighing of Sir Launcelot's horse and, changing direction, rode up to the apple tree, where they discovered the sleeping knight. And as each of the queens gazed at the handsome Sir Launcelot, so each wanted him for her own.

"Let us not quarrel," said Morgan le Fay.[3] "Instead, I will cast a spell over him so that he remains asleep while we take him to my castle and make him our prisoner. We can then oblige him to choose one of us for his paramour."

Sir Launcelot was laid on his shield and borne by two of the knights to the Castle Charyot, which was Morgan le Fay's stronghold. He awoke to find himself in a cold cell, where a young noblewoman was serving him supper.

"What cheer?" she asked.

"My lady, I hardly know, except that I must have been brought here by means of an enchantment."

"Sir, if you are the knight you appear to be,

---

3. **Morgan le Fay:** King Arthur's wicked half sister, an enchantress.

Morgan Le Fay. Oil painting by Anthony Frederick Sandys (1829-1904).
Birmingham Museums and Art Galley.

you will learn your fate at dawn tomorrow." And with that the young noblewoman left him. Sir Launcelot spent an uncomfortable night but at dawn the four queens presented themselves and Morgan le Fay spoke to him:

"Sir Launcelot, I know that Queen Gwynevere loves you, and you her. But now you are my prisoner, and you will have to choose: either to take one of us for your paramour, or to die miserably in this cell—just as you please. Now I will tell you who we are: I am Morgan le Fay, Queen of Gore; my companions are the Queens of North Galys, of Estelonde, and of the Outer Isles. So make your choice."

"A hard choice! Understand that I choose none of you, lewd sorceresses that you are; rather will I die in this cell. But were I free, I would take pleasure in proving it against any who would champion you that Queen Gwynevere is the finest lady of this land."

"So, you refuse us?" asked Morgan le Fay.

"On my life, I do," Sir Launcelot said finally, and so the queens departed.

Sometime later, the young noblewoman who had served Sir Launcelot's supper reappeared.

"What news?" she asked.

"It is the end," Sir Launcelot replied.

"Sir Launcelot, I know that you have refused the four queens, and that they wish to kill you out of spite. But if you will be ruled by me, I can save you. I ask that you will champion my father at a tournament next Tuesday, when he has to combat the King of North Galys, and three knights of the Round Table, who last Tuesday defeated him ignominiously."

"My lady, pray tell me, what is your father's name?"

"King Bagdemagus."

"Excellent, my lady, I know him for a good king and a true knight, so I shall be happy to serve him."

"May God reward you! And tomorrow at dawn I will release you, and direct you to an abbey which is ten miles from here, and where the good monks will care for you while I fetch my father."

"I am at your service, my lady."

As promised, the young noblewoman released Sir Launcelot at dawn. When she had led him through the twelve doors to the castle entrance, she gave him his horse and armor, and directions for finding the abbey.

"God bless you, my lady; and when the time comes, I promise I shall not fail you."

Sir Launcelot rode through the forest in search of the abbey, but at dusk had still failed to find it, and coming upon a red silk pavilion, apparently unoccupied, decided to rest there overnight, and continue his search in the morning.

Launcelot Enters a Tournament

As soon as it was daylight, Sir Launcelot armed, mounted, and rode away in search of the abbey, which he found in less than two hours. King Bagdemagus' daughter was waiting for him, and as soon as she heard his horse's footsteps in the yard ran to the window, and, seeing that it was Sir Launcelot, herself ordered the servants to stable his horse. She then led him to her chamber, disarmed him, and gave him a long gown to wear, welcoming him warmly as she did so.

King Bagdemagus' castle was twelve miles away, and his daughter sent for him as soon as she had settled Sir Launcelot. The king arrived with his retinue and embraced Sir Launcelot, who then described his recent enchantment, and the great obligation he was under to his daughter for releasing him.

"Sir, you will fight for me on Tuesday next?"

"Sire, I shall not fail you; but please tell me the names of the three Round Table knights whom I shall be fighting."

"Sir Modred, Sir Madore de la Porte, and Sir Gahalantyne. I must admit that last Tuesday they defeated me and my knights completely."

"Sire, I hear that the tournament is to be fought within three miles of the abbey. Could you send me three of your most trustworthy knights, clad in plain armor, and with no device, and a fourth suit of armor which I myself shall wear? We will take up our position just outside the tournament field and watch while you and the King of North Galys enter into combat with your followers; and then, as soon as you are in difficulties, we will come to your rescue and show your opponents what kind of knights you command."

This was arranged on Sunday, and on the following Tuesday Sir Launcelot and the three knights of King Bagdemagus waited in a copse,[4] not far from the pavilion which had been erected for the lords and ladies who were to judge the tournament and award the prizes.

The King of North Galys was the first on the field, with a company of ninescore knights; he was followed by King Bagdemagus with fourscore knights, and then by the three knights of the Round Table, who remained apart from both companies. At the first encounter King Bagdemagus lost twelve knights, all killed, and the King of North Galys six.

With that, Sir Launcelot galloped onto the field, and with his first spear unhorsed five of the King of North Galys' knights, breaking the backs of four of them. With his next spear he charged the king, and wounded him deeply in the thigh.

---

4. **copse:** group of small trees or bushes.

"That was a shrewd blow," commented Sir Madore, and galloped onto the field to challenge Sir Launcelot. But he too was tumbled from his horse, and with such violence that his shoulder was broken.

Sir Modred was the next to challenge Sir Launcelot, and he was sent spinning over his horse's tail. He landed head first, his helmet became buried in the soil, and he nearly broke his neck, and for a long time lay stunned.

Finally Sir Gahalantyne tried; at the first encounter both he and Sir Launcelot broke their spears, so both drew their swords and hacked vehemently at each other. But Sir Launcelot, with mounting wrath, soon struck his opponent a blow on the helmet which brought the blood streaming from eyes, ears, and mouth. Sir Gahalantyne slumped forward in the saddle, his horse panicked, and he was thrown to the ground, useless for further combat.

Sir Launcelot took another spear, and unhorsed sixteen more of the King of North Galys' knights, and with his next, unhorsed another twelve; and in each case with such violence that none of the knights ever fully recovered. The King of North Galys was forced to admit defeat, and the prize was awarded to King Bagdemagus.

That night Sir Launcelot was entertained as the guest of honor by King Bagdemagus and his daughter at their castle, and before leaving was loaded with gifts.

"My lady, please, if ever again you should need my services, remember that I shall not fail you."

The Battle of Sir Launcelot and Sir Tarquine

The next day Sir Launcelot rode once more through the forest, and by chance came to the apple tree where he had previously slept. This

ir Launcelot doeth battle with Sir Turquine.

time he met a young noblewoman riding a white palfrey.[5]

"My lady, I am riding in search of adventure; pray tell me if you know of any I might find hereabouts."

"Sir, there are adventures hereabouts if you believe that you are equal to them; but please tell me, what is your name?"

"Sir Launcelot du Lake."

"Very well, Sir Launcelot, you appear to be a sturdy enough knight, so I will tell you. Not far away stands the castle of Sir Tarquine, a knight who in fair combat has overcome more than sixty opponents whom he now holds prisoner. Many are from the court of King Arthur."

"My lady, please lead me to Sir Tarquine."

When they arrived at the castle, Sir Launcelot watered his horse at the ford, and then beat the caldron until the bottom fell out. However, none came to answer the challenge, so they waited by the castle gate for half an hour or so. Then Sir Tarquine appeared, riding toward the castle with a wounded prisoner slung over his horse, whom Sir Launcelot recognized as Sir Gaheris, Sir Gawain's brother and a knight of the Round Table.

"Good knight," said Sir Launcelot, "it is known to me that you have put to shame many of the knights of the Round Table. Pray allow your prisoner, who I see is wounded, to recover, while I vindicate the honor of the knights whom you have defeated."

"I defy you, and all your fellowship of the Round Table," Sir Tarquine replied.

"You boast!" said Sir Launcelot.

At the first charge the backs of the horses were broken and both knights stunned. But they soon recovered and set to with their swords, and both struck so lustily that neither shield nor armor could resist, and within two

hours they were cutting each other's flesh, from which the blood flowed liberally. Finally they paused for a moment, resting on their shields.

"Worthy knight," said Sir Tarquine, "pray hold your hand for a while, and if you will, answer my question."

"Sir, speak on."

"You are the most powerful knight I have fought yet, but I fear you may be the one whom in the whole world I most hate. If you are not, for the love of you I will release all my prisoners and swear eternal friendship."

"What is the name of the knight you hate above all others?"

"Sir Launcelot du Lake; for it was he who slew my brother, Sir Carados of the Dolorous Tower, and it is because of him that I have killed a hundred knights, and maimed as many more, apart from the sixty-four I still hold prisoner. And so, if you are Sir Launcelot, speak up, for we must then fight to the death."

"Sir, I see now that I might go in peace and good fellowship, or otherwise fight to the death; but being the knight I am, I must tell you: I am Sir Launcelot du Lake, son of King Ban of Benwick, of Arthur's court, and a knight of the Round Table. So defend yourself!"

"Ah! this is most welcome."

Now the two knights hurled themselves at each other like two wild bulls; swords and shields clashed together, and often their swords drove into the flesh. Then sometimes one, sometimes the other, would stagger and fall, only to recover immediately and resume the contest. At last, however, Sir Tarquine grew faint, and unwittingly lowered his shield. Sir Launcelot was swift to follow up his advantage, and dragging the other down to his knees, unlaced his helmet and beheaded him.

---

5. **palfrey:** horse.

Millefleurs tapestry with
horseman. Montacute House,
Somerset, England.
Courtesy, The National Trust.

FOR STUDY AND DISCUSSION

1. In Sir Thomas Malory's *Morte d' Arthur*, Launcelot is the ideal knight. Three of the principal duties of a knight, according to the code of chivalry, were to correct wrongs, to honor his word, and to serve his "lady." Find examples from this selection that show how Launcelot fulfills these knightly duties.

2. Why might Launcelot have felt divided in his loyalties when he fought for King Bagdemagus? Which loyalty did Launcelot obviously put first? Why do you think he did this?

3. Malory writes that Launcelot was first among the knights of the Round Table not only in arms but in "nobility of bearing" as well. How does Launcelot show "nobility of bearing" in this selection?

4. Malory's reading public liked duels and tournaments just as people today like the action in Westerns. What other kinds of stories popular today are similar to these knightly adventures—in characterization as well as in plot? How do you account for their appeal?

5. What aspects of these knightly stories lend themselves to parody? What parodies have you seen or read of such chivalrous tales?

The Tale of Sir Launcelot du Lake 447

LANGUAGE AND VOCABULARY

Identifying Word Origins

After the Normans from France conquered England in 1066, French was instituted as the official language of the ruling classes in England. For two centuries, French was used in court, government, military affairs, commerce, the arts, and religion. The result is that thousands of words in English today are French in origin.

Because it was the language of the ruling classes, French was considered more "elegant" than plain English. This might be one reason why this story was called "Morte d'Arthur," instead of "the death of Arthur." *Death* is an English word that goes back to Old Saxon; *morte* is French. You can see how strong the French influence has been when you consider all the other English words related to *morte: mortality, mortal, mortify, mortgage.*

It is interesting to look at the French influence on words used to name foods. While they were in the barnyard, animals kept their plain English names, but they became French when they were served on the table. In a dictionary, look up the derivations of the following words. Which are French in origin, and which are English? Could they be used interchangeably?

swine, pig, boar, pork, bacon
cow, beef
sheep, lamb, mutton
deer, venison
veal, calf

FOR COMPOSITION

Writing a Romance

From reading Launcelot's adventures, you have an idea of the patterns typically found in a medieval romance or adventure story. Make up a brief story about Sir Launcelot or any other knight, in which you show the hero fighting to uphold the ideals of chivalry. Although knights were always men in medieval romances, you might want to imagine a woman in the role.

The hero's enemy may be either human or nonhuman (a dragon, fiend, or monster). If the enemy is human, he or she must be depicted as very evil.

Add dialogue and details to make your story exciting. Some of the Arthurian romances show touches of humor and exaggeration. Use these devices in your own story if you wish to. If you feel so inclined, make your "romance" a parody.

Besides the tales of King Arthur and Sir Launcelot, Malory's *Morte d'Arthur* includes tales of other knights who gallop off to slay monsters, rescue women in danger, and search, as Sir Galahad does, for the Holy Grail. "The Tale of Sir Gareth," which follows, is a story of one knight's trial and adventure. Gareth's story is enlivened with touches of robust humor. As with many heroes of the Arthurian legends, Gareth is in disguise when he first appears on the scene.

The Tale of Sir Gareth

Sir Thomas Malory, retold by Keith Baines

It happened one Pentecost[1] when King Arthur and his knights of the Round Table had all assembled at the castle of Kynke Kenadonne and were waiting, as was customary, for some unusual event to occur before settling down to the feast, that Sir Gawain saw through the

window three gentlemen riding toward the castle, accompanied by a dwarf. The gentlemen dismounted, and giving their horses into the care of the dwarf, started walking toward the castle gate.

"My lords," Sir Gawain shouted, "we can sit down to the feast, for here come three gentlemen and a dwarf who are certain to bring strange tidings."

---

1. **Pentecost:** a Christian festival held on the seventh Sunday after Easter.

The king and his knights sat down at the great Round Table, which provided seats for a hundred and fifty knights; but this year, as in most, several were vacant because their owners had either been killed in the course of their adventures, or else taken prisoner.

The three gentlemen entered the hall, and there was complete silence as they approached the king. All three were richly clothed; and the one who walked in the center was obviously young, but taller than his companions by eighteen inches, strongly built, of noble features, and with large and beautiful hands. He leaned heavily on his companions' shoulders and did not stand up to his full height until he was confronting the king. Then he spoke:

"Most noble king, may God bless you and your knights of the Round Table! I come to ask you for three gifts, and none of them is unreasonable or such as to give you cause to repent. The first of the gifts I will ask for now, the other two at the next Pentecost."

"The three gifts shall be yours for the asking," Arthur replied.

"Sire, today I ask that you shall give me food and drink for twelve months, until the next Pentecost, when I shall ask for the other two."

"My dear son, this is a simple thing to ask for. I have never denied food and drink either to my friends or to my enemies. Can you ask for no worthier gift? For you have the appearance of a man nobly born and bred."

"Sire, for the present I ask nothing more."

"Very well, then; but pray tell me your name."

"Sire, that I cannot tell you."

"It is strange indeed that you should not know your name."

King Arthur then commanded Sir Kay, his steward, to serve the young gentleman with the best fare available throughout the coming year, and to treat him with the courtesy due to a nobleman.

"Sire, that is unnecessary," Sir Kay answered sourly, "for were he of noble birth he would have asked for a horse and for armor. No! he is nothing but a great loafer born of a serving wench, you may be sure. However, I will keep him in the kitchen and feed him until he is as fat as any pig, and the kitchen shall be his sty. And since he has neither name nor purpose, I shall call him Beaumains."[2]

And so Beaumains' companions duly delivered him into the charge of Sir Kay, who lost no opportunity to gibe and jeer at him. Both Sir Gawain and Sir Launcelot were deeply ashamed of Sir Kay's cavalier behavior, and Sir Launcelot spoke his mind:

"Sir Kay, take warning! Beaumains may yet prove to be of noble birth, and win fame for himself and for our liege."

Throughout the next twelve months, while Sir Kay remained irate and contemptuous, both Sir Launcelot and Sir Gawain treated Beaumains with the greatest courtesy, inviting him frequently to their quarters to dine, and urging him to accept money for his needs. With Sir Launcelot this was due to his habitually gentle nature; but with Sir Gawain it was more, for he had an unexplained feeling of kinship with Beaumains. However, Beaumains always refused them, remaining in the kitchen to work and eat with the servants, and meekly obedient to Sir Kay. Only when the knights were jousting would he leave the kitchen to watch them, or when games were played, then he participated, and by virtue of his natural strength and skill, was always the champion; and only then would Sir Kay take pride in his charge, and say: "Well, what do you think of my kitchen lad now?"

---

2. **Beaumains** (bō-mănz´): in French, "Fair Hands."

Once more the feast of Pentecost came around, and once more King Arthur and his knights waited for an unusual occurrence before sitting down to the banquet. This time a squire came running into the hall, and straight up to Arthur:

"Sire, you may take your seats at the Round Table, for a lady is approaching the castle, with strange tidings to relate."

As soon as the king and his knights were seated at the table the lady entered the hall, and kneeling before Arthur, begged his aid.

"Lady, pray tell us your story," Arthur responded.

"Sire, I have a sister, of noble birth and wide dominion, who for two years has been held captive by a most audacious and tyrannical knight; so now I beseech Your Majesty, who is said to command the flower of the chivalry, to dispatch one of your knights to her rescue."

"My lady, pray tell me her name and where she lives, also the name of the knight who holds her prisoner."

"Sire, I may not reveal her name or where she lives; I can only plead that she is a lady of great worth. The knight who holds her prisoner while extorting wealth from her estates is known as the Red Knight of the Red Lands."

"Then I do not know him."

"Sire, I do!" cried Sir Gawain. "He is a knight who is said to have the strength of seven men, and I can believe it, because I fought him once and barely escaped with my life."

"My lady," said Arthur, "I can send a knight to rescue your sister only if I know her name and where she lives; otherwise you can have no help from this court."

"Alas! I thought you would not fail me; so now I must resume my search."

But then Beaumains spoke up: "Sire, for twelve months I have eaten in your kitchen;

now the time has come for me to ask you for the other two gifts."

"You ask at your peril, Beaumains," said the king.

"The first is that I pursue the quest besought by this lady, for I believe that it is my appointed one. The second, that Sir Launcelot should follow us, and when I have proved myself worthy, make me a knight, for it is only by him, who is peerless among all knights, that I should wish to be sworn into the order."

"I grant you both gifts, Beaumains."

"Sire, you shame me! To send a kitchen boy on such a noble quest! I will have none of it," said the lady, and walked angrily from the hall.

Meanwhile Beaumains' two companions and the dwarf had arrived, leading a fine charger with gold trappings, and an excellent sword and suit of armor; only a spear and shield were lacking. Beaumains armed at once and mounted; and Arthur's knights were astonished to discover him the possessor of such fine equipment and to see how nobly he bore himself, once clad in it. Beaumains returned to the hall, took his leave of Arthur and of Sir Gawain, and then set off after the lady, followed by Sir Launcelot.

Just as they were leaving the court, Sir Kay appeared, fully armed and mounted. "I too am going to follow this kitchen lout," he said grimly.

"Sir Kay, you would do better to remain here," said Sir Launcelot.

But Sir Kay was not to be dissuaded, and he galloped up to Beaumains and shouted: "Well, Beaumains, do you still recognize your master?"

"I know you for the most ungracious knight at the court, Sir Kay, so now beware!"

Sir Kay couched his spear and charged at him. Beaumains, having neither shield nor spear, drew his sword, and as Sir Kay bore down on him, made two rapid strokes. With the first he knocked the spear out of Sir Kay's grasp, and with the second lunged at Sir Kay and drove the sword into his side, wounding him deeply so that he fell to the ground as though dead.

Beaumains dismounted, took possession of Sir Kay's spear and shield, and then remounted and instructed his dwarf to take the spare horse. At this point Sir Launcelot rode up to him, and Beaumains asked if he would like to joust, to which Sir Launcelot agreed.

They drew apart and then galloped together, and the collision sent both men and horses tumbling to the ground. Recovering quickly, both drew their swords and attacked each other with the ferocity of wild boars. Sir Launcelot, who had hitherto been unmatched, was astonished at Beaumains' strength and skill, and felt as if he were fighting a giant rather than an ordinary man. Each succeeded in delivering blows that sent his opponent staggering to the ground, only to recover immediately. After a while, however, Sir Launcelot began to realize that his strength was not equal to that of Beaumains, and fearing an ignominious defeat, called a halt.

"My friend, pray hold off! for we have no quarrel," he said.

"That is true, Sir Launcelot, yet it does me good to feel your strength, though I have not yet fought to my uttermost."

"Then you are matchless: I called a halt just now for fear that I should be shamed into begging for mercy!"

"Sir Launcelot, will you make me a knight?"

"Certainly, but first you must reveal to me your true name, and of whom you were born."

"Sir, if you will pledge yourself to absolute secrecy, I will tell you."

"I shall not betray you."

"My name is Gareth of Orkney; I am Sir Gawain's brother, born of the same parents."

"Gareth, that gladdens my heart, for I guessed that you were of noble birth."

Sir Launcelot then knighted Gareth and left him. Sir Kay was still lying senseless, so he laid him on his shield and brought him to the court, where the other knights, especially Sir Gawain, taunted him without mercy. However, Sir Launcelot excused Sir Kay on the grounds that he was young and ignorant of Beaumains' birth and of his purpose in serving in the kitchen for a year.

Sir Gareth, meanwhile, had ridden after the lady, and as soon as he caught up with her she rounded on him:

"Why do you follow me, you wretched lackey? Your clothes still stink of tallow and grease; and I know from Sir Kay that you are nameless and have to be called Beaumains, and how treacherously you overcame that excellent knight! Now leave me, I command you; have done!"

"Madame, I have come to serve you, and your words shall not deter me."

"Lewd little knave! Well, before long we shall meet a knight who will frighten you back to your kitchen quickly enough."

At this moment a man came running frantically out of the forest.

"My good fellow, what is your trouble?" asked Sir Gareth.

"My lord, six thieves have attacked my master; they have him bound and at any moment will kill him."

"Pray lead me to them."

Sir Gareth killed three of the thieves as soon as they came upon them. The other three fled, and Sir Gareth chased them until they turned about and attacked him fiercely, but before long he had killed them all. Returning to the knight, he released him from his bonds, and the knight begged Sir Gareth to accompany him to his castle, where he would be able to reward him as he deserved.

"Sir, I need no reward for doing as a knight should; and today I have been knighted by the peerless Sir Launcelot, so I am content enough. Pray forgive me now if I return to my lady, whose quest I am pursuing."

Sir Gareth returned to the lady, and she turned on him again:

"Misshapen wretch! What pleasure do you expect me to take in your cumbrous deeds? Now leave me, get back to your kitchen, I say!"

The knight whom Sir Gareth had rescued now rode up to them both and offered them hospitality for the night. It was already dusk,

and the lady accepted. At dinner she found herself sitting opposite to Sir Gareth, and protested at once: "Sir, forgive me, but I cannot possibly dine in company with this stinking kitchen knave; why, he is fit only for sticking pigs."

Thereupon the knight set Sir Gareth at a side table, and excusing himself, removed his own place there as well.

In the morning, after thanking their host, Sir Gareth and the lady resumed their journey. Soon they came to a broad stream, and on the further bank were two knights.

"Now," said the lady, "I think you had better fly, and save your bacon."

"My lady, were there six knights, I should not fly."

The first of the knights and Sir Gareth galloped their horses into the stream, and both broke their spears as they collided. They drew their swords, and soon Sir Gareth stunned his opponent with a blow on the helmet, and he fell into the water and was drowned. Urging his horse through the stream, Sir Gareth met the second knight on the far bank; and again both spears were broken, and again Sir Gareth struck his opponent on the helmet, this time with a blow that killed him outright.

"It is strange," said the lady when Sir Gareth had joined her once more, "that fortune should favor so vile a wretch as you. But do not suppose for one moment that it was either by skill or daring that you overcame those two excellent knights. No, I watched you closely. The first was thrown into the water by his horse stumbling, and so unhappily drowned. The second you won by a cowardly blow when he was not expecting it. However, had you not better turn back now? For the next knight we meet will certainly cut you down without mercy or remorse."

"My lady, I shall not turn back. So far I have

fought with such ability as God gave me, and trusting in His protection. My only discouragement has been your own extraordinary abuse.''

All day they rode together, and the lady's villainous tongue never ceased to wag. In the evening they came to the Black Land. By a black hawthorne on which was hung a black shield, and by the side of which was a black rock, stood a black standard. Under the tree stood a knight in black armor, who was Knight of the Black Lands.

''Now fly,'' said the lady to Gareth, ''for here is a knight before whom even the brave might tremble.''

''I am not a coward, my lady.''

''My lady!'' shouted the Black Knight, ''are you come with your champion from King Arthur's court?''

''Sir, unhappily not! This ill-gotten lout has pursued me from King Arthur's kitchen, and continues to force his odious presence upon me. Purely by mischance, and by treachery, he has overcome a few knights on the way; but I beg you to rid me of him.''

''My lady, that I will happily do. I thought for a moment that since he was accompanying you, he must be of noble birth. Now let us see: it would be degrading to fight him, so I will just strip him of his armor and horse, and then he can run back to his kitchen.''

''Sir, I shall pass through this country as it pleases me, and whether you will or no. It appears that you covet my horse and my armor.

Very well, let us see if you can win them! Now—defend yourself!"

And with that, both knights, in a black rage, galloped thunderously at each other. Both broke their spears, but while Sir Gareth was unharmed, the point of his own spear was embedded deeply in the body of his opponent. They fought with their swords, and for an hour and a half the Black Knight held out, but then he fell dead from his horse.

Noticing the fine quality of the Black Knight's armor, Sir Gareth stripped him of it, and exchanged it for his own. He then remounted and joined his lady.

"Alas! the lackey still lives. Shall I never be rid of him? Tell me, cockroach, why do you not run off now? You could boast to everyone that you have overcome all these knights, who, entirely through misfortune, have fallen to you."

"My lady, I shall accompany you until I have accomplished my quest or died in the attempt. This, whether you will or no."

Next they came upon the Green Knight, clad in green armor, who, seeing Sir Gareth's black armor, inquired if it were not his brother, the Black Knight.

"Alas! no," the lady replied. "This is but a fat pauper from King Arthur's kitchen, who has treacherously murdered your noble brother. I pray you, avenge him!"

"My lady, this is most shameful; certainly I will avenge him."

"This is slander," said Sir Gareth. "I killed him in fair combat; so now defend yourself!"

The Green Knight blew three times on his horn, and two maids appeared, who handed him his green spear and green shield.

They jousted and both broke their spears, then continued the fight with swords, still on horseback, until Sir Gareth wounded his opponent's horse and it collapsed under him. They both leaped clear and resumed the

fight on foot. The Green Knight was powerful, and both were soon liberally wounded. At last the lady spoke up:

"Why, sir, for shame! Does it take so long to dispatch a mere scullery boy! Surely you can finish him off; this is the weed overshooting the corn!"

The Green Knight, deeply ashamed, redoubled his blows, and succeeded in splintering Sir Gareth's shield. Sir Gareth then exerted his full strength, and striking his opponent on the helmet, sent him reeling to the ground, where he unlaced his helmet in order to behead him; and the Green Knight cried for mercy.

"Mercy you shall not have, unless this lady pleads for you," Sir Gareth replied.

"And that I should be beholden to a servant? Never!" the lady replied.

"Very well, sweet lady, he shall die."

"Not so fast, knave!"

"Good knight, I pray you, do not kill me for want of a good word from the lady. Spare me, and not only shall I forgive you the death of my brother, but I will myself swear you allegiance, together with that of the thirty knights at my command."

"In the devil's name! The Green Knight and his thirty followers at the command of a scullery boy! For shame, I say!"

For answer, Sir Gareth raised his sword, and made as if to behead the Green Knight.

"Hold, you dog, or you will repent it!" said the lady.

"My lady's command is a pleasure, and I shall obey her in this as in all things; for surely I would do nothing to displease her."

With that Sir Gareth released the Green Knight, who at once swore him homage.

The two knights and the lady rode to the Green Knight's castle, and as ever, the lady unbridled her flow of invective against Sir Gareth, and once more refused to dine at the same table with him. The Green Knight removed both his own and Sir Gareth's places to a side table, and the two knights ate merrily together. Then the Green Knight addressed the lady:

"My lady, it astonishes me that you can behave in such unseemly fashion before this noble knight, who has proved himself worthier than I—and believe me, I have encountered the greatest knights of my time. He is surely rendering you an honorable service, and I warn you that whatever mystery he pretends concerning his birth, it will be proved in the end that he is of noble, if not royal, blood."

"My lord, you make me sick," the lady responded.

Before retiring to their chambers, the Green Knight commanded thirty of his retainers to watch over Sir Gareth while he slept, and to be on their guard against treachery.

In the morning, after Mass and breakfast, the Green Knight accompanied Sir Gareth and the lady through the forest, and when he came to take leave of them, spoke to Sir Gareth:

"Noble knight, please remember that I and my thirty knights are sworn to your service, to command when you will."

"Sir, I thank you; when the time comes, I shall request you to make your allegiance to King Arthur."

"Sir, we shall be ready at all times," said the Green Knight.

"For shame! For shame!" cried the lady.

They parted, and then the lady spoke to Sir Gareth:

"Now, you greasy knave, surely you have run to the end of your leash. Ahead of us lies the Passage Perelous, and it would take a true-born knight, and one of the quality of Sir Launcelot, Sir Tristram, or Sir Lamerok, to pass through this stage of the journey without losing courage. And so I advise you to run for it now!"

"Perhaps, my lady, I shall not run," Sir Gareth replied.

They were approaching a castle comprising a fine white tower, surrounded by machicolated walls[3] and double ditches. Leading up to the gate was a large jousting field, with a pavilion in process of erection for a coming tournament; and hung above the gate were fifty shields bearing different devices. The lord of the castle, seeing Sir Gareth approach with the lady and his dwarf, decided to challenge him, so he clad himself in puce[4] armor, for he was the Puce Knight, and then rode out to meet them.

"Sir, are you not my brother, the Black Knight?" he asked.

"Sir, indeed he is not. He is a nameless servant from King Arthur's kitchen, called Beaumains. Purely by treachery and mischance he has killed your brother the Black Knight, and obtained the allegiance of your excellent brother the Green Knight. I beg you to avenge them, and rid me of his odious presence once and for all."

"My lady, it shall be done," the Puce Knight replied.

They jousted and both horses collapsed, and they continued the fight on foot. After two hours the lady could contain herself no longer:

"Sir, for shame that you should dally so long with a mere scullery boy. Pray do me the goodness to finish him off."

The Puce Knight was duly ashamed, and redoubled his strokes, but to no avail; for Sir

---

3. **machicolated** (mə-chĭk'ə-lāt'ĭd) **walls:** castle walls with openings (machicolations) through which stones or hot liquids could be dropped upon attackers.
4. **puce** (pyo͞os): brownish purple or dull red.

Gareth, using only a little more strength, struck him to the ground, then, straddling him, dragged off his helmet to behead him. The Puce Knight pleaded for mercy.

"Mercy you shall not have unless my lady pleads for you."

"Leave him be, Beaumains; he is a noble knight," said the lady.

"Then, my lady, he shall thank you for his life," said Sir Gareth.

The Puce Knight rose, and begged them to accept hospitality in his castle for the night. The lady accepted and that evening they dined well and then went to bed; but as ever she continued to abuse Sir Gareth. Distrusting her, the Puce Knight commanded his sixty knights to keep watch over him while he slept. In the morning, after hearing Mass and breakfasting, the lady and Sir Gareth took leave of their host; and before parting the Puce Knight swore his allegiance, and that of his sixty knights, to Sir Gareth, who, as before, said that in due course he would require him to make his allegiance to King Arthur.

They resumed their journey, and by noon had come in sight of a beautiful city. Before it stretched a plain, the grass was newly mown, and many splendid pavilions had been erected. But one in particular caught the eye, being the color of indigo, and arranged about it were armor and equipment of the same color; so also were the adornments of the ladies who passed to and fro.

"Yonder lies the pavilion of Sir Persaunte, the Indigo Knight, and lord of this city. But for one, he is the greatest knight living, and when the weather is good he pitches his pavilions on the plain and spends his time in jousting and tournaments, and other pastimes suitable to the nobility. He has at his command a hundred and fifty knights, and it is his custom to challenge every knight who passes through his terrain. And so now, filthy knave, had you

not better think twice and flee, before Sir Persaunte chastises you with the ignominy that you deserve?"

"My lady, if he is noble, as you say he is, he will not dispatch his knights to murder me, but fight with me in single combat; and if he has won honor as you say he has, the greater glory will be mine if I overcome him. Before each combat you yourself chasten me with your abuse; and after each you deny flatly what I have truly accomplished, distorting the event so that it serves only to augment the hatred you bear me!"

"Sir, your courteous speech and brave deeds astound me. I have with my own eyes witnessed what you have already accomplished, and I am becoming convinced that you must indeed be of noble birth. But this time I would save you, so please offer no challenge to the Indigo Knight, for both you and your horse have already suffered much in your previous combats. Up to now we have come safely through this difficult journey, but here we are within seven miles of the castle where my sister is held captive; and to combat the knight who holds her, you will need all your strength, for his is seven times that of ordinary men."

"My lady, I should be ashamed to withdraw from combat with the Indigo Knight now; but with God's grace, we shall be able to continue our journey in two hours."

"Ah Jesu!" exclaimed the lady. "Worthy knight, you must indeed be of noble blood to have borne for so long and with such courtesy the terrible way in which I have reviled you."

"My lady, it would be an unworthy knight indeed who was unable to bear the chastisement of a lady. The anger your insults inspired in me I turned against my opponents, and so overcame them more readily. Always have I been determined to prove my own worth: I served in King Arthur's kitchen in order to discover who were my true friends, and who my enemies. What my blood may be shall be revealed in due course; but at present I wish to prove myself by my deeds alone. And so, my lady, I shall continue to serve you as I have already."

"I beg you, gentle knight, can you forgive me my terrible words?"

"My lady, you are forgiven; and if formerly anger made me strong, may joy now make me invincible!"

Meanwhile, the Indigo Knight had seen Sir Gareth and the lady approach, and sent a messenger to inquire whether they came in war or in peace. Sir Gareth replied that he offered a challenge only if the Indigo Knight wished to receive one. The Indigo Knight decided to accept the challenge and fight to his uttermost, so he mounted and rode out to meet Sir Gareth.

They charged at each other with equal determination, and both broke their spears into three pieces, while their horses tumbled to the ground.

The sword fight lasted for two hours, and in the course of it Sir Gareth wounded the Indigo Knight deeply in the side; however, he continued to fight bravely. At last, though somewhat loath because of his opponent's bravery, Sir Gareth delivered his crushing blow on the helmet, and the Indigo Knight was sent spinning to the ground. Once more Sir Gareth straddled his opponent and unlaced his helmet to behead him, and the Indigo Knight yielded. The lady at once begged that Sir Gareth should spare his life.

"My lady, that I will gladly do, for he is a noble knight."

"May God reward you!" said the Indigo Knight. "Now I understand well enough how it was that you killed my brother Sir Perarde the Black Knight, and won the allegiance of my other two brothers, Sir Pertolope the

Green Knight and Sir Perymones the Puce Knight."

Sir Persaunte then led Sir Gareth and the lady to his pavilion, where he refreshed them with wine and spices, and insisted that Sir Gareth should rest both before and after supper.

In the morning Sir Persaunte asked the lady where she was leading Sir Gareth.

"To the Castle Dangerous."

"Ah ha! that is where the Red Knight of the Red Lands lives, and holds the Lady Lyoness prisoner, is it not? But tell me, you are surely her sister, Lady Lynet?"

"Sir, that is my name," the lady replied.

"Well, sir, you must prepare yourself for an ordeal, for it is said that the Red Knight has the strength of seven ordinary men. But you will be fighting for a worthy cause, for this knight has held the Lady Lyoness prisoner for

two years now. He has been waiting for a challenge from one of four knights from King Arthur's court: Sir Launcelot, the most powerful of all, Sir Tristram, Sir Gawain, or Sir Lamerok. And although many other knights have achieved much fame—for example, Sir Palomides, Sir Safere, Sir Bleobris, Sir Blamoure, Sir Bors, Sir Ector, Sir Percivale, and so on—it is one of these four he wishes to fight. So, now, let me wish you God's speed, and strength for the coming battle."

"Sir Persaunte, would you have the goodness of heart to make my companion a knight? It would please me greatly to see this done before he fights the Red Knight of the Red Lands."

"My lady, I will gladly, if he will accept the order from so simple a man as I."

"Sir, I thank you for your gracious offer, but I have already been knighted by Sir Launcelot,

for I wished it to be from no other hands than his. And if you will both swear to keep the secret, I will now reveal to you my name, and of whom I was born."

"We swear," they said together.

"I am Sir Gareth, Sir Gawain's brother, and the youngest son of King Lot of Lowthean and Orkney; my mother is Margawse, King Arthur's sister. But neither King Arthur, Sir Gawain, nor any other at his court, with the exception of Sir Launcelot, knows who I am."

In the morning, after Mass and breakfast, Sir Gareth and the lady rode through the forest, and then across a wide plain, to the Castle Dangerous, which stood on the seashore. The Red Knight had pitched his pavilions beneath the walls of the castle, and to one side Sir Gareth noticed a copse of tall trees, and from the branches hung forty knights. They were in full armor, with their swords in their hands, shields, and spurs at their heels. Sir Gareth was horrified.

"Tell, my lady, what is the meaning of this?"

"Sir Gareth, those are the knights who hitherto have attempted to rescue my sister, so take heed! The Red Knight is a formidable warrior, and lord of many marches,[5] but once he has overcome a knight in battle, he always puts him to this murderous end; and that is one reason why no gentlewoman can love him."

"May Jesu preserve me from such a death! Certainly I should prefer to die fighting. But how strange that no knight from King Arthur's court has yet defeated him!"

"My lord, take courage; he is a powerful knight."

The castle moats were formed by two dikes which ran around from the sea. Several ships were at anchor and everywhere were signs of activity. On board the ships, in the Red Knight's pavilions, and from within the castle could be heard the merry sounds of minstrelsy,[6] while lords and their ladies walked upon the castle walls. Just by the gate grew a large sycamore tree, and on this was hung an elephant's horn for those who wished to challenge the Red Knight. Sir Gareth was about to blow it when the lady cautioned him:

"Sir Gareth, do not sound your challenge yet. Until noon the Red Knight's strength increases, after then it wanes, so if you will wait for a little the advantage will be yours."

"My lady, I should be ashamed not to challenge him at his greatest strength." And with that Sir Gareth blew a tremendous blast on the horn.

Immediately knights and ladies came run-

ning from all directions, to the castle walls and windows, or out of their pavilions, in order to witness the coming battle. The Red Knight hastily armed, assisted by his earls and barons. One of them laced on his helmet while another buckled on his spurs and a third handed him his blood-red shield and spear. He then mounted, rode out to a small hollow which could be easily viewed from the castle, and awaited his challenger.

"My lord, here comes your mortal enemy, and at the tower window stands your lady."

"Pray, tell me where," asked Sir Gareth.

The lady pointed with her finger, and Sir Gareth looked up and saw a lady whose beauty filled him with awe. She curtsied to him, and then held out her hands in supplication.

"Truly, she is the most beautiful lady on earth. My quarrel could not be better chosen," he said.

"Sir, you may cease looking at the lady, and look to your arms instead. She is not for you, nor shall she be," said the Red Knight grimly.

"Sir, it would seem that although you hold the lady, she is not yours, and therefore your love for her is nothing but folly. Now that I have seen her and I know that I love her, by the grace of God, I shall win her for myself."

"Sir, are you not warned by the array of corpses hung from the trees—your predecessors, who spoke as you do?"

"No, I am not. Rather am I filled with anger and contempt, and understand well why the lady does not love you. And for myself, I wish only to fight you to the death and put an end to your murderous ways. Nor shall I feel any of that remorse in overcoming you which I have felt in the past for more honorable opponents."

"Sir, make ready—enough of your words!"

They jousted, and both crashed to the ground with such violence, and lay stunned

---

5. **marches:** borderlands.
6. **sounds of minstrelsy:** music (sounds made by minstrels, or musicians).

for so long, that the onlookers supposed that they had broken their necks. However, they recovered, and drawing their swords, chopped at each other with heavy, deliberate blows, beneath which one or the other would occasionally stagger. So they fought until well past noon, when they paused for a moment to recover their breath. Both were streaming with blood from their wounds, panting, and momentarily exhausted as they leaned on their shields.

Beneath the steady rain of blows their shields were chipped and their armor and mail had given way in many places; and Sir Gareth soon learned, to his cost, to defend them from the shrewd blows of his opponent. Several times one or the other fell to the ground, half stunned by a blow, whereon the other would leap on top of him; and more than once in the ensuing scuffle they exchanged swords.

At eventide they agreed to rest, and sat on two molehills while their pages unlaced their helmets so that they should be refreshed by the cool breeze. Sir Gareth looked up to the tower, and seeing the lady, was inspired with fresh courage:

"Sir, let us continue; to the death!"

"To the death!" the Red Knight responded.

Despite their many wounds, they continued the fight with fresh vigor, until with two skillful blows the Red Knight first knocked the sword from Sir Gareth's hand, and then sent him spinning to the ground, Leaping on top of him, the Red Knight started unlacing his helmet, when suddenly Lady Lynet cried out:

"Alas! Sir Gareth, your lady weeps with despair, and my own heart is heavy."

Sir Gareth responded with a tremendous thrust of his body and succeeded in overturning his opponent, then, reaching swiftly for his sword, confronted him once more. A new

and desperate battle ensued, as each strained to the limits of his strength to overmatch the other. Then it was Sir Gareth who sent his opponent's sword flying from his hand, and following it up with a hail of blows on the helmet, knocked him senseless to the ground, where he sprang on top of him. He had just unlaced his helmet to behead him when the Red Knight cried aloud:

"Most noble knight, I beg for mercy!"

"Sir, how can I honorably spare you, when you have murdered so many courageous knights who yielded to you?"

"Sir, there was a reason for that, if you will only allow me to tell you."

"Speak on."

"Once I loved a lady whose brethren had all been killed by Sir Launcelot or Sir Gawain; and it was at her bidding that I fought with every knight who passed this way from King Arthur's court, and hung by the neck those whom I overcame. And to this day I have been waiting for either Sir Launcelot or Sir Gawain to mete[7] her final revenge. And to accomplish this purpose, I have been enchanted, so that each day my strength increases until noon, when it is seven times that of other men, after which it wanes again."

Meanwhile the Red Knight's earls and barons had gathered round, and now they threw themselves on their knees and begged Sir Gareth to spare him:

"Sir, surely nothing can be gained by his death, nor can the dead be brought to life again. But spare him and he shall pay you homage, and learn to atone for his misdeeds."

"My lords, for your asking I will spare the Red Knight; and in my heart I can find some room for forgiveness, since what he did was at his lady's bidding. But these are my condi-

---

7. **mete:** dole out.

tions: that first he shall yield to Lady Lyoness, making full redress for the damage done to her, and then go to King Arthur's court and yield to Sir Launcelot and Sir Gawain, confessing his enmity toward them."

"Sir, I thank you, and will most certainly fulfill your conditions."

For the next ten days, the Red Knight entertained Sir Gareth and the lady in his pavilion, where the lady treated their wounds. Then, in accordance with his oath, he first yielded to Lady Lyoness and then rode to King Arthur's court, where, in the presence of all, he yielded to Sir Launcelot and Sir Gawain, recounting fully his own misdeeds and defeat at the hands of Sir Gareth, whose progress through the Passage Perelous he also described.

"I wonder," said Arthur, "of whose blood he was born, for certainly he has proved himself a noble knight since he ate in our kitchen."

"Sire, it is no marvel, for such courage and endurance as his surely stem from noble blood," said Sir Launcelot.

"Sir Launcelot, it would seem that you already know the secret of his birth?"

"Sire, I must admit that I do. I demanded to know before making him a knight, but I have been sworn to secrecy."

Sir Gareth, meanwhile, had asked Lady Lynet if he could not see her sister.

"Sir, most certainly you shall," she replied.

Sir Gareth armed and mounted and rode toward the castle, but as he did so, he was astonished to see the gate being closed and the drawbridge raised. Then Lady Lyoness spoke to him from one of the castle windows:

"Go your way, good knight, for you shall not have my love until you have won further fame; therefore you must strive for another year. Return to me then, and I will tell you more."

"My lady, I had not expected such thanks

from one for whom I have already striven so hard, and for whom, alas! I was willing to shed the last drop of my blood."

"Worthy knight, be assured that I love you for your brave deeds, and go forth with a glad heart. Soon the twelve months will pass, and, in the meantime, do not doubt that I shall be faithful to you."

Sir Gareth rode into the forest, bitterly unhappy and careless of direction, his dwarf following. That night he lodged in a humble cottage, but was unable to sleep. He continued his aimless journey all the next day, and that night came to a marsh where, feeling sleepy, he lay on his shield, while his dwarf watched over him.

crept up on the dwarf, seized him suddenly, and tucked him under his arm. However, the dwarf roared lustily, and Sir Gareth awoke in time to see him disappearing in the arms of a black knight.

Arming himself hastily, Sir Gareth mounted and pursued them as best he could, but with great difficulty, owing to his ignorance of the lay of the land. All night he rode across wild moors, over steep hills, and through dense forest, and frequently his horse stumbled, nearly throwing him. But at dawn he came to a woodland path, and seeing a forester, asked him if he had seen a black knight riding that way, with a dwarf behind him.

"Sir, I have. It was Sir Gryngamour, whose castle lies two miles further on. But I should beware of him, for once provoked he is a dangerous enemy."

Meanwhile Sir Gryngamour had taken the dwarf to his castle, where Lady Lyoness was cross-examining him.

"Dwarf, we wish to know the secret of your master's birth; and if you would prefer not to starve in the castle dungeon, you had better tell us. Who was his father, and who his mother, and whence does he come?"

"My lady, I am not ashamed to tell you that my master is Sir Gareth, the son of King Lot of Orkney and Queen Margawse, King Arthur's sister. Furthermore he is such a knight that he will soon destroy your lands and bring this castle tumbling about your ears if you do not release me."

"As for that, I think we need not trouble ourselves," said Lady Lyoness. "But let us go now and dine."

In honor of his sister's visit, Sir Gryngamour had ordered a splendid banquet, so they all sat down and dined merrily.

"My dear sister," said Lady Lynet, "you know I can well believe that your paramour is of noble birth, for throughout our journey

As soon as Sir Gareth had ridden into the forest, the Lady Lyoness had summoned her brother, Sir Gryngamour.

"My dear brother, I need your help. Would you ride after Sir Beaumains, and when you find an opportunity, kidnap his dwarf? I am in difficulties because I do not know whether or not Sir Beaumains is of noble birth, and until I know, naturally, I cannot love him. But I feel certain that we can frighten his dwarf into telling us."

Sir Gryngamour prepared to do as his sister asked, and cladding himself entirely in black armor, and mounting a black horse, followed them faithfully until they came to the marsh. Then, as soon as Sir Gareth was asleep, he

through the Passage Perelous, in scorn of what I assumed to be his low birth, I taunted him unmercifully, and never once did he rebuke me. And certainly, as you yourself have witnessed, his feats at arms are unexampled."

At this moment Sir Gareth rode up to the castle gate with his sword drawn, and shouted in a tremendous voice:

"Sir Gryngamour, treacherous knight that you are, deliver my dwarf to me at once."

"Sir, that I shall not," Sir Gryngamour replied through the window.

"Coward! Come out and fight for him, then."

"Very well," Sir Gryngamour said.

"My dear brother, not so fast!" said Lady Lyoness. "I think Sir Gareth could have his dwarf. Now that I know who he is, I can love him, and certainly I am indebted to him for releasing me from the Red Knight. Therefore let us entertain him, but I shall disguise myself so that he will not know me."

"My dear sister, just as you wish," said Sir Gryngamour, and then to Sir Gareth: "Sir, I beg your pardon for taking your dwarf. Now we know that your name, as well as your deeds, commends you, we invite you to accept hospitality at the castle."

"And my dwarf?" Sir Gareth shouted.

"Most certainly you shall have him," Sir Gryngamour replied; and then, accompanied by the dwarf, he went to the castle gate and, taking Sir Gareth by the hand, led him into the hall, where his wife welcomed him.

"Ah, my good dwarf, what a hunt I have had for you!" said Sir Gareth.

Presently Lady Lynet appeared with her sister, who had dressed in all her finery, and disguised herself as a princess. Minstrels were summoned, and amid dancing and singing Lady Lyoness set out to win the love of Sir Gareth. She succeeded, and was herself enrap-
tured by him, so that before long ardent looks and tender words passed between them. Sir Gareth was completely deceived by her disguise, and several times wished secretly to himself that his paramour at the Castle Dangerous were as beautiful and as gracious.

At supper neither of the young lovers could eat, both being hungry only for the looks and words of the other. Sir Gryngamour noticed this, and after supper took Lady Lyoness aside and spoke to her:

"Dear sister, it appears that you love the young Sir Gareth, and certainly his noble blood and valor commend him. If you wish to pledge yourself to him, and I could think of none worthier, I will persuade him to stay at my castle."

"Dear brother, not only is what you say true, but also I am beholden to him more than to any man living."

Then Sir Gryngamour went to Sir Gareth and spoke to him:

"Sir, I could not but observe the semblance of love between you and my sister; and if this should be founded on true feeling on your part, as it is on hers, I should like to welcome you to stay in my castle for as long as it please you."

"Sir, you make me the happiest man on earth; I thank you."

"Good! Then that is arranged; and I can promise you that my sister will be here to entertain you, both day and night."

"Sir, again I thank you. In fact I have sworn to remain in this country for twelve months, and your castle has the advantage that should King Arthur, my liege, wish to find me, he will be able to do so readily."

Sir Gareth returned to Lady Lyoness, and she now revealed to him her true identity, and admitted that it was at her instigation that his dwarf had been kidnapped, so that she could discover the secret of his birth before declaring herself. Sir Gareth was overjoyed, and there followed an exchange of vows.

At Pentecost, each of the knights whom Sir Gareth had overcome went to Caerleon to surrender to Arthur: Sir Pertolope, the Green Knight, with his fifty retainers; Sir Perymones, the Puce Knight, with his sixty retainers; Sir Persaunte, the Indigo Knight, with his hundred and fifty retainers; and Sir Ironside, the Red Knight, with his five hundred retainers.

Arthur's amazement grew as each of the brothers in turn related how he had been overcome by the knight called Beaumains; also Arthur was delighted, for the five brothers had been among his most implacable enemies. Then he noticed that Sir Perarde, the Black Knight, had not come, and the Green Knight went on to describe how Beaumains had killed him in combat; also the two brothers, Sir Arnolde and Sir Gerarde le Brewse, whom Beaumains had killed at the river. The death of the Black Knight was regretted by all, and Arthur promised to make the four remaining brothers fellows of the Round Table as soon as Sir Beaumains returned.

The whole company now sat down to enjoy the banquet, but no sooner were they seated than Queen Margawse of Orkney arrived, attended by her royal suite. Her sons—Sir Gawain, Sir Aggravayne, and Sir Gaheris—at once left their places and knelt down to receive her blessing, as none of them had seen her for twelve years.

When all were seated once more, Queen Margawse inquired after her youngest son, Sir Gareth, and told Arthur frankly that word had reached her that he had been kept in the kitchen for a year in the charge of Sir Kay, who had dubbed him Beaumains and treated him with the utmost disrespect.

It was now clear to Arthur that Beaumains was none other than Sir Gareth, and so he described to his sister how Sir Gareth had come without revealing his identity and asked for the three gifts: to eat in his kitchen, to pursue the quest of Lady Lyoness, and to be knighted by Sir Launcelot.

"Dear brother," said Queen Margawse, "I can well believe it of him, for even as a child he always displayed a remarkable wit, and was wont to go his own way. And perhaps Sir Kay's scornful name is not so inept after all, for certainly since he was knighted he has won great honor by the use of his hands. But now how shall we find him again?"

"I pray you, let me go in search of him," cried Sir Gawain, "for I too was in complete ignorance of the fact that he was my brother."

"I think that will not be necessary," said Sir Launcelot. "Surely our best plan would be to send for Lady Lyoness, who is certain to know his whereabouts."

On Michaelmas Day[8] the Archbishop of Canterbury married Sir Gareth to Lady Lyoness and, at Arthur's request, Sir Gaheris to Lady Lynet (or Lady Saveage), and Sir Aggravayne to their niece, Lady Lawrell. When the triple wedding was over, the knights whom Sir Gareth had overcome arrived with their followers to swear him allegiance.

---

8. **Michaelmas** (mĭk′əl-məs) **Day**: feast of the archangel Michael, held on September 29.

FOR STUDY AND DISCUSSION

1. According to the code of chivalry, a knight was expected at all times to be courteous. How do Launcelot and Gawain fulfill this requirement by their treatment of Beaumains? How does Kay show himself, by his treatment of Beaumains, to be unchivalrous?

2. Even as a mere scullery boy, Beaumains demonstrates abilities that hint at his true identity. What noble traits of character and physical prowess does the young Beaumains exhibit?

3. One aspect of medieval society pictured in this tale is the sharp division that existed between social classes. The upper class, made up of knights, ladies, and royalty, was the master of the lower class, made up of common working people. Socializing and marriage between classes was almost never allowed. How is this division between classes illustrated by the attitudes of Sir Kay, Lady Lynet, and Lady Lyoness toward Beaumains?

4. What other stories or films can you name in which the hero or heroine disguises his or her true identity? Why do you think this kind of story has such wide appeal?

5. What is comic about this old story?

THE MEDIEVAL ROMANCE

Malory's tales are *romances*, a form of literature popular throughout Europe during the Middle Ages. Certain features characterize the medieval romance:

1. A romance is about the adventures of knights and the institution of chivalry. Romances are concerned with the exploits of kings, queens, and knights—not with common, ordinary people.

2. A romance does not take place in a realistic setting, but in idealized worlds—in imaginary castles, gardens, and forests. (No one in a romance has to worry about the price of potatoes or catching a cold.)

3. A romance contains mysterious, magical, and supernatural events.

4. A romance hero or heroine is braver, nobler, and more honorable than an ordinary human. Often the hero or heroine has the use of magic or other extraordinary powers.

5. A romance hero or heroine will often put on a lowly disguise to conceal his or her true identity.

6. A romance hero or heroine is often motivated by romantic love.

7. A romance pits the forces of good against the forces of evil.

Look back at the two excerpts you have just read from Malory's *Morte d'Arthur.* See if you can find examples in the text of each of these characteristics.

Some of these characteristics of the medieval romance survive even today. Perhaps you can name some present-day stories or movies that reflect the qualities of a medieval romance.

LANGUAGE AND VOCABULARY

Reading Midland Dialect

When Sir Thomas Malory wrote the story of King Arthur, he used the language spoken by the people of London during the fifteenth century. These people spoke a form of Midland dialect. For several centuries before Malory's time, English was divided into several dialects. By writing in the Midland dialect, Malory helped that dialect become the basis for modern English.

William Caxton, the first Englishman to use the new printing press, published an edition of Malory's *Morte d'Arthur* in 1485. Here is a sample of Malory's prose as Caxton printed it.

It befel in the dayes of Vther Pendragon when he was kynge of all Englond/ and ſo regned that there was a myȝty duke of Cornewaill that helde warre ageynſt hym long tyme/ And the duke was called the duke of Tyntagil/ and ſo by meanes kynge Vther ſend for this duk/

Read this paragraph aloud, if you can. Then try to rewrite it in modern English. Note that the writers of the Midland dialect used an alphabet somewhat different from ours. They wrote a v for *u*, a ſ for *s*, and a ȝ for *gh*.

FOR COMPOSITION

Writing an Explanation

These two selections by Malory give an ideal picture of chivalry. The idea of chivalry was developed in France as a code of conduct for horse soldiers, or cavalry. In fact, the word *chivalry* is derived from the French word for horse, *cheval*. Chivalry in practice did not always work as ideally as Malory pictures it. Malory's tales, however, do give the modern reader a good idea of the civilizing goals that chivalry stood for. The idea of chivalry was kept alive even after the medieval world vanished, and was glorified in the works of later writers such as Edmund Spenser, Sir Walter Scott, and Alfred, Lord Tennyson.

Drawing upon what you have learned from these tales by Malory, write a short essay in which you explain what you think chivalry meant. If you wish to look further into the subject, refer to an encyclopedia or history book. Tell which aspects of chivalry, if any, you think are still alive today. Which aspects of chivalry do you think are gone forever?

ABOUT THE AUTHOR

Sir Thomas Malory (?–1471), who led an adventurous life but apparently not a chivalrous one, has been the subject of considerable research. Modern scholars have been able to piece together a number of the facts of his life. They have found, for example, that he was a knight who fought in the Hundred Years' War in France, and that he was a member of the British Parliament in 1445.

The greatest impact on Malory's life came from the series of disastrous civil wars fought from 1455 to 1485 between the supporters of the two great families that claimed the right to rule all of England, the House of Lancaster and the House of York. Malory was caught up in the violence of this political conflict. In 1451 he was imprisoned for a long list of offenses. Though he escaped twice, he spent the last years of his life in prison, and there, in 1469–1470, he compiled *Morte d'Arthur*.

Each age has read its own concerns into the King Arthur legend, and a main concern of Victorian England—Tennyson's England—was morality. It is not surprising, then, that when Tennyson wrote about Arthur in *Idylls of the King*, he told the story as the rise and fall of a moral hero and of a moral idea.

In Tennyson's version of the legend, as in Malory's, the fall of the Round Table begins when the love between Lancelot and Guinevere is discovered. For Tennyson, this disloyal love is a destructive force that undermines the high moral standards of Arthur's court. How can others keep the faith, Tennyson asks, if the noblest man and woman do not? The knights begin to quarrel among themselves, and Arthur's

The castle of Camelot. From a nineteenth-century edition of *Idylls of the King*, illustrated by Gustave Doré (1832–1883).

nephew, Sir Modred, plots to overthrow him. Lancelot and Guinevere are forced to flee, he to his castle in France and she to a convent. Arthur is challenged by the rebel Modred and goes forth to meet him in his last great battle.

This selection takes up the story after Arthur's battle with Modred. All the knights of the Round Table have been killed except the faithful Sir Bedivere. Arthur has killed Modred in combat but has himself been mortally wounded. Close to death, Arthur is moved by Bedivere to a chapel near a lake. The selection begins just after Arthur has commanded Sir Bedivere to take his sword Excalibur and throw it into the water. This brilliant sword had been given to Arthur by a magical Lady of the Lake.

The Passing of Arthur

Alfred, Lord Tennyson

To him replied the bold Sir Bedivere:
"It is not meet,° Sir King, to leave thee thus,
Aidless, alone, and smitten through the helm—
A little thing may harm a wounded man;
Yet I thy hest° will all perform at full, 5
Watch what I see, and lightly bring thee word."

So saying, from the ruined shrine he stepped,
And in the moon athwart° the place of tombs,
Where lay the mighty bones of ancient men,
Old knights, and over them the sea-wind sang 10
Shrill, chill, with flakes of foam. He, stepping down
By zigzag paths, and juts of pointed rock,
Came on the shining levels of the lake.

There drew he forth the brand° Excalibur,
And o'er him, drawing it, the winter moon, 15
Brightening the skirts of a long cloud, ran forth
And sparkled keen with frost against the hilt;
For all the haft° twinkled with diamond sparks,
Myriads of topaz-lights, and jacinth°-work

2. **meet:** right.

5. **hest:** command.

8. **athwart:** across.

14. **brand:** sword.

18. **haft:** handle.

19. **jacinth:** semiprecious stone, orange in color.

Of subtlest jewelry. He gazed so long   20
That both his eyes were dazzled as he stood,
This way and that dividing the swift mind,
In act to throw: but at the last it seemed
Better to leave Excalibur concealed
There in the many-knotted waterflags,°   25   **25. waterflags:** a kind of iris.
That whistled stiff and dry about the marge.°   **26. marge:** margin (edge) of the
So strode he back slow to the wounded King.   lake.

    Then spake King Arthur to Sir Bedivere:
"Hast thou performed my mission which I gave?
What is it thou hast seen? or what hast heard?"   30

    And answer made the bold Sir Bedivere:
"I heard the ripple washing in the reeds,
And the wild water lapping on the crag."

    To whom replied King Arthur, faint and pale:
"Thou hast betrayed thy nature and thy name,   35
Not rendering true answer, as beseemed
Thy fealty,° nor like a noble knight;   **37. fealty:** duty.
For surer sign had followed, either hand,
Or voice, or else a motion of the mere.°   **39. mere:** body of water.
This is a shameful thing for men to lie.   40
Yet now, I charge thee, quickly go again,
As thou art lief° and dear, and do the thing   **42. lief:** loved.
I bade thee, watch, and lightly bring me word."

    Then went Sir Bedivere the second time
Across the ridge, and paced beside the mere,   45
Counting the dewy pebbles, fixed in thought;
But when he saw the wonder of the hilt,
How curiously° and strangely chased,° he smote   **48. curiously:** wondrously; skill-
His palms together, and he cried aloud: fully.   **chased:** decorated with a
                                                                         raised design.

    "And if indeed I cast the brand away,   50
Surely a precious thing, one worthy note,
Should thus be lost for ever from the earth,
Which might have pleased the eyes of many men.
What good should follow this, if this were done?
What harm, undone? Deep harm to disobey,   55
Seeing obedience is the bond of rule.
Were it well to obey then, if a king demand

An act unprofitable, against himself?
The King is sick, and knows not what he does.
What record, or what relic of my lord   60
Should be to aftertime, but empty breath
And rumors of a doubt? But were this kept,
Stored in some treasure-house of mighty kings,
Someone might show it at a joust of arms,
Saying: 'King Arthur's sword, Excalibur,   65
Wrought by the lonely maiden of the Lake.
Nine years she wrought it, sitting in the deeps
Upon the hidden bases of the hills.'
So might some old man speak in the aftertime
To all the people, winning reverence.   70
But now much honor and much fame were lost."

   So spake he, clouded with his own conceit,°   72. **conceit**: idea; thought.
And hid Excalibur the second time,
And so strode back slow to the wounded King.

   Then spoke King Arthur, breathing heavily: 75
"What is it thou hast seen? or what hast heard?"

   And answer made the bold Sir Bedivere:
"I heard the water lapping on the crag,
And the long ripple washing in the reeds."

   To whom replied King Arthur, much in wrath: 80
"Ah miserable and unkind, untrue,
Unknightly, traitor-hearted! Woe is me!
Authority forgets a dying king,
Laid widowed of the power in his eye
That bowed the will. I see thee what thou art,   85
For thou, the latest-left of all my knights,
In whom should meet the offices of all,
Thou wouldst betray me for the precious hilt;
Either from lust of gold, or like a girl
Valuing the giddy pleasure of the eyes.   90
Yet, for a man may fail in duty twice,
And the third time may prosper, get thee hence;
But, if thou spare to fling Excalibur,
I will arise and slay thee with my hands."

Then quickly rose Sir Bedivere, and ran, 95
And, leaping down the ridges lightly, plunged
Among the bulrush beds, and clutched the sword,
And strongly wheeled and threw it. The great brand
Made lightnings in the splendor of the moon,
And flashing round and round, and whirled in an arch, 100
Shot like a streamer of the northern morn,°
Seen where the moving isles of winter shock°
By night, with noises of the Northern Sea.
So flashed and fell the brand Excalibur:
But ere he dipped the surface, rose an arm 105
Clothed in white samite,° mystic, wonderful,
And caught him° by the hilt, and brandished him
Three times, and drew him under in the mere.
And lightly went the other to the King.

Then spoke King Arthur, drawing thicker breath: 110
"Now see I by thine eyes that this is done.
Speak out: what is it thou hast heard, or seen?"

And answer made the bold Sir Bedivere:
"Sir King, I closed mine eyelids, lest the gems
Should blind my purpose, for I never saw, 115
Nor shall see, here or elsewhere, till I die,
Not though I live three lives of mortal men,
So great a miracle as yonder hilt.
Then with both hands I flung him, wheeling him;
But when I looked again, behold an arm, 120
Clothed in white samite, mystic, wonderful,
That caught him by the hilt, and brandished him
Three times, and drew him under in the mere."

And answer made King Arthur, breathing hard:
"My end draws nigh; 'tis time that I were gone. 125
Make broad thy shoulders to receive my weight,
And bear me to the margin; yet I fear
My wound hath taken cold, and I shall die."

So saying, from the pavement he half rose,
Slowly, with pain, reclining on his arm, 130
And looking wistfully with wide blue eyes
As in a picture. Him Sir Bedivere
Remorsefully regarded through his tears,

101. **streamer . . . morn:** the aurora borealis, or "northern lights."
102. **where . . . shock:** where the icebergs collide.

106. **samite:** heavy silk cloth woven with gold and silver.
107. **him:** Excalibur.

And would have spoken, but he found not words;
Then took with care, and kneeling on one knee,   135
O'er both his shoulders drew the languid hands,
And rising bore him through the place of tombs.

But, as he walked, King Arthur panted hard,
Like one that feels a nightmare on his bed
When all the house is mute. So sighed the King,   140
Muttering and murmuring at his ear, "Quick, quick!
I fear it is too late, and I shall die."
But the other swiftly strode from ridge to ridge,
Clothed with his breath, and looking, as he walked,
Larger than human on the frozen hills.   145
He heard the deep° behind him, and a cry   146. **deep:** open sea.
Before. His own thought drove him like a goad.
Dry clashed his harness° in the icy caves   148. **harness:** armor and other
And barren chasms, and all to left and right   equipment.
The bare black cliff clanged round him, as he based   150
His feet on juts of slippery crag that rang
Sharp-smitten with the dint° of armèd° heels—   152. **dint:** blow. **armèd:** He wore
And on a sudden, lo, the level lake,   steel boots.
And the long glories of the winter moon!

Then saw they how there hove° a dusky barge,   155   155. **hove:** moved into sight.
Dark as a funeral scarf from stem to stern,
Beneath them; and descending they were ware
That all the decks were dense with stately forms,
Black-stoled, black-hooded, like a dream—by° these   159. **by:** beside.
Three Queens with crowns of gold—and from them rose   160
A cry that shivered to the tingling stars,
And, as it were one voice, an agony
Of lamentation, like a wind that shrills
All night in a waste land, where no one comes,
Or hath come, since the making of the world.   165

Then murmured Arthur, "Place me in the barge."
So to the barge they came. There those three Queens
Put forth their hands, and took the King, and wept.
But she that rose the tallest of them all
And fairest, laid his head upon her lap,   170
And loosed the shattered casque,° and chafed his hands,   171. **casque:** helmet.
And called him by his name, complaining loud.
And dropping bitter tears against a brow

Striped with dark blood: for all his face was white
And colorless, and like the withered moon   175
Smote by the fresh beam of the springing east;
And all his greaves° and cuisses° dashed with drops
Of onset;° and the light and lustrous curls—
That made his forehead like a rising sun
High from the dais-throne°—were parched with dust;   180
Or, clotted into points and hanging loose,
Mixed with the knightly growth that fringed his lips.
So like a shattered column lay the King;
Not like that Arthur who, with lance in rest,
From spur to plume a star of tournament,   185
Shot through the lists° at Camelot, and charged
Before the eyes of ladies and of kings.

   Then loudly cried the bold Sir Bedivere:
"Ah! my Lord Arthur, whither shall I go?
Where shall I hide my forehead and my eyes?   190
For now I see the true old times are dead,
When every morning brought a noble chance,
And every chance brought out a noble knight.
Such times have been not since the light that led
The holy Elders° with the gift of myrrh.   195
But now the whole Round Table is dissolved
Which was an image of the mighty world;
And I, the last, go forth companionless,
And the days darken round me, and the years,
Among new men, strange faces, other minds."   200

   And slowly answered Arthur from the barge:
"The old order changeth, yielding place to new,
And God fulfills himself in many ways,
Lest one good custom should corrupt the world.
Comfort thyself; what comfort is in me?   205
I have lived my life, and that which I have done
May He within himself make pure! but thou,
If thou shouldst never see my face again,
Pray for my soul. More things are wrought by prayer
Than this world dreams of. Wherefore, let thy voice   210
Rise like a fountain for me night and day.
For what are men better than sheep or goats
That nourish a blind life within the brain,
If, knowing God, they lift not hands of prayer

177. **greaves:** armor that covers the shins. **cuisses** (kwĭs′əz): armor that covers the thighs.
178. **onset:** blood, or the "onset" of death.
180. **dais-throne:** throne raised on a low platform.

186. **lists:** here, the jousting field. .

195. **The holy Elders:** the Magi, who brought gold and frankincense and myrrh to the infant Jesus (see Matthew 2:1–12).

Both for themselves and those who call them friend? 215
For so the whole round earth is every way
Bound by gold chains about the feet of God.
But now farewell. I am going a long way
With these thou seest—if indeed I go
(For all my mind is clouded with a doubt)— 220
To the island-valley of Avilion;°

221. **Avilion:** Paradise, in Celtic mythology.

Where falls not hail, or rain, or any snow,
Nor ever wind blows loudly; but it lies
Deep-meadowed, happy, fair with orchard lawns
And bowery hollows crowned with summer sea, 225
Where I will heal me of my grievous wound."

So said he, and the barge with oar and sail
Moved from the brink, like some full-breasted swan
That, fluting a wild carol° ere her death,
Ruffles her pure cold plume, and takes the flood° 230

229. **wild carol:** The swan is believed to sing just before death.
230. **flood:** deep water.

With swarthy webs. Long stood Sir Bedivere
Revolving many memories, till the hull
Looked one black dot against the verge of dawn,
And on the mere the wailing died away.

But when that moan had passed for evermore, 235
The stillness of the dead world's winter dawn
Amazed him, and he groaned, "The King is gone."
And therewithal came on him the weird rhyme,
"From the great deep to the great deep he goes."

Whereat he slowly turned and slowly clomb 240
The last hard footstep of that iron crag;
Thence marked the black hull moving yet, and cried,
"He passes to be King among the dead,
And after healing of his grievous wound
He comes again; but—if he come no more— 245
O me, be yon dark Queens in yon black boat,
Who shrieked and wailed, the three whereat we gazed
On that high day, when, clothed with living light,
They stood before his throne in silence, friends
Of Arthur, who should help him at his need?" 250

Then from the dawn it seemed there came, but faint
As from beyond the limit of the world,
Like the last echo born of a great cry,

Sounds as if some fair city were one voice
Around a king returning from his wars.   255

　　Thereat once more he moved about, and clomb
Ev'n to the highest he could climb, and saw,
Straining his eyes beneath an arch of hand,
Or thought he saw, the speck that bare the King,
Down that long water opening on the deep   260
Somewhere far off, pass on and on, and go
From less to less and vanish into light.
And the new sun rose bringing the new year.

FOR STUDY AND DISCUSSION

1. What reasons does Bedivere give for not throwing Excalibur into the lake? What motives does Arthur accuse Bedivere of having? How close to the truth is Arthur?

2. After Bedivere fails a second time to carry out Arthur's command, Arthur laments: "Authority forgets a dying king." What emotion does this line convey? How does it represent a major point of the poem?

3. As Tennyson describes Arthur being placed in the barge, he writes: "So like a shattered column lay the King." How is the wounded Arthur like a "shattered column"?

4. What does Bedivere fear will be lost when Arthur dies? What does Arthur say to comfort him?

5. In the next-to-last line of the poem, Tennyson says that the barge bearing Arthur vanished into light. This light then becomes a new sun, in the last line, bringing in a new year. With this image, what does the poet suggest about the future of Arthur and the ideals he stood for?

FOR COMPOSITION

Supporting an Opinion

In early Celtic legend it was said that Arthur would someday return to lead his people in battle once again against their enemies. This idea of the leader who will return is echoed in lines 243–245 of Tennyson's poem, where Bedivere says:

> "He passes to be King among the dead,
> And after healing of his grievous wound
> He comes again . . ."

These lines express a feeling of optimism about the future that has always been a part of the Arthur legend. But many readers have pointed out that a strong note of pessimism or doubt is also struck in Tennyson's poem.

Write a short essay in which you give your overall impression of this story of the death of Arthur. Is it optimistic, or pessimistic and doubtful? Quote lines from the poem to support your opinion. Consider specifically the implications of lines 202–204, 234, and 245.

ABOUT THE AUTHOR

Alfred, Lord Tennyson (1809–1892) was brought up, with his seven brothers and four sisters, in the comfortable rectory of an English country town. The children were encouraged to draw on the family's extensive library, and they grew up knowing far more about knights, giants, and princesses than about the busy world a few miles distant.

At seven, young Alfred was sent to a grammar school. He was unhappy there and later returned home, where his father prepared him for college. At Cambridge, Tennyson was not an exceptional student, and in fact never received a degree, but he read widely and soon established himself as a masterful poet.

All his life Tennyson tended to withdraw from society. He devoted himself to reading, to enjoying nature, but above all, to writing poetry. Besides *Idylls of the King,* Tennyson wrote such great poems as *In Memoriam,* "The Lady of Shalott," and "Ulysses." Eight years before his death he was made a lord, a title he valued highly. Tennyson was England's chief spokesman during the reign of Queen Victoria, and was poet laureate for over forty years.

Practice in Reading and Writing

READING AND WRITING ABOUT LITERATURE

As you have read in the introduction to this unit, the
account of Arthur and his knights is one of the central
stories in Western literature. You have seen how three
writers turned to the Arthurian legend and told it in their
own words: Malory in the fifteenth century, Tennyson
in the nineteenth century, and White in our own twentieth
century.

John Steinbeck, an American writer who won both the
Pulitzer Prize and the Nobel Prize for literature, also wrote a
book about Arthur, which he called *The Acts of King Arthur
and His Noble Knights* (1976). Though Steinbeck's famous
realistic novels seem far removed from the romantic world
of knights and chivalry, the stories of Arthur had a dramatic
effect on Steinbeck.

A portion of Steinbeck's introduction to his version of the
Arthurian tales follows. After you have read these comments,
write a brief essay of your own, in which you explain
your own reactions to the Arthurian stories in this unit.
Perhaps you agree with Steinbeck; if so, cite the specific
stories and characters that appeal to you and explain why
they do so. Perhaps you disagree with Steinbeck and have
had an entirely different reaction to the Arthurian stories. If
this is the case, write a brief essay explaining what your own
reaction is, and tell why you feel this way.

> I remember that words—written or printed—were
> devils, and books, because they gave me pain, were my
> enemies.
>
> Some literature was in the air around me. The Bible I ab-
> sorbed through my skin. My uncles exuded Shakespeare, and
> *Pilgrim's Progress* was mixed with my mother's milk. But
> these things came into my ears. They were sounds, rhythms,
> figures. Books were printed demons—the tongs and thumb-

screws of outrageous persecution. And then, one day, an aunt gave me a book and fatuously ignored my resentment. I stared at the black print with hatred, and then, gradually, the pages opened and let me in. The magic happened. The Bible and Shakespeare and *Pilgrim's Progress* belonged to everyone. But this was mine— It was a cut version of the Caxton *Morte d'Arthur* of Thomas Malory. I loved the old spelling of the words—and the words no longer used. Perhaps a passionate love for the English language opened to me from this one book. I was delighted to find out paradoxes—that *cleave* means both to stick together and to cut apart; that *host* means both an enemy and a welcoming friend; that *king* and *gens* (people) stem from the same root. For a long time, I had a secret language—*yclept* and *hyght*, *wist*—and *accord* meaning peace, and *entente* meaning purpose, and *fyaunce* meaning promise. . . . But beyond the glorious and secret words—"And when the chylde is borne lete it be delyvered to me at yonder privy posterne uncrystened"—oddly enough I knew the words from whispering them to myself. The very strangeness of the language dyd me enchante, and vaulted me into an ancient scene.

And in that scene were all the vices that ever were—and courage and sadness and frustration, but particularly gallantry—perhaps the only single quality of man that the West has invented. I think my sense of right and wrong, my feeling of noblesse oblige, and any thought I may have against the oppressor and for the oppressed, came from this secret book. It did not outrage my sensibilities as nearly all the children's books did. . . . I was not frightened to find that there were evil knights, as well as noble ones. In my own town there were men who wore the clothes of virtue whom I knew to be bad. In pain or sorrow or confusion, I went back to my magic book. Children are violent and cruel—and good—and I was all of these—and all of these were in the secret book. If I could not choose my way at the crossroads of love and loyalty, neither could Lancelot. I could understand the darkness of Mordred because he was in me too; and there was some Galahad in me, but perhaps not enough. The Grail feeling was there, however, deep-planted, and perhaps always will be.

John Steinbeck
The Acts of King Arthur

For Further Reading

Baines, Keith, *Le Morte d'Arthur: King Arthur and the Knights of the Round Table* (paperback, Mentor, 1962)

All the tales of Arthur are included here, as told by Sir Thomas Malory and retold by Keith Baines in a modern idiom. The book includes the rousing adventures of Sir Launcelot du Lake, Sir Gareth, and Sir Tristram; the quest for the Holy Grail; the story of Launcelot and Gwynevere's tragic love affair; and, finally, the death of the king and the destruction of his noble ideal.

Jenkins, Elizabeth, *The Mystery of King Arthur* (Coward-McCann, 1975)

This beautifully illustrated book traces the development of the legend and proves its enduring popularity with artists and writers.

Lerner, Alan Jay, and Frederick Loewe, *Camelot* (Random House, 1961)

This musical comedy, based on T. H. White's *The Once and Future King*, had a successful Broadway run and was later made into a popular motion picture.

Picard, Barbara, *Stories of King Arthur and His Knights* (Walck, 1955)

This illustrated collection of the Arthurian romances is retold in lively contemporary language, especially for high-school readers.

Pyle, Howard, *Story of King Arthur and His Knights* (Grosset & Dunlap; paperback, Dover)

Pyle's illustrated version of the legend is now a classic.

Steinbeck, John, *The Acts of King Arthur and His Noble Knights* (Farrar, Straus and Giroux, 1976; paperback, Ballantine, 1977)

Steinbeck's aim was to keep the magic and wonder of the legend, but to set down the Arthur stories in plain, present-day speech for his own children. He also hoped to compete with the movies, comic strips, and TV serials, often the only places where young people find the Arthur tales today.

Stewart, Mary, *The Crystal Cave* (William Morrow, 1970; paperback, Fawcett, 1978)

This best-selling romantic novel centers on the life story of Merlin, the mysterious magician of King Arthur's court. According to legend, Merlin, as an old man, was seduced by a girl who robbed him of his powers and left him shut in his cave till the end of time.

Stewart, Mary, *The Hollow Hills* (William Morrow, 1973; paperback, Fawcett, 1978)

This novel tells how a king risked everything to produce an heir—and then rejected his only son. Here is the story of Arthur's perilous growth to manhood in fifth-century Britain, a world of fear and superstition, of flights to secret places in the hollow hills, and of sudden death.

Sutcliff, Rosemary, *Tristan and Iseult* (paperback, Penguin, 1976)

A gifted storyteller retells this tragic love story. Young Tristan, a knight of Arthur's court, falls in love with the beautiful Iseult, who is pledged to marry an older man.

Tennyson, Alfred, Lord, *Idylls of the King* (available in several paperback editions)

Tennyson wrote his own poetic versions of twelve of the Arthurian tales. These stories include "Merlin and Vivien," "Lancelot and Elaine," and "The Holy Grail." Many of Tennyson's idylls picture the wasteland of a once-ideal civilization, without conscience or love.

Twain, Mark, *A Connecticut Yankee in King Arthur's Court* (available in several paperback editions)

Twain's comic burlesque of the Arthurian romances tells of Hank Morgan's attempts to transform fifth-century Britain—a world of filth, superstition, poverty, and tyranny—into an enlightened republic.

White, T. H., *The Once and Future King* (Putnam's, 1958; paperback, Berkley Medallion)

The best-selling modernization of the Arthur legend, this book has become a contemporary classic. White's story, tragic and comic at the same time, traces Arthur's life from his boyhood days as a servant; to his triumphant days at Camelot, where his Queen eventually betrays him; to his last battle on the Salisbury plain.

History of the Drama

The origins of drama are obscure, but the form is probably as old as language itself. The first theater might have been a Stone Age campfire; the first actor-playwright, a person retelling the story of a hunt to other members of the tribe. All the ingredients were probably there: the suspenseful story, the conflict between hero and enemy, the tense hush in the audience, the climax, the satisfying ending.

Drama evolved through the ages. The drama of the early Greeks began as simple religious celebrations, but by the sixth and fifth centuries B.C., the Greeks were presenting their plays in huge, open-air amphitheaters. Costumed performers acted out the old Greek myths and legends, and the large audience spent all day at the theater, viewing a series of tragedies interspersed with comedies. When the center of Mediterranean civilization shifted from Greece to Rome,

DRAMA

A scene from *Medea*, an ancient Greek tragedy written by Euripides. A production of the Comedie Française.

An actor prepares for a production of *The Book of Job*.

there was a decline in the range and scope of the drama. Although the Romans enjoyed comedies and some tragedies, many of their plays were copied from those of the Greeks.

During the Middle Ages, drama was for a while confined to strolling minstrels and players, who sang or mimed their tales to small groups in marketplaces, fairs, or courts. Gradually, from the rich ceremonies of the medieval church grew another form of drama. As with the Greeks, this drama was connected at first to religious rituals. Bible stories were acted out, first by priests before the altar and later by actors on the steps of the cathedral. Biblical plays gave way to what were called "morality plays," in which actors pretended to be abstract qualities, such as vice, greed, or charity. These plays were enacted to teach certain morals or lessons. Eventually, as Greek and Roman manuscripts began to be rediscovered, the classical dramas were copied and restaged. By the end of the sixteenth century, the folk, religious, and classical elements of the theater had culminated in the dramas of William Shakespeare.

Since Shakespeare's time, drama has continued to take on varied forms, and certain forms have been associated with particular countries. Ever since the seventeenth century, the English have often used the stage to laugh at themselves and to criticize their own society. The Italians have produced grand opera. The French have produced plays that are, for the most part, cool, objective, and ironic—a theater of the mind. Toward the end of the nineteenth century, the Scandinavians produced a series of "social" dramas that were angry, hardheaded attacks on middle-class society. Americans became famous for the development of popular dramatic forms—musical comedies and movies, which made Broadway and Hollywood practically household terms.

Tragedy and Comedy

Over the centuries, plays have generally clustered around two poles: tragedy and comedy. These terms were first established by the Greeks. *Tragos* in Greek means "goat," and *oide,* "song," thus "goatsong." This suggests a primitive play in which an actor, dressed in goatskin, sang his lines. We do not

The actor Menander and three dramatic masks. A Roman relief based on a Greek original.
The Art Museum, Princeton University.

know much about these ancient "goatsongs," but we do know that as Greek drama developed, the word *tragedy* came to be applied to serious plays that depicted the fall and death of a noble character in conflict with forces beyond his or her control. It is not easy to say exactly what tragedy is, but it is clear that tragedy must have something to do with thought, with human decisions. A person who makes a series of foolish decisions and gets into trouble doesn't seem tragic. Tragedy requires that the hero or heroine make choices that lead to a situation from which there is no escape. Tragedy is the confrontation of human intelligence with forces that intelligence cannot cope with. We admire the tragic heroes and heroines for their struggles; we feel that perhaps we might do the same things; and we weep when we see them fall. When we leave a tragic play, our feeling is one of profound sadness. Yet we also feel our hearts lifted, because we have been reminded of the fact that people are capable of nobility of spirit, even in the face of overwhelming disaster.

The Greek word *komos* suggests a festive procession, and *oide,* as already mentioned, is a song. Most likely, in ancient Greece, this song was sung by a daring peasant who, with temporary immunity, poked fun at his ruler and let him know a few of his faults. It is thought that classical Greek comedy rose from these primitive beginnings, and eventually developed into a special form of theater in which a comic hero acted out a story that mocked social customs and procedures. The best comedy of all ages seems to have continued in this tradition. Comedy usually takes aim at society, advocates changes, and makes us laugh at its boldness and truthfulness. Both tragic and comic figures struggle against authority of some sort. In tragedy, the odds are usually unconquerable; in comedy, the hero or heroine is usually able to overthrow the authority figure and the play ends happily. One of the most popular comic plots is the one involving two lovers. In this plot, one of the lovers must overcome some obstacle—social or personal—to their marriage. Hollywood has been capable of finding endless variations on this popular comic plot.

In this unit you will find two tragedies: Sophocles' *Antigone,* first performed around 440 B.C. in Athens, and William Shakespeare's *Julius Caesar,* first performed in 1599 in London. Though tragedy and comedy are useful generalizations, literature refuses to be easily pigeonholed, as you will see from the American dramas included here. The famous American radio play *Invasion from Mars* was first broadcast on the Mercury Theater on the Air the night before Halloween 1938. Robert Anderson's realistic American drama *I Never Sang for My Father* opened on Broadway in January 1968.

Comedian Charlie Chaplin (1889–1977).

Sophocles and His Theater

Antigone

Irene Pappas as Antigone.

The theater for which *Antigone* was written was very different from the one we attend today. It resembled more what we would call a stadium. It was outdoors, and plays were presented during the daylight hours only. The Greeks were careful in choosing sites for their theaters, which were built on hillsides, preferably on those with a slight inward slope. This provided a natural semicircle, or amphitheater. Seats were built up in rows, either of earth and stone or of wood, to provide an arena, at the base of which plays could be performed. The area at the base was called the *orchestra*. The orchestra (so named because it was the place where the chorus chanted and danced) was also the place where the actors performed. There was no raised stage as there was later in Roman times.

The acoustics in these theaters were usually very fine, and people had little trouble hearing even in the highest rows of seats. The sound was also amplified by the large masks the actors wore. The chanting of the chorus also helped to carry the sound further. To aid viewing, the actors wore oversized, well-padded costumes, and boots with raised soles to add to their height. The masks not only were oversized but also had exaggerated features so that they could be seen clearly at large distances. Behind the orchestra was a painted wall called a *skene* (our word *scenery* comes from this word), through which the actors entered and exited. The actors, all of whom were men, masked and padded, moved in a stately and controlled fashion. We might think these actors were performing some stately ritual if we compared their acting to the realistic acting style of today's theater. The chorus would also strike us as artificial, and their chanting and dancing would add to our feeling of ritual. The chorus consisted of fifteen men with one spokesman, or leader, called the *choragos*. The chorus, usually representing the city elders, took part in the action of the play, reacting to what was happening as citizens might. But the chorus also commented on the action of the play and interpreted its meaning for the audience in a series of chanted poems, or odes.

The Greeks took their theater very seriously and we would be right to see it as part of a religious ritual. In fact, the plays were written for performance at great festivals held seasonally in honor of the god Dionysos, whose altar stood in the orchestra. New plays were written specifically for these festivals, competitions were held, and prizes awarded. Many playwrights entered the competitions, and plays were performed continuously for several days.

Sophocles (496?–406 B.C.) first competed for the prize in tragedy when he was twenty-seven; he won, defeating the great Aeschylus, then the most famous playwright in Athens. Sophocles is said to have had a fortunate life. He was born at Colonus of a wealthy family. He was given a traditional education in music, dancing, and gymnastics. When the Greeks defeated the Persians in 480 B.C., young Sophocles led the chorus in singing and dancing at the victory celebration. He is said to have been graceful and handsome, and to have had musical as well as dramatic gifts. Sophocles was also active in public life. He was twice elected general, served as a priest of the god Asclepius, and at eighty-three was appointed to a commission studying a revision of Athens' constitution.

It is probable that Sophocles wrote over one hundred twenty tragedies in his lifetime. Only seven remain to us today, but they are among the greatest plays ever written. Sophocles won many victories for his plays and was greatly respected by his fellow citizens; at his death he was given the honors of a hero. It is hard to imagine, given his tranquil and successful life, how Sophocles came by his great and deep understanding of human grief and suffering. It may be that the ancient myths of his people provided him with insight into the depths of human nature and its relationship to fate and to the gods.

Background of the Play

The story of the ill-fated royal house of Thebes is one of the mythical stories that Sophocles looked into most deeply. Three of his surviving plays are based on this tragic story: *Oedipus* (ĕd′ə-pəs) *the King*, *Oedipus at Colonus*, and *Antigone* (ăn-tĭg′ə-nē′).

An actor in *Oedipus the King*, at the Tyrone Guthrie Theater, Minneapolis.

The story begins when Laios (lā′əs), grandson of the founder of Thebes, is king, and Iocaste (yō-kăs′tə) the queen. Because of an impiety Laios has committed, an oracle proclaims that he will be slain by his own son. In an attempt to avoid this fate, Laios pierces and binds the feet of his infant son and abandons him on a nearby mountain. But the child is found by the shepherds of King Polybus (pä′lə-bəs) of Corinth. They bring the baby to their master who adopts him as his own son and names him Oedipus, which means "swollen foot." Polybus raises Oedipus as his heir. When Oedipus grows to manhood, he is told by another oracle that he is destined to slay his own father and marry his mother. As Laios had done, Oedipus attempts to avoid this fate. He leaves Corinth, but at a crossroads he meets a stranger; they quarrel, and Oedipus kills the man, not realizing that the stranger is his father, Laios.

In the meantime, a celebrated Sphinx has appeared at Thebes. This winged monster with the body of a lion and the face of a woman has been preying on travelers whom she challenges with a riddle. If they are unable to answer the riddle, they are thrown into the sea. The riddle goes like this: What creature has four feet, two feet, then three feet, but only one voice, and when it has the most feet, it is the weakest? Oedipus' answer (the correct one) is "man," who crawls on all fours as an infant, walks on two feet when grown, and needs a cane when old. Defeated by Oedipus, the Sphinx throws herself into the sea, and the Theban people welcome Oedipus as their savior. He learns that their king has recently died. They offer to make him king and give him Iocaste, their queen, for his wife. Thus Oedipus unknowingly marries his own mother, and the oracles he and Laios had tried to avoid are fulfilled.

Oedipus visits the Sphinx.
Base of an Attic cup.
The Vatican Museum.

Iocaste and Oedipus have four children—two daughters, Antigone and Ismene (ĭs-mē′nē), and two sons, Eteocles (ĭ-tē′ə-klēz′) and Polyneices (päl′ə-nī′sēz). They reign in Thebes in harmony for many years until a plague strikes the city. Oedipus sends his wife's brother, Creon, to consult the oracle to discover the cause of the plague. Creon brings word that Thebes is unclean because the murderer of the former king still lives there. Oedipus rashly promises that he will again make hidden things known, assuming that he can solve this problem as easily as he solved the riddle of the Sphinx. The blind Teiresias (tī-rē′sē-əs), a seer (or prophet), advises Oedipus not to seek for the murderer lest he discover that it is himself.

But Oedipus goes ahead with the investigation anyway, and gradually he learns the truth: that he has indeed murdered his father and married his own mother. Iocaste, in horror, commits suicide, and Oedipus blinds himself because he has failed to see the truth that could have saved him. Oedipus then asks to be sent into exile, but Creon says he must stay until the will of the gods has been revealed. Oedipus remains

A scene from *Oedipus the King*, performed at Epidaurus, Greece.

in Thebes for some years until Creon and the Theban elders decide he should be exiled. By this time, Oedipus wants to remain in Thebes, but his sons do nothing to help him. Oedipus goes off with his two daughters to wander as a beggar, cursing his ungrateful sons. The old man finally dies at peace in Colonus. When his daughters are assured that no mortal may approach the hidden tomb of their father, they return to Thebes.

Creon rules in Thebes until Oedipus' sons decide that they should have their father's throne. Creon sides with Eteocles, and Polyneices is exiled. But in exile, he raises a force among the Argives, his wife's people. These troops storm the seven gates of Thebes. At one of the gates, the brothers meet and slay each other, fulfilling their father's curse. Creon, still siding with Eteocles, has him buried with full state honors. But he decrees that Polyneices shall go unburied as an enemy of the state. This was a very harsh sentence in the eyes of the ancient Greeks because their holiest law required the performance of certain burial rites. The soul of a person whose corpse was left to decay in the open, and on whose behalf no wine was poured out for the gods, was condemned to eternal unrest.

As the play begins, it is the day after the battle. Antigone decides to defy Creon's decree and bury her brother.

The photographs that illustrate this play are scenes from Greek tragedies performed at Epidaurus, Greece, by the National Theater Group.

Antigone

Sophocles *Translated by Dudley Fitts and Robert Fitzgerald*

Characters

Antigone (ăn-tĭg′ə-nē′)⎫
Ismene (ĭs-mē′nē)   ⎬ daughters of Oedipus, former king of Thebes
Creon, king of Thebes, uncle of Antigone and Ismene
Haimon (hī′mən), Creon's son, engaged to Antigone
Eurydice (yōō-rĭd′ə-sē′), wife of Creon
Teiresias (tī-rē′sē-əs), a blind prophet
Chorus, made up of about fifteen elders of Thebes
Choragos, leader of the Chorus
A Boy, who leads Teiresias
A Sentry
Guards
Servants
A Messenger

Scene: *Before the palace of* Creon, *king of Thebes. A central double door, and two doors at the side. A platform extends the length of the stage, and from this platform three steps lead down into the orchestra, or chorus-ground.*
Time: *Dawn of the day after the repulse of the Argive army from the assault on Thebes.*

Prologue

[Antigone *and* Ismene *enter from the central door of the palace.*]

Antigone. Ismene, dear sister,
   You would think that we had already suffered enough
   For the curse on Oedipus:
   I cannot imagine any grief
   That you and I have not gone through. And now —   5
   Have they told you of the new decree of our King Creon?
Ismene. I have heard nothing: I know
   That two sisters lost two brothers, a double death
   In a single hour; and I know that the Argive army
   Fled in the night; but beyond this, nothing.   10

Antigone. I thought so. And that is why I wanted you
    To come out here with me. There is something we must do.
Ismene. Why do you speak so strangely?
Antigone. Listen, Ismene:
    Creon buried our brother Eteocles   15
    With military honors, gave him a soldier's funeral,
    And it was right that he should; but Polyneices,
    Who fought as bravely and died as miserably—
    They say that Creon has sworn
    No one shall bury him, no one mourn for him,   20
    But his body must lie in the fields, a sweet treasure
    For carrion birds to find as they search for food.
    That is what they say, and our good Creon is coming here
    To announce it publicly; and the penalty—
    Stoning to death in the public square!
                                        There it is,   25
    And now you can prove what you are:
    A true sister, or a traitor to your family.
Ismene. Antigone, you are mad! What could I possibly do?
Antigone. You must decide whether you will help me or not.
Ismene. I do not understand you. Help you in what?   30
Antigone. Ismene, I am going to bury him. Will you come?
Ismene. Bury him! You have just said the new law forbids it.
Antigone. He is my brother. And he is your brother, too.
Ismene. But think of the danger! Think what Creon will do!
Antigone. Creon is not strong enough to stand in my way.   35
Ismene. Ah sister!
    Oedipus died, everyone hating him
    For what his own search brought to light, his eyes
    Ripped out by his own hand; and Iocaste died,
    His mother and wife at once: she twisted the cords   40
    That strangled her life; and our two brothers died,
    Each killed by the other's sword. And we are left:
    But oh, Antigone,
    Think how much more terrible than these
    Our own death would be if we should go against Creon   45
    And do what he has forbidden! We are only women,
    We cannot fight with men, Antigone!
    The law is strong, we must give in to the law
    In this thing, and in worse. I beg the dead
    To forgive me, but I am helpless: I must yield   50
    To those in authority. And I think it is dangerous business
    To be always meddling.

Antigone.   If that is what you think,
  I should not want you, even if you asked to come.
  You have made your choice, you can be what you want to be.
  But I will bury him; and if I must die,   55
  I say that this crime is holy: I shall lie down
  With him in death, and I shall be as dear
  To him as he to me.
                      It is the dead,
  Not the living, who make the longest demands:
  We die forever . . .
                      You may do as you like,   60
  Since apparently the laws of the gods mean nothing to you.
Ismene. They mean a great deal to me; but I have no strength
  To break laws that were made for the public good.
Antigone. That must be your excuse, I suppose. But as for me,
  I will bury the brother I love.
Ismene.   Antigone,   65
  I am so afraid for you!
Antigone.   You need not be:
  You have yourself to consider, after all.
Ismene. But no one must hear of this, you must tell no one!
  I will keep it a secret, I promise!
Antigone.   Oh tell it! Tell everyone!
  Think how they'll hate you when it all comes out   70
  If they learn that you knew about it all the time!
Ismene. So fiery! You should be cold with fear.
Antigone. Perhaps. But I am doing only what I must.
Ismene. But can you do it? I say that you cannot.
Antigone. Very well: when my strength gives out, I shall do no more.   75
Ismene. Impossible things should not be tried at all.
Antigone. Go away, Ismene:
  I shall be hating you soon, and the dead will, too,
  For your words are hateful. Leave me my foolish plan:
  I am not afraid of the danger; if it means death,   80
  It will not be the worst of deaths—death without honor.
Ismene. Go then, if you feel that you must.
  You are unwise,
  But a loyal friend indeed to those who love you.

[*Exit into the palace.* Antigone *goes off, left. Enter the* Chorus *and* Choragos.]

Chorus. Now the long blade of the sun, lying   85
  Level east to west, touches with glory

Thebes of the Seven Gates. Open, unlidded
Eye of golden day! O marching light
Across the eddy and rush of Dirce's stream,°
Striking the white shields of the enemy 90
Thrown headlong backward from the blaze of morning!

Choragos. Polyneices their commander
Roused them with windy phrases,
He the wild eagle screaming
Insults above our land, 95
His wings their shields of snow,
His crest their marshaled helms.

Chorus. Against our seven gates in a yawning ring
The famished spears came onward in the night;
But before his jaws were sated with our blood, 100
Or pinefire took the garland of our towers,
He was thrown back; and as he turned, great Thebes—
No tender victim for his noisy power—
Rose like a dragon behind him, shouting war.

Choragos. For God hates utterly 105
The bray of bragging tongues;
And when he beheld their smiling,
Their swagger of golden helms,
The frown of his thunder blasted
Their first man from our walls.° 110

Chorus. We heard his shout of triumph high in the air
Turn to a scream; far out in a flaming arc
He fell with his windy torch, and the earth struck him.
And others storming in fury no less than his
Found shock of death in the dusty joy of battle. 115

Choragos. Seven captains at seven gates
Yielded their clanging arms to the god
That bends the battle line and breaks it.
These two only, brothers in blood,
Face to face in matchless rage, 120
Mirroring each the other's death,
Clashed in long combat.

---

89. **Dirce's stream:** Dirce, an early queen of Thebes, was murdered and her body thrown into the stream that bears her name.   105–110. **For God . . . walls:** Zeus threw a thunderbolt that killed the first Argive attackers.

Chorus. But now in the beautiful morning of victory
    Let Thebes of the many chariots sing for joy!
    With hearts for dancing we'll take leave of war: 125
    Our temples shall be sweet with hymns of praise,
    And the long night shall echo with our chorus.

Scene 1

Choragos. But now at last our new king is coming:
    Creon of Thebes, Menoikeus'° son.
    In this auspicious dawn of his reign
    What are the new complexities
    That shifting fate has woven for him?   5
    What is his counsel? Why has he summoned
    The old men to hear him?

[*Enter* Creon *from the palace, center. He addresses the* Chorus *from the top step.*]

Creon. Gentlemen: I have the honor to inform you that our ship of state, which recent
storms have threatened to destroy, has come safely to harbor at last, guided by the
merciful wisdom of heaven. I have summoned you here this morning because I know   10
that I can depend upon you: your devotion to King Laios was absolute; you never hesitated in your duty to our late ruler Oedipus; and when Oedipus died, your loyalty was
transferred to his children. Unfortunately, as you know, his two sons, the princes
Eteocles and Polyneices, have killed each other in battle, and I, as the next in blood,
have succeeded to the full power of the throne.   15
    I am aware, of course, that no ruler can expect complete loyalty from his subjects
until he has been tested in office. Nevertheless, I say to you at the very outset that I
have nothing but contempt for the kind of governor who is afraid, for whatever reason,
to follow the course that he knows is best for the state; and as for the man who sets
private friendship above the public welfare — I have no use for him, either. I call God to   20
witness that if I saw my country headed for ruin, I should not be afraid to speak out
plainly; and I need hardly remind you that I would never have any dealings with an
enemy of the people. No one values friendship more highly than I; but we must
remember that friends made at the risk of wrecking our ship are not real friends at all.
    These are my principles, at any rate, and that is why I have made the following   25
decisions concerning the sons of Oedipus: Eteocles, who died as a man should die,

---

2. **Menoikeus** (mĕ-noi′kē-əs).

fighting for his country, is to be buried with full military honors, with all the ceremony that is usual when the greatest heroes die; but his brother Polyneices, who broke his exile to come back with fire and sword against his native city and the shrines of his fathers' gods, whose one idea was to spill the blood of his blood and sell his own people into slavery—Polyneices, I say, is to have no burial: no man is to touch him or say the least prayer for him; he shall lie on the plain, unburied; and the birds and the scavenging dogs can do with him whatever they like. 30

This is my command, and you can see the wisdom behind it. As long as I am king, no traitor is going to be honored with the loyal man. But whoever shows by word and deed that he is on the side of the state—he shall have my respect while he is living and my reverence when he is dead. 35

Choragos. If that is your will, Creon, son of Menoikeus,
    You have the right to enforce it: we are yours.
Creon. That is my will. Take care that you do your part. 40

Choragos. We are old men: let the younger ones carry it out.

Creon. I do not mean that: The sentries have been appointed.

Choragos. Then what is it that you would have us do?

Creon. You will give no support to whoever breaks this law.

Choragos. Only a crazy man is in love with death!　　　　　　　　　45

Creon. And death it is; yet money talks, and the wisest
    Have sometimes been known to count a few coins too many.

[Enter Sentry *from left.]*

Sentry. I'll not say that I'm out of breath from running, King, because every time I stopped
    to think about what I have to tell you, I felt like going back. And all the time a voice
    kept saying, "You fool, don't you know you're walking straight into trouble?"; and　50
    then another voice: "Yes, but if you let somebody else get the news to Creon first, it
    will be even worse than that for you!" But good sense won out, at least I hope it was
    good sense, and here I am with a story that makes no sense at all; but I'll tell it any-
    how, because, as they say, what's going to happen's going to happen, and —

Creon. Come to the point. What have you to say?　　　　　　　　　55

Sentry. I did not do it. I did not see who did it. You must not punish me for what someone
    else has done.

Creon. A comprehensive defense! More effective, perhaps,
    If I knew its purpose. Come: what is it?

Sentry. A dreadful thing . . . I don't know how to put it —　　　　　60

Creon. Out with it!

Sentry. 　　　　　　　　Well, then;
    The dead man —
          Polyneices —

[Pause. The Sentry *is overcome, fumbles for words.* Creon *waits impassively.]*

            out there —
                someone —
New dust on the slimy flesh!

[Pause. No sign from Creon.*]*

Someone has given it burial that way, and
Gone —　　　　　　　　　　　　　　　　　　　65

[Long pause. Creon *finally speaks with deadly control.]*

Creon. And the man who dared do this?

Sentry.   I swear I
    Do not know! You must believe me!
                         Listen:
    The ground was dry, not a sign of digging, no,
    Not a wheeltrack in the dust, no trace of anyone.
    It was when they relieved us this morning; and one of them,   70
    The corporal, pointed to it.
                     There it was,
    The strangest——
             Look:
    The body, just mounded over with light dust: you see?
    Not buried really, but as if they'd covered it
    Just enough for the ghost's peace. And no sign   75
    Of dogs or any wild animal that had been there.

    And then what a scene there was! Every man of us
    Accusing the other: we all proved the other man did it,
    We all had proof that we could not have done it.
    We were ready to take hot iron in our hands,   80
    Walk through fire, swear by all the gods,
    It was not I!
    I do not know who it was, but it was not I!

[*Creon's rage has been mounting steadily, but the* Sentry *is too intent upon his story to notice it.*]

    And then, when this came to nothing, someone said
    A thing that silenced us and made us stare   85
    Down at the ground: You had to be told the news,
    And one of us had to do it! We threw the dice,
    And the bad luck fell to me. So here I am,
    No happier to be here than you are to have me:
    Nobody likes the man who brings bad news.   90
Choragos. I have been wondering, King: can it be that the gods have done this?
Creon *(furiously).* Stop!
    Must you doddering wrecks
    Go out of your heads entirely? "The gods!"
    Intolerable!   95
    The gods favor this corpse? Why? How had he served them?
    Tried to loot their temples, burn their images,
    Yes, and the whole state, and its laws with it!
    Is it your senile opinion that the gods love to honor bad men?
    A pious thought!—

No, from the very beginning   100
There have been those who have whispered together,
Stiff-necked anarchists,° putting their heads together,
Scheming against me in alleys. These are the men,
And they have bribed my own guard to do this thing.
(Sententiously°)   105
Money!
There's nothing in the world so demoralizing as money.
Down go your cities,
Homes gone, men gone, honest hearts corrupted,
Crookedness of all kinds, and all for money!
                    (To Sentry*)* But you—!
I swear by God and by the throne of God,   110
The man who has done this thing shall pay for it!
Find that man, bring him here to me, or your death
Will be the least of your problems: I'll string you up
Alive, and there will be certain ways to make you
Discover your employer before you die;   115
And the process may teach you a lesson you seem to have missed:
The dearest profit is sometimes all too dear:
That depends on the source. Do you understand me?
A fortune won is often misfortune.

Sentry. King, may I speak?

Creon.   Your very voice distresses me.   120

Sentry. Are you sure that it is my voice, and not your conscience?

Creon. By God, he wants to analyze me now!

Sentry. It is not what I say, but what has been done, that hurts you.

Creon. You talk too much.

Sentry.   Maybe; but I've done nothing.

Creon. Sold your soul for some silver: that's all you've done.   125

Sentry. How dreadful it is when the right judge judges wrong!

Creon. Your figures of speech
   May entertain you now; but unless you bring me the man,
   You will get little profit from them in the end.

                               [Exit Creon *into the palace.]*

Sentry. "Bring me the man"—!   130
   I'd like nothing better than bringing him the man!
   But bring him or not, you have seen the last of me here.
   At any rate, I am safe!

                                          [Exit Sentry*.]*

---

102. **anarchists:** people who believe that law and organized government should be done away with. S.D. **Sententiously:** speaking in a way that is especially trite or moralistic.

Ode 1°

Chorus. Numberless are the world's wonders, but none
    More wonderful than man; the storm-gray sea
    Yields to his prows, the huge crests bear him high;
    Earth, holy and inexhaustible, is graven
    With shining furrows where his plows have gone   5
    Year after year, the timeless labor of stallions.

    The lightboned birds and beasts that cling to cover,
    The lithe fish lighting their reaches of dim water,
    All are taken, tamed in the net of his mind;
    The lion on the hill, the wild horse windy-maned,   10
    Resign to him; and his blunt yoke has broken
    The sultry shoulders of the mountain bull.

    Words also, and thought as rapid as air,
    He fashions to his good use; statecraft is his,
    And his the skill that deflects the arrows of snow,   15
    The spears of winter rain: from every wind
    He has made himself secure—from all but one:
    In the late wind of death he cannot stand.

    O clear intelligence, force beyond all measure!
    O fate of man, working both good and evil!   20
    When the laws are kept, how proudly his city stands!   *Proverb*
    When the laws are broken, what of his city then?
    Never may the anarchic man° find rest at my hearth,
    Never be it said that my thoughts are his thoughts.

a sigh   *Full stop. Question*
                            2

Scene 2

               [*Reenter* Sentry, *leading* Antigone.]

Choragos. What does this mean? Surely this captive woman
    Is the princess, Antigone. Why should she be taken?

  °**Ode:** a song chanted by the Chorus. An ode separates one scene from the next. (There was no curtain in the Greek theater.)   23. **anarchic** (ăn-är′kĭk) **man:** an anarchist.

Sentry. Here is the one who did it! We caught her
    In the very act of burying him. — Where is Creon?
Choragos. Just coming from the house.

[Enter Creon, center.]

Creon.   What has happened?   5
    Why have you come back so soon?
Sentry *(expansively)*.   O King,
    A man should never be too sure of anything:
    I would have sworn
    That you'd not see me here again: your anger
    Frightened me so, and the things you threatened me with;   10
    But how could I tell then
    That I'd be able to solve the case so soon?

    No dice-throwing this time: I was only too glad to come!

    Here is this woman. She is the guilty one:
    We found her trying to bury him.   15
    Take her, then; question her; judge her as you will.
    I am through with the whole thing now, and glad of it.
Creon. But this is Antigone! Why have you brought her here?
Sentry. She was burying him, I tell you!
Creon *(severely)*.   Is this the truth?
Sentry. I saw her with my own eyes. Can I say more?   20
Creon. The details: Come, tell me quickly!
Sentry.   It was like this: Stop Question
    After those terrible threats of yours, King,
    We went back and brushed the dust away from the body.
    The flesh was soft by now, and stinking,
    So we sat on a hill to windward and kept guard.   25
    No napping this time! We kept each other awake.
    But nothing happened until the white round sun
    Whirled in the center of the round sky over us:
    Then, suddenly,
    A storm of dust roared up from the earth, and the sky   30
    Went out, the plain vanished with all its trees
    In the stinging dark. We closed our eyes and endured it.
    The whirlwind lasted a long time, but it passed;
    And then we looked, and there was Antigone!
    I have seen   35
    A mother bird come back to a stripped nest, heard

Her crying bitterly a broken note or two
For the young ones stolen. Just so, when this girl
Found the bare corpse, and all her love's work wasted,
She wept, and cried on heaven to damn the hands
That had done this thing.

               And then she brought more dust
And sprinkled wine three times for her brother's ghost.

We ran and took her at once. She was not afraid,
Not even when we charged her with what she had done.
She denied nothing.

             And this was a comfort to me,
And some uneasiness: for it is a good thing
To escape from death, but it is no great pleasure
To bring death to a friend.

                Yet I always say
There is nothing so comfortable as your own safe skin!

Creon (*slowly, dangerously*). And you, Antigone,
    You with your head hanging—do you confess this thing?
Antigone. I do. I deny nothing.
Creon (*to* Sentry).   You may go.   [*Exit* Sentry.]
    (*To* Antigone) Tell me, tell me briefly:
    Had you heard my proclamation touching this matter?
Antigone. It was public. Could I help hearing it?
Creon. And yet you dared defy the law.
Antigone.   I dared.
    It was not God's proclamation. That final justice
    That rules the world below makes no such laws.

Your edict, King, was strong,
But all your strength is weakness itself against
The immortal unrecorded laws of God.
They are not merely now: they were, and shall be,
Operative forever, beyond man utterly.

I knew I must die, even without your decree:
I am only mortal. And if I must die
Now, before it is my time to die,
Surely this is no hardship: can anyone
Living, as I live, with evil all about me,
Think death less than a friend? This death of mine
Is of no importance; but if I had left my brother
Lying in death unburied, I should have suffered.

Now I do not.
              You smile at me. Ah Creon,
Think me a fool, if you like; but it may well be
That a fool convicts me of folly.

Choragos. Like father, like daughter: both headstrong, deaf to reason! 75
She has never learned to yield.

Creon.   She has much to learn.
The inflexible heart breaks first, the toughest iron
Cracks first, and the wildest horses bend their necks
At the pull of the smallest curb.

                                   Pride? In a slave?
This girl is guilty of a double insolence, 80
Breaking the given laws and boasting of it.
Who is the man here,
She or I, if this crime goes unpunished?
Sister's child, or more than sister's child,
Or closer yet in blood—she and her sister 85
Win bitter death for this!
            (*To* Servants) Go, some of you,
Arrest Ismene. I accuse her equally.
Bring her: You will find her sniffling in the house there.

Her mind's a traitor: crimes kept in the dark
Cry for light, and the guardian brain shudders; 90
But how much worse than this
Is brazen boasting of barefaced anarchy!

Antigone. Creon, what more do you want than my death?

Creon.   Nothing.
That gives me everything.

Antigone.   Then I beg you: kill me.
This talking is a great weariness: your words 95
Are distasteful to me, and I am sure that mine
Seem so to you. And yet they should not seem so:
I should have praise and honor for what I have done.
All these men here would praise me
Were their lips not frozen shut with fear of you. 100
(*Bitterly*)
Ah the good fortune of kings,
Licensed to say and do whatever they please!

Creon. You are alone here in that opinion.

Antigone. No, they are with me. But they keep their tongues in leash.

Creon. Maybe. But you are guilty, and they are not. 105

Antigone. There is no guilt in reverence for the dead.

Creon. But Eteocles—was he not your brother too?

Antigone. My brother too.

Creon.   And you insult his memory?

Antigone *(softly).* The dead man would not say that I insult it.

Creon. He would: for you honor a traitor as much as him.   110

Antigone. His own brother, traitor or not, and equal in blood.

Creon. He made war on his country. Eteocles defended it.

Antigone. Nevertheless, there are honors due all the dead.

Creon. But not the same for the wicked as for the just.

Antigone. Ah Creon, Creon,   115
    Which of us can say what the gods hold wicked?

Creon. An enemy is an enemy, even dead.

Antigone. It is my nature to join in love, not hate.

Creon *(finally losing patience).* Go join them, then; if you must have your love,
    Find it in hell!   120

Choragos. But see, Ismene comes:

[Enter Ismene, *guarded.]*

    Those tears are sisterly, the cloud
    That shadows her eyes rains down gentle sorrow.

Creon. You too, Ismene,
    Snake in my ordered house, sucking my blood   125
    Stealthily—and all the time I never knew
    That these two sisters were aiming at my throne!
                                        Ismene,
    Do you confess your share in this crime, or deny it?
    Answer me.

Ismene. Yes, if she will let me say so. I am guilty.   130

Antigone *(coldly).* No, Ismene. You have no right to say so.
    You would not help me, and I will not have you help me.

Ismene. But now I know what you meant; and I am here
    To join you, to take my share of punishment.

Antigone. The dead man and the gods who rule the dead   135
    Know whose act this was. Words are not friends.

Ismene. Do you refuse me, Antigone? I want to die with you:
    I too have a duty that I must discharge to the dead.

Antigone. You shall not lessen my death by sharing it.

Ismene. What do I care for life when you are dead?   140

Antigone. Ask Creon. You're always hanging on his opinions.

Ismene. You are laughing at me. Why, Antigone?

Antigone. It's a joyless laughter, Ismene.

Ismene.   But can I do nothing?

Antigone. Yes. Save yourself. I shall not envy you.
    There are those who will praise you; I shall have honor, too.   145
Ismene. But we are equally guilty!
Antigone.   No more, Ismene.
    You are alive, but I belong to death.
Creon *(to the* Chorus*).* Gentlemen, I beg you to observe these girls:
    One has just now lost her mind; the other,
    It seems, has never had a mind at all.   150
Ismene. Grief teaches the steadiest minds to waver, King.
Creon. Yours certainly did, when you assumed guilt with the guilty!
Ismene. But how could I go on living without her?
Creon.   You are.
    She is already dead.
Ismene.   But your own son's bride!
Creon. There are places enough for him to push his plow.   155
    I want no wicked women for my sons!
Ismene. O dearest Haimon, how your father wrongs you!

Creon. I've had enough of your childish talk of marriage!

Choragos. Do you really intend to steal this girl from your son?

Creon. No; death will do that for me.

Choragos.   Then she must die?   160

Creon *(ironically).* You dazzle me.

                    —But enough of this talk!

(To Guards*)* You, there, take them away and guard them well:

For they are but women, and even brave men run

When they see death coming.

                    [*Exeunt* Ismene, Antigone, *and* Guards.]

stop Question 3

Ode 2

Chorus. Fortunate is the man who has never tasted God's vengeance!
    Where once the anger of heaven has struck, that house is shaken
    Forever: damnation rises behind each child
    Like a wave cresting out of the black northeast,
    When the long darkness under sea roars up   5
    And bursts drumming death upon the windwhipped sand.
    I have seen this gathering sorrow from time long past

    Loom upon Oedipus' children: generation from generation
    Takes the compulsive rage of the enemy god.
    So lately this last flower of Oedipus' line   10
    Drank the sunlight! but now a passionate word
    And a handful of dust have closed up all its beauty.

stop question 1

      What mortal arrogance
      Transcends the wrath of Zeus?
    Sleep cannot lull him,° nor the effortless long months   15
    Of the timeless gods: but he is young forever,
    And his house is the shining day of high Olympos.°
      And that is and shall be,
      And all the past, is his.
    No pride on earth is free of the curse of heaven.   20

    The straying dreams of men
    May bring them ghosts of joy:

---

  15. **him:** Zeus, king of the gods. 17. **Olympos:** a mountain in northern Greece, legendary home of the gods and goddesses.

But as they drowse, the waking embers burn them;
Or they walk with fixed eyes, as blind men walk.
But the ancient wisdom speaks for our own time: 25
    Fate works most for woe
    With folly's fairest show.
Man's little pleasure is the spring of sorrow.   *stop Question 2*

Scene 3

Choragos. But here is Haimon, King, the last of all your sons.
    Is it grief for Antigone that brings him here,
    And bitterness at being robbed of his bride?

                  [*Enter* Haimon.]

Creon. We shall soon see, and no need of diviners.°
                          —Son,
    You have heard my final judgment on that girl: 5
    Have you come here hating me, or have you come
    With deference and with love, whatever I do?
Haimon. I am your son, Father. You are my guide.
    You make things clear for me, and I obey you.
    No marriage means more to me than your continuing wisdom.   10
Creon. Good. That is the way to behave: subordinate
    Everything else, my son, to your father's will.
    This is what a man prays for, that he may get
    Sons attentive and dutiful in his house,
    Each one hating his father's enemies,   15
    Honoring his father's friends. But if his sons
    Fail him, if they turn out unprofitably,
    What has he fathered but trouble for himself
    And amusement for the malicious?
                  So you are right
    Not to lose your head over this woman.   20
    Your pleasure with her would soon grow cold, Haimon,
    And then you'd have a hellcat in bed and elsewhere.
    Let her find her husband in hell!
    Of all the people in this city, only she
    Has had contempt for my law and broken it.   25

---

4. **diviners:** persons who could predict the future.

Do you want me to show myself weak before the people?
Or to break my sworn word? No, and I will not.
The woman dies.
I suppose she'll plead "family ties." Well, let her.
If I permit my own family to rebel,
How shall I earn the world's obedience? 30
Show me the man who keeps his house in hand,
He's fit for public authority.

                     I'll have no dealings
With lawbreakers, critics of the government:
Whoever is chosen to govern should be obeyed—
Must be obeyed, in all things, great and small, 35
Just and unjust! O Haimon,
The man who knows how to obey, and that man only,
Knows how to give commands when the time comes.
You can depend on him, no matter how fast
The spears come: He's a good soldier, he'll stick it out. 40

Anarchy, anarchy! Show me a greater evil!
This is why cities tumble and the great houses rain down,
This is what scatters armies!

No, no: Good lives are made so by discipline.
We keep the laws then, and the lawmakers, 45
And no woman shall seduce us. If we must lose,
Let's lose to a man, at least! Is a woman stronger than we?
Choragos. Unless time has rusted my wits,
   What you say, King, is said with point and dignity.
Haimon *(boyishly earnest)*. Father: 50
   Reason is God's crowning gift to man, and you are right
To warn me against losing mine. I cannot say—
I hope that I shall never want to say!—that you
Have reasoned badly. Yet there are other men
Who can reason, too; and their opinions might be helpful. 55
You are not in a position to know everything
That people say or do, or what they feel:
Your temper terrifies them—everyone
Will tell you only what you like to hear.
But I, at any rate, can listen; and I have heard them 60
Muttering and whispering in the dark about this girl.
They say no woman has ever, so unreasonably,
Died so shameful a death for a generous act:
"She covered her brother's body. Is this indecent?
65

She kept him from dogs and vultures. Is this a crime?
Death?—She should have all the honor that we can give her!"

This is the way they talk out there in the city.

You must believe me:
Nothing is closer to me than your happiness.   70
What could be closer? Must not any son
Value his father's fortune as his father does his?
I beg you, do not be unchangeable:
Do not believe that you alone can be right.
The man who thinks that,   75
The man who maintains that only he has the power
To reason correctly, the gift to speak, the soul—
A man like that, when you know him, turns out empty.

It is not reason never to yield to reason!

In flood time you can see how some trees bend,   80
And because they bend, even their twigs are safe,
While stubborn trees are torn up, roots and all.
And the same thing happens in sailing:
Make your sheet fast, never slacken,—and over you go,
Head over heels and under: and there's your voyage.   85
Forget you are angry! Let yourself be moved!
I know I am young; but please let me say this:
The ideal condition
Would be, I admit, that men should be right by instinct;
But since we are all too likely to go astray,   90
The reasonable thing is to learn from those who can teach.
Choragos. You will do well to listen to him, King,
      If what he says is sensible. And you, Haimon,
      Must listen to your father—both speak well.
Creon. You consider it right for a man of my years and experience   95
      To go to school to a boy?
Haimon.   It is not right
      If I am wrong. But if I am young, and right,
      What does my age matter?
Creon. You think it right to stand up for an anarchist?
Haimon. Not at all. I pay no respect to criminals.   100
Creon. Then she is not a criminal?
Haimon. The city would deny it, to a man.
Creon. And the city proposes to teach me how to rule?

Haimon. Ah. Who is it that's talking like a boy now?

Creon. My voice is the one voice giving orders in this city!   105

Haimon. It is no city if it takes orders from one voice.

Creon. The state is the king!

Haimon.   Yes, if the state is a desert.

[*Pause.*]

Creon. This boy, it seems, has sold out to a woman.

Haimon. If you are a woman: My concern is only for you.

Creon. So? Your "concern"! In a public brawl with your father!   110

Haimon. How about you, in a public brawl with justice?

Creon. With justice, when all that I do is within my rights?

Haimon. You have no right to trample on God's right.

Creon (*completely out of control*). Fool, adolescent fool! Taken in by a woman!

Haimon. You'll never see me taken in by anything vile.   115

Creon. Every word you say is for her!

Haimon (*quietly, darkly*).   And for you.
    And for me. And for the gods under the earth.

Creon. You'll never marry her while she lives.

Haimon. Then she must die—But her death will cause another.

Creon. Another?   120
    Have you lost your senses? Is this an open threat?

Haimon. There is no threat in speaking to emptiness.

Creon. I swear you'll regret this superior tone of yours!
    You are the empty one!

Haimon.   If you were not my father,
    I'd say you were perverse.°   125

Creon. You girlstruck fool, don't play at words with me!

Haimon. I am sorry. You prefer silence.

Creon.   Now, by God—!
    I swear, by all the gods in heaven above us,
    You'll watch it, I swear you shall!
                    (*To the* Servants) Bring her out!
    Bring the woman out! Let her die before his eyes!   130
    Here, this instant, with her bridegroom beside her!

Haimon. Not here, no; she will not die here, King.
    And you will never see my face again.
    Go on raving as long as you've a friend to endure you.

[*Exit* Haimon.]

---

125. **perverse:** here, stubbornly refusing to yield to reason.

Choragos. Gone, gone.

 Creon, a young man in a rage is dangerous!

Creon. Let him do, or dream to do, more than a man can.

 He shall not save these girls from death.

Choragos.   These girls?

 You have sentenced them both?

Creon.   No, you are right.

 I will not kill the one whose hands are clean.

Choragos. But Antigone?

Creon (somberly).   I will carry her far away

 Out there in the wilderness and lock her

 Living in a vault of stone. She shall have food,

 As the custom is, to absolve the state of her death.

 And there let her pray to the gods of hell:

 They are her only gods:

 Perhaps they will show her an escape from death,

 Or she may learn,

     though late,

 That piety shown the dead is pity in vain.   [*Exit* Creon.]

Ode 3

Chorus. Love, unconquerable

 Waster of rich men, keeper

 Of warm lights and all-night vigil

 In the soft face of a girl:

 Sea-wanderer, forest-visitor!

 Even the pure Immortals cannot escape you,

 And mortal man, in his one day's dusk,

 Trembles before your glory.

 Surely you swerve upon ruin

 The just man's consenting heart,

 As here you have made bright anger

 Strike between father and son—

 And none has conquered but love!

 A girl's glance working the will of Heaven:

 Pleasure to her alone who mocks us,

 Merciless Aphrodite.°

---

16. **Aphrodite:** goddess of love and beauty.

Scene 4

Choragos (*as* Antigone *enters, guarded*). But I can no longer stand in awe of this,
    Nor, seeing what I see, keep back my tears.
    Here is Antigone, passing to that chamber
    Where all find sleep at last.

Antigone. Look upon me, friends, and pity me   5
    Turning back at the night's edge to say
    Goodbye to the sun that shines for me no longer;
    Now sleepy death
    Summons me down to Acheron,° that cold shore:
    There is no bridesong there, nor any music.   10

Chorus. Yet not unpraised, not without a kind of honor,
    You walk at last into the underworld;
    Untouched by sickness, broken by no sword.
    What woman has ever found your way to death?

Antigone. How often I have heard the story of Niobe,°   15
    Tantalos'° wretched daughter, how the stone
    Clung fast about her, ivy-close; and they say
    The rain falls endlessly
    And sifting soft snow; her tears are never done.
    I feel the loneliness of her death in mine.   20

Chorus. But she was born of heaven, and you
    Are woman, woman-born. If her death is yours,
    A mortal woman's, is this not for you
    Glory in our world and in the world beyond?

Antigone. You laugh at me. Ah, friends, friends,   25
    Can you not wait until I am dead? O Thebes,
    O men many-charioted, in love with fortune,
    Dear springs of Dirce, sacred Theban grove,
    Be witnesses for me, denied all pity,
    Unjustly judged! and think a word of love   30
    For her whose path turns
    Under dark earth, where there are no more tears.

Chorus. You have passed beyond human daring and come at last
    Into a place of stone where justice sits.

---

9. **Acheron** (ăk′ə-rŏn): in Greek mythology, one of the rivers surrounding Hades.   15. **Niobe** (nī′ə-bē): an ancient queen of Thebes who boasted that she was greater than the goddess Leto because she had seven sons and seven daughters while Leto had only two children. To punish her for her arrogance, the gods killed all of Niobe's children, and Zeus turned the weeping woman into a column of stone from which her tears, in the form of a stream, continued to flow.   16. **Tantalos** (tăn′tə-ləs): Niobe's father, who suffered eternal hunger and thirst in the underworld. In Greek mythology, the underworld was not primarily a place of punishment. All dead souls wandered there as ghosts, or shades. Antigone looks forward to a reunion there with her family.

I cannot tell 35
What shape of your father's guilt appears in this.
Antigone. You have touched it at last: that bridal bed
Unspeakable, horror of son and mother mingling:
Their crime, infection of all our family!
O Oedipus, father and brother! 40
Your marriage strikes from the grave to murder mine.
I have been a stranger here in my own land:
All my life
The blasphemy of my birth has followed me.
Chorus. Reverence is a virtue, but strength 45
Lives in established law: That must prevail.
You have made your choice,
Your death is the doing of your conscious hand.
Antigone. Then let me go, since all your words are bitter,
And the very light of the sun is cold to me. 50
Lead me to my vigil, where I must have
Neither love nor lamentation; no song, but silence.

[Creon *interrupts impatiently.*]

Creon. If dirges and planned lamentations could put off death,
Men would be singing forever.
(To the Servants) Take her, go!
You know your orders: take her to the vault 55
And leave her alone there. And if she lives or dies,
That's her affair, not ours: Our hands are clean.
Antigone. O tomb, vaulted bride-bed in eternal rock,
Soon I shall be with my own again
Where Persephone° welcomes the thin ghosts underground: 60
And I shall see my father again, and you, Mother,
And dearest Polyneices—
dearest indeed
To me, since it was my hand
That washed him clean and poured the ritual wine;
And my reward is death before my time! 65

And yet, as men's hearts know, I have done no wrong,
I have not sinned before God. Or if I have,
I shall know the truth in death. But if the guilt

---

60. **Persephone** (pər-sĕf'ə-nē): queen of Hades, or the underworld.

Lies upon Creon who judged me, then, I pray,
May his punishment equal my own.

Choragos. O passionate heart, 70
Unyielding, tormented still by the same winds!

Creon. Her guards shall have good cause to regret their delaying.

Antigone. Ah! That voice is like the voice of death!

Creon. I can give you no reason to think you are mistaken.

Antigone. Thebes, and you my fathers' gods, 75
And rulers of Thebes, you see me now, the last
Unhappy daughter of a line of kings,
Your kings, led away to death. You will remember
What things I suffer, and at what men's hands,
Because I would not transgress the laws of heaven. 80
(To the Guards, *simply)* Come: let us wait no longer.

[*Exit* Antigone, *left, guarded.*]

Ode 4

Chorus. All Danae's beauty° was locked away
In a brazen cell where the sunlight could not come:
A small room, still as any grave, enclosed her.
Yet she was a princess, too,
And Zeus in a rain of gold poured love upon her. 5
O child, child,
No power in wealth or war
Or tough sea-blackened ships
Can prevail against untiring destiny!

And Dryas' son° also, that furious king, 10
Bore the god's prisoning anger for his pride:
Sealed up by Dionysos in deaf stone,
His madness died among echoes.
So at the last he learned what dreadful power
His tongue had mocked: 15
For he had profaned the revels,

---

1. **Danae's beauty:** Danae (dăn'ə-ē') was a princess whose father imprisoned her in a bronze tower because it was predicted that the son she would one day bear would kill him. Zeus loved Danae, visited her in the form of a shower of gold, and gave her a son. 10. **Dryas' son:** a king named Lycurgos, who disapproved of the worship of Dionysos, god of wine and revelry. Lycurgos attacked the god, who, as punishment, drove him mad and imprisoned him in stone.

And fired the wrath of the nine
Implacable Sisters° that love the sound of the flute.

And old men tell a half-remembered tale°   20
Of horror done where a dark ledge splits the sea
And a double surf beats on the gray shores:
How a king's new woman, sick
With hatred for the queen he had imprisoned,
Ripped out his two sons' eyes with her bloody hands   25
While grinning Ares° watched the shuttle plunge
Four times: four blind wounds crying for revenge,

Crying, tears and blood mingled—piteously born,
Those sons whose mother was of heavenly birth!
Her father was the god of the North Wind   30
And she was cradled by gales,
She raced with young colts on the glittering hills
And walked untrammeled in the open light;
But in her marriage deathless Fate found means
To build a tomb like yours for all her joy.

Scene 5

[*Enter blind* Teiresias, *led by a* Boy. *The opening speeches of* Teiresias *should be in singsong contrast to the realistic lines of* Creon.]

Teiresias. This is the way the blind man comes, Princes, Princes,
    Lock-step, two heads lit by the eyes of one.
Creon. What new thing have you to tell us, old Teiresias?
Teiresias. I have much to tell you: Listen to the prophet, Creon.
Creon. I am not aware that I have ever failed to listen.   5
Teiresias. Then you have done wisely, King, and ruled well.
Creon. I admit my debt to you.° But what have you to say?
Teiresias. This, Creon: You stand once more on the edge of fate.
Creon. What do you mean? Your words are a kind of dread.

17–18. **nine Implacable Sisters:** the Muses, goddesses of the arts and sciences. *Implacable* means that once offended, they cannot be appeased.   19. **a half-remembered tale:** The details that follow refer to an ancient myth about King Phineus of Thrace, who imprisoned his first wife, Cleopatra, daughter of the North Wind god. Cleopatra's two sons were blinded by the king's new wife.   25. **Ares:** god of war and strife.
    7. **my debt to you:** Teiresias served as an instrument of the gods in foretelling Odeipus' fate and was thus indirectly responsible for Creon's ascension to the throne.

Teiresias. Listen, Creon:

    I was sitting in my chair of augury,° at the place 10
    Where the birds gather about me. They were all a-chatter,
    As is their habit, when suddenly I heard
    A strange note in their jangling, a scream, a
    Whirring fury; I knew that they were fighting, 15
    Tearing each other, dying
    In a whirlwind of wings clashing. And I was afraid.
    I began the rites of burnt-offering at the altar,
    But Hephaistos° failed me: Instead of bright flame,
    There was only the sputtering slime of the fat thighflesh 20
    Melting: The entrails dissolved in gray smoke,
    The bare bone burst from the welter. And no blaze!

    This was a sign from heaven. My boy described it,
    Seeing for me as I see for others.

    I tell you, Creon, you yourself have brought 25
    This new calamity upon us. Our hearths and altars
    Are stained with the corruption of dogs and carrion birds
    That glut themselves on the corpse of Oedipus' son.
    The gods are deaf when we pray to them, their fire
    Recoils from our offering, their birds of omen 30
    Have no cry of comfort, for they are gorged
    With the thick blood of the dead.
                   O my son,
    These are no trifles! Think: all men make mistakes,
    But a good man yields when he knows his course is wrong,
    And repairs the evil. The only crime is pride. 35

    Give in to the dead man, then: Do not fight with a corpse—
    What glory is it to kill a man who is dead?
    Think, I beg you:
    It is for your own good that I speak as I do.
    You should be able to yield for your own good. 40
Creon. It seems that prophets have made me their especial province.
    All my life long
    I have been a kind of butt for the dull arrows
    Of doddering fortunetellers!

---

11. **chair of augury:** the place where Teiresias interpreted omens. Among the omens he interpreted were certain sounds from birds. 19. **Hephaistos** (hĭ-fĭs′təs): Greek god of fire.

No, Teiresias:

If your birds—if the great eagles of God himself   45
Should carry him stinking bit by bit to heaven,
I would not yield. I am not afraid of pollution:
No man can defile the gods.

Do what you will,

Go into business, make money, speculate
In India gold or that synthetic gold from Sardis,°   50
Get rich otherwise than by my consent to bury him.
Teiresias, it is a sorry thing when a wise man
Sells his wisdom, lets out his words for hire!

Teiresias. Ah Creon! Is there no man left in the world—

Creon. To do what?—Come, let's have the aphorism!°   55

Teiresias. No man who knows that wisdom outweighs any wealth?

Creon. As surely as bribes are baser than any baseness.

Teiresias. You are sick, Creon! You are deathly sick!

Creon. As you say: It is not my place to challenge a prophet.

Teiresias. Yet you have said my prophecy is for sale.   60

Creon. The generation of prophets has always loved gold.

Teiresias. The generation of kings has always loved brass.

Creon. You forget yourself! You are speaking to your king.

Teiresias. I know it. You are a king because of me.

Creon. You have a certain skill; but you have sold out.   65

Teiresias. King, you will drive me to the words that—

Creon.   Say them, say them!

Only remember: I will not pay you for them.

Teiresias. No, you will find them too costly.

Creon.   No doubt. Speak:

Whatever you say, you will not change my will.

Teiresias. Then take this, and take it to heart!   70
The time is not far off when you shall pay back
Corpse for corpse, flesh of your own flesh.
You have thrust the child of this world into living night,
You have kept from the gods below the child that is theirs:
The one in a grave before her death, the other,   75
Dead, denied the grave. This is your crime;
And the Furies° and the dark gods of hell
Are swift with terrible punishment for you.

---

50. **Sardis:** In Sardis, the capital of ancient Lydia, the first metal coins were produced from a natural alloy of gold that contained 20 to 35 percent silver.   55. **aphorism** (ăf′ə-rĭz′əm): wise saying, used ironically here.   77. **Furies:** three winged goddesses who avenge unpunished crimes, especially those that go against the ties of kinship.

Do you want to buy me now, Creon?
                                   Not many days,
And your house will be full of men and women weeping,   80
And curses will be hurled at you from far
Cities grieving for sons unburied, left to rot
Before the walls of Thebes.

These are my arrows, Creon: They are all for you.

(To Boy*)* But come, child: Lead me home.   85
Let him waste his fine anger upon younger men.
Maybe he will learn at last
To control a wiser tongue in a better head.   [*Exit* Teiresias.]

Choragos. The old man has gone, King, but his words
Remain to plague us. I am old, too, 90
But I cannot remember that he was ever false.
Creon. That is true . . . It troubles me.
Oh it is hard to give in! But it is worse
To risk everything for stubborn pride.
Choragos. Creon: Take my advice.
Creon. What shall I do? 95
Choragos. Go quickly: free Antigone from her vault
And build a tomb for the body of Polyneices.
Creon. You would have me do this?
Choragos. Creon, yes!
And it must be done at once: God moves
Swiftly to cancel the folly of stubborn men. 100
Creon. It is hard to deny the heart! But I
Will do it: I will not fight with destiny.
Choragos. You must go yourself, you cannot leave it to others.
Creon. I will go.
—Bring axes, servants:
Come with me to the tomb. I buried her, I 105
Will set her free.
Oh quickly!
My mind misgives—
The laws of the gods are mighty, and a man must serve them
To the last day of his life! [*Exit* Creon.]

Exodos°

[*Enter* Messenger, *left.*]

Messenger. Men of the line of Kadmos,° you who live
Near Amphion's° citadel:
I cannot say
Of any condition of human life "This is fixed,
This is clearly good, or bad." Fate raises up,
And fate casts down the happy and unhappy alike: 5
No man can foretell his fate.
Take the case of Creon:
Creon was happy once, as I count happiness;

°**Exodos:** the final, or exit, scene.   1. **Kadmos:** the founder of Thebes.   2. **Amphion** (ăm-fī′ən): Niobe's husband, former ruler of Thebes.

Victorious in battle, sole governor of the land,
Fortunate father of children nobly born.
And now it has all gone from him! Who can say   10
That a man is still alive when his life's joy fails?
He is a walking dead man. Grant him rich,
Let him live like a king in his great house:
If his pleasure is gone, I would not give
So much as the shadow of smoke for all he owns.   15

Choragos. Your words hint at sorrow; what is your news for us?
Messenger. They are dead. The living are guilty of their death.
Choragos. Who is guilty? Who is dead? Speak!
Messenger.   Haimon.
    Haimon is dead; and the hand that killed him
    Is his own hand.
Choragos.   His father's? or his own?   20
Messenger. His own, driven mad by the murder his father had done.
Choragos. Teiresias, Teiresias, how clearly you saw it all!
Messenger. This is my news; you must draw what conclusions you can from it.
Choragos. But look: Eurydice, our queen:
    Has she overheard us?   25

[*Enter* Eurydice *from the palace, center.*]

Eurydice. I have heard something, friends:
    As I was unlocking the gate of Pallas'° shrine,
    For I needed her help today, I heard a voice
    Telling of some new sorrow. And I fainted
    There at the temple with all my maidens about me.   30
    But speak again; whatever it is, I can bear it:
    Grief and I are not strangers.°
Messenger.   Dearest lady,
    I will tell you plainly all that I have seen.
    I shall not try to comfort you: What is the use,
    Since comfort could lie only in what is not true?   35
    The truth is always best.
                        I went with Creon
    To the outer plain where Polyneices was lying,
    No friend to pity him, his body shredded by dogs.
    We made our prayers in that place to Hecate
    And Pluto,° that they would be merciful. And we bathed 40

---

27. **Pallas:** Pallas Athena, goddess of wisdom.   43. **Grief . . . strangers:** Megareus, the older son of Eurydice and Creon, had died in the battle for Thebes.   39–40. **Hecate** (hĕk'ə-tē) and **Pluto:** divinities associated with the dead and the underworld.

The corpse with holy water, and we brought
Fresh-broken branches to burn what was left of it,
And upon the urn we heaped up a towering barrow
Of the earth of his own land.

                     When we were done, we ran
To the vault where Antigone lay on her couch of stone.   45
One of the servants had gone ahead,
And while he was yet far off he heard a voice
Grieving within the chamber, and he came back
And told Creon. And as the king went closer,
The air was full of wailing, the words lost,   50
And he begged us to make all haste. "Am I a prophet?"
He said weeping. "And must I walk this road,
The saddest of all that I have gone before?
My son's voice calls me on. Oh quickly, quickly!
Look through the crevice there, and tell me   55
If it is Haimon, or some deception of the gods!"

We obeyed; and in the cavern's farthest corner
We saw her lying:
She had made a noose of her fine linen veil
And hanged herself. Haimon lay beside her,   60
His arms about her waist, lamenting her,
His love lost under ground, crying out
That his father had stolen her away from him.

When Creon saw him the tears rushed to his eyes
And he called to him: "What have you done, child? Speak to me.   65
What are you thinking that makes your eyes so strange?
O my son, my son, I come to you on my knees!"
But Haimon spat in his face. He said not a word,
Staring—
        And suddenly drew his sword
And lunged. Creon shrank back, the blade missed; and the boy,   70
Desperate against himself, drove it half its length
Into his own side and fell. And as he died
He gathered Antigone close in his arms again,
Choking, his blood bright red on her white cheek.
And now he lies dead with the dead, and she is his   75
At last, his bride in the houses of the dead.   [*Exit* Eurydice *into the palace.*]

Choragos. She has left us without a word. What can this mean?
Messenger. It troubles me, too; yet she knows what is best.

Her grief is too great for public lamentation,
And doubtless she has gone to her chamber to weep   80
For her dead son, leading her maidens in his dirge.
Choragos. It may be so; but I fear this deep silence.

[*Pause.*]

Messenger. I will see what she is doing. I will go in.

[*Exit* Messenger *into the palace.*]

[*Enter* Creon *with attendants, bearing* Haimon's *body.*]

Choragos. But here is the king himself: oh look at him,
Bearing his own damnation in his arms.   85
Creon. Nothing you say can touch me any more.
My own blind heart has brought me
From darkness to final darkness. Here you see
The father murdering, the murdered son—
And all my civic wisdom!   90

Haimon my son, so young, so young to die,
I was the fool, not you; and you died for me.
Choragos. That is the truth; but you were late in learning it.
Creon. This truth is hard to bear. Surely a god
Has crushed me beneath the hugest weight of heaven,   95
And driven me headlong a barbaric way
To trample out the thing I held most dear.

The pains that men will take to come to pain!

[*Enter* Messenger *from the palace.*]

Messenger. The burden you carry in your hands is heavy,
But it is not all: You will find more in your house.   100
Creon. What burden worse than this shall I find there?
Messenger. The queen is dead.
Creon. O port of death, deaf world,
Is there no pity for me? And you, angel of evil,
I was dead, and your words are death again.   105
Is it true, boy? Can it be true?
Is my wife dead? Has death bred death?
Messenger. You can see for yourself.

[The doors are opened, and the body of Eurydice *is disclosed within.]*

Creon. Oh pity!
    All true, all true, and more than I can bear!   110
    O my wife, my son!
Messenger. She stood before the altar, and her heart
    Welcomed the knife her own hand guided,
    And a great cry burst from her lips for Megareus dead,
    And for Haimon dead, her sons; and her last breath   115
    Was a curse for their father, the murderer of her sons.
    And she fell, and the dark flowed in through her closing eyes.
Creon. O God, I am sick with fear.
    Are there no swords here? Has no one a blow for me?
Messenger. Her curse is upon you for the deaths of both.   120
Creon. It is right that it should be. I alone am guilty.
    I know it, and I say it. Lead me in
    Quickly, friends.
    I have neither life nor substance. Lead me in.
Choragos. You are right, if there can be right in so much wrong.   125
    The briefest way is best in a world of sorrow.
Creon. Let it come,
    Let death come quickly, and be kind to me.
    I would not ever see the sun again.
Choragos. All that will come when it will; but we, meanwhile,   130
    Have much to do. Leave the future to itself.
Creon. All my heart was in' that prayer!
Choragos. Then do not pray any more: the sky is deaf.
Creon. Lead me away. I have been rash and foolish.
    I have killed my son and my wife.   135
    I look for comfort; my comfort lies here dead.
    Whatever my hands have touched has come to nothing.
    Fate has brought all my pride to a thought of dust.

[As Creon *is being led into the house, the* Choragos *advances and speaks directly to the audience.]*

Choragos. There is no happiness where there is no wisdom;
    No wisdom but in submission to the gods.   140
    Big words are always punished,
    And proud men in old age learn to be wise.

FOR STUDY AND DISCUSSION

Prologue

1. The action of the play begins immediately with a conflict between Antigone and Ismene. What is the cause of the conflict?

2. Ismene and Antigone are strongly contrasted in this scene. What can you tell of Antigone's character? Of Ismene's?

3. The speeches of the Chorus and Choragos interrupt the action of the play to describe the battle to the audience. What do these city elders look forward to in the future?

Scene 1

1. What have we already learned about Creon before he appears onstage? What is revealed of Creon's character in this scene? (Remember that characters may reveal their own motives in the motives they attribute to others.)

2. What reason does Creon give for his ruling concerning the bodies of Polyneices and Eteocles? How does the Chorus react?

3. The Sentry is a very ordinary person, even somewhat humorous. What does he want Creon to think about him?

Ode 1

1. This ode presents a portrait of human existence—its wonders and its limitations. Restate its main idea in your own words.

2. How does the ode comment on the problem of the play as it has been developed so far?

Scene 2

1. Since Greek dramas usually do not move from one setting to another, many of their important actions take place offstage. What major event has taken place before this scene opens? How does Sophocles help the audience picture what has happened?

2. How does Antigone defend her actions?

3. Look back at the comments of the Choragos in this scene. Does he seem to side with Antigone or with Creon? Explain.

4. How has Ismene changed since we first saw her in the Prologue? How does Antigone treat her?

Ode 2

1. What grave fears for Oedipus' children does this ode express?

2. How would you explain the ancient wisdom in line 28: "Man's little pleasure is the spring of sorrow"?

Scene 3

1. Haimon is caught in a conflict of loyalties in this scene. What methods and arguments does he use to try to persuade Creon to change his mind? For example, how does he appeal to his father's self-interest?

2. How does Creon react to Haimon's arguments? What attitudes does Creon seem to take toward women?

3. What function does the Choragos have in this scene? Whose side, if any, is he on?

Ode 3

The first ode was about human strengths and limitations, the second was about fate and the vengeance of the gods. What is the subject of this ode? Which lines allude to specific characters in the play?

Scene 4

1. What comfort does the Chorus offer Antigone in this scene? Antigone thinks (in line 25) that the Chorus is making fun of her. Do you agree or disagree? Explain.

2. As Antigone faces her death, does she seem in any way changed from the way she has been in previous scenes? Explain your answer.

3. Antigone is not to be stoned to death as originally planned. Why does the form of her punishment suit Creon?

Ode 4

In this ode the Chorus alludes to three Greek myths that were familiar to the ancient Greek audiences. How are the fates of the characters in these myths related to Antigone's fate?

Scene 5

1. Creon has refused to yield to the arguments of Antigone and Haimon, and at first he refuses to listen to Teiresias. Of what does he accuse Teiresias?

2. Teiresias tells Creon that the only crime is pride. How has Creon shown that he is guilty of pride?

3. Why does Creon finally give in? What part does the Choragos play in Creon's decision?

4. How has the character of the Chorus (or its leader, the Choragos) changed throughout the play? Where in the play do you think the Chorus speaks for Sophocles himself?

Exodos

1. Violence is certainly a part of Greek drama, but it was never portrayed onstage. How does Sophocles tell us what happens to Antigone, Haimon, and Eurydice?

2. How is Teiresias' prophecy from Scene 5 fulfilled in this scene?

3. How has Creon changed since the beginning of the play? What does he finally come to recognize?

THE PLAY AS A WHOLE

1. In his last words, the Choragos states one of the major themes of the play:

> There is no happiness where there is no
>   wisdom;
> No wisdom but in submission to the gods.
> Big words are always punished,
> And proud men in old age learn to be wise.

What other lines in the play also refer to the idea that human pride can be destructive?

2. Other important themes appear in *Antigone*. Try to state in a few sentences what the play says about the individual conscience in conflict with the authority of the state. What does the play say about the conflict between human and divine laws? About loyalty to the family versus loyalty to the state?

3. The conflict in a tragedy is rarely between absolute good and absolute evil. How can Creon's conflict be seen as a conflict between two choices that seem equally "good" — that is, between the stability of the state and obedience to divine law?

4. What errors in judgment does Creon make in the course of the play? By the end of the play, do you find him a sympathetic or an unsympathetic character? Tell why.

5. Discuss whether Antigone is admirable and worthy to be honored, or whether she is foolish and just as proud as Creon. Where in the play does the Chorus accuse Antigone of pride?

6. Discuss the idea of fate as it is expressed in *Antigone*. Are Antigone and Creon the helpless victims of fate, or do they freely choose their own destinies? Explain your answer.

THE TRAGIC HERO OR HEROINE

The Greek philosopher Aristotle (384–322 B.C.) formulated ideas about tragedy that have influenced writers and critics for centuries. Aristotle based his ideas on the tragedies produced in his own day.

Aristotle defines the tragic hero as a person who is neither completely virtuous nor utterly villainous. The downfall of this tragic figure is brought about "not by vice or depravity but by some error in judgment or frailty." The tragic hero or heroine is "highly renowned or prosperous" so that the fall from good fortune to disaster will arouse strong emotions in the audience.

Aristotle felt that it was good to arouse these strong feelings in the audience. He thought that the release of these upsetting emotions—called *catharsis* (or "cleansing")— was helpful politically because it cleansed people of their urges to defy authority the way the tragic hero or heroine did.

Who is the tragic figure in *Antigone?* Some critics argue that Creon is the real tragic hero. To support their position, they offer the following evidence: Creon undergoes a dramatic change, whereas Antigone's fate is determined in the first scene and she disappears from stage halfway through the play. The deaths of Haimon and Eurydice are meaningful only to Creon, not to Antigone. And it is the body of Creon's son that is carried onstage, not Antigone's body.

The classical scholar H. D. F. Kitto has suggested that *Antigone* is built on a "double foundation," and that the play's "center of gravity does not lie in one person, but between two." Kitto says that "of the two, the significant one to Sophocles was always Creon." What do you think? Are there two tragic figures in this play, or only one? If you think there is only one, who is it?

To help you decide, apply each of the following questions to Antigone and to Creon:

1. What error in judgment or frailty in character did the tragic figure display?
2. At what point in the play might the character have saved himself or herself from a tragic downfall?
3. Define the character's downfall. How did he or she change during the course of the play?
4. What emotions did the character's downfall arouse in you?

FOR COMPOSITION

Supporting an Opinion

The characters in *Antigone* make many statements that sound like proverbs, or wise sayings. If you look closely, you will see that these statements express the speaker's view about life. None are factual statements that can be definitely proved or disproved, though they do invite agreement or disagreement. Choose one of the following statements from the play and in a brief essay tell whether you agree or disagree with it. Support your opinion with at least three good reasons.

We are only women, we cannot fight with men, Antigone!

Impossible things should not be tried at all.

Money! There's nothing in the world so demoralizing as money.

Good lives are made so by discipline.

The only crime is pride.

There is no happiness where there is no wisdom.

The Tragedy of Julius Caesar

At the beginning of *Julius Caesar*, the Roman Republic is at peace after three years of civil war. By the end of the play, one man has been assassinated in public, another has been torn to pieces by an angry mob, a woman has killed herself by swallowing hot coals, thousands of soldiers lie dead on a battlefield, a government has changed hands, and several of Rome's most respected citizens have killed themselves rather than face dishonor.

These are historical events of the first century B.C., which William Shakespeare used to write *Julius Caesar*. The facts of this story can be found in an encyclopedia. In 1599, when Shakespeare was writing the play, he found his facts in a translation of *Plutarch's Lives of the Noble Greeks and Romans*. (Plutarch was a Greek historian who wrote during the first century A.D.) But the play *Julius Caesar* is more than a collection of facts. Historians can tell you about facts; playwrights must find ways of dramatizing and re-creating events before your eyes.

Julius Cæfar.

Catherine A *Clajwatt*

TRAGEDY.

As it is Now ACTED

AT THE

Theatre Royal.

WRITTEN

By *William Shakefpeare*.

✠✠✠✠✠
✠✠✠✠
✠✠✠

LONDON,

Printed by *H. H.* Jun. for *Hen. Heringman* and *R. Bentley* in *Ruffel-ftreet* in *Covent-Garden*, and fold by *Jofeph Knight* and *Francis Saunders* at the *Blew Anchor* in the Lower Walk of the *New Exchange* in the *Strand*. 1 6 8 4 .

Shakespeare's Life and Times

Since his death over three hundred and sixty years ago, Shakespeare has been regarded as the greatest writer in the English language. Not only did he express himself in language unsurpassed for richness and beauty, but perhaps better than any other writer before or after him, Shakespeare understood human concerns—the joys, fears, hopes, passions, and weaknesses common to all of us, in all ages.

Few facts are known about Shakespeare's life. In April 1564, in the early part of Queen Elizabeth's reign, William Shakespeare was born at Stratford-on-Avon, a small market town in the county of Warwickshire. William was the oldest son of John Shakespeare, one of the most prosperous men of Stratford, and of Mary Arden, the daughter of a gentleman. At the age of eighteen, William Shakespeare married Anne Hathaway, the daughter of a nearby farmer, and within a few years their three children were born. Sometime after this, Shakespeare left Stratford for London. By 1592, when he was twenty-eight, he was firmly established as an actor and a playwright. Two years later, Shakespeare became a full sharer in the profits of the acting company known as the Lord Chamberlain's Company. By the time he was thirty-two, he was generally considered "the most excellent" of the writers of both tragedy and comedy for the stage. By the time he was thirty-six, he had behind him such masterpieces as *Romeo and Juliet* (a tragedy), *A Midsummer Night's Dream* (a comic farce and fantasy), and *As You Like It* (a mixture of comedy and satire—to be taken "as you like it").

Early in 1599 the Chamberlain's Men moved into a new theater, built to their own specifications, just south of London. One of the first plays performed in this theater (called the Globe) was *The Tragedy of Julius Caesar*. Within a few years, Shakespeare produced a series of great tragedies: *Hamlet, Othello, King Lear, Macbeth,* and *Antony and Cleopatra.* Many of these plays were performed at the royal court, for when Queen Elizabeth died in 1603, Shakespeare's company received the enthusiastic patronage of her successor, King James I. Known thereafter as the King's Men, the company at the Globe rose to even greater prominence.

A scene from Shakespeare's comedy *A Midsummer Night's Dream*, performed at the Stratford Shakespearean Festival, Ontario, with Maggie Smith as Titania and Alan Scarfe as Bottom (under the donkey's head).

In his mid-forties, Shakespeare retired from the stage and returned to his home in Stratford-on-Avon, a prosperous man and one of the town's most honored citizens. He died in Stratford on April 23, 1616.

Shakespeare lived near the end of the historical period called the Renaissance, which lasted from about 1350 to 1600. During the Renaissance (a French word meaning "rebirth"), Europeans made their first great expeditions to the New World, technology advanced at an unprecedented rate, the arts flourished, and the great classical civilizations of Greece and Rome were rediscovered. The grammar school of Shakespeare's day taught the Bible, Latin grammar, and Ovid's *Metamorphoses*, and educated its students to look to the past for lessons about their own times.

During the reign of Queen Elizabeth (1558–1603), England developed into one of the great powers of the world. This was the age of growing English sea power, of English exploration, and of continuing growth in English scholarship. Nevertheless, most Englishmen had little reliable information about life beyond their own island, much less of life in ancient Rome in the first century B.C. Thus, in *Julius Caesar*, you will find many details of Elizabethan life mixed in with Roman history. Such out-of-place objects, customs, and beliefs are called *anachronisms*, which means literally "out of time." Shakespeare's Romans mention striking clocks, nightcaps, chimneys, hats, and doublets (which are heavy Elizabethan jackets). None of these existed in ancient Rome. There are also references to bearbaiting, an Elizabethan sport in which chained bears were attacked by dogs. Even Elizabethan and Roman superstitions are mixed in *Julius Caesar*.

Shakespeare's Theater

A model of the original Globe Theater.
Folger Shakespeare Library, Washington, D.C.

In September of 1599, a Swiss doctor visiting London wrote in his diary that he crossed the river Thames "and there in the house with the thatched roof witnessed an excellent performance of the tragedy of the first emperor Julius." The house with the thatched roof was the Globe, a theater which had just opened that summer. Fourteen years later that thatch caught fire and the Globe burned to the ground. The Swiss doctor's diary entry is one of the few pieces of information about the original Globe that has survived.

WOOD NEAR ATHENS

An artist's conception of an Elizabethan production of *A Midsummer Night's Dream*.

The Globe opened only twenty-three years after the first permanent theater had been built in England. Before that, plays had been performed in the courtyards of inns and on wagons in the street. The Globe contained many reminders of its courtyard origins. It was an eight-sided building with a central yard. About a third of the yard was occupied by a six-foot-high platform stage. The spectators paid one penny to stand in the yard around the stage, two pennies to sit in the second- or third-floor galleries that surrounded the yard, or three pennies to sit in the first-floor galleries. Those who paid the least and stood in the yard were called *groundlings* — the noisiest and perhaps most vocally critical members of the audience.

The stage of the Globe had no front curtain and no artificial lighting. (Performances took place in the afternoon.) The back wall of the stage had at least two doors for entrances and exits. There was a balcony, used for scenes that took place on a hilltop, on the walls of a town, or on a second story.

From various bills and receipts that have survived, we know that Elizabethan theaters used many props: swords, lanterns, trees, rocks, and even a Mouth of Hell. The heavier props were probably raised and lowered through trapdoors in the stage. But there were no settings of the sort used in many modern theaters. The realistic, boxlike set with the audience spying through an imaginary fourth wall did not come into being until the late nineteenth century. Because there were no elaborate sets or a curtain in Shakespeare's time, each scene could follow the other with little interruption. To make up for the lack of scenery, Elizabethan costumes were lavish and expensive. Having costumes appropriate to the historical period of a play is also a modern idea: for example, Shakespeare's Caesar wore an Elizabethan doublet, not a Roman toga.

A performance of *Julius Caesar* included realistic sound effects for thunder and battle noises. The actor playing Caesar probably had a pig's bladder filled with blood hidden in his costume; when he was stabbed, he and the conspirators were drenched with gore.

Plays at the Globe were acted on the repertory system. A different play was presented every afternoon, and the company kept on its program a series of plays to which it was constantly adding. The average life of a play was about ten performances, although popular plays were generally acted more often. In a given season, an actor might have had to memorize half a dozen or more parts. About fifteen men played all the roles in *Julius Caesar*, with the women's parts taken by boy apprentices. The senior actors were also shareholders in the company. Since the Puritans of Elizabethan England considered the theater sinful, an acting company often had to seek the legal protection of a noble patron. Shakespeare's company was protected by the Lord Chamberlain at first, and later by King James I.

The picture you now have of a performance at the Globe may seem a little unusual. How could the plays be convincing without actresses and sets?

But no play, movie, or television show is truly realistic. Imagine how Shakespeare would have felt if he could have seen a

A scene from Shakespeare's comedy *As You Like It*, performed at the Stratford Shakespearean Festival, Ontario, with Maggie Smith as Rosalind (disguised as a boy) and Jack Wetherall as Orlando.

A scene from *As You Like It*, performed at the American Shakespeare Theater, Stratford, Connecticut, with William Larson as Corin (a shepherd) and George Hearn as Touchstone (a clown).

fade-out in a modern movie. He might have thought that the actor or actress was a disappearing ghost. Because we have seen movies all our lives, we understand that a fade-out indicates the passage of time. In a way, we have made a silent agreement with the filmmakers that in this make-believe world a fade-out will stand for a time lapse. These kinds of agreements between the artist and audience are called *conventions*. Shakespeare and his audience also accepted certain conventions.

One of these conventions involves the use of *verse*. The characters in *Julius Caesar* express themselves in poetry. Occasionally, Shakespeare will have his characters speak in prose, often for coarse, comic effects. Casca, in Act One, for example, is addressed in poetry, but he answers in prose because he wants to be blunt. When a character speaks alone on the stage, we call the speech a *soliloquy*. The soliloquy is used to convey a character's thoughts directly to the audience. Sometimes a character will make a remark during a scene that is meant to be heard by the audience and perhaps by one other character, but by no one else onstage. These remarks are called *asides*. Asides are often used for an ironic effect, informing the audience of something that another character is ignorant of.

Historical Background
of the Play

Julius Caesar (100?–44 B.C.) was the foremost Roman of his day and, because of the great influence of Rome, one could say he was then the most powerful man in the known world. He was born into a prominent family and was for most of his career close to the centers of power. He led an active and adventuresome life. As a young man, he had been banished from Rome because of an unpopular marriage. After he had been pardoned, he decided to prepare for a political career by studying oratory or rhetoric, the usual training for public life in his day. On his way to Rhodes to study, he was captured by pirates. After his ransom was paid, Caesar manned ships, set out in pursuit of the pirates, overtook and overcame them, and had them executed.

When he returned to Rome, he set about systematically to win the favor of the people. Caesar spent great sums of money on popular causes and was rewarded with a succession of high offices. He used these high offices to cement his relationship with the people. He raised many persons to positions of wealth and power—Marcus Brutus was one. Caesar also became a brilliant military strategist. His conquests in Gaul and Britain made him even more popular with the people and gained him the loyalty of the army as well. All of these favors and gifts, however, made him unpopular with his former political allies, who became jealous of him. United under Pompey, these enemies persuaded the Roman Senate to pass a resolution commanding Caesar to disband his army and return to Rome as a private citizen. Caesar refused to comply. Instead, he marched on Rome with his army. Many members of the force sent to stop him deserted their commander, Pompey, and joined Caesar's army. Pompey fled to Greece, and then to Egypt, where he was murdered before Caesar could capture him.

Caesar then did battle in Asia Minor, announcing his victory to the Senate with the now famous words: "*Veni. Vidi. Vici.*" ("I came. I saw. I conquered.") After defeating the remaining Pompeian forces in Africa and Spain, he returned to Rome,

Trajan's Column in Rome, showing Roman military victories. Constructed in A.D. 113 by the Emperor Trajan.

the undisputed master of the Roman world. Caesar was made dictator for life and probably wanted to be named king, though he was uncertain about how popular this would be with the people. In the sixth century B.C., the Romans had expelled their last king and set up a republican government. Since then, they had had a lasting hatred of the office and title of king. There was good reason for this: the last king, Tarquin, came to the throne by murder and held it by tyranny.

This is the situation as Shakespeare's play begins. On the one hand is Caesar, recently arrived in Rome with great favor among the populace. On the other hand are those who envy him and who fear for the republic should he be named king.

Julius Caesar   *William Shakespeare*

Characters

Julius Caesar
Octavius Caesar ⎫ triumvirs after
Marcus Antonius ⎬ the death of
M. Aemilius Lepidus ⎭ Julius Caesar
Cicero ⎫
Publius ⎬ Senators
Popilius Lena ⎭
Marcus Brutus ⎫
Cassius ⎪
Casca ⎪ conspirators
Trebonius ⎬ against Julius
Ligarius ⎪ Caesar
Decius Brutus ⎪
Metellus Cimber ⎪
Cinna ⎭
Flavius and Marullus, tribunes of
the people
Artemidorus of Cnidos, a teacher
of rhetoric

A Soothsayer
Cinna, a poet
Another Poet

Lucilius ⎫
Titinius ⎬ friends of Brutus
Messala ⎬ and Cassius
Young Cato ⎪
Volumnius ⎭
Varro ⎫
Clitus ⎪
Claudius ⎬ servants of Brutus
Strato ⎪
Lucius ⎪
Dardanius ⎭
Pindarus, servant of Cassius

Calpurnia, wife of Caesar
Portia, wife of Brutus

Senators, Citizens, Guards, Attendants, etc.

Scene: Rome; the neighborhood of Sardis; the neighborhood of Philippi

The photographs that illustrate *Julius Caesar*
are from the MGM film production, with James
Mason as Brutus, Deborah Kerr as Portia, Louis
Calhern as Caesar, Marlon Brando as Antony,
and John Gielgud as Cassius.

Act One

Scene 1

[*A street in Rome. It is the fifteenth of February, Lupercalia, a Roman festival celebrated with dancing, feasting, and public games. Caesar has recently returned to Rome.*
As the play opens, Flavius *and* Marullus, *tribunes of the people, meet a group of* Commoners *on their way to the Forum. The tribunes are angered by the people's eagerness to celebrate* Caesar's *triumph.*]

Flavius. Hence! Home, you idle creatures, get you home.
    Is this a holiday? What! Know you not,
    Being mechanical,° you ought not walk
    Upon a laboring day without the sign
    Of your profession?° [*Stopping one*] Speak, what trade art thou?   5
First Commoner. Why, sir, a carpenter.
Marullus. Where is thy leather apron and thy rule?
    What dost thou with thy best apparel on?
    [*To another*] You, sir, what trade are you?
Second Commoner. Truly, sir, in respect of a fine workman,° I am but, as you would say, a   10
    cobbler.°
Marullus. But what trade art thou? Answer me directly.
Second Commoner. A trade, sir, that I hope I may use with a safe conscience, which is indeed, sir, a mender of bad soles.
Marullus. What trade, thou knave? Thou naughty knave, what trade?   15
Second Commoner. Nay, I beseech you, sir, be not out° with me. Yet if you be out, sir, I can mend you.
Marullus. What mean'st thou by that? Mend me, thou saucy fellow!
Second Commoner. Why, sir, cobble you.
Flavius. Thou art a cobbler, art thou?   20
Second Commoner. Truly, sir, all that I live by is with the awl. I meddle with no tradesman's matters, nor women's matters, but with awl. I am indeed, sir, a surgeon to old shoes. When they are in great danger, I re-cover them. As proper men as ever trod upon neat's leather° have gone upon my handiwork.
Flavius. But wherefore art not in thy shop today? Why dost thou lead these men about the   25
    streets?
Second Commoner. Truly, sir, to wear out their shoes, to get myself into more work. But indeed, sir, we make holiday, to see Caesar and to rejoice in his triumph.

---

3. **mechanical:** workmen. 4–5. **sign . . . profession:** tools and work clothes. 10. **in . . . workman:** as far as good work is concerned. 11. **cobbler:** a shoemaker. (In Shakespeare's time, the word also meant "bungler.") 16. **out:** This first *out* means "out of temper, angry." The next one means "down at the heel." 24. **neat's leather:** oxhide.

Marullus. Wherefore rejoice? What conquest brings he home?
    What tributaries° follow him to Rome,   30
    To grace in captive bonds his chariot wheels?
    You blocks, you stones, you worse than senseless things!
    O you hard hearts, you cruel men of Rome,
    Knew you not Pompey? Many a time and oft
    Have you climbed up to walls and battlements,   35
    To towers and windows, yea, to chimney tops,
    Your infants in your arms, and there have sat
    The livelong day with patient expectation
    To see great Pompey pass the streets of Rome.
    And when you saw his chariot but appear,   40
    Have you not made a universal shout,
    That Tiber° trembled underneath her banks
    To hear the replication° of your sounds
    Made in her concave shores?
    And do you now put on your best attire?   45
    And do you now cull out° a holiday?
    And do you now strew flowers in his way
    That comes in triumph over Pompey's blood?°
    Be gone!
    Run to your houses, fall upon your knees,   50
    Pray to the gods to intermit° the plague
    That needs must light on this ingratitude.
Flavius. Go, go, good countrymen, and for this fault
    Assemble all the poor men of your sort.
    Draw them to Tiber banks and weep your tears   55
    Into the channel till the lowest stream
    Do kiss the most exalted shores of all.

                                      [Exeunt all the Commoners.]

    See whether their basest metal° be not moved.
    They vanish tongue-tied in their guiltiness.
    Go you down that way toward the Capitol,   60
    This way will I. Disrobe the images°
    If you do find them decked with ceremonies.°
Marullus. May we do so?
    You know it is the feast of Lupercal.°
Flavius. It is no matter. Let no images   65
    Be hung with Caesar's trophies. I'll about,

---

30. **tributaries:** captives, prisoners. 42. **Tiber:** the river that runs through Rome. 43. **replication:** echo. 46. **cull out:** choose to take. 48. **Pompey's blood:** Caesar has killed Pompey's sons in Spain. 51. **intermit:** prevent. 58. **metal:** material, stuff of which they are made. 61. **Disrobe the images:** strip the statues. 62. **ceremonies:** decorations. 64. **Lupercal** (lōō′pər-kăl): Roman god of fertility.

And drive away the vulgar° from the streets.
So do you too, where you perceive them thick.
These growing feathers plucked from Caesar's wing
Will make him fly an ordinary pitch,°   70
Who else would soar above the view of men
And keep us all in servile fearfulness.

                                                            [*Exeunt.*]

Scene 2

[*A public square near the Forum. A flourish of trumpets announces the approach of
Caesar. A crowd of* Commoners *gathers, among them an old man, a* Soothsayer. *Enter*
Caesar, *his wife* Calpurnia, Portia, Decius, Cicero, Brutus, Cassius, Casca, *and* Antony,
who is stripped for running in the games.]

Caesar. Calpurnia!
Casca.   Peace, ho! Caesar speaks.
Caesar.   [*Music ceases.*] Calpurnia!
Calpurnia. Here, my lord.
Caesar. Stand you directly in Antonius'° way
    When he doth run his course. Antonius!
Antonius. Caesar, my lord?   5
Caesar. Forget not, in your speed, Antonius,
    To touch Calpurnia, for our elders say
    The barren, touchèd in this holy chase,
    Shake off their sterile curse.°
Antonius.   I shall remember:
    When Caesar says "Do this," it is performed.   10
Caesar. Set on, and leave no ceremony out.

                [*Flourish of trumpets. Caesar starts to leave.*]

Soothsayer. Caesar!
Caesar. Ha! Who calls?
Casca. Bid every noise be still—peace yet again!
Caesar. Who is it in the press° that calls on me?   15

---

67. **vulgar:** common people.   70. **pitch:** height of a soaring falcon. Flavius is saying that without the common people
("these growing feathers"), Caesar will not be able to soar so high.
    3. **Antonius:** Mark Antony is sometimes referred to as Marcus Antonius.   7–9. **Calpurnia . . . curse:** Caesar's wife
has been unable to bear children. The Romans believed that women would bear children if touched by a whip of goat's
hide carried by a racer during this feast in celebration of the return of spring. Caesar asks Antony to touch Calpurnia
with his whip, hoping that this will enable her to give him a son   15. **press:** crowd.

I hear a tongue, shriller than all the music,
Cry "Caesar." Speak. Caesar is turned to hear.
Soothsayer. Beware the ides of March.°
Caesar.   What man is that?
Brutus. A soothsayer bids you beware the ides of March.
Caesar. Set him before me. Let me see his face.   20
Cassius. Fellow, come from the throng. Look upon Caesar.
Caesar. What say'st thou to me now? Speak once again.
Soothsayer. Beware the ides of March.
Caesar. He is a dreamer. Let us leave him—pass.

[Trumpets sound. Exeunt all but Brutus *and* Cassius.]

Cassius. Will you go see the order of the course?   25
Brutus. Not I.
Cassius. I pray you, do.
Brutus. I am not gamesome.° I do lack some part
Of that quick spirit that is in Antony.
Let me not hinder, Cassius, your desires.   30
I'll leave you.
Cassius. Brutus, I do observe you now of late.
I have not from your eyes that gentleness
And show of love as I was wont to° have.
You bear too stubborn and too strange a hand   35
Over your friend that loves you.
Brutus.   Cassius,
Be not deceived. If I have veiled my look,
I turn the trouble of my countenance
Merely upon myself. Vexèd I am
Of late with passions of some difference,°   40
Conceptions only proper to myself,
Which give some soil° perhaps to my behaviors.
But let not therefore my good friends be grieved—
Among which number, Cassius, be you one—
Nor construe° any further my neglect   45
Than that poor Brutus, with himself at war,
Forgets the shows of love to other men.
Cassius. Then, Brutus, I have much mistook your passion,
By means whereof° this breast of mine hath buried

---

18. **ides of March:** March 15. 28. **gamesome:** fond of games. 34. **was wont to:** used to. 40. **passions . . . difference:** conflicting feelings. 42. **soil:** blemish, stain. 45. **construe:** interpret, guess at. 49. **By means whereof:** because of which.

Thoughts of great value, worthy cogitations. 50
Tell me, good Brutus, can you see your face?
Brutus. No, Cassius, for the eye sees not itself
But by reflection, by some other things.
Cassius. 'Tis just.°
And it is very much lamented, Brutus, 55
That you have no such mirrors as will turn
Your hidden worthiness into your eye,
That you might see your shadow.° I have heard
Where many of the best respect in Rome,
Except immortal° Caesar, speaking of Brutus, 60
And groaning underneath this age's yoke,
Have wished that noble Brutus had his eyes.
Brutus. Into what dangers would you lead me, Cassius,
That you would have me seek into myself
For that which is not in me? 65
Cassius. Therefore, good Brutus, be prepared to hear.
And since you know you cannot see yourself
So well as by reflection, I your glass°
Will modestly discover to yourself
That of yourself which you yet know not of. 70
And be not jealous on° me, gentle Brutus.
Were I a common laugher, or did use
To stale with ordinary oaths my love
To every new protester;° if you know
That I do fawn on men and hug them hard, 75
And after scandal them; or if you know
That I profess° myself in banqueting
To all the rout°—then hold me dangerous.

[*Flourish and shout.*]

Brutus. What means this shouting? I do fear the people
Choose Caesar for their king.
Cassius.   Aye, do you fear it? 80
Then must I think you would not have it so.
Brutus. I would not, Cassius, yet I love him well.
But wherefore do you hold me here so long?

---

54. **just:** true. 58. **shadow:** reflection. 60. **immortal:** Cassius speaks sarcastically. 68. **glass:** mirror. 71. **jealous on:** suspicious of. 72–74. **Were . . . protester:** if I were an ordinary jester (laugher), in the habit of swearing common oaths to everyone who swears them to me, and thereby cheapening my gift of friendship. 77. **profess:** proclaim friendship. 78. **rout:** mob.

What is it that you would impart to me?
If it be aught toward the general good,   85
Set honor in one eye and death i' the other,
And I will look on both indifferently;
For let the gods so speed me° as I love
The name of honor more than I fear death.

Cassius. I know that virtue to be in you, Brutus,   90
As well as I do know your outward favor.°
Well, honor is the subject of my story.
I cannot tell what you and other men
Think of this life, but for my single self
I had as lief not be° as live to be   95
In awe of such a thing as I myself.
I was born free as Caesar; so were you.
We both have fed as well, and we can both
Endure the winter's cold as well as he.
For once, upon a raw and gusty day,   100
The troubled Tiber chafing with her shores,
Caesar said to me "Darest thou, Cassius, now
Leap in with me into this angry flood
And swim to yonder point?" Upon the word,
Accoutered° as I was, I plungèd in   105
And bade him follow. So indeed he did.
The torrent roared, and we did buffet it
With lusty sinews, throwing it aside
And stemming it with hearts of controversy.°
But ere we could arrive the point proposed,   110
Caesar cried, "Help me, Cassius, or I sink!"
I, as Aeneas° our great ancestor
Did from the flames of Troy upon his shoulder
The old Anchises bear, so from the waves of Tiber
Did I the tired Caesar—and this man   115
Is now become a god, and Cassius is
A wretched creature, and must bend his body
If Caesar carelessly but nod on him.
He had a fever when he was in Spain,
And when the fit was on him, I did mark   120
How he did shake. 'Tis true, this god did shake.
His coward lips did from their color fly,°

---

88. **speed me:** give me good fortune. 91. **favor:** appearance. 95. **I . . . be:** I would prefer not to exist. 105. **Accoutered:** dressed in armor. 109. **controversy:** competition. 112. **Aeneas:** according to legend, the founder of Rome. As the Greeks destroyed Troy, Aeneas escaped, carrying his aged father, Anchises, on his back. 122. **His . . . fly:** Caesar's lips lost their color.

And that same eye whose bend doth awe the world
Did lose his luster. I did hear him groan.
Aye, and that tongue of his that bade the Romans   125
Mark him and write his speeches in their books,
Alas, it cried, "Give me some drink, Titinius,"
As a sick girl. Ye gods! It doth amaze me
A man of such a feeble temper should
So get the start of° the majestic world   130
And bear the palm° alone.

[*Shout. Flourish.*]

Brutus. Another general shout!
    I do believe that these applauses are
    For some new honors that are heaped on Caesar.
Cassius. Why, man, he doth bestride the narrow world   135
    Like a Colossus,° and we petty men
    Walk under his huge legs and peep about
    To find ourselves dishonorable graves.
    Men at some time are masters of their fates.
    The fault, dear Brutus, is not in our stars   140
    But in ourselves, that we are underlings.
    Brutus, and Caesar. What should be in that Caesar?
    Why should that name be sounded more than yours?
    Write them together, yours is as fair a name.
    Sound them, it doth become the mouth as well.   145
    Weigh them, it is as heavy. Conjure° with 'em,
    Brutus will start a spirit as soon as Caesar.
    Now, in the names of all the gods at once,
    Upon what meat doth this our Caesar feed
    That he is grown so great? Age, thou art shamed!   150
    Rome, thou hast lost the breed of noble bloods!
    When went there by an age, since the great flood,
    But it was famed with more than with one man?
    When could they say till now that talked of Rome
    That her wide walls encompassed but one man?   155
    Now is it Rome indeed, and room° enough,
    When there is in it but one only man.
    Oh, you and I have heard our fathers say

---

130. **get . . . of:** get a headstart on. 131. **palm:** prize of victory. 136. **Colossus:** The Colossus of Rhodes, one of the seven wonders of the ancient world, was a gigantic statue whose legs straddled the entrance of the harbor of Rhodes. 146. **Conjure:** call up spirits. 156. **Rome . . . room:** a pun. Both words were pronounced and spelled alike in Shakespeare's time.

There was a Brutus° once that would have brooked°
The eternal Devil to keep his state in Rome   160
As easily as a king.
Brutus. That you do love me, I am nothing jealous.°
What you would work me to, I have some aim.°
How I have thought of this and of these times,
I shall recount hereafter; for this present,   165
I would not, so with love I might entreat you,
Be any further moved. What you have said
I will consider. What you have to say
I will with patience hear, and find a time
Both meet° to hear and answer such high things.   170
Till then, my noble friend, chew upon this:
Brutus had rather be a villager
Than to repute himself a son of Rome
Under these hard conditions as this time
Is like to lay upon us.   175
Cassius. I am glad that my weak words
Have struck but thus much show of fire from Brutus.

[Voices and music are heard approaching.]

Brutus. The games are done, and Caesar is returning.
Cassius. As they pass by, pluck Casca by the sleeve,
And he will, after his sour fashion, tell you   180
What hath proceeded worthy note today.

[Reenter Caesar and his train of followers.]

Brutus. I will do so. But look you, Cassius.
The angry spot doth glow on Caesar's brow,
And all the rest look like a chidden train.°
Calpurnia's cheek is pale, and Cicero°   185
Looks with such ferret° and such fiery eyes
As we have seen him in the Capitol,
Being crossed in conference by some Senators.
Cassius. Casca will tell us what the matter is.

[Caesar looks at Cassius and turns to Antony.]

---

159. **a Brutus:** Lucius Junius Brutus expelled the last king from Rome and established the Republic in the sixth century B.C. Marcus Brutus believed he was descended from this patriot. **brooked:** put up with. 162. **am . . . jealous:** have no doubt. 163. **aim:** idea. 170. **meet:** appropriate. 184. **a chidden train:** scolded followers. 185. **Cicero:** a Roman senator. 186. **ferret:** a weasel-like animal with tiny red eyes. Here, sharp, nervous.

Caesar. Antonius! 190
Antonius. Caesar?
Caesar. Let me have men about me that are fat,
    Sleek-headed men, and such as sleep o' nights.
    Yond Cassius has a lean and hungry look.
    He thinks too much, such men are dangerous. 195
Antonius. Fear him not, Caesar. He's not dangerous,
    He is a noble Roman, and well given.°
Caesar. Would he were fatter! But I fear him not.
    Yet if my name were liable to fear,
    I do not know the man I should avoid 200
    So soon as that spare Cassius. He reads much,
    He is a great observer, and he looks
    Quite through the deeds of men. He loves no plays
    As thou dost, Antony; he hears no music.
    Seldom he smiles, and smiles in such a sort 205
    As if he mocked himself, and scorned his spirit
    That could be moved to smile at anything.
    Such men as he be never at heart's ease
    While they behold a greater than themselves,
    And therefore are they very dangerous. 210
    I rather tell thee what is to be feared
    Than what I fear, for always I am Caesar.
    Come on my right hand, for this ear is deaf,
    And tell me truly what thou think'st of him.

    [*Trumpets sound. Exeunt* Caesar *and all his train except* Casca, *who stays behind.*]

Casca. You pulled me by the cloak. Would you speak with me? 215
Brutus. Aye, Casca. Tell us what hath chanced today
    That Caesar looks so sad.°
Casca. Why, you were with him, were you not?
Brutus. I should not then ask Casca what had chanced.
Casca. Why, there was a crown offered him; and being offered him, he put it by with the 220
    back of his hand, thus. And then the people fell a-shouting.
Brutus. What was the second noise for?
Casca. Why, for that too.
Cassius. They shouted thrice. What was the last cry for?
Casca. Why, for that too. 225
Brutus. Was the crown offered him thrice?
Casca. Aye, marry,° was 't, and he put it by thrice, every time gentler than other. And at
    every putting-by mine honest neighbors shouted.

---

197. **well given:** well disposed (toward Caesar).   217. **sad:** serious.   227. **marry:** indeed.

Cassius. Who offered him the crown?

Casca. Why, Antony.   230

Brutus. Tell us the manner of it, gentle Casca.

Casca. I can as well be hanged as tell the manner of it. It was mere foolery—I did not mark it. I saw Mark Antony offer him a crown, yet 'twas not a crown neither, 'twas one of these coronets;° and, as I told you, he put it by once. But for all that, to my thinking, he would fain° have had it. Then he offered it to him again, then he put it by again. But, to   235 my thinking, he was very loath to lay his fingers off it. And then he offered it the third time, he put it the third time by. And still as he refused it the rabblement° hooted and clapped their chopped° hands and threw up their sweaty nightcaps and uttered such a deal of stinking breath because Caesar refused the crown that it had almost choked Caesar; for he swounded° and fell down at it. And for mine own part, I durst not laugh,   240 for fear of opening my lips and receiving the bad air.

Cassius. But soft,° I pray you. What, did Caesar swound?

Casca. He fell down in the market place and foamed at mouth and was speechless.

Brutus. 'Tis very like—he hath the falling sickness.°

Cassius. No, Caesar hath it not. But you, and I,   245
And honest Casca, we have the falling sickness.

Casca. I know not what you mean by that, but I am sure Caesar fell down. If the tagrag° people did not clap him and hiss him according as he pleased and displeased them, as they use to do the players in the theater, I am no true man.

Brutus. What said he when he came unto himself?   250

Casca. Marry, before he fell down, when he perceived the common herd was glad he refused the crown, he plucked me ope his doublet° and offered them his throat to cut. An I had been a man of any occupation,° if I would not have taken him at a word, I would I might go to Hell among the rogues. And so he fell. When he came to himself again, he said if he had done or said anything amiss, he desired Their Worships to   255 think it was his infirmity. Three or four wenches where I stood cried, "Alas, good soul!" and forgave him with all their hearts: but there's no heed to be taken of them. If Caesar had stabbed their mothers, they would have done no less.

Brutus. And after that, he came, thus sad, away?

Casca. Aye.   260

Cassius. Did Cicero say anything?

Casca. Aye, he spoke Greek.

Cassius. To what effect?

Casca. Nay, an I tell you that, I'll ne'er look you i' the face again. But those that understood him smiled at one another and shook their heads—but for mine own part, it was Greek   265 to me. I could tell you more news too. Marullus and Flavius, for pulling scarfs off

---

234. **coronets:** small crowns wreathed with laurel. 235. **fair:** gladly. 237. **rabblement:** common people. 238. **chopped:** chapped. 240. **swounded:** fainted. 242. **soft:** slowly. 244. **falling sickness:** epilepsy. Cassius picks up the term and gives it quite another meaning. 247. **tagrag:** shabbily dressed. 252. **ope his doublet:** open his short coat. Note that the actors were dressed in Elizabethan costumes. 253. **An . . . occupation:** if I had been a craftsman who carried cutting tools.

Caesar's images, are put to silence.° Fare you well. There was more foolery yet, if I
could remember it.

Cassius. Will you sup with me tonight, Casca?

Casca. No, I am promised forth.   270

Cassius. Will you dine with me tomorrow?

Casca. Aye, if I be alive, and your mind hold, and your dinner worth the eating.

Cassius. Good. I will expect you.

Casca. Do so. Farewell, both.

                                    [*Exit.*]

Brutus. What a blunt fellow is this grown to be!   275
He was quick mettle° when he went to school.

Cassius. So is he now in execution
Of any bold or noble enterprise,
However he puts on this tardy form.°
This rudeness is a sauce to his good wit,   280
Which gives men stomach to digest his words
With better appetite.

Brutus. And so it is. For this time I will leave you.
Tomorrow, if you please to speak with me,
I will come home to you, or, if you will,   285
Come home to me and I will wait for you.

                                    [*Exit* Brutus.]

Cassius. I will do so. Till then, think of the world.
Well, Brutus, thou art noble. Yet I see
Thy honorable mettle may be wrought
From that it is disposed.° Therefore it is meet   290
That noble minds keep ever with their likes,
For who so firm that cannot be seduced?
Caesar doth bear me hard,° but he loves Brutus.
If I were Brutus now and he were Cassius,
He should not humor° me. I will this night,   295
In several hands,° in at his windows throw,
As if they came from several citizens,
Writings, all tending to the great opinion
That Rome holds of his name, wherein obscurely
Caesar's ambition shall be glancèd° at.   300
And after this let Caesar seat him° sure,
For we will shake him, or worse days endure.

                                    [*Exit.*]

---

267. **put to silence:** banished. 276. **quick mettle:** lively spirited. 279. **tardy form:** appearance of stupidity.
289–290. **wrought . . . disposed:** changes from its natural inclinations. 293. **bear me hard:** dislikes me. 295. **humor:**
influence, persuade. 296. **several hands:** several different handwritings. 300. **glancèd:** hinted. 301. **him:** himself.

Scene 3

[*A street. Thunder and lightning. Enter, from opposite sides,* Casca, *with his sword drawn,*
and Cicero. *It is the night before the ides of March.*]

Cicero. Good even, Casca. Brought you Caesar home?
    Why are you breathless? And why stare you so?
Casca. Are not you moved, when all the sway° of earth
    Shakes like a thing unfirm? O Cicero,
    I have seen tempests when the scolding winds   5
    Have rived° the knotty oaks, and I have seen
    The ambitious ocean swell and rage and foam,
    To be exalted with° the threatening clouds.
    But never till tonight, never till now,
    Did I go through a tempest dropping fire.   10
    Either there is a civil strife in Heaven,
    Or else the world too saucy with the gods
    Incenses° them to send destruction.
Cicero. Why, saw you anything more wonderful?
Casca. A common slave—you know him well by sight—   15
    Held up his left hand, which did flame and burn
    Like twenty torches joined, and yet his hand,
    Not sensible of fire, remained unscorched.
    Besides—I ha' not since put up my sword—
    Against the Capitol I met a lion,   20
    Who glazed° upon me and went surly by
    Without annoying me. And there were drawn
    Upon a heap° a hundred ghastly women
    Transformèd with their fear, who swore they saw
    Men all in fire walk up and down the streets.   25
    And yesterday the bird of night° did sit
    Even at noonday upon the market place,
    Hooting and shrieking. When these prodigies°
    Do so conjointly meet, let not men say
    "These are their reasons, they are natural."   30
    For I believe they are portentous things
    Unto the climate that they point upon.°
Cicero. Indeed, it is a strange-disposèd time.
    But men may construe things after their fashion,

---

3. **sway:** natural order. 6. **rived:** split. 8. **exalted with:** raised up to the level of. 13. **Incenses:** angers.
21. **glazed:** glared. 22-23. **drawn...heap:** huddled together. 26. **bird of night:** screech owl. 28. **prodigies:** wonders.
31-32. **portentous...upon:** ominous things, foretelling disaster for Rome.

    Clean from the purpose° of the things themselves.   35
    Comes Caesar to the Capitol tomorrow?
Casca. He doth, for he did bid Antonius
    Send word to you he would be there tomorrow.
Cicero. Good night then, Casca. This disturbèd sky
    Is not to walk in.
Casca.   Farewell, Cicero.   40

                                     [*Exit* Cicero.]

                  [*Enter* Cassius.]

Cassius. Who's there?
Casca.   A Roman.
Cassius.   Casca, by your voice.
Casca. Your ear is good. Cassius, what night is this!
Cassius. A very pleasing night to honest men.
Casca. Who ever knew the heavens menace so?
Cassius. Those that have known the earth so full of faults.   45
    For my part, I have walked about the streets,
    Submitting me unto the perilous night,
    And thus unbraced,° Casca, as you see,
    Have bared my bosom to the thunder stone.°
    And when the cross° blue lightning seemed to open   50
    The breast of Heaven, I did present myself
    Even in the aim and very flash of it.
Casca. But wherefore did you so much tempt the heavens?
    It is the part of men to fear and tremble
    When the most mighty gods by tokens send   55
    Such dreadful heralds to astonish us.
Cassius. You are dull, Casca, and those sparks of life
    That should be in a Roman you do want,°
    Or else you use not. You look pale and gaze
    And put on fear and cast yourself in wonder,   60
    To see the strange impatience of the heavens.
    But if you would consider the true cause
    Why all these fires, why all these gliding ghosts,
    Why birds and beasts from quality and kind,°
    Why old men fool and children calculate,°   65
    Why all these things change from their ordinance,°

---

35. **Clean . . . purpose:** opposite to the real meaning.   48. **unbraced:** with clothes blowing open.   49. **thunder stone:** thunderbolt.   50. **cross:** forked.   58. **want:** lack.   64. **from . . . kind:** acting contrary to their natures.   65. **calculate:** prophesy.   66. **ordinance:** natural order.

Their natures and preformèd faculties,
To monstrous quality, why, you shall find
That Heaven hath infused them with these spirits
To make them instruments of fear and warning   70
Unto some monstrous state.
Now could I, Casca, name to thee a man
Most like this dreadful night
That thunders, lightens, opens graves, and roars
As doth the lion in the Capitol —   75
A man no mightier than thyself or me
In personal action, yet prodigious grown
And fearful, as these strange eruptions are.
Casca. 'Tis Caesar that you mean, is it not, Cassius?
Cassius. Let it be who it is. For Romans now   80
    Have thews° and limbs like to their ancestors.
    But, woe the while!° our father's minds are dead,
    And we are governed with our mothers' spirits,
    Our yoke and sufferance show us womanish.
Casca. Indeed they say the Senators tomorrow   85
    Mean to establish Caesar as a king,
    And he shall wear his crown by sea and land
    In every place save here in Italy.
Cassius. I know where I will wear this dagger then.
    Cassius from bondage will deliver Cassius.   90
    Therein, ye gods, you make the weak most strong.
    Therein, ye gods, you tyrants do defeat.
    Nor stony tower, nor walls of beaten brass,
    Nor airless dungeon, nor strong links of iron,
    Can be retentive to the strength of spirit;   95
    But life, being weary of these worldly bars,
    Never lacks power to dismiss itself.
    If I know this, know all the world besides,
    That part of tyranny that I do bear
    I can shake off at pleasure.

                       [Thunder still.]

Casca.   So can I.   100
    So every bondman in his own hand bears
    The power to cancel his captivity.

---

81. **thews:** sinews, strength. 82. **woe the while:** alas for our time.

Cassius. And why should Caesar be a tyrant, then?
    Poor man! I know he would not be a wolf
    But that he sees the Romans are but sheep.   105
    He were no lion were not Romans hinds.°
    Those that with haste will make a mighty fire
    Begin it with weak straws. What trash is Rome,
    What rubbish and what offal,° when it serves
    For the base matter to illuminate   110
    So vile a thing as Caesar! But, O Grief,
    Where hast thou led me? I perhaps speak this
    Before a willing bondman;° then I know
    My answer must be made. But I am armed,
    And dangers are to me indifferent.   115
Casca. You speak to Casca, and to such a man
    That is no fleering° telltale. Hold, my hand
    Be factious for redress of all these griefs,°
    And I will set this foot of mine as far
    As who goes farthest.
Cassius.   There's a bargain made.   120
    Now know you, Casca, I have moved already
    Some certain of the noblest-minded Romans
    To undergo with me an enterprise
    Of honorable-dangerous consequence.
    And I do know, by this they stay° for me   125
    In Pompey's porch;° for now, this fearful night,
    There is no stir or walking in the streets,
    And the complexion of the element
    In favor's° like the work we have in hand,
    Most bloody, fiery, and most terrible.   130

                    [*Enter* Cinna.]

Casca. Stand close° awhile, for here comes one in haste.
Cassius. 'Tis Cinna, I do know him by his gait—
    He is a friend. Cinna, where haste you so?
Cinna. To find out you. Who's that? Metellus Cimber?
Cassius. No, it is Casca, one incorporate   135
    To our attempts.° Am I not stayed for, Cinna?

---

106. **hinds:** female deer.   109. **offal** (ô'fəl): garbage.   113. **bondman:** slave (that is, of Caesar).   117. **fleering:** sneering.   118. **Be factious . . . griefs:** Form a faction, or conspiracy, with me to right these wrongs.   125. **stay:** wait.   126. **Pompey's porch:** the covered entrance to the theater built by Pompey.   128–129. **element in favor's:** sky (element) in appearance (favor) is.   131. **close:** hidden.   135–136. **incorporate . . . attempts:** involved in our conspiracy.

Cinna. I am glad on 't.° What a fearful night is this!

There's two or three of us have seen strange sights.

Cassius. Am I not stayed for? Tell me.

Cinna.   Yes, you are.

O Cassius, if you could   140

But win the noble Brutus to our party——

Cassius. Be you content. Good Cinna, take this paper,

And look you lay it in the praetor's chair,°

Where Brutus may but find it, and throw this

In at his window; set this up with wax   145

Upon old Brutus'° statue. All this done,

Repair to Pompey's porch, where you shall find us.

Is Decius Brutus and Trebonius there?

Cinna. All but Metellus Cimber, and he's gone

To seek you at your house. Well, I will hie,°   150

And so bestow these papers as you bade me.

Cassius. That done, repair to Pompey's theater.

[Exit Cinna.]

Come, Casca, you and I will yet ere day

See Brutus at his house. Three parts of him

Is ours already, and the man entire   155

Upon the next encounter yields him ours.

Casca. Oh, he sits high in all the people's hearts,

And that which would appear offense in us

His countenance, like richest alchemy,°

Will change to virtue and to worthiness.   160

Cassius. Him and his worth and our great need of him

You have right well conceited.° Let us go,

For it is after midnight, and ere day

We will awake him and be sure of him.

[Exeunt.]

---

137. **I . . . on 't:** that is, that Casca is involved.   143. **praetor's** (prē'tərz) **chair:** Brutus was a praetor, a high-ranking Roman judge, second in power only to Caesar's rank of consul.   146. **old Brutus:** Brutus' ancestor, Lucius Junius Brutus.   150. **hie:** hurry.   159. **alchemy** (ăl'kə-mē): an ancient science that attempted to change lesser metals into gold.   162. **conceited:** understood.

FOR STUDY AND DISCUSSION

1. The play begins with a humorous scene that provides important background information. How are the conflicting attitudes toward Caesar shown? What information about Caesar and Pompey is revealed?

2. The commoners (the mob) are a major force in the play. What does Scene 1 tell you about how fickle the mob is in its loyalty? How does it show that the mob is easily influenced by people in authority?

3. In line 46 of Scene 2, Brutus says that he is at war with himself. What are the two sides of the "war" that is going on in Brutus' mind?

4. In the early part of Scene 2, Cassius attempts to get Brutus to join the conspiracy against Caesar. Why doesn't he ask Brutus directly? What tactics does he use?

5. What is Caesar's emotional state when he reenters in Scene 2? What do you think he means by the word *hungry* in line 194?

6. What personal defects and weaknesses of Caesar does Shakespeare emphasize in Act One? Do you think these frailties make him unsuitable as a leader? Explain.

7. According to lines 162–170 of Scene 2, how eager is Brutus to continue his conversation with Cassius? Brutus' attitude has changed by lines 283–286. Why?

8. What does Cassius do and say that makes us suspicious of his motives and his cause? Do his actions seem to support Caesar's opinion of him?

9. In what ways is Cassius the opposite of Brutus?

10. Scene 3 begins with a frightening storm. What attitude does each of the following characters have toward the storm and its causes: Cicero, Casca, Cassius? How does Cassius use the storm to support his political views?

11. In Scene 3 Cassius sounds out Casca on joining the conspiracy, just as in Scene 2 he sounded out Brutus. How is his approach to Casca different from his approach to Brutus? How is it similar?

12. Why is it necessary to the conspirators that Brutus join them? Cite lines from Scene 3 that show their attitudes toward Brutus.

13. What is the mood of Scene 3?

DRAMATIC STRUCTURE: CHARACTERIZATION

In Act One, Scene 2, Shakespeare brings all of his major characters onstage. By the end of this scene, we have come to know them as individuals with distinct traits, beliefs, and ways of speaking. Even characters with little to say in this scene—Antony and Casca, for example—are distinct persons in a way that the minor characters Flavius and Marullus are not.

The playwright's basic method for building several characterizations economically is this: when a character speaks, he or she will often give information about three people. These three people are the character being discussed, the character being addressed, and the character speaking.

To illustrate, look at one of Caesar's early speeches:

> Forget not, in your speed, Antonius,
> To touch Calpurnia, for our elders say
> The barren, touchèd in this holy chase,
> Shake off their sterile curse.
> (2, 6–9)

Caesar is discussing Calpurnia, his wife, and we learn that Antony is a friend of Caesar's: the words "Forget not" make it clear that Antony and Caesar have already had a conversation on the subject.

And what does Caesar tell us about himself? First, we learn that he is superstitious and concerned about his public image. It is "our elders" who believe in this magic cure, he says, not me; nevertheless, he is saying, don't forget to touch my wife in case the magic works. Second, Caesar gives us what may be a clue about his ambitions. One of the differences between a king and a dictator is that a king passes on his title to his offspring. If Caesar wants to be a king, he will also want to have an heir.

Read again each of the following speeches in its context. What does each tell about its speaker, its subject, and its listener?

Brutus. I am not gamesome. I do lack some part
  Of that quick spirit that is in Antony.
  Let me not hinder, Cassius, your desires.
  I'll leave you.

  (2, 28–31)

Cassius.   I have heard
  Where many of the best respect in Rome,
  Except immortal Caesar, speaking of Brutus,
  And groaning underneath this age's yoke,
  Have wished that noble Brutus had his eyes.

  (2, 58–62)

Caesar. I rather tell thee what is to be feared
  Than what I fear, for always I am Caesar.
  Come on my right hand, for this ear is deaf,
  And tell me truly what thou think'st of him.

  (2, 211–214)

LANGUAGE AND VOCABULARY

Understanding the Function of Puns

"Truly, sir, in respect of a fine workman, I am but, as you would say, a cobbler." Ten lines into *Julius Caesar*, Shakespeare has his cobbler make the first of several puns. Some puns are jokes that depend for their humor on words that sound alike but mean different things. Other puns play on different meanings of a single word. In the line quoted above, *cobbler* means both "shoemaker" and "bungler." It is hard for us to understand this pun because in the years since Shakespeare wrote this line, "bungler" as a meaning for *cobbler* has become archaic, that is, gone out of use.

Puns have a practical purpose in getting an audience into a good-humored mood. From accounts of Shakespeare's time, we know that his audiences were rowdier and more vocal in their approval and disapproval than a typical theater audience is today. Look back at Casca's remarks in Act One, Scene 2, lines 247–249; they describe an Elizabethan audience as well as a Roman one.

Shakespeare's use of puns at the start of his play is also a way of alerting his audience to the fact that words are tricky. As the play continues, words get trickier and soon become treacherous. Even in the first scene, puns are used by the cobbler to undercut the authority of the tribunes.

Puns have a metaphoric use as well. The cobbler lives by the *awl*, a tool for punching holes, which also sounds like the *All*, that is, the universe. The cobbler calls himself "a mender of bad soles" (souls). To what occupation is he comparing his own? The cobbler also says that he is a "surgeon" to old shoes. Where do the ideas of a body in bad health and souls in trouble come up again in Cassius' speeches to Brutus in Scene 2?

Act Two

Scene 1

[Rome. Brutus' orchard.]

Brutus. What, Lucius, ho! *[To himself]*
    I cannot, by the progress of the stars,
    Give guess how near to day. *[Calling]* Lucius, I say!
    I would it were my fault to sleep so soundly.
    When, Lucius, when? Awake, I say! What, Lucius!   5

[Enter Lucius from the house.]

Lucius. Called you, my lord?
Brutus. Get me a taper° in my study, Lucius.
    When it is lighted, come and call me here.
Lucius. I will, my lord.

                                                    [Exit.]

[Brutus returns to his brooding.]

Brutus. It must be by his° death and for my part   10
    I know no personal cause to spurn at him,
    But for the general.° He would be crowned.
    How that might change his nature, there's the question.
    It is the bright day that brings forth the adder,°
    And that craves wary walking. Crown him? — That —   15
    And then, I grant, we put a sting in him,
    That at his will he may do danger with.
    The abuse of greatness is when it disjoins
    Remorse° from power; and to speak truth of Caesar,
    I have not known when his affections swayed°   20
    More than his reason. But 'tis a common proof
    That lowliness is young ambition's ladder,
    Whereto the climber-upward turns his face.
    But when he once attains the upmost round,°
    He then unto the ladder turns his back,   25
    Looks in the clouds, scorning the base degrees
    By which he did ascend. So Caesar may.

---

7. **taper:** candle. 10. **his:** Caesar's. 12. **the general:** the general good. 14. **adder:** poisonous snake. 19. **Remorse:** pity. 20. **his affections swayed:** his personal desires ruled. 24. **round:** rung.

Then, lest he may, prevent.° And since the quarrel
Will bear no color° for the thing he is,
Fashion it thus: that what he is, augmented,
Would run to these and these extremities.   30
And therefore think him as a serpent's egg
Which hatched would as his kind grow mischievous,
And kill him in the shell.

[Reenter Lucius *with a letter.]*

Lucius. The taper burneth in your closet,° sir.   35
    Searching the window for a flint, I found
    This paper thus sealed up, and I am sure
    It did not lie there when I went to bed.

[Gives him the letter.]

Brutus. Get you to bed again. It is not day.
    Is not tomorrow, boy, the ides of March?   40
Lucius. I know not, sir.
Brutus. Look in the calendar and bring me word.
Lucius. I will, sir.

                                                                [Exit.]

Brutus. The exhalations° whizzing in the air
    Give so much light that I may read by them.   45

[Opens the letter and reads.]

"Brutus, thou sleep'st. Awake and see thyself.
Shall Rome, etc.° Speak, strike, redress."°
"Brutus, thou sleep'st. Awake."
Such instigations have been often dropped
Where I have took them up.   50
"Shall Rome, etc." Thus must I piece it out—
Shall Rome stand under one man's awe? What, Rome?
My ancestors did from the streets of Rome
The Tarquin° drive, when he was called a king.
"Speak, strike, redress." Am I entreated   55
To speak and strike? O Rome, I make thee promise,

---

28. **prevent:** he must be stopped. 29. **Will . . . color:** is unconvincing. 35. **closet:** a small room. 44. **exhalations:** meteors. 47. **etc.:** The letter continues, but Shakespeare did not include it in the manuscript. **redress:** right a wrong. 54. **Tarquin:** the last king of Rome, expelled by Brutus' ancestor.

556 *Drama*

If the redress will follow, thou receivest
Thy full petition at the hand of Brutus!

[*Reenter* Lucius.]

Lucius. Sir, March is wasted fifteen days.

[*Knocking within.*]

Brutus. 'Tis good. Go to the gate. Somebody knocks.   60

[*Exit* Lucius.]

Since Cassius first did whet me against Caesar
I have not slept.
Between the acting of a dreadful thing
And the first motion,° all the interim is
Like a phantasma or a hideous dream.   65
The Genius and the mortal instruments°
Are then in council, and the state of man,
Like to a little kingdom, suffers then
The nature of an insurrection.°

[*Reenter* Lucius.]

Lucius. Sir, 'tis your brother° Cassius at the door,   70
Who doth desire to see you.
Brutus.   Is he alone?
Lucius. No, sir, there are more with him.
Brutus.   Do you know them?
Lucius. No, sir. Their hats are plucked about their ears,
And half their faces buried in their cloaks,
That by no means I may discover them   75
By any mark of favor.°
Brutus.   Let 'em enter.

[*Exit* Lucius.]

They are the faction. O Conspiracy,
Shamest thou to show thy dangerous brow by night,
When evils are most free? Oh, then by day
Where wilt thou find a cavern dark enough   80
To mask thy monstrous visage? Seek none, Conspiracy—

---

64. **motion:** hint of the idea.   66. **The Genius . . . mortal instruments:** the mind (Genius) and the body.   69. **insurrec-tion:** revolution, civil war.   70. **brother:** brother-in-law. Cassius had married Brutus' sister.   76. **favor:** appearance.

Hide it in smiles and affability.
For if thou path, thy native semblance on,°
Not Erebus° itself were dim enough
To hide thee from prevention.°   85

[*Enter the conspirators,* Cassius, Casca, Decius, Cinna, Metellus Cimber, *and* Trebonius.]

Cassius. I think we are too bold upon your rest.
    Good morrow, Brutus. Do we trouble you?
Brutus. I have been up this hour, awake all night.
    Know I these men that come along with you?
Cassius. Yes, every man of them, and no man here   90
    But honors you, and every one doth wish
    You had but that opinion of yourself
    Which every noble Roman bears of you.
    This is Trebonius.
Brutus.   He is welcome hither.
Cassius. This, Decius Brutus.
Brutus.   He is welcome too.   95
Cassius. This, Casca, this, Cinna, and this, Metellus Cimber.
Brutus. They are all welcome.
    What watchful cares do interpose themselves
    Betwixt your eyes and night?
Cassius. Shall I entreat a word?   100

[*They whisper.*]

Decius. Here lies the east. Doth not the day break here?
Casca. No.
Cinna. Oh, pardon, sir, it doth, and yon gray lines
    That fret° the clouds are messengers of day.
Casca. You shall confess that you are both deceived.   105
    Here, as I point my sword, the sun arises,
    Which is a great way growing on the south,
    Weighing° the youthful season of the year.
    Some two months hence up higher toward the north
    He first presents his fire, and the high east   110
    Stands as the Capitol, directly here.

[Brutus *and* Cassius *rejoin the others.*]

---

83. **path . . . on:** walk openly in your usual way.   84. **Erebus** (ĕr′ə-bəs): in Greek mythology, a dim region of the underworld.   85. **prevention:** discovery.   104. **fret:** lace, ornament.   108. **Weighing:** considering.

Brutus. Give me your hands all over, one by one.

Cassius. And let us swear our resolution.

Brutus. No, not an oath. If not the face of men,
The sufferance of our souls, the time's abuse — 115
If these be motives weak, break off betimes,°
And every man hence to his idle bed.
So let high-sighted° tyranny range on
Till each man drop by lottery.° But if these,
As I am sure they do, bear fire enough 120
To kindle cowards and to steel with valor
The melting spirits of women, then, countrymen,
What need we any spur but our own cause
To prick us to redress? What other bond
Than secret Romans that have spoke the word, 125
And will not palter?° And what other oath
Than honesty to honesty engaged
That this shall be or we will fall for it?
Swear priests and cowards and men cautelous,°
Old feeble carrions° and such suffering souls 130
That welcome wrongs; unto bad causes swear
Such creatures as men doubt; but do not stain
The even virtue of our enterprise,
Nor the insuppressive mettle of our spirits,
To think that or our cause or° our performance 135
Did need an oath when every drop of blood
That every Roman bears, and nobly bears,
Is guilty of a several bastardy°
If he do break the smallest particle
Of any promise that hath passed from him. 140

Cassius. But what of Cicero? Shall we sound him?
I think he will stand very strong with us.

Casca. Let us not leave him out.

Cinna.   No, by no means.

Metellus. Oh, let us have him, for his silver hairs
Will purchase us a good opinion, 145
And buy men's voices to commend our deeds.
It shall be said his judgment ruled our hands.
Our youths and wildness shall no whit appear,
But all be buried in his gravity.

Brutus. Oh, name him not. Let us not break with him,° 150

---

116. **betimes:** right now.   118. **high-sighted:** proud-eyed.   119. **lottery:** chance.   126. **palter:** play false.   129. **cautelous:** crafty, cunning.   130. **carrions:** carcasses.   135. **or . . . or:** either . . . or.   138. **several bastardy:** individual betrayal.   150. **break with him:** disclose our plot to him.

For he will never follow anything
That other men begin.
Cassius.   Then leave him out.
Casca. Indeed he is not fit.
Decius. Shall no man else be touched but only Caesar?
Cassius. Decius, well urged. I think it is not meet   155
Mark Antony, so well beloved of Caesar,
Should outlive Caesar. We shall find of him
A shrewd contriver;° and you know his means,
If he improve them, may well stretch so far
As to annoy° us all. Which to prevent,   160
Let Antony and Caesar fall together.
Brutus. Our course will seem too bloody, Caius Cassius,
To cut the head off and then hack the limbs,
Like wrath in death and envy afterward.
For Antony is but a limb of Caesar.   165
Let us be sacrificers, but not butchers, Caius.
We all stand up against the spirit of Caesar,
And in the spirit of men there is no blood.
Oh, that we then could come by Caesar's spirit,
And not dismember Caesar! But, alas,   170
Caesar must bleed for it! And, gentle° friends,
Let's kill him boldly, but not wrathfully.
Let's carve him as a dish fit for the gods,
Not hew him as a carcass fit for hounds.
And let our hearts, as subtle masters do,   175
Stir up their servants° to an act of rage
And after seem to chide 'em. This shall make
Our purpose necessary and not envious,°
Which so appearing to the common eyes,
We shall be called purgers, not murderers.   180
And for Mark Antony, think not of him,
For he can do no more than Caesar's arm
When Caesar's head is off.
Cassius.   Yet I fear him,
For in the ingrafted love he bears to Caesar—
Brutus. Alas, good Cassius, do not think of him.   185
If he love Caesar, all that he can do
Is to himself, take thought and die for Caesar.

---

158. **contriver:** plotter.   160. **annoy:** harm.   171. **gentle:** noble.   176. **their servants:** our hands.   178. **envious:** full of malice.

And that were much he should, for he is given
To sports, to wildness and much company.
Trebonius. There is no fear° in him. Let him not die,   190
For he will live and laugh at this hereafter.

[*Clock strikes.*]

Brutus. Peace! Count the clock.
Cassius.   The clock hath stricken three.
Trebonius. 'Tis time to part.
Cassius.   But it is doubtful yet
Whether Caesar will come forth today or no,
For he is superstitious grown of late,   195
Quite from the main opinion he held once
Of fantasy, of dreams and ceremonies.°
It may be these apparent prodigies,
The unaccustomed terror of this night
And the persuasion of his augurers,°   200
May hold him from the Capitol today.
Decius. Never fear that. If he be so resolved,
I can o'ersway him. For he loves to hear
That unicorns may be betrayed with trees
And bears with glasses, elephants with holes,   205
Lions with toils° and men with flatterers—
But when I tell him he hates flatterers,
He says he does, being then most flattered.
Let me work,
For I can give his humor the true bent,°   210
And I will bring him to the Capitol.
Cassius. Nay, we all of us be there to fetch him.
Brutus. By the eighth hour.° Is that the uttermost?°
Cinna. Be that the uttermost, and fail not then.
Metellus. Caius Ligarius doth bear Caesar hard,   215
Who rated° him for speaking well of Pompey.
I wonder none of you have thought of him.
Brutus. Now, good Metellus, go along by him.
He loves me well, and I have given him reasons.
Send him but hither and I'll fashion° him.   220

---

190. **no fear:** nothing to fear. 197. **ceremonies:** supernatural signs. 200. **augurers:** officials who predicted the future by means of signs and omens. 204–206. **unicorns . . . toils:** It was believed that unicorns could be trapped by having a hunter stand in front of a tree, provoke the unicorn into charging, and then step quickly aside. Bears were supposed to be vain and easily lured by mirrors. Elephants can still be caught in pits and lions in snares (toils). 210. **humor . . . bent:** put him in the right mood. 213. **eighth hour:** the hour that business usually started in Shakespeare's day. **uttermost:** latest. 216. **rated:** rebuked. 220. **fashion:** mold.

Cassius. The morning comes upon 's. We'll leave you, Brutus.
　　And friends, disperse yourselves, but all remember
　　What you have said, and show yourselves true Romans.
Brutus. Good gentlemen, look fresh and merrily.
　　Let not our looks put on our purposes,　　　　　　　　　　225
　　But bear it as our Roman actors do,
　　With untired spirits and formal constancy.°
　　And so, good morrow to you every one.

　　　　　　　　　　　　　　　　　　[Exeunt all but Brutus.]

　　Boy! Lucius! Fast asleep! It is no matter.
　　Enjoy the honey-heavy dew of slumber.　　　　　　　　　　230
　　Thou hast no figures° nor no fantasies
　　Which busy care draws in the brains of men,
　　Therefore thou sleep'st so sound.

　　　　　　　　　[Enter Portia, Brutus' *wife.]*

Portia.　　　　　　　　　　　　Brutus, my lord!
Brutus. Portia, what mean you? Wherefore rise you now?
　　It is not for your health thus to commit　　　　　　　　　235
　　Your weak condition to the raw cold morning.
Portia. Nor for yours neither. You've ungently, Brutus,
　　Stole from my bed. And yesternight at supper
　　You suddenly arose and walked about,
　　Musing and sighing, with your arms across.　　　　　　　240
　　And when I asked you what the matter was,
　　You stared upon me with ungentle looks.
　　I urged you further, then you scratched your head,
　　And too impatiently stamped with your foot.
　　Yet I insisted, yet you answered not,　　　　　　　　　245
　　But with an angry wafture° of your hand
　　Gave sign for me to leave you. So I did,
　　Fearing to strengthen that impatience
　　Which seemed too much enkindled, and withal°
　　Hoping it was but an effect of humor,°　　　　　　　　250
　　Which sometime hath his hour with every man.
　　It will not let you eat, nor talk, nor sleep,
　　And, could it work so much upon your shape

---

227. **formal constancy:** calm self-control.　231. **figures:** dreams, visions.　246. **wafture:** motion.　249. **withal:** in addition.　250. **humor:** moodiness.

As it hath much prevailed on your condition,
I should not know you, Brutus. Dear my lord,   255
Make me acquainted with your cause of grief.
Brutus. I am not well in health, and that is all.
Portia. Brutus is wise, and were he not in health,
He would embrace the means to come by it.
Brutus. Why, so I do. Good Portia, go to bed.   260
Portia. Is Brutus sick, and is it physical°
To walk unbraced and suck up the humors°
Of the dank morning? What, is Brutus sick,
And will he steal out of his wholesome bed
To dare the vile contagion of the night,°   265
And tempt the rheumy and unpurgèd air

---

261. **physical:** good for your health.   262. **humors:** mists.   265. **contagion . . . night:** It was thought that night air was unhealthy, since it was moist (rheumy) and unpurified (unpurged) by the sun.

To add unto his sickness? No, my Brutus;
You have some sick offense within your mind,
Which by the right and virtue of my place
I ought to know of. And, upon my knees, 270
I charm you, by my once commended beauty,
By all your vows of love and that great vow
Which did incorporate and make us one,
That you unfold to me, yourself, your half,
Why you are heavy, and what men tonight 275
Have had resort to you; for here have been
Some six or seven who did hide their faces
Even from darkness.
Brutus.   Kneel not, gentle Portia.
Portia. I should not need if you were gentle Brutus.
Within the bond of marriage, tell me, Brutus, 280
Is it excepted I should know no secrets
That appertain to you? Am I yourself°
But,° as it were, in sort or limitation,
To keep with you at meals, comfort your bed,
And talk to you sometimes? Dwell I but in the suburbs 285
Of your good pleasure? If it be no more,
Portia is Brutus' harlot, not his wife.
Brutus. You are my true and honorable wife,
As dear to me as are the ruddy drops°
That visit my sad heart. 290
Portia. If this were true, then should I know this secret.
I grant I am a woman, but withal
A woman that Lord Brutus took to wife.
I grant I am a woman, but withal
A woman well reputed, Cato's daughter.° 295
Think you I am no stronger than my sex,
Being so fathered and so husbanded?
Tell me your counsels, I will not disclose 'em.
I have made strong proof of my constancy,
Giving myself a voluntary wound 300
Here in the thigh. Can I bear that with patience
And not my husband's secrets?
Brutus.   O ye gods,
Render me worthy of this noble wife!

---

282. **yourself:** part of you (by marriage). 283. **But:** only. 289. **ruddy drops:** blood. 295. **Cato's daughter:** Cato of Utica, Portia's father. Famous for his honesty and courage, Cato killed himself after Caesar defeated Pompey because he would not live under a tyrant's rule.

Hark, hark! One knocks. Portia, go in awhile,
And by and by thy bosom shall partake   305
The secrets of my heart.
All my engagements I will construe° to thee,
All the charactery° of my sad brows.
Leave me with haste. [*Exit* Portia.] Lucius, who's that knocks?

[*Reenter* Lucius *with* Ligarius.]

Lucius. Here is a sick man that would speak with you.   310
Brutus. Caius Ligarius, that Metellus spake of.
    Boy, stand aside. Caius Ligarius! How?
Ligarius. Vouchsafe° good morrow from a feeble tongue.
Brutus. Oh, what a time have you chose out, brave Caius,
    To wear a kerchief!° Would you were not sick!   315
Ligarius. I am not sick if Brutus have in hand
    Any exploit worthy the name of honor.
Brutus. Such an exploit have I in hand, Ligarius,
    Had you a healthful ear to hear of it.
Ligarius. By all the gods that Romans bow before,   320
    I here discard my sickness! Soul of Rome!
    Brave son, derived from honorable loins!
    Thou, like an exorcist,° hast conjured up
    My mortified spirit. Now bid me run,
    And I will strive with things impossible,   325
    Yea, get the better of them. What's to do?
Brutus. A piece of work that will make sick men whole.
Ligarius. But are not some whole that we must make sick?
Brutus. That must we also. What it is, my Caius,
    I shall unfold to thee as we are going   330
    To whom it must be done.
Ligarius.   Set on your foot,
    And with a heart new-fired I follow you,
    To do I know not what, but it sufficeth
    That Brutus leads me on.
Brutus.   Follow me, then.

                                           [*Exeunt.*]

---

307. **construe:** explain. 308. **charactery:** written lines. 313. **Vouchsafe:** please accept. 315. **kerchief:** a muffler, worn by the sick. 323. **exorcist:** summoner of dead (mortified) spirits to walk again.

Scene 2

[Caesar's house. Thunder and lightning. Enter Caesar *in his nightgown.]*

Caesar. Nor Heaven nor earth have been at peace tonight.
    Thrice hath Calpurnia in her sleep cried out,
    "Help, ho! They murder Caesar!" *[Calling.]* Who's within?

[Enter a Servant.*]*

Servant. My lord?
Caesar. Go bid the priests do present° sacrifice,   5
    And bring me their opinions of success.
Servant. I will, my lord.

                                                     [Exit.]

[Calpurnia, Caesar's wife, enters, alarmed.]

Calpurnia. What mean you, Caesar? Think you to walk forth?
    You shall not stir out of your house today.
Caesar. Caesar shall forth. The things that threatened me   10
    Ne'er looked but on my back. When they shall see
    The face of Caesar, they are vanishèd.
Calpurnia. Caesar, I never stood on ceremonies,°
    Yet now they fright me. There is one within,
    Besides the things that we have heard and seen,   15
    Recounts most horrid sights seen by the watch.°
    A lioness hath whelpèd° in the streets.
    And graves have yawned and yielded up their dead.
    Fierce fiery warriors fight upon the clouds,
    In ranks and squadrons and right form of war,   20
    Which drizzled blood upon the Capitol.
    The noise of battle hurtled in the air,
    Horses did neigh and dying men did groan,
    And ghosts did shriek and squeal about the streets.
    O Caesar! these things are beyond all use,°   25
    And I do fear them.
Caesar.   What can be avoided
    Whose end is purposed by the mighty gods?

---

5. **present:** immediate. 13. **stood on ceremonies:** paid much attention to omens. 16. **the watch:** night watchmen. 17. **whelpèd:** given birth. 25. **use:** custom, usual events.

Yet Caesar shall go forth, for these predictions
Are to the world in general as to Caesar.
Calpurnia. When beggars die, there are no comets seen.   30
The heavens themselves blaze forth the death of princes.
Caesar. Cowards die many times before their deaths,
The valiant never taste of death but once.
Of all the wonders that I yet have heard,
It seems to me most strange that men should fear,   35
Seeing that death, a necessary end,
Will come when it will come.

[*Reenter* Servant.]

What say the augurers?
Servant. They would not have you to stir forth today.
Plucking the entrails of an offering forth,
They could not find a heart within the beast.°   40
Caesar. The gods do this in shame of cowardice.
Caesar should be a beast without a heart
If he should stay at home today for fear.
No, Caesar shall not. Danger knows full well
That Caesar is more dangerous than he,   45
We are two lions littered° in one day,
And I the elder and more terrible.
And Caesar shall go forth.
Calpurnia.   Alas, my lord,
Your wisdom is consumed in confidence.
Do not go forth today. Call it my fear   50
That keeps you in the house, and not your own.
We'll send Mark Antony to the Senate House,
And he shall say you are not well today.
Let me, upon my knee, prevail in this.
Caesar. Mark Antony shall say I am not well,   55
And, for thy humor,° I will stay at home.

[*Enter* Decius.]

Here's Decius Brutus. He shall tell them so.
Decius. Caesar, all hail! Good morrow, worthy Caesar.
I come to fetch you to the Senate House.

---

40. **heart ... beast:** Roman augurers predicted the future by examining the insides of animals killed for sacrifice. In this case, the lack of the heart, the most important organ, suggests that the state soon will lack its most important citizen. Caesar, however, finds another explanation.   46. **littered:** born.   56. **humor:** whim, wish.

Caesar. And you are come in very happy time,   60
    To bear my greeting to the Senators
    And tell them that I will not come today.
    Cannot is false, and that I dare not, falser—
    I will not come today. Tell them so, Decius.
Calpurnia. Say he is sick.
Caesar.   Shall Caesar send a lie?   65
    Have I in conquest stretched mine arm so far,
    To be afeared to tell graybeards the truth?
    Decius, go tell them Caesar will not come.
Decius. Most mighty Caesar, let me know some cause,
    Lest I be laughed at when I tell them so.   70
Caesar. The cause is in my will—I will not come.
    That is enough to satisfy the Senate.
    But, for your private satisfaction,
    Because I love you, I will let you know.
    Calpurnia here, my wife, stays me at home.   75
    She dreamt tonight she saw my statue,
    Which like a fountain with a hundred spouts
    Did run pure blood, and many lusty Romans
    Came smiling and did bathe their hands in it.
    And these does she apply for warnings and portents   80
    And evils imminent, and on her knee
    Hath begged that I will stay at home today.
Decius. This dream is all amiss interpreted.
    It was a vision fair and fortunate.
    Your statue spouting blood in many pipes,   85
    In which so many smiling Romans bathed,
    Signifies that from you great Rome shall suck
    Reviving blood, and that great men shall press
    For tinctures, stains, relics, and cognizance.°
    This by Calpurnia's dream is signified.   90
Caesar. And this way have you well expounded° it.
Decius. I have, when you have heard what I can say.
    And know it now—the Senate have concluded
    To give this day a crown to mighty Caesar.
    If you shall send them word you will not come,   95
    Their minds may change. Besides, it were a mock
    Apt to be rendered, for someone to say
    "Break up the Senate till another time,
    When Caesar's wife shall meet with better dreams."

---

89. **tinctures . . . cognizance:** souvenirs of your greatness. 91. **expounded:** explained.

If Caesar hide himself, shall they not whisper   100
"Lo, Caesar is afraid"?
Pardon me, Caesar, for my dear dear love
To your proceeding bids me tell you this,
And reason to my love is liable.°

Caesar. How foolish do your fears seem now, Calpurnia!   105
I am ashamèd I did yield to them.
Give me my robe, for I will go.

[*Enter* Publius, Brutus, Ligarius, Metellus, Casca, Trebonius, *and* Cinna.]

And look where Publius is come to fetch me.
Publius. Good morrow, Caesar.
Caesar.   Welcome, Publius.
What, Brutus, are you stirred so early too?   110
Good morrow, Casca. Caius Ligarius,
Caesar was ne'er so much your enemy°
As that same ague° which hath made you lean.
What is 't o'clock?
Brutus.   Caesar, 'tis strucken eight.
Caesar. I thank you for your pains and courtesy.   115

[*Enter* Antony.]

See! Antony, that revels long o' nights,
Is notwithstanding up. Good morrow, Antony.
Antony. So to most noble Caesar.
Caesar.   Bid them prepare within.
I am to blame to be thus waited for.
Now, Cinna, now, Metellus. What, Trebonius!   120
I have an hour's talk in store for you.
Remember that you call on me today.
Be near me, that I may remember you.
Trebonius. Caesar, I will. [*Aside*] And so near will I be
That your best friends shall wish I had been further.   125
Caesar. Good friends, go in and taste some wine with me,
And we like friends will straightway go together.
Brutus. [*Aside*] That every like is not the same, O Caesar,
The heart of Brutus yearns° to think upon!

[*Exeunt.*]

---

104. **And reason . . . liable:** and my love requires that I speak the truth to you.   112. **Caesar . . . enemy:** Ligarius sided with Pompey during the civil war.   113. **ague:** feverish sickness.   129. **yearns:** grieves.

Scene 3

[*A street near the Capitol. Enter* Artemidorus, *reading a paper.*]

Artemidorus. "Caesar, beware of Brutus; take heed of Cassius; come not near Casca; have
an eye to Cinna; trust not Trebonius; mark well Metellus Cimber; Decius Brutus loves
thee not; thou has wronged Caius Ligarius. There is but one mind in all these men,
and it is bent against Caesar. If thou beest not immortal, look about you. Security°
gives way to conspiracy. The mighty gods defend thee!   5

Thy lover,° Artemidorus."

Here will I stand till Caesar pass along,
And as a suitor° will I give him this.
My heart laments that virtue cannot live
Out of the teeth of emulation.°   10
If thou read this, O Caesar, thou mayst live;
If not, the Fates with traitors do contrive.°

[*Exit.*]

Scene 4

[*Another part of the same street, before the house of* Brutus. *Enter* Portia *and* Lucius.]

Portia. I prithee,° boy, run to the Senate House.
Stay not to answer me, but get thee gone.
Why dost thou stay?
Lucius.   To know my errand, madam.
Portia. I would have had thee there, and here again,
Ere I can tell thee what thou shouldst do there.   5
O Constancy, be strong upon my side!
Set a huge mountain 'tween my heart and tongue!
I have a man's mind, but a woman's might.
How hard it is for women to keep counsel!
Art thou here yet?
Lucius.   Madam, what should I do?   10
Run to the Capitol, and nothing else?
And so return to you, and nothing else?
Portia. Yes, bring me word, boy, if thy lord look well,
For he went sickly forth. And take good note

---

4. **Security:** overconfidence.   6. **lover:** friend.   8. **suitor:** one who seeks a favor.   10. **emulation:** envy.   12. **con-trive:** plot.
1. **prithee:** pray thee.

What Caesar doth, what suitors press to him.   15
    Hark, boy! What noise is that?
Lucius. I hear none, madam.
Portia.   Prithee, listen well.
    I heard a bustling rumor like a fray,°
    And the wind brings it from the Capitol.
Lucius. Sooth,° madam, I hear nothing.

[*Enter the* Soothsayer.]

Portia.   Come hither, fellow.   20
    Which way hast thou been?
Soothsayer.   At mine own house, good lady.
Portia. What is 't o'clock?
Soothsayer.   About the ninth hour, lady.
Portia. Is Caesar yet gone to the Capitol?
Soothsayer. Madam, not yet. I go to take my stand
    To see him pass on to the Capitol.   25
Portia. Thou hast some suit to Caesar, hast thou not?
Soothsayer. That I have, lady. If it will please Caesar
    To be so good to Caesar as to hear me,
    I shall beseech him to befriend himself.
Portia. Why, know'st thou any harm's intended toward him?   30
Soothsayer. None that I know will be, much that I fear may chance.
    Good morrow to you. Here the street is narrow,
    The throng that follows Caesar at the heels,
    Of Senators, of praetors, common suitors,
    Will crowd a feeble man almost to death.   35
    I'll get me to a place more void,° and there
    Speak to great Caesar as he comes along.

                                                                          [*Exit.*]

Portia. I must go in. Aye me, how weak a thing
    The heart of women is! O Brutus,
    The heavens speed thee in thine enterprise!   40
    Sure, the boy heard me. Brutus hath a suit
    That Caesar will not grant. Oh, I grow faint.
    Run, Lucius, and commend me to my lord.
    Say I am merry. Come to me again,
    And bring me word what he doth say to thee.   45

                                                              [*Exeunt severally.*°]

---

18. **rumor . . . fray:** noise like a battle.   20. **Sooth:** truly.   36. **void:** empty.   S.D. **severally:** by different exits.

FOR STUDY AND DISCUSSION

1. As Brutus begins his soliloquy in Scene 1, it is clear he has already decided that Caesar must die. What reasons does he give for his decision? From what you have seen of Caesar, are they good reasons? Tell why or why not.

2. Lucius is the only important character in the play whom Shakespeare did not find in Plutarch's *Lives*. What function does Lucius serve in Scene 1? Watch for Lucius again in Act Four, and see if you can decide why Shakespeare put him in the play.

3. Why does Brutus believe there is no need for the conspirators to swear an oath? What does this suggest about his character?

4. In Scene 1, what two changes does Brutus make in the plans of the conspirators? Are his reasons noble and high-minded? Are they realistic and practical? Explain.

5. Portia appears at the end of Scene 1 right after the conspirators leave. What does the scene reveal about the characters of Brutus and Portia and about their relationship?

6. Brutus follows a philosophy called Stoicism. Stoics believed that individuals should lead lives of virtue, reason, and duty, mastering all emotions and submitting to fate. So far in the play, how does Brutus show his Stoicism? How does Portia show she is a Stoic?

7. In Scene 2, what impression do you get of Caesar? What strengths does he show? What weaknesses?

8. Scene 2 focuses on the question of whether or not Caesar will attend the Senate. How does Shakespeare build suspense? What feelings do you have as you watch Caesar try to make up his mind?

9. Both Portia and Calpurnia try to exert influence on their husbands. How do their methods differ? How does Caesar's treatment of Calpurnia differ from Brutus' treatment of Portia?

10. Reread lines 58–107 in Scene 2. To what aspects of Caesar's personality is Decius appealing as he tries to persuade him to go to the Senate?

11. Lines 32–37 in Scene 2 contain one of the most famous speeches in all of Shakespeare's work. Explain what Caesar means in this speech. Why is this speech ironic to the audience?

12. How does Scene 3 add to the suspense of the play?

13. In Scene 4, why does Portia send Brutus the message that she is merry? Describe her actual state of mind in this scene and tell how you know what it is.

14. Why do you think Shakespeare has the soothsayer reappear in Scene 4? In line 29 he says that Caesar is his own enemy. How is this so?

DRAMATIC STRUCTURE: SUSPENSE AND ACTION

Film director Alfred Hitchcock has said that the difference between surprise and suspense is that surprise makes you wonder *what* will happen, but suspense makes you wonder *how* it will happen. You know that Julius Caesar will be dead before the play is over. What questions remain unanswered at this point in the play to keep you in suspense? Put your answer in the form of a list of questions, each beginning with "How."

What is the *action* of this play? Clearly, there will be some violence before it is over. Violence is action. But other things are action too. There has been no violence in the first two acts, but this does not mean that nothing has happened. Action is whatever keeps a play moving forward. Thinking can be action. Talking can be action. But if characters think and do not change their minds, if characters talk but do not reach a decision, then the play stops moving.

Make a list of the people who have changed their minds thus far in the play. Jot down what they thought before the change and what they thought afterward. (Think of the citizens as one person.)

Have you changed your mind about anything so far? Has your impression of certain characters changed? How does this make you part of the action, in a way?

IMAGERY

One of Shakespeare's greatest talents is his ability to take a simple, familiar image and give it many shades of meaning and feeling. Let's look at the way the image of *blood* is used in Act Two, Scene 1:

In line 136, *blood* means "the honor of a Roman."
In line 162, *bloody* means "senselessly brutal."
In line 168, *blood* means "red fluid in the body."
In line 171, *bleed* means "die."

Notice that one image—blood—pulls together the contradictory concepts of life and death, honor and brutality. How do these contradictions reflect the moral problem of the assassination?

Shakespeare also uses images of *sleep, sickness,* and *fire.* Select one of these words, locate its appearances (including its variants) in Act Two, and prepare a list similar to the one above.

Act Three

Scene 1

[*Rome. Before the Capitol, a great crowd. On a higher level, the Senate sits, waiting for* Caesar *to appear. The* Soothsayer *and* Artemidorus *are among the crowd.*
A flourish of trumpets. Enter Caesar, Brutus, Cassius, Casca, Decius, Metellus, Trebonius, Cinna, Antony, Lepidus, Popilius, Publius, *and others.* Caesar *stops in front of the* Soothsayer *and smiles.*]

Caesar. The ides of March are come.
Soothsayer. Aye, Caesar, but not gone.

[Artemidorus *steps up to* Caesar *with his warning.*]

Artemidorus. Hail, Caesar! Read this schedule.°

[Decius *steps forward quickly with another paper.*]

Decius. Trebonius doth desire you to o'erread,
    At your best leisure, this his humble suit. 5
Artemidorus. O Caesar, read mine first, for mine's a suit
    That touches Caesar nearer. Read it, great Caesar.
Caesar. What touches us ourself shall be last served.

[Caesar *pushes the paper aside and turns away.*]

Artemidorus. Delay not, Caesar. Read it instantly.
Caesar. What, is the fellow mad?
Publius.   Sirrah,° give place. 10

[Publius *and the other conspirators force* Artemidorus *away from* Caesar.]

Cassius. What, urge you your petitions in the street?
    Come to the Capitol.

[Caesar *goes up into the Senate House, the rest following.* Popilius *speaks to* Cassius *in a low voice.*]

Popilius. I wish your enterprise today may thrive.
Cassius. What enterprise, Popilius?

---

3. **schedule:** paper. 10. **Sirrah:** an insulting way of addressing an inferior.

Popilius.   Fare you well.

[*Advances to* Caesar.]

Brutus. What said Popilius Lena?   15
Cassius. He wished today our enterprise might thrive.
    I fear our purpose is discovered.
Brutus. Look how he makes to° Caesar. Mark him.
Cassius.   Casca,
    Be sudden, for we fear prevention.
    Brutus, what shall be done? If this be known,   20
    Cassius or Caesar never shall turn back,
    For I will slay myself.
Brutus.   Cassius, be constant.
    Popilius Lena speaks not of our purposes,
    For look he smiles and Caesar doth not change.
Cassius. Trebonius knows his time, for look you, Brutus,   25
    He draws Mark Antony out of the way.

[*Exeunt* Antony *and* Trebonius.]

Decius. Where is Metellus Cimber? Let him go,
    And presently prefer his suit to Caesar.
Brutus. He is addressed.° Press near and second him.
Cinna. Casca, you are the first that rears your hand.   30

[Caesar *seats himself in his high Senate chair.*]

Caesar. Are we all ready? What is now amiss
    That Caesar and his Senate must redress?
Metellus. Most high, most mighty, and most puissant° Caesar,
    Metellus Cimber throws before thy seat
    A humble heart——

[*Kneeling.*]

Caesar.   I must prevent thee, Cimber.   35
    These couchings° and these lowly courtesies
    Might fire the blood of ordinary men,
    And turn preordinance and first decree
    Into the law of children.° Be not fond,°
    To think that Caesar bears such rebel blood   40

---

18. **makes to:** goes toward. 29. **addressed:** ready. 33. **puissant** (pwĭs′ənt): powerful. 36. **couchings:** low bowings. 38–39. **And . . . children:** and turn established laws (preordinance) and penalties (first decree) into laws or rules that change at whim. 39. **fond:** foolish.

That will be thawed from the true quality
With that which melteth fools—I mean sweet words,
Low-crookèd° curtsies, and base spaniel fawning.
Thy brother by decree is banished.
If thou dost bend and pray and fawn for him, 45
I spurn thee like a cur out of my way.
Know, Caesar doth not wrong, nor without cause
Will he be satisfied.

Metellus. Is there no voice more worthy than my own,
To sound more sweetly in great Caesar's ear 50
For the repealing of my banished brother?

Brutus. I kiss thy hand, but not in flattery, Caesar,
Desiring thee that Publius Cimber may
Have an immediate freedom of repeal.

Caesar. What, Brutus!

Cassius.   Pardon, Caesar, Caesar, pardon. 55
As low as to thy foot doth Cassius fall,
To beg enfranchisement° for Publius Cimber.

Caesar. I could be well moved, if I were as you.
If I could pray to move, prayers would move me;
But I am constant as the Northern Star, 60
Of whose true-fixed and resting quality
There is no fellow in the firmament.°
The skies are painted with unnumbered sparks,
They are all fire, and every one doth shine,
But there's but one in all doth hold his place. 65
So in the world. 'Tis furnished well with men,
And men are flesh and blood, and apprehensive;°
Yet in the number I do know but one
That unassailable holds on his rank,
Unshaked of motion. And that I am he, 70
Let me a little show it, even in this,
That I was constant Cimber should be banished,
And constant do remain to keep him so.

Cinna. O Caesar—

Caesar.   Hence! Wilt thou lift up Olympus?°

Decius. Great Caesar—

Caesar.   Doth not Brutus bootless° kneel? 75

Casca. Speak, hands, for me!

---

43. **Low-crookèd:** low-bending.   57. **enfranchisement:** restoration of rights as a citizen.   62. **no . . . firmament:** no equal in the heavens.   67. **apprehensive:** capable of thought and feeling.   74. **Olympus:** a mountain in Greece, the legendary home of the gods.   75. **bootless:** in vain.

[Casca *first, then the other conspirators and* Marcus Brutus *stab* Caesar.]

Caesar. *Et tu, Brute?*° Then fall, Caesar! [*Dies.*]
Cinna. Liberty! Freedom! Tyranny is dead!
    Run hence, proclaim, cry it about the streets.
Cassius. Some to the common pulpits, and cry out
    "Liberty, freedom, and enfranchisement!"
Brutus. People, and Senators, be not affrighted.
    Fly not, stand still. Ambition's debt is paid.

80

---

77. *Et tu, Brute?* (brōō'tā): Latin for "And you (too), Brutus?"

Casca. Go to the pulpit, Brutus.
Decius. And Cassius too.
Brutus. Where's Publius?°
Cinna. Here, quite confounded° with this mutiny.   85
Metellus. Stand fast together, lest some friend of Caesar's
    Should chance——
Brutus. Talk not of standing. Publius, good cheer.
    There is no harm intended to your person,
    Nor to no Roman else. So tell them, Publius.   90
Cassius. And leave us, Publius, lest that the people
    Rushing on us should do your age some mischief.
Brutus. Do so, and let no man abide° this deed
    But we the doers.

[Reenter Trebonius.]

Cassius. Where is Antony?
Trebonius. Fled to his house amazed.   95
    Men, wives, and children stare, cry out, and run
    As it were Doomsday.
Brutus. Fates, we will know your pleasures.
    That we shall die, we know; 'tis but the time,
    And drawing days out, that men stand upon.°   100
Casca. Why, he that cuts off twenty years of life
    Cuts off so many years of fearing death.
Brutus. Grant that, and then is death a benefit.
    So are we Caesar's friends that have abridged
    His time of fearing death. Stoop, Romans, stoop,
    And let us bathe our hands in Caesar's blood   105
    Up to the elbows, and besmear our swords.
    Then walk we forth, even to the market place,
    And waving our red weapons o'er our heads,
    Let's all cry "Peace, freedom, and liberty!"
Cassius. Stoop then, and wash. How many ages hence   110
    Shall this our lofty scene be acted over
    In states unborn and accents yet unknown!
Brutus. How many times shall Caesar bleed in sport,
    That now on Pompey's basis lies along°
    No worthier than the dust!   115

---

85. **Publius:** an elderly senator; not Publius Cimber who is in exile.   86. **confounded:** confused.   94. **abide:** pay the penalty for.   100. **stand upon:** worry about.   115. **Pompey's . . . along:** lies stretched out on the base of Pompey's statue.

Cassius.   So oft as that shall be,
      So often shall the knot of us be called
      The men that gave their country liberty.
Decius. What, shall we forth?
Cassius.   Aye, every man away.
      Brutus shall lead, and we will grace his heels   120
      With the most boldest and best hearts of Rome.

                              [*Enter a* Servant.]

Brutus. Soft! Who comes here? A friend of Antony's.
Servant. Thus, Brutus, did my master bid me kneel,
      Thus did Mark Antony bid me fall down,
      And, being prostrate, thus he bade me say: 125
      Brutus is noble, wise, valiant, and honest,
      Caesar was mighty, bold, royal, and loving.
      Say I love Brutus and I honor him,
      Say I feared Caesar, honored him, and loved him.
      If Brutus will vouchsafe° that Antony   130
      May safely come to him and be resolved°
      How Caesar hath deserved to lie in death,
      Mark Antony shall not love Caesar dead
      So well as Brutus living, but will follow
      The fortunes and affairs of noble Brutus   135
      Through the hazards of this untrod state
      With all true faith. So says my master Antony.
Brutus. Thy master is a wise and valiant Roman—
      I never thought him worse.
      Tell him, so please him come unto this place,   140
      He shall be satisfied and, by my honor,
      Depart untouched.
Servant.   I'll fetch him presently.°
                                                                        [*Exit.*]

Brutus. I know that we shall have him well to friend.°
Cassius. I wish we may, but yet have I a mind
      That fears him much, and my misgiving still   145
      Falls shrewdly to the purpose.°

                              [*Reenter* Antony.]

---

130. **vouchsafe:** permit.   131. **resolved:** convinced.   142. **presently:** immediately.   143. **well to friend:** as a good
friend.   145–146. **my misgiving . . . purpose:** my worries are usually justified.

Brutus. But here comes Antony. Welcome, Mark Antony.

Antony. O mighty Caesar, dost thou lie so low?
    Are all thy conquests, glories, triumphs, spoils,
    Shrunk to this little measure? Fare thee well.   150
    I know not, gentlemen, what you intend,
    Who else must be let blood, who else is rank.°
    If I myself, there is no hour so fit
    As Caesar's death's hour, nor no instrument
    Of half that worth as those your swords, made rich   155
    With the most noble blood of all this world.
    I do beseech ye, if you bear me hard,
    Now, whilst your purpled hands do reek and smoke,
    Fulfill your pleasure. Live a thousand years,
    I shall not find myself so apt to die.   160
    No place will please me so, no mean° of death,
    As here by Caesar, and by you cut off,
    The choice and master spirits of this age.

Brutus. O Antony, beg not your death of us.
    Though now we must appear bloody and cruel,   165
    As by our hands and this our present act
    You see we do. Yet see you but our hands
    And this the bleeding business they have done.
    Our hearts you see not. They are pitiful,
    And pity to the general wrong of Rome—   170
    As fire drives out fire, so pity pity—
    Hath done this deed on Caesar. For your part,
    To you our swords have leaden° points, Mark Antony.
    Our arms in strength of malice,° and our hearts
    Of brothers' temper, do receive you in   175
    With all kind love, good thoughts, and reverence.

Cassius. Your voice shall be as strong as any man's
    In the disposing of new dignities.°

Brutus. Only be patient till we have appeased
    The multitude, beside themselves with fear,   180
    And then we will deliver you the cause
    Why I, that did love Caesar when I struck him,
    Have thus proceeded.

Antony.   I doubt not of your wisdom.
    Let each man render me his bloody hand.
    First, Marcus Brutus, will I shake with you.   185

---

152. **rank:** in need of bleeding to cure an illness.   161. **mean:** means, method.   173. **leaden:** blunt.   174. **in . . . mal-ice:** with power to hurt you.   178. **disposing . . . dignities:** deciding who should hold high public office.

Next, Caius Cassius, do I take your hand.
Now, Decius Brutus, yours, now yours, Metellus;
Yours, Cinna, and, my valiant Casca, yours—
Though last, not least in love, yours, good Trebonius.
Gentlemen all—alas, what shall I say?   190
My credit° now stands on such slippery ground
That one of two bad ways you must conceit° me,
Either a coward or a flatterer.
That I did love thee, Caesar, oh, 'tis true.
If then thy spirit look upon us now,   195
Shall it not grieve thee dearer than thy death
To see thy Antony making his peace,
Shaking the bloody fingers of thy foes,
Most noble! in the presence of thy corse?°
Had I as many eyes as thou hast wounds,   200
Weeping as fast as they stream forth thy blood,
It would become me better than to close
In terms of friendship with thine enemies.
Pardon me, Julius! Here wast thou bayed,° brave hart,°
Here didst thou fall, and here thy hunters stand,   205
Signed in thy spoil° and crimsoned in thy lethe.°
O world, thou wast the forest to this hart,
And this, indeed, O world, the heart of thee.
How like a deer strucken by many princes
Dost thou here lie!   210
Cassius. Mark Antony——
Antony.   Pardon me, Caius Cassius.
The enemies of Caesar shall say this;
Then, in a friend, it is cold modesty.
Cassius. I blame you not for praising Caesar so,
But what compact mean you to have with us?   215
Will you be pricked in number° of our friends,
Or shall we on, and not depend on you?
Antony. Therefore I took your hands, but was indeed
Swayed from the point by looking down on Caesar.
Friends am I with you all and love you all,   220
Upon this hope that you shall give me reasons
Why and wherein Caesar was dangerous.
Brutus. Or else were this a savage spectacle.

---

191. **credit:** reputation. 192. **conceit:** think of. 199. **corse:** corpse. 204. **bayed:** brought to bay, surrounded by hounds. **hart:** deer. 206. **Signed . . . spoil:** stained with your slaughter. **lethe:** blood, death. 216. **pricked in number:** marked in the list, counted on.

Our reasons are so full of good regard
That were you, Antony, the son of Caesar,   225
You should be satisfied.
Antony.   That's all I seek.
And am moreover suitor that I may
Produce his body to the market place,
And in the pulpit, as becomes a friend,
Speak in the order of his funeral.   230
Brutus. You shall, Mark Antony.
Cassius.   Brutus, a word with you.
[*Aside to* Brutus] You know not what you do. Do not consent
That Antony speak in his funeral.
Know you how much the people may be moved
By that which he will utter?
Brutus.   By your pardon,   235
I will myself into the pulpit first,
And show the reason of our Caesar's death.
What Antony shall speak, I will protest
He speaks by leave and by permission,
And that we are contented Caesar shall   240
Have all true rites and lawful ceremonies.
It shall advantage more than do us wrong.
Cassius. I know not what may fall. I like it not.
Brutus. Mark Antony, here, take you Caesar's body.
You shall not in your funeral speech blame us,   245
But speak all good you can devise of Caesar,
And say you do 't by our permission.
Else shall you not have any hand at all
About his funeral. And you shall speak
In the same pulpit whereto I am going—   250
After my speech is ended.
Antony.   Be it so.
I do desire no more.
Brutus. Prepare the body then, and follow us.

[*Exeunt all but* Antony, *who looks down at* Caesar's body.]

Antony. O, pardon me, thou bleeding piece of earth,
That I am meek and gentle with these butchers!   255
Thou art the ruins of the noblest man
That ever livèd in the tide of times.
Woe to the hand that shed this costly blood!
Over thy wounds now do I prophesy,

Which like dumb mouths do ope their ruby lips   260
To beg the voice and utterance of my tongue,
A curse shall light upon the limbs of men.
Domestic fury and fierce civil strife
Shall cumber° all the parts of Italy.
Blood and destruction shall be so in use,   265
And dreadful objects so familiar,
That mothers shall but smile when they behold
Their infants quartered° with the hands of war,
All pity choked with custom of fell° deeds.
And Caesar's spirit ranging for revenge,   270
With Até° by his side come hot from Hell,
Shall in these confines with a monarch's voice
Cry "Havoc,"° and let slip the dogs of war,
That this foul deed shall smell above the earth
With carrion men, groaning for burial.   275

[*Enter a* Servant.]

You serve Octavius Caesar,° do you not?
Servant. I do, Mark Antony.
Antony. Caesar did write for him to come to Rome.
Servant. He did receive his letters, and is coming,
    And bid me say to you by word of mouth —   280
    [*Seeing the body*] O Caesar!
Antony. Thy heart is big. Get thee apart and weep.
    Passion, I see, is catching, for mine eyes,
    Seeing those beads of sorrow stand in thine,
    Began to water. Is thy master coming?   285
Servant. He lies tonight within seven leagues of Rome.
Antony. Post° back with speed, and tell him what hath chanced.
    Here is a mourning Rome, a dangerous Rome,
    No Rome of safety for Octavius yet.
    Hie hence, and tell him so. Yet stay awhile.   290
    Thou shalt not back till I have borne this corse
    Into the market place. There shall I try,°
    In my oration, how the people take
    The cruel issue° of these bloody men,

---

264. **cumber:** encumber, weigh down. 268. **quartered:** torn apart. 269. **fell:** cruel. 271. **Até:** Greek goddess of vengeance and strife. 273. **"Havoc":** a signal for general slaughter, meaning that no prisoners be taken but all enemies killed. 276. **Octavius Caesar:** the grandson of Caesar's sister, adopted by Caesar as his official heir. 287. **Post:** ride. 292. **try:** test, find out. 294. **issue:** action, deed.

According to the which, thou shalt discourse   295
To young Octavius of the state of things.
Lend me your hand.

> [*Exeunt with* Caesar's *body.*]

Scene 2

[*The Forum. Enter* Brutus *and* Cassius, *and a throng of* Citizens, *disturbed by the death of* Caesar.]

Citizens. We will be satisfied. Let us be satisfied.
Brutus. Then follow me, and give me audience, friends.
    Cassius, go you into the other street,
    And part the numbers.°
    Those that will hear me speak, let 'em stay here,   5
    Those that will follow Cassius, go with him,
    And public reasons shall be rendered
    Of Caesar's death.
First Citizen.   I will hear Brutus speak.
Second Citizen. I will hear Cassius, and compare their reasons
    When severally° we hear them rendered.   10

> [*Exit* Cassius, *with some of the* Citizens. Brutus *goes into the pulpit.*]

Third Citizen. The noble Brutus is ascended. Silence!
Brutus. Be patient till the last.
    Romans, countrymen, and lovers! Hear me for my cause, and be silent, that you may
    hear. Believe me for mine honor, and have respect to mine honor, that you may
    believe. Censure° me in your wisdom, and awake your senses, that you may the better   15
    judge. If there be any in this assembly, any dear friend of Caesar's, to him I say that
    Brutus' love to Caesar was no less than his. If then that friend demand why Brutus rose
    against Caesar, this is my answer—not that I loved Caesar less, but that I loved Rome
    more. Had you rather Caesar were living, and die all slaves, than that Caesar were dead,
    to live all freemen? As Caesar loved me, I weep for him; as he was fortunate, I rejoice   20
    at it; as he was valiant, I honor him. But as he was ambitious, I slew him. There is tears
    for his love, joy for his fortune, honor for his valor, and death for his ambition. Who is
    here so base that would be a bondman?° If any, speak, for him have I offended. Who is
    here so rude° that would not be a Roman? If any, speak, for him have I offended. Who
    is here so vile that will not love his country? If any, speak, for him have I offended.   25
    I pause for a reply.

---

   4. **part the numbers:** divide the crowd. 10. **severally:** separately. 15. **Censure:** judge. 23. **bondman:** slave.
24. **rude:** uncivilized.

All. None, Brutus, none.

Brutus. Then none have I offended. I have done no more to Caesar than you shall do to Brutus. The question of his death is enrolled in the Capitol,° his glory not extenuated,° wherein he was worthy, nor his offenses enforced,° for which he suffered death. 30

[*Enter* Antony *and others, with* Caesar's *body.*]

Here comes his body, mourned by Mark Antony, who, though he had no hand in his death, shall receive the benefit of his dying, a place in the commonwealth—as which of you shall not? With this I depart—that, as I slew my best lover for the good of Rome, I have the same dagger for myself when it shall please my country to need my death. 35

All. Live, Brutus! Live, live!

First Citizen. Bring him with triumph home unto his house.

Second Citizen. Give him a statue with his ancestors.

---

29. **The question . . . Capitol:** The reasons for Caesar's death are written in the public archives. **extenuated:** belittled.   30. **enforced:** exaggerated.

Third Citizen. Let him be Caesar.

Fourth Citizen.   Caesar's better parts
   Shall be crowned in Brutus.   40

First Citizen. We'll bring him to his house with shouts and clamors.

Brutus. My countrymen——

Second Citizen.   Peace! Silence! Brutus speaks.

First Citizen. Peace, ho!

Brutus. Good countrymen, let me depart alone,
   And, for my sake, stay here with Antony.   45
   Do grace to Caesar's corpse, and grace his speech
   Tending to Caesar's glories, which Mark Antony
   By our permission is allowed to make.

I do entreat you, not a man depart,
Save I alone, till Antony have spoke.   50

                                                      [*Exit.*]

First Citizen. Stay, ho, and let us hear Mark Antony!
Third Citizen. Let him go up into the public chair.
    We'll hear him. Noble Antony, go up.
Antony. For Brutus' sake, I am beholding° to you.

                    [*Goes into the pulpit.*]

Fourth Citizen. What does he say of Brutus?
Third Citizen.   He says, for Brutus' sake,   55
    He finds himself beholding to us all.
Fourth Citizen. 'Twere best he speak no harm of Brutus here.
First Citizen. This Caesar was a tyrant.
Third Citizen.   Nay, that's certain.
    We are blest that Rome is rid of him.
Second Citizen. Peace! Let us hear what Antony can say.   60
Antony. You gentle Romans —
All.   Peace, ho! Let us hear him.
Antony. Friends, Romans, countrymen, lend me your ears.
    I come to bury Caesar, not to praise him.
    The evil that men do lives after them,
    The good is oft interrèd° with their bones.   65
    So let it be with Caesar. The noble Brutus
    Hath told you Caesar was ambitious.
    If it were so, it was a grievous fault.
    And grievously hath Caesar answered it.
    Here, under leave of Brutus and the rest —   70
    For Brutus is an honorable man,
    So are they all, all honorable men —
    Come I to speak in Caesar's funeral.
    He was my friend, faithful and just to me.
    But Brutus says he was ambitious,   75
    And Brutus is an honorable man.
    He hath brought many captives home to Rome,
    Whose ransoms did the general coffers° fill.
    Did this in Caesar seem ambitious?
    When that the poor have cried, Caesar hath wept —   80
    Ambition should be made of sterner stuff.
    Yet Brutus says he was ambitious,

---

54. **beholding:** indebted.   65. **interrèd:** buried.   78. **general coffers:** public treasury.

And Brutus is an honorable man.
You all did see that on the Lupercal
I thrice presented him a kingly crown,   85
Which he did thrice refuse. Was this ambition?
Yet Brutus says he was ambitious,
And, sure, he is an honorable man.
I speak not to disprove what Brutus spoke,
But here I am to speak what I do know.   90
You all did love him once, not without cause.
What cause withholds you then to mourn for him?
O judgment, thou art fled to brutish beasts,
And men have lost their reason! Bear with me,
My heart is in the coffin there with Caesar,   95
And I must pause till it come back to me.

First Citizen. Methinks there is much reason in his sayings.

Second Citizen. If thou consider rightly of the matter,
Caesar has had great wrong.

Third Citizen.   Has he, masters?
I fear there will a worse come in his place.   100

Fourth Citizen. Marked ye his words? He would not take the crown,
Therefore 'tis certain he was not ambitious.

First Citizen. If it be found so, some will dear abide it.°

Second Citizen. Poor soul! His eyes are red as fire with weeping.

Third Citizen. There's not a nobler man in Rome than Antony.   105

Fourth Citizen. Now mark him, he begins again to speak.

Antony. But yesterday the word of Caesar might
Have stood against the world. Now lies he there,
And none so poor to do him reverence.°
O masters, if I were disposed to stir   110
Your hearts and minds to mutiny and rage,
I should do Brutus wrong and Cassius wrong,
Who, you all know, are honorable men.
I will not do them wrong; I rather choose
To wrong the dead, to wrong myself and you,   115
Than I will wrong such honorable men.
But here's a parchment with the seal of Caesar—
I found it in his closet—'tis his will.
Let but the commons hear this testament—
Which, pardon me, I do not mean to read—   120
And they would go and kiss dead Caesar's wounds

---

103. **dear abide it:** pay for it dearly.   109. **And . . . reverence:** And you think that honoring Caesar is beneath your dignity.

And dip their napkins° in his sacred blood,
Yea, beg a hair of him for memory,
And, dying, mention it within their wills,
Bequeathing it as a rich legacy   125
Unto their issue.°

Fourth Citizen. We'll hear the will. Read it, Mark Antony.

All. The will, the will! We will hear Caesar's will.

Antony. Have patience, gentle friends. I must not read it.
It is not meet you know how Caesar loved you.   130
You are not wood, you are not stones, but men;
And, being men, hearing the will of Caesar,
It will inflame you, it will make you mad.
'Tis good you know not that you are his heirs,
For if you should, oh, what would come of it!   135

Fourth Citizen. Read the will. We'll hear it, Antony.
You shall read us the will, Caesar's will.

Antony. Will you be patient? Will you stay awhile?
I have o'ershot myself to tell you of it.
I fear I wrong the honorable men   140
Whose daggers have stabbed Caesar. I do fear it.

Fourth Citizen. They were traitors—honorable men!

All. The will! The testament!

Second Citizen. They were villains, murderers. The will! Read the will.

Antony. You will compel me then to read the will?   145
Then make a ring about the corpse of Caesar.
And let me show you him that made the will.
Shall I descend? And will you give me leave?

All. Come down.

Second Citizen. Descend.   150

[He comes down from the pulpit.]

Third Citizen. You shall have leave.

Fourth Citizen. A ring. Stand round.

First Citizen. Stand from the hearse, stand from the body.

Second Citizen. Room for Antony, most noble Antony.

Antony. Nay, press not so upon me. Stand far off.   155

All. Stand back. Room! Bear back.

Antony. If you have tears, prepare to shed them now.
You all do know this mantle. I remember
The first time ever Caesar put it on.

---

122. **napkins:** handkerchiefs.   126. **issue:** children.

'Twas on a summer's evening, in his tent, 160
That day he overcame the Nervii.°
Look, in this place ran Cassius' dagger through.
See what a rent the envious Casca made.
Through this the well-belovèd Brutus stabbed,
And as he plucked his cursèd steel away, 165
Mark how the blood of Caesar followed it,
As rushing out of doors, to be resolved
If Brutus so unkindly knocked, or no.
For Brutus, as you know, was Caesar's angel.
Judge, O you gods, how dearly Caesar loved him! 170
This was the most unkindest cut of all,
For when the noble Caesar saw him stab,
Ingratitude, more strong than traitors' arms,
Quite vanquished him. Then burst his mighty heart,
And, in his mantle muffling up his face, 175
Even at the base of Pompey's statue,
Which all the while ran blood, great Caesar fell.
Oh, what a fall was there, my countrymen!
Then I, and you, and all of us fell down,
Whilst bloody treason flourished over us. 180
Oh, now you weep, and I perceive you feel
The dint° of pity. These are gracious drops.
Kind souls, what weep you when you but behold
Our Caesar's vesture wounded?° Look you here—
Here is himself, marred, as you see, with traitors. 185

[*He pulls the cloak off* Caesar's body.]

First Citizen. Oh, piteous spectacle!
Second Citizen. Oh, noble Caesar!
Third Citizen. Oh, woeful day!
Fourth Citizen. Oh, traitors, villains!
First Citizen. Oh, most bloody sight! 190
Second Citizen. We will be revenged.
All. Revenge! About! Seek! Burn! Fire! Kill! Slay!
    Let not a traitor live!
Antony. Stay, countrymen.
First Citizen. Peace there! Hear the noble Antony. 195
Second Citizen. We'll hear him, we'll follow him, we'll die with him.

---

161. **Nervii:** fierce tribe in Belgium, conquered in 57 B.C.   182. **dint:** blow.   184. **vesture wounded:** clothing torn.

Antony. Good friends, sweet friends, let me not stir you up
    To such a sudden flood of mutiny.
    They that have done this deed are honorable.
    What private griefs they have, alas, I know not,   200
    That made them do it. They are wise and honorable,
    And will, no doubt, with reasons answer you.
    I come not, friends, to steal away your hearts.
    I am no orator, as Brutus is,
    But, as you know me all, a plain blunt man   205
    That love my friend; and that they know full well
    That gave me public leave to speak of him.
    For I have neither wit, nor words, nor worth,
    Action, nor utterance, nor the power of speech,
    To stir men's blood. I only speak right on,   210
    I tell you that which you yourselves do know,
    Show you sweet Caesar's wounds, poor poor dumb mouths,
    And bid them speak for me. But were I Brutus,
    And Brutus Antony, there were an Antony
    Would ruffle up your spirits, and put a tongue   215
    In every wound of Caesar that should move
    The stones of Rome to rise and mutiny.
All. We'll mutiny.
First Citizen. We'll burn the house of Brutus.
Third Citizen. Away, then! Come, seek the conspirators.   220
Antony. Yet hear me, countrymen, yet hear me speak.
All. Peace, ho! Hear Antony. Most noble Antony!
Antony. Why, friends, you go to do you know not what.
    Wherein hath Caesar thus deserved your loves?
    Alas, you know not. I must tell you, then—   225
    You have forgot the will I told you of.
All. Most true, the will! Let's stay and hear the will.
Antony. Here is the will, and under Caesar's seal.
    To every Roman citizen he gives,
    To every several° man, seventy-five drachmas.°   230
Second Citizen. Most noble Caesar! We'll revenge his death.
Third Citizen. Oh, royal Caesar!
Antony. Hear me with patience.
All. Peace, ho!
Antony. Moreover, he hath left you all his walks,   235
    His private arbors and new-planted orchards,

---

230. **several**: individual. **drachmas**: Greek silver coins.

On this side Tiber. He hath left them you,
And to your heirs forever—common pleasures,
To walk abroad and recreate yourselves.
Here was a Caesar! When comes such another?   240
First Citizen. Never, never. Come, away, away!
    We'll burn his body in the holy place,
    And with the brands fire the traitors' houses.
    Take up the body.
Second Citizen. Go fetch fire.   245
Third Citizen. Pluck down benches.
Fourth Citizen. Pluck down forms, windows,° anything.

                          [*Exeunt* Citizens *with the body.*]

Antony. Now let it work. Mischief, thou art afoot,
    Take thou what course thou wilt.

                   [*Enter a* Servant.]

                 How now, fellow?
Servant. Sir, Octavius is already come to Rome.   250
Antony. Where is he?
Servant. He and Lepidus° are at Caesar's house.
Antony. And thither will I straight to visit him.
    He comes upon a wish.° Fortune is merry,
    And in this mood will give us anything.   255
Servant. I heard him say Brutus and Cassius
    Are rid like madmen through the gates of Rome.
Antony. Belike° they had some notice of the people,
    How I had moved them. Bring me to Octavius.

                                 [*Exeunt.*]

Scene 3

             [*A street. Enter* Cinna *the poet.*]

Cinna. I dreamt tonight that I did feast with Caesar,
    And things unluckily charge my fantasy.°
    I have no will to wander forth of doors,
    Yet something leads me forth.

---

247. **forms, windows:** benches and shutters.   252. **Lepidus:** one of Caesar's generals and one of the three chief leaders
of Caesar's party.   254. **upon a wish:** just when I wanted him.   258. **Belike:** probably.
  2. **unluckily charge my fantasy:** ominously fill my imagination.

[A mob of Citizens, *armed with sticks, spears, and swords, enters and surrounds him.]*

First Citizen. What is your name? 5
Second Citizen. Whither are you going?
Third Citizen. Where do you dwell?
Fourth Citizen. Are you a married man or a bachelor?
Second Citizen. Answer every man directly.
First Citizen. Aye, and briefly. 10
Fourth Citizen. Aye, and wisely.
Third Citizen. Aye, and truly, you were best.
Cinna. What is my name? Whither am I going? Where do I dwell? Am I a married man or a
    bachelor? Then, to answer every man directly and briefly, wisely and truly, wisely I
    say I am a bachelor. 15
Second Citizen. That's as much as to say they are fools that marry. You'll bear me a bang°
    for that, I fear. Proceed, directly.
Cinna. Directly, I am going to Caesar's funeral.
First Citizen. As a friend or an enemy?
Cinna. As a friend. 20
Second Citizen. That matter is answered directly.
Fourth Citizen. For your dwelling, briefly.
Cinna. Briefly, I dwell by the Capitol.
Third Citizen. Your name, sir, truly.
Cinna. Truly, my name is Cinna. 25
First Citizen. Tear him to pieces. He's a conspirator.
Cinna. I am Cinna the poet, I am Cinna the poet.
Fourth Citizen. Tear him for his bad verses, tear him for his bad verses.
Cinna. I am not Cinna the conspirator.
Fourth Citizen. It is no matter, his name's Cinna. Pluck but his name out of his heart, and 30
    turn him going.
Third Citizen. Tear him, tear him! Come, brands. Ho, firebrands – to Brutus', to Cassius'!
    Burn all. Some to Decius' house, and some to Casca's, some to Ligarius'. Away, go!

[Exeunt.]

---

16. **bear me a bang:** get a wallop from me.

FOR STUDY AND DISCUSSION

1. You have seen Caesar three times onstage and heard many characters talk about him. What is your opinion of him? Is he likable?

2. What are Caesar's dying words? How did you feel as these words were spoken?

3. Describe the mood of the conspirators immediately after the assassination. What is the idea they claim to have killed?

4. In lines 116–118 of Scene 1, what side of Cassius' character is seen for the first time?

5. With Caesar murdered, Antony's position is perilous. Look carefully at his words in Scene 1. What impression does he wish to give the conspirators? Where in the scene do you learn how he really feels?

6. Cassius' loyalty to Brutus, like his resentment of Caesar, is personal. Does Brutus have any personal loyalties? Explain your answer.

7. Notice that Brutus' speech in Scene 2 is in prose whereas Antony's is in verse. How does Brutus' speech show that he addresses himself more to the citizens' reason than to their emotions? What values does he assume the citizens cherish?

8. Which remarks by the citizens show that they have not understood Brutus at all?

9. What does Antony say in his speech to make the crowd feel (a) sorry for him? (b) guilty about having thought Caesar a tyrant? (c) angry at the conspirators? What props does he use to produce these reactions?

10. By the end of Scene 2, whose personal leadership has replaced Caesar's?

11. What does Scene 3 show about the nature of a mob?

12. In what way is Scene 3 humorous? Does the use of humor increase or lessen the horror of the mob's attack on an innocent man? Explain your answer.

DRAMATIC STRUCTURE: PLOT

Act One of *Julius Caesar* presents the basic conflict of the play, the conflict between Caesar and his party and a group of dissatisfied citizens who either resent or fear Caesar's great power. This conflict is obvious from the first scene between the tribunes, Flavius and Marullus, and the citizens who are celebrating Caesar's triumph. Most of the major characters are presented in this act. Because this act exposes or sets forth the problem in the play, we say it contains the *exposition*.

Acts Two and Three constitute the *rising action* of the play, which means the action that leads us to the *turning point*, the crisis of the play, when the fate of the hero is sealed. Brutus joins the dissatisfied citizens, a full-scale conspiracy is planned, and Caesar is assassinated. All of these complications come finally to the turning point. In Shakespeare's plays, the turning point almost always takes place in the third act, and *Julius Caesar* is no exception. Here, in Act Three, it is decided that Mark Antony will *not* be assassinated, but that he will be allowed to deliver a funeral oration for his dead friend. Find the moment when this fact becomes clear. This marks the turning point of the play because in this decision lie the seeds of destruction for the conspirators. We know now that Caesar's power will be passed on not to the high-minded and naive Brutus, but to the shrewd and revengeful Antony and those who join him.

Acts Four and Five will constitute the *falling action* of the play. Watch for a reversal of roles and the final inevitable catastrophe.

IRONY

When Antony in his famous funeral oration for Caesar says one thing and means something else ("Brutus is an honorable man"), he is using *verbal irony*. Antony's words are ironic rather than deceptive, because his true meaning is clear to his audience.

Another type of irony is *irony of situation*. This occurs when a situation turns out differently from the way we expect it to turn out. Brutus expects that Antony will not blame the conspirators in his oration. Ironically, while Antony does not literally break his promise to Brutus, the result of his speech is the same as if he had.

Another type of irony is *dramatic irony*. Dramatic irony occurs in a story or play when the reader or audience has a better understanding of what is going on than the individual characters do. When Caesar calls the conspirators "good friends" near the end of Scene 2 in Act Two, we in the audience find this ironic, even though Caesar means exactly what he says. We know better than he does how "good" his friends are.

Tell why the following passages are ironic:

Brutus. And for Mark Antony, think not of him,
For he can do no more than Caesar's arm
When Caesar's head is off.
(II, 1, 181–183)

Antony. I come to bury Caesar, not to praise him.   (III, 2, 63)

Antony. O masters, if I were disposed to stir
Your hearts and minds to mutiny and rage,
I should do Brutus wrong and Cassius wrong,
Who, you all know, are honorable men.
I will not do them wrong . . .
(III, 2, 110–114)

Act Four

Scene 1

[*A house in Rome.* Antony, Octavius, *and* Lepidus, *seated at a table.*]

Antony. These many then shall die, their names are pricked.°
Octavius. Your brother too must die. Consent you, Lepidus?
Lepidus. I do consent.
Octavius.   Prick him down, Antony.
Lepidus. Upon condition Publius shall not live,
Who is your sister's son, Mark Antony.
Antony. He shall not live. Look, with a spot I damn him.   5
But, Lepidus, go you to Caesar's house.
Fetch the will hither, and we shall determine
How to cut off some charge in legacies.°

---

1. **pricked:** marked (on a wax tablet) by punching a hole next to the names.   9. **cut . . . legacies:** reduce the amount of money given in some bequests.

Lepidus. What, shall I find you here?   10
Octavius. Or here or at the Capitol.

                                                          [*Exit* Lepidus.]

Antony. This is a slight unmeritable man,
  Meet to be sent on errands. Is it fit,
  The threefold world divided, he should stand
  One of the three to share it?
Octavius.   So you thought him,   15
  And took his voice who should be pricked to die
  In our black sentence and proscription.°
Antony. Octavius, I have seen more days than you.
  And though we lay these honors on this man,
  To ease ourselves of divers slanderous loads,   20
  He shall but bear them as the ass bears gold,
  To groan and sweat under the business,
  Either led or driven, as we point the way.
  And having brought our treasure where we will,
  Then take we down his load and turn him off,   25
  Like to the empty ass, to shake his ears
  And graze in commons.°
Octavius.   You may do your will.
  But he's a tried and valiant soldier.
Antony. So is my horse, Octavius, and for that
  I do appoint him store of provender.°   30
  It is a creature that I teach to fight,
  To wind,° to stop, to run directly on,
  His corporal° motion governed by my spirit.
  And, in some taste,° is Lepidus but so.
  He must be taught, and trained, and bid go forth,   35
  A barren-spirited fellow, one that feeds
  On abjects, orts,° and imitations,
  Which, out of use and staled by other men,
  Begin his fashion. Do not talk of him
  But as a property.° And now, Octavius,   40
  Listen great things. Brutus and Cassius
  Are levying powers.° We must straight make head.°
  Therefore let our alliance be combined,
  Our best friends made, our means stretched,
  And let us presently go sit in council   45

---

17. **proscription:** accusation of treason, the death list. 27. **in commons:** on public pastures. 30. **store of provender:** supply of food. 32. **wind:** turn. 33. **corporal:** bodily. 34. **in some taste:** to some extent. 37. **abjects, orts:** worthless things, scraps. 40. **property:** tool. 42. **levying powers:** gathering armies. **make head:** make headway.

How covert matters may be best disclosed,
And open perils surest answered.
Octavius. Let us do so, for we are at the stake,°
And bayed about with many enemies.
And some that smile have in their hearts, I fear,   50
Millions of mischiefs.

                                                    [*Exeunt.*]

Scene 2

[*A camp near Sardis, in Greece. In front of* Brutus' *tent. A sound of drums. Enter* Brutus,
   Lucilius, Lucius, *and* Soldiers. Titinius *and* Pindarus, *from* Cassius' *army, meet them.*
   Brutus *halts his men.*]

Brutus. Stand, ho!
Lucilius. Give the word, ho, and stand!
Brutus. What now, Lucilius! Is Cassius near?
Lucilius. He is at hand, and Pindarus is come
   To do you salutation from his master.   5
Brutus. He greets me well.° Your master, Pindarus,
   In his own change, or by ill officers,°
   Hath given me some worthy cause to wish
   Things done undone. But if he be at hand,
   I shall be satisfied.°
Pindarus.   I do not doubt   10
   But that my noble master will appear
   Such as he is, full of regard and honor.
Brutus. He is not doubted. A word, Lucilius,
   How he received you. Let me be resolved.
Lucilius. With courtesy and with respect enough,   15
   But not with such familiar instances,°
   Nor with such free and friendly conference,
   As he hath used of old.
Brutus.   Thou hast described
   A hot friend cooling. Ever note, Lucilius,
   When love begins to sicken and decay,   20
   It useth an enforcèd ceremony.

---

48. **at the stake:** like a bear tied to a stake and "bayed about" by dogs.
   6. **greets me well:** sends his greetings with a worthy man.   7. **In . . . officers:** because of some change of heart in him-self or because of the deeds of unworthy subordinates.   10. **be satisfied:** find out the truth.   16. **familiar instances:** friendly behavior.

There are no tricks in plain and simple faith.
But hollow men, like horses hot at hand,°
Make gallant show and promise of their mettle,
But when they should endure the bloody spur,   25
They fall their crests° and like deceitful jades°
Sink in the trial. Comes his army on?
Lucilius. They mean this night in Sardis to be quartered.
The greater part, the horse in general,°
Are come with Cassius.

[Low march within.]

Brutus.   Hark! He is arrived.   30
March gently cn to meet him.

[Enter Cassius and his army.]

Cassius. Stand, ho!
Brutus. Stand, ho! Speak the word along.
First Soldier. Stand!
Second Soldier. Stand!   35
Third Soldier. Stand!
Cassius. Most noble brother, you have done me wrong.
Brutus. Judge me, you gods! Wrong I mine enemies?
And if not so, how should I wrong a brother?
Cassius. Brutus, this sober° form of yours hides wrongs,   40
And when you do them—
Brutus.   Cassius, be content,
Speak your griefs softly. I do know you well.
Before the eyes of both our armies here,
Which should perceive nothing but love from us,
Let us not wrangle. Bid them move away,   45
Then in my tent, Cassius, enlarge your griefs,
And I will give you audience.
Cassius.   Pindarus,
Bid our commanders lead their charges off
A little from this ground.
Brutus. Lucilius, do you the like, and let no man   50
Come to our tent till we have done our conference.
Let Lucius and Titinius guard our door.

[Exeunt.]

---

23. **hot at hand:** eager before the race begins.   26. **crests:** proud necks.   **jades:** worn-out nags.   29. **the horse in general:** all the cavalry.   40. **sober:** composed.

Scene 3

[*Inside* Brutus' *tent. Enter* Brutus *and* Cassius.]

Cassius. That you have wronged me doth appear in this:
You have condemned and noted° Lucius Pella
For taking bribes here of the Sardians,
Wherein my letters, praying on his side,
Because I knew the man, were slighted off.   5
Brutus. You wronged yourself to write in such a case.
Cassius. In such a time as this it is not meet
That every nice offense should bear his comment.°
Brutus. Let me tell you, Cassius, you yourself
Are much condemned to have an itching palm,   10
To sell and mart your offices° for gold
To undeservers.
Cassius.   I an itching palm!
You know that you are Brutus that speaks this,
Or, by the gods, this speech were else your last.
Brutus. The name of Cassius honors this corruption,   15
And chastisement doth therefore hide his head.
Cassius. Chastisement!
Brutus. Remember March, the ides of March remember.
Did not great Julius bleed for justice' sake?
What villain touched his body that did stab,   20
And not for justice? What, shall one of us,
That struck the foremost man of all this world
But for supporting robbers, shall we now
Contaminate our fingers with base bribes,
And sell the mighty space of our large honors   25
For so much trash as may be graspèd thus?
I had rather be a dog and bay the moon
Than such a Roman.
Cassius.   Brutus, bait° not me,
I'll not endure it. You forget yourself,
To hedge me in. I am a soldier, I,   30
Older in practice, abler than yourself
To make conditions.°
Brutus.   Go to. You are not, Cassius.
Cassius. I am.

---

 2. **noted:** publicly disgraced. 7–8. **not meet . . . comment:** not necessary for every trivial offense to be strictly punished. 11. **mart your offices:** trade your services. 28. **bait:** antagonize. 32. **conditions:** rules.

Brutus. I say you are not.

Cassius. Urge me no more, I shall forget myself. 35
    Have mind upon your health, tempt me no farther.

Brutus. Away, slight man!

Cassius. Is 't possible?

Brutus.   Hear me, for I will speak.
    Must I give way and room to your rash choler?°
    Shall I be frighted when a madman stares? 40

Cassius. O ye gods, ye gods! Must I endure all this?

Brutus. All this! Aye, more. Fret till your proud heart break.
    Go show your slaves how choleric you are,
    And make your bondmen tremble. Must I budge?
    Must I observe you? Must I stand and crouch 45
    Under your testy humor?° By the gods,
    You shall digest the venom of your spleen,°
    Though it do split you; for, from this day forth,
    I'll use you for my mirth, yea, for my laughter,
    When you are waspish.

Cassius.   Is it come to this? 50

Brutus. You say you are a better soldier.
    Let it appear so, make your vaunting° true
    And it shall please me well. For mine own part,
    I shall be glad to learn of noble men.

Cassius. You wrong me every way, you wrong me, Brutus. 55
    I said an elder soldier, not a better.
    Did I say better?

Brutus.   If you did, I care not.

Cassius. When Caesar lived, he durst° not thus have moved me.

Brutus. Peace, peace! You durst not so have tempted him.

Cassius. I durst not! 60

Brutus. No.

Cassius. What, durst not tempt him!

Brutus.   For your life you durst not.

Cassius. Do not presume too much upon my love.
    I may do that I shall be sorry for.

Brutus. You have done that you should be sorry for. 65
    There is no terror, Cassius, in your threats,
    For I am armed so strong in honesty
    That they pass by me as the idle wind
    Which I respect not. I did send to you

---

39. **choler:** anger. 46. **testy humor:** bad temper. 47. **spleen:** rage, temper. 52. **vaunting:** boasting. 58. **durst:** dared.

For certain sums of gold, which you denied me.   70
For I can raise no money by vile means—
By heaven, I had rather coin my heart,
And drop my blood for drachmas, than to wring
From the hard hands of peasants their vile trash
By any indirection.° I did send   75
To you for gold to pay my legions,
Which you denied me. Was that done like Cassius?
Should I have answered Caius Cassius so?
When Marcus Brutus grows so covetous,
To lock such rascal counters° from his friends,   80
Be ready, gods, with all your thunderbolts,
Dash him to pieces!

Cassius.   I denied you not.

Brutus. You did.

Cassius.   I did not. He was but a fool
That brought my answer back. Brutus hath rived° my heart.
A friend should bear his friend's infirmities.   85
But Brutus makes mine greater than they are.

Brutus. I do not, till you practice them on me.

Cassius. You love me not.

Brutus.   I do not like your faults.

Cassius. A friendly eye could never see such faults.

Brutus. A flatterer's would not, though they do appear   90
As huge as high Olympus.

Cassius. Come, Antony, and young Octavius, come,
Revenge yourselves alone° on Cassius,
For Cassius is aweary of the world—
Hated by one he loves, braved° by his brother,   95
Checked like a bondman,° all his faults observed,
Set in a notebook, learned and conned by rote,°
To cast into my teeth. Oh, I could weep
My spirit from mine eyes! There is my dagger,
And here my naked breast; within, a heart   100
Dearer than Plutus' mine,° richer than gold.
If that thou be'st a Roman, take it forth,
I, that denied thee gold, will give my heart.
Strike, as thou didst at Caesar; for I know
When thou didst hate him worst, thou lovedst him better   105
Than ever thou lovedst Cassius.

---

75. **indirection:** underhanded means. 80. **rascal counters:** filthy coins. 84. **rived:** split. 93. **alone:** only. 95. **braved:** mocked. 96. **Checked like a bondman:** scolded like a slave. 97. **conned by rote:** learned by heart. 101. **Plutus' mine:** Plutus was the Greek god of wealth and precious metals.

Brutus.   Sheathe your dagger.

    Be angry when you will, it shall have scope;°
    Do what you will, dishonor shall be humor.°
    O Cassius, you are yokèd with a lamb
    That carries anger as the flint bears fire,   110
    Who, much enforcèd, shows a hasty spark
    And straight is cold again.

Cassius.   Hath Cassius lived

    To be but mirth and laughter to his Brutus,
    When grief and blood ill-tempered vexeth him?

Brutus. When I spoke that, I was ill-tempered too.   115

Cassius. Do you confess so much? Give me your hand.

Brutus. And my heart too.

Cassius.   O Brutus!

Brutus.   What's the matter?

Cassius. Have not you love enough to bear with me
    When that rash humor which my mother gave me
    Makes me forgetful?

Brutus.   Yes, Cassius, and from henceforth,   120
    When you are overearnest with your Brutus,
    He'll think your mother chides, and leave you so.

Poet. [*Within*] Let me go in to see the generals.
    There is some grudge between 'em, 'tis not meet
    They be alone.   125

Lucilius. [*Within*] You shall not come to them.

Poet. [*Within*] Nothing but death shall stay me.

[*Enter* Poet, *followed by* Lucilius, Titinius, *and* Lucius.]

Cassius. How now! What's the matter?

Poet. For shame, you generals! What do you mean?
    Love and be friends, as two such men should be,
    For I have seen more years, I'm sure, than ye.   130

Cassius. Ha, ha! How vilely doth this cynic° rhyme!

Brutus. Get you hence, sirrah. Saucy fellow, hence!

Cassius. Bear with him, Brutus. 'Tis his fashion.

Brutus. I'll know his humor when he knows his time.°   135
    What should the wars do with these jigging fools?
    Companion,° hence!

---

107. **scope:** free range.   108. **dishonor . . . humor:** your insults shall be considered just a mood or whim.   132. **cynic:** ill-mannered fellow.   135. **I'll . . . time:** I'll be patient with his whims if he knows the right time to speak.   137. **Companion:** fellow, used with contempt.

Cassius. Away, away, be gone!

[Exit Poet.]

Brutus. Lucilius and Titinius, bid the commanders
    Prepare to lodge their companies tonight.

Cassius. And come yourselves, and bring Messala with you   140
    Immediately to us.

[Exeunt Lucilius and Titinius.]

Brutus. Lucius, a bowl of wine!

[Exit Lucius.]

Cassius. I did not think you could have been so angry.

Brutus. O Cassius, I am sick of many griefs.

Cassius. Of your philosophy you make no use
    If you give place to accidental evils.   145

Brutus. No man bears sorrow better. Portia is dead.

Cassius. Ha! Portia!

Brutus. She is dead.

Cassius. How 'scaped I killing when I crossed you so?
    Oh, insupportable and touching loss!   150
    Upon what sickness?

Brutus.   Impatient of my absence,
    And grief that young Octavius with Mark Antony
    Have made themselves so strong—for with her death
    That tidings came—with this she fell distract,°
    And, her attendants absent, swallowed fire.   155

Cassius. And died so?

Brutus.   Even so.

Cassius.   O ye immortal gods!

[Reenter Lucius, with wine and taper.]

Brutus. Speak no more of her. Give me a bowl of wine.
    In this I bury all unkindness, Cassius. [Drinks.]

Cassius. My heart is thirsty for that noble pledge.
    Fill, Lucius, till the wine o'erswell the cup.   160
    I cannot drink too much of Brutus' love. [Drinks.]

Brutus. Come in, Titinius!

[Exit Lucius.]

[Reenter Titinius, with Messala.]

Welcome, good Messala.

---

154. **distract:** mad.

Now sit we close about this taper here,
And call in question our necessities.°
Cassius. Portia, art thou gone?
Brutus.   No more, I pray you.   165
    Messala, I have here receivèd letters
    That young Octavius and Mark Antony
    Come down upon us with a mighty power,
    Bending their expedition toward Philippi.°
Messala. Myself have letters of the selfsame tenor.   170
Brutus. With what addition?

---

164. **call . . . necessities:** discuss what must be done.   169. **Philippi:** city in northern Greece.

Messala. That by proscription and bills of outlawry
    Octavius, Antony, and Lepidus
    Have put to death a hundred Senators.
Brutus. Therein our letters do not well agree. 175
    Mine speak of seventy Senators that died
    By their proscriptions, Cicero being one.
Cassius. Cicero one!
Messala.   Cicero is dead,
    And by that order of proscription.
    Had you your letters from your wife, my lord? 180
Brutus. No, Messala.
Messala. Nor nothing in your letters writ of her?
Brutus. Nothing, Messala.
Messala.   That, methinks, is strange.
Brutus. Why ask you? Hear you aught of her in yours?
Messala. No, my lord. 185
Brutus. Now, as you are a Roman, tell me true.
Messala. Then like a Roman bear the truth I tell—
    For certain she is dead, and by strange manner.
Brutus. Why, farewell, Portia. We must die, Messala.
    With meditating that she must die once 190
    I have the patience to endure it now.
Messala. Even so great men great losses should endure.
Cassius. I have as much of this in art° as you,
    But yet my nature could not bear it so.
Brutus. Well, to our work alive. What do you think 195
    Of marching to Philippi presently?
Cassius. I do not think it good.
Brutus.   Your reason?
Cassius.   This it is:
    'Tis better that the enemy seek us.
    So shall he waste his means, weary his soldiers,
    Doing himself offense, whilst we lying still 200
    Are full of rest, defense, and nimbleness.
Brutus. Good reasons must of force give place to better.
    The people 'twixt Philippi and this ground
    Do stand in a forced affection,
    For they have grudged us contribution. 205
    The enemy, marching along by them,
    By them shall make a fuller number up,

---

193. **art:** theory, philosophical belief.

Come on refreshed, new-added, and encouraged.
For which advantage shall we cut him off
If at Philippi we do face him there,   210
These people at our back.
Cassius.   Hear me, good brother——
Brutus. Under your pardon. You must note beside
That we have tried the utmost of our friends,
Our legions are brimful, our cause is ripe.
The enemy increaseth every day,   215
We, at the height, are ready to decline.
There is a tide in the affairs of men
Which taken at the flood leads on to fortune;
Omitted, all the voyage of their life
Is bound in shallows and in miseries.   220
On such a full sea are we now afloat,
And we must take the current when it serves,
Or lose our ventures.
Cassius.   Then, with your will, go on.
We'll along ourselves and meet them at Philippi.
Brutus. The deep of night is crept upon our talk,   225
And nature must obey necessity,
Which we will niggard° with a little rest.
There is no more to say?
Cassius.   No more. Good night.
Early tomorrow will we rise and hence.
Brutus. Lucius! [*Reenter* Lucius.] My gown. [*Exit* Lucius.] Farewell, good Messala.   230
Good night, Titinius. Noble, noble Cassius,
Good night, and good repose.
Cassius.   O my dear brother!
This was an ill beginning of the night.
Never come such division 'tween our souls!
Let it not, Brutus.
Brutus.   Everything is well.   235
Cassius. Good night, my lord.
Brutus.   Good night, good brother.
Titinius *and* **Messala.** Good night, Lord Brutus.
Brutus.   Farewell, everyone.

                                              [*Exeunt all but* Brutus.]

        [*Reenter* Lucius, *with the gown.*]

---

227. **niggard:** satisfy reluctantly.

Give me the gown. Where is thy instrument?

Lucius. Here in the tent.

Brutus.   What, thou speak'st drowsily?

Poor knave,° I blame thee not, thou art o'erwatched.°   240

Call Claudius and some other of my men.

I'll have them sleep on cushions in my tent.

Lucius. Varro and Claudius!

[*Enter* Varro *and* Claudius.]

Varro. Calls my lord?

Brutus. I pray you, sirs, lie in my tent and sleep.   245

It may be I shall raise you by and by

On business to my brother Cassius.

Varro. So please you, we will stand and watch your pleasure.°

Brutus. I will not have it so. Lie down, good sirs.

It may be I shall otherwise bethink me.   250

Look, Lucius, here's the book I sought for so,

I put it in the pocket of my gown.

[Varro *and* Claudius *lie down.*]

Lucius. I was sure your lordship did not give it me.

Brutus. Bear with me, good boy, I am much forgetful.

Canst thou hold up thy heavy eyes awhile,   255

And touch thy instrument a strain or two?

Lucius. Aye, my lord, an 't please you.

Brutus.   It does, my boy.

I trouble thee too much, but thou art willing.

Lucius. It is my duty, sir.

Brutus. I should not urge thy duty past thy might—   260

I know young bloods look for a time of rest.

Lucius. I have slept, my lord, already.

Brutus. It was well done, and thou shalt sleep again,

I will not hold thee long. If I do live,

I will be good to thee.   265

[*Music, and a song.* Lucius *falls asleep as he sings.*]

---

240. **knave:** servant boy. **o'erwatched:** worn out from too much watching. 248. **watch your pleasure:** await your command.

This is a sleepy tune. O murderous slumber,
Lay'st thou thy leaden mace° upon my boy,
That plays thee music? Gentle knave, good night.
I will not do thee so much wrong to wake thee.
If thou dost nod, thou break'st thy instrument,   270
I'll take it from thee, and, good boy, good night.
Let me see, let me see, is not the leaf turned down
Where I left reading? Here it is, I think.

[*Sits down and begins to read. Enter the* Ghost of Caesar.]

How ill this taper burns! Ha! Who comes here?
I think it is the weakness of mine eyes   275
That shapes this monstrous apparition.
It comes upon me. Art thou anything?
Art thou some god, some angel, or some devil,
That makest my blood cold, and my hair to stare?°
Speak to me what thou art.   280
Ghost. Thy evil spirit, Brutus.
Brutus.   Why comest thou?
Ghost. To tell thee thou shalt see me at Philippi.
Brutus. Well, then I shall see thee again?
Ghost. Aye, at Philippi.
Brutus. Why, I will see thee at Philippi then.   285

                                                    [*Exit* Ghost.]

Now I have taken heart, thou vanishest.
Ill spirit, I would hold more talk with thee.
Boy, Lucius! Varro! Claudius! Sirs, awake!
Claudius!
Lucius. [*Sleepily*] The strings, my lord, are false.   290
Brutus. He thinks he still is at his instrument.
    Lucius, awake!
Lucius. My lord?
Brutus. Didst thou dream, Lucius, that thou so criedst out?
Lucius. My lord, I do not know that I did cry.
Brutus. Yes, that thou didst. Didst thou see anything?   295
Lucius. Nothing, my lord.
Brutus. Sleep again, Lucius. Sirrah Claudius!
    [*To* Varro] Fellow thou, awake!

---

267. **mace:** club. Morpheus, Greek god of dreams, was said to carry a leaden mace that caused sleep. 279. **stare:** stand up.

Varro. My lord?   300

Claudius. My lord?

Brutus. Why did you so cry out, sirs, in your sleep?

Varro *and* **Claudius.** Did we, my lord?

Brutus.   Aye, Saw you anything?

Varro. No, my lord, I saw nothing.

Claudius.   Nor I, my lord.

Brutus. Go and commend me to my brother Cassius.   305
    Bid him set on his powers betimes before,°
    And we will follow.

Varro *and* **Claudius.** It shall be done, my lord.

                                                          [Exeunt.]

---

306. **set . . . before:** lead his army on ahead of ours right away.

FOR STUDY AND DISCUSSION

1. Find the lines in Scene 1 that indicate Antony has decided to change Caesar's will. What new aspect of his character does this reveal?

2. How does Antony's behavior in Scene 1 affect your opinion of him?

3. What does Scene 1 reveal about Octavius? Of the three men in power, which do you think is the most worthy leader? Why?

4. In Scene 2, what do we learn of the relationship between Brutus and Cassius?

5. Brutus and Cassius are so different that conflict between them seems inevitable. State briefly the concrete issues that Brutus and Cassius quarrel about in Scene 3. What accusations do they each make?

6. Being forced from Rome is the first great loss Brutus suffers in the play. Portia's death is the second. Is Brutus' reaction to Portia's death characteristic or uncharacteristic of his behavior throughout the play so far? Explain your answer.

7. Compare the meeting of Brutus and Cassius in Scene 3 with the meeting of the Triumvirate in the first scene of this act. Look for similarites as well as differences. For example, what does Cassius say that is similar to Antony's "Octavius, I have seen more days than you"? Which characters in each scene are shown to be corrupt?

8. Once against a course of action must be decided, and Brutus and Cassius have different opinions. So far in the play what have we learned about Brutus' judgment? Why does Cassius yield to Brutus' opinion?

9. Although Caesar has been dead for more than two years, in what sense does he still have an important role in the play? What do you think the appearance of his ghost in Scene 3 signifies? What does his reaction to the ghost reveal about Brutus?

10. Scene 3, one of the longest in the play, begins with an argument and ends with the visitation of a ghost. Describe the mood (or moods) of this scene. What details of setting and action contribute to the mood?

METAPHOR

A *metaphor* is a figure of speech that compares two things which are basically dissimilar. The purpose of a metaphor is to give added meaning to one of the things being compared.

An extended metaphor extends the points of comparison throughout several lines of a poem. Here is an extended metaphor from Act Two, Scene 1, where Brutus is talking about Caesar's ambition. Note that he starts by directly stating that lowliness is a ladder:

> But 'tis a common proof
> That lowliness is young ambition's ladder,
> Whereto the climber-upward turns his face.
> But when he once attains the upmost
>   round,
> He then unto the ladder turns his back,
> Looks in the clouds, scorning the base de-
>   grees
> By which he did ascend.   (21–27)

The two terms of the metaphor are lowliness and a ladder. The overall similarity is that they both reach for a higher place. Shakespeare extends the metaphor by saying that when the ambitious person gets to the top rung, he turns his back on the ladder and the lowliness it helped him escape.

Identify the metaphors in the following lines from *Julius Caesar.* What is being compared in each one? Are any of these metaphors extended to show several points of comparison?

Caesar. Caesar should be a beast without a
    heart
  If he should stay at home today for fear.
  No, Caesar shall not. Danger knows full
    well
  That Caesar is more dangerous than he,
  We are two lions littered in one day,
  And I the elder and more terrible.
                       (II, 2, 42–47)

Brutus. There is a tide in the affairs of men
  Which taken at the flood leads on to for-
    tune;
  Omitted, all the voyage of their life
  Is bound in shallows and in miseries.
  On such a full sea are we now afloat,
  And we must take the current when it
    serves,
  Or lose our ventures.   (IV, 3, 217–223)

Act Five

Scene 1

[The plains of Philippi in Greece. Enter Octavius, Antony, *and their* Army.]

Octavius. Now, Antony, our hopes are answerèd.
  You said the enemy would not come down,
  But keep the hills and upper regions.
  It proves not so, their battles° are at hand,
  They mean to warn° us at Philippi here,   5
  Answering before we do demand of them.
Antony. Tut, I am in their bosoms,° and I know
  Wherefore they do it. They could be content
  To visit other places, and come down
  With fearful bravery,° thinking by this face   10
  To fasten in our thoughts that they have courage.
  But 'tis not so.

[Enter a Messenger.]

Messenger.   Prepare you, generals.
  The enemy comes on in gallant show.
  Their bloody sign° of battle is hung out,
  And something to be done immediately.   15
Antony. Octavius, lead your battle softly on,
  Upon the left hand of the even field.

---

4. **battles:** armies drawn up for battle. 5. **warn:** challenge. 7. **bosoms:** inner thoughts. 10. **bravery:** brave
show. 14. **bloody sign:** red flag.

Octavius. Upon the right hand I. Keep thou the left.
Antony. Why do you cross me in this exigent?°
Octavius. I do not cross you, but I will do so.   20

[*March. Drum. Enter from the other side of the stage* Brutus, Cassius, *and their* Army;
   Lucilius, Titinius, Messala, *and others.*]

Brutus. They stand, and would have parley.
Cassius. Stand fast, Titinius. We must out and talk.
Octavius. Mark Antony, shall we give sign of battle?
Antony. No, Caesar, we will answer on their charge.
   Make forth, the generals would have some words.   25
Octavius. Stir not until the signal.

         [Brutus, Cassius, Octavius, *and* Antony *meet in the center of the stage.*]

Brutus. Words before blows. Is it so, countrymen?
Octavius. Not that we love words better, as you do.
Brutus. Good words are better than bad strokes, Octavius.
Antony. In your bad strokes, Brutus, you give good words.   30
   Witness the hole you made in Caesar's heart,
   Crying "Long live! Hail, Caesar!"
Cassius.   Antony,
   The posture of your blows are yet unknown,
   But for your words, they rob the Hybla° bees,
   And leave them honeyless.
Antony.   Not stingless too.   35
Brutus. Oh, yes, and soundless too,
   For you have stol'n their buzzing, Antony,
   And very wisely threat before you sting.
Antony. Villains, you did not so when your vile daggers
   Hacked one another in the sides of Caesar.   40
   You showed your teeth like apes, and fawned like hounds,
   And bowed like bondmen, kissing Caesar's feet,
   Whilst damnèd Casca, like a cur, behind
   Struck Caesar on the neck. O you flatterers!
Cassius. Flatterers! Now, Brutus, thank yourself.   45
   This tongue had not offended so today
   If Cassius might have ruled.°

───

19. **exigent:** critical moment.   34. **Hybla:** a mountain in Sicily famous for the honey produced there.   47. **ruled:** had
his way in wanting to slay Antony.

Octavius. Come, come, the cause. If arguing make us sweat,
The proof of it will turn to redder drops.
Look,
I draw a sword against conspirators.
When think you that the sword goes up° again?
Never, till Caesar's three and thirty wounds
Be well avenged, or till another Caesar
Have added slaughter to the sword of traitors.

Brutus. Caesar, thou canst not die by traitors' hands,
Unless thou bring'st them with thee.

Octavius.   So I hope.
I was not born to die on Brutus' sword.

Brutus. Oh, if thou wert the noblest of thy strain,
Young man, thou couldst not die more honorable.

Cassius. A peevish schoolboy, worthless of such honor,
Joined with a masker° and a reveler!

Antony. Old Cassius still!

Octavius.   Come, Antony, away!
Defiance, traitors, hurl we in your teeth.
If you dare fight today, come to the field;
If not, when you have stomachs.°

[*Exeunt* Octavius, Antony, *and their* Army.]

Cassius. Why, now, blow wind, swell billow, and swim bark!°
The storm is up, and all is on the hazard.°

Brutus. Ho, Lucilius! Hark, a word with you.

Lucilius.   [*Standing forth*] My lord?

[Brutus *and* Lucilius *converse apart.*]

Cassius. Messala!

Messala. [*Standing forth*] What says my general?

Cassius. Messala,
This is my birthday, as this very day
Was Cassius born. Give me thy hand, Messala.
Be thou my witness that, against my will,
As Pompey was, am I compelled to set
Upon one battle all our liberties.
You know that I held Epicurus° strong,

50

55

60

65

70

75

---

52. **up:** back in its scabbard. 62. **masker:** actor. 66. **stomachs:** appetites. 67. **bark:** ship. 68. **on the hazard:** at stake. 77. **Epicurus:** a philosopher who taught that supernatural omens were simply superstition.

And his opinion. Now I change my mind,
And partly credit things that do presage.°
Coming from Sardis, on our former ensign°   80
Two mighty eagles fell, and there they perched,
Gorging and feeding from our soldiers' hands,
Who to Philippi here consorted° us.
This morning are they fled away and gone,
And in their steads do ravens, crows, and kites°   85
Fly o'er our heads and downward look on us,
As we were sickly prey. Their shadows seem
A canopy most fatal, under which
Our army lies, ready to give up the ghost.

Messala. Believe not so.

Cassius.   I but believe it partly,   90
For I am fresh of spirit and resolved
To meet all perils very constantly.

             [Brutus *and* Lucilius *end their conversation.*]

Brutus. Even so, Lucilius.

Cassius.   Now, most noble Brutus,
The gods today stand friendly, that we may,
Lovers in peace, lead on our days to age!   95
But since the affairs of men rest still incertain,
Let's reason with the worst that may befall.
If we do lose this battle, then is this
The very last time we shall speak together.
What are you then determinèd to do?   100

Brutus. Even by the rule of that philosophy
By which I did blame Cato° for the death
Which he did give himself—I know not how,
But I do find it cowardly and vile,
For fear of what might fall, so to prevent   105
The time of life°—arming myself with patience
To stay° the providence of some high powers
That govern us below.

Cassius.   Then, if we lose this battle,
You are contented to be led in triumph
Thorough the streets of Rome?   110

Brutus. No, Cassius, no. Think not, thou noble Roman,

---

79. **presage** (prĭ-sāj′): foretell what is to come. 80. **former ensign:** foremost battle flag. 83. **consorted:** accompanied. 85. **kites:** hawks. 102. **Cato:** Portia's father, a Stoic, killed himself when Caesar defeated Pompey. 105–106. **prevent . . . life:** anticipate the natural end of life. 107. **stay:** await.

That ever Brutus will go bound to Rome.
He bears too great a mind. But this same day
Must end that work the ides of March begun,
And whether we shall meet again I know not.   115
Therefore our everlasting farewell take.
Forever and forever, farewell, Cassius!
If we do meet again, why, we shall smile;
If not, why then this parting was well made.
Cassius. Forever and forever farewell, Brutus!   120
If we do meet again, we'll smile indeed;
If not, 'tis true this parting was well made.
Brutus. Why then, lead on. Oh, that a man might know
The end of this day's business ere it come!
But it sufficeth that the day will end,   125
And then the end is known. Come, ho! Away!

[Exeunt.]

Scene 2

[The field of battle. Alarum.° Enter Brutus _and_ Messala.]

Brutus. Ride, ride, Messala, ride, and give these bills°
Unto the legions on the other side.

[Loud alarum.]

Let them set on at once, for I perceive
But cold demeanor° in Octavius' wing,
And sudden push gives them the overthrow.   5
Ride, ride, Messala. Let them all come down.

[Exeunt.]

Scene 3

[Another part of the field. Alarums. Enter Cassius _and_ Titinius, _dismayed._]

Cassius. Oh, look, Titinius, look, the villains fly!
Myself have to mine own turned enemy.
This ensign° here of mine was turning back.

S.D. **Alarum:** drum or trumpet call to arms.   1. **bills:** orders.   4. **cold demeanor:** lack of spirit.
3. **ensign:** flag bearer.

I slew the coward, and did take it from him.

Titinius. O Cassius, Brutus gave the word too early, 5
    Who, having some advantage on Octavius,
    Took it too eagerly. His soldiers fell to spoil°
    Whilst we by Antony are all enclosed.

                      [*Enter* Pindarus.]

Pindarus. Fly further off, my lord, fly further off.
    Mark Antony is in your tents, my lord.
    Fly, therefore, noble Cassius, fly far off. 10

Cassius. This hill is far enough. Look, look, Titinius,
    Are those my tents where I perceive the fire?

Titinius. They are, my lord.

Cassius.   Titinius, if thou lovest me,
    Mount thou my horse and hide thy spurs in him
    Till he have brought thee up to yonder troops 15
    And here again, that I may rest assured
    Whether yond troops are friend or enemy.

Titinius. I will be here again, even with° a thought.

                                  [*Exit.*]

Cassius. Go, Pindarus, get higher on that hill— 20
    My sight was ever thick.° Regard Titinius,
    And tell me what thou notest about the field.

              [Pindarus *ascends the hill.*]

    This day I breathèd first. Time is come round,
    And where I did begin, there shall I end,
    My life is run his compass. Sirrah, what news? 25

Pindarus. [*Above*] O my lord!

Cassius. What news?

Pindarus. [*Above*] Titinius is enclosèd round about
    With horsemen that make to him on the spur,
    Yet he spurs on. Now they are almost on him. 30
    Now, Titinius! Now some light.° Oh, he lights too.
    He's ta'en. [*Shout*] And, hark! They shout for joy.

Cassius. Come down, behold no more.
    Oh, coward that I am, to live so long,
    To see my best friend ta'en before my face! 35

---

7. **spoil:** looting. 19. **even with:** as quickly as. 21. **thick:** weak. 31. **light:** dismount.

[Pindarus *descends*.]

Come hither, sirrah.
In Parthia° did I take thee prisoner,
And then I swore thee, saving of thy life,
That whatsoever I did bid thee do
Thou shouldst attempt it. Come now, keep thine oath. 40
Now be a free man, and with this good sword,
That ran through Caesar's bowels, search this bosom.
Stand not to answer. Here, take thou the hilts,
And when my face is covered, as 'tis now,
Guide thou the sword.

[Pindarus *stabs him*.]

                    Caesar, thou art revenged, 45
Even with the sword that killed thee. [*Dies*.]
Pindarus. So, I am free, yet would not so have been,
Durst I have done my will. O Cassius!
Far from this country Pindarus shall run,
Where never Roman shall take note of him. 50

[*He throws down the sword and runs. Reenter* Titinius *with* Messala.]

Messala. It is but change,° Titinius, for Octavius
Is overthrown by noble Brutus' power,
As Cassius' legions are by Antony.
Titinius. These tidings will well comfort Cassius.
Messala. Where did you leave him?
Titinius.   All disconsolate, 55
With Pindarus his bondman, on this hill.
Messala. Is not that he that lies upon the ground?
Titinius. He lies not like the living. Oh, my heart!
Messala. Is not that he?
Titinius.   No, this was he, Messala,
But Cassius is no more. O setting sun, 60
As in thy red rays thou dost sink to night,
So in his red blood Cassius' day is set,
The sun of Rome is set! Our day is gone,

---

37. **Parthia:** ancient country in Asia.   51. **change:** even exchange.

Clouds, dews, and dangers come. Our deeds are done!
Mistrust of my success hath done this deed.   65
Messala. Mistrust of good success hath done this deed.
O hateful error, melancholy's child,
Why dost thou show to the apt° thoughts of men
The things that are not? O error, soon conceived,
Thou never comest unto a happy birth,   70
But kill'st the mother that engendered thee!
Titinius. What, Pindarus! Where art thou, Pindarus?
Messala. Seek him, Titinius, whilst I go to meet
The noble Brutus, thrusting this report
Into his ears. I may say "thrusting" it,   75
For piercing steel and darts envenomèd
Shall be as welcome to the ears of Brutus
As tidings of this sight.
Titinius.   Hie you, Messala,
And I will seek for Pindarus the while.

                                                                [*Exit* Messala.]

                              [Titinius *looks at* Cassius.]

Why didst thou send me forth, brave Cassius?   80
Did I not meet thy friends? And did not they
Put on my brows this wreath of victory,
And bid me give it thee? Didst thou not hear their shouts?
Alas, thou has misconstrued° everything!
But hold thee, take this garland on thy brow.   85
Thy Brutus bid me give it thee, and I
Will do his bidding. Brutus, come apace,°
And see how I regarded Caius Cassius.
By your leave, gods, this is a Roman heart.
Come, Cassius' sword, and find Titinius' heart.   90

                                                                [*Kills himself.*]

        [*Alarum. Reenter* Messala, *with* Brutus, *young* Cato, Lucilius, *and others.*]

Brutus. Where, where, Messala, doth his body lie?
Messala. Lo, yonder, and Titinius mourning it.
Brutus. Titinius' face is upward.
Cato.   He is slain.

---

68. **apt:** ready to be deceived.   84. **misconstrued:** misinterpreted.   87. **apace:** quickly.

Brutus. O Julius Caesar, thou art mighty yet!
Thy spirit walks abroad, and turns our swords   95
In our own proper entrails.

[*Low alarums.*]

Cato.   Brave Titinius!
Look whether he have not crowned dead Cassius!
Brutus. Are yet two Romans living such as these?
The last of all the Romans, fare thee well!
It is impossible that ever Rome   100
Should breed thy fellow. Friends, I owe more tears
To this dead man than you shall see me pay.
I shall find time, Cassius, I shall find time.
Come therefore, and to Thasos° send his body.
His funerals shall not be in our camp,   105
Lest it discomfort us.° Lucilius, come,
And come, young Cato. Let us to the field.
Labeo and Flavius, set our battles on.
'Tis three o'clock, and, Romans, yet ere night
We shall try fortune in a second fight.   110

[*Exeunt.*]

Scene 4

[*Another part of the field. Alarum. Enter, fighting,* Soldiers *of both armies; then* Brutus,
young Cato, Lucilius, *and others in retreat.*]

Brutus. Yet, countrymen, oh, yet hold up your heads!
Cato. What fellow doth not? Who will go with me?
I will proclaim my name about the field.
I am the son of Marcus Cato, ho! —
A foe to tyrants, and my country's friend.   5
I am the son of Marcus Cato, ho!

[*He runs off, followed by several* Soldiers.]

---

104. **Thasos:** Greek island in the Aegean Sea.   106. **discomfort us:** make us all lose heart.

Brutus. And I am Brutus, Marcus Brutus, I—
　　Brutus, my country's friend. Know me for Brutus!

[*He runs off in another direction, followed by all but* Lucilius, *who looks off in the direction taken by young* Cato. *A loud cry offstage.*]

Lucilius. O young and noble Cato, art thou down?
　　Why, now thou diest as bravely as Titinius,
　　And mayst be honored, being Cato's son.　　　　　　　　　　　　　　　10

[*Soldiers of* Antony's *army enter behind him with drawn swords.*]

First Soldier. Yield, or thou diest.
Lucilius.　　　　　　　　　　Only I yield to die.
　　[*Offering money*] There is so much that thou wilt kill me straight.
　　Kill Brutus, and be honored in his death.
First Soldier. We must not. A noble prisoner!　　　　　　　　　　15
Second Soldier. Room, ho! Tell Antony, Brutus is ta'en.
First Soldier. I'll tell the news. Here comes the general.

[*Enter* Antony.]

　　Brutus is ta'en, Brutus is ta'en, my lord.
Antony. Where is he?
Lucilius. Safe, Antony, Brutus is safe enough　　　　　　　　　　20
　　I dare assure thee that no enemy
　　Shall ever take alive the noble Brutus.
　　The gods defend him from so great a shame!
　　When you do find him, or alive or dead,
　　He will be found like Brutus, like himself.　　　　　　　　　　　25
Antony. This is not Brutus, friend, but, I assure you,
　　A prize no less in worth. Keep this man safe,
　　Give him all kindness. I had rather have
　　Such men my friends than enemies. Go on,
　　And see whether Brutus be alive or dead,　　　　　　　　　　30
　　And bring us word unto Octavius' tent
　　How everything is chanced.

[*Exeunt.*]

Scene 5

[*Another part of the field. Enter* Brutus, Dardanius, Clitus, Strato, *and* Volumnius, *weary and defeated.*]

Brutus. Come, poor remains of friends, rest on this rock.
Clitus. Statilius showed the torchlight,° but, my lord,
   He came not back. He is or ta'en or slain.
Brutus. Sit thee down, Clitus. Slaying is the word,
   It is a deed in fashion. Hark thee, Clitus. [*Whispering*]   5
Clitus. What, I, my lord? No, not for all the world.
Brutus. Peace then, no words.
Clitus.   I'll rather kill myself.
Brutus. Hark thee, Dardanius. [*Whispering*]
Dardanius.   Shall I do such a deed?
Clitus. O Dardanius!
Dardanius. O Clitus!   10
Clitus. What ill request did Brutus make to thee?
Dardanius. To kill him, Clitus. Look, he meditates.
Clitus. Now is that noble vessel full of grief,
   That it runs over even at his eyes.
Brutus. Come hither, good Volumnius, list° a word.   15
Volumnius. What says my lord?
Brutus.   Why, this, Volumnius.
   The ghost of Caesar hath appeared to me
   Two several° times by night – at Sardis once,
   And this last night here in Philippi fields.
   I know my hour is come.
Volumnius.   Not so, my lord.   20
Brutus. Nay, I am sure it is, Volumnius.
   Thou seest the world, Volumnius, how it goes,
   Our enemies have beat us to the pit.°

[*Low alarums.*]

   It is more worthy to leap in ourselves
   Than tarry till they push us. Good Volumnius,   25
   Thou know'st that we two went to school together.

---

2. **showed the torchlight:** gave the signal.   15. **list:** listen to.   18. **several:** different.   23. **Our . . . pit:** a reference to the method hunters used, encircling and driving their prey into a pit.

Even for that our love of old, I prithee
    Hold thou my sword hilts whilst I run on it.
Volumnius. That's not an office for a friend, my lord.

                    [*Alarum still.*]

Clitus. Fly, fly, my lord, there is no tarrying here. 30
Brutus. Farewell to you, and you, and you, Volumnius.
    Strato, thou hast been all this while asleep—
    Farewell to thee too, Strato. Countrymen,
    My heart doth joy that yet in all my life
    I found no man but he was true to me. 35
    I shall have glory by this losing day,
    More than Octavius and Mark Antony
    By this vile conquest shall attain unto.
    So, fare you well at once, for Brutus' tongue
    Hath almost ended his life's history. 40
    Night hangs upon mine eyes, my bones would rest
    That have but labored to attain this hour.

        [*Alarum. Cry within,* "Fly, fly, fly!"]

Clitus. Fly, my lord, fly!
Brutus.   Hence! I will follow.

        [*Exeunt* Clitus, Dardanius, *and* Volumnius.]

    I prithee, Strato, stay thou by thy lord.
    Thou art a fellow of a good respect, 45
    Thy life hath had some smatch° of honor in it.
    Hold then my sword, and turn away thy face
    While I do run upon it. Wilt thou, Strato?
Strato. Give me your hand first. Fare you well, my lord.
Brutus. Farewell, good Strato. [*Runs on his sword.*] Caesar, now be still. 50
    I killed not thee with half so good a will. [*Dies.*]

    [*Alarum. Retreat. Enter* Octavius, Antony, Messala, Lucilius, *and the* Army.]

Octavius. What man is that?
Messala. My master's man. Strato, where is thy master?

---

46. **smatch**: taste.

Strato. Free from the bondage you are in, Messala.
    The conquerors can but make a fire of him,   55
    For Brutus only overcame himself,
    And no man else hath honor by his death.
Lucilius. So Brutus should be found. I thank thee, Brutus,
    That thou hast proved Lucilius' saying true.
Octavius. All that served Brutus, I will entertain them.°   60
    Fellow, wilt thou bestow thy time with me?
Strato. Aye, if Messala will prefer° me to you.
Octavius. Do so, good Messala.
Messala. How died my master, Strato?
Strato. I held the sword, and he did run on it.
Messala. Octavius, then take him to follow thee   65
    That did the latest° service to my master.
Antony. This was the noblest Roman of them all.
    All the conspirators, save only he,
    Did that they did in envy of great Caesar.
    He only, in a general honest thought   70
    And common good to all, made one of them.
    His life was gentle, and the elements
    So mixed in him that Nature might stand up
    And say to all the world, "This was a man."
Octavius. According to his virtue let us use° him,   75
    With all respect and rites of burial.
    Within my tent his bones tonight shall lie,
    Most like a soldier, ordered honorably.
    So call the field to rest, and let's away,
    To part° the glories of this happy day.   80

                                              [Exeunt.]

---

60. **entertain them**: give them a place in my service. 62. **prefer**: recommend. 67. **latest**: last. 76. **use**: treat. 81. **part**: divide up.

FOR STUDY AND DISCUSSION

1. In Scene 1, the enemies meet to talk before they fight. Evaluate the behavior of the four main characters: Antony and Octavius versus Brutus and Cassius. What has united the two pairs on either side? Which of the four seem most in control of their emotions?

2. Who is the other Caesar that Octavius mentions in line 54 of Scene 1?

3. In lines 77–89 of Scene 1, Cassius reports some omens which, for the first time in his life, he "partly credits." How do these omens, together with Brutus' and Cassius' parting speeches, affect the mood of the scene?

4. What function does Scene 2 have? How does it affect your expectation of the battle's outcome?

5. Explain how Messala's speech on error and melancholy (lines 67–71, Scene 3) applies to Cassius' death.

6. In lines 94–96 of Scene 3, Brutus addresses Julius Caesar. How is Caesar present in this scene?

7. What does Scene 4 reveal about the progress of the battle offstage?

8. Look back at the actions of Cassius, Pindarus, and Titinius in Scene 3, and at the actions of Lucilius in Scene 4. How does each one deal with what seems to be defeat at the hands of the enemy?

9. What are the reasons for the suicides of Cassius and Brutus? Who dies for loyalty? Who for honor?

10. In your opinion, is Antony's speech in Scene 5 an accurate description of Brutus' character? Is Antony being sincere or ironic? Explain.

11. How does Octavius show himself to be a good politician in Scene 5? Why do you think Shakespeare gives him the closing lines of the play?

THE PLAY AS A WHOLE

1. Suppose you were going to direct a production of *Julius Caesar*. You would want to decide which character (if any) should be the focus of the play. Who is the tragic hero in this play? One of the following comments may help you in finding your answer.

Caesar vanquishes Brutus and Cassius at Philippi as truly as he vanquishes Pompey at Pharsalus. Antony and Octavius are not Caesar's avengers; they are merely Caesar's agents; he avenges himself . . . Caesar, alive or dead, pervades and operates the drama—and not less after his death than in his life.

George Lyman Kittredge
Introduction to *Julius Caesar*

Brutus is the dramatic hero of *Julius Caesar*. He is the most prominent figure, and at almost every stage our interest is focused on his deliberations and decisions. Obviously Shakespeare was greatly interested in the mind of Brutus.

T. S. Dorsch
Introduction to *Julius Caesar*

2. Some critics have suggested that *Julius Caesar* tends to be misinterpreted by modern audiences because of their belief in democracy and liberty. According to these critics, Shakespeare had quite a different point of view, living as he did under a legitimate and respected ruler in a time of peace and prosperity, not so long after a series of bloody civil wars. Shakespeare, these critics say, intended Brutus to be the villain of his play, not the hero, since he kills a popular ruler and disrupts the social order. Do you agree? What evidence is there in the play that Shakespeare thought of Brutus as a hero? As a villain?

3. Brutus is an idealist; he desires perfection in himself and in the society he lives in. Brutus is also the only character in the play who consistently says what he really thinks. What do Brutus' actions and decisions show about the virtues and shortcomings of idealism? Are there any occasions where Cassius seems more likable and human than Brutus?

4. *Julius Caesar* is a play about politics and power. What kind of person, does the play suggest, is most likely to come out on top in a power struggle? Discuss whether or not you think this is necessarily true.

DRAMATIC STRUCTURE: TRAGEDY

Everyone has some idea of what tragedy means when it applies to something other than plays. Tragic plays, however, are so called because they have similar structures. The Greeks called tragic characters "dying ones," a term which is much more vivid than our term *mortal*, though it means the same thing. The simplest ingredient of a tragic structure is an unhappy ending. In this respect, tragedy is the opposite of comedy. In comedy, events go from bad to worse, but finally there is an upturn and a happy ending. By contrast, most tragedies start with a hero or heroine at the height of power and prestige and then plunge that person into defeat.

Many people who have written about tragedy refer to the hero's or heroine's *tragic flaw*. This may be pride, arrogance, lust for power, or something else. In many tragedies, the flaw is lack of insight, the inability to see circumstances as they really are, or to understand one's own nature properly. Frequently, this flaw, combined with ill luck or blind fate, brings about the downfall of the principal character, called the *protagonist*. The protagonist is usually opposed by the *antagonist*, who also may contribute to the downfall.

Generally, along with suffering, the protagonist comes to a *recognition*, a discovery, insight, enlightenment, or understanding. The suffering that the protagonist goes through is the price that must be paid and the means by which enlightenment comes.

Elizabethan audiences particularly liked a kind of tragedy that dealt with *revenge*. These plays often dealt with personal vendettas in which the protagonist, revenging a murder, brought about general destruction. Shakespeare's revenge plays are almost always set in a larger social context. In his plays, there is usually a strong *ruling figure* who is brought down by a *rebel*, or usurping figure, who in turn is defeated by an *avenger*.

You might want to consider what characters or group of characters in *Julius Caesar* take these three roles of ruling figure, rebel, and avenger. You might also want to consider the following questions in your discussion of the play:

Is this Caesar's tragedy, the story of a man whose ambition brings about his fall? Is this Brutus' tragedy, the story of a man whose lack of insight brings chaos to his society and his own death? Is this a revenge tragedy, the story of a man who avenges the death of his friend?

BLANK VERSE

English is an accented language, which means that its speakers put more stress on some words and syllables than on others. In English, meaning is often determined by accent: "Did you ASK?" is one question, but "Did YOU ask?" is another. English poetry, as you know, makes deliberate use of accents, and many poems are worked out so that they have a regular pattern of stressed and unstressed syllables.

In this line from *Julius Caesar*, an unstressed syllable is regularly followed by a stressed syllable. The unstressed syllable is marked (˘) and the stressed (´):

Whў, mán, hĕ dóth bĕstrídĕ thĕ nárrŏw wórld

This unit of rhythm—an unstressed syllable followed by a stressed one—is called an *iamb*. Unrhymed poetry that uses five iambs to a line is called *blank verse*. Blank verse is the verse form used by Shakespeare as well as by other major English poets. The natural cadence of the English language lends itself to the rhythm of the iamb, which might explain its widespread use in English poetry.

In reading blank verse aloud, actors and actresses must not overemphasize the iambs, or the speeches will take on a singsong rhythm and their meaning will be blunted. The best way to read blank verse is to look first for meaning, and then read each speech to bring the meaning out. The forceful iambs will take care of themselves, in the background, as steady and essential as a heartbeat.

Poetry, of course, can be read in different ways, with accents placed on different words, depending on how individual readers interpret the meaning. In the line quoted above, for example, some readers might stress the word *he*. In what different ways could the rest of this speech be recited aloud?

Cassius. Why, man, he doth bestride the narrow world
  Like a Colossus, and we petty men
  Walk under his huge legs and peep about
  To find ourselves dishonorable graves.
  Men at some time are masters of their fates.
  The fault, dear Brutus, is not in our stars
  But in ourselves, that we are underlings.
  (I, 2, 135–141)

FOR COMPOSITION

Comparing Two Literary Works

Shakespeare based his play *The Tragedy of Julius Caesar* largely on what he read in Plutarch's history. In a short essay, compare Shakespeare's dramatization of Calpurnia's dream (Act Two, Scene 2); of the attempts of Artemidorus to warn Caesar (Act Two, Scene 3); and of the assassination scene (Act Three, Scene 1) with what you have read in Plutarch. What specific facts has Shakespeare taken from Plutarch? What additions has Shakespeare made to Plutarch's story? Discuss how Shakespeare has developed Plutarch's narrative to suit his own dramatic purposes.

On the night before Halloween in 1938, a woman ran into an Indianapolis church screaming, "New York destroyed; it's the end of the world! You might as well go home to die! I just heard it on the radio!" All over the country that night, thousands of panic-stricken Americans were fleeing from Martian monsters who had invaded Earth. How did they know about the invasion? They'd heard it on the radio.

What they'd heard was the play *Invasion from Mars*, by Howard Koch. Koch's radio drama was suggested by H. G. Wells's short novel *The War of the Worlds.*

Orson Welles, a young actor, producer, writer, and director, was in charge of the hour-length dramatizations heard every Sunday night on CBS's Mercury Theater. Each week, Welles and his co-producer John Houseman assigned a novel or short story to Howard Koch, a young playwright on his first professional job. Koch had six days to write a radio script based on the novel or short story. When he read *The War of the Worlds,*

Invasion from Mars

Orson Welles.

Koch realized he could use practically nothing of Wells's book except the idea of the Martian invasion and the description of the Martians and their machines. Koch decided to tell the story in a series of news bulletins. The broadcast format conveyed such a sense of reality that it caused a panic.

"This is Glub, sitting in for Tom Dunn on the 'Eleven O'Clock News,' and I wish to announce that there has been a rather sudden and sweeping change in your government."

Drawing by Alan Dunn; © 1968. The New Yorker Magazine, Inc.

Radio Drama

Up until the mid-1950's, radio drama enjoyed great popularity in America. The radio dramatists did not have to work under the limitations imposed by stage or movie sets. They could move around freely in time and space. They could use words and sound to suggest all kinds of settings and characters. Old-time listeners remember the various places evoked by words and sound on radio: dismal moors, city streets, Western ranches, even the inside of a brain.

By the mid-1950's, radio was giving way to television. In the end, radio, for all its promise, failed to produce many lasting dramas. Producers and sponsors were afraid to lose audiences, so they gave people what they thought they wanted: easy stories with happy endings. Few of these were durable.

Invasion from Mars

Howard Koch

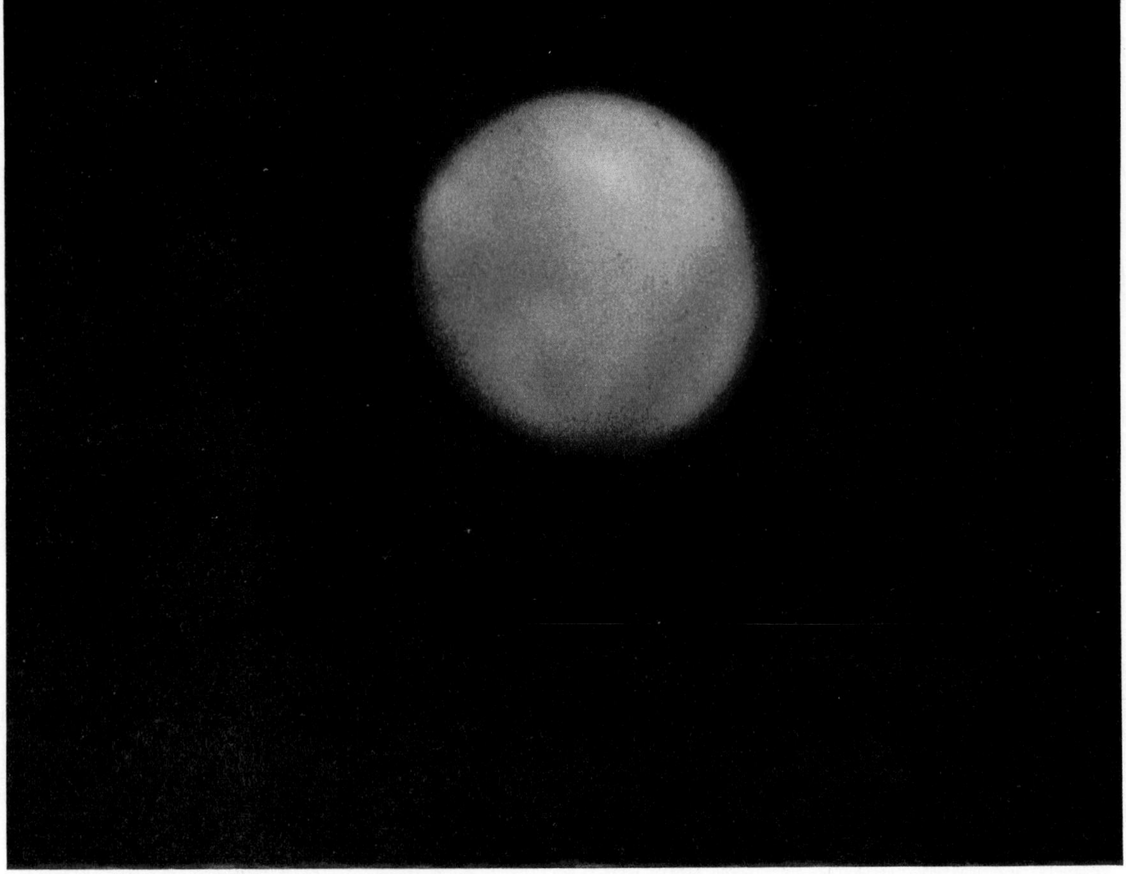

Characters

Orson Welles
Three Announcers
Carl Phillips, radio commentator
Professor Richard Pierson, astronomer
A Policeman
Mr. Wilmuth, a farmer
Brigadier General Montgomery Smith
Harry McDonald

Captain Lansing
Secretary of the Interior
An Officer ⎫
A Gunner ⎬ 22nd Field Artillery
An Observer ⎭
Commander Voght
Five Radio Operators
A Stranger

Columbia Broadcasting System
Orson Welles and Mercury Theater
on the Air
Sunday, October 30, 1938
8:00 to 9:00 P.M.

Announcer One. The Columbia Broadcasting System and its affiliated stations present Orson Welles and the Mercury Theater on the Air in a radio play by Howard Koch suggested by the H. G. Wells novel *The War of the Worlds.*

[*Mercury Theater musical theme.*]

Announcer One. Ladies and gentlemen: the director of the Mercury Theater and star of these broadcasts, Orson Welles . . .

Orson Welles. We know now that in the early years of the twentieth century this world was being watched closely by intelligences greater than man's and yet as mortal as his own. We know now that as human beings busied themselves about their various concerns, they were scrutinized and studied, perhaps almost as narrowly as a man with a microscope might scrutinize the transient creatures that swarm and multiply in a drop of water. With infinite complacence, people went to and fro over the earth about their little affairs, serene in the assurance of their dominion over this small spinning fragment of solar driftwood, which by chance or design man has inherited out of the dark mystery of Time and Space. Yet across an immense ethereal gulf, minds that are to our minds as ours are to the beasts in the jungle, intellects vast, cool, and unsympathetic, regarded this earth with envious eyes and slowly and surely drew their plans against us. In the thirty-eighth year of the twentieth century came the great disillusionment.

It was near the end of October. Business was better.[1] The war was over. More men were back at work. Sales were picking up. On this particular evening, October 30, the Crossley service estimated that thirty-two million people were listening in on radios.

Announcer Two. . . . for the next twenty-four hours not much change in temperature. A slight atmospheric disturbance of undetermined origin is reported over Nova Scotia, causing a low pressure area to move down rather rapidly over the northeastern states, bringing a forecast of rain, accompanied by winds of light gale force. Maximum temperature 66; minimum 48. This weather report comes to you from the Government Weather Bureau.

. . . We now take you to the Meridian Room in the Hotel Park Plaza in downtown New York, where you will be entertained by the music of Ramón Raquello and his orchestra.

[*Spanish theme song . . . fades.*]

Announcer Three. Good evening, ladies and gentlemen. From the Meridian Room in the Park Plaza in New York City, we bring you the music of Ramón Raquello and his orchestra. With a touch of the Spanish, Ramón Raquello leads off with "La Cumparsita."

[*Piece starts playing.*]

Announcer Two. Ladies and gentlemen, we interrupt our program of dance music to bring you a special bulletin from the Intercontinental Radio News. At twenty minutes before eight, Central Time, Professor Farrell of the

---

1. **Business was better:** During the Depression of the 1930's, banks and businesses failed and there was mass unemployment. By 1938 the economy had begun to improve.

Mount Jennings Observatory, Chicago, Illinois, reports observing several explosions of incandescent gas, occurring at regular intervals on the planet Mars.

The spectroscope indicates the gas to be hydrogen and moving towards the earth with enormous velocity. Professor Pierson of the observatory at Princeton confirms Farrell's observation, and describes the phenomenon as (quote) like a jet of blue flame shot from a gun (unquote). We now return you to the music of Ramón Raquello, playing for you in the Meridian Room of the Park Plaza Hotel, situated in downtown New York.

[*Music plays for a few moments until piece ends . . . sound of applause.*]

Now a tune that never loses favor, the ever popular "Star Dust." Ramón Raquello and his orchestra . . .

[*Music.*]

Announcer Two. Ladies and gentlemen, following on the news given in our bulletin a moment ago, the Government Meteorological Bureau has requested the large observatories of the country to keep an astronomical watch on any further disturbances occurring on the planet Mars. Due to the unusual nature of this occurrence, we have arranged an interview with the noted astronomer, Professor Pierson, who will give us his views on this event. In a few moments we will take you to the Princeton Observatory at Princeton, New Jersey. We return you until then to the music of Ramón Raquello and his orchestra.

[*Music . . .*]

Announcer Two. We are ready now to take you to the Princeton Observatory at Princeton where Carl Phillips, our commentator, will interview Professor Richard Pierson, famous astronomer. We take you now to Princeton, New Jersey.

[*Echo chamber.*[2]]

Phillips. Good evening, ladies and gentlemen. This is Carl Phillips, speaking to you from the observatory at Princeton. I am standing in a large semicircular room, pitch-black except for an oblong split in the ceiling. Through this opening I can see a sprinkling of stars that cast a kind of frosty glow over the intricate mechanism of the huge telescope. The ticking sound you hear is the vibration of the clockwork. Professor Pierson stands directly above me on a small platform, peering through the giant lens. I ask you to be patient, ladies and gentlemen, during any delay that may arise during our interview. Besides his ceaseless watch of the heavens, Professor Pierson may be interrupted by telephone or other communications. During this period he is in constant touch with the astronomical centers of the world . . . Professor, may I begin our questions?

Pierson. At any time, Mr. Phillips.

Phillips. Professor, would you please tell our radio audience exactly what you see as you observe the planet Mars through your telescope?

Pierson. Nothing unusual at the moment, Mr. Phillips. A red disk swimming in a blue sea. Transverse stripes across the disk. Quite distinct now because Mars happens to be at the point nearest the earth . . . in opposition, as we call it.

---

2. **Echo chamber:** a room used in a broadcasting studio to produce the sound of an echo. Here, the echo chamber is used to suggest the sounds of people speaking in a high-ceilinged room, such as an observatory.

Phillips. In your opinion, what do these transverse stripes signify, Professor Pierson?

Pierson. Not canals, I can assure you, Mr. Phillips, although that's the popular conjecture of those who imagine Mars to be inhabited. From a scientific viewpoint the stripes are merely the result of atmospheric conditions peculiar to the planet.

Phillips. Then you're quite convinced as a scientist that living intelligence as we know it does not exist on Mars?

Pierson. I should say the chances against it are a thousand to one.

Phillips. And yet how do you account for these gas eruptions occurring on the surface of the planet at regular intervals?

Pierson. Mr. Phillips, I cannot account for it.

Phillips. By the way, Professor, for the benefit of our listeners, how far is Mars from the earth?

Pierson. Approximately forty million miles.

Phillips. Well, that seems a safe enough distance.

Just a moment, ladies and gentlemen, someone has just handed Professor Pierson a message. While he reads it, let me remind you that we are speaking to you from the observatory in Princeton, New Jersey, where we are interviewing the world-famous astronomer, Professor Pierson . . . One moment, please. Professor Pierson has passed me a message which he has just received . . . Professor, may I read the message to the listening audience?

Pierson. Certainly, Mr. Phillips.

Phillips. Ladies and gentlemen, I shall read you a wire addressed to Professor Pierson from Dr. Gray of the Natural History Museum, New York: "9:15 P.M. Eastern Standard Time. Seismograph registered shock of almost earthquake intensity occurring within a radius of twenty miles of Princeton. Please investigate. Signed, Lloyd Gray, Chief of Astronomical Division." . . . Professor Pierson,

could this occurrence possibily have something to do with the disturbances observed on the planet Mars?

Pierson. Hardly, Mr. Phillips. This is probably a meteorite of unusual size and its arrival at this particular time is merely a coincidence. However, we shall conduct a search, as soon as daylight permits.

Phillips. Thank you, Professor. Ladies and gentlemen, for the past ten minutes we've been speaking to you from the observatory at Princeton, bringing you a special interview with Professor Pierson, noted astronomer. This is Carl Phillips speaking. We now return you to our New York studio.

[Fade in piano playing.]

Announcer Two. Ladies and gentlemen, here is the latest bulletin from the Intercontinental Radio News. Montreal, Canada: Professor Morse of McGill University reports observing a total of three explosions on the planet Mars between the hours of 7:45 P.M. and 9:20 P.M. Eastern Standard Time. This confirms earlier reports received from American observatories. Now, nearer home, comes a special announcement from Trenton, New Jersey. It is reported that at 8:50 P.M. a huge, flaming object, believed to be a meteorite, fell on a farm in the neighborhood of Grovers Mill, New Jersey, twenty-two miles from Trenton. The flash in the sky was visible within a radius of several hundred miles and the noise of the impact was heard as far north as Elizabeth.

We have dispatched a special mobile unit to the scene, and will have our commentator, Mr. Phillips, give you a word description as soon as he can reach there from Princeton. In the meantime, we take you to the Hotel Martinet in Brooklyn, where Bobby Millette and his orchestra are offering a program of dance music.

[*Swing band for twenty seconds . . . then cut.*]

Announcer Two. We take you now to Grovers Mill, New Jersey.

[*Crowd noises . . . police sirens.*]

Phillips. Ladies and gentlemen, this is Carl Phillips again, at the Wilmuth farm, Grovers Mill, New Jersey. Professor Pierson and myself made the eleven miles from Princeton in ten minutes. Well, I . . . I hardly know where to begin, to paint for you a word picture of the strange scene before my eyes, like something out of a modern *Arabian Nights*.[3] Well, I just got here. I haven't had a chance to look around yet. I guess that's it. Yes, I guess that's the . . . thing, directly in front of me, half buried in a vast pit. Must have struck with terrific force. The ground is covered with splinters of a tree it must have struck on its way down. What I can see of the . . . object itself doesn't look very much like a meteor, at least not the meteors I've seen. It looks more like a huge cylinder. It has a diameter of . . . what would you say, Professor Pierson?
Pierson (*off*). About thirty yards.
Phillips. About thirty yards . . . The metal on the sheath is . . . well, I've never seen anything like it. The color is sort of yellowish-white. Curious spectators now are pressing close to the object in spite of the efforts of the police to keep them back. They're getting in front of my line of vision. Would you mind standing on one side, please?
Policeman. One side, there, one side.
Phillips. While the policemen are pushing the crowd back, here's Mr. Wilmuth, owner of the

farm here. He may have some interesting facts to add . . . Mr. Wilmuth, would you please tell the radio audience as much as you remember of this rather unusual visitor that dropped in your backyard? Step closer, please. Ladies and gentlemen, this is Mr. Wilmuth.
Wilmuth. I was listenin' to the radio.
Phillips. Closer and louder, please.
Wilmuth. Pardon me!
Phillips. Louder, please, and closer.
Wilmuth. Yes, sir — while I was listening to the radio and kinda drowsin', that professor fellow was talkin' about Mars, so I was half dozin' and half . . .
Phillips. Yes, Mr. Wilmuth. Then what happened?
Wilmuth. As I was sayin', I was listenin' to the radio kinda halfways . . .
Phillips. Yes, Mr. Wilmuth, and then you saw something?
Wilmuth. Not first off. I heard something.
Phillips. And what did you hear?
Wilmuth. A hissing sound. Like this: sssssss . . . kinda like a fourt' of July rocket.
Phillips. Then what?
Wilmuth. Turned my head out the window and would have swore I was to sleep and dreamin'.
Phillips. Yes?
Wilmuth. I seen a kinda greenish streak and then zingo! Somethin' smacked the ground. Knocked me clear out of my chair!
Phillips. Well, were you frightened, Mr. Wilmuth?
Wilmuth. Well, I — I ain't quite sure. I reckon I — I was kinda riled.
Phillips. Thank you, Mr. Wilmuth. Thank you.
Wilmuth. Want me to tell you some more?
Phillips. No . . . That's quite all right, that's plenty.

Ladies and gentlemen, you've just heard Mr. Wilmuth, owner of the farm where this

---

3. *Arabian Nights:* a collection of ancient Persian, Indian, and Arabian tales, full of adventure and fantasy.

thing has fallen. I wish I could convey the atmosphere . . . the background of this . . . fantastic scene. Hundreds of cars are parked in a field in back of us. Police are trying to rope off the roadway leading into the farm. But it's no use. They're breaking right through. Their headlights throw an enormous spot on the pit where the object's half buried. Some of the more daring souls are venturing near the edge. Their silhouettes stand out against the metal sheen.

[*Faint humming sound.*]

One man wants to touch the thing . . . he's having an argument with a policeman. The policeman wins . . . Now, ladies and gentlemen, there's something I haven't mentioned in all this excitement, but it's becoming more distinct. Perhaps you've caught it already on your radio. Listen: (*Long pause*) . . . Do you hear it? It's a curious humming sound that seems to come from inside the object. I'll move the microphone nearer. Here. (*Pause*) Now we're not more than twenty-five feet away. Can you hear it now? Oh, Professor Pierson!

Pierson. Yes, Mr. Phillips?

Phillips. Can you tell us the meaning of that scraping noise inside the thing?

Pierson. Possibly the unequal cooling of its surface.

Phillips. Do you still think it's a meteor, Professor?

Pierson. I don't know what to think. The metal casing is definitely extraterrestrial . . . not found on this earth. Friction with the earth's atmosphere usually tears holes in a meteorite. This thing is smooth and, as you can see, of cylindrical shape.

Phillips. Just a minute! Something's happening! Ladies and gentlemen, this is terrific!

This end of the thing is beginning to flake off! The top is beginning to rotate like a screw! The thing must be hollow!

Voices. She's a movin'!

Look, the darn thing's unscrewing!

Keep back, there! Keep back, I tell you!

Maybe there's men in it trying to escape!

It's red hot, they'll burn to a cinder!

Keep back there. Keep those idiots back!

[*Suddenly the clanking sound of a huge piece of falling metal.*]

Voices. She's off! The top's loose!

Look out there! Stand back!

Phillips. Ladies and gentlemen, this is the most terrifying thing I have ever witnessed . . . Wait a minute! *Someone's crawling out of the hollow top.* Someone or . . . something. I can see peering out of that black hole two luminous disks . . . Are they eyes? It might be a face. It might be . . .

[*Shout of awe from the crowd.*]

Phillips. Good heavens, something's wriggling out of the shadow like a gray snake. Now it's another one, and another. They look like tentacles to me. There, I can see the thing's body. It's large as a bear and it glistens like wet leather. But that face. It . . . it's indescribable. I can hardly force myself to keep looking at it. The eyes are black and gleam like a serpent. The mouth is V-shaped with saliva dripping from its rimless lips that seem to quiver and pulsate. The monster or whatever it is can hardly move. It seems weighed down by . . . possibly gravity or something. The thing's rising up. The crowd falls back. They've seen enough. This is the most extraordinary experience. I can't find words . . .

War's Over
How U. S. Met Mars

The radio's "end of the world," as some listeners understood it, produced repercussions throughout the United States. Samples, as reported by the Associated Press, follow:

Woman Tries Suicide

Pittsburgh.—A man returned home in the midst of the broadcast and found his wife, a bottle of poison in her hand, screaming: "I'd rather die this way than like that."

Man Wants to Fight Mars

San Francisco.—An offer to volunteer in stopping an invasion from Mars came among hundreds of telephone inquiries to police and newspapers during the radio dramatization of H. G. Wells' story. One excited man called Oakland police and shouted: "My God! Where can I volunteer my services? We've got to stop this awful thing!"

Church Lets Out

Indianapolis.—A woman ran into a church screaming: "New York destroyed; it's the end of the world. You might as well go home to die. I just heard it on the radio." Services were dismissed immediately.

College Boys Faint

Brevard, N. C.—Five Brevard College students fainted and panic gripped the campus for a half hour with many students fighting for telephones to inform their parents to come and get them.

It's a Massacre

Providence, R. I.—Weeping and hysterical women swamped the switchboard of the Providence Journal for details of the "massacre." The electric company received scores of calls urging it to turn off all lights so that the city would be safe from the "enemy."

She Sees "the Fire"

Boston.—One woman declared she could "see the fire" and told the Boston Globe she and many others in her neighborhood were "getting out of here."

"Where Is It Safe?"

Kansas City.—One telephone informant said he had loaded all his children into his car, had filled it with gasoline, and was going somewhere. "Where it is safe?" he wanted to know. The Associated Press bureau received queries on the "meteors" from Los Angeles, Salt Lake City, Beaumont, Tex., and St. Joseph, Mo.

Prayers in Richmond

Richmond, Va.—The Times-Dispatch reported some of its telephone calls came from persons who said they were praying.

Atlanta's "Monsters"

Atlanta—Listeners throughout the Southeast called newspapers reporting that "a planet struck in New Jersey, with monsters and almost everything, and anywhere from 40 to 7,000 people were killed." Editors said responsible persons, known to them, were among the anxious information seekers.

Rushes Home From Reno

Reno.—Marion Leslie Thorgaard, here for a divorce from Hilsce Robert Thorgaard, of New York, collapsed, fearing her mother and children in New York had been killed. One man immediately started East in hope of aiding the wife he was here to divorce.

I'm pulling this microphone with me as I talk. I'll have to stop the description until I've taken a new position. Hold on, will you please, I'll be back in a minute.

[*Fade into piano.*]

Announcer Two. We are bringing you an eyewitness account of what's happening on the Wilmuth farm, Grovers Mill, New Jersey. (*More piano*) We now return you to Carl Phillips at Grovers Mill.

Phillips. Ladies and gentlemen. (Am I on?) Ladies and gentlemen, here I am, back of a stone wall that adjoins Mr. Wilmuth's garden. From here I get a sweep of the whole scene. I'll give you every detail as long as I can talk. As long as I can see. More state police have arrived. They're drawing up a cordon in front of the pit, about thirty of them. No need to push the crowd back now. They're willing to keep their distance. The captain is conferring with someone. We can't quite see who. Oh yes, I believe it's Professor Pierson. Yes, it is. Now they've parted. The professor moves around one side, studying the object, while the captain and two policemen advance with something in their hands. I can see it now. It's a white handkerchief tied to a pole . . . a flag of truce. If those creatures know what that means . . . what anything means! . . . *Wait!* Something's happening!

[*Hissing sound followed by a humming that increases in intensity.*]

A humped shape is rising out of the pit. I can make out a small beam of light against a mirror. What's that? There's a jet of flame springing from that mirror, and it leaps right at the advancing men. It strikes them head on! Good Lord, they're turning into flame!

[*Screams and unearthly shrieks.*]

Now the whole field's caught fire. (*Explosion*) The woods . . . the barns . . . the gas tanks of automobiles . . . it's spreading everywhere. It's coming this way. About twenty yards to my right . . .

[*Crash of microphone . . . then dead silence.*]

Announcer Two. Ladies and gentlemen, due to circumstances beyond our control, we are unable to continue the broadcast from Grovers Mill. Evidently there's some difficulty with our field transmission. However, we will return to that point at the earliest opportunity. In the meantime, we have a late bulletin from San Diego, California. Professor Indellkoffer, speaking at a dinner of the California Astronomical Society, expressed the opinion that the explosions on Mars are undoubtedly nothing more than severe volcanic disturbances on the surface of the planet. We continue now with our piano interlude.

[*Piano . . . then cut.*]

Ladies and gentlemen, I have just been handed a message that came in from Grovers Mill by telephone. Just a moment. At least forty people, including six state troopers, lie dead in a field east of the village of Grovers Mill, their bodies burned and distorted beyond all possible recognition. The next voice you hear will be that of Brigadier General Montgomery Smith, commander of the state militia at Trenton, New Jersey.

Smith. I have been requested by the governor of New Jersey to place the counties of Mercer and Middlesex as far west as Princeton, and east to Jamesburg, under martial law. No one will be permitted to enter this area except by special pass issued by state or military authorities. Four companies of state militia are proceeding from Trenton to Grovers Mill, and will aid in the evacuation of homes within the range of military operations. Thank you.

Announcer Two. You have just been listening to General Montgomery Smith, commanding the state militia at Trenton. In the meantime, further details of the catastrophe at Grovers Mill are coming in. The strange creatures, after unleashing their deadly assault, crawled back in their pit and made no attempt to prevent the efforts of the firemen to recover the bodies and extinguish the fire. Combined fire departments of Mercer County are fighting the flames which menace the entire countryside.

We have been unable to establish any contact with our mobile unit at Grovers Mill, but we hope to be able to return you there at the earliest possible moment. In the meantime we take you — uh, just one moment, please.

[*Long pause.*]

(*Whisper*) Ladies and gentlemen, I have just been informed that we have finally established communication with an eyewitness of the tragedy. Professor Pierson has been located at a farmhouse near Grovers Mill where he has established an emergency observation post. As a scientist, he will give you his explanation of the calamity. The next voice you hear will be that of Professor Pierson, brought to you by direct wire. Professor Pierson.

Pierson. Of the creatures in the rocket cylinder at Grovers Mill, I can give you no authoritative information — either as to their nature, their origin, or their purposes here on earth. Of their destructive instrument I might venture some conjectural explanation. For want of a better term, I shall refer to the mysterious weapon as a heat ray. It's all too evident that these creatures have scientific knowledge far in advance of our own. It is my guess that in some way they are able to generate an intense heat in a chamber of practically absolute non-conductivity. This intense heat they project in a parallel beam against any object they choose, by means of a polished parabolic mirror of unknown composition, much as the mirror of a lighthouse projects a beam of light. That is my conjecture of the origin of the heat ray . . .

Announcer Two. Thank you, Professor Pierson. Ladies and gentlemen, here is a bulletin from Trenton. It is a brief statement informus that the charred body of Carl Phillips has been identified in a Trenton hospital. Now here's another bulletin from Washington, D.C.

Office of the director of the National Red Cross reports ten units of Red Cross

Illustration from H. G. Wells's novel *The War of the Worlds*

emergency workers have been assigned to the headquarters of the state militia stationed outside of Grovers Mill, New Jersey. Here's a bulletin from state police, Princeton Junction: The fires at Grovers Mill and vicinity now under control. Scouts report all quiet in the pit, and no sign of life appearing from the mouth of the cylinder . . . And now, ladies and gentlemen, we have a special statement from Mr. Harry McDonald, vice president in charge of operations.

McDonald. We have received a request from the militia at Trenton to place at their disposal our entire broadcasting facilities. In view of the gravity of the situation, and believing that radio has a definite responsibility to serve in the public interest at all times, we are turning over our facilities to the state militia at Trenton.

Announcer Two. We take you now to the field headquarters of the state militia near Grovers Mill, New Jersey.

Captain. This is Captain Lansing of the signal corps, attached to the state militia now engaged in military operations in the vicinity of Grovers Mill. Situation arising from the reported presence of certain individuals of unidentified nature is now under complete control.

The cylindrical object which lies in a pit directly below our position is surrounded on all sides by eight battalions of infantry, without heavy fieldpieces, but adequately armed with rifles and machine guns. All cause for alarm, if such cause ever existed, is now entirely unjustified. The things, whatever they are, do not even venture to poke their heads above the pit. I can see their hiding place plainly in the glare of the searchlights here. With all their reported resources, these creatures can scarcely stand up against heavy machine-gun fire. Anyway, it's an interesting outing for the troops. I can make out their khaki uniforms, crossing back and forth in front of the lights. It looks almost like a real war. There appears to be some slight smoke in the woods bordering the Millstone River. Probably fire started by campers. Well, we ought to see some action soon. One of the companies is deploying on the left flank. A quick thrust and it will all be over. Now wait a minute! I see something on top of the cylinder. No, it's nothing but a shadow. Now the troops are on the edge of the Wilmuth farm. Seven thousand armed men closing in on an old metal tube. Wait, that wasn't a shadow! It's something moving . . . solid metal . . . kind of a shieldlike affair rising up out of the cylinder . . . It's going higher and higher. Why, it's standing on legs . . . actually rearing up on a sort of metal framework. Now it's reaching above the trees and the searchlights are on it! Hold on!

Announcer Two. Ladies and gentlemen, I have a grave announcement to make. Incredible as it may seem, both the observations of science and the evidence of our eyes lead to the inescapable assumption that those strange beings who landed in the Jersey farmlands tonight are the vanguard of an invading army from the planet Mars. The battle which took place tonight at Grovers Mill has ended in one of the most startling defeats ever suffered by an army in modern times; seven thousand men armed with rifles and machine guns pitted against a single fighting machine of the invaders from Mars. One hundred and twenty known survivors. The rest strewn over the battle area from Grovers Mill to Plainsboro, crushed and trampled to death under the metal feet of the monster, or burned to cinders by its heat ray. The monster is now in control of the middle section of New Jersey and has effectively cut the state through its center. Communication lines are down from Pennsylvania to the Atlantic Ocean. Railroad tracks are torn and service from New York to Philadelphia discontinued except routing some of the trains through Allentown and Phoenixville. Highways to the north, south, and west are clogged with frantic human traffic. Police and army reserves are unable to control the mad flight. By morning the fugitives will have swelled Philadelphia, Camden, and Trenton, it is estimated, to twice their normal population.

At this time martial law prevails throughout New Jersey and eastern Pennsylvania. We take you now to Washington for a special broadcast on the national emergency . . . the Secretary of the Interior . . .

Secretary. Citizens of the nation: I shall not try to conceal the gravity of the situation that confronts the country, nor the concern of

Illustration from H. G. Wells's novel *The War of the Worlds.*

your government in protecting the lives and property of its people. However, I wish to impress upon you—private citizens and public officials, all of you—the urgent need of calm and resourceful action. Fortunately, this formidable enemy is still confined to a comparatively small area, and we may place our faith in the military forces to keep them there. In the meantime, placing our faith in God, we must continue the performance of our duties, each and every one of us, so that we may confront this destructive adversary with a nation united, courageous, and consecrated to the preservation of human supremacy on this earth. I thank you.

Announcer Two. You have just heard the Secretary of the Interior speaking from Washington. Bulletins too numerous to read are piling up in the studio here. We are informed that the central portion of New Jersey is blacked out from radio communication due to the effect of the heat ray upon power lines and electrical equipment. Here is a special bulletin from New York. Cables received from English, French, German scientific bodies offering assistance. Astronomers report continued gas outbursts at regular intervals on planet Mars. Majority voice opinion that enemy will be reinforced by additional rocket machines. Attempts made to locate Professor Pierson of Princeton, who has observed Martians at close range. It is feared he was lost in recent battle. Langham Field, Virginia: Scouting planes report three Martian machines visible above treetops, moving north towards Somerville with population fleeing ahead of them. Heat ray not in use; although advancing at express-train speed, invaders pick their way carefully. They seem to be making conscious effort to avoid destruction of cities and countryside. However, they stop to uproot power lines, bridges, and railroad tracks. Their apparent objective is to crush resistance, paralyze communication, and disorganize human society.

Here is a bulletin from Basking Ridge, New Jersey: Coon hunters have stumbled on a second cylinder similar to the first embedded in the great swamp twenty miles south of Morristown. U. S. Army fieldpieces are proceeding from Newark to blow up second invading unit before cylinder can be opened and the fighting machine rigged. They are taking up position in the—foothills of Watchung Mountains. Another bulletin from Langham Field, Virginia: Scouting planes report enemy machines, now three in number, increasing speed northward, kicking over houses and trees in their evident haste to form a conjunction with their allies south of Morristown. Machines also sighted by telephone operator east of Middlesex within ten miles of Plainfield. Here's a bulletin from Winston Field, Long Island: Fleet of army bombers carrying heavy explosives flying north in pursuit of enemy. Scouting planes act as guides. They keep speeding enemy in sight. Just a moment, please. Ladies and gentlemen, we've run special wires to the artillery line in adjacent villages to give you direct reports in the zone of the advancing enemy. First we take you to the battery of the Twenty-Second Field Artillery, located in the Watchung Mountains.

Officer. Range, thirty-two meters.

Gunner. Thirty-two meters.

Officer. Projection, thirty-nine degrees.

Gunner. Thirty-nine degrees.

Officer. Fire!

[Boom of heavy gun . . . pause.]

Observer. One hundred and forty yards to the right, sir.

Officer. Shift range . . . thirty-one meters.

Gunner. Thirty-one meters.

Officer. Projection . . . thirty-seven degrees.

Gunner. Thirty-seven degrees.
Officer. Fire!

[*Boom of heavy gun . . . pause.*]

Observer. A hit, sir! We got the tripod of one of them. They've stopped. The others are trying to repair it.
Officer. Quick, get the range! Shift thirty meters.
Gunner. Thirty meters.
Officer. Projection . . . twenty-seven degrees.
Gunner. Twenty-seven degrees.
Officer. Fire!

[*Boom of heavy gun . . . pause.*]

Observer. Can't see the shell land, sir. They're letting off a smoke.
Officer. What is it?
Observer. A black smoke, sir. Moving this way. Lying close to the ground. It's moving fast.
Officer. Put on gas masks. (*Pause*) Get ready to fire. Shift to twenty-four meters.
Gunner. Twenty-four meters.
Officer. Projection, twenty-four degrees.
Gunner. Twenty-four degrees.
Officer. Fire!

[*Boom.*]

Observer. Still can't see, sir. The smoke's coming nearer.
Officer. Get the range. (*Coughs*)
Observer. Twenty-three meters. (*Coughs*)
Officer. Twenty-three meters. (*Coughs*)
Gunner. Twenty-three meters. (*Coughs*)
Observer. Projection, twenty-two degrees. (*Coughing*)
Officer. Twenty-two degrees. (*Fade in coughing*)

[*Fading in . . . sound of airplane motor.*]

Commander. Army bombing plane, V-8-43, off Bayonne, New Jersey, Lieutenant Voght, commanding eight bombers. Reporting to Commander Fairfax, Langham Field . . . This is Voght, reporting to Commander Fairfax, Langham Field . . . Enemy tripod machines now in sight. Reinforced by three machines from the Morristown cylinder . . . Six altogether. One machine partially crippled. Believed hit by shell from army gun in Watchung Mountains. Guns now appear silent. A heavy black fog hanging close to the earth . . . of extreme density, nature unknown. No sign of heat ray. Enemy now turns east, crossing Passaic River into the Jersey marshes. Another straddles the Pulaski Skyway. Evident objective is New York City. They're pushing down a high-tension power station. The machines are close together now, and we're ready to attack. Planes circling, ready to strike. A thousand yards and we'll be over the first—eight hundred yards . . . six hundred . . . four hundred . . . two hundred . . . There they go! The giant arm raised . . . Green flash! They're spraying us with flame! Two thousand feet. Engines are giving out. No chance to release bombs. Only one thing left . . . drop on them, plane and all. We're diving on the first one. Now the engine's gone! Eight . . .
Operator One. This is Bayonne, New Jersey, calling Langham Field . . .
   This is Bayonne, New Jersey, calling Langham Field . . .
   Come in, please . . . Come in, please . . .
Operator Two. This is Langham Field . . . go ahead . . .
Operator One. Eight army bombers in engagement with enemy tripod machines over Jersey flats. Engines incapacitated by heat ray. All crashed. One enemy machine destroyed. Enemy now discharging heavy black smoke in direction of —

Operator Three. This is Newark, New Jersey . . .

This is Newark, New Jersey . . .

Warning! Poisonous black smoke pouring in from Jersey marshes. Reaches South Street. Gas masks useless. Urge population to move into open spaces . . . automobiles use Routes 7, 23, 24 . . . Avoid congested areas. Smoke now spreading over Raymond Boulevard . . .

Operator Four. 2X2L . . . calling CQ . . .

2X2L . . . calling CQ . . .

2X2L . . . calling 8X3R . . .

Come in, please . . .

Operator Five. This is 8X3R . . . coming back at 2X2L.

Operator Four. How's reception? How's reception? K, please. Where are you, 8X3R?

What's the matter? Where are you?

[*Bells ringing over city, gradually diminishing.*]

Announcer Two. I'm speaking from the roof of Broadcasting Building, New York City. The bells you hear are ringing to warn the people to evacuate the city as the Martians approach. Estimated in last two hours three million people have moved out along the roads to the north, Hutchison River Parkway still kept open for motor traffic. Avoid bridges to Long Island . . . hopelessly jammed. All communication with Jersey shore closed ten minutes ago. No more defenses. Our army wiped out . . . artillery, air force, everything wiped out. This may be the last broadcast. We'll stay here to the end . . . People are holding service below us . . . in the cathedral.

[*Voices singing hymn.*]

Now I look down the harbor. All manner of boats, overloaded with fleeing population, pulling out from docks.

[*Sound of boat whistles.*]

Streets are all jammed. Noise in crowds like New Year's Eve in city. Wait a minute . . . Enemy now in sight above the Palisades. Five great machines. First one is crossing river. I can see it from here, wading the Hudson like a man wading through a brook . . . A bulletin's handed me . . . Martian cylinders are falling all over the country. One outside Buffalo, one in Chicago, St. Louis . . . seem to be timed and spaced . . . Now the first machine reaches the shore. He stands watching, looking over the city. His steel, cowlish head is even with the skyscrapers. He waits for the others. They rise like a line of new towers on the city's west side . . . Now they're lifting their metal hands. This is the end now. Smoke comes out . . . black smoke, drifting over the city. People in the streets see it now. They're running towards the East River . . . thousands of them, dropping in like rats. Now the smoke's spreading faster. It's reached Times Square. People trying to run away from it, but it's no use. They're falling like flies. Now the smoke's crossing Sixth Avenue . . . Fifth Avenue . . . one hundred yards away . . . it's fifty feet . . .

Operator Four. 2X2L calling CQ . . .

2X2L calling CQ . . .

2X2L calling CQ . . . New York.

Isn't there anyone on the air?

Isn't there anyone . . .

2X2L—

Announcer One. You are listening to a CBS presentation of Orson Welles and the Mercury Theater on the Air in an original dramatization of *The War of the Worlds* by H. G. Wells. The performance will continue after a brief intermission.

This is the Columbia . . . Broadcasting System.

[*Music.*]

Orson Welles.

Pierson. As I set down these notes on paper, I'm obsessed by the thought that I may be the last living man on earth. I have been hiding in this empty house near Grovers Mill — a small island of daylight cut off by the black smoke from the rest of the world. All that happened before the arrival of these monstrous creatures in the world now seems part of another life . . . a life that has no continuity with the present, furtive existence of the lonely derelict who pencils these words on the back of some astronomical notes bearing the signature of Richard Pierson. I look down at my blackened hands, my torn shoes, my tattered clothes, and I try to connect them with a professor who lives at Princeton, and who, on the night of October 30, glimpsed through his telescope an orange splash of light on a distant planet. My wife, my colleagues, my students, my books, my observatory, my . . . my world . . . where are they? Did they ever exist? Am I Richard Pierson? What day is it? Do days exist without calendars? Does time pass when there are no human hands left to wind the clocks? . . . In writing down my daily life, I tell myself I shall preserve human history between the dark covers of this little book that was meant to record the movements of the stars . . . But to write I must live, and to live I must eat . . . I find moldy bread in the kitchen, and an orange not too spoiled to swallow. I keep watch at the window. From time to time I catch sight of a Martian above the black smoke.

The smoke still holds the house in its black coil . . . But at length there is a hissing sound and suddenly I see a Martian mounted on his machine, spraying the air with a jet of steam, as if to dissipate the smoke. I watch in a corner as his huge metal legs nearly brush against the house. Exhausted by terror, I fall asleep . . . It's morning. Sun streams in the window. The black cloud of gas has lifted, and the scorched meadows to the north look as though a black snowstorm has passed over them. I venture from the house. I make my way to a road. No traffic. Here and there a wrecked car, baggage overturned, a blackened skeleton. I push on north. For some reason I feel safer trailing these monsters than running away from them. And I keep a careful watch. I have seen the Martians feed. Should one of their machines appear over the top of trees, I am ready to fling myself flat on the earth. I come to a chestnut tree. October, chestnuts are ripe. I fill my pockets. I must keep alive. Two days I wander in a vague northerly direction through a desolate world. Finally I notice a living creature . . . a small red squirrel in a beech tree. I stare at him, and wonder. He stares back at me. I believe at that moment the animal and I shared the same emotion . . . the joy of finding another living being . . . I push on north. I find dead cows in a brackish field. Beyond, the charred ruins of a dairy. The silo remains standing guard over the wasteland like a lighthouse deserted by the sea. Astride the silo perches a weathercock. The arrow points north.

Next day I came to a city vaguely familiar in its contours, yet its buildings strangely dwarfed and leveled off, as if a giant had sliced off its highest towers with a capricious sweep of his hand. I reached the outskirts. I found Newark, undemolished, but humbled by some whim of the advancing Martians. Presently, with an odd feeling of being watched, I caught sight of something crouching in a doorway. I made a step towards it, and it rose up and became a man — a man, armed with a large knife.

Stranger. Stop . . . Where did you come from?

Pierson. I come from . . . many places. A long time ago from Princeton.

Stranger. Princeton, huh? That's near Grovers Mill!

Pierson. Yes.

Stranger. Grovers Mill . . . (*Laughs as at a great joke*) There's no food here. This is my country . . . all this end of town down to the river. There's only food for one . . . Which way are you going?

Pierson. I don't know. I guess I'm looking for — for people.

Stranger (*nervously*). What was that? Did you hear something just then?

Pierson. Only a bird . . . (*Marvels*) A live bird!

Stranger. You get to know that birds have shadows these days . . . Say, we're in the open here. Let's crawl into this doorway and talk.

Pierson. Have you seen any Martians?

Stranger. They've gone over to New York. At night the sky is alive with their lights. Just as if people were still living in it. By daylight you can't see them. Five days ago a couple of them carried something big across the flats from the airport. I believe they're learning how to fly.

Pierson. Fly!

Stranger. Yeah, fly.

Pierson. Then it's all over with humanity. Stranger, there's still you and I. Two of us left.

Stranger. They got themselves in solid; they wrecked the greatest country in the world. Those green stars, they're probably falling somewhere every night. They've only lost one machine. There isn't anything to do. We're done. We're licked.

Pierson. Where were you? You're in a uniform.

Stranger. What's left of it. I was in the militia —National Guard . . . That's good! Wasn't any war any more than there's war between men and ants.

Pierson. And we're edible ants. I found that out . . . What will they do to us?

Stranger. I've thought it all out. Right now we're caught as we're wanted. The Martian only has to go a few miles to get a crowd on the run. But they won't keep doing that. They'll begin catching us systematic like— keeping the best and storing us in cages and things. They haven't begun on us yet!

Pierson. Not begun!

Stranger. Not begun. All that's happened so far is because we don't have sense enough to keep quiet . . . bothering them with guns and such stuff and losing our heads and rushing off in crowds. Now instead of our rushing around blind we've got to fix ourselves up according to the way things are now. Cities, nations, civilization, progress . . . done.

Pierson. But if that's so, what is there to live for?

Stranger. There won't be any more concerts for a million years or so, and no nice little dinners at restaurants. If it's amusement you're after, I guess the game's up.

Pierson. And what is there left?

Stranger. Life . . . that's what! I want to live. And so do you! We're not going to be exterminated. And I don't mean to be caught, either, and tamed, and fattened, and bred like an ox.

Pierson. What are you going to do?

Stranger. I'm going on . . . right under their feet. I gotta plan. We men as men are finished. We don't know enough. We gotta learn plenty before we've got a chance. And we've got to live and keep free while we learn. I've thought it all out, see.

Pierson. Tell me the rest.

Stranger. Well, it isn't all of us that are made for wild beasts, and that's what it's got to be. That's why I watched you. All these little office workers that used to live in these houses —they'd be no good. They haven't any stuff to 'em. They just used to run off to work. I've seen hundreds of 'em, running wild to catch their commuters' train in the morning for fear that they'd get canned if they didn't; running back at night afraid they won't be in time for dinner. Lives insured and a little invested in case of accidents. And on Sundays, worried about the hereafter. The Martians will be a godsend for those guys. Nice roomy cages, good food, careful breeding, no worries. After a week or so chasing about the fields on empty stomachs they'll come and be glad to be caught.

Pierson. You've thought it all out, haven't you?

Stranger. You bet I have! And that isn't all. These Martians will make pets of some of them, train 'em to do tricks. Who knows? Get sentimental over the pet boy who grew up and had to be killed. And some, maybe, they'll train to hunt us.

Pierson. No, that's impossible. No human being . . .

Stranger. Yes they will. There's men who'll do it gladly. If one of them ever comes after me . . .

Pierson. In the meantime, you and I and others like us . . . where are we to live when the Martians own the earth?

Stranger. I've got it all figured out. We'll live

underground. I've been thinking about the sewers. Under New York are miles and miles of 'em. The main ones are big enough for anybody. Then there's cellars, vaults, underground storerooms, railway tunnels, subways. You begin to see, eh? And we'll get a bunch of strong men together. No weak ones, that rubbish, out.

Pierson. And you meant me to go?

Stranger. Well, I gave you a chance, didn't I?

Pierson. We won't quarrel about that. Go on.

Stranger. And we've got to make safe places for us to stay in, see, and get all the books we can—science books. That's where men like you come in, see? We'll raid the museums, we'll even spy on the Martians. It may not be so much we have to learn before—just imagine this: four or five of their own fighting machines suddenly start off—heat rays right and left and not a Martian in 'em. Not a Martian in 'em! But *men*—men who have learned the way how. It may even be in our time. Gee! Imagine having one of them lovely things with its heat ray wide and free. We'd turn it on Martians, we'd turn it on men. We'd bring everybody down to their knees.

Pierson. That's your plan?

Stranger. You and me and a few more of us, we'd own the world.

Pierson. I see.

Stranger. Say, what's the matter? Where are you going?

Pierson. Not to your world . . . Goodbye, stranger . . .

After parting with the artilleryman, I came at last to the Holland Tunnel. I entered that silent tube anxious to know the fate of the great city on the other side of the Hudson. Cautiously I came out of the tunnel and made my way up Canal Street.

I reached Fourteenth Street, and there again were black powder and several bodies, and an evil ominous smell from the gratings of the cellars of some of the houses. I wandered up through the Thirties and Forties; I stood alone on Times Square. I caught sight of a lean dog running down Seventh Avenue with a piece of dark brown meat in his jaws, and a pack of starving mongrels at his heels. He made a wide circle around me, as though he feared I might prove a fresh competitor. I walked up Broadway in the direction of that strange powder—past silent shopwindows, displaying their mute wares to empty sidewalks—past the Capitol Theater, silent, dark—past a shooting gallery, where a row of empty guns faced an arrested line of wooden ducks. Near Columbus Circle I noticed models of 1939 motorcars in the showrooms facing empty streets. From over the top of the General Motors Building, I watched a flock of black birds circling in the sky. I hurried on. Suddenly I caught sight of the hood of a Martian machine, standing somewhere in Central Park, gleaming in the late afternoon sun. An insane idea! I rushed recklessly across Columbus Circle and into the park. I climbed a small hill above the pond at Sixtieth Street. From there I could see, standing in a silent row along the mall, nineteen of those great metal Titans,[4] their cowls empty, their steel arms hanging listlessly by their sides. I looked in vain for the monsters that inhabit those machines.

Suddenly, my eyes were attracted to the immense flock of black birds that hovered directly below me. They circled to the ground, and there before my eyes, stark and silent, lay the Martians, with the hungry birds pecking and tearing brown shreds of flesh from their dead bodies. Later when their bodies were examined in laboratories, it was found that they

---

4. **Titans:** The Martians are compared to a race of giants in Greek mythology. The Titans ruled the universe until Zeus and the other Olympians seized power.

were killed by the putrefactive and disease bacteria against which their systems were unprepared . . . slain, after all man's defenses had failed, by the humblest thing that God in His wisdom put upon this earth.

Before the cylinder fell there was a general persuasion that through all the deep of space no life existed beyond the petty surface of our minute sphere. Now we see further. Dim and wonderful is the vision I have conjured up in my mind of life spreading slowly from this little seedbed of the solar system throughout the inanimate vastness of sidereal space. But that is a remote dream. It may be that the destruction of the Martians is only a reprieve. To them, and not to us, is the future ordained perhaps.

Strange it now seems to sit in my peaceful study at Princeton writing down this last chapter of the record begun at a deserted farm in Grovers Mill. Strange to see from my window the university spires dim and blue through an April haze. Strange to watch children playing in the streets. Strange to see young people strolling on the green, where the new spring grass heals the last black scars of a bruised earth. Strange to watch the sightseers enter the museum where the disassembled parts of a Martian machine are kept on public view. Strange when I recall the time when I first saw it, bright and clean-cut, hard and silent, under the dawn of that last great day.

[Music.]

Orson Welles. This is Orson Welles, ladies and gentlemen, out of character to assure you that the War of the Worlds has no further significance than as the holiday offering it was intended to be. The Mercury Theater's own radio version of dressing up in a sheet and jumping out of a bush and saying Boo! Starting now, we couldn't soap all your windows and steal all your garden gates, by tomorrow night . . . so we did the next best thing. We annihilated the world before your very ears, and utterly destroyed the Columbia Broadcasting System. You will be relieved, I hope, to learn that we didn't mean it, and that both institutions are still open for business. So goodbye, everybody, and remember, please, for the next day or so, the terrible lesson you learned tonight. That grinning, glowing, globular invader of your living room is an inhabitant of the pumpkin patch, and if your doorbell rings and nobody's there, that was no Martian . . . it's Halloween.

FOR STUDY AND DISCUSSION

1. To make the play seem authentic, the dramatist uses techniques commonly used by news broadcasters. How are "news bulletins" used to create the impression that the regular programming has been interrupted? How does the "regular program" contrast with the content of these news flashes?

2. A second reporting technique is the interview. What is the purpose of the interview with Professor Pierson, beginning on page 632? Find two other on-the-spot interviews in the play. What does each interview contribute to the action?

3. A third reporting technique is the eyewitness accounts in the play. How do they add suspense and tension to the "broadcast"?

4. The fourth news-reporting device used by the playwright is the official statement. Identify the authority figures who make official statements in the play. Do their messages to the public sound authentic? Explain.

5. In the second section of the play, after the break for station identification (page 642), Professor Pierson begins to write in his diary. What important facts does he tell us?

6. The play moves from diary entries to dialogue. What contrasting attitudes toward disaster and responsibility are revealed in the conversation between Professor Pierson and the Stranger?

7. In most dramas, a main character is engaged in a conflict with an enemy of some sort. How would you describe the conflict in the play? How does the dramatist resolve the conflict?

8. At the end of the play, Welles says to the audience: "We annihilated the world before your very ears." What other witty remarks bring this *Invasion from Mars* broadcast to a conclusion? What dramatic purpose do you think these remarks serve?

Orson Welles interviewed by members of the press after the panic.

RADIO DRAMA

To create a radio drama, a playwright depends solely on dialogue, sound effects, and the listeners' imaginations. Settings, characters, and actions may be described, but not shown. The radio dramatists let their characters describe settings and actions. For example, what does the following speech help you visualize?

Phillips. Good heavens, something's wriggling out of the shadow like a gray snake. Now it's another one, and another. They look like tentacles to me. There, I can see the thing's body. It's large as a bear and it glistens like wet leather. But that face. It . . . it's indescribable. I can hardly force myself to keep looking at it. The eyes are black and gleam like a serpent. The mouth is V-shaped with saliva dripping from its rimless lips that seem to quiver and pulsate. The monster or whatever it is can hardly move. It seems weighed down by . . . possibly gravity or something. . . .

Find the speeches in the play that help the listener visualize the following: the Martian machines; the countryside after the Martians' black smoke clears away; New York City as the Martians approach; New York City later.

Besides words, the radio dramatist can use sound effects. Where is music used in this play to set a mood or to indicate a change of scene? What is the dramatic effect of each of the following sound effects?

boom of heavy gun (page 640)
coughs (page 641)
sound of airplane motor (page 641)
bells ringing over city, gradually diminishing (page 642)
voices singing hymn (page 642)
sound of boat whistles (page 642)

The Modern Theater

One major trend that has developed in the modern theater is the trend toward realism. Realism in drama, like realism in novels and short stories, attempts to present life as it actually is, not as we wish it would be. Realism explores in detail the characters of ordinary people and the world they live in. Another trend in modern drama is experimentalism. Modern playwrights have experimented with traditional dramatic elements, trying to find new ways of presenting action and character on the stage. Some playwrights have abandoned plot altogether. Some have only a few planks of wood for scenery. One playwright has his characters speak while sitting inside trash cans.

I Never Sang for My Father

Poster advertising a new production of Anton Chekhov's great realistic drama *The Cherry Orchard,* starring Irene Worth.

Robert Anderson's *I Never Sang for My Father* is a realistic play that uses certain experimental touches. Anderson's play has no scenery but uses lighting as the chief means for setting the stage. It makes sudden shifts in time and place, and it has a character who steps out of the action to speak directly to the audience. Anderson has stripped away all the nonessentials in order to focus our attention on the real problem faced by one American family. As you remember, the tragedies of ancient Greece and Elizabethan England were concerned with the downfall of noble characters, and with how their downfall affected a larger society. Anderson's play is different: it is about ordinary people involved in a very personal problem. The characters do not speak in verse but in the ordinary language and disjointed rhythms of everyday conversation. When death comes to characters in realistic dramas like Anderson's, it does not come from the avenging gods or from the designs of fate; it comes from things like old age or car accidents.

In many modern dramas, the conflict is caused by social or emotional factors—war, sickness, poverty, loneliness, and so on. Some modern plays do not even present any resolution to the conflict. Unlike the endings of the Greek or Shakespearean tragedies, the conflict in a modern play might remain unresolved, even as the last curtain is coming down.

What the modern theater shares with the theater of the past is a basic concern with the ideas, needs, fears, and joys that matter to all of us. Sophocles, in *Antigone*, and Shakespeare, in *Julius Caesar*, were interested in the universal problems of power, authority, and the conscience of the individual. Robert Anderson, in *I Never Sang for My Father*, is interested in our need for love.

The photographs that illustrate *I Never Sang for My Father* are from the original Broadway production, with Hal Holbrook as Gene, Lillian Gish as Margaret, Alan Webb as Tom, and Teresa Wright as Alice.
Photographs by Martha Swope.

I Never Sang for My Father

Robert Anderson

Characters

Gene Garrison
Porter
Tom Garrison
Margaret Garrison
Mary
Nurse

Reverend Pell
Marvin Scott
Waiter
Dr. Mayberry
Alice

The time is the present and the past. The places are New York City and a town in Westchester County.

There are no sets. Lighting is the chief means for setting the stage.

Act One

A man comes from the shadows in the rear. He is Gene Garrison, *age forty. He checks his watch. A* Porter *passes through with a baggage cart.*

Gene. I wonder if you could help me. (*The* Porter *stops.*) My father and mother are coming in on the Seaboard Express from Florida. I'd like a wheelchair for my mother if I could get one.
Porter. You have the car number?
Gene. Yes. (*He checks a slip of paper.*) One-oh-seven.
Porter. Due in at three ten. I'll meet you on the platform.
Gene. Thank you. (*The* Porter *moves away and off.* Gene *comes down and addresses the audience.*) Death ends a life, but it does not end a relationship, which struggles on in the survivor's mind toward some final resolution, some clear meaning, which it perhaps never finds. (*He changes the mood.*) Pennsylvania Station, New York, a few years ago. My mother and father were returning from Florida. They were both bored in Florida, but they had been going each winter for a number of years. If they didn't go, my father came down with pneumonia and my mother's joints stiffened cruelly with arthritis. My mother read a great deal, liked to play bridge and chatter and laugh gaily with "the girls" . . . make her eyes sparkle in a way she had and pretend that she had not had two operations for cancer, three heart attacks and painful arthritis . . . She used to say, "Old age takes courage." She had it. My father, though he had never been in the service, had the air of a retired brigadier general. He read the newspapers, all editions, presumably to help him make decisions about his investments. He watched Westerns on television and told anyone who would listen the story of his life. I loved my mother . . . I wanted to love my father . . .

[*The lights come up on another area of the stage, where the* Porter *is already standing with the wheelchair and baggage cart.* Tom Garrison *is standing amid the suitcases which have been piled up on the platform. He is a handsome man, almost eighty, erect in his bearing, neat in his dress. He speaks distinctly, and when he is irritated, his voice takes on a hard, harsh edge. At the moment he is irritated, slightly bewildered, on the brink of exasperation.*]

Tom. We had four bags. I don't see any of them. We had one in the compartment with us. That can't have been lost.

[*He fumes for a moment. As* Gene *watches his father for a moment, we can see in his face something of his feelings of tension. On the surface he shows great kindness and consideration for the old man. Underneath there is usually considerable strain.*]

Gene. Hello, Dad.
Tom (*beaming*). Well, Gene, as I live and breathe. This is a surprise.
Gene. I wrote you I'd be here.
Tom. Did you? Well, my mind is like a sieve. (*They have shaken hands and kissed each other on the cheek.*) Am I glad to see you! They've lost all our bags.

Gene. I'm sure they're somewhere, Dad.

Tom (*firmly*). No. I've looked. It's damnable!

Gene. Well, let's just take it easy. I'll handle it. (*He looks around at the luggage piled on the platform.*)

Tom. I'm confident we had four bags.

Gene (*quietly showing the redcap*). There's one . . . They'll show up. Where's Mother?

Tom. What? . . . Oh, she's still on the train. Wait a minute. Are you sure that's ours? (*He looks around for bags, fussing and fuming. He shakes his head in exasperation with the world.*)

Gene. Yes, Dad. You just relax now.

[Tom *is seized with a fit of coughing.*]

Tom (*is exasperated at the cough*). Damnable cough. You know the wind never stops blowing down there.

Gene. Don't worry about anything now, Dad. We've got a porter, and everything's under control. (Tom *snorts at this idea. The redcap proceeds in a quiet, efficient and amused way to work the luggage.*) I brought a wheelchair for Mother.

Tom. Oh. That's very considerate of you.

Gene. I'll go get her.

Tom. I didn't hear you.

Gene (*raising his voice*). I said I'll go get Mother.

Tom. Yes, you do that. I've got to get these bags straightened out. (*His rage and confusion are rising.*)

Gene (*to the* Porter). There's one. The gray one.

Tom. That's not ours.

Gene (*patient but irritated*). Yes, it is, Dad.

Tom. No. Now wait. We don't want to get the wrong bags. Mine is brown.

Gene. The old one was brown, Dad. I got you a new one this year for the trip.

Tom (*smiling reasonably*). Now. Gene. I've had the bag in Florida all winter. I should know.

Gene. Dad. Please . . . Please let me handle this.

Tom (*barks out an order to his son without looking at him*). You go get your mother. I'll take care of the bags.

[Gene's *mouth thins to a line of annoyance. He points out another bag to the* Porter, *who is amused.* Gene *moves with the wheelchair to another area of the stage, where his mother,* Margaret Garrison, *is sitting.* Margaret *is waiting patiently. She is seventy-eight, still a pretty woman. She has great spirit and a smile that lights up her whole face. She is a good sport about her problems. When she is put out, she says "darn." She is devoted to her son, but she is not the possessive and smothering mother. She is wearing a white orchid on her mink stole.*]

Gene. Hello, Mother.

Margaret (*Her face lights up*). Well, Gene. (*She opens her arms, but remains seated. They embrace.*) Oh, my, it's good to see you. (*This with real feeling as she holds her son close to her.*)

Gene (*when he draws away*). You look wonderful.

Margaret. What?

Gene (*raises his voice slightly. His mother wears a hearing aid*). You look wonderful.

Margaret (*little-girl coy*). Oh . . . a little rouge . . . This is your Easter orchid. I had them keep it in the icebox in the hotel. This is the fourth time I've worn it.

Gene. You sure get mileage out of those things.

Margaret (*raising her voice slightly*). I say it's the fourth time I've worn it . . . Some of the other ladies had orchids for Easter, but mine was the only white one. (*She knows she is* *being snobbishly proud and smiles as she pokes at the bow.*) I was hoping it would last so you could see it.

Gene. How do you feel?

Margaret (*serious, pouting*). I'm all right, but your father . . . did you see him out there?

Gene. Yes.

Margaret. He's sick and he won't do anything about it.

Gene. I heard his cough.

Margaret. It makes me so darned mad. I couldn't get him to see a doctor.

Gene. Why not?

Margaret. Oh, he's afraid they'd send him a big bill. He says he'll see Mayberry tomorrow . . . But I can't tell you what it's been like. You tell him. Tell him he's got to see a doctor. He's got me sick with worry. (*She starts to cry.*)

Gene (*comforts her*). I'll get him to a doctor, Mother. Don't you worry.

Margaret. He makes me so mad. He coughs all night and keeps us both awake. Poor man, he's skin and bone . . . And he's getting so forgetful. This morning he woke up here on the train and he asked me where we were going.

Gene. Well, Mother, he's almost eighty.

Margaret. Oh, I know. And he's a remarkable man. Stands so straight. Everyone down there always comments on how handsome your father is . . . But I've given up. You get him to a doctor.

Gene. I've got a wheelchair for you, Mother. Save you the long walk up the ramp.

Margaret. Oh, my precious. What would we ever do without you?

Gene (*He is always embarrassed by these expressions of love and gratitude*). Oh, you manage pretty well.

[*He helps her up from the chair, and she gives him a big hug as she stands . . . and looks at him.*]

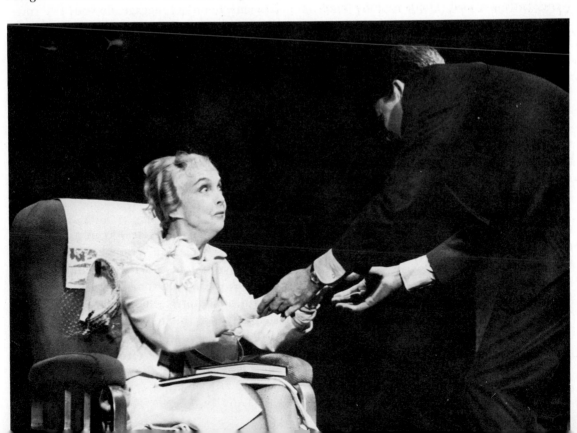

Margaret. Oh, you're a sight for sore eyes.

Gene (*embarrassed by the intensity*). It's good to see you.

Margaret (*She sits in the wheelchair*). You know, much as we appreciate your coming to meet us . . . I say, much as we appreciate your coming like this, the last thing in the world I'd want to do is take you away from your work.

Gene. You're not, Mother.

[*Father coughs his hacking cough.*]

Margaret. Do you hear that? I'm so worried and so darned mad.

[*They arrive at the platform area.*]

Tom. Oh, Gene, this is damnable. They've lost a suitcase. We had four suitcases.

Gene. Let's see, Dad. There are four there.

Tom. Where?

Gene. Under the others. See?

Tom. That's not ours.

Gene. Yes. Your new one.

Tom. Well, I'm certainly glad you're here. My mind's like a sieve. (*Low, to* Gene) It's the confusion and worrying about your mother.

Gene. Well, everything's under control now, Dad, so let's go. We'll take a cab to my apartment, where I've got the car parked, and then I'll drive you out home.

Tom. Your mother can't climb the stairs to your apartment.

Gene. She won't have to. We'll just change from the cab to my car.

Tom. But she might have to use the facilities.

Margaret. No. No. I'm all right.

Tom (*with a twinkle in his eye . . . the operator*). You know, if you handle it right, you can get away with parking right out there in front of the station. When I used to come to meet the Senator . . .

Gene. I know, but I'd prefer to do it this way. I'm not very good at that sort of thing.

Tom. Well, all right. You're the boss. It's just that you can get right on the West Side Drive.

Gene. It's easier for me to go up the Major Deegan.

Tom. Rather than the Cross County?

Gene. Yes.

Tom. I don't like to question you, old man, but I'm sure if you clocked it, you'd find it shorter to go up the West Side Drive and —

Margaret (*annoyed with him*). Father, now come on. Gene is handling this.

Tom. All right. All right. Just a suggestion.

Gene. Come on, Dad.

Tom. You go along with your mother. I'll keep an eye on this luggage.

Gene (*trying to be patient*). It will be all right.

Tom (*clenching his teeth and jutting out his jaw, sarcastic*). You don't mind if I want to keep an eye on my luggage, do you? I've traveled a good deal more than you have in my day, old man, and I know what these guys will do if you let them out of your sight. (Gene *is embarrassed. The* Porter *smiles and starts moving off.*) Hey, not so fast there.

[*And he strides after the* Porter *and the bags.* Gene *moves to the front of the stage again, as the lights dim on the retreating wheelchair and luggage, and on* Tom *and* Margaret.]

Gene. My father's house was in a suburb of New York City, up in Westchester County. It had been a quiet town with elms and chestnut trees, lawns and old sprawling houses with a certain nondescript elegance. My father had been mayor of this town, a long time ago . . . Most of the elms and chestnut trees had gone, and the only elegance left was in the pretentious names of the developments and ugly apartment houses . . . Parkview Meadows Estates . . . only there was no meadow, and no park, and no view except of the neon signs of the chain stores. Some old houses remained, like slightly frowzy dowagers. The lawns were not well kept, and the houses were not painted as often as they should have been, but they remained. My father's house was one of these.

[Tom *and* Margaret *have now started coming in from the back.*]

Tom. Just look at this town.

Margaret. What, dear?

Tom (*raises his voice in irritation*). Do you have that thing turned on?

Margaret. Yes.

Tom. I said just look at this town.

Margaret. I know, dear, but time marches on.

Tom. Junky, ugly mess. When we came here . . .

Margaret. Don't get started on that. You can't play the show over again.

Tom. I can make a comment, can't I?

Margaret. But you always dwell on the gloomy side. Look at the good things.

Tom. Like what? . . . I'll bet you Murphy didn't bring the battery back for the Buick. I wrote him we'd be home today. (*He heads for the garage.*)

Margaret (*to* Gene). I don't know what we're going to do about that car. Your father shouldn't be driving any more. But they just keep renewing his license by mail. (*She moves stiffly, looking at her garden and trees and lawn.*) I must say, there's no place like home. *Mmmmm.* Just smell the grass.

Gene (*taking his mother's arm*). You all right?

Margaret. It's just my mean old joints getting adjusted. I want to look at my garden. I think I see some crocuses. (*And she moves into the shadows to see her garden.*)

Tom (*coming back*). Well, he did bring it back.

Gene. Good.

Tom. Can't count on anyone these days. Where's your mother?

Gene. She's walking around her garden.

Tom. What?

Gene. She's walking around her garden.

Tom. You know, Gene, I don't mean to criticize, but I notice you're mumbling a great deal. It's getting very difficult to understand you.

Gene (*friendly, his hand on his father's shoulder*). I think you need a hearing aid, Dad.

Tom. I can hear perfectly well if people would only enunciate. "Mr. Garrison, if you would only *E-NUN-CIATE.*" Professor Aurelio, night school. Didn't you ever have to take any public speaking?

Gene. No, Dad.

Tom. All your education. Well . . . Where did you say your mother was?

Gene. Walking around her garden.

Tom (*intense. He has been waiting for someone to say this to*). I tell you, the strain has been awful.

Gene. She looks well.

Tom. I know. But you never know when she might get another of those damnable seizures. (*He looks at the ground and shakes his head at the problem of it all.*)

Gene (*pats his father's shoulder*). It's rough. I know.

Tom. Well, we'll manage. She's a good soldier. But you know, she eats too fast. The doctor said she must slow down. But not your mother. Incidentally, don't forget she has a birthday coming up.

Gene (*who knows his mother's birthday and hates being reminded of it each year*). Yes, I know.

Tom. Before you go, I want to give you some money. Go get something nice for me to give her. Handkerchiefs. You know what she likes.

Gene (*who has done this every Christmas and birthday for years . . . smiles*). All right. (*Tom coughs, deep and thick.*) We're going to have to get that cough looked into.

Tom. I fully intend to, now I'm home. But I wasn't going to let them get their hands on me down there. If you're a tourist, they just soak you.

Gene. With the problems you've had with pneumonia . . .

Tom. I can take care of myself. Don't worry about me.

Gene. Let's go see if Dr. Mayberry can see you.

Tom. First thing tomorrow.

Gene. Why not make the appointment today?

Tom (*irked*). Now, look, I'm perfectly able to take care of myself.

Gene. Mother would feel better if——

Tom (*that smile again*). Now, Gene, don't you think I have the sense to take care of myself?

Gene (*smiling, but a little angry*). Sometimes, no.

Tom (*considers this, but is mollified by the smile*). Well, I appreciate your solicitude, old man. Why don't you stay for supper?

Gene. I was planning to take you to Schrafft's.

Tom. Hooray for our side! (*Gene starts out toward the garden.*) Oh, Gene. I want to talk to you a minute. We received your four letters from California . . .

Gene. I'm sorry I didn't write more often.

Tom. Well, we *do* look forward to your letters. But this girl, this woman you mentioned several times . . .

Gene. Yes?

Tom. You seemed to see a lot of her.

Gene. Yes. I did.

Tom. Carol's been dead now, what is it? . . .

Gene. About a year.

Tom. And there's no reason why you shouldn't go out with other women. (*Gene just waits.*) I was in California with the Senator, and before that. It's a perfectly beautiful place. I can understand your enthusiasm for it. Gorgeous place.

Gene. Yes. I like it a lot.

Tom. But listen, Gene . . . (*He bites his upper lip, and his voice is heavy with emotion.*) If you were to go out there, I mean, to live, it would kill your mother. (*He looks at his son with piercing eyes, tears starting. This has been in the nature of a plea and an order. Gene says nothing. He is angry at this order, that his father would say such a thing.*) You know you're her whole life. (*Gene is further embarrassed and troubled by this statement of what he knows to be the truth from his father.*) Yes, you are! Oh, she likes your sister. But you . . . are . . . her . . . life!

Gene. Dad, we've always been fond of each other, but——

Tom. Just remember what I said.

[Margaret *can now be heard reciting to herself, very emotionally.*]

Margaret. "Loveliest of trees, the cherry now / Is hung with bloom along the bough, / And stands about the woodland ride, / Wearing white for Eastertide."[1] (*She opens her eyes.*) Oh, Gene, I've just been looking at your garden. Give me a real hug. You haven't given me a real hug yet. (*Gene hugs her, uncomfortable, but loving and dutiful. It is, after all, a small thing. Margaret looks at him, then kisses him on the lips.*) Mmmmmmm. (*She smiles, making a playful thing of it.*) Oh, you're a sight for sore eyes.

---

1. **"Loveliest . . . Eastertide"**: lines from a poem called "Loveliest of Trees" by A. E. Housman.

[Tom *has watched this, and looks significantly at* Gene.]

Tom (*moving off*). Gene is staying for dinner. We're going to Schrafft's.
Margaret. Oh. Can you give us all that time?
Tom. He said he would. Now come along. You shouldn't be standing so long. You've had a long trip. (*He exits.*)
Margaret. He worries so about me. I suppose it is a strain, but he makes me nervous reminding me I should be sitting or lying down . . . Oh, well . . . (*She takes* Gene's *arm.*) How are you, my precious?
Gene. Fine.
Margaret. We haven't talked about your trip to California.
Gene. No.
Margaret (*raising her voice*). I say, we haven't talked about your trip.
Gene. We will.
Margaret (*low*). Did you speak to your father about seeing a doctor?
Gene. He promised me tomorrow.
Margaret. I'll believe it when I see it. He's so darned stubborn. Alice takes after him.
Gene. Oh, I got a piece of it too.
Margaret (*her tinkling laugh*). You? You don't have a stubborn bone in your body.

[*We fade, as they move up and into the shadows.*

Immediately the lights come up on another part of the stage—Schrafft's.]

Mary (*A pretty Irish waitress, she is just finishing setting up her table as* Tom *enters*). Well, good evening, Mr. Garrison. Welcome back.
Tom (*the charmer*). Greetings and salutations.
Mary. We've missed you.
Tom. It's mutual. Is this your table?

Mary. Yes.
Tom. Is there a draft here? I like to keep Mrs. Garrison out of drafts.

[*He looks around for windows.* Margaret *and* Gene *come into the area. He is helping her, as she moves slowly and deliberately.*]

Mary. Good evening, Mrs. Garrison. Nice to have you back.
Tom. You remember Mary?
Margaret (*polite but reserved*). Yes. Good evening, Mary.
Mary. You're looking well, Mrs. Garrison.
Margaret (*as* Tom *holds the chair for her*). But look at him. (*She nods at* Tom.)
Mary. We'll fatten him up.
Tom (*smiling, flirtatiously*). Will you do that now? Oh, we've missed you. We've had a girl down there in Florida, no sense of humor. Couldn't get a smile out of her.
Mary. Well, we'll have some jokes. Dry martini?
Tom (*a roguish twinkle*). You twist my arm. Six to one. (*He says this as though he were being quite a man to drink his martini so dry.* Gene *finds all this byplay harmless, but uncomfortable.*) You remember my son, Gene.
Mary (*smiles*). Yes.

[Gene *smiles back.*]

Tom. What's your pleasure, Gene . . . Dubonnet?
Gene. I'll have a martini too, please.
Tom. But not six to one.
Gene. Yes. The same.
Tom. Well!
Gene. Mother?
Margaret. No, nothing. My joints would be stiff as a board.
Tom (*with a twinkle in his eye*). You said you'd be stiff?

Margaret. What?

Tom (*raising his voice*). You said you'd be stiff?

Margaret. My joints. My joints.

Tom. Oh, wouldn't want you stiff. (*He thinks he's being very funny, and tries to share his laugh with Gene, who smiles reluctantly. Mary exits. To Gene*) Have I ever shown you this ring?

Margaret. Oh, Tom, you've shown it to him a hundred times.

Tom (*ignoring her reminder*). I never thought I'd wear a diamond ring, but when the Senator died, I wanted something of his. Last time I had it appraised, they told me it was worth four thousand.

Margaret. It's his favorite occupation, getting that ring appraised.

Tom (*again ignoring her*). Don't let anyone ever tell you it's a yellow diamond. It's a golden diamond. Of course, when I go to see a doctor, I turn it around. (*He gives a sly smile. The others look embarrassed.*)

Margaret (*looking at the menu*). What are you going to have?

Tom (*taking out his glasses*). Now, this is my dinner, understand?

Gene. No. I invited you.

Tom. Uh-uh. You had all the expenses of coming to get us.

Gene. No, it's mine. And order what you want. Don't go reading down the prices first.

Tom (*smiles at the idea, though he knows he does it*). What do you mean?

Gene. Whenever I take you out to dinner, you always read down the prices first.

Margaret. Oh, he does that anyway.

Tom. I do not. But I think it's ridiculous to pay, look, three seventy-five for curried shrimp.

Gene. You like shrimp. Take the shrimp.

Tom. If you'll let me pay for it.

Gene (*getting annoyed*). No! Now, come on.

Tom. Look, I appreciate it, Gene, but on what you make . . .

Gene. I can afford it. Now let's not argue.

Margaret. Tell me, lovey, do you get paid your full salary on your sabbatical?[2]

Gene. No. Fifty percent.

Tom. Well, then, look . . .

Margaret. Now, Father, he wants to pay. Let him pay. (*They consult their menus.*) Incidentally, Tom, you should go over and say hello to Bert Edwards. Gene and I stopped on our way in.

Tom. Why?

Margaret. While we were gone, he lost his wife.

Tom. Where'd he lose her?

Margaret. Tom!

Tom. Just trying to get a rise.

Margaret. And Mrs. Bernard. She looks terrible.

Tom. Always did.

Margaret. She lost her husband six months ago. She told me, just before we left for Florida, "I hope I go soon."

Tom. Why are you so morbid tonight?

Margaret. I'm not morbid. They're just there. We really should see them, have them in.

Tom. Phooey! Who needs them?

Margaret. Oh, Tom! I can't have anyone in.

Your father won't play bridge or do anything. He just wants to watch Westerns or tell the story of his life.

Tom. Now, wait a minute.

Margaret. I can't invite people to come over to watch Westerns or to listen to you go on and on. You embarrass me so. You insist on going into the most gruesome details of your life.

Tom. People seem to be interested.

Margaret. What?

Tom. Have you got that turned up?

Margaret. Yes. (*She adjusts the volume.*)

Tom. I said they seem to be interested.

[*He tries to take* Gene *in on an exasperated shaking of the head, but* Gene *looks the other way.*]

Margaret. I admit it's a remarkable story, your life. But there are other things to talk about. People want to talk about art or music or books.

Tom. Well, let them.

Margaret. He keeps going over and over the old times. Other people have had miserable childhoods, and they don't keep going over and over them . . . That story of your mother's funeral. And you say I'm morbid.

Gene. What was that? I don't remember that.

Margaret. Oh, don't get him started.

Tom. Your mother wants me to play cards with a lot of women who just want to gossip and chatter about styles. That's why I won't play.

Margaret. You won't play because you can't follow the play of the cards any more.

Tom. I beg to disagree.

Gene. Please! Don't fight . . . don't fight. (*He's said this in a mock-serious singsong.*)

Margaret. He kept telling everyone how he wouldn't allow his father to come to his mother's funeral.

---

2. **sabbatical:** leave of absence.

Tom (*defensively angry*). Are you implying that I should have let him?

Margaret. I'm not saying——

Tom. He'd run out on us when we were kids, and I told him——

Margaret. I'm not saying you were wrong. You're so defensive about it. I'm saying you're wrong to keep bringing it up.

Tom. You brought it up this time.

Margaret. Well, I'm sorry. Imagine going around telling everyone he shoved his father off the funeral coach. (*She is consulting the menu.*)

Tom. And I'd do it again. I was only ten, but I'd do it again. We hadn't seen him in over a year, living, the four of us, in a miserable two-room tenement, and suddenly he shows up weeping and begging, and drunk, as usual. And I shoved him off! (*He almost relives it.*) I never saw him again till some years later when he was dying in Bellevue . . . of drink. (*The hatred and anger are held in, but barely.*)

Margaret (*She has been studying the menu*). What looks good to you?

Tom (*a hard, sharp edge to his voice*). I have not finished! I went down to see him, to ask him if he wanted anything. He said he wanted an orange. I sent him in a half-dozen oranges. I would have sent more, except I knew he was dying, and there was no point in just giving a lot of oranges to the nurses. The next morning he died.

[*There is a silence for a moment, while* Gene *and* Margaret *look at the menu, and* Tom *grips and ungrips his hand in memory of his hatred for his father.*]

Margaret (*gently*). Look at your menu now, Father. What are you going to eat?

Tom. I don't feel like anything. I have no appetite. (*He lights a cigarette.*)

Margaret (*to* Gene). This is the way it's been.

Gene. He'll see a doctor tomorrow. Don't get upset.

[Mary *arrives with the martinis.*]

Tom. Ah, here we are.

Mary. Six to one. (*She puts the martini in front of him.*)

Tom. Oh . . . ! (*He shakes his head in exasperation and fishes out the lemon peel.*)

Mary. But you always ask for lemon peel.

Tom (*demonstrating*). Twisted over it, not dumped in it. It's all right. It's all right. (*With an Irish accent*) Well, to your smilin' Irish eyes.

Mary. He hasn't changed, has he?

Tom. What county are you from, did you say?

Mary. Armagh.

Tom. I knew there was something I liked about you. That's where my people came from, County Armagh. (*He drinks.*) Do you have any burnt ice cream tonight?

Mary. Ah, you.

Tom (*smiling*). No, I mean it. (*To* Gene) They have burnt ice cream here.

Mary. I'll be back. (*And she exits.* Margaret *sits embarrassed and piqued by this kind of flirtation which has gone on all their lives.*)

Tom (*the sport, to* Gene). I like to get a rise out of them. If they kid with me, I give them a good tip. If they don't, a straight ten percent. (*He draws a line on the tablecloth to emphasize this. He looks at* Margaret.) What's the matter?

Margaret. If you want to make a fool of yourself, go right ahead.

[Tom *is angry, hurt and exasperated. He looks at her, and then tries to include* Gene, *to make him share his anger. But* Gene *looks away and to the menu.* Tom *stares at his glass, and his jaw muscles start to work. The scene dims in the Schrafft's area, and* Gene *moves from the table to another side of the stage.*]

Gene. We hurried through the last part of our dinner. My father ate only his dessert, burnt almond ice cream. We hurried through to rush home to one of my father's rituals, the television Western. He would sit in front of them hour after hour, falling asleep in one and waking up in the middle of the next one, never knowing the difference. When my father fell in love with a program, it was forever. All during my childhood we ate our dinner to the accompaniment of Lowell Thomas and Amos and Andy.[3] If anyone dared to talk, Father would storm away from the table and have his dinner served at the radio . . . I say, we rushed away from Schrafft's. Actually, my father rushed. We just lived down the street. I walked my mother home very slowly, stopping every fifty yards or so.

[Margaret *has joined* Gene *and taken his arm.*]

Margaret. I don't know how he can sit through hour after hour of those Westerns.
Gene. I think he always wished he'd been a cowboy. "Take 'em out and shoot 'em!"
Margaret. He won't listen to the things I want to hear. Down in Florida there's only one TV in the lounge, and he rode herd on it. And then he'd fall asleep in three minutes . . . Still, he's a remarkable man.
Gene. Good old Mom.
Margaret. Well, he is. Not many boys have fathers they could be as proud of.

Gene. I know that, Mom. I'm very . . . proud of him.
Margaret (*She catches his tone*). Everything he's done, he's done for his family. (Gene *just looks at her, smiling.*) So he didn't dance with me at parties. (*She smiles at* Gene.) You took care of that.
Gene. You were just a great dancer, Mother.
Margaret. I was a terrible dancer. You just couldn't stand seeing me sitting alone at a table at the club while your father was . . . (*She stops, realizing she's about to make* Gene's *point.*)
Gene. . . . off dancing with various other people, table-hopping or playing poker with the boys in the locker room.
Margaret. What a shame that children can't see their parents when they're young and courting, and in love. All they see them being is tolerant, sympathetic, forbearing and devoted. All the qualities that are so unimportant to passionate young people.

[Tom *appears.*]

Tom. Gene . . . Gene . . . Come watch this one. This is a real shoot-'em-up.
Gene. In a minute, Dad.
Margaret. Gene, I want to talk to you.
Gene. You should be in bed. You've had a big day. (*They move to another part of the stage.*)
Margaret. I took another nitro.[4] And I've had something on my mind for a long time now. You remember you gave me that heart-shaped pillow when I was in the hospital once, when you were a boy? (*She sits on the chaise longue.*)

---

3. **Lowell Thomas and Amos and Andy:** radio shows popular in the 1930's and 1940's. Lowell Thomas was a commentator, and Amos and Andy were comics.

4. **nitro:** short for nitroglycerine, a medication that relieves heart pains.

Gene. Yes.

Margaret. Fidget used to curl up here. (*She indicates the crook in her leg.*) And you'd sit over there, and we'd listen to the Metropolitan Opera broadcasts.

[Gene *is made uncomfortable by this attempt to evoke another time, another kind of relationship, but he doesn't show it.*]

Gene. Yes. I remember.

Margaret. You'd dress up in costumes and act in front of that mirror. I remember you were marvelous as D'Artagnan in *The Three Musketeers*. (*For the fun of it, a forty-year-old man, he assumes the dueling stance, and* thrusts *at his image in an imaginary mirror.* Gene *sits on a footstool and watches her adjust herself in her chaise. After a moment*) Tell me about California.

Gene (*a little taken by surprise. Here is the subject*). I loved it.

Margaret. And the girl, the woman with the children? The doctor? (Gene *doesn't say anything. He frowns, wondering what to say.*) You love her too, don't you?

Gene. I think so.

Margaret. I know when Carol died, you said you'd never marry again. But I hoped you would. I know it's hard, but I think Carol would have wanted you to.

Gene. I don't know.

Margaret. Gene, your sabbatical is over soon, isn't it?

Gene. A few more months.

Margaret. I think you want to move to California and get a job teaching there and marry this woman.

Gene (*after a moment*). Yes. I think I do. I wasn't sure while I was there. I suddenly felt I should get away and think. But when I walked into my old apartment, with all Carol's things there . . .

Margaret. I think it would be the best thing in the world for you to get away, to marry this girl.

Gene (*touched . . . very simply*). Thanks.

Margaret. A new place, a new wife, a new life. I would feel just terrible if you didn't go because of me. There are still planes, trains and telephones, and Alice comes from Chicago once or twice a year and brings the children.

Gene. Thanks, Mother. You've always made things very easy. I think you'll like Peggy.

Margaret. I'm sure I will. You have good taste in women. And they have good taste when they like you.

Gene. I'm not so sure. I never really knew if I made Carol happy . . . If I did make her happy, I wish she'd let me know it.

Margaret. I guess a lot of us forget to say thank you until it's too late. (*She takes his hand and smiles at him.*) Thank you . . . You have such nice hands. I've always loved your hands . . . You've been so good to me, Gene, so considerate. Perhaps I've let you be too considerate. But it was your nature, and your father just withdrew behind his paper and his investments and his golf. And our interests seem to go together. You liked to sing, and I played the piano, oh, miserably, but I played. (*She strokes his hand.*) I tried not to be one of those possessive mothers, Gene. If I did things wrong, I just did the best I knew how.

Gene. You did everything just fine. (*He pats his mother's hand before he draws his own away.*)

Margaret. And your father has done the best he knew how.

Gene (*with no conviction*). Yes.

[*This is her old song. She knows that Gene knows it's probably true, but he gets no satisfaction from the knowledge.*]

Margaret. Of course you know your father will object to your going away.

Gene. He already has. He said it would kill you.

Margaret. How sad. Why can't he say it would kill him? He doesn't think it would hold you or mean anything to you. (*She shakes her head.*) He dotes on your letters down there. Reads them and rereads them. Tells everyone what a fine relationship he has with you. "My door is always open . . . Anything he wants, he can have . . . We have always had each others' confidence . . ." (*Gene smiles at this and sadly shakes his head.*) Well, you go to California. Your father and I can take care of each other. I'll remember where he put his checkbook, and he'll make the beds, which is the only thing I'm really not supposed to do. And, for your information, I have my old-lady's home all picked out. That's what I want, so I won't be a burden to any of you.

Gene. You a burden!

Margaret (*wisely*). Oh, yes! Now don't mention this business to your father tonight. He's not well, and it's been such a nice day. In the next few days I'll talk to him, tell him it's important for you to—

Gene. No, I'll do it. (*He kisses her on the cheek.*)

Margaret. Good night, my precious.

Gene. Where would you like to celebrate your birthday?

Margaret. Oh, lovey, you've already given me so much time. Just call me on the phone.

Gene. No . . . We can at least have dinner . . . I'll make some plans.

Margaret. Gene, if your father gives you money to buy his present for me, please, no more handkerchiefs.

Gene. He always says handkerchiefs.

Margaret. I know, but I've got dozens and dozens from my past birthdays and Christmases.

Gene. What would you like?

Margaret: Get me some perfume. You choose the kind, except I don't like lily of the valley, or gardenia.

Gene. You're a hard woman to please . . . Good night . . . You look great.

Margaret. Oh, a little rouge and lipstick. Thanks for coming to meet us. Tell your father I've gone to bed, and don't let him keep you there to all hours watching television. (*Calling after him*) I don't like carnation either.

[Gene *waves back affectionately and moves away, as the lights dim on* Margaret's *area.* Gene *moves, then stands and looks at the back of his father's chair as the TV sounds come up, and lights come on in that area.* Gene *moves to his father's chair and gently touches his arm while turning the knob of the TV volume.*]

Tom (*stirring*). What? . . . What? (*He comes to slowly, shakes his head and looks at* Gene, *bewildered.*)

Gene (*gently*). I'm going now, Dad.

Tom. Oh, so soon?

Gene (*controls his irritation. This has always been his father's response, no matter how long he has been with him*). Yes. I have to go.

Tom. Where's your mother?

Gene. She's upstairs. She's fine. (Tom *starts to cough.*) You see about that in the morning, Dad.

Tom (*getting up, steadying himself*). I fully intend to. I would have done it down there, but I wasn't going to be charged outrageous prices. (*He glances at the TV screen.*) Oh, this is a good one. Why don't you just stay for this show?

Gene (*the anger building*). No, Dad. I've got to run along.

Tom. Well, all right. We see so little of you.

Gene. I'm up at least once a week, Dad.

Tom. Oh, I'm not complaining. (*But he is.*) There just doesn't seem to be any time. And when you are here, your mother's doing all the talking. The way she interrupts. She just doesn't listen. And I say, "Margaret, please." . . . But she goes right on . . . Well, "all's lost, all's spent, when we our desires get without content . . . 'tis better to be that which we destroy, than by destruction dwell with doubtful joy."[5]

Gene (*He is always puzzled by his father's frequent use of this quotation. It never is immediately appropriate, but it indicates such unhappiness that it is sad and touching to him*). We'll get a chance to talk, Dad. (*He moves toward the porch.*)

Tom. I can't tell you what a comfort it is knowing you are just down in the city. Don't know what we'd do without you. No hat or coat?

Gene. No.

Tom. It's still chilly. You should be careful.

Gene (*kissing his father on the cheek*). Good night, Dad. I'll call you tomorrow to see if you've gone to the doctor's.

Tom. Well, I may and I may not. I've looked

---

5. **"all's lost . . . doubtful joy"**: These lines expressing tragic regret are spoken by Lady Macbeth in Act Three, Scene 2, of William Shakespeare's *Macbeth*.

after myself pretty well for almost eighty years. I guess I can judge if I need to see the doctor or not.

Gene (*angry*). Look, Dad . . .

Tom. Seventy years ago, when I was a snot-nosed kid up in Harlem, a doctor looked at me and said if I were careful, I'd live to be twenty. That's what I think about doctors. Ten dollars to look at your tongue. Phooey! Out! Who needs them?

Gene. Look, Dad, you're worrying Mother to death with that cough.

Tom. All right, all right. I'll go. I'll be a good soldier . . . You're coming up for your mother's birthday, aren't you?

Gene. Yes.

Tom. And don't forget, Mother's Day is coming up.

Gene. Well . . .

Tom. Why don't we make reservations at that restaurant in Connecticut where you took us last Mother's Day?

Gene. We'll see.

Tom. It will be my party. And, Gene, remember what I said about California!

Gene (*straining to get away from all the encirclements*). Good night, Dad. (*He moves off.*)

Tom. Drive carefully. I noticed you were inclined to push it up there a little. (*Gene burns.*) Make a full stop going out the driveway, then turn right.

Gene (*angry, moves further down*). Yes, Dad.

Tom (*calling after him*). Traffic is terrible out there now. Used to be a quiet little street. Take your first left, and your second right.

Gene (*He has driven this route for many years*). Yes.

Tom. Then left under the bridge. It's a little tricky down there. (*When he gets no response, he calls.*) Gene?

Gene (*in a sudden outburst*). Dad, I've driven this road for twenty years! (*He is immediately*

sorry, and turns away from his father's direction.*)

Tom. Just trying to be helpful.

[*The lights fade on* Tom *as he goes back into the house.* Gene *is now downstage.*]

Gene. Take your first left and your second right. Then turn left under the bridge. But do not go as far as California, because it would kill your mother . . . I hated him for that, for sending up warning flares that if I left, it would not be with his blessing, but with a curse . . . as he had banished my sister Alice years ago for marrying someone he didn't approve of . . . and the scene so terrified me at fourteen, I was sick . . . He knew his man . . . that part of me at least . . . a gentleman who gave way at intersections . . . And yet, when I looked at those two old people, almost totally dependent on me for their happiness . . . This is the way the world ends, all right . . .

[*A phone rings. A light picks out* Tom *holding the phone.*]

Tom. I was downstairs in the kitchen, and suddenly I heard your mother scream . . . "Tom! Tom!" . . . I ran up the stairs . . . (*He is seized with a fit of coughing.*) I ran up the stairs, and there she was stretched out on the floor of the bedroom . . . "Nitro" . . . "nitro" . . . That's all she could say. You know we have nitroglycerine all over the house.

[*A* Nurse *comes to* Tom *as the lights come up; she leads him into a hospital waiting-room area.* Gene *joins them.*].

Gene. Dad. (*He shakes his hand and kisses him on the cheek.*)

Tom. Am I glad to see you! Have you seen your mother?

Gene. Yes. She's sleeping.

[Tom *starts to cough.*]

Gene. That doesn't sound any better.

Tom. Well, I've had a shot. After your mother got settled over here, the doctor took me to his office and gave me a shot. I *would* have gone down there in Florida, you know, but . . . well . . . (*shakes his head*) I just don't know. I was in the kitchen getting breakfast . . . You know I've been getting the breakfasts, when suddenly I heard her scream, "Tom, Tom." I went running up the stairs, and there she was stretched out on the floor. She'd had an attack. "Nitro," she whispered. We've got it all over the house, you know. She'd had attacks before, but I knew at once that this was something more. I gave her the pills and called the doctor . . . "This is an emergency. Come quick." . . . The doctor came, gave her a shot . . . and called the ambulance . . . and here we are. (*He shakes his head, partly in sorrow, but also partly in exasperation that such a thing could happen.*) She had a good time in Florida. I don't understand it. She ate too fast, you know. And the doctor had said she should do everything more slowly.

Gene. There's no explaining these things, Dad.

Tom. I suppose I could have seen more of her down there. But she just wanted to play bridge, and I didn't play, because the ladies just chattered all the time about styles and shops . . . And I met some very interesting people. Oh, some of them were bores and just wanted to tell you the story of their life. But there were others. You know, I met a man from Waterbury, Connecticut, used to know Helen Moffett . . . I've told you about Helen Moffett, haven't I? When I was a kid, when the clouds were low and dark, my grandfather'd take me up there sometimes on Sun-

days . . . a city slum kid in that lovely country . . . And Helen and I . . . oh . . . it never amounted to much. We'd go to church, and then we'd take a walk and sit in a hammock or under an apple tree. I think she liked that. But I didn't have any money, and I couldn't go up there often. Her mother didn't like me . . . "That young man will end up the same way as his father." . . . And that scared her off . . . This man in Florida, I've got his name somewhere . . . (*He fishes out a notebook and starts to go through it.*) He said Helen had never married . . . Said she'd been in love as a kid . . . and had never married. (*Tears come to his eyes.*) Well, I can't find it. No matter. (Gene *doesn't know what to say. He is touched by this naked and unconscious revelation of an early and deeply meaningful love. But it seems so incongruous under the circumstances.*) Someday we might drive out there and look him up . . . Helen's dead now, but it's nice country. I was a kid with nothing . . . living with my grandfather . . . Maybe if she hadn't been so far away . . . Well, that's water over the dam.

Gene (*After a long pause, he touches his father*). Yes.

Tom (*just sits for a few moments, then seems to come back to the present, and takes out his watch*). You know, I'd like to make a suggestion.

Gene. What, Dad?

Tom. If we move right along, we might be able to make the Rotary Club for dinner. (Gene *frowns in bewilderment.*) I've been away for three months. They don't like that very much if you're absent too often. They drop you or fine you. How about it? (*He asks this with a cocked head and a twinkle in his eye.*)

Gene. I thought we might eat something around here in the hospital.

Tom. I had lunch in the coffee shop down-

stairs, and it's terrible. It will only take a little longer. We won't stay for the speeches, though sometimes they're very good, very funny. We'll just say hello to the fellows and get back . . . Your mother's sleeping now. That's what they want her to do.
Gene (*bewildered by this, but doesn't want to get into an argument*). Let's drop by and see Mother first.
Tom. They want her to rest. We'd only disturb her.
Gene. All right.
Tom (*As they turn to go, he puts his arm around Gene's shoulder*). I don't know what I'd do without you, old man.

[*As the lights shift, and Tom and Gene head away, we move to the Rotary gathering, held in the grill room of one of the local country clubs. A piano is heard offstage, playing old-fashioned singing-type songs—badly. A tinkle of glasses . . . a hum of men talking and laughing. This area is presumably an anteroom with two comfortable leather chairs. A man enters, wearing a large name button and carrying a glass. This is the minister, Reverend Pell, a straightforward, middle-aged man.*]

Reverend Pell. Hello, Tom, good to see you back.
Tom (*His face lights up in a special "greeting the fellows" type grin*). Hello, Sam.
Reverend Pell. Did you have a good trip?
Tom. All except for the damnable wind down there. You know my son, Gene. Reverend Pell.
Reverend Pell. Yes, of course. Hello, Gene. (*They shake hands.*)
Tom. Gene was a Marine. (Gene *frowns.*) You were a Marine, weren't you, Sam?
Reverend Pell. No. Navy.
Tom. Well, same thing.
Reverend Pell. Don't say that to a Marine.

[Gene *and* Reverend Pell *smile.*]

Tom. Gene saw the flag go up on Iwo.[6]
Gene (*embarrassed by all this inappropriate line*). Let's order a drink, Dad.
Tom. Sam, I've been wanting to talk to you. Now is not the appropriate time, but some bozo has been crowding into our pew at church. You know Margaret and I sit up close because she doesn't hear very well. Well, this guy has been there in our pew. I've given him a pretty sharp look several times, but it doesn't seem to faze him. Now, I don't want to seem unreasonable, but there is a whole church for him to sit in.
Reverend Pell. Well, we'll see what we can do, Tom.
Tom (*calling to a bartender*). A martini, George. Six to one. (*To Gene*) Dubonnet?
Gene. A martini.
Tom. Six to one?
Gene. Yes. Only make mine vodka.
Tom. Vodka? Out! Phooey!
Reverend Pell. What have you got against vodka, Tom?
Tom. It's Russian, isn't it? However, I don't want to influence you. Make his vodka. Six to one, now! These fellows like to charge you extra for a six to one, and then they don't give you all the gin you've got coming to you.
Reverend Pell. I hope you don't drink many of those, Tom, six to one.
Tom. My grandmother used to give me, every morning before I went to school, when I was knee-high to a grasshopper . . . she used to give me a jigger of gin with a piece of garlic in it, to keep away colds. I wonder what the teacher thought. Phew. I must have stunk to high heaven . . . She used to put a camphor

---

6. **Iwo:** Iwo Jima, a tiny island in the Pacific, taken in March 1945 by the United States Marines after fierce fighting.

ball in my necktie too. That was for colds, too, I think . . . But they were good people. They just didn't know any better. That's my grandfather and my grandmother. I lived with them for a while when I was a little shaver, because my father . . . well, that's another story . . . but my grandfather——

Reverend Pell (*He puts his hand on* Tom's *arm*). I don't mean to run out on you, Tom, but I was on my way to the little boy's room. I'll catch up with you later.

Tom. Go ahead. We don't want an accident.

Reverend Pell (*as he is going, to* Gene). You got a great dad there. (*And he disappears.*)

Tom. I don't really know these fellows any more. (*Indicating people offstage*) All new faces. Most of them are bores. All they want to do is tell you the story of their lives. But sometimes you hear some good jokes . . . Now, here's someone I know. Hello, Marvin.

[Marvin Scott, *a man about sixty-five, enters.*]

Marvin Scott. Hello, Tom. Good to see you back.

Tom. You remember my son, Gene.

Marvin Scott. Yes. Hello.

Gene. Hello, Mr. Scott.

Marvin Scott (*to* Tom). Well, young feller, you're looking great!

Tom. Am I? Well, thank you.

Marvin Scott. How's Margaret?

[Tom *goes very dramatic, pauses for a moment and bites his lip.* Marvin *looks at* Gene.]

Gene. Mother's . . .

Tom. Margaret's in an oxygen tent in the hospital.

Marvin Scott (*Surprised that* Tom *is here, he looks at* Gene, *then at* Tom). I'm terribly sorry to hear that, Tom.

Tom. Heart. (*He shakes his head and starts to get emotional.*)

Gene (*embarrassed*). We're just going to grab a bite and get back. Mother's sleeping, and if we were there, she'd want to talk.

Marvin Scott. I'm sorry to hear that, Tom. When did it happen?

Tom (*striving for control. His emotion is as much anger that it could happen, and self-pity, as anything else*). This morning . . . I was in the kitchen, getting something for Margaret, when suddenly I heard her scream . . . "Tom . . . Tom . . ." and I ran upstairs . . . and there she was stretched out on the bedroom floor . . . "Nitro . . . nitro" . . . she said . . . We have nitroglycerine all over the house, you know . . . since her last two attacks . . . So, I get her the nitro and call the doctor . . . and now she's in an oxygen tent in the hospital . . . (*The bell starts to ring to call them to dinner.*)

Marvin Scott. Well, I hope everything's all right, Tom.

Gene. Thank you.

Tom. What happened to those martinis? We've got to go into dinner and we haven't gotten them yet.

Gene. We can take them to the table with us.

Tom. I have to drink mine before I eat anything. It brings up the gas. Where are they? (*And he heads off.*)

Marvin Scott (*to* Gene). He's quite a fella.

[*And they move off as Rotarians start singing to the tune of* "Auld Lang Syne," "We're awfully glad you're here," *etc.*

As the lights fade on this group they come up on the hospital bed and Margaret. *The* Nurse *is sitting there, reading a movie magazine. The oxygen tent has been moved away.* Tom *and* Gene *enter quietly, cautiously. The* Nurse *gets up.* Gene *approaches the bed.*]

Gene (*whispers to the* Nurse). Anything?

Nurse. The doctor was just here. He said things looked much better.

Tom (*too loud*). Hooray for our side.

Margaret (*stirs*). Hm . . . What? (*She looks around.*)

Gene. Hello, Mother.

Margaret. Oh, Gene. (*She reaches as though to touch him.*) Look where I ended up.

Gene. The doctor says you're better tonight.

Margaret (*her eyes flashing*). You know how this happened, don't you? Why it happened? (*She nods her head in the direction of* Tom, *who is at the foot of the bed chatting with the* Nurse.)

Gene (*quieting*). Now, Mother. Take it easy. He's seen the doctor. He's had his shot.

Margaret. Well!

Gene. You should be sleeping.

Margaret. That's all I've been doing. (*She takes his hand.*) It makes me so mad. I was feeling so well. All the ladies down in Florida said I've never looked so well.

Gene. You've had these before, Mother. Easy does it.

Margaret. He's seen the doctor for himself?

Gene. Yes. Just a bad cold. He's had a shot.

Margaret. Why wouldn't he have that down there?

Gene. Mother, we'll have to go if you talk like this, because you should be resting.

Tom (*leaving the* Nurse, *cheerful*). Well, how goes it?

Margaret. How do I know?

Tom (*takes her hand and smiles*). You look better.

Margaret. You know I came without anything. I've still got my stockings on.

Tom (*kidding. Very gentle*). Well, it all happened pretty quick, my darling.

Margaret. I'll need some things.

Tom. Your wish is our command.

Gene. I'll write it down. But don't talk too much.

Margaret. Toothbrush . . . some night clothes. I'm still in my slip . . . a hairbrush.

Tom. We'll collect some things.

Margaret (*joshing*). Oh, you. You wouldn't know what to bring. Gene, you look around.

Gene. Yes. Now, take it easy.

Margaret. I hate being seen this way.

Tom. We think you look beautiful.

Gene. Mother, we're just going to sit here now, because you're talking too much. You're being a bad girl. (Margaret *makes a childlike face at him, puckering her lips and wrinkling her nose. She reaches out for his hand.*) Those are lovely flowers Alice sent. She knows your favorites. I called her. I'll keep in touch with her. She said she'd come on, but I said I didn't think she had to.

Margaret. Did you have any dinner?

Tom. We went to Rotary. Everyone asked for you.

Margaret. That's nice.

[Dr. Mayberry *comes into the room, in the shadows of the entrance.* Gene *spots him and goes to him.*]

Dr. Mayberry. Hello, Gene. How are you?

Gene (*trying to catch him before he enters the room entirely*). I'd like to—

Dr. Mayberry (*pleasant and hearty*). We can talk right here. She seems to be coming along very well.

Gene. Good.

Tom. That's wonderful news.

Dr. Mayberry (*kidding her*). She's tough. (Margaret *smiles and makes a face at him.*) We won't know the extent of it until we're able to take a cardiogram tomorrow. It was nothing to toss off lightly, but it looks good now.

Gene. Well . . . thank you. (Tom *coughs.*) What about that?

Dr. Mayberry. He'll be all right. Just a deep cough. He'll get another shot tomorrow.

Gene (*low*). You don't think we should . . . stay around?

Dr. Mayberry. I wouldn't say so. And she should rest.

Gene. Thanks, Doctor. (*They shake hands.*)

Dr. Mayberry. Do I have your number in New York? I'll keep in touch with you. Your dad's a little vague about things. (Gene *jots the number on a slip of paper.*) Good night, Mrs. Garrison. I'm going to kick your family out now so that you can get some rest.

Margaret (*smiles and makes a small wave of the fingers*). Take care of Tom.

Dr. Mayberry. He's going to be fine. (*To* Tom) Drop into the office for another shot tomorrow.

Tom (*kidding*). Will you ask that girl of yours to be a little more considerate next time?

Dr. Mayberry. Oh, you can take it.

Tom. Oh, I'm a good soldier. But, wow! (*He indicates a sore rump.*)

Dr. Mayberry. Good night. (*He waves his hand and disappears.*)

Gene. We'll run along now, Mother.

[*She reaches her hand out.*]

Margaret. My precious.

Gene (*leans down and kisses her hand*). Good night. Sleep well.

Tom. Well, my dearest, remember what we used to say to the children. "When you wake up, may your cheeks be as red as roses and your eyes as bright as diamonds."

Margaret (*pouts, half-kidding*). Just you take care of yourself. And get the laundry ready for Annie tomorrow.

Tom (*with a flourish*). Your wish is my command.

Margaret. I put your dirty shirts from Florida

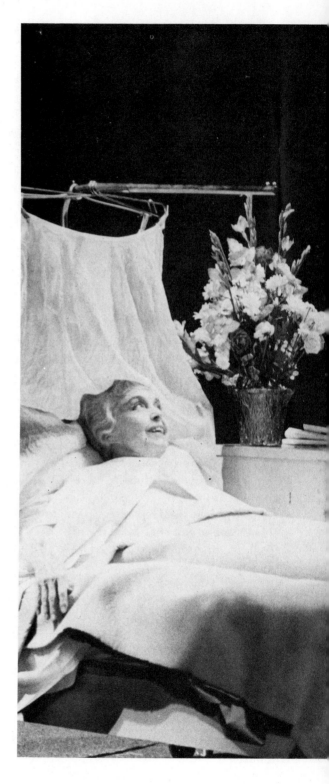

in the hamper in the guest bathroom, and my things are——

Gene (*trying to stop her talking*). We'll find them.

Margaret (*to Gene*). Thanks for coming. Don't bother to come tomorrow. Father will keep in touch with you.

Gene. We'll see. Good night.

[*He stops at the door for a little wave. She wiggles her fingers in a small motion. The lights dim on the hospital scene as* Tom *and* Gene *move away.*]

Tom. Well, that's good news.

Gene. Yes.

Tom. She looks a lot better than when they brought her in here this morning, I can tell you that.

Gene. She looked pretty good.

Tom. She's a good soldier. Do you remember what she asked us to bring her? My mind is like a sieve.

Gene. I'll come along and get the bag ready and round up the laundry.

Tom. We should get the laundry ready tonight because Annie arrives at eight sharp, and she starts getting paid the minute she enters the door. But we could leave the bag till morning.

Gene (*uneasy*). I've got an early appointment at college tomorrow, Dad. I'll have to run along after we have a nightcap.

Tom. Oh, I thought you might spend the night.

Gene. I . . . uh . . . I've got an early appointment at college tomorrow.

Tom. I thought you were on your sabbatical.

Gene. I am . . . But I arranged a meeting with someone there, Dad.

Tom. You could stay and still make it.

Gene. It's very early, Dad.

Tom. We've got an alarm. Alarm clocks all over the house.

Gene. I want to change before the appointment . . . Shirt . . .

Tom. I've got plenty of shirts . . . underwear . . . socks . . .

Gene (*more uncomfortable*). I don't wear your sizes, Dad.

Tom. I could get you up earlier, then. I don't sleep beyond five these days.

Gene (*tense*). No, Dad . . . I just . . . No. I'll come by and——

Tom. There may be something good on television . . . Wednesday night. I think there is . . .

Gene. . . . We'll watch a little television, Dad . . . and have some drinks . . . But then I'll have to go.

Tom (*after a moment*). All right, old man.

[Gene *instinctively reaches out to touch his father's arm, to soften the rejection. They look at each other a moment; then* Tom *drifts off into the dark, as* Gene *moves directly downstage.*]

Gene. I sat with my father much longer than I meant to . . . Because I knew I should stay the night. But . . . I couldn't . . . We watched television. He's slept on and off . . . and I went home . . . The next morning, around nine thirty, my mother died . . . (Gene *turns and walks upstage, as the lights dim.*)

[*Curtain.*]

FOR STUDY AND DISCUSSION

1. This play is told mainly from the point of view of Gene. He functions as a narrator, guiding us through the action and commenting on it. Look at Gene's first speech to the audience (page 652). What problem central to the play is introduced in this speech?

2. The characters of Tom and Margaret Garrison are revealed in a succession of scenes, which move from a railroad station, to their home, to Schrafft's restaurant, to a hospital, to a Rotary Club meeting. What actions show that Tom can be bossy and self-centered? Do you feel sympathy for Tom in any of these scenes? Explain.

3. In the stage directions on page 654, the playwright tells us that Margaret Garrison is "devoted to her son." Which of Margaret's actions reveal this characteristic? How does Margaret serve as a contrast to Tom?

4. The stage directions often tell us that Gene is irritated or angry with his father. Where does Gene also show sympathy for the older man?

5. The playwright lets Tom Garrison tell about his childhood for certain purposes. What have you learned in Act One of Tom's relationship with his own father? How do these details affect the way you feel about Tom?

6. At the end of Act One, Margaret Garrison dies. What new problems do you think this will introduce into the play?

7. What are your feelings for each of these characters at this stage of the action? Did your feelings about any of them change as the action progressed?

Act Two

Gene *and* Dr. Mayberry *enter from the rear.* Gene *is carrying a small overnight case containing his mother's things.*

Gene. Thank you for all you've done for her over the years. It's been a great comfort to her, to us all.

Dr. Mayberry. I was very fond of her.

Gene. She was terribly worried about my father's health. Yesterday she said to me, "You know what put me here."

Dr. Mayberry. Well, Gene, I think that's a little too harsh. She's been living on borrowed time for quite a while, you know.

Gene. Yes . . . Where's Dad?

Dr. Mayberry. He's gone along to the undertaker's. He wanted to wait for you, but since we couldn't reach you this morning, he went along. We sent your mother's nurse to be with him till you arrived.

Gene. Thank you.

Dr. Mayberry. He's all right. You know, Gene, old people live with death. He's been prepared for this for years. It may in some way be a relief. He's taken wonderful care of her.

Gene. Yes, he has.

Dr. Mayberry. Alice will be coming on, I suppose.

Gene. I've called her.

Dr. Mayberry. He shouldn't be staying in that house alone. (Gene *nods.*) Now, you have the suitcase and the envelope with your mother's things.

Gene. Yes. I think she should have her wedding ring.

Dr. Mayberry. Maybe you ought to check with your father . . .

Gene. No . . . Will you? . . .

[*He hands the ring to* Dr. Mayberry *and moves away. The lights come up on the undertaker's office.* Tom *and the* Nurse *are there.*]

Tom. I find that constant wind down there very annoying. Every year I think it's going to be different, but it isn't. You get a little overheated in the sun, and when you walk out from behind some shelter, it knifes into you.

Gene (*He has stood looking at his father for a moment. He now comes to him with tenderness, to share the experience*). Dad.

Tom (*looks up in the middle of his story*). Oh, Gene.

[*He gets up shakily. They embrace.* Gene *pats him on the back.* Tom *steps away and shakes his head. His mouth contorts, showing emotion and anger that this should have happened. He looks at the floor in moments like this.*]

Nurse. We've given him a little sedative.

Tom (*looks up*). What?

Nurse. I said we'd given you a little sedative.

Tom (*at once the charmer*). Oh, yes. This lovely lady has taken wonderful care of me.

Gene (*to the* Nurse). Thank you.

Tom. It turns out she's been to Florida, very near to where we go.

Gene (*a little surprised at this casual conversation, but playing along*). Oh, really?

Tom. I was telling her it was too bad we didn't have the pleasure of meeting her down there. But she goes in the summer. Isn't it terribly hot down there in the summer?

Nurse. The trade winds are always blowing.

Tom. Oh, yes, those damnable winds. We wanted this young man to come join us there, but he went to California instead. (*To* Gene) You'll have to come down to Florida sometime. See what lovely girls you'd meet there!

Gene (*baffled and annoyed by this chatter, but passes it off*). I will.

Tom. What was your name again? My mind's like a sieve.

Nurse. Halsey.

Tom (*courtly*). Miss Halsey . . . My son, Gene.

Gene. How do you do?

Tom. Miss Halsey and I are on rather intimate terms. She . . . uh . . . gave me my shot.

Gene. Good.

Tom (*to the* Nurse). I had this terrible cough down there. The winds. But I'll be all right. Don't worry about me. If I can get some regular exercise, get over to the club.

[*For a moment they all just sit there. Obviously there is to be no sharing of the experience of the mother's death.*]

Gene. I called Alice.

Tom. Oh. Thank you. (*To the* Nurse) Alice was my daughter. She . . . uh . . . lives in Chicago.

Nurse (*shaking his hand, kindly*). Goodbye, Mr. Garrison.

Tom. Oh, are you going?

Nurse. Yes. Take good care of yourself.

Tom. Oh, well. Thank you very much my dear. You've been very kind.

Gene. Thank you.

[*The* Nurse *exits.*]

Marvin Scott (*entering with some forms and papers*). Now, Tom, all we have to do is—(*He looks up from papers and sees* Gene.) Oh, hello, Gene.

Gene. Mr. Scott.

Marvin Scott. I'm terribly sorry.

Gene. Thank you.

Marvin Scott. Now, the burial is to be where, Tom? (*Throughout he is simple, considerate and decent.*)

Tom. The upper burial ground. I've got the deed at home in my file cabinet, if I can ever find it. For years I've meant to clean out that file cabinet. But I'll find it.

Marvin Scott (*to* Gene). Will you see that I get it? At least the number of the plot?

Gene. It's 542.

Marvin Scott. You're sure of that?

Gene. My wife was buried there last year.

Tom (*suddenly remembering*). That's right. (*He reaches out and puts his hand on* Gene's *arm, implying that they have something to share.* Gene *doesn't really want to share his father's kind of emotionalism.*)

Marvin Scott (*He has been making notes*). We'll need some clothes . . . uh . . .

Gene (*quickly*). Yes, all right. I'll take care of that.

Marvin Scott. Do you want the casket open or closed while she's resting here?

[*There is a pause.*]

Gene. Dad?

Tom. What was that?

Gene. Do you want the casket open or closed?

Tom. Oh . . . open, I think.

[Gene *would have preferred it closed.*]

Marvin Scott. Now, an obituary. Perhaps you would like to prepare something, Tom.

Tom. Yes. Well . . . Gene? Gene was very close to his mother.

[Marvin Scott *looks at* Gene.]

Gene. Yes, I'll work something up.

Marvin Scott. If you could by this afternoon, so that it would catch the—

Tom. She was my inspiration. When I met her the clouds hung low and dark. I was going to night school, studying shorthand and typing and *elocution* . . . and working in a lumberyard in the daytime . . . wearing a cutaway coat, if you please, someone at the church had given me . . . I was making a home for my brother and sister . . . My mother had died, and my father had deserted us . . . (*He has gone hard on his father . . . and stops a moment.*) "He did not know the meaning of the word 'quit.' " They said that some years ago when The Schoolboys of Old Harlem gave me an award. You were there, Gene.

Gene. Yes.

Tom. "Obstructions, yes. But go through them or over them, but never around them." Teddy Roosevelt said that. I took it down in shorthand for practice . . . Early in life I developed a will of iron . . . (*You can feel the iron in the way he says it.*) Any young man in this country who has a sound mind and a sound body, who will set himself an objective, can achieve anything he wants, within reason. (*He has said all this firmly, as though lecturing or giving a speech. He now looks at his cigarette.*) Ugh . . . Filthy habit. Twenty years ago a doctor told me to give these things up, and I did. But when things pile up . . . Well . . . All's lost, all's spent, when we our desires get without content . . . (*He looks around. There is a pause.*)

Gene. I'll write something.

Tom. About what?

Gene. Mother. For an obituary.

Tom. Oh, yes, you do that. He's the lit'ry member of the family. You'll use the church, won't you? Not the chapel. I imagine there'll be hundreds of people there . . . Garden Club . . . Woman's Club . . . Mother's Club.

Marvin Scott. I'm sure that Reverend Pell will use whichever you want. (*He shuffles some papers.*) Now, Tom, the only thing that's left is the most difficult. We have to choose a coffin.

Tom. Do we have to do that now?

Marvin Scott. It's easier now, Tom. To get it over with.

Tom (*firm*). I want the best. That's one thing. I want the best!

Marvin Scott (*moves across the stage with* Tom *and* Gene). There are many kinds.

Tom (*As he takes a few steps, he takes* Gene's *arm*). I don't know what I'd do without this young fellow. (*This kind of word-bribery disturbs* Gene. *In the coffin area, overhead lights suddenly come on. Shafts of light in the darkness indicate the coffins.* Tom *claps his hand to his forehead*) Do I have to look at all these?

Marvin Scott (*gently*). It's the only way, Tom. The best way is to just let you wander around alone and look at them. The prices are all marked on the cards inside the caskets. (*He lifts an imaginary card.*)

Tom (*puts on his glasses to look*). Nine hundred? For the casket?

Marvin Scott. That includes everything, Tom. All our services, and one car for the mourners. Other cars are extra.

Tom (*to* Gene, *who is standing back*). Well, we'll have your car, so we shouldn't need another. Anybody else wants to come, let them drive their own car. (*Looks back at the caskets*) Oh, dear . . . Gene! (Gene *comes alongside. He is tender and considerate to the part of his father that is going through a difficult time, though irritated by the part that has always angered him. They walk silently among the caskets for a few moments.* Tom *lifts a price tag and looks at it.*) Two thou-sand! (*He taps an imaginary casket.*) What are these made of?

Marvin Scott (*coming forward*). They vary, Tom . . . Steel, bronze . . . wood.

Tom. What accounts for the variation in prices?

Marvin Scott. Material . . . workmanship . . . The finish inside. You see, this is all silk.

Tom. I suppose the metal stands up best.

Marvin Scott. Well, yes. (Tom *shakes his head, confused.*) Of course the casket does not go directly into the ground. We first sink a concrete outer vault.

Tom. Oh?

Marvin Scott. That prevents seepage, et cetera.

Tom. That's included in the price?

Marvin Scott. Yes.

[Tom *walks on.* Gene *stays in the shadows.*]

Tom. How long do any of these stand up?

[Gene *closes his eyes.*]

Marvin Scott. It's hard to say, Tom. It depends on the location. Trees, roots, and so on.

Tom. I suppose these metal ones are all welded at the seams?

Marvin Scott. Oh, yes.

Tom. Our plot up there is on a small slope. I suppose that's not so good for wear. I didn't think of that when I bought it . . . And the trees looked so lovely . . . I never thought.

Marvin Scott (*gently*). I don't think it makes that much difference, Tom.

Tom (*moves along, stops*). For a child?

Marvin Scott. Yes.

Tom (*shakes his head, moved*). My mother would have fit in that. She was a little bit of a thing . . . Died when I was ten. (*Tears come to his eyes.*) I don't remember much about her funeral except my father . . . He'd run out on us, but he came back when she died . . . and I wouldn't let him come to the cemetery. (*He gets angry all over again . . . then*) Oh, well . . . water over the dam. But this made me think of her . . . a little bit of a thing. (Gene *is touched by his father's memory of his own mother, but still upset at this supermarket type of shopping.*) Five hundred. What do you think of this one, Gene? (Gene *comes up.*) I like the color of the silk. Did you say that was silk or satin?

Marvin Scott. Silk.

Gene. I don't think it makes much difference, Dad. Whatever you think.

Tom. I mean, they all go into this concrete business. (*He senses some disapproval on Gene's part and moves on, then adjusts his glasses.*) This one is eight hundred. I don't see the difference. Marvin, what's the difference?

Marvin Scott. It's mostly finish and workmanship. They're both steel.

Tom. I don't like the browns or blacks. Gray seems less somber. Don't you agree, Gene?

Gene. Yes, I do.

Tom. Eight hundred. Is there a tax, Marvin?

[Gene *turns away.*]

Marvin Scott. That includes the tax, Tom.

Tom. All right. Let's settle for that, then, and get out of here. (*He shivers.*)

Marvin Scott. Fine. (*To* Gene) And you'll send some clothes over?

Gene. Yes. (Gene *bobs his head up and down, annoyed with the details, though* Marvin *has been considerate and discreet.*)

Marvin Scott. I'd estimate that Mrs. Garrison should be . . . that is, if people want to come to pay their respects, about noon tomorrow.

Gene. All right.

Marvin Scott. Would you like to see where Mrs. Garrison will be resting?

Gene (*definite*). No, thank you. I think we'll be moving along.

Marvin Scott. I assume your sister Alice will be coming on?

Gene. She arrives this evening. (*He looks around for his father and sees him standing in front of the child's coffin, staring at it. He goes over to his father and takes him gently by the arm.*) Shall we go, Dad?

Tom (*nods his head, far away*). She was just a little bit of a thing.

[*And they start moving out of the room, as the lights dim out.*

As the lights come up again on another part of the stage, Alice, Gene's *older sister, is coming on. She is in her early forties, attractive, brisk, realistic, unsentimental.*]

Alice. Shouldn't we be getting home to Dad?

Gene (*carrying two highballs. He is blowing off steam*). I suppose so, but I'm not ready to go home yet . . . Let's sit over here, where we can get away from the noise at the bar.

Alice. You've had quite a day.

Gene. I'm sorry for blowing off, but . . . (*shakes his head*) Alice, our mother died this morning, and I've wanted to talk about her, but she hasn't been mentioned except as "my inspiration," which is his cue to start the story of his life.

Alice. I'm sorry you've had to take it all alone.

Gene. Well, I'm glad you're here, and I'm glad of the chance to get out of the house to come to meet you . . . I'm so tired of hearing about "when the clouds hung low and dark" . . . I'm so tired of people coming up to me and saying, "Your dad's a remarkable man." Nobody talks about Mother. Just "He's a remarkable man." You'd think he died! . . . I want to say to them, "My mother was a remarkable woman . . . You don't know my father. You only know the man in the newspapers. He's a

selfish man who's lived on the edge of exasperation all his life. You don't know the bite of his sarcasm. The night he banished my sister for marrying someone he didn't approve of did not get into the papers."

Alice. *Shhh . . .*

Gene. What a night that was! Mother running from the room sobbing. You shouting at him and storming out, and the two of us, father and son, left to finish dinner, in silence. Afterward I threw up.

Alice. I shouted and you threw up. That was pretty much the pattern.

Gene. I know I'm being unfair. But I'm in the mood to be unfair. I've wanted to turn to him all day and say, "Will you for once shut up about your miserable childhood and say something about Mother?" (*A little ashamed of his outburst*) But I can't say that. He's an old man and my father, and his wife has died, and he may be experiencing something, somewhere, I know nothing about. (*He shakes his head for going on like this.*) I'm sorry.

Alice. It's all right.

Gene. No. (*He touches her arm, smiles.*) Mother loved your flowers.

Alice. I've felt guilty about Mother all the way coming here. I should have seen her more, invited her more often, brought the kids more often. Instead I sent flowers.

Gene. I guess that's an inevitable feeling when a person dies. I feel the same way.

Alice. But you were so good to her. You made her life.

Gene (*He has always hated that phrase. Slowly, quietly*). A son is not supposed to make his mother's life . . . Oh, I loved Mother. You know that. But to be depended on to make her life . . . Dad says, he boasts, he never knew the meaning of the word *quit*. Well, he quit on her all right. And I . . . I was just there. (Alice *looks at this sudden revelation of his feelings, his resentment that he was left to save his mother from loneliness and unhappiness.*) Still, wait till you see him. There's something that comes through . . . the old Tiger. Something that reaches you and makes you want to cry . . . He'll probably be asleep when we get home, in front of the television. And you'll see. The Old Man . . . the Father. But then he wakes up and becomes Tom Garrison, and I'm in trouble . . . Last night he asked me to stay with him, and I didn't . . . I couldn't. I'm ashamed of that now.

Alice (*Touched by the complexity of Gene's feelings, she looks at him a long moment, then*). Have you called California?

Gene (*frowns. A problem*). No. (*He takes a drink, wanting to avoid the subject.*)

Alice. I suppose we have enough problems for the next few days, but . . .

Gene. After?

Alice. Yes. We'll have to start thinking about Dad, about what we're going to do.

Gene (*nods his head*). I don't know. (*They look at each other a moment, then*) Well, let's go home. (*He rises.*) Thanks for listening to all this, Alice. You had to pay good money to get someone to listen to you. I appreciate it. (*He smiles.*) I thought I wanted to talk to you about Mother, but all I've done is talk about him, just like the others.

Alice. We'll talk. There'll be time.

[*And they leave. The lights dim out on the bar area and come up on the home area.* Tom *is asleep, his head forward, his glasses on, some legal papers in his lap. Quiet like this, he is a touching picture of old age. The strong face . . . the good but gnarled hands. He is the symbol of* Father. *The television is on. As* Gene *and* Alice *come in, they pause and look. They are impressed by the sad dignity. Finally* Gene *approaches and gently puts his hand on his father's arm, then turns down the television.*]

Gene. Dad?

Tom (*barely stirs*). Hm?

Gene. Dad?

Tom. Mm? Margaret? (*Coming to a little more and looking up at* Gene) . . . Oh, Gene . . . I must have dozed off.

Gene. Alice is here.

Tom. Alice? . . . What for? (*He is genuinely confused.*)

Alice (*comes from the shadows*). Hello, Dad.

Tom (*looks around, a bit panicky, confused. Then he remembers*). Oh . . . Oh, yes.

[*He bites his upper lip, and with his gnarled hands grips theirs for a moment of affection and family strength.* Alice *kisses him on the cheek. They help him from the chair and start putting on his coat. As the lights dim on the home area, they come up on a graveyard area.* Tom, Gene *and* Alice *and all the people we have met, are gathering as* Reverend Pell *starts his eulogy.*]

Reverend Pell. Margaret Garrison was a loving wife and a kind and generous mother, and a public-spirited member of the community. The many people who were touched by her goodness can attest to the pleasure and joy she brought them through her love of life and her power to communicate this love to others. The many children, now grown . . .

Gene (*turns from the family group*). Only a dozen or so people were at my mother's funeral. Most of her friends were dead, or had moved to other cities, or just couldn't make it. Fifteen years earlier the church would have been filled. There were a few men sent from Rotary, a few women from the Garden Club, the Mother's Club, the Woman's Club, and a few of the members of her bridge club were there . . . The hundreds of children who had listened to her tell stories year after year on Christmas Eve were all gone, or had forgotten . . . Perhaps some of them who were still in the neighborhood looked up from their evening papers to say, "I see Mrs. Garrison died. She was nice . . . Well, she was an old lady." (*He turns to rejoin the family group.*)

Reverend Pell. Earth to earth . . . ashes to ashes . . . dust to dust . . . The Lord giveth and the Lord taketh away . . . Blessed be the name of the Lord . . . Amen.

[Tom *comes to shake hands with* Reverend Pell. *The others drift about, exchanging nods, and gradually leave during the following.*]

Tom. Well, it's a nice place up here.

Gene (*who has wandered over to look at another grave*). Yes.

Tom. Your mother and I bought it soon after we were married. She thought it a strange thing to do, but we bought it. (*He looks at the grave* Gene *is looking at.*) Now, let's see, that's . . .

Gene. Carol.

Tom. Who?

Gene. Carol. My wife.

Tom. Oh, yes. (*He reaches out a sympathetic hand toward* Gene, *then moves away.*) There's room for three more burials up here, as I remember. There . . . there . . . and there. I'm to go there, when the time comes. (*He looks around for a moment.*) This plot is in terrible shape . . . I paid three hundred dollars some years ago for perpetual care, and now look at it. Just disgraceful . . . I'm going to talk to that superintendent.

[*And he strides off. The lights change.* Alice *and* Gene *move into another area, what might be a garden with a bench. For a moment neither says anything.* Gene *lights a cigarette and sits on the grass.*]

Alice. I don't know how you feel, but I'd like to figure out some kind of memorial for Mother . . . Use some of the money she left.

Gene. Yes, definitely.

Alice. Maybe some shelves of books for the children's library. Christmas books with the stories she liked to tell.

Gene. That's a good idea.

[*There is a long and awkward pause.*]

Alice. Well, Gene, what are we going to do?

Gene (*frowns*). Mother always said to put her in an old-people's home. She had one all picked out.

Alice. Sidney's mother and father saw it coming and arranged to be in one of those cottage colonies for old people.

Gene. Mother and Dad didn't.

Alice. I think you should go ahead and get married and move to California . . . But . . . I might as well get this off my chest, it would be murder if he came to live with us. In the first place, he wouldn't do it, feeling as he does about Sid, and the kids can't stand how he tells them how to do everything.

Gene. I think you're right. That would never work. (*There is a pause.* Gene *looks out at the garden.*) I can't tell you what it does to me as a man . . . to see someone like that . . . a man who was distinguished, remarkable . . . just become a nuisance.

Alice (*She is disturbed at what her brother may be thinking*). I know I sound hard, but he's had his life . . . and as long as we can be assured that he's taken care of . . . Oh, I'll feel some guilt, and you, maybe more. But my responsibility is to my husband and my children.

Gene. Yes. That's *your* responsibility.

Alice. And your responsibility is to yourself . . . to get married again, to get away from memories of Carol and her whole world. Have you called California?

Gene (*frowns*). No.

Alice. If I were the girl you were planning to marry, and you didn't call me to tell me your mother had died . . .

Gene (*gets up, disturbed*). I just haven't wanted to go into it all with her.

Alice (*understanding, but worried*). Gene, my friend . . . my brother . . . Get out of here!

Gene. Look, Alice, your situation is quite different. Mine is very complex. You fortunately see things very clearly, but it's not so easy for me. (Alice *looks at* Gene, *troubled by what his thinking seems to be leading to. After a moment . . . reflective*) We always remember the terrible things about Dad. I've been trying to remember some of the others . . . How much he *did* do for us.

Alice. I'm doing a lot for my kids. I don't expect them to pay me back at the other end.

(Gene *wanders around, thinking, scuffing the grass.*) I'm sure we could find a full-time housekeeper. He can afford it.

Gene. He'd never agree.

Alice. It's that or finding a home. (*Gene frowns.*) Sidney's folks like where they are. Also, we might as well face it, his mind's going. Sooner or later, we'll have to think about powers of attorney, perhaps committing him to an institution.

Gene (*shaking his head*). It's all so ugly.

Alice (*smiling*). Yes, my gentle Gene, a lot of life is.

Gene. Now, look, don't go trying to make me out some softhearted . . . (*He can't find the word.*) I know life is ugly.

Alice. Yes, I think you know it. You've lived through a great deal of ugliness. But you work like a Trojan to deny it, to make it not so. (*After a moment, not arguing*) He kicked me out. He said he never wanted to see me again. He broke Mother's heart over that for years. He was mean, unloving. He beat you when you were a kid . . . You've hated and feared him all your adult life . . .

Gene (*cutting in*). Still he's my father, and a man. And what's happening to him appalls me as a man.

Alice. We have a practical problem here.

Gene. It's not as simple as all that.

Alice. To me it is. I don't understand this mystical haze you're casting over it. I'm going to talk to him tomorrow, after the session with the lawyer, about a housekeeper. (*Gene reacts but says nothing.*) Just let me handle it. He can visit us, and we can take turns coming to visit him. Now, I'll do the dirty work. Only when he turns to you, don't give in.

Gene. I can't tell you how ashamed I feel . . . not to say with open arms, "Poppa, come live with me . . . I love you, Poppa, and I want to take care of you." . . . I need to love him. I've always wanted to love him.

[*He drops his arms and wanders off. Alice watches her brother drift off into the garden as the lights go down in that area. The lights come up in the living-room area. Tom is seated in his chair, writing. Alice comes into the room. Small packing boxes are grouped around.*]

Alice. How are you coming?

Tom. Oh, Alice, I've written out receipts for you to sign for the jewelry your mother left you. And if you'll sign for the things she left the children.

Alice. All right.

[*Signs.* Gene *comes into the room carrying a box full of his mother's things. He exchanges a look with* Alice, *knowing the time has come for the discussion.*]

Tom. It may not be necessary, but as executor, I'll be held responsible for these things.

Alice. Dad, I'd like to talk a little . . . with you . . . about—

Tom. Yes, all right. But first I'd like to read you this letter I've written to Harry Hall . . . He and I used to play golf out in New Jersey . . . He wrote a very nice letter to me about your mother . . . and I've written him as follows . . . It will only take a minute . . . If I can read my own shorthand . . . (*He adjusts his glasses.*) "Dear Harry . . . How thoughtful of you to write me on the occasion of Margaret's death. It was quite a blow. As you know, she was my inspiration, and had been ever since that day fifty-five years ago when I met her . . . when the clouds hung low and dark for me. At that time I was supporting my younger brother and my sister and my aged grandfather in a two-room flat . . . going to work every day in a lumber mill. Providence, which has always guided me, prompted me to take a night course in shorthand and typing, and also

prompted me to go to the Underwood Type-writing Company seeking a position as stenographer. They sent me, God be praised, to the office of T. J. Parks . . . and a job that started at five dollars a week, ended in 1929 when I retired, at fifty thousand a year . . ." That's as far as I've gotten at the moment. (*He looks up for approval.*)

Gene. Dad, I don't think financial matters are particularly appropriate in answering a letter of condolence.

Tom. Oh? (*He looks at the letter.*) But it's true. You see, it follows. I'm saying she was my inspiration . . . and it seems entirely appropriate to explain that.

Gene. Well, it's your letter, Dad.

Tom (*looks it over*). Well . . .

Alice. Dad, I'm leaving tomorrow . . . and . . .

Tom (*looking up*). What?

Alice. I'm going home tomorrow.

Tom (*formal*). Well, Alice, I'm grateful you came. I know it was difficult for you, leaving home. Your mother would have appreciated it. She was very fond of you, Alice.

Alice. I think we ought to talk over, maybe, what your plans are.

Tom. My plans? I have many letters to answer, and a whole mess in my files and accounts. If the income-tax people ever asked me to produce my books . . .

Gene. They're not likely to, Dad. Your income is no longer of that size.

Tom (*with a twinkle in his eye*). Don't be too sure.

Alice. I didn't mean exactly that kind of plans. I meant . . . Well, you haven't been well.

Tom (*belligerent*). Who said so?

Alice. Mother was worried to death about— (*She stops.*)

Tom. I was under a strain. Your mother's health . . . never knowing when it might happen. Trying to get her to take care of herself,

to take it easy. You know, the doctor said if she didn't eat more slowly, this might happen.

Alice. You plan to keep the house?

Tom. Oh, yes. All my things are here . . . It's a . . . It's a . . . I'll be back on my feet, and my . . . (*Points to his head*) . . . will clear up. Now this strain is over, I'm confident I'll be in shape any day now.

Alice. I worry, leaving you in this house . . . alone, Dad.

Tom (*looks around, very alert, defensively*). I'm perfectly all right. Now don't worry about me . . . either of you. Why, for the last year, since your mother's first attack, I've been getting the breakfast, making the beds, using a dust rag . . . (*He makes quite a performance of this. It is a gallant struggle.*) And the laundress comes in once a week and cleans up for me . . . And Gene here . . . if Gene will keep an eye on me, drop in once or twice a week . . .

Alice. That's the point.

Gene (*low*). Alice!

Alice. We think you should have a full-time housekeeper, Dad. To live here.

Tom (*trying to kid it off, but angry*). Alone here with me? That wouldn't be very proper, would it?

Alice (*smiling*). Nevertheless . . .

Tom. No. Now that's final!

Alice. Dad, Gene and I would feel a lot better about it if—

Tom. Look, you don't have to worry about me.

Alice. Dad, you're forgetting things more and more.

Tom. Who says so?

Alice. Mother wrote me, and—

Tom. I was under a strain. I just finished telling you. Look, Alice, you can go, leave with a clear mind. I'm all right. (*Gene is touched and moved by his father's effort, his desperate effort to maintain his dignity, his* standing as a functioning man.) Of course, I will appreciate Gene's dropping in. But I'm all right.

Alice. We still would like to get a full-time housekeeper.

Tom (*bristling*). What do you mean, you would get? I've hired and fired thousands of people in my day. I don't need anyone *getting* someone for me.

Alice. Will you do it yourself, then?

Tom. No, I told you. No! (*He gets very angry. His voice sharpens and hardens.*) Since I was eight years old I've taken care of myself. What do you two know about it? You were given everything on a platter. At an age when you two were swinging on that tree out there, breaking the branches, I was selling newspapers five hours a day, and at night dancing a jig in saloons for pennies . . . And you're trying to tell me I can't take care of myself . . . If I want a housekeeper, and I don't, I'll hire one . . . I've hired and fired thousands of people in my time. When I was vice president of Colonial Brass at fifty thousand a year . . . Two thousand people. And you tell me I'm incompetent . . . to hire a housekeeper. And how many people have you hired? (*To* Gene) You teach . . . Well, all right. That's your business, if that's what you want to do. But don't talk to me about hiring and firing.

[*The children are saddened and perhaps a little cowed by this naked outburst, the defense of a man who knows that he is slipping, and an angry outburst of hatred and jealousy for his own children. Everyone is quiet for a moment . . . then.*]

Alice. Dad, you might fall down.

Tom. Why fall down? There's nothing wrong with my balance.

[Gene *is sick at this gradual attempt to bring*

to a man's consciousness the awareness that he is finished.]

Alice. Sometimes, when you get up, you're dizzy.

Tom. Nonsense. (*He gets up abruptly. He makes great effort and stands for a moment, then one foot moves slightly to steady his balance . . . and the children both look away.*) Now, I appreciate your concern . . . (*Very fatherly*) But I'm perfectly able to carry on by myself. As I said, with Gene's help from time to time. I imagine we could have dinner every once in a while, couldn't we, Gene . . . once a week or so? Take you up to Rotary. Some of the speakers are quite amusing.

[Alice *looks at* Gene *to see if he is going to speak up.*]

Gene. Sure, Dad.

Tom. Give us some time together at last. Get to know each other.

Alice (*quietly but firmly*). Gene wants to get married.

Gene. Alice!

Tom. What?

Alice. Gene wants to move to California and get married.

Gene. Alice, shut up.

Alice (*almost in tears*). I can't help it. You've never faced up to him. You'd let him ruin your life.

Gene (*angry*). I can take care of my own life.

Alice. You can't!

Tom (*loud*). Children! . . . Children! (*They stop arguing and turn to their father at his command.* Tom *speaks with a note of sarcasm.*) I have no desire to interfere with either of your lives. I took care of myself at eight. I can take care of myself at eighty. I have never wanted to be a burden to my children.

Gene. I'm going to hang around, Dad.

Tom. There's no need to.

Gene. I'll move in here at least till you're feeling better.

[Alice *turns away, angry and despairing.*]

Tom (*sarcastically*). I don't want to ruin your life.

Gene (*angry now at his father*). I didn't say that.

Tom. I have long gotten the impression that my only function in this family is to supply the money to——

Gene (*anguished*). Dad!

Tom. —— to supply the funds for your education, for your——

Gene. Dad, stop it!

[Tom *staggers a little, dizzy.* Gene *goes to his side to steady him.* Tom *breathes heavily in and out in rage. The rage of this man is a terrible thing to see, old as he is. He finally gets some control of himself.*]

Tom. As far as I am concerned, this conversation is ended. Alice, we've gotten along very well for some years now without your attention.

Gene (*protesting, but hating the fight*). Dad!

Alice. You sent me away. Don't forget that.

Tom. You chose to lead your own life. Well, we won't keep you now.

Gene. Dad . . .

Tom (*rage again*). I was competent to go into the city year after year to earn money for your clothes, your food, the roof over your head. Am I now incompetent? Is that what you're trying to tell me?

[*He looks at* Alice *with a terrible look. He breathes heavily for a moment or two; then, shaking his head, he turns away from both of*

them and leaves, disappearing into the shadows.]

Gene (*angry, troubled*). Alice!

Alice. I'm only trying to get a practical matter accomplished.

Gene. You don't have to destroy him in the process.

Alice. I wasn't discussing his competence. Although that will be a matter for discussion soon.

Gene. Look, Alice, just leave it now, the way it is. Don't say any more.

Alice. With you staying on.

Gene. Yes. You can go with a clear conscience.

Alice. My conscience is clear.

Gene. I am doing this because I want to.

Alice. You're doing it because you can't help yourself.

Gene. Look, when I want to be analyzed, I'll pay for it.

Alice (*pleading*). But I saw you. Didn't you see yourself there, when he started to rage? Didn't you feel youself pull in? You shrank.

Gene. I shrank at the ugliness of what was happening.

Alice. You're staying because you can't stand his wrath the day you say, "Dad, I'm leaving." You've never been able to stand up to his anger. He's cowed you.

Gene. Look, Alice . . .

Alice. He'll call you ungrateful, and you'll believe him. He'll lash out at you with his sarcasm, and that will kill this lovely, necessary image you have of yourself as the good son. Can't you see that?

Gene (*lashing out*). What do you want us to do? Shall we get out a white paper?[1] Let it be known that we, Alice and Gene, have done all that we can to make this old man happy in his

---

1. **white paper:** official report.

old age, without inconveniencing ourselves, of course. And he has refused our help. So, if he falls and hits his head and lies there until he rots, it is not our fault. Is that it?

Alice. You insist on——

Gene. (*running on*). Haven't you learned on the couch[2] that people do *not* always do what you want them to do? It is sometimes *we* who have to make the adjustments?

Alice. The difference between us is that I accept the inevitable sadness of this world without an acute sense of personal guilt. You don't. I don't think anyone expects either of us to ruin our lives for an unreasonable old man.

Gene. It's not going to ruin my life.

Alice. It is.

Gene. A few weeks, a month.

Alice. Forever!

Gene. Alice, let's not go on discussing it. I know what I am going to do. Maybe I can't explain my reasons to you. I just know I can't do anything else. Maybe there isn't the same thing between a mother and a daughter, but the "old man" in me feels something very deep, wants to extend some kind of mercy to that old man. I never had a father. I ran away from him. He ran away from me. Maybe he's right. Maybe it is time we found each other.

Alice. Excuse me for saying so, but I find that sentimental slop! I think this is all rationalization to make tolerable a compulsion you have to stay here. You hate the compulsion, so you've dressed it up to look nice.

Gene. How do you know what you're saying isn't a rationalization to cover up a callousness, a selfishness, a coldness in yourself. To make *it* smell nice?

Alice. What do you think you'll find?

Gene. I don't know.

Alice. You hope to find love. Couldn't you tell

_____
2. **on the couch:** on the psychiatrist's couch.

from what he just said what you're going to find? Don't you understand he's got to hate you? He may not think it in his head or feel it in his heart, but you are his enemy! From the moment you were born a boy, you were a threat to this man and his enemy.

Gene. That sounds like the textbooks, Alice.

Alice. He wanted your guts, and he's had them! When has he ever regarded you as a man, an equal, a male? When you were a Marine. And that you did for him. Because even back there you were looking for his love. You didn't want to be a Marine. "Now, Poppa, will you love me?" And he did. No, not love. But he was proud and grateful because you gave him an extension of himself he could boast about, with his phony set of values. When was he ever proud about the thing *you* do? The things *you* value? When did he ever mention your teaching or your books, except in scorn?

Gene. You don't seem to have felt the absence of a father. But I feel incomplete, deprived. I just do not want to let my father die a stranger to me.

Alice. You're looking for something that isn't there, Gene. You're looking for a mother's love in a father. Mothers are soft and yielding. Fathers are hard and rough, to teach us the way of the world, which is rough, which is mean, which is selfish and prejudiced.

Gene. All right. That's your definition. And because of what he did to you, you're entitled to it.

Alice. I've always been grateful to him for what he did. He taught me a marvelous lesson, and has made me able to face a lot. And there has been a lot to face, and I'm grateful to him. Because if I couldn't get the understanding and compassion from a father, who could I expect it from in the world? Who in the world, if not from a father? So I learned, and didn't expect it, and I've found very little, and

so I'm grateful to him. I'm grateful to him. (*The growing intensity ends in tears, and she turns her head.*)

Gene (*looks in pity at the involuntary revelation of her true feeling. He moves to her and touches her*). I'll stay, Alice . . . for a while, at least . . . for whatever reasons. Let's not argue any more.

Alice. And Peggy?

Gene. She'll be coming in a week or two, we'll see.

Alice. Don't lose her, Gene. Maybe I'm still fouled up on myself, but I think I've spoken near the truth about you.

Gene. I keep wondering why I haven't called her, or wanted to call her. Why I seem so much closer to Carol at the moment.

Alice (*gently, tentatively*). The image . . . of the eternally bereaved husband . . . forgive me . . . the dutiful son . . . They're very appealing and seductive . . . But they're not living. (Gene *just stands, looking at her, thinking about what she has said.* Alice *kisses him on the cheek.*) Good night, Gene.

Gene (*his hands on her shoulders*). Good night.

Alice (*She suddenly puts her head tight against his shoulder and holds him*). Suddenly I miss Mother so. (*She sobs. He just holds her and strokes her back.*)

Gene. Yes. (*And he holds her, comforting her, as the lights dim.*)

[*After a few moments of darkness the lights come up on* Tom *in his bedroom in pajamas and bathrobe, kneeling by his bed, praying. On his bed is a small top drawer of a bureau, filled with mementos.* Gene *comes in. He stands in the shadows and watches his father at his prayers.* Gene *does not pray any more, and he has always been touched by the sight of his father praying.* Tom *gets up and starts to untie his bathrobe.*]

Gene. You ready to be tucked in?

Tom (*smiling*). Yes. (*Loosening his robe*) Look at the weight I've lost.

Gene (*troubled at the emaciated body, which is pathetic. The face is ruddy and strong, the body that of an old man*). Since when?

Tom. Oh, I don't know.

Gene (*tapping his father's stomach*). Well, you had quite a little pot there, Dad.

Tom (*smiling*). Did I?

Gene. Yes.

Tom. But look, all through here, through my chest.

Gene. Well, we'll put some back on you. You've been eating pretty well this last week.

Tom (*looking at his own chest*). You know, I never had hair on my chest. I don't understand it. You have hair on your chest. I just didn't have any. Well, I'm confident if I could get some exercise . . . Do you remember when I used to get you up in the morning, and we'd go down and do calisthenics to the radio?

Gene (*smiling*). Yes.

Tom (*stands very straight, swings his arms*). One-two-three-four . . . One-two-three-four . . .

Gene. Hey, take it easy.

Tom. I used to swing the Indian clubs every day at lunchtime. I gave you a set once, didn't I?

Gene. I think so.

Tom. We'll have to dig them out. (*Starts bending exercises*) One-two-three-four . . . one-two-three-four.

Gene. Why don't you wait till morning for that?

Tom. Remember when we used to put on the gloves and spar down on the side porch? . . . I don't think you ever liked it very much. (*He crouches in boxing position.*) The manly art of self-defense . . . Gentleman Jim Corbett . . . Now it's something else again . . . Oh, well, things to worry about. But I intend to get over to the club, play some golf, sit around and swap stories with the boys. Too bad you never took up golf. Alice could have played a good game of golf. But she had a temper. Inherited it from your mother's father. (*He fishes in the bureau drawer on the bed.*) I was looking through my bureau drawer . . . I don't know, just going over things . . . Did you ever see this? (*He takes out a small revolver.*)

Gene. Yes.

Tom. Never had occasion to use it. Oh, I took it out West one winter when we went to Arizona instead of Florida. Shot at rattlesnakes in a rock pile. (*Takes potshots*) I don't have a permit for this any more. (*Starts putting it back in its box*) I suppose they wouldn't give me one. I don't know anyone up there any more. When I was Mayor, cops on every corner would wave . . . "Hello, Mr. Garrison . . . 'Morning, Mr. Garrison." Now, one of the young whippersnappers gave me a ticket, just before we left for Florida. Said I'd passed a full-stop sign. That's what *he* said. First ticket I had in forty or more years of driving, so keep this quiet. (*He takes out a packet of photographs wrapped in tissue paper.*) Pictures . . . I think you've seen most of them . . . The family.

Gene (*very tentatively*). You know, Dad, I've never seen a picture of your father. (*Tom looks at him a long time. Then finally, with his hatred showing on his face, he unwraps another tissue and hands over a small picture.* Gene *looks at it a long moment.*) He's just a boy.

Tom. That was taken about the time he was married.

Gene. I'd always thought of him as . . . the way you talked about him . . . as . . . (Gene *is obviously touched by the picture.*)

Tom. Oh, he was a fine-looking man before he started to drink. Big, square, high color. But he became my mortal enemy . . . Did I ever show you that? (*He takes out a small piece of paper.*) Careful . . . When I set up a home for my brother and sister, one day we were all out, and he came around and ripped up all my sister's clothes and shoes. Drunk, of course. A few days later he came around to apologize and ask for some money, and I threw him out . . . The next day he left this note . . . "You are welcome to your burden."

Gene. And you kept it?

Tom. Yes. I never saw him again until many years later he was dying, in Bellevue, and someone got word to me, and I went down and asked him if he wanted anything. He said he'd like some fruit. So I sent him in a few oranges. He died the next day.

Gene. There must have been something there to love, to understand.

Tom. In my father? (*Shakes his head "no."* Then he shows Gene *another card.*) Do you remember this? (*He reads.*) "To the best dad in the world on Father's Day." That was in . . . (*Turns over and reads the notation*) 1946 . . . Yes. (*Emotional*) I appreciate that, Gene. That's a lovely tribute. I think I have all your Father's Day cards here. You know, your

mother used to talk of you children as her jewels. Maybe because my interests were different, I've always said you were my dividends . . . You know, I didn't want children, coming from the background I did . . . and we didn't have Alice for a long time. But your mother finally persuaded me. She said they would be a comfort in our old age. And you are, Gene.

Gene (*touched, but embarrassed and uncomfortable*). Well . . .

Tom (*fishes in the drawer and brings out a sheet of paper*). A program of yours from college . . . some glee club concert . . . I've got everything but the kitchen stove in here. (*Looks over the program*) Do you still sing?

Gene (*smiling*). Not in years.

Tom. That's too bad. You had a good voice. But we can't do everything . . . I remember your mother would sit at the piano, hour after hour, and I'd be up here at my desk, and I'd hear you singing.

Gene. You always asked me to sing "When I Grow Too Old to Dream."

Tom. Did I? . . . I don't remember your ever singing that . . . You always seemed to be just finishing when I came into the room . . . (*Looks at* Gene) Did you used to sing that for me?

Gene (*not a joke any more*). No . . . But you always asked me to sing it for you.

Tom. Oh . . . (*Puts the program away*) Well, I enjoyed sitting up here and listening. (*He pokes around in his box and takes something out . . . in tissue paper. He unwraps a picture carefully.*) And that's my mother.

Gene (*gently*). Yes. I've seen that, Dad. It's lovely.

Tom. She was twenty-five when that was taken. She died the next year . . . I carried it in my wallet for years . . . And then I felt I was wearing it out. So I put it away . . . Just a little bit of a thing . . . (*He starts to cry, and the*

deep, deep, sobs finally come and his emaciated body is wracked by them. It is a terrible, almost soundless sobbing. Gene comes
to his father and puts his arms around him
and holds him. After moments) I didn't think
it would be this way . . . I always thought I'd
go first. (He sobs again, gasping for air. Gene
continues to hold him, inevitably moved and
touched by this genuine suffering. Finally,
Tom gets a stern grip on himself.) I'm sorry . . .
(Tries to shake it off) It just comes over me . . .
It'll pass . . . I'll get a hold of myself.
Gene. Don't try, Dad . . . Believe me, it's best.
Tom (angry with himself). No . . . It's just

that . . . I'll be all right. (He turns and blows
his nose.)
Gene. It's rough, Dad . . . It's bound to be
rough.
Tom (shakes his head to snap out of it). It'll
pass . . . it'll pass . . . (Starts to wrap up the
picture of his mother)
Gene. Can I help you put these things away,
Dad?
Tom. No . . . No . . . I can . . . (He seems to be
looking for something he can't find.) Well, if
you would. (Gene helps him wrap the pictures.) I don't know what we'd do without
you . . .

[*And together they put the things back in the box. As they do so,* Gene *is deeply moved with feelings of tenderness for his father. After a few moments he starts, with great consideration.*]

Gene. Dad?

Tom. Yes?

Gene (*carefully*). You remember . . . I wrote you about California . . . and Peggy?

Tom. What?

Gene. The girl . . . in California.

Tom (*on guard*). Oh, yes.

Gene (*putting it carefully, and slowly*). I'm thinking very seriously, Dad . . . of going out there . . . to marry . . . and to live. (Tom *straightens up a little.*) Now, I know this is your home, where you're used to . . . But I'd like you to come out there with me, Dad . . . It's lovely out there, as you said, and we could find an apartment for you, near us. (*This is the most loving gesture* Gene *has made to his father in his life.*)

Tom (*thinks for a moment, then looks at* Gene *with a smile*). You know, I'd like to make a suggestion . . . Why don't you all come live here?

Gene (*explaining calmly*). Peggy has a practice out there.

Tom. A what?

Gene. She's a doctor. I told you. And children with schools and friends.

Tom. We have a big house here. You always liked this house. It's wonderful for children. You used to play baseball out back, and there's that basketball thing.

Gene. Dad, I'd like to get away from this part of the country for a while. It's been rough here ever since Carol died. It would be good for you too, getting away.

Tom. Your mother would be very happy to have the house full of children again. I won't be around long, and then it would be all yours.

Gene. That's very kind of you, Dad. But I don't think that would work. Besides her work and the children, all Peggy's family is out there.

Tom. Your family is here.

Gene. Yes, I know.

Tom. Just me, of course.

Gene. You see, the children's father is out there, and they're very fond of him and see him a lot.

Tom. Divorced?

Gene. Yes.

Tom. You know, Gene, I'm only saying this for your own good, but you went out there very soon after Carol's death, and you were exhausted from her long illness, and well, naturally, very susceptible . . . I was wondering if you've really waited long enough to know your own mind.

Gene. I know my own mind.

Tom. I mean, taking on another man's children. You know, children are far from the blessing they're supposed to be . . . And then there's the whole matter of discipline, of keeping them in line. You may rule them with a rod of iron, but if this father—

Gene (*cutting in*). I happen to love Peggy.

Tom (*looks at* Gene *a long moment*). Did you mention this business of California to your mother?

Gene (*gets the point, but keeps level*). She mentioned it to me, and told me to go ahead, with her blessings.

Tom. She would say that, of course . . . But I warned you.

Gene (*turns away*). For God's sake—

Tom (*giving up, angry*). All right, go ahead. I can manage . . . (*His sarcasm*) Send me a Christmas card . . . if you remember.

Gene (*enraged*). Dad!

Tom. What?

Gene. I've asked you to come with me!

Tom. And I've told you I'm not going.

Gene. I understand that, but not this "send me a Christmas card, if you remember."

Tom. I'm very sorry if I offended you. Your mother always said I mustn't raise my voice to you. (*Suddenly hard and vicious*) Did you want me to make it easy for you the way your mother did? Well, I won't. If you want to go, go!

Gene. Dad!

Tom (*running on*). I've always known it would come to this when your mother was gone. I was tolerated around this house because I paid the bills and——

Gene. Shut up!

Tom (*coming at him*). Don't you——

Gene (*shouting*). Shut up! I asked you to come with me. What do you want? For God's sake, what do you want? If I lived here the rest of my life, it wouldn't be enough for you. I've tried, I've tried to be the dutiful son, to maintain the image of the good son . . . Commanded into your presence on every conceivable occasion . . . Easter, Christmas, birthdays, Thanksgiving . . . Even that Thanksgiving when Carol was dying, and I was staying with her in the hospital. "We miss you so. Our day is nothing without you. Couldn't you come up for an hour or two after you leave Carol?" You had no regard for what was really going on . . . My wife was dying!

Tom. Is it so terrible to want to see your own son?

Gene. It is terrible to want to possess him . . . entirely and completely!

Tom (*coldly . . . after a moment*). There will be some papers to sign for your mother's estate. Be sure you leave an address with my lawyer . . .

Gene (*cutting in*). Dad!

Tom (*cutting, with no self-pity*). From tonight on, you can consider me dead. (*Turns on him in a rage of resentment*) I gave you everything. Since I was a snot-nosed kid I've worked my fingers to the bone. You've had everything and I had nothing. I put a roof over your head, clothes on your back——

Gene. Food on the table.

Tom. ——things I never had.

Gene. I know!

Tom. You ungrateful . . . !

Gene (*seizes him, almost as though he would hit him*). What do you want for gratitude? Nothing, nothing would be enough. You have resented everything you ever gave me. The orphan boy in you has resented everything. I'm sorry about your miserable childhood. When I was a kid, and you told me those stories, I used to go up to my room at night and cry. But there is nothing I can do about it . . . and it does not excuse everything . . . I *am* grateful to you. I also admire you and respect you, and stand in awe of what you have done with your life. I will never be able to touch it. (Tom *looks at him with contempt.*) But it does not make me love you. And I wanted to love you. (Tom *snorts his disbelief.*) You hated your father. I saw what it did to you. I did not want to hate you.

Tom. I don't care what you feel about me.

Gene. I do! (*He moves away from his father.*) I came so close to loving you tonight . . . I'd never felt so open to you. You don't know what it cost me to ask you to come with me . . . when I have never been able to sit in a room alone with you . . . Did you really think your door was always open to me?

Tom. It was not my fault if you never came in.

Gene (*starts to move out*). Goodbye, Dad. I'll arrange for someone to come in.

Tom (*shouting*). I don't want anyone to come in! I can take care of myself! I have always had to take care of myself. Who needs you? Get out!

[*This last, wildly at* Gene. *The lights dim out quickly, except for a lingering light on* Gene.]

Gene (*after a few moments*). That night I left my father's house forever . . . I took the first right and the second left . . . and this time I went as far as California . . . Peggy and I visited him once or twice . . . and then he came to California to visit us, and had a fever and swollen ankles, and we put him in a hospital, and he never left . . . The reason we gave, and which he could accept, for not leaving . . . the swollen ankles. But the real reason . . . the arteries were hardening, and he gradually over several years slipped into complete and speechless senility . . . with all his life centered in his burning eyes. (*A Nurse wheels in* Tom, *dressed in a heavy, warm bathrobe, and wearing a white linen golf cap to protect his head from drafts. The* Nurse *withdraws into the shadows.*) When I would visit him, and we would sit and look at each other, his eyes would mist over and his nostrils would pinch with emotion . . . But I never could learn what the emotion was . . . anger . . . or love . . . or regret . . . One day, sitting in his wheelchair and staring without comprehension at television . . . he died . . . alone . . . without even an orange in his hand. (*The light fades on* Tom.) Death ends a life . . . but it does not end a relationship, which struggles on in the survivor's mind . . . toward some resolution, which it never finds. Alice said I would not accept the sadness of the world . . . What did it matter if I never loved him, or if he never loved me? . . . Perhaps she was right . . . But, still, when I hear the word *father* . . . (*He cannot express it . . . there is still the longing, the emotion. He looks around . . . out . . . as though he would finally be able to express it, but he can only say . . .*) It matters. (*He turns and walks slowly away, into the shadows . . . as the lights dim.*)

[*Curtain.*]

FOR STUDY AND DISCUSSION

1. The tension between Tom and Gene mounts steadily in Act Two. How do Tom's reactions to Margaret's death differ from Gene's?

2. Why do Tom's actions make Gene angry? Where do you also learn that Gene is sometimes touched by his father and wants to feel love for him?

3. Although she is mentioned in Act One, Alice does not appear in the play until Act Two. How is Alice's character a contrast, or a foil, to Gene's? What new problem does Alice force into the open?

4. In the scene beginning on page 684, Tom is angry and hurt by his children's attempts to arrange for his care. What do you think of each character in this important scene? What truths are revealed about each one?

5. The major conflict in this play takes place between Gene and his father, but there is also a conflict between Gene and his sister. Look at the scene that begins on page 688, where Alice tries to make Gene see their father the way she sees him. What does Alice want Gene to think of his father? What is Gene's response?

6. At what points in the final scene of the play does it seem that Gene and his father might be able to change and begin to show their love for each other? When does the play reach its climax—that point when you know that this will not happen as Gene hopes it will?

7. Find the lines in which the play's title is explained.

8. What is the significance of Gene's saying that his father died "without even an orange in his hand"?

THE PLAY AS A WHOLE

1. In classical Greek tragedies, a father and a son like Tom and Gene might have suffered because they were cursed by the gods. Modern dramatists often look for other explanations for human problems. How is Tom's basic problem explained in this play? How is Tom's feeling for his own father like a "curse" that is passed on to another generation?

2. This play, like many works of literature, is about a search. On page 689, Gene says:

> . . . the "old man" in me feels something very deep, wants to extend some kind of mercy to that old man. I never had a father. I ran away from him. He ran away from me. . . . Maybe it is time we found each other.

How would you explain Gene's statement in your own words? What has happened to Gene's search by the end of the play, and how does this ending make you feel?

3. In Act One (page 663), Margaret makes this speech to Gene:

> What a shame that children can't see their parents when they're young and courting, and in love. All they see them being is tolerant, sympathetic, forbearing and devoted. All the qualities that are so unimportant to passionate young people.

In what ways are Gene and Alice able to show tolerance, sympathy, forbearing, and devotion to their father? In what ways do they fail? What accounts for their failure?

4. How would you define the theme of this play—the central truth about life that the playwright is revealing?

FOR DRAMATIZATION

Imagine that you are an actor or actress in *I Never Sang for My Father*. You must convey to the audience the characters' feelings and thoughts as they speak these lines of dialogue:

Gene (*the anger building*). No, Dad, I've got to run along.

Gene (*bewildered by this, but doesn't want to get into an argument*). Let's drop by and see Mother first.

Alice (*almost in tears*). I can't help it. You've never faced up to him. You'd let him ruin your life.

Tom (*sarcastically*). I don't want to ruin your life.

Alice (*pleading*). But I saw you. Didn't you see yourself there, when he started to rage? Didn't you feel yourself pull in? You shrank.

How can you use your voice to convey emotion? Practice reading aloud each of these lines from the play, experimenting with volume, pitch, emphasis, and pauses. Then choose one scene from the play, and work with another student (or other students) in reading aloud the dialogue to convey the feelings you think the author intends.

ABOUT THE AUTHOR

Robert Anderson (1917–   ) has been an important American dramatist since 1953, when his play *Tea and Sympathy* became a Broadway hit. Anderson was born in New York City and graduated from Harvard University. He has written numerous plays for the stage, radio, and television. He has also taught courses in drama and playwriting, and advises aspiring dramatists to follow his example: "All I can tell you—if you really want to learn to do something, try teaching it. That's how I learned to write plays." Anderson's notable successes include a comedy called *You Know I Can't Hear You When the Water's Running* and the screenplay for the movie *The Nun's Story*.

Practice in Reading and Writing

READING AND WRITING ABOUT LITERATURE

As in a short story or novel, the *theme* of a play is its central meaning—the truth or insight about life or human nature that the play expresses or illuminates. Below is one critic's opinion on the meaning of *Antigone*. In a brief essay, tell whether you agree or disagree with this comment. Use evidence from the play to support your opinion.

> A careful reading of *Antigone* shows that neither Antigone nor Creon singly is the true subject, but that the play is designed to show a pattern of events, a pattern that emerges in the life of Antigone *and* in the life of Creon, as well as in the lives of the brothers Eteocles and Polyneices and a number of other figures mentioned, chiefly by the Chorus, during the course of the action. Choose one good to the exclusion of another—and it seems to be the nature of great men to do so—the play shows, and *this* will inevitably happen. *This* is the plot of the play, and the play is shaped in all its parts to reveal and define this plot.
>
> Alvin B. Kernan
> *Character and Conflict*

Three critical opinions about the theme of the play *Julius Caesar* follow. Choose one of the opinions and write at least one paragraph to support or dispute it. Use evidence from the play to defend your opinion.

> [Brutus'] death is but a symbol of a greater disaster, the death of liberty. And the defeat is brought about, not at Philippi, but through the corruption and instability of human nature.
>
> John Dover Wilson
> Introduction to *Julius Caesar*

Brutus best interprets the play's theme: Do evil that good
may come, and see what does come!

Harley Granville-Barker
Prefaces to Shakespeare

We are asked to see that while a just man in private life is to
be praised, a just man in public life may very well bring
about catastrophe. The wicked—or, like Caesar, the conceited and superstitious—may be the genius as a ruler.

William and Barbara Rosen
Introduction to *Julius Caesar*

I Never Sang for My Father is a good example of contemporary American drama. The first quotation that follows is
from the text introduction to that play. The second is a comment from a critic. Referring directly to the play itself, write
a brief essay telling whether you think these statements do
or do not apply to Anderson's drama, and why. Before you
begin, of course, be sure you know what a "static emotional
impasse" is.

In many modern dramas, the conflict is caused by social or
emotional factors. . . . Some modern plays do not even
present any resolution to the conflict.

Sometimes poignant, sometimes sentimental, always earnest, it [*I Never Sang for My Father*] presents a static emotional impasse . . .

Time magazine

For Further Reading

Anouilh, Jean, *Antigone* (included in *Anouilh: Five Plays*, paperback, Hill & Wang, 1958)
 Anouilh's adaptation of this ancient Greek drama was first performed in 1944 in Nazi-occupied Paris. Anouilh concentrates on the character of Antigone, the heroic individual who says no to a chief of state who values law more than freedom.

Bolt, Robert, *A Man for All Seasons* (paperback, Vintage, 1966)
 This tragedy focuses on the conflict faced by Thomas More, the popular Chancellor of England, who obeyed his conscience instead of his King (Henry VIII) and who paid for his convictions with his life. The play was made into an Academy Award-winning movie.

Hewes, Henry, editor, *Famous American Plays of the 1940's* (paperback, Dell, 1960)
 Five memorable American plays are included in this book: *The Skin of Our Teeth* by Thornton Wilder; *Home of the Brave* by Arthur Laurents; *All My Sons* by Arthur Miller; *Lost in the Stars* by Maxwell Anderson; and *The Member of the Wedding* by Carson McCullers.

Gibson, William, *The Miracle Worker* (Knopf, 1957; paperback, Bantam)
 Gibson's appealing realistic drama tells how Annie Sullivan taught the blind and deaf Helen Keller to speak. The play has appeared on television, on stage, and in the movies.

Hansberry, Lorraine, *A Raisin in the Sun* (paperback, Signet, 1961)
 Winner of the New York Drama Critics Circle Award for the 1958–1959 season, this realistic play shows the tensions that erupt as a Chicago family tries to start a new life after coming into a legacy.

Kaufman, George, and Moss Hart, *The Man Who Came to Dinner* (included in *Six Modern American Plays*, paperback, Modern Library, 1966)
 This comedy is based on a hilarious possibility: what if someone came for dinner and just never went home?

Kesserling, Joseph, *Arsenic and Old Lace* (in *Comedy Tonight! Broadway Picks Its Favorite Plays*, edited by Mary Sherwin, Doubleday, 1977)
 This comedy features two kindly Victorian ladies who kill lonely old men with poisoned elderberry wine, as their frantic nephew tries to put a stop to the mayhem.

Lindsay, Howard, and Russel Crouse, *Life with Father* and *Life with Mother* (Knopf, 1953)
 This is an illustrated edition of two great comedies about family life in America.

Shaw, George Bernard, *The Portable Bernard Shaw* (paperback, Penguin, 1977)
 This collection of some of the works of the great Irish satirist includes *The Devil's Disciple*, a comedy set during the American Revolution, and *Pygmalion*, a comedy and love story about a poor Cockney flower-seller who is transformed by her tutor, Henry Higgins.

Sweetkind, Morris, editor, *Ten Great One Act Plays* (paperback, Bantam)
 The Bear, a boisterous farce by the Russian dramatist Anton Chekhov, and *Riders to the Sea*, a brooding tragedy by the Irish dramatist John Millington Synge, are among the one-act dramas included here.

Williams, Tennessee, *The Glass Menagerie* (included in *Six Modern American Plays*, paperback, Modern Library, 1966)
 An American classic, Williams' play dramatizes the efforts of a mother to push her withdrawn, sensitive daughter into the "real" world of boyfriends and jobs. The poignant story of Laura's trembling efforts to please her first "gentleman caller" is remembered by her brother Tom.

Van Druten, John, *I Remember Mama* (included in *Eight American Ethnic Plays*, edited by Francis Griffith and Joseph Mersand, paperback, Scribner's, 1974)
 Based on Kathryn Forbes's novel *Mama's Bank Account*, this comedy tells of a Norwegian family living in San Francisco, whose security for years is based on a mythical "bank account."

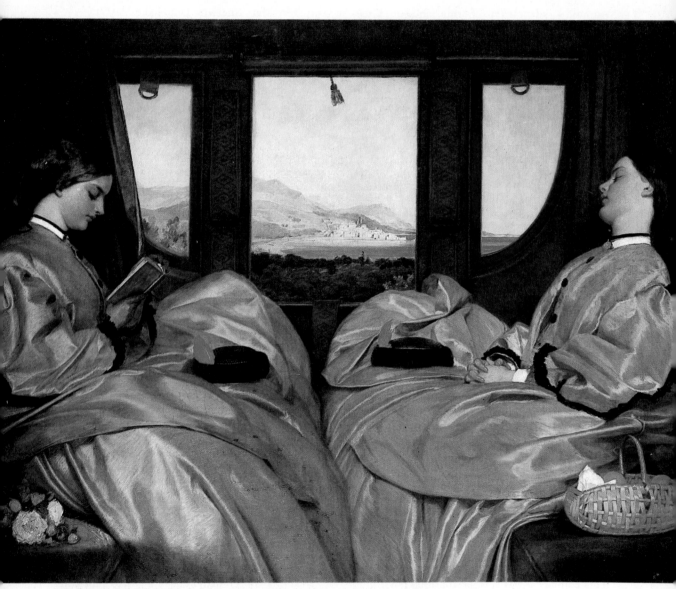

The Traveling Companions. Oil painting by Augustus Leopold Egg (1816-1863). Birmingham Museums and Art Gallery.

THE NOVEL

The novel is one of the most popular and familiar of all literary forms. Down through the ages, people have always enjoyed a good story. The novel—a long, fictional prose narrative which usually has many characters and a strong plot or story line—has allowed readers the pleasure of becoming involved with new people and identifying with problems and feelings that are very much like their own.

The novel is a comparative newcomer to English literature. It appeared in England after a major political and social revolution that took place in the mid-seventeenth century. In the course of that revolution, the English monarchy in the person of King Charles I was overthrown by the followers of Oliver Cromwell, who sought a more democratic form of government. Though the monarchy was restored in 1660, a new social class—the middle class of merchants, bankers, and shopkeepers—had started its rise to power. This new social class firmly established itself by the eighteenth century.

Before this, only a handful of the population could read, and the art of printing was crude and expensive. But by the eighteenth century, education had spread, and printing was so vastly improved that books could be produced more rapidly and inexpensively. Up to this time, most stories in English literature had been about elevated characters—kings, queens, princes, knights, and larger-than-life heroes—and the dominant writing style had been poetic, dignified, and often elaborate. The new middle class was more interested in stories of ordinary people like themselves, and they wanted the stories told in the language of their own everyday speech.

One of the first writers to meet this demand was Daniel Defoe. The hero of his story *Robinson Crusoe* (1719) is an ordinary trader who tells about his adventures in the everyday language of the shop, street, and trading ship. Defoe's books are basically adventure or travel stories, in which the hero or heroine becomes involved in one episode after another. There is little or no plot—that is, there is no development of a major conflict, with a beginning, a middle, and an end.

In 1740 a printer named Samuel Richardson published a pious, sentimental story called *Pamela; or Virtue Rewarded.* The story is told as a series of letters which a servant girl writes to her friends. The letters tell how the master pursues the girl, how she succeeds in foiling his schemes, and how she eventually reforms him and marries him. *Pamela* is often regarded as the first English novel. It has a definite shape or plot, in which a single theme—here, the idea of virtue getting its reward—is introduced, developed, and resolved.

Elements of the Novel

The novel has taken on many variations since Richardson's day, but it has retained certain fundamental elements. The *plot* is the pattern of related events that make up the story. The plot entangles the characters in a *conflict*—a struggle that might take place between two characters, or within a character's mind. As the conflict becomes more involved, the story moves toward a *climax*, or moment of great emotional intensity. The novel ends with a *resolution*, or disentanglement of the conflict. In many long and complex novels, you will find several related plots and conflicts in operation, though one plot and its conflict are usually dominant.

Effective *characterization*, the creation of interesting, believable characters, is another important element of the novel. One way to create characters is to describe their physical appearance and give each person a single outstanding trait. Generally, however, novelists have the leisure to create characters in more depth—by looking inside them, by examining their thoughts, feelings, and motivations. Novelists can create characters by describing their actions, their gestures, their talk, and sometimes their physical surroundings. For example, the people in the novels of Ernest Hemingway are characterized mainly by what they say, rather than by detailed physical descriptions.

Like all major works of literature, the novel has a *theme*—the idea or truth about life that the story reveals. For example, the theme of Mark Twain's great novel *The Adventures of Huckleberry Finn* might be expressed in this way: the spirit of youth will break down social and physical boundaries to discover new ideas and uncharted territories. In some novels, theme is immediately apparent and may even be stated directly by the writer. In others, theme is introduced and devel-

Illustration from Daniel Defoe's *Robinson Crusoe*.

Manuscript page from the *Autobiography* of American novelist Mark Twain.

oped more subtly. Sometimes the reader can get a hint of the theme from the images or symbols used over and over again by the writer. In *The Adventures of Huckleberry Finn,* for example, the Mississippi River — exciting, untamed, and free — can be seen as a symbol of Huck's restless desire to "light out" for new territories.

The Bookseller and the Author (1784). Caricature by Thomas Rowlandson (1757-1827).

Copyright reserved. Reproduced by gracious permission of Her Majesty Queen Elizabeth II.

Novelists approach and write their stories in many different ways. They will select techniques that best suit their own particular skills, as well as the content and nature of their own particular stories. For example, they can make use of one or more of the three major *points of view.* In the *omniscient,* or all-knowing, point of view, the writer stands outside the novel and reveals the unspoken thoughts and feelings of all the characters. In the *first-person* point of view, the writer pretends to be a character in the story and narrates the events through the voice of this character. In the *limited third-person* point of view, the writer stands outside the story but narrates all events from the vantage point of one character only.

A writer's characteristic form of expression is known as his or her *style*. Some writers use an elaborate, formal style; others may write in plain, informal language or even in slang. Some novelists include long poetic passages of description; some use a great deal of dialogue; and so on.

To some extent, style determines a novel's *tone*—the attitude the writer takes toward the story and its characters. Satiric novelists may ridicule their characters in a scornful, biting manner. Comic novelists, on the other hand, tend to laugh sympathetically with their characters, rather than at them. Other writers may be detached and objective, or nostalgic and personal. Style and tone are closely linked. Together they make up the writer's voice, a personal signature, tying the work together and making it unmistakably the writer's own.

Le Quai Conti (1846). Oil painting by William Parrot. Musée Carnavalet, Paris.

John Steinbeck

Two qualities mark the work of American writer John Steinbeck (1902–1968): a deep feeling for nature and a profound sympathy for people. With the detachment of a scientist, Steinbeck can view his characters as living on a purely instinctual level, moved by forces they can hardly understand or control. But we also find his characters striving toward wisdom, struggling, even under the most brutal conditions, to realize their decency and dignity as human beings.

Steinbeck was born in Salinas, California, a state that has provided the settings for many of his stories. He attended Stanford University where he specialized in marine biology. He worked at odd laboring jobs after he left college, and he wrote. Until the publication of *Tortilla Flat* in 1935, however, his writing earned him little money. In 1937 Steinbeck achieved literary success with *Of Mice and Men*, which he followed two years later with his masterpiece, *The Grapes of Wrath. The Grapes of Wrath,* a novel set in the Great Depression, depicts the tragic plight of the "Okies"—Oklahoma farmers who fled from the Dust Bowl and migrated to California to seek jobs as fruit pickers. It is a work of epic scope and was quickly recognized as one of the great American novels. *The Grapes of Wrath* was awarded the Pulitzer Prize and made Steinbeck one of the most widely known writers of our time. His career was capped in 1962, when he was awarded the Nobel Prize for literature. In announcing the award, the Swedish Academy said of Steinbeck: ". . . he had no mind to be an unoffending comforter and entertainer. Instead, the topics he chose were serious and denunciatory . . . ."

In 1940, Steinbeck sailed in a sardine boat with his friend the biologist Edward F. Ricketts to collect marine invertebrates from the beaches of the Gulf of California. The expedition was described by the two men in a book called *The Sea of Cortez.* In one part of *The Sea of Cortez,* Steinbeck describes how, while stopping off in the harbor town of La Paz in Mexico, he heard a story about a poor Indian boy who found a magnificent pearl. Steinbeck later transformed this story into a novel that he calls a *parable*—a tale that is told to present a moral lesson of universal significance, a story that speaks to all people, everywhere.

The Pearl

John Steinbeck

"In the town they tell the story of the great pearl—how it was found and how it was lost again. They tell of Kino, the fisherman, and of his wife, Juana, and of the baby, Coyotito.[1] And because the story has been told so often, it has taken root in every man's mind. And, as with all retold tales that are in people's hearts, there are only good and bad things and black and white things and good and evil things and no in-between anywhere.

"If this story is a parable, perhaps everyone takes his own meaning from it and reads his own life into it. In any case, they say in the town that . . ."

---

1. **Kino** (kē′nō); **Juana** (hwä′nä); **Coyotito** (kō′yō-tē′tō).

I

Kino awakened in the near dark. The stars still shone and the day had drawn only a pale wash of light in the lower sky to the east. The roosters had been crowing for some time, and the early pigs were already beginning their ceaseless turning of twigs and bits of wood to see whether anything to eat had been over-looked. Outside the brush house in the tuna[1] clump, a covey of little birds chittered and flurried with their wings.

Kino's eyes opened, and he looked first at the lightening square which was the door and

---

1. **tuna:** a prickly-pear plant found in the tropics.

then he looked at the hanging box where Coyotito slept. And last he turned his head to Juana, his wife, who lay beside him on the mat, her blue head shawl over her nose and over her breasts and around the small of her back. Juana's eyes were open too. Kino could never remember seeing them closed when he awakened. Her dark eyes made little reflected stars. She was looking at him as she was always looking at him when he awakened.

Kino heard the little splash of morning waves on the beach. It was very good — Kino closed his eyes again to listen to his music. Perhaps he alone did this and perhaps all of his people did it. His people had once been great makers of songs so that everything they saw or thought or did or heard became a song. That was very long ago. The songs remained; Kino knew them, but no new songs were added. That does not mean that there were no personal songs. In Kino's head there was a song now, clear and soft, and if he had been able to speak it, he would have called it the Song of the Family.

His blanket was over his nose to protect him from the dank air. His eyes flicked to a rustle beside him. It was Juana arising, almost soundlessly. On her hard bare feet she went to the hanging box where Coyotito slept, and she leaned over and said a little reassuring word. Coyotito looked up for a moment and closed his eyes and slept again.

Juana went to the fire pit and uncovered a coal and fanned it alive while she broke little pieces of brush over it.

Now Kino got up and wrapped his blanket about his head and nose and shoulders. He slipped his feet into his sandals and went outside to watch the dawn.

Outside the door he squatted down and gathered the blanket ends about his knees. He saw the specks of Gulf clouds flame high in the air. And a goat came near and sniffed at him and stared with its cold yellow eyes. Behind him Juana's fire leaped into flame and threw spears of light through the chinks of the brush-house wall and threw a wavering square of light out the door. A late moth blustered in to find the fire. The Song of the Family came now from behind Kino. And the rhythm of the family song was the grinding stone where Juana worked the corn for the morning cakes.

The dawn came quickly now, a wash, a glow, a lightness, and then an explosion of fire as the sun arose out of the Gulf. Kino looked down to cover his eyes from the glare. He could hear the pat of the corncakes in the house and the rich smell of them on the cooking plate. The ants were busy on the ground, big black ones with shiny bodies, and little dusty quick ants. Kino watched with the detachment of God while a dusty ant frantically tried to escape the sand trap an ant lion[2] had dug for him. A thin, timid dog came close and, at a soft word from Kino, curled up, arranged its tail neatly over its feet, and laid its chin delicately on the pile. It was a black dog with yellow-gold spots where its eyebrows should have been. It was a morning like other mornings and yet perfect among mornings.

Kino heard the creak of the rope when Juana took Coyotito out of his hanging box and cleaned him and hammocked him in her shawl in a loop that placed him close to her breast. Kino could see these things without looking at them. Juana sang softly an ancient song that had only three notes and yet endless variety of interval. And this was part of the family song too. It was all part. Sometimes it rose to an aching chord that caught the throat, saying this is safety, this is warmth, this is the *Whole*.

---

2. **ant lion:** a large insect whose larvae trap ants in pits.

Across the brush fence were other brush houses, and the smoke came from them too, and the sound of breakfast, but those were other songs, their pigs were other pigs, their wives were not Juana. Kino was young and strong and his black hair hung over his brown forehead. His eyes were warm and fierce and bright and his mustache was thin and coarse. He lowered his blanket from his nose now, for the dark poisonous air was gone and the yellow sunlight fell on the house. Near the brush fence two roosters bowed and feinted at each other with squared wings and neck feathers ruffed out. It would be a clumsy fight. They were not game chickens. Kino watched them for a moment, and then his eyes went up to a flight of wild doves twinkling inland to the hills. The world was awake now, and Kino arose and went into his brush house.

As he came through the door Juana stood up from the glowing fire pit. She put Coyotito back in his hanging box and then she combed her black hair and braided it in two braids and tied the ends with thin green ribbon. Kino squatted by the fire pit and rolled a hot corncake and dipped it in sauce and ate it. And he drank a little pulque[3] and that was breakfast. That was the only breakfast he had ever known outside of feast days and one incredible fiesta on cookies that had nearly killed him. When Kino had finished, Juana came back to the fire and ate her breakfast. They had spoken once, but there is not need for speech if it is only a habit anyway. Kino sighed with satisfaction—and that was conversation.

The sun was warming the brush house, breaking through its crevices in long streaks. And one of the streaks fell on the hanging box where Coyotito lay, and on the ropes that held it.

It was a tiny movement that drew their eyes to the hanging box. Kino and Juana froze in their positions. Down the rope that hung the baby's box from the roof support a scorpion moved slowly. His stinging tail was straight out behind him, but he could whip it up in a flash of time.

Kino's breath whistled in his nostrils and he opened his mouth to stop it. And then the startled look was gone from him and the rigidity from his body. In his mind a new song had come, the Song of Evil the music of the enemy, of any foe of the family, a savage, secret, dangerous melody, and underneath, the Song of the Family cried plaintively.

The scorpion moved delicately down the rope toward the box. Under her breath Juana repeated an ancient magic to guard against such evil, and on top of that she muttered a Hail Mary[4] between clenched teeth. But Kino was in motion. His body glided quietly across the room, noislessly and smoothly. His hands were in front of him, palms down, and his eyes were on the scorpion. Beneath it in the hanging box Coyotito laughed and reached up his hand toward it. It sensed danger when Kino was almost within reach of it. It stopped, and its tail rose up over its back in little jerks and the curved thorn on the tail's end glistened.

Kino stood perfectly still. He could hear Juana whispering the old magic again, and he could hear the evil music of the enemy. He could not move until the scorpion moved, and it felt for the source of the death that was coming to it. Kino's hand went forward very slowly, very smoothly. The thorned tail

---

3. **pulque** (pōōl'kä'): a fermented, milky drink made from the juice of a desert plant.

4. **Hail Mary:** a prayer to the Virgin Mary.

jerked upright. And at that moment the laughing Coyotito shook the rope and the scorpion fell.

Kino's hand leaped to catch it, but it fell past his fingers, fell on the baby's shoulder, landed and struck. Then, snarling, Kino had it, had it in his fingers, rubbing it to a paste in his hands. He threw it down and beat it into the earth floor with his fist, and Coyotito screamed with pain in his box. But Kino beat and stamped the enemy until it was only a fragment and a moist place in the dirt. His teeth were bared and fury flared in his eyes and the Song of the Enemy roared in his ears.

But Juana had the baby in her arms now. She found the puncture with redness starting from it already. She put her lips down over the puncture and sucked hard and spat and sucked again while Coyotito screamed.

Kino hovered; he was helpless, he was in the way.

The screams of the baby brought the neighbors. Out of their brush houses they poured — Kino's brother Juan Tomás and his fat wife Apolonia and their four children crowded in the door and blocked the entrance, while behind them others tried to look in, and one small boy crawled among legs to have a look. And those in front passed the word back to those behind — "Scorpion. The baby has been stung."

Juana stopped sucking the puncture for a moment. The little hole was slightly enlarged and its edges whitened from the sucking, but the red swelling extended farther around it in a hard lymphatic mound.[5] And all of these people knew about the scorpion. An adult might be very ill from the sting, but a baby could easily die from the poison. First, they knew, would come swelling and fever and

---

5. **lymphatic mound:** a swelling caused by infection.

tightened throat, and then cramps in the stomach, and then Coyotito might die if enough of the poison had gone in. But the stinging pain of the bite was going away. Coyotito's screams turned to moans.

Kino had wondered often at the iron in his patient, fragile wife. She, who was obedient and respectful and cheerful and patient, she could arch her back in child pain with hardly a cry. She could stand fatigue and hunger almost better than Kino himself. In the canoe she was like a strong man. And now she did a most surprising thing.

"The doctor," she said. "Go to get the doctor."

The word was passed out among the neighbors where they stood close packed in the little yard behind the brush fence. And they repeated among themselves, "Juana wants the doctor." A wonderful thing, a memorable thing, to want the doctor. To get him would be a remarkable thing. The doctor never came to the cluster of brush houses. Why should he, when he had more than he could do to take care of the rich people who lived in the stone and plaster houses of the town.

"He would not come," the people in the yard said.

"He would not come," the people in the door said, and the thought got into Kino.

"The doctor would not come," Kino said to Juana.

She looked up at him, her eyes as cold as the eyes of a lioness. This was Juana's first baby—this was nearly everything there was in Juana's world. And Kino saw her determination and the music of the family sounded in his head with a steely tone.

"Then we will go to him," Juana said, and with one hand she arranged her dark blue shawl over her head and made of one end of it a sling to hold the moaning baby and made of the other end of it a shade over his eyes to pro-

tect him from the light. The people in the door pushed against those behind to let her through. Kino followed her. They went out of the gate to the rutted path and the neighbors followed them.

The thing had become a neighborhood affair. They made a quick soft-footed procession into the center of the town, first Juana and Kino, and behind them Juan Tomás and Apolonia, her big stomach jiggling with the strenuous pace, then all the neighbors with the children trotting on the flanks. And the yellow sun threw their black shadows ahead of them so that they walked on their own shadows.

They came to the place where the brush houses stopped and the city of stone and plaster began, the city of harsh outer walls and inner cool gardens where a little water played and the bougainvillea[6] crusted the walls with purple and brick-red and white. They heard from the secret gardens the singing of caged birds and heard the splash of cooling water on hot flagstones. The procession crossed the blinding plaza and passed in front of the church. It had grown now, and on the outskirts the hurrying newcomers were being softly informed how the baby had been stung by a scorpion, how the father and mother were taking it to the doctor.

And the newcomers, particularly the beggars from the front of the church who were great experts in financial analysis, looked quickly at Juana's old blue skirt, saw the tears in her shawl, appraised the green ribbon on her braids, read the age of Kino's blanket and the thousand washings of his clothes, and set them down as poverty people and went along to see what kind of drama might develop. The four beggars in front of the church knew ev-

---

6. **bougainvillea** (boo′gən-vĭl′ē-ə): a vine covered with bright flowers.

erything in the town. They were students of the expressions of young women as they went into confession, and they saw them as they came out and read the nature of the sin. They knew every little scandal and some very big crimes. They slept at their posts in the shadow of the church so that no one crept in for consolation without their knowledge. And they knew the doctor. They knew his ignorance, his cruelty, his avarice, his appetites, his sins. They knew his clumsy operations and the little brown pennies he gave sparingly for alms. They had seen his corpses go into the church. And, since early Mass was over and business was slow, they followed the procession, these endless searchers after perfect knowledge of their fellow men, to see what the fat lazy doctor would do about an indigent baby with a scorpion bite.

The scurrying procession came at last to the big gate in the wall of the doctor's house. They could hear the splashing water and the singing of caged birds and the sweep of the long brooms on the flagstones. And they could smell the frying of good bacon from the doctor's house.

Kino hesitated a moment. This doctor was not of his people. This doctor was of a race which for nearly four hundred years had beaten and starved and robbed and despised Kino's race, and frightened it too, so that the indigene[7] came humbly to the door. And as always when he came near to one of this race, Kino felt weak and afraid and angry at the same time. Rage and terror went together. He could kill the doctor more easily than he could talk to him, for all of the doctor's race spoke to all of Kino's race as though they were simple animals. And as Kino raised his right hand to the iron ring knocker in the gate, rage swelled in him, and the pounding music of the enemy beat in his ears, and his lips drew tight against his teeth—but with his left hand he reached to take off his hat. The iron ring pounded against the gate. Kino took off his hat and stood waiting. Coyotito moaned a little in Juana's arms and she spoke softly to him. The procession crowded close the better to see and hear.

After a moment the big gate opened a few inches. Kino could see the green coolness of the garden and little splashing fountain through the opening. The man who looked out at him was one of his own race. Kino spoke to him in the old language. "The little one—the firstborn—has been poisoned by the scorpion," Kino said. "He requires the skill of the healer."

The gate closed a little, and the servant refused to speak in the old language. "A little moment," he said. "I go to inform myself," and he closed the gate and slid the bolt home. The glaring sun threw the bunched shadows of the people blackly on the white wall.

In his chamber the doctor sat up in his high bed. He had on his dressing gown of red watered silk that had come from Paris, a little tight over the chest now if it was buttoned. On his lap was a silver tray with a silver chocolate pot and a tiny cup of eggshell china, so delicate that it looked silly when he lifted it with his big hand, lifted it with the tips of thumb and forefinger and spread the other three fingers wide to get them out of the way His eyes rested in puffy little hammocks of flesh and his mouth drooped with discontent. He was growing very stout, and his voice was hoarse with the fat that pressed on his throat. Beside him on a table was a small Oriental gong and a bowl of cigarettes. The furnishings of the room were heavy and dark and gloomy. The pictures were religious, even the large

---

7. **indigene** (ĭn′də-jən): a native or original inhabitant of an area.

tinted photograph of his dead wife, who, if Masses willed and paid for out of her own estate could do it, was in Heaven. The doctor had once for a short time been a part of the great world and his whole subsequent life was memory and longing for France. "That," he said, "was civilized living" — by which he meant that on a small income he had been able to keep a mistress and eat in restaurants. He poured his second cup of chocolate and crumbled a sweet biscuit in his fingers. The servant from the gate came to the open door and stood waiting to be noticed.

"Yes?" the doctor asked.

"It is a little Indian with a baby. He says a scorpion stung it."

The doctor put his cup down gently before he let his anger rise.

"Have I nothing better to do than cure insect bites for 'little Indians'? I am a doctor, not a veterinary."

"Yes, *Patron*,"[8] said the servant.

"Has he any money?" the doctor demanded. "No, they never have any money. I, I alone in the world am supposed to work for nothing — and I am tired of it. See if he has any money!"

At the gate the servant opened the door a trifle and looked out at the waiting people. And this time he spoke in the old language.

---

8. *Patron* (pä-trōn'): master; boss.

"Have you money to pay for the treatment?"

Now Kino reached into a secret place somewhere under his blanket. He brought out a paper folded many times. Crease by crease he unfolded it, until at last there came to view eight small misshapen seed pearls,[9] as ugly and gray as little ulcers, flattened and almost valueless. The servant took the paper and closed the gate again, but this time he was not gone long. He opened the gate just wide enough to pass the paper back.

"The doctor has gone out," he said. "He was called to a serious case." And he shut the gate quickly out of shame.

And now a wave of shame went over the whole procession. They melted away. The beggars went back to the church steps, the stragglers moved off, and the neighbors departed so that the public shaming of Kino would not be in their eyes.

For a long time Kino stood in front of the gate with Juana beside him. Slowly he put his suppliant hat on his head. Then, without warning, he struck the gate a crushing blow with his fist. He looked down in wonder at his split knuckles and at the blood that flowed down between his fingers.

---

9. **seed pearls:** very small, irregularly shaped pearls.

FOR STUDY AND DISCUSSION

1. Steinbeck introduces his major characters and their setting in this first chapter. What details suggest that Kino and Juana are good people who live in harmony with their world?

2. Kino's songs are used to reveal his emotions. For example, the Song of the Family says to Kino: "this is the Whole." What do you think the word *whole* signifies here?

3. A new song intrudes into the Song of the Family when the scorpion appears. What does Kino identify the scorpion with? What events does the scorpion bite set into motion?

4. The doctor is introduced on page 714. How does he contrast with Kino in appearance, in way of life, and in values? What details does Steinbeck use to make the doctor seem evil?

5. What larger social conflict has existed for centuries between the doctor's people and Kino's? How is this larger conflict underscored by the doctor's saying, "I am a doctor, not a veterinary" (page 715)?

II

The town lay on a broad estuary,[1] its old yellow plastered buildings hugging the beach. And on the beach the white and blue canoes that came from Nayarit[2] were drawn up, canoes preserved for generations by a hard shell-like waterproof plaster whose making was a secret of the fishing people. They were high and graceful canoes with curving bow and stern and a braced section midships where a mast could be stepped to carry a small lateen sail.[3]

The beach was yellow sand, but at the water's edge a rubble of shell and algae took its place. Fiddler crabs bubbled and sputtered in their holes in the sand, and in the shallows little lobsters popped in and out of their tiny homes in the rubble and sand. The sea bottom was rich with crawling and swimming and growing things. The brown algae waved in the gentle currents and the green eel grass swayed and little sea horses clung to its stems. Spotted botete,[4] the poison fish, lay on the bottom in the eel-grass beds, and the bright-colored swimming crabs scampered over them.

On the beach the hungry dogs and the hungry pigs of the town searched endlessly for any dead fish or sea bird that might have floated in on a rising tide.

Although the morning was young, the hazy mirage was up. The uncertain air that magnified some things and blotted out others hung over the whole Gulf so that all sights were unreal and vision could not be trusted; so that sea and land had the sharp clarities and the vagueness of a dream. Thus it might

be that the people of the Gulf trust things of the spirit and things of the imagination, but they do not trust their eyes to show them distance or clear outline or any optical exactness. Across the estuary from the town one section of mangroves stood clear and telescopically defined, while another mangrove clump was a hazy black-green blob. Part of the far shore disappeared into a shimmer that looked like water. There was no certainty in seeing, no proof that what you saw was there or was not there. And the people of the Gulf expected all places were that way, and it was not strange to them. A copper haze hung over the water, and the hot morning sun beat on it and made it vibrate blindingly.

The brush houses of the fishing people were back from the beach on the right-hand side of the town, and the canoes were drawn up in front of this area.

Kino and Juana came slowly down to the beach and to Kino's canoe, which was the one thing of value he owned in the world. It was very old. Kino's grandfather had brought it from Nayarit, and he had given it to Kino's father, and so it had come to Kino. It was at once property and source of food, for a man with a boat can guarantee a woman that she will eat something. It is the bulwark against starvation. And every year Kino refinished his canoe with the hard shell-like plaster by the secret method that had also come to him from his father. Now he came to the canoe and touched the bow tenderly as he always did. He laid his diving rock and his basket and the two ropes in the sand by the canoe. And he folded his blanket and laid it in the bow.

Juana laid Coyotito on the blanket, and she placed her shawl over him so that the hot sun could not shine on him. He was quiet now, but the swelling on his shoulder had continued up his neck and under his ear and his face was puffed and feverish. Juana went to

---

1. **estuary:** an inlet of the sea.
2. **Nayarit** (nä′yä-rēt′): a small state in western Mexico, northwest of Mexico City.
3. **lateen** (lă-tēn′) **sail:** a triangular sail hung from a long pole attached to a short mast.
4. **botete** (bō-tā′tā).

the water and waded in. She gathered some brown seaweed and made a flat damp poultice[5] of it, and this she applied to the baby's swollen shoulder, which was as good a remedy as any and probably better than the doctor could have done. But the remedy lacked his authority because it was simple and didn't cost anything. The stomach cramps had not come to Coyotito. Perhaps Juana had sucked out the poison in time, but she had not sucked out her worry over her firstborn. She had not prayed directly for the recovery of the baby—she had prayed that they might find a pearl with which to hire the doctor to cure the

baby, for the minds of people are as unsubstantial as the mirage of the Gulf.

Now Kino and Juana slid the canoe down the beach to the water, and when the bow floated, Juana climbed in, while Kino pushed the stern in and waded beside it until it floated lightly and trembled on the little breaking waves. Then in coordination Juana and Kino drove their double-bladed paddles into the sea, and the canoe creased the water and hissed with speed. The other pearlers were gone out long since. In a few moments Kino could see them clustered in the haze, riding over the oyster bed.

Light filtered down through the water to the bed where the frilly pearl oysters lay fastened to the rubbly bottom, a bottom strewn with shells of broken, opened oysters. This

---

5. **poultice** (pōl'tĭs): a soft, moist substance applied to the body as a remedy.

was the bed that had raised the King of Spain to be a great power in Europe in past years, had helped to pay for his wars, and had decorated the churches for his soul's sake. The gray oysters with ruffles like skirts on the shells, the barnacle-crusted oysters with little bits of weed clinging to the skirts and small crabs climbing over them. An accident could happen to these oysters, a grain of sand could lie in the folds of muscle and irritate the flesh until in self-protection the flesh coated the grain with a layer of smooth cement. But once started, the flesh continued to coat the foreign body until it fell free in some tidal flurry or until the oyster was destroyed. For centuries men had dived down and torn the oysters from the beds and ripped them open, looking for the coated grains of sand. Swarms of fish lived near the bed to live near the oysters thrown back by the searching men and to nibble at the shining inner shells. But the pearls were accidents, and the finding of one was luck, a little pat on the back by God or the gods or both.

Kino had two ropes, one tied to a heavy stone and one to a basket. He stripped off his shirt and trousers and laid his hat in the bottom of the canoe. The water was oily smooth. He took his rock in one hand and his basket in the other, and he slipped feet first over the side and the rock carried him to the bottom. The bubbles rose behind him until the water cleared and he could see. Above, the surface of the water was an undulating mirror of brightness, and he could see the bottoms of the canoes sticking through it.

Kino moved cautiously so that the water would not be obscured with mud or sand. He hooked his foot in the loop on his rock and his hands worked quickly, tearing the oysters loose, some singly, others in clusters. He laid them in his basket. In some places the oysters clung to one another so that they came free in lumps.

Now, Kino's people had sung of everything that happened or existed. They had made songs to the fishes, to the sea in anger and to the sea in calm, to the light and the dark and the sun and the moon, and the songs were all in Kino and in his people—every song that had ever been made, even the ones forgotten. And as he filled his basket the song was in Kino, and the beat of the song was his pounding heart as it ate the oxygen from his held breath, and the melody of the song was the gray-green water and the little scuttling animals and the clouds of fish that flitted by and were gone. But in the song there was a secret little inner song, hardly perceptible, but always there, sweet and secret and clinging, almost hiding in the countermelody, and this was the Song of the Pearl That Might Be, for every shell thrown in the basket might contain a pearl. Chance was against it, but luck and the gods might be for it. And in the canoe above him Kino knew that Juana was making the magic of prayer, her face set rigid and her muscles hard to force the luck, to tear the luck out of the god's hands, for she needed the luck for the swollen shoulder of Coyotito. And because the need was great and the desire was great, the little secret melody of the pearl that might be was stronger this morning. Whole phrases of it came clearly and softly into the Song of the Undersea.

Kino, in his pride and youth and strength, could remain down over two minutes without strain, so that he worked deliberately, selecting the largest shells. Because they were disturbed, the oyster shells were tightly closed. A little to his right a hummock of rubbly rock stuck up, covered with young oysters not ready to take. Kino moved next to the hummock, and then, beside it, under a little overhang, he saw a very large oyster lying by itself, not covered with its clinging brothers. The shell was partly open, for the overhang protected this ancient oyster, and in the liplike muscle Kino saw a ghostly gleam, and then the shell closed down. His heart beat out a heavy rhythm and the melody of the maybe pearl shrilled in his ears. Slowly he forced the oyster loose and held it tightly against his breast. He kicked his foot free from the rock loop, and his body rose to the surface and his black hair gleamed in the sunlight. He reached over the side of the canoe and laid the oyster in the bottom.

Then Juana steadied the boat while he climbed in. His eyes were shining with excitement, but in decency he pulled up his rock, and then he pulled up his basket of oysters and lifted them in. Juana sensed his excitement, and she pretended to look away. It is not good to want a thing too much. It sometimes drives the luck away. You must want it just enough, and you must be very tactful with God or the gods. But Juana stopped breathing. Very deliberately Kino opened his short strong knife. He looked speculatively at the basket. Perhaps it would be better to open *the* oyster last. He took a small oyster from the basket, cut the muscle, searched the folds of flesh, and threw it in the water. Then he seemed to see the great oyster for the first time. He squatted in the bottom of the canoe, picked up the shell and examined it. The flutes were shining black to brown, and only a few small barnacles adhered to the shell. Now Kino was reluctant to open it. What he had seen, he knew, might be a reflection, a piece of flat shell accidentally drifted in or a complete illusion. In this Gulf of uncertain light there were more illusions than realities.

But Juana's eyes were on him and she could not wait. She put her hand on Coyotito's covered head. "Open it," she said softly.

Kino deftly slipped his knife into the edge of the shell. Through the knife he could feel the muscle tighten hard. He worked the blade leverwise and the closing muscle parted and the shell fell apart. The liplike flesh writhed up and then subsided. Kino lifted the flesh, and there it lay, the great pearl, perfect as the moon. It captured the light and refined it and gave it back in silver incandescence. It was as large as a sea gull's egg. It was the greatest pearl in the world.

Juana caught her breath and moaned a little. And to Kino the secret melody of the maybe pearl broke clear and beautiful, rich and warm and lovely, glowing and gloating and triumphant. In the surface of the great pearl he could see dream forms. He picked the pearl from the dying flesh and held it in his palm, and he turned it over and saw that its curve was perfect. Juana came near to stare at it in his hand, and it was the hand he had smashed against the doctor's gate, and the torn flesh of the knuckles was turned grayish white by the sea water.

Instinctively Juana went to Coyotito where he lay on his father's blanket. She lifted the poultice of seaweed and looked at the shoulder. "Kino," she cried shrilly.

He looked past his pearl, and he saw that the swelling was going out of the baby's shoulder, the poison was receding from its body. Then Kino's fist closed over the pearl and his emotion broke over him. He put back his head and howled. His eyes rolled up and he screamed and his body was rigid. The men in the other canoes looked up, startled, and then they dug their paddles into the sea and raced toward Kino's canoe.

FOR STUDY AND DISCUSSION

1. In the opening paragraphs of this chapter, Steinbeck describes the story's setting. How has the setting become part of the people's ways of seeing and thinking?

2. Why does Juana feel that it is "not good to want a thing too much"? What does this reveal about the villagers' attitude toward life?

3. Two of Kino's and Juana's desires seem to be fulfilled at the end of this chapter. One is the finding of the pearl. What other "miracle" has accompanied the discovery of the pearl? Do you think that Kino links the two events? Why or why not?

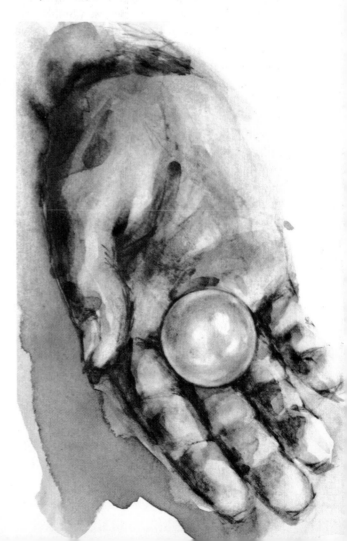

III

A town is a thing like a colonial animal. A town has a nervous system and a head and shoulders and feet. A town is a thing separate from all other towns, so that there are no two towns alike. And a town has a whole emotion. How news travels through a town is a mystery not easily to be solved. News seems to move faster than small boys can scramble and dart to tell it, faster than women can call it over the fences.

Before Kino and Juana and the other fishers had come to Kino's brush house, the nerves of the town were pulsing and vibrating with the news—Kino had found the Pearl of the World. Before panting little boys could strangle out the words, their mothers knew it. The news swept on past the brush houses, and it washed in a foaming wave into the town of stone and plaster. It came to the priest walking in his garden, and it put a thoughtful look in his eyes and a memory of certain repairs necessary to the church. He wondered what the pearl would be worth. And he wondered whether he had baptized Kino's baby, or married him for that matter. The news came to the shopkeepers, and they looked at men's clothes that had not sold so well.

The news came to the doctor where he sat with a woman whose illness was age, though neither she nor the doctor would admit it. And when it was made plain who Kino was, the doctor grew stern and judicious at the same time. "He is a client of mine," the doctor said. "I'm treating his child for a scorpion sting." And the doctor's eyes rolled up a little in their fat hammocks and he thought of Paris. He remembered the room he had lived in there as a great and luxurious place, and he remembered the hard-faced woman who had lived with him as a beautiful and kind girl, although she had been none of these three. The doctor looked past his aged patient and saw himself sitting in a restaurant in Paris and a waiter was just opening a bottle of wine.

The news came early to the beggars in front of the church, and it made them giggle a little with pleasure, for they knew that there is no almsgiver in the world like a poor man who is suddenly lucky.

Kino has found the Pearl of the World. In the town, in little offices, sat the men who bought pearls from the fishers. They waited in their chairs until the pearls came in, and then they cackled and fought and shouted and threatened until they reached the lowest price the fisherman would stand. But there was a price below which they dared not go, for it had happened that a fisherman in despair had given his pearls to the church. And when the buying was over, these buyers sat alone and their fingers played restlessly with the pearls, and they wished they owned the pearls. For there were not many buyers really—there was only one, and he kept these agents in separate offices to give a semblance of competition. The news came to these men, and their eyes squinted and their fingertips burned a little, and each one thought how the patron could not live forever and someone had to take his place. And each one thought how with some capital he could get a new start.

All manner of people grew interested in Kino—people with things to sell and people with favors to ask. Kino had found the Pearl of the World. The essence of pearl mixed with essence of men and a curious dark residue was precipitated. Every man suddenly became related to Kino's pearl, and Kino's pearl went into the dreams, the speculations, the schemes, the plans, the futures, the wishes, the needs, the lusts, the hungers, of everyone, and only one person stood in the way and that was Kino, so that he became curiously every man's enemy. The news stirred up something

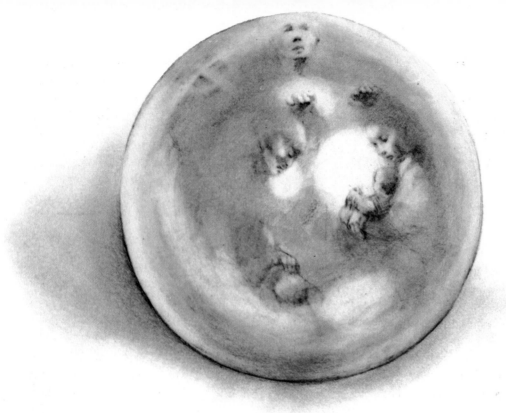

infinitely black and evil in the town; the black distillate was like the scorpion, or like hunger in the smell of food, or like loneliness when love is withheld. The poison sacs of the town began to manufacture venom, and the town swelled and puffed with the pressure of it.

But Kino and Juana did not know these things. Because they were happy and excited they thought everyone shared their joy. Juan Tomás and Apolonia did, and they were the world too. In the afternoon, when the sun had gone over the mountains of the Peninsula to sink in the outward sea, Kino squatted in his house with Juana beside him. And the brush house was crowded with neighbors. Kino held the great pearl in his hand, and it was warm and alive in his hand. And the music of the pearl had merged with the music of the family so that one beautified the other. The neighbors looked at the pearl in Kino's hand and they wondered how such luck could come to any man.

And Juan Tomás, who squatted on Kino's right hand because he was his brother, asked, "What will you do now that you have become a rich man?"

Kino looked into his pearl, and Juana cast her eyelashes down and arranged her shawl to cover her face so that her excitement could not be seen. And in the incandescence of the pearl the pictures formed of the things Kino's mind had considered in the past and had given up as impossible. In the pearl he saw Juana and Coyotito and himself standing and kneeling at the high altar, and they were being married now that they could pay. He spoke softly, "We will be married—in the church."

In the pearl he saw how they were dressed —Juana in a shawl stiff with newness and a new skirt, and from under the long skirt Kino could see that she wore shoes. It was in the pearl—the picture glowing there. He himself was dressed in new white clothes, and he carried a new hat—not of straw but of fine black felt—and he too wore shoes—not sandals but shoes that laced. But Coyotito—he was the one—he wore a blue sailor suit from the United States and a little yachting cap such as Kino had seen once when a pleasure boat put into the estuary. All of these things Kino saw in the lucent[1] pearl and he said, "We will have new clothes."

And the music of the pearl rose like a chorus of trumpets in his ears.

Then to the lovely gray surface of the pearl came the little things Kino wanted: a harpoon to take the place of one lost a year ago, a new harpoon of iron with a ring in the end of the shaft; and—his mind could hardly make the leap—a rifle—but why not, since he was so rich. And Kino saw Kino in the pearl, Kino holding a Winchester carbine. It was the wildest daydreaming and very pleasant. His lips moved hesitantly over this—"A rifle," he said. "Perhaps a rifle."

It was the rifle that broke down the barriers. This was an impossibility, and if he could think of having a rifle whole horizons were burst and he could rush on. For it is said that humans are never satisfied, that you give them one thing and they want something more. And this is said in disparagement, whereas it is one of the greatest talents the species has and one that has made it superior to animals that are satisfied with what they have.

The neighbors, close pressed and silent in the house, nodded their heads at his wild imaginings. And a man in the rear murmured, "A rifle. He will have a rifle."

But the music of the pearl was shrilling with triumph in Kino. Juana looked up, and her eyes were wide at Kino's courage and at his imagination. And electric strength had come to him now the horizons were kicked out. In the pearl he saw Coyotito sitting at a little desk in a school, just as Kino had once seen it through an open door. And Coyotito was dressed in a jacket, and he had on a white collar and a broad silken tie. Moreover, Coyotito was writing on a big piece of paper. Kino looked at his neighbors fiercely. "My son will go to school," he said, and the neighbors were hushed. Juana caught her breath sharply. Her eyes were bright as she watched him, and she looked quickly down at Coyotito in her arms to see whether this might be possible.

But Kino's face shone with prophecy. "My son will read and open the books, and my son will write and will know writing. And my son will make numbers, and these things will make us free because he will know—he will know and through him we will know." And in the pearl Kino saw himself and Juana squatting by the little fire in the brush hut while Coyotito read from a great book. "This is what the pearl will do," said Kino. And he had never said so many words together in his life. And suddenly he was afraid of his talking. His hand closed down over the pearl and cut the light away from it. Kino was afraid as a man is afraid who says, "I will,"[2] without knowing.

Now the neighbors knew they had witnessed a great marvel. They knew that time would now date from Kino's pearl, and that they would discuss this moment for many years to come. If these things came to pass, they would recount how Kino looked and what he said and how his eyes shone, and they would say, "He was a man transfigured. Some power was given to him, and there it started. You see what a great man he has become, starting from that moment. And I myself saw it."

And if Kino's planning came to nothing,

---

1. **lucent** (lo͞o'sənt): shiny; luminous.

2. **"I will"**: the promise made in the wedding ceremony.

those same neighbors would say, "There it started. A foolish madness came over him so that he spoke foolish words. God keep us from such things. Yes, God punished Kino because he rebelled against the way things are. You see what has become of him. And I myself saw the moment when his reason left him."

Kino looked down at his closed hand and the knuckles were scabbed over and tight where he had struck the gate.

Now the dusk was coming. And Juana looped her shawl under the baby so that he hung against her hip, and she went to the fire hole and dug a coal from the ashes and broke a few twigs over it and fanned a flame alive. The little flames danced on the faces of the neighbors. They knew they should go to their own dinners, but they were reluctant to leave.

The dark was almost in, and Juana's fire threw shadows on the brush walls when the whisper came in, passed from mouth to mouth. "The Father is coming—the priest is coming." The men uncovered their heads and stepped back from the door, and the women gathered their shawls about their faces and cast down their eyes. Kino and Juan Tomás, his brother, stood up. The priest came in—a graying, aging man with an old skin and a young sharp eye. Children, he considered these people, and he treated them like children.

"Kino," he said softly, "thou art named after a great man—and a great Father of the Church."[3] He made it sound like a benediction. "Thy namesake tamed the desert and sweetened the minds of thy people, didst thou know that? It is in the books."

Kino looked quickly down at Coyotito's head, where he hung on Juana's hip. Some

day, his mind said, that boy would know what things were in the books and what things were not. The music had gone out of Kino's head, but now, thinly, slowly, the melody of the morning, the music of evil, of the enemy sounded, but it was faint and weak. And Kino looked at his neighbors to see who might have brought this song in.

But the priest was speaking again. "It has come to me that thou hast found a great fortune, a great pearl."

Kino opened his hand and held it out, and the priest gasped a little at the size and beauty of the pearl. And then he said, "I hope thou wilt remember to give thanks, my son, to Him who has given thee this treasure, and to pray for guidance in the future."

---

3. **Father of the Church:** Kino is named after Eusebius Kino, a great seventeenth-century missionary-explorer.

Kino nodded dumbly, and it was Juana who spoke softly. "We will, Father. And we will be married now. Kino has said so." She looked at the neighbors for confirmation, and they nodded their heads solemnly.

The priest said, "It is pleasant to see that your first thoughts are good thoughts. God bless you, my children." He turned and left quietly, and the people let him through.

But Kino's hand had closed tightly on the pearl again, and he was glancing about suspiciously, for the evil song was in his ears, shrilling against the music of the pearl.

The neighbors slipped away to go to their houses, and Juana squatted by the fire and set her clay pot of boiled beans over the little flame. Kino stepped to the doorway and looked out. As always, he could smell the smoke from many fires, and he could see the hazy stars and feel the damp of the night air so that he covered his nose from it. The thin dog came to him and threshed itself in greeting like a windblown flag, and Kino looked down at it and didn't see it. He had broken through the horizons into a cold and lonely outside. He felt alone and unprotected, and scraping crickets and shrilling tree frogs and croaking toads seemed to be carrying the melody of evil. Kino shivered a little and drew his blanket more tightly against his nose. He carried the pearl still in his hand, tightly closed in his palm, and it was warm and smooth against his skin.

Behind him he heard Juana patting the cakes before she put them down on the clay cooking sheet. Kino felt all the warmth and security of his family behind him, and the Song of the Family came from behind him like the purring of a kitten. But now, by saying what his future was going to be like, he had created it. A plan is a real thing, and things projected are experienced. A plan once made and visualized becomes a reality along with other realities—never to be destroyed but easily to be attacked. Thus Kino's future was real, but having set it up, other forces were set up to destroy it, and this he knew, so that he had to prepare to meet the attack. And this Kino knew also—that the gods do not love men's plans, and the gods do not love success unless it comes by accident. He knew that the gods take their revenge on a man if he be successful through his own efforts. Consequently Kino was afraid of plans, but having made one, he could never destroy it. And to meet the attack, Kino was already making a hard skin for himself against the world. His eyes and his mind probed for danger before it appeared.

Standing in the door, he saw two men approach; and one of them carried a lantern which lighted the ground and the legs of the men. They turned in through the opening of Kino's brush fence and came to his door. And Kino saw that one was the doctor and the other the servant who had opened the gate in the morning. The split knuckles on Kino's right hand burned when he saw who they were.

The doctor said, "I was not in when you came this morning. But now, at the first chance, I have come to see the baby."

Kino stood in the door, filling it, and hatred raged and flamed in back of his eyes, and fear too, for the hundreds of years of subjugation were cut deep in him.

"The baby is nearly well now," he said curtly.

The doctor smiled, but his eyes in their little lymph-lined hammocks did not smile.

He said, "Sometimes, my friend, the scorpion sting has a curious effect. There will be apparent improvement, and then without warning—pouf!" He pursed his lips and made a little explosion to show how quick it could be, and he shifted his small black doctor's bag

about so that the light of the lamp fell upon it, for he knew that Kino's race love the tools of any craft and trust them. "Sometimes," the doctor went on in a liquid tone, "sometimes there will be a withered leg or a blind eye or a crumpled back. Oh, I know the sting of the scorpion, my friend, and I can cure it."

Kino felt the rage and hatred melting toward fear. He did not know, and perhaps this doctor did. And he could not take the chance of putting his certain ignorance against this man's possible knowledge. He was trapped as his people were always trapped, and would be until, as he had said, they could be sure that the things in the books were really in the books. He could not take a chance—not with the life or with the straightness of Coyotito. He stood aside and let the doctor and his man enter the brush hut.

Juana stood up from the fire and backed away as he entered, and she covered the baby's face with the fringe of her shawl. And when the doctor went to her and held out his hand, she clutched the baby tight and looked at Kino where he stood with the fire shadows leaping on his face.

Kino nodded, and only then did she let the doctor take the baby.

"Hold the light," the doctor said, and when the servant held the lantern high, the doctor looked for a moment at the wound on the baby's shoulder. He was thoughtful for a moment and then he rolled back the baby's eyelid and looked at the eyeball. He nodded his head while Coyotito struggled against him.

"It is as I thought," he said. "The poison has gone inward and it will strike soon. Come look!" He held the eyelid down. "See—it is blue." And Kino, looking anxiously, saw that indeed it was a little blue. And he didn't know whether or not it was always a little blue. But the trap was set. He couldn't take the chance.

The doctor's eyes watered in their little hammocks. "I will give him something to try to turn the poison aside," he said. And he handed the baby to Kino.

Then from his bag he took a little bottle of white powder and a capsule of gelatine. He filled the capsule with the powder and closed it, and then around the first capsule he fitted a second capsule and closed it. Then he worked very deftly. He took the baby and pinched its lower lip until it opened its mouth. His fat fingers placed the capsule far back on the baby's tongue, back of the point where he could spit it out, and then from the floor he picked up the little pitcher of pulque and gave Coyotito a drink, and it was done. He looked again at the baby's eyeball and he pursed his lips and seemed to think.

At last he handed the baby back to Juana, and he turned to Kino. "I think the poison will attack within the hour," he said. "The medicine may save the baby from hurt, but I will come back in an hour. Perhaps I am in time to save him." He took a deep breath and went out of the hut, and his servant followed him with the lantern.

Now Juana had the baby under her shawl, and she stared at it with anxiety and fear. Kino came to her, and he lifted the shawl and stared at the baby. He moved his hand to look under the eyelid, and only then saw that the pearl was still in his hand. Then he went to a box by the wall, and from it he brought a piece of rag. He wrapped the pearl in the rag, then went to the corner of the brush house and dug a little hole with his fingers in the dirt floor, and he put the pearl in the hole and covered it up and concealed the place. And then he went to the fire where Juana was squatting, watching the baby's face.

The doctor, back in his house, settled into his chair and looked at his watch. His people brought him a little supper of chocolate and sweet cakes and fruit, and he stared at the food discontentedly.

In the houses of the neighbors the subject that would lead all conversations for a long time to come was aired for the first time to see how it would go. The neighbors showed one another with their thumbs how big the pearl was, and they made little caressing gestures to show how lovely it was. From now on they would watch Kino and Juana very closely to see whether riches turned their heads, as riches turn all people's heads. Everyone knew why the doctor had come. He was not good at dissembling and he was very well understood.

Out in the estuary a tight-woven school of small fishes glittered and broke water to escape a school of great fishes that drove in to eat them. And in the houses the people could hear the swish of the small ones and the bouncing splash of the great ones as the slaughter went on. The dampness arose out of the Gulf and was deposited on bushes and cacti and on little trees in salty drops. And the night mice crept about on the ground and the little night hawks hunted them silently.

The skinny black puppy with flame spots over his eyes came to Kino's door and looked in. He nearly shook his hind quarters loose when Kino glanced up at him, and he subsided when Kino looked away. The puppy did not enter the house, but he watched with frantic interest while Kino ate his beans from the little pottery dish and wiped it clean with a corncake and ate the cake and washed the whole down with a drink of pulque.

Kino was finished and was rolling a cigarette when Juana spoke sharply. "Kino." He glanced at her and then got up and went quickly to her for he saw fright in her eyes. He stood over her, looking down, but the light was very dim. He kicked a pile of twigs into the fire hole to make a blaze, and then he could see the face of Coyotito. The baby's face was flushed and his throat was working and a little thick drool of saliva issued from his lips. The spasm of the stomach muscles began, and the baby was very sick.

Kino knelt beside his wife. "So the doctor knew," he said, but he said it for himself as well as for his wife, for his mind was hard and suspicious and he was remembering the white powder. Juana rocked from side to side and moaned out the little Song of the Family as though it could ward off the danger, and the baby vomited and writhed in her arms. Now uncertainty was in Kino, and the music of evil throbbed in his head and nearly drove out Juana's song.

The doctor finished his chocolate and nibbled the little fallen pieces of sweet cake. He brushed his fingers on a napkin, looked at his watch, arose, and took up his little bag.

The news of the baby's illness traveled quickly among the brush houses, for sickness is second only to hunger as the enemy of poor people. And some said softly, "Luck, you see, brings bitter friends." And they nodded and got up to go to Kino's house. The neighbors scuttled with covered noses through the dark until they crowded into Kino's house again. They stood and gazed, and they made little comments on the sadness that this should happen at a time of joy, and they said, "All things are in God's hands." The old women squatted down beside Juana to try to give her aid if they could and comfort if they could not.

Then the doctor hurried in, followed by his man. He scattered the old women like chickens. He took the baby and examined it and felt its head. "The poison it has worked," he said. "I think I can defeat it. I will try my best." He asked for water, and in the cup of it he put three drops of ammonia, and he pried open the baby's mouth and poured it down. The baby spluttered and screeched under the treatment, and Juana watched him with haunted eyes. The doctor spoke a little as he worked. "It is lucky that I know about the poison of the scorpion, otherwise——" and he shrugged to show what could have happened.

But Kino was suspicious, and he could not take his eyes from the doctor's open bag, and from the bottle of white powder there. Gradually the spasms subsided and the baby relaxed under the doctor's hands. And then Coyotito sighed deeply and went to sleep, for he was very tired with vomiting.

The doctor put the baby in Juana's arms. "He will get well now," he said. "I have won the fight." And Juana looked at him with adoration.

The doctor was closing his bag now. He said, "When do you think you can pay this bill?" He said it even kindly.

"When I have sold my pearl I will pay you," Kino said.

"You have a pearl? A good pearl?" the doctor asked with interest.

And then the chorus of the neighbors broke in. "He has found the Pearl of the World," they cried, and they joined forefinger with thumb to show how great the pearl was.

"Kino will be a rich man," they clamored. "It is a pearl such as one has never seen."

The doctor looked surprised. "I had not heard of it. Do you keep this pearl in a safe place? Perhaps you would like me to put it in my safe?"

Kino's eyes were hooded now, his cheeks were drawn taut. "I have it secure," he said. "Tomorrow I will sell it and then I will pay you."

The doctor shrugged, and his wet eyes never left Kino's eyes. He knew the pearl would be buried in the house, and he thought Kino might look toward the place where it was buried. "It would be a shame to have it stolen before you could sell it," the doctor said, and he saw Kino's eyes flick involuntarily to the floor near the side post of the brush house.

When the doctor had gone and all the neighbors had reluctantly returned to their houses, Kino squatted beside the little glowing coals in the fire hole and listened to the night sound, the soft sweep of the little waves on the shore and the distant barking of dogs, the creeping of the breeze through the brush house roof and the soft speech of his neighbors in their houses in the village. For these people do not sleep soundly all night; they awaken at intervals and talk a little and then go to sleep again. And after a while Kino got up and went to the door of his house.

He smelled the breeze and he listened for any foreign sound of secrecy or creeping, and his eyes searched the darkness, for the music of evil was sounding in his head and he was fierce and afraid. After he had probed the night with his senses he went to the place by the side post where the pearl was buried, and he dug it up and brought it to his sleeping mat, and under his sleeping mat he dug another little hole in the dirt floor and buried his pearl and covered it up again.

And Juana, sitting by the fire hole, watched him with questioning eyes, and when he had buried his pearl she asked, "Who do you fear?"

Kino searched for a true answer, and at last he said, "Everyone." And he could feel a shell of hardness drawing over him.

After a while they lay down together on the sleeping mat, and Juana did not put the baby in his box tonight, but cradled him on her arms and covered his face with her head shawl. And the last light went out of the embers in the fire hole.

But Kino's brain burned, even during his sleep, and he dreamed that Coyotito could read, that one of his own people could tell him the truth of things. And in his dream, Coyotito was reading from a book as large as a house, with letters as big as dogs, and the words galloped and played on the book. And then darkness spread over the page, and with the darkness came the music of evil again, and Kino stirred in his sleep; and when he stirred, Juana's eyes opened in the darkness. And then Kino awakened, with the evil music pulsing in him, and he lay in the darkness with his ears alert.

Then from the corner of the house came a sound so soft that it might have been simply a thought, a little furtive movement, a touch of a foot on earth, the almost inaudible purr of controlled breathing. Kino held his breath to listen, and he knew that whatever dark thing was in his house was holding its breath too, to listen. For a time no sound at all came from the corner of the brush house. Then Kino might have thought he had imagined the sound. But Juana's hand came creeping over to him in warning, and then the sound came again! the whisper of a foot on dry earth and the scratch of fingers in the soil.

And now a wild fear surged in Kino's breast, and on the fear came rage, as it always did. Kino's hand crept into his breast where his knife hung on a string, and then he sprang like an angry cat, leaped striking and spitting for the dark thing he knew was in the corner of the house. He felt cloth, struck at it with his knife and missed, and struck again and felt his knife go through cloth, and then his head crashed with lightning and exploded with pain. There was a soft scurry in the doorway, and running steps for a moment, and then silence.

Kino could feel warm blood running down from his forehead, and he could hear Juana calling to him. "Kino! Kino!" And there was terror in her voice. Then coldness came over him as quickly as the rage had, and he said, "I am all right. The thing has gone."

He groped his way back to the sleeping mat. Already Juana was working at the fire. She uncovered an ember from the ashes and shredded little pieces of cornhusk over it and blew a little flame into the cornhusks so that a tiny light danced through the hut. And then from a secret place Juana brought a little piece of consecrated candle and lighted it at the flame and set it upright on a fireplace stone. She worked quickly, crooning as she moved about. She dipped the end of her head shawl in water and swabbed the blood from Kino's bruised forehead. "It is nothing," Kino said, but his eyes and his voice were hard and cold and a brooding hate was growing in him.

Now the tension which had been growing in Juana boiled up to the surface and her lips were thin. "This thing is evil," she cried harshly. "This pearl is like a sin! It will destroy us," and her voice rose shrilly. "Throw it away, Kino. Let us break it between stones. Let us bury it and forget the place. Let us throw it back into the sea. It has brought evil. Kino, my husband, it will destroy us." And in the firelight her lips and her eyes were alive with her fear.

But Kino's face was set, and his mind and his will were set. "This is our one chance," he said. "Our son must go to school. He must break out of the pot that holds us in."

"It will destroy us all," Juana cried. "Even our son."

"Hush," said Kino. "Do not speak any more. In the morning we will sell the pearl, and then the evil will be gone, and only the good remain. Now hush, my wife." His dark eyes scowled into the little fire, and for the first time he knew that his knife was still in his hands, and he raised the blade and looked at it and saw a little line of blood on the steel. For a moment he seemed about to wipe the blade on his trousers but then he plunged the knife into the earth and so cleansed it.

The distant roosters began to crow and the air changed and the dawn was coming. The wind of the morning ruffled the water of the estuary and whispered through the mangroves, and the little waves beat on the rubbly beach with an increased tempo. Kino raised the sleeping mat and dug up his pearl and put it in front of him and stared at it.

And the beauty of the pearl, winking and glimmering in the light of the little candle, cozened[4] his brain with its beauty. So lovely it was, so soft, and its own music came from it—its music of promise and delight, its guarantee of the future, of comfort, of security. Its warm lucence promised a poultice against illness and a wall against insult. It closed a door on hunger. And as he stared at it Kino's eyes softened and his face relaxed. He could see the little image of the consecrated candle reflected in the soft surface of the pearl, and he heard again in his ears the lovely music of the undersea, the tone of the diffused green light of the sea bottom. Juana, glancing secretly at him, saw him smile. And because they were in some way one thing and one purpose, she smiled with him.

And they began this day with hope.

---

4. **cozened** (kŭz'ənd): beguiled; deluded.

FOR STUDY AND DISCUSSION

1. The poison of the scorpion infected Coyotito in the first chapter, but another kind of poison now infects the town. Steinbeck describes this evil with a metaphor: "the town swelled and puffed with the pressure of it." How would you describe what is actually happening in the town?

2. What are the reactions of these people to Kino's discovery: the priest, the shopkeepers, the doctor, the beggars, the pearl buyers?

3. How do Kino's dreams for the pearl differ from those of the townspeople?

4. Why do you think Kino hears the evil song when the first outsider, the priest, comes to see the pearl?

5. On page 726 we read of the first changes taking place in Kino: "He had broken through the horizons," and he "was already making a hard skin for himself against the world." What do these metaphors mean? How would you explain what is causing the change in Kino?

6. Why does the doctor come to Kino's house after refusing to see the baby that morning? What do you think he actually does to Coyotito?

7. What experiences make Kino realize that his innocence and lack of knowledge have put him at the mercy of other people?

IV

It is wonderful the way a little town keeps track of itself and of all its units. If every single man and woman, child and baby, acts and conducts itself in a known pattern and breaks no walls and differs with no one and experiments in no way and is not sick and does not endanger the ease and peace of mind or steady unbroken flow of the town, then that unit can disappear and never be heard of. But let one man step out of the regular thought or the known and trusted pattern, and the nerves of the townspeople ring with nervousness and communication travels over the nerve lines of the town. Then every unit communicates to the whole.

Thus, in La Paz, it was known in the early morning through the whole town that Kino was going to sell his pearl that day. It was known among the neighbors in the brush huts, among the pearl fishermen; it was known among the Chinese grocery-store owners; it was known in the church, for the altar boys whispered about it. Word of it crept in among the nuns; the beggars in front of the church spoke of it, for they would be there to take the tithe[1] of the first fruits of the luck. The little boys knew about it with excitement, but most of all the pearl buyers knew about it, and when the day had come, in the offices of the pearl buyers, each man sat alone with his little black velvet tray, and each man rolled the pearls about with his fingertips and considered his part in the picture.

It was supposed that the pearl buyers were individuals acting alone, bidding against one another for the pearls the fishermen brought in. And once it had been so. But this was a wasteful method, for often, in the excitement of bidding for a fine pearl, too great a price had been paid to the fishermen. This was extravagant and not to be countenanced. Now there was only one pearl buyer with many hands, and the men who sat in their offices and waited for Kino knew what price they would offer, how high they would bid, and what method each one would use. And although these men would not profit beyond their salaries, there was excitement among the pearl buyers, for there was excitement in the hunt, and if it be a man's function to break down a price, then he must take joy and satisfaction in breaking it as far down as possible. For every man in the world functions to the best of his ability, and no one does less than his best, no matter what he may think about it. Quite apart from any reward they might get, from any word of praise, from any promotion, a pearl buyer was a pearl buyer, and the best and happiest pearl buyer was he who bought for the lowest prices.

The sun was hot yellow that morning, and it drew the moisture from the estuary and from the Gulf and hung it in shimmering scarves in the air so that the air vibrated and vision was insubstantial. A vision hung in the air to the north of the city—the vision of a mountain that was over two hundred miles away, and the high slopes of this mountain were swaddled with pines and a great stone peak arose above the timber line.

And the morning of this day the canoes lay lined up on the beach; the fishermen did not go out to dive for pearls, for there would be too much happening, too many things to see when Kino went to sell the great pearl.

In the brush houses by the shore Kino's neighbors sat long over their breakfasts, and they spoke of what they would do if they had found the pearl. And one man said that he

---

1. **tithe** (tīth): literally a tenth, but popularly any small portion given to charity.

would give it as a present to the Holy Father in Rome. Another said that he would buy Masses for the souls of his family for a thousand years. Another thought he might take the money and distribute it among the poor of La Paz; and a fourth thought of all the good things one could do with the money from the pearl, of all the charities, benefits, of all the rescues one could perform if one had money. All of the neighbors hoped that sudden wealth would not turn Kino's head, would not make a rich man of him, would not graft onto him the evil limbs of greed and hatred and coldness. For Kino was a well-liked man; it would be a shame if the pearl destroyed him. "That good wife Juana," they said, "and the beautiful baby Coyotito, and the others to come. What a pity it would be if the pearl should destroy them all."

For Kino and Juana this was the morning of mornings of their lives, comparable only to the day when the baby was born. This was to be the day from which all other days would take their arrangement. Thus they would say, "It was two years before we sold the pearl," or, "It was six weeks after we sold the pearl." Juana, considering the matter, threw caution to the winds, and she dressed Coyotito in the clothes she had prepared for his baptism, when there would be money for his baptism. And Juana combed and braided her hair and tied the ends with two little bows of red ribbon, and she put on her marriage skirt and waist. The sun was quarter high when they were ready. Kino's ragged white clothes were clean at least, and this was the last day of his raggedness. For tomorrow, or even this afternoon, he would have new clothes.

The neighbors, watching Kino's door through the crevices in their brush houses, were dressed and ready too. There was no self-consciousness about their joining Kino and Juana to go pearl selling. It was expected, it was an historic moment, they would be crazy if they didn't go. It would be almost a sign of unfriendship.

Juana put on her head shawl carefully, and she draped one end under her right elbow and gathered it with her right hand so that a hammock hung under her arm, and in this little hammock she placed Coyotito, propped up against the head shawl so that he could see everything and perhaps remember. Kino put on his large straw hat and felt it with his hand to see that it was properly placed, not on the back or side of his head, like a rash, unmarried, irresponsible man, and not flat as an elder would wear it, but tilted a little forward to show aggressiveness and seriousness and vigor. There is a great deal to be seen in the tilt of a hat on a man. Kino slipped his feet into his sandals and pulled the thongs up over his heels. The great pearl was wrapped in an old soft piece of deerskin and placed in a little leather bag, and the leather bag was in a pocket in Kino's shirt. He folded his blanket carefully and draped it in a narrow strip over his left shoulder, and now they were ready.

Kino stepped with dignity out of the house, and Juana followed him, carrying Coyotito. And as they marched up the freshet-washed alley toward the town, the neighbors joined them. The houses belched people; the doorways spewed out children. But because of the seriousness of the occasion, only one man walked with Kino, and that was his brother, Juan Tomás.

Juan Tomás cautioned his brother. "You must be careful to see they do not cheat you," he said.

And, "Very careful," Kino agreed.

"We do not know what prices are paid in other places," said Juan Tomás. "How can we know what is a fair price, if we do not know what the pearl buyer gets for the pearl in another place?"

"That is true," said Kino, "but how can we know? We are here, we are not there."

As they walked up toward the city the crowd grew behind them, and Juan Tomás, in pure nervousness, went on speaking.

"Before you were born, Kino," he said, "the old ones thought of a way to get more money for their pearls. They thought it would be better if they had an agent who took all the pearls to the capital and sold them there and kept only his share of the profit."

Kino nodded his head. "I know," he said. "It was a good thought."

"And so they got such a man," said Juan Tomás, "and they pooled the pearls, and they started him off. And he was never heard of again and the pearls were lost. Then they got another man, and they started him off, and he was never heard of again. And so they gave the whole thing up and went back to the old way."

"I know," said Kino. "I have heard our father tell of it. It was a good idea, but it was against religion, and the Father made that very clear. The loss of the pearl was a punishment visited on those who tried to leave their station. And the Father made it clear that each man and woman is like a soldier sent by God to guard some part of the castle of the Universe. And some are in the ramparts and some far deep in the darkness of the walls. But each one must remain faithful to his post and must not go running about, else the castle is in danger from the assaults of Hell."

"I have heard him make that sermon," said Juan Tomás. "He makes it every year."

The brothers, as they walked along, squinted their eyes a little, as they and their grandfathers and their great-grandfathers had done for four hundred years, since first the strangers came with arguments and authority and gunpowder to back up both. And in the four hundred years Kino's people had learned

only one defense—a slight slitting of the eyes and a slight tightening of the lips and a retirement. Nothing could break down this wall, and they could remain whole within the wall.

The gathering procession was solemn, for they sensed the importance of this day, and any children who showed a tendency to scuffle, to scream, to cry out, to steal hats and rumple hair, were hissed to silence by their elders. So important was this day that an old man came to see, riding on the stalwart shoulders of his nephew. The procession left the brush huts and entered the stone and plaster city where the streets were a little wider and there were narrow pavements beside the buildings. And as before, the beggars joined them as they passed the church; the grocers looked out at them as they went by; the little saloons lost their customers and the owners closed up shop and went along. And the sun beat down on the streets of the city and even tiny stones threw shadows on the ground.

The news of the approach of the procession ran ahead of it, and in their little dark offices the pearl buyers stiffened and grew alert. They got out papers so that they could be at work when Kino appeared, and they put their pearls in the desks, for it is not good to let an inferior pearl be seen beside a beauty. And word of the loveliness of Kino's pearl had come to them. The pearl buyers' offices were clustered together in one narrow street, and they were barred at the windows, and wooden slats cut out the light so that only a soft gloom entered the offices.

A stout slow man sat in an office waiting. His face was fatherly and benign, and his eyes twinkled with friendship. He was a caller of good mornings, a ceremonious shaker of hands, a jolly man who knew all jokes and yet who hovered close to sadness, for in the midst of a laugh he could remember the death of your aunt, and his eyes could become wet

with sorrow for your loss. This morning he had placed a flower in a vase on his desk, a single scarlet hibiscus, and the vase sat beside the black velvet-lined pearl tray in front of him. He was shaved close to the blue roots of his beard, and his hands were clean and his nails polished. His door stood open to the morning, and he hummed under his breath while his right hand practiced legerdemain.[2] He rolled a coin back and forth over his knuckles and made it appear and disappear, made it spin and sparkle. The coin winked into sight and as quickly slipped out of sight, and the man did not even watch his own performance. The fingers did it all mechanically, precisely, while the man hummed to himself and peered out the door. Then he heard the tramp of feet of the approaching crowd, and the fingers of his right hand worked faster and faster until, as the figure of Kino filled the doorway, the coin flashed and disappeared.

"Good morning, my friend," the stout man said. "What can I do for you?"

Kino stared into the dimness of the little office, for his eyes were squeezed from the outside glare. But the buyer's eyes had become as steady and cruel and unwinking as a hawk's eyes, while the rest of his face smiled in greeting. And secretly, behind his desk, his right hand practiced with the coin.

"I have a pearl," said Kino. And Juan Tomás stood beside him and snorted a little at the understatement. The neighbors peered around the doorway, and a line of little boys clambered on the window bars and looked through. Several little boys, on their hands and knees, watched the scene around Kino's legs.

"You have a pearl," the dealer said. "Sometimes a man brings in a dozen. Well, let us see your pearl. We will value it and give you the best price." And his fingers worked furiously with the coin.

Now Kino instinctively knew his own dramatic effects. Slowly he brought out the leather bag, slowly took from it the soft and dirty piece of deerskin, and then he let the great pearl roll into the black velvet tray, and instantly his eyes went to the buyer's face. But there was no sign, no movement, the face did not change, but the secret hand behind the desk missed in its precision. The coin stumbled over a knuckle and slipped silently into the dealer's lap. And the fingers behind the desk curled into a fist. When the right hand came out of hiding, the forefinger touched the great pearl, rolled it on the black velvet; thumb and forefinger picked it up and brought it near to the dealer's eyes and twirled it in the air.

Kino held his breath, and the neighbors held their breath, and the whispering went back through the crowd. "He is inspecting it—No price has been mentioned yet—They have not come to a price."

Now the dealer's hand had become a personality. The hand tossed the great pearl back to the tray, the forefinger poked and insulted it, and on the dealer's face there came a sad and contemptuous smile.

"I am sorry, my friend," he said, and his shoulders rose a little to indicate that the misfortune was no fault of his.

"It is a pearl of great value," Kino said.

The dealer's fingers spurned the pearl so that it bounced and rebounded softly from the sides of the velvet tray.

"You have heard of fool's gold," the dealer said. "This pearl is like fool's gold. It is too large. Who would buy it? There is no market for such things. It is a curiosity only. I am sorry. You thought it was a thing of value, and it is only a curiosity."

---

2. **legerdemain** (lĕj′ər-də-mān′): tricks or magic done with the hands.

Now Kino's face was perplexed and worried. "It is the Pearl of the World," he cried. "No one has ever seen such a pearl."

"On the contrary," said the dealer, "it is large and clumsy. As a curiosity it has interest; some museum might perhaps take it to place in a collection of seashells. I can give you, say, a thousand pesos."[3]

Kino's face grew dark and dangerous. "It is worth fifty thousand," he said. "You know it. You want to cheat me."

And the dealer heard a little grumble go through the crowd as they heard his price. And the dealer felt a little tremor of fear.

"Do not blame me," he said quickly. "I am only an appraiser. Ask the others. Go to their offices and show your pearl—or better let them come here, so that you can see there is no collusion.[4] Boy," he called. And when his servant looked through the rear door, "Boy, go to such a one, and such another one and such a third one. Ask them to step in here and do not tell them why. Just say that I will be pleased to see them." And his right hand went behind the desk and pulled another coin from his pocket, and the coin rolled back and forth over his knuckles.

Kino's neighbors whispered together. They had been afraid of something like this. The pearl was large, but it had a strange color. They had been suspicious of it from the first. And after all, a thousand pesos was not to be thrown away. It was comparative wealth to a man who was not wealthy. And suppose Kino took a thousand pesos. Only yesterday he had nothing.

But Kino had grown tight and hard. He felt the creeping of fate, the circling of wolves, the hover of vultures. He felt the evil coagulating about him, and he was helpless to protect himself. He heard in his ears the evil music. And on the black velvet the great pearl glistened, so that the dealer could not keep his eyes from it.

The crowd in the doorway wavered and broke and let the three pearl dealers through. The crowd was silent now, fearing to miss a word, to fail to see a gesture or an expression. Kino was silent and watchful. He felt a little tugging at his back, and he turned and looked in Juana's eyes, and when he looked away he had renewed strength.

The dealers did not glance at one another nor at the pearl. The man behind the desk said, "I have put a value on this pearl. The owner here does not think it fair. I will ask you to examine this—this thing and make an offer. Notice," he said to Kino, "I have not mentioned what I have offered."

The first dealer, dry and stringy, seemed now to see the pearl for the first time. He took it up, rolled it quickly between thumb and forefinger, and then cast it contemptuously back into the tray.

"Do not include me in the discussion," he said dryly. "I will make no offer at all. I do not want it. This is not a pearl—it is a monstrosity." His thin lips curled.

Now the second dealer, a little man with a shy soft voice, took up the pearl, and he examined it carefully. He took a glass from his pocket and inspected it under magnification. Then he laughed softly.

"Better pearls are made of paste," he said. "I know these things. This is soft and chalky, it will lose its color and die in a few months. Look—." He offered the glass to Kino, showed him how to use it, and Kino, who had never seen a pearl's surface magnified, was shocked at the strange-looking surface.

The third dealer took the pearl from Kino's

---

3. **a thousand pesos:** eighty dollars. The peso was then worth about eight cents.

4. **collusion:** secret agreement made for the purpose of fraud; conspiracy.

hands. "One of my clients likes such things," he said. "I will offer five hundred pesos, and perhaps I can sell it to my client for six hundred."

Kino reached quickly and snatched the pearl from his hand. He wrapped it in the deerskin and thrust it inside his shirt.

The man behind the desk said, "I'm a fool, I know, but my first offer stands. I still offer one thousand. What are you doing?" he asked, as Kino thrust the pearl out of sight.

"I am cheated," Kino cried fiercely. "My pearl is not for sale here. I will go, perhaps even to the capital."

Now the dealers glanced quickly at one another. They knew they had played too hard; they knew they would be disciplined for their failure, and the man at the desk said quickly, "I might go to fifteen hundred."

But Kino was pushing his way through the crowd. The hum of talk came to him dimly, his rage blood pounded in his ears, and he burst through and strode away. Juana followed, trotting after him.

When the evening came, the neighbors in the brush houses sat eating their corncakes and beans, and they discussed the great theme of the morning. They did not know, it seemed a fine pearl to them, but they had never seen such a pearl before, and surely the dealers knew more about the value of pearls than they. "And mark this," they said. "Those dealers did not discuss these things. Each of the three knew the pearl was valueless."

"But suppose they had arranged it before?"

"If that is so, then all of us have been cheated all of our lives."

Perhaps, some argued, perhaps it would

have been better if Kino took the one thousand five hundred pesos. That is a great deal of money, more than he has ever seen. Maybe Kino is being a pigheaded fool. Suppose he should really go to the capital and find no buyer for his pearl. He would never live that down.

And now, said other fearful ones, now that he had defied them, those buyers will not want to deal with him at all. Maybe Kino has cut off his own head and destroyed himself.

And others said, Kino is a brave man, and a fierce man; he is right. From his courage we may all profit. These were proud of Kino.

In his house Kino squatted on his sleeping mat, brooding. He had buried his pearl under a stone of the fire hole in his house, and he stared at the woven tules[5] of his sleeping mat until the crossed design danced in his head. He had lost one world and had not gained another. And Kino was afraid. Never in his life had he been far from home. He was afraid of strangers and of strange places. He was terrified of that monster of strangeness they called the capital. It lay over the water and through the mountains, over a thousand miles, and every strange terrible mile was frightening. But Kino had lost his old world and he must clamber on to a new one. For his dream of the future was real and never to be destroyed, and he had said "I will go," and that made a real thing too. To determine to go and to say it was to be halfway there.

Juana watched him while he buried his pearl, and she watched him while she cleaned Coyotito and nursed him, and Juana made the corncakes for supper.

Juan Tomás came in and squatted down beside Kino and remained silent for a long time, until at last Kino demanded, "What else could I do? They are cheats."

Juan Tomás nodded gravely. He was the elder, and Kino looked to him for wisdom. "It is hard to know," he said, "We do know that we are cheated from birth to the overcharge on our coffins. But we survive. You have defied not the pearl buyers, but the whole structure, the whole way of life, and I am afraid for you."

"What have I to fear but starvation?" Kino asked.

But Juan Tomás shook his head slowly. "That we must all fear. But suppose you are correct — suppose your pearl is of great value — do you think then the game is over?"

"What do you mean?"

"I don't know," said Juan Tomás, "but I am afraid for you. It is new ground you are walking on, you do not know the way."

"I will go. I will go soon," said Kino.

"Yes," Juan Tomás agreed. "That you must do. But I wonder if you will find it any different in the capital. Here, you have friends and me, your brother. There, you will have no one."

"What can I do?" Kino cried. "Some deep outrage is here. My son must have a chance. That is what they are striking at. My friends will protect me."

"Only so long as they are not in danger or discomfort from it," said Juan Tomás. He arose, saying, "Go with God."

And Kino said, "Go with God," and did not even look up, for the words had a strange chill in them.

Long after Juan Tomás had gone Kino sat brooding on his sleeping mat. A lethargy had settled on him, and a little gray hopelessness. Every road seemed blocked against him. In his head he heard only the dark music of the enemy. His senses were burningly alive, but his mind went back to the deep participation with all things, the gift he had from his people. He heard every little sound of the gather-

---

5. **tules** (tōō′lēs): reeds or rushes.

ing night, the sleepy complaint of settling birds, the love agony of cats, the strike and withdrawal of little waves on the beach, and the simple hiss of distance. And he could smell the sharp odor of exposed kelp from the receding tide. The little flare of the twig fire made the design on his sleeping mat jump before his entranced eyes.

Juana watched him with worry, but she knew him and she knew she could help him best by being silent and by being near. And as though she too could hear the Song of Evil, she fought it, singing softly the melody of the family, of the safety and warmth and wholeness of the family. She held Coyotito in her arms and sang the song to him, to keep the evil out, and her voice was brave against the threat of the dark music.

Kino did not move nor ask for his supper. She knew he would ask when he wanted it. His eyes were entranced, and he could sense the wary, watchful evil outside the brush house; he could feel the dark creeping things waiting for him to go out into the night. It was shadowy and dreadful, and yet it called to him and threatened him and challenged him. His right hand went into his shirt and felt his knife; his eyes were wide; he stood up and walked to the doorway.

Juana willed to stop him; she raised her hand to stop him, and her mouth opened with terror. For a long moment Kino looked out into the darkness and then he stepped outside. Juana heard the little rush, the grunting struggle, the blow. She froze with terror for a moment, and then her lips drew back from her teeth like a cat's lips. She set Coyotito down on the ground. She seized a stone from the fireplace and rushed outside, but it was over by then. Kino lay on the ground, struggling to rise, and there was no one near him. Only the shadows and the strike and rush of waves and the hiss of distance. But the evil

was all about, hidden behind the brush fence, crouched beside the house in the shadow, hovering in the air.

Juana dropped her stone, and she put her arms around Kino and helped him to his feet and supported him into the house. Blood oozed down from his scalp and there was a long deep cut in his cheek from ear to chin, a deep, bleeding slash. And Kino was only half conscious. He shook his head from side to side. His shirt was torn open and his clothes half pulled off. Juana sat him down on his sleeping mat and she wiped the thickening blood from his face with her skirt. She brought him pulque to drink in a little pitcher, and still he shook his head to clear out the darkness.

"Who?" Juana asked.

"I don't know," Kino said. "I didn't see."

Now Juana brought her clay pot of water and she washed the cut on his face while he stared dazed ahead of him.

"Kino, my husband," she cried, and his eyes stared past her. "Kino, can you hear me?"

"I hear you," he said dully.

"Kino, this pearl is evil. Let us destroy it before it destroys us. Let us crush it between two stones. Let us—let us throw it back in the sea where it belongs. Kino, it is evil, it is evil!"

And as she spoke the light came back in Kino's eyes so that they glowed fiercely and his muscles hardened and his will hardened.

"No," he said. "I will fight this thing. I will

win over it. We will have our chance." His fist pounded the sleeping mat. "No one shall take our good fortune from us," he said. His eyes softened then and he raised a gentle hand to Juana's shoulder. "Believe me," he said. "I am a man." And his face grew crafty.

"In the morning we will take our canoe and we will go over the sea and over the mountains to the capital, you and I. We will not be cheated. I am a man."

"Kino," she said huskily, "I am afraid. A man can be killed. Let us throw the pearl back into the sea."

"Hush," he said fiercely. "I am a man. Hush." And she was silent, for his voice was command. "Let us sleep a little," he said. "In the first light we will start. You are not afraid to go with me?"

"No, my husband."

His eyes were soft and warm on her then, his hand touched her cheek. "Let us sleep a little," he said.

FOR STUDY AND DISCUSSION

1. The central event in this chapter is Kino's attempt to sell the pearl. What details reveal how the pearl buyers have deceived the pearl divers for centuries?

2. The pearl buyer's face is described as "fatherly and benign," but one detail—the way the buyer plays tricks with a coin—reveals the true nature of his character. What does this detail suggest about the pearl buyer? After Kino shows him the pearl, what happens to the coin? How does this show the reader—but not Kino—the buyer's true reaction?

3. Reread the paragraph that opens this chapter. By the end of the chapter, how has Kino broken "walls" and stepped out of "known and trusted patterns"?

V

The late moon arose before the first rooster crowed. Kino opened his eyes in the darkness, for he sensed movement near him, but he did not move. Only his eyes searched the darkness, and in the pale light of the moon that crept through the holes in the brush house Kino saw Juana arise silently from beside him. He saw her move toward the fireplace. So carefully did she work that he heard only the lightest sound when she moved the fireplace stone. And then like a shadow she glided toward the door. She paused for a moment beside the hanging box where Coyotito lay, then for a second she was back in the doorway, and then she was gone.

And rage surged in Kino. He rolled up to his feet and followed her as silently as she had gone, and he could hear her quick footsteps going toward the shore. Quietly he tracked her, and his brain was red with anger. She burst clear of the brush line and stumbled over the little boulders toward the water, and

then she heard him coming and she broke into a run. Her arm was up to throw when he leaped at her and caught her arm and wrenched the pearl from her. He struck her in the face with his clenched fist and she fell among the boulders, and he kicked her in the side. In the pale light he could see the little waves break over her, and her skirt floated about and clung to her legs as the water receded.

Kino looked down at her and his teeth were bared. He hissed at her like a snake, and Juana stared at him with wide unfrightened eyes, like a sheep before the butcher. She knew there was murder in him, and it was all right; she had accepted it, and she would not resist or even protest. And then the rage left him and a sick disgust took its place. He turned away from her and walked up the beach and through the brush line. His senses were dulled by his emotion.

He heard the rush, got his knife out and lunged at one dark figure and felt his knife go home, and then he was swept to his knees and swept again to the ground. Greedy fingers went through his clothes, frantic fingers searched him, and the pearl, knocked from his hand, lay winking behind a little stone in the pathway. It glinted in the soft moonlight.

Juana dragged herself up from the rocks on the edge of the water. Her face was a dull pain and her side ached. She steadied herself on her knees for a while and her wet skirt clung to her. There was no anger in her for Kino. He had said, "I am a man," and that meant certain things to Juana. It meant that he was half insane and half god. It meant that Kino would drive his strength against a mountain and plunge his strength against the sea. Juana, in her woman's soul, knew that the mountain would stand while the man broke himself; that the sea would surge while the man drowned in it. And yet it was this thing that made him a man, half insane and half god, and Juana had need of a man; she could not live without a man. Although she might be puzzled by these differences between man and woman, she knew them and accepted them and needed them. Of course she would follow him, there was no question of that. Sometimes the quality of woman, the reason, the caution, the sense of preservation, could cut through Kino's manness and save them all. She climbed painfully to her feet, and she dipped her cupped palms in the little waves and washed her bruised face with the stinging salt water, and then she went creeping up the beach after Kino.

A flight of herring clouds had moved over the sky from the south. The pale moon dipped in and out of the strands of clouds so that Juana walked in darkness for a moment and in light the next. Her back was bent with pain and her head was low. She went through the line of brush when the moon was covered, and when it looked through she saw the glimmer of the great pearl in the path behind the rock. She sank to her knees and picked it up, and the moon went into the darkness of the clouds again. Juana remained on her knees while she considered whether to go back to the sea and finish her job, and as she considered, the light came again, and she saw two dark figures lying in the path ahead of her. She leaped forward and saw that one was Kino and the other a stranger with dark shiny fluid leaking from his throat.

Kino moved sluggishly, arms and legs stirred like those of a crushed bug, and a thick muttering came from his mouth. Now, in an instant, Juana knew that the old life was gone forever. A dead man in the path and Kino's knife, dark bladed beside him, convinced her. All of the time Juana had been trying to rescue something of the old peace, of the time before the pearl. But now it was gone, and there was no retrieving it. And knowing this, she abandoned the past instantly. There was nothing to do but to save themselves.

Her pain was gone now, her slowness. Quickly she dragged the dead man from the pathway into the shelter of the brush. She went to Kino and sponged his face with her wet skirt. His senses were coming back and he moaned.

"They have taken the pearl. I have lost it. Now it is over," he said. "The pearl is gone."

Juana quieted him as she would quiet a sick child. "Hush," she said. "Here is your pearl. I found it in the path. Can you hear me now? Here is your pearl. Can you understand? You have killed a man. We must go away. They will come for us, can you understand? We must be gone before the daylight comes."

"I was attacked," Kino said uneasily. "I struck to save my life."

"Do you remember yesterday?" Juana asked. "Do you think that will matter? Do you remember the men of the city? Do you think your explanation will help?"

Kino drew a great breath and fought off his weakness. "No," he said. "You are right." And his will hardened and he was a man again.

"Go to our house and bring Coyotito," he said, "and bring all the corn we have. I will drag the canoe into the water and we will go."

He took his knife and left her. He stumbled toward the beach and he came to his canoe. And when the light broke through again he saw that a great hole had been knocked in the bottom. And a searing rage came to him and gave him strength. Now the darkness was closing in on his family; now the evil music filled the night, hung over the mangroves, skirled[1] in the wave beat. The canoe of his grandfather, plastered over and over, and a splintered hole broken in it. This was an evil beyond thinking. The killing of a man was not so evil as the killing of a boat. For a boat does not have sons, and a boat cannot protect itself, and a wounded boat does not heal. There was sorrow in Kino's rage, but this last thing had tightened him beyond breaking. He was an animal now, for hiding, for attacking, and he lived only to preserve himself and his family. He was not conscious of the pain in his head. He leaped up the beach, through the brush line toward his brush house, and it did not occur to him to take one of the canoes of his neighbors. Never once did the thought enter his head, any more than he could have conceived breaking a boat.

The roosters were crowing and the dawn was not far off. Smoke of the first fires seeped out through the walls of the brush houses, and the first smell of cooking corncakes was in the air. Already the dawn birds were scampering in the bushes. The weak moon was losing its light and the clouds thickened and curdled to the southward. The wind blew freshly into the estuary, a nervous, restless wind with the smell of storm on its breath, and there was change and uneasiness in the air.

Kino, hurrying toward his house, felt a surge of exhilaration. Now he was not confused, for there was only one thing to do, and Kino's hand went first to the great pearl in his shirt and then to his knife hanging under his shirt.

He saw a little glow ahead of him, and then without interval a tall flame leaped up in the dark with a crackling roar, and a tall edifice of fire lighted the pathway. Kino broke into a run; it was his brush house, he knew. And he knew that these houses could burn down in a very few moments. And as he ran a scuttling figure ran toward him—Juana, with Coyotito in her arms and Kino's shoulder blanket

---

1. **skirled** (skûrld): made a shrill, piercing sound.

clutched in her hand. The baby moaned with fright, and Juana's eyes were wide and terrified. Kino could see the house was gone, and he did not question Juana. He knew, but she said, "It was torn up and the floor dug—even the baby's box turned out, and as I looked they put the fire to the outside."

The fierce light of the burning house lighted Kino's face strongly. "Who?" he demanded.

"I don't know," she said. "The dark ones."

The neighbors were tumbling from their houses now, and they watched the falling sparks and stamped them out to save their own houses. Suddenly Kino was afraid. The light made him afraid. He remembered the man lying dead in the brush beside the path, and he took Juana by the arm and drew her into the shadow of a house away from the light, for light was danger to him. For a mo-

ment he considered and then he worked among the shadows until he came to the house of Juan Tomás, his brother, and he slipped into the doorway and drew Juana after him. Outside, he could hear the squeal of children and the shouts of the neighbors, for his friends thought he might be inside the burning house.

The house of Juan Tomás was almost exactly like Kino's house; nearly all the brush houses were alike, and all leaked light and air, so that Juana and Kino, sitting in the corner of the brother's house, could see the leaping flames through the wall. They saw the flames tall and furious, they saw the roof fall and watched the fire die down as quickly as a twig fire dies. They heard the cries of warning of their friends, and the shrill, keening[2] cry of Apolonia, wife of Juan Tomás. She, being the nearest woman relative, raised a formal lament for the dead of the family.

Apolonia realized that she was wearing her second-best head shawl and she rushed to her house to get her fine new one. As she rummaged in a box by the wall, Kino's voice said quietly, "Apolonia, do not cry out. We are not hurt."

"How do you come here?" she demanded.

"Do not question," he said. "Go now to Juan Tomás and bring him here and tell no one else. This is important to us, Apolonia."

She paused, her hands helpless in front of her, and then, "Yes, my brother-in-law," she said.

In a few moments Juan Tomás came back with her. He lighted a candle and came to them where they crouched in a corner and he said, "Apolonia, see to the door, and do not let anyone enter." He was older, Juan Tomás, and he assumed the authority. "Now, my brother," he said.

---

2. **keening:** wailing.

"I was attacked in the dark," said Kino. "And in the fight I have killed a man."

"Who?" asked Juan Tomás quickly.

"I do not know. It is all darkness—all darkness and shape of darkness."

"It is the pearl," said Juan Tomás. "There is a devil in this pearl. You should have sold it and passed on the devil. Perhaps you can still sell it and buy peace for yourself."

And Kino said, "Oh, my brother, an insult has been put on me that is deeper than my life. For on the beach my canoe is broken, my house is burned, and in the brush a dead man lies. Every escape is cut off. You must hide us, my brother."

And Kino, looking closely, saw deep worry come into his brother's eyes and he forestalled him in a possible refusal. "Not for long," he said quickly. "Only until a day has passed and the new night has come. Then we will go."

"I will hide you," said Juan Tomás.

"I do not want to bring danger to you," Kino said. "I know I am like a leprosy. I will go tonight and then you will be safe."

"I will protect you," said Juan Tomás, and he called, "Apolonia, close up the door. Do not even whisper that Kino is here."

They sat silently all day in the darkness of the house, and they could hear the neighbors speaking of them. Through the walls of the house they could watch their neighbors raking the ashes to find the bones. Crouching in the house of Juan Tomás, they heard the shock go into their neighbors' minds at the news of the broken boat. Juan Tomás went out among the neighbors to divert their suspicions, and he gave them theories and ideas of what had happened to Kino and to Juana and to the baby. To one he said, "I think they have gone south along the coast to escape the evil that was on them." And to another, "Kino would never leave the sea. Perhaps he found another boat." And he said, "Apolonia is ill with grief."

And in that day the wind rose up to beat the Gulf and tore the kelps and weeds that lined the shore, and the wind cried through the brush houses and no boat was safe on the water. Then Juan Tomás told among the neighbors, "Kino is gone. If he went to the sea, he is drowned by now." And after each trip among the neighbors Juan Tomás came back with something borrowed. He brought a little woven straw bag of red beans and a gourd full of rice. He borrowed a cup of dried peppers and a block of salt, and he brought in a long working knife, eighteen inches long and heavy, as a small ax, a tool and a weapon. And when Kino saw this knife his eyes lighted up, and he fondled the blade and his thumb tested the edge.

The wind screamed over the Gulf and turned the water white, and the mangroves plunged like frightened cattle, and a fine sandy dust arose from the land and hung in a stifling cloud over the sea. The wind drove off the clouds and skimmed the sky clean and drifted the sand of the country like snow.

Then Juan Tomás, when the evening approached, talked long with his brother. "Where will you go?"

"To the north," said Kino. "I have heard that there are cities in the north."

"Avoid the shore," said Juan Tomás. "They are making a party to search the shore. The men in the city will look for you. Do you still have the pearl?"

"I have it," said Kino. "And I will keep it. I might have given it as a gift, but now it is my misfortune and my life and I will keep it." His eyes were hard and cruel and bitter.

Coyotito whimpered and Juana muttered little magics over him to make him silent.

"The wind is good," said Juan Tomás. "There will be no tracks."

They left quietly in the dark before the moon had risen. The family stood formally in the house of Juan Tomás. Juana carried Coyotito on her back, covered and held in by her head shawl, and the baby slept, cheek turned sideways against her shoulder. The head shawl covered the baby, and one end of it came across Juana's nose to protect her from the evil night air. Juan Tomás embraced his brother with the double embrace and kissed him on both cheeks. "Go with God," he said, and it was like a death. "You will not give up the pearl?"

"This pearl has become my soul," said Kino. "If I give it up I shall lose my soul. Go thou also with God."

FOR STUDY AND DISCUSSION

1. At the opening of the novel, Kino and Juana were "one thing and one purpose." But the pearl has changed all this. What event dramatizes how greatly they have been divided? How do you account for Juana's reactions to her husband's brutal behavior?

2. Steinbeck frequently uses animal imagery in this story to suggest a cruel world where people prey on one another. What animals are Kino and Juana compared to in the scene on the beach (page 742)?

3. The *turning point* of a story is that moment when the fate of the main character is sealed, when the events of the story must turn in one direction or another. What event marks the turning point of this novel, as Juana realizes the peace of the past is gone forever?

4. Look back at the end of this chapter where Kino says that the pearl has become his "soul." What do you think "soul" means here? If Kino really believes this at this point in the story, what does it reveal about him?

VI

The wind blew fierce and strong, and it pelted them with bits of sticks, sand, and little rocks. Juana and Kino gathered their clothing tighter about them and covered their noses and went out into the world. The sky was brushed clean by the wind and the stars were cold in a black sky. The two walked carefully, and they avoided the center of town where some sleeper in a doorway might see them pass. For the town closed itself in against the night, and anyone who moved about in the darkness would be noticeable. Kino threaded his way around the edge of the city and turned north, north by the stars, and found the rutted sandy road that led through the brushy country toward Loreto where the miraculous Virgin has her station.[1]

Kino could feel the blown sand against his ankles and he was glad, for he knew there would be no tracks. The little light from the stars made out for him the narrow road through the brushy country. And Kino could hear the pad of Juana's feet behind him. He went quickly and quietly, and Juana trotted behind him to keep up.

Some ancient thing stirred in Kino. Through his fear of dark and the devils that haunt the night, there came a rush of exhilaration; some animal thing was moving in him so that he was cautious and wary and dangerous; some ancient thing out of the past of his people was alive in him. The wind was at his back and the stars guided him. The wind cried and whisked in the brush, and the family went on monotonously, hour after hour. They passed no one and saw no one. At last, to their right, the waning moon arose, and when it came up the wind died down, and the land was still.

---

1. **station:** shrine.

Now they could see the little road ahead of them, deep cut with sand-drifted wheel tracks. With the wind gone there would be footprints, but they were a good distance from the town and perhaps their tracks might not be noticed. Kino walked carefully in a wheel rut, and Juana followed in his path. One big cart, going to the town in the morning, could wipe out every trace of their passage.

All night they walked and never changed their pace. Once Coyotito awakened, and Juana shifted him in front of her and soothed him until he went to sleep again. And the evils of the night were about them. The coyotes cried and laughed in the brush, and the owls screeched and hissed over their heads. And once some large animal lumbered away, crackling the undergrowth as it went. And Kino gripped the handle of the big working knife and took a sense of protection from it.

The music of the pearl was triumphant in Kino's head, and the quiet melody of the family underlay it, and they wove themselves into the soft padding of sandaled feet in the dusk. All night they walked, and in the first dawn Kino searched the roadside for a covert to lie in during the day. He found his place near to the road, a little clearing where deer might have lain, and it was curtained thickly with the dry brittle trees that lined the road. And when Juana had seated herself and had settled to nurse the baby, Kino went back to the road. He broke a branch and carefully swept the footprints where they had turned from the roadway. And then, in the first light, he heard the creak of a wagon, and he crouched beside the road and watched a heavy two-wheeled cart go by, drawn by slouching oxen. And when it had passed out of sight, he went back to the roadway and looked at the rut and found that the footprints were gone. And again he swept out his traces and went back to Juana.

She gave him the soft corncakes Apolonia had packed for them, and after a while she slept a little. But Kino sat on the ground and stared at the earth in front of him. He watched the ants moving, a little column of them near to his foot, and he put his foot in their path. Then the column climbed over his instep and continued on its way, and Kino left his foot there and watched them move over it.

The sun arose hotly. They were not near the Gulf now, and the air was dry and hot so that the brush cricked[2] with heat and a good resinous smell came from it. And when Juana awakened, when the sun was high, Kino told her things she knew already.

"Beware of that kind of tree there," he said, pointing. "Do not touch it, for if you do and then touch your eyes, it will blind you. And beware of the tree that bleeds. See, that one over there. For if you break it the red blood will flow from it, and it is evil luck." And she nodded and smiled at him, for she knew these things.

"Will they follow us?" she asked. "Do you think they will try to find us?"

"They will try," said Kino. "Whoever finds us will take the pearl. Oh, they will try."

And Juana said, "Perhaps the dealers were right and the pearl has no value. Perhaps this has all been an illusion."

Kino reached into his clothes and brought out the pearl. He let the sun play on it until it burned in his eyes. "No," he said, "they would not have tried to steal it if it had been valueless."

"Do you know who attacked you? Was it the dealers?"

"I do not know," he said. "I didn't see them."

He looked into his pearl to find his vision. "When we sell it at last, I will have a rifle," he said, and he looked into the shining surface for his rifle, but he saw only a huddled dark body on the ground with shining blood dripping from its throat. And he said quickly, "We will be married in a great church." And in the pearl he saw Juana with her beaten face crawling home through the night. "Our son must learn to read," he said frantically. And there in the pearl Coyotito's face, thick and feverish from the medicine.

And Kino thrust the pearl back into his clothing, and the music of the pearl had become sinister in his ears and it was interwoven with the music of evil.

The hot sun beat on the earth so that Kino and Juana moved into the lacy shade of the brush, and small gray birds scampered on the ground in the shade. In the heat of the day Kino relaxed and covered his eyes with his hat and wrapped his blanket about his face to keep the flies off, and he slept.

But Juana did not sleep. She sat quiet as a stone and her face was quiet. Her mouth was still swollen where Kino had struck her, and big flies buzzed around the cut on her chin. But she sat as still as a sentinel, and when Coyotito awakened she placed him on the ground in front of her and watched him wave his arms and kick his feet, and he smiled and gurgled at her until she smiled too. She picked up a little twig from the ground and tickled him, and she gave him water from the gourd she carried in her bundle.

Kino stirred in a dream, and he cried out in a guttural voice, and his hand moved in symbolic fighting. And then he moaned and sat up suddenly, his eyes wide and his nostrils flaring. He listened and heard only the cricking heat and the hiss of distance.

"What is it?" Juana asked.

"Hush," he said.

"You were dreaming."

"Perhaps." But he was restless, and when

---

2. **cricked**: turned or twisted.

she gave him a corncake from her store he paused in his chewing to listen. He was uneasy and nervous; he glanced over his shoulder; he lifted the big knife and felt its edge. When Coyotito gurgled on the ground Kino said, "Keep him quiet."

"What is the matter?" Juana asked.

"I don't know."

He listened again, an animal light in his eyes. He stood up then, silently; and crouched low, he threaded his way through the brush toward the road. But he did not step into the road; he crept into the cover of a thorny tree and peered out along the way he had come.

And then he saw them moving along. His body stiffened and he drew down his head and peeked out from under a fallen branch. In the distance he could see three figures, two on foot and one on horseback. But he knew what they were, and a chill of fear went through him. Even in the distance he could see the two on foot moving slowly along, bent low to the ground. Here, one would pause and look at the earth, while the other joined him. They were the trackers, they could follow the trail of a bighorn sheep in the stone mountains. They were as sensitive as hounds. Here, he and Juana might have stepped out of the wheel rut, and these people from the inland, these hunters, could follow, could read a broken straw or a little tumbled pile of dust. Behind them, on a horse, was a dark man, his nose covered with a blanket, and across his saddle a rifle gleamed in the sun.

Kino lay as rigid as the tree limb. He barely breathed, and his eyes went to the place where he had swept out the track. Even the sweeping might be a message to the trackers. He knew these inland hunters. In a country where there is little game they managed to live because of their ability to hunt, and they were hunting him. They scuttled over the ground like animals and found a sign and

crouched over it while the horseman waited.

The trackers whined a little, like excited dogs on a warming trail. Kino slowly drew his big knife to his hand and made it ready. He knew what he must do. If the trackers found the swept place, he must leap for the horseman, kill him quickly and take the rifle. That was his only chance in the world. And as the three drew nearer on the road, Kino dug little pits with his sandaled toes so that he could leap without warning, so that his feet would not slip. He had only a little vision under the fallen limb.

Now Juana, back in her hidden place, heard the pad of the horse's hoofs, and Coyotito gurgled. She took him up quickly and put him under her shawl and gave him her breast and he was silent.

When the trackers came near, Kino could see only their legs and only the legs of the horse from under the fallen branch. He saw the dark horny feet of the men and their ragged white clothes, and he heard the creak of leather of the saddle and the clink of spurs. The trackers stopped at the swept place and studied it, and the horseman stopped. The horse flung his head up against the bit and the

bit-roller clicked under his tongue and the horse snorted. Then the dark trackers turned and studied the horse and watched his ears.

Kino was not breathing, but his back arched a little and the muscles of his arms and legs stood out with tension and a line of sweat formed on his upper lip. For a long moment the trackers bent over the road, and they moved on slowly, studying the ground ahead of them, and the horseman moved after them. The trackers scuttled along, stopping, looking, and hurrying on. They would be back, Kino knew. They would be circling and seaching, peeping, stooping, and they would come back sooner or later to his covered track.

He slid backward and did not bother to cover his tracks. He could not; too many little signs were there, too many broken twigs and scuffed places and displaced stones. And there was a panic in Kino now, a panic of flight. The trackers would find his trail, he knew it. There was no escape, except in flight. He edged away from the road and went quickly and silently to the hidden place where Juana was. She looked up at him in question.

"Trackers," he said. "Come!"

And then a helplessness and a hopelessness swept over him, and his face went black and his eyes were sad. "Perhaps I should let them take me."

Instantly Juana was on her feet and her hand lay on his arm. "You have the pearl," she cried hoarsely. "Do you think they would take you back alive to say they had stolen it?"

His hand strayed limply to the place where the pearl was hidden under his clothes. "They will find it," he said weakly.

"Come," she said. "Come!"

And when he did not respond, "Do you think they would let me live? Do you think they would let the little one here live?"

Her goading struck into his brain; his lips snarled and his eyes were fierce again. "Come," he said. "We will go into the mountains. Maybe we can lose them in the mountains."

Frantically he gathered the gourds and the little bags that were their property. Kino carried a bundle in his left hand, but the big knife swung free in his right hand. He parted the brush for Juana and they hurried to the west, toward the high stone mountains. They trotted quickly through the tangle of the undergrowth. This was panic flight. Kino did not try to conceal his passages; he trotted, kicking the stones, knocking the telltale leaves from the little trees. The high sun streamed down on the dry creaking earth so that even vegetation ticked in protest. But ahead were the naked granite mountains, rising out of erosion rubble and standing monolithic against the sky. And Kino ran for the high place, as nearly all animals do when they are pursued.

This land was waterless, furred with the cacti which could store water and with the great-rooted brush which could reach deep into the earth for a little moisture and get along on very little. And underfoot was not soil but broken rock, split into small cubes, great slabs, but none of it water-rounded. Little tufts of sad dry grass grew between the stones, grass that had sprouted with one single rain and headed,[3] dropped its seed, and died. Horned toads watched the family go by and turned their little pivoting dragon heads. And now and then a great jackrabbit, disturbed in his shade, bumped away and hid behind the nearest rock. The singing heat lay over this desert country, and ahead the stone mountains looked cool and welcoming.

And Kino fled. He knew what would happen. A little way along the road the trackers would become aware that they had missed the path, and they would come back, searching and judging, and in a little while they would find the place where Kino and Juana had rested. From there it would be easy for them—these little stones, the fallen leaves and the whipped branches, the scuffed places where a foot had slipped. Kino could see them in his mind, slipping along the track, whining a little with eagerness, and behind them, dark and half disinterested, the horseman with the rifle. His work would come last, for he would not take them back. Oh, the music of evil sang loud in Kino's head now, it sang with the whine of heat and with the dry ringing of snake rattles. It was not large and overwhelming now, but secret and poisonous, and the pounding of his heart gave it undertone and rhythm.

The way began to rise, and as it did the rocks grew larger. But now Kino had put a little distance between his family and the trackers. Now, on the first rise, he rested. He climbed a great boulder and looked back over the shimmering country, but he could not see his enemies, not even the tall horseman riding through the brush. Juana had squatted in the shade of the boulder. She raised her bottle of water to Coyotito's lips; his little dried tongue sucked greedily at it. She looked up at Kino when he came back; she saw him examine her ankles, cut and scratched from the stones and brush, and she covered them quickly with her skirt. Then she handed the bottle to him, but he shook his head. Her eyes were bright in her tired face. Kino moistened his cracked lips with his tongue.

"Juana," he said, "I will go on and you will hide. I will lead them into the mountains, and when they have gone past, you will go north to Loreto or to Santa Rosalia.[4] Then, if I can escape them, I will come to you. It is the only safe way."

She looked full into his eyes for a moment.

---

3. **headed:** grew to a head.

4. **Santa Rosalia** (sän'tä rō-zä'lē-ä): a town on the west coast of Baja California.

752   *The Novel*

"No," she said. "We go with you."

"I can go faster alone," he said harshly. "You will put the little one in more danger if you go with me."

"No," said Juana.

"You must. It is the wise thing and it is my wish," he said.

"No," said Juana.

He looked then for weakness in her face, for fear or irresolution, and there was none. Her eyes were very bright. He shrugged his shoulders helplessly then, but he had taken strength from her. When they moved on it was no longer panic flight.

The country, as it rose toward the mountains, changed rapidly. Now there were long outcroppings of granite with deep crevices between, and Kino walked on bare unmarkable stone when he could and leaped from ledge to ledge. He knew that wherever the trackers lost his patch they must circle and lose time before they found it again. And so he did not go straight for the mountains any more; he moved in zigzags, and sometimes he cut back to the south and left a sign and then went toward the mountains over bare stone again. And the path rose steeply now, so that he panted a little as he went.

The sun moved downward toward the bare stone teeth of the mountains, and Kino set his direction for a dark and shadowing cleft in the range. If there were any water at all, it would be there where he could see, even in the distance, a hint of foliage. And if there were any passage through the smooth stone range, it would be by this same deep cleft. It had its danger, for the trackers would think of it too, but the empty water bottle did not let that consideration enter. And as the sun lowered, Kino and Juana struggled wearily up the steep slope toward the cleft.

High in the gray stone mountains, under a frowning peak, a little spring bubbled out of a rupture in the stone. It was fed by shade-preserved snow in the summer, and now and then it died completely and bare rocks and dry algae were on its bottom. But nearly always it gushed out, cold and clean and lovely. In the times when the quick rains fell, it might become a freshet and send its column of white water crashing down the mountain cleft, but nearly always it was a lean little spring. It bubbled out into a pool and then fell a hundred feet to another pool, and this one, overflowing, dropped again, so that it continued, down and down, until it came to the rubble of the upland, and there it disappeared altogether. There wasn't much left of it then anyway, for every time it fell over an escarpment the thirsty air drank it, and it splashed from the pools to the dry vegetation. The animals from miles around came to drink from the little pools, and the wild sheep and the deer, the pumas and raccoons, and the mice—all came to drink. And the birds which spent the day in the brushland came at night to the little pools that were like steps in the mountain cleft. Beside this tiny stream, wherever enough earth collected for root-hold, colonies of plants grew, wild grape and little palms, maidenhair fern, hibiscus, and tall pampas grass with feathery rods raised above the spike leaves. And in the pool lived frogs and waterskaters, and waterworms crawled on the bottom of the pool. Everything that loved water came to these few shallow places. The cats took their prey there, and strewed feathers and lapped water through their bloody teeth. The little pools were places of life because of the water, and places of killing because of the water, too.

The lowest step, where the stream collected before it tumbled down a hundred feet and disappeared into the rubbly desert, was a little platform of stone and sand. Only a pencil of water fell into the pool, but it was

enough to keep the pool full and to keep the ferns green in the underhang of the cliff, and wild grape climbed the stone mountain and all manner of little plants found comfort here. The freshets had made a small sandy beach through which the pool flowed, and bright green watercress grew in the damp sand. The beach was cut and scarred and padded by the feet of animals that had come to drink and to hunt.

The sun had passed over the stone mountains when Kino and Juana struggled up the steep broken slope and came at last to the water. From this step they could look out over the sunbeaten desert to the blue Gulf in the distance. They came utterly weary to the pool, and Juana slumped to her knees and first washed Coyotito's face and then filled her bottle and gave him a drink. And the baby was weary and petulant, and he cried softly until Juana gave him her breast, and then he gurgled and clucked against her. Kino drank long and thirstily at the pool. For a moment, then, he stretched out beside the water and relaxed all his muscles and watched Juana feeding the baby, and then he got to his feet and went to the edge of the step where the water slipped over, and he searched the distance carefully. His eyes set on a point and he became rigid. Far down the slope he could see the two trackers; they were little more than dots or scurrying ants and behind them a larger ant.

Juana had turned to look at him and she saw his back stiffen.

"How far?" she asked quietly.

"They will be here by evening," said Kino. He looked up the long steep chimney of the cleft where the water came down. "We must go west," he said, and his eyes searched the stone shoulder behind the cleft. And thirty feet up on the gray shoulder he saw a series of little erosion caves. He slipped off his sandals and clambered up to them, gripping the bare stone with his toes, and he looked into the shallow caves. They were only a few feet deep, wind-hollowed scoops, but they sloped slightly downward and back. Kino crawled into the largest one and lay down and knew that he could not be seen from the outside. Quickly he went back to Juana.

"You must go up there. Perhaps they will not find us there," he said.

Without question she filled her water bottle to the top, and then Kino helped her up to the shallow cave and brought up the packages of food and passed them to her. And Juana sat in the cave entrance and watched him. She saw that he did not try to erase their tracks in the sand. Instead, he climbed up the brush cliff beside the water, clawing and tearing at the ferns and wild grape as he went. And when he had climbed a hundred feet to the next bench, he came down again. He looked carefully at the smooth rock shoulder toward the cave to see that there was no trace of passage, and last he climbed up and crept into the cave beside Juana.

"When they go up," he said, "we will slip away, down to the lowlands again. I am afraid only that the baby may cry. You must see that he does not cry."

"He will not cry," she said, and she raised the baby's face to her own and looked into his eyes and he stared solemnly back at her.

"He knows," said Juana.

Now Kino lay in the cave entrance, his chin braced on his crossed arms, and he watched the blue shadow of the mountain move out across the brushy desert below until it reached the Gulf, and the long twilight of the shadow was over the land.

The trackers were long in coming, as though they had trouble with the trail Kino had left. It was dusk when they came at last to the little pool. And all three were on foot now, for a horse could not climb the last steep slope. From above they were thin figures in the evening. The two trackers scurried about on the little beach, and they saw Kino's progress up the cliff before they drank. The man with the rifle sat down and rested himself, and the trackers squatted near him, and in the evening the points of their cigarettes glowed and receded. And then Kino could see that they were eating, and the soft murmur of their voices came to him.

Then darkness fell, deep and black in the mountain cleft. The animals that used the pool came near and smelled men there and drifted away again into the darkness.

He heard a murmur behind him. Juana was whispering, "Coyotito." She was begging him to be quiet. Kino heard the baby whimper, and he knew from the muffled sounds that Juana had covered his head with her shawl.

Down on the beach a match flared, and in its momentary light Kino saw that two of the men were sleeping, curled up like dogs, while the third watched, and he saw the glint of the rifle in the match light. And then the match died, but it left a picture on Kino's eyes. He could see it, just how each man was, two sleeping curled and the third squatting in the sand with the rifle between his knees.

Kino moved silently back into the cave. Juana's eyes were two sparks reflecting a low star. Kino crawled quietly close to her and he put his lips near to her cheek.

"There is a way," he said.

"But they will kill you."

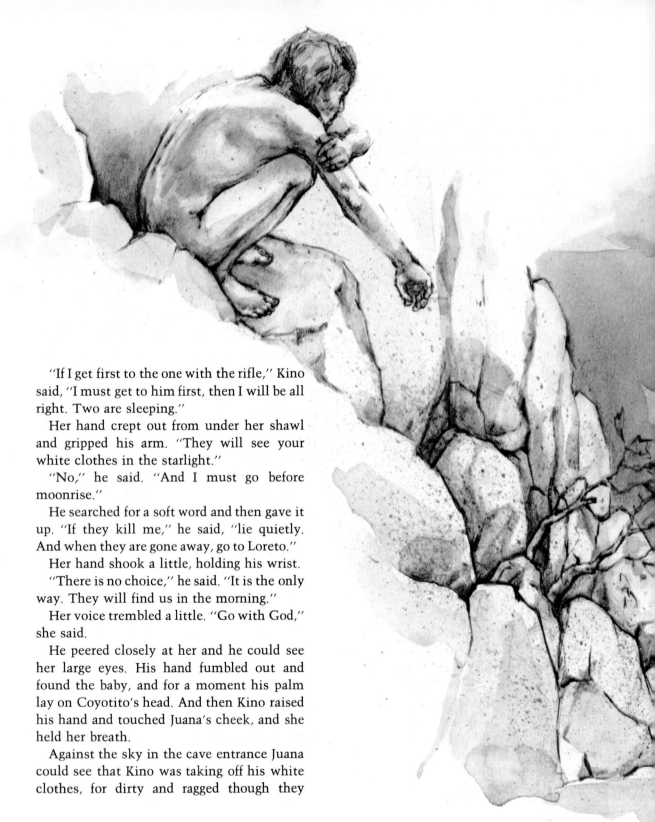

"If I get first to the one with the rifle," Kino said, "I must get to him first, then I will be all right. Two are sleeping."

Her hand crept out from under her shawl and gripped his arm. "They will see your white clothes in the starlight."

"No," he said. "And I must go before moonrise."

He searched for a soft word and then gave it up. "If they kill me," he said, "lie quietly. And when they are gone away, go to Loreto."

Her hand shook a little, holding his wrist.

"There is no choice," he said. "It is the only way. They will find us in the morning."

Her voice trembled a little. "Go with God," she said.

He peered closely at her and he could see her large eyes. His hand fumbled out and found the baby, and for a moment his palm lay on Coyotito's head. And then Kino raised his hand and touched Juana's cheek, and she held her breath.

Against the sky in the cave entrance Juana could see that Kino was taking off his white clothes, for dirty and ragged though they

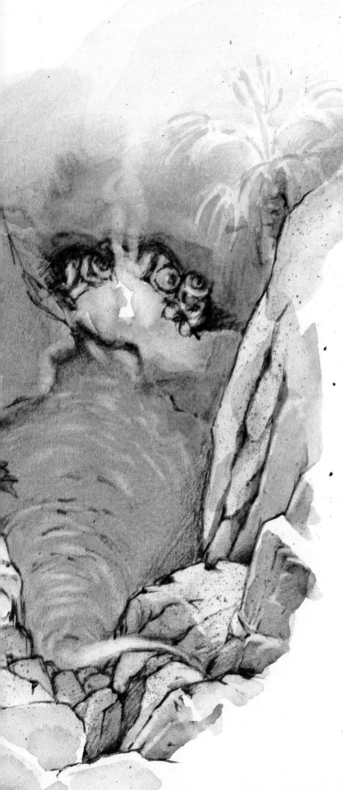

were, they would show up against the dark night. His own brown skin was a better protection for him. And then she saw how he hooked his amulet[5] neck-string about the horn handle of his great knife, so that it hung down in front of him and left both hands free. He did not come back to her. For a moment his body was black in the cave entrance, crouched and silent, and then he was gone.

Juana moved to the entrance and looked out. She peered like an owl from the hole in the mountain, and the baby slept under the blanket on her back, his face turned sideways against her neck and shoulder. She could feel his warm breath against her skin, and Juana whispered her combination of prayer and magic, her Hail Marys and her ancient intercession, against the black unhuman things.

The night seemed a little less dark when she looked out, and to the east there was a lightning in the sky, down near the horizon where the moon would show. And, looking down, she could see the cigarette of the man on watch.

Kino edged like a slow lizard down the smooth rock shoulder. He had turned his

---

5. **amulet** (ăm′yə-lĭt): a charm or magic ornament, usually worn around the neck.

neck-string so that the great knife hung down from his back and could not clash against the stone. His spread fingers gripped the mountain, and his bare toes found support through contact, and even his chest lay against the stone so that he would not slip. For any sound, a rolling pebble or a sign, a little slip of flesh on rock, would rouse the watchers below. Any sound that was not germane to the night would make them alert. But the night was not silent; the little tree frogs that lived near the stream twittered like birds, and the high metallic ringing of the cicadas filled the mountain cleft. And Kino's own music was in his head, the music of the enemy, low and pulsing, nearly asleep. But the Song of the Family had become as fierce and sharp and feline as the snarl of a female puma. The family song was alive now and driving him down on the dark enemy. The harsh cicada seemed to take up its melody, and the twittering tree frogs called little phrases of it.

And Kino crept silently as a shadow down the smooth mountain face. One bare foot moved a few inches and the toes touched the stone and gripped, and the other foot a few inches, and then the palm of one hand a little downward, and then the other hand, until the whole body, without seeming to move, had moved. Kino's mouth was open so that even his breath would make no sound, for he knew that he was not invisible. If the watcher, sensing movement, looked at the dark place against the stone which was his body, he could see him. Kino must move so slowly he would not draw the watcher's eyes. It took him a long time to reach the bottom and to crouch behind a little dwarf palm. His heart thundered in his chest and his hands and face were wet with sweat. He crouched and took slow long breaths to calm himself.

Only twenty feet separated him from the enemy now, and he tried to remember the ground between. Was there any stone which might trip him in his rush? He kneaded his legs against cramp and found that his muscles were jerking after their long tension. And then he looked apprehensively to the east. The moon would rise in a few moments now, and he must attack before it rose. He could see the outline of the watcher, but the sleeping men were below his vision. It was the watcher Kino must find — must find quickly and without hesitation. Silently he drew the amulet string over his shoulder and loosened the loop from the horn handle of his great knife.

He was too late, for as he rose from his crouch the silver edge of the moon slipped above the eastern horizon, and Kino sank back behind his bush.

It was an old and ragged moon, but it threw hard light and hard shadow into the mountain cleft, and now Kino could see the seated figure of the watcher on the little beach beside the pool. The watcher gazed full at the moon, and then he lighted another cigarette, and the match illumined his dark face for a moment. There could be no waiting now; when the watcher turned his head, Kino must leap. His legs were as tight as wound springs.

And then from above came a little murmuring cry. The watcher turned his head to listen and then he stood up, and one of the sleepers stirred on the ground and awakened and asked quietly, "What is it?"

"I don't know," said the watcher. "It sounded like a cry, almost like a human — like a baby."

The man who had been sleeping said, "You can't tell. Some coyote bitch with a litter. I've heard a coyote pup cry like a baby."

The sweat rolled in drops down Kino's forehead and fell into his eyes and burned them. The little cry came again and the watcher looked up the side of the hill to the dark cave.

"Coyote maybe," he said, and Kino heard the harsh click as he cocked the rifle.

"If it's a coyote, this will stop it," the watcher said as he raised the gun.

Kino was in midleap when the gun crashed and the barrel-flash made a picture on his eyes. The great knife swung and crunched hollowly. It bit through neck and deep into chest, and Kino was a terrible machine now. He grasped the rifle even as he wrenched free his knife. His strength and his movement and his speed were a machine. He whirled and struck the head of the seated man like a melon. The third man scrabbled away like a crab, slipped into the pool, and then he began to climb frantically, to climb up the cliff where the water penciled down. His hands and feet threshed in the tangle of the wild grapevine, and he whimpered and gibbered as he tried to get up. But Kino had become as cold and deadly as steel. Deliberately he threw the lever of the rifle, and then he raised the gun and aimed deliberately and fired. He saw his enemy tumble backward into the pool, and Kino strode to the water. In the moonlight he could see the frantic frightened eyes, and Kino aimed and fired between the eyes.

And then Kino stood uncertainly. Something was wrong, some signal was trying to get through to his brain. Tree frogs and cicadas were silent now. And then Kino's brain cleared from its red concentration and he knew the sound—the keening, moaning, rising hysterical cry from the little cave in the side of the stone mountain, the cry of death.

Everyone in La Paz remembers the return of the family; there may be some old ones who saw it, but those whose fathers and whose grandfathers told it to them remember it nevertheless. It is an event that happened to everyone.

It was late in the golden afternoon when the first little boys ran hysterically in the town and spread the word that Kino and Juana were coming back. And everyone hurried to see them. The sun was settling toward the western mountains and the shadows on the ground were long. And perhaps that was what left the deep impression on those who saw them.

The two came from the rutted country road into the city, and they were not walking in single file, Kino ahead and Juana behind, as usual, but side by side. The sun was behind them and their long shadows stalked ahead, and they seemed to carry two towers of darkness with them. Kino had a rifle across his arm and Juana carried her shawl like a sack over her shoulder. And in it was a small limp heavy bundle. The shawl was crusted with dried blood, and the bundle swayed a little as she walked. Her face was hard and lined and leathery with fatigue and with the tightness with which she fought fatigue. And her wide eyes stared inward on herself. She was as remote and as removed as Heaven. Kino's lips were thin and his jaws tight, and the people say that he carried fear with him, that he was as dangerous as a rising storm. The people say that the two seemed to be removed from human experience; that they had gone through pain and had come out on the other side; that there was almost a magical protection about them. And those people who had rushed to see them crowded back and let them pass and did not speak to them.

Kino and Juana walked through the city as though it were not there. Their eyes glanced neither right nor left nor up nor down, but stared only straight ahead. Their legs moved a little jerkily, like well-made wooden dolls, and they carried pillars of black fear about them. And as they walked through the stone and plaster city brokers peered at them from barred windows and servants put one eye to a slitted gate and mothers turned the faces of their youngest children inward against their skirts. Kino and Juana strode side by side through the stone and plaster city and down among the brush houses, and the neighbors stood back and let them pass. Juan Tomás raised his hand in greeting and did not say the greeting and left his hand in the air for a moment uncertainly.

In Kino's ears the Song of the Family was as fierce as a cry. He was immune and terrible, and his song had become a battle cry. They trudged past the burned square where their house had been without even looking at it. They cleared the brush that edged the beach and picked their way down the shore toward the water. And they did not look toward Kino's broken canoe.

And when they came to the water's edge they stopped and stared out over the Gulf. And then Kino laid the rifle down, and he dug among his clothes, and then he held the great pearl in his hand. He looked into its surface and it was gray and ulcerous. Evil faces peered from it into his eyes, and he saw the light of burning. And in the surface of the pearl he saw the frantic eyes of the man in the pool. And in the surface of the pearl he saw Coyotito lying in the little cave with the top of his head shot away. And the pearl was ugly; it was gray, like a malignant growth. And Kino heard the music of the pearl, distorted and insane. Kino's hand shook a little, and he turned slowly to Juana and held the pearl out to her. She stood beside him, still holding her dead bundle over her shoulder. She looked at the pearl in his hand for a moment and then she looked into Kino's eyes and said softly, "No, you."

And Kino drew back his arm and flung the pearl with all his might. Kino and Juana watched it go, winking and glimmering under the setting sun. They saw the little splash in the distance, and they stood side by side watching the place for a long time.

And the pearl settled into the lovely green water and dropped toward the bottom. The waving branches of the algae called to it and beckoned to it. The lights on its surface were green and lovely. It settled down to the sand bottom among the fernlike plants. Above, the surface of the water was a green mirror. And the pearl lay on the floor of the sea. A crab scampering over the bottom raised a little cloud of sand, and when it settled the pearl was gone.

And the music of the pearl drifted to a whisper and disappeared.